FILM

AN INTRODUCTION

SECOND EDITION

William H. Phillips

University of Wisconsin–Eau Claire

BEDFORD/ST. MARTIN'S   Boston ◆ New York

FOR BEDFORD/ST. MARTIN'S
Communication Editor: Jennifer Bartlett
Developmental Editor: Michael Bagnulo
Senior Production Editor: Michael Weber
Senior Production Supervisor: Joe Ford
Marketing Manager: Richard Cadman
Art Director: Lucy Krikorian
Text Design: Wanda Kossak
Cover Design: Lucy Krikorian
Composition and Layout: DeNee Reiton Skipper
Printing and Binding: R. R. Donnelley and Sons

President: Charles H. Christensen
Editorial Director: Joan E. Feinberg
Publisher for History and Communication: Patricia Rossi
Director of Marketing: Karen R. Melton
Director of Editing, Design, and Production: Marcia Cohen
Managing Editor: Erica T. Appel

Library of Congress Catalog Card Number: 2001087206

Manufactured in the United States of America.

7 6 5 4 3 2
f e d c b

For information, write: Bedford/St. Martin's, 75 Arlington Street, Boston, MA 02116 (617-399-4000)

ISBN: 0–312–25896–8

Published and distributed outside North America by
PALGRAVE
Houndmills, Basingstoke, Hampshire RG21 2XS and London
Companies and representatives throughout the world.
PALGRAVE is the new global academic imprint of St. Martin's Press LLC
Scholarly and Reference Division and Palgrave Publishers Ltd. (formerly
Macmillan Press Ltd.).
ISBN: 0-333-97226-0

A catalog record for this book is available from the British Library.

Preface to the Second Edition

THE BOOK BEFORE YOU represents the culmination of more than twenty-five years of research, experimentation in teaching, and writing. I developed and wrote *Film: An Introduction* in the twofold hope that its readers will better understand and appreciate individual films and gain a fuller understanding of the film medium's variety, achievements, and possibilities. The many film courses using the first edition and the positive reactions to it have been extremely gratifying. In addition, suggestions from film instructors and students have helped shape this major revision, which I have undertaken in the hope that this new book may even more successfully meet faculty and student needs.

AN EXTENSIVE, REVISED ART PROGRAM ENSURES STUDENTS SEE THE CONCEPTS COVERED Approximately half the photographs are new to this edition. Compared with those in the first edition of *Film*, the photographs are more varied, detailed, plentiful, and visually faithful to the original films. Whenever possible (most of the time), photographs representing films are presented in the same shape (aspect ratio) in which the images were first shown. Furthermore, this edition of *Film* is the only introductory text to place frame enlargements from consecutive shots, sometimes consecutive frames, side by side, allowing readers to understand more clearly many of the film techniques discussed. Even by themselves, the many varied, expressive photographs and accompanying extensive captions could function as a clear, vivid, and comprehensive yet brief introduction to the film medium.

NEW CHAPTERS SHOW THE EXTENDED APPLICATION OF FILM TERMS AND CONCEPTS In this edition, each of the book's three parts is now followed by a new chapter that demonstrates how the information and concepts from that part can be applied to better understand and appreciate any film. Chapter 5 offers students an exploration of expressive film techniques employed in the classic *The Third Man*. Chapter 10 provides students an opportunity to explore some of the immense variety of film: in this example, the sources, types, narrative components, and documentary aspects of the narrative documentary *Hearts of Darkness: A Filmmaker's Apocalypse*. Chapter 13 uses *The Player* to illustrate some of the ways viewers can understand a film, including consideration of contexts, viewer expectations and interactions as they watch a film, and possible meanings.

EXTENSIVE REVISED COVERAGE KEEPS READERS UP TO DATE AND INFORMED IN DEPTH   Besides the three new chapters, much else is new to the second edition. All chapters include updated examples, both in the text and photos, that today's students are more likely to recognize. To prevent students from feeling overwhelmed with too many examples, some sections now include fewer examples but more detail about those that remain. All chapters in the second edition have new sections, sections that have been extensively revised, or both.

There are new sections of chapters on storyboards as a source for fictional films, on TV as a source for fictional films and films as a source for TV, and on multiple sources for a fictional film. Related to this last point, in various places there is now much more emphasis on the intertexuality of films and other texts. A new section on possible sources for documentaries has also been added. And there are new sections on the contexts in which a film can be seen (from nickelodeons to theaters with stadium seating) and on some of the many possible influences on the ways people react to and think about films.

Many existing chapter sections have been extensively revised, updated, and rewritten, including the sections on settings and costumes, film stocks and digital filmmaking, and history and plays as sources for fictional films. The section on the western has been pruned and reorganized. Other chapter sections have been reorganized and further developed: Italian neorealism, the celebratory documentary, and the mediated characteristic of the documentary. Because of their growing prominence, documentary films and animation are now covered in more detail. The sections on the changing representation of gays in cinema and on how technology affects the types of films made have been reorganized along historical lines. (Compared with the first edition, this edition contains more film history and more sections organized chronologically.) *Tarzan* movies have been used to show how different times and places produce different versions of the same basic story. To illustrate how viewers form changing expectations and reactions, I have included the example of viewers watching "Bambi Meets Godzilla" for the first time. The definitions of *style, magic realism, explicit meaning*, and a few other terms have been refined and the corresponding discussions rewritten. There is new material on how expectations and interactions function differently for the cult film than for a film viewers are seeing for the first time. The Japanese film *Shall We Dance?* and *Gladiator* are now included as examples of how a film can be symptomatic of a culture's beliefs and values.

FILM'S STRUCTURE ALLOWS INSTRUCTORS TO TAILOR THE TEXT TO THEIR CLASS-ROOM NEEDS   The structure of *Film* makes possible a more comprehensive introduction to the film medium than that provided by other introductory film texts. The book's structure also leads its readers from the most familiar and accessible material (the expressiveness of film techniques) to increasingly unfamiliar and somewhat more demanding theoretical issues. Part One considers many of the techniques used in making a film and, more important, the consequences for viewers of the filmmakers' choices. Part Two considers the variety of films, including their sources, types, and components. Part Three examines ways to understand viewer responses to a film: how viewers can better understand a film when they consider its contexts, how their expectations of a film and their changing interactions with it influence their responses to the film, and how viewers formulate meanings.

Many instructors will find that the arrangement of chapters reflects the order of the topics they cover in class. Others might want to read or teach the book's chapters in a different order. I have made the book flexible to fit the different ways introductory material can be approached.

THE APPENDICES HAVE BEEN EXPANDED AND REVISED   The book concludes with four appendices that offer some of its most distinctive features. (1) "Studying Films" consists of a concise discussion of writing strategies; guidelines for writing definitions; advice on improving reading comprehension; exercises for examining films; revised questions for thought, discussion, and writing; and an updated annotated list of film resources available in print. (Information on digital resources can be accessed through the Web page for this book.) (2) "A Chronology: Film in Context (1895–2000)" (revised and updated) is a four-column chronology revealing some of the contexts of major historical events, the arts, mass media developments, and a variety of films and videos. The chronology is also a place to find a date or other fact, check a spelling, and, I hope, be enticed into reading histories. (Other uses of the chronology are explained in its introduction.) (3) "How to Read Film Credits" reprints the end credits from a movie and explains what they mean. This feature encourages students to examine a film's credits and helps them appreciate the work and creativity involved in making a feature-length film. (4) The extensive and extensively revised illustrated glossary—now with nearly three times the photographs of the first edition glossary—defines terms used in the text, gives examples, and refers students to the in-text discussion. Students can use this glossary as a reference long after the course is over.

CAREFUL ATTENTION TO FILM LANGUAGE ARMS STUDENTS WITH ESSENTIAL VOCABULARY
In addition to providing an expanded and revised illustrated glossary, the
second edition of *Film* helps students learn the terms and concepts essential to
a critical understanding of the film medium. To aid reading comprehension,
key terms for each chapter are defined and illustrated in the text or glossed
in the margin. These marginal glosses also reinforce major concepts from other
chapters and make it easy for instructors to assign chapters in any order.

Boldface and Marginal Definitions

Each chapter includes words that are set off in **boldface** and words that
are defined briefly in the margin.

Words in boldface are explained in the glossary. Sometimes they are explained briefly in the margins of the chapter pages. Sometimes words in
boldface are explained briefly within the same sentence of the text (and
thus no marginal explanation is necessary). Occasionally they go unexplained in the sentence because their meanings will be clear enough from
the context. (If not, readers can check the word's entry in the glossary.)

Marginal explanations are intended to help readers read a chapter
with few or no interruptions. To speed the reading, they are kept as brief
as possible. For all terms, fuller explanations and examples are provided in
the glossary, which the reader is urged to study often—before or after
reading a chapter.

A BROAD RANGE OF FILMS EXPANDS STUDENTS' UNDERSTANDING OF THE FILM
MEDIUM   The book discusses films that students know (movies through
summer 2001) and a wider range of films that instructors believe students should
know (including films made by ethnic, international, and women filmmakers;
historical films; documentaries; experimental films; and short films). Although
an even wider variety of films are cited in this edition than in the first edition,
the focus remains on the fictional and documentary films most often seen today because most beginning film students will more likely be drawn into the
study of film if they begin with something familiar and enjoyable.

ABUNDANT PEDAGOGICAL APPARATUS HELPS STUDENTS LEARN AND REMEMBER
This book was designed as a teaching tool to help students learn, study, write,
answer questions, and formulate their own questions. Chapter summaries
highlight each chapter's key concepts. The second edition of *Film* includes
fifteen feature sections, seven of which are new. The features contain a variety
of engaging supplementary material, including descriptions of films; descriptions and analyses of particular aspects of a film, such as the editing in a
clip from *High Noon;* and factual information such as excerpts from the Production Code of the Motion Picture Producers and Directors of America.

Updated works cited and annotated reading lists at the end of each chapter acquaint students with some of the rich array of film scholarship and provide a variety of useful sources for undergraduates to consult for more information or for research projects.

For clarity, throughout the book titles of short films (those less than sixty minutes long) are set off by quotation marks; titles of films sixty or more minutes long are in italics.

THE INSTRUCTOR'S MANUAL HAS BEEN REVISED   The Instructor's Manual includes an expanded section on teaching strategies, revised test questions and an answer key to accompany each chapter, a revised sample syllabus, and assignments for essays, journals, group presentations, a sample quiz, and two types of final examinations. The IM also includes a section written expressly for teachers on how to help students write more effectively about film, a new section on the course review, and useful updated sources for film teachers: film and video distributors, books, and articles.

THE WEB SITE HAS BEEN UPDATED   The Web site for this book includes many resources for both instructors and students. Student self-testing with instructor tracking; sample student essays; selected outlines for films discussed in the second edition; information about the author and e-mail access to him; and many annotated links to useful film sites, such as film reviews and film journals, all serve to make the new *Film* Web site an even more useful tool for both teaching and learning about film. The site is at <http://www.bedfordstmartins.com/phillips-film>.

Acknowledgments

The following libraries and archives have aided me in my research: McIntyre Library, University of Wisconsin–Eau Claire; L. E. Phillips Memorial Public Library, Eau Claire, Wisconsin; Pacific Film Archive, Berkeley; Library and Film Center, Museum of Modern Art; and Motion Pictures, Broadcasting, and Recorded Sound Division, U.S. Library of Congress. The following film distributors have also cooperated: Anthology Film Archives, California Newsreel, Canyon Cinema, Chicago Filmmakers, Creative Thinking International, Filmmakers' Cooperative, Flower Films, International Film Bureau, Kino International, Michael Wiese Productions, National Film Board of Canada, New Line Productions, New Video Group, New Yorker Films, Pyramid Film and Video, and Women Make Movies.

REVIEWERS   Over the many years I wrote and rewrote this text, I consulted scores of professional filmmakers and film scholars about the accuracy and clarity of various sections of the book. The following people, generous professionals all, gave of their precious time and provided feedback appropriate for my introductory audience: Les Blank, Flower Films, El Cerrito, California; Rose Bond, Gaea Graphics, Portland, Oregon; Stan Brakhage, University of Colorado, Boulder; Jim Gardner, Sound One, New York; Cecelia Hall, executive sound director, Paramount Pictures; Michael B. Hoggan, past president, American Cinema Editors and now adjunct professor of filmmaking, University of Southern California and California State University, Northridge; Ken Jacobs, Independent Filmmakers, New York; George Kuchar, independent filmmaker, San Francisco, California; Tak Miyagishima, Panavision International, L.P.; Errol Morris, Fourth Floor Productions, Cambridge, Massachusetts; J. J. Murphy, University of Wisconsin, Madison; Robert Orlando, Coppola Pictures, New York; Lee Parker, Daedalus Corporation, Turlock, California; Jeff Wall, University of British Columbia; and technical representatives of the Imax Corporation, Toronto. These professional filmmakers supplied information or photographs (or both) or corrections, suggestions, and encouragement about different sections of the manuscript.

Many people have read the entire manuscript or parts of it and made helpful suggestions and corrections: Barbara L. Baker, Central Missouri State University; Bob Baron, Mesa Community College; Frank Beaver, University of Michigan; Peter Bondanella, Indiana University; Christine Catanzarite, Illinois State University; Jeffrey Chown, Northern Illinois State University; Marshall Deutelbaum, Purdue University; Carol Dole, Ursinus College; Bernard Duyfhuizen, University of Wisconsin–Eau Claire; Charles Eidsvik, University of Georgia; Jack Ellis, Northwestern University; Douglas Gomery, University of Maryland; Charles Harpole, University of Central Florida; Ken Harrow, Michigan State University; William H. Hayes, professor emeritus of philosophy, California State University, Stanislaus; Ron Heiss, Spokane Community College; Nel Hellenberg, Spokane Falls Community College; Tim Hirsch, University of Wisconsin–Eau Claire; Deborah Holdstein, Governors State University; Barbara Klinger, Indiana University; Ira Konigsberg, University of Michigan; Don Kunz, University of Rhode Island; Karen Mann, Western Illinois University; Mike McBrine, Amherst College; Scott MacDonald, Utica College; Dale Melgaard, University of Nevada, Las Vegas; Avis Meyer, St. Louis University; Wayne Miller, Franklin University; James Naremore, Indiana University; David Natharius, Arizona State University; Martin F. Norden, University of Massachusetts, Amherst; Samuel Oppenheim, California State University, Stanislaus; Kimberly M. Radek, Illinois Valley Community College; August Rubrecht, University of Wisconsin–Eau Claire; Eva L. Santos-Phillips, University of Wisconsin–Eau Claire; Paul Scherer, Indiana University, South Bend; Carol Schrepfer, Waubonsee Community College; John Schultheiss, California State University, Northridge; John W. Spalding, Wayne State University; Terry Steiner, Spokane Falls Community College; Sonja Swenson, Taft College; Kristin Thompson, University of Wisconsin–Madison; Frank Tomasulo, Georgia State University; and Tricia Welsch, Bowdoin College.

QUESTIONNAIRE RESPONDENTS   The following instructors of an introduction to film course responded to a Bedford/St. Martin's questionnaire, sharing strategies for teaching the course and their requirements in a textbook: Richard Abel, Drake University; Marilyn K. Ackerman, Foothill College; Dr. Robert Adubato, Essex County College; William A. Allman, Baldwin-Wallace College; Ann Alter, Humboldt State University; Bob Alto, University of San Francisco; Victoria Amador, Western New Mexico University; Lauri Anderson, Suomi College; Robert Arnett, Mississippi State University; Bob Arnold, University of Toledo; Paul Arthur, Montclair State University; Dr. Maureen Asten, Worcester State College; Ray Barcia, Goucher College; Dr. Bob Baron, Mesa Community College; Karen Becker, Richland Community College; Edward I. Benintende, County College of Morris; John Bernstein, Macalester College; Robin Blaetz, Emory University; James Bozan, University of Missouri, Rolla; Bruce C. Browne, University of Wisconsin, Sheboygan; Carolyn R. Bruder, University of Southwestern Louisiana; Lawrence Budner, Rhode Island College; Ken Burke, Mills College; George Butte, Colorado College; Jim Carmody, University of California, San Diego; Ray Carney, Boston University; Harold Case, Allan Hancock College; Lisa Cartwright, University of Rochester; Dr. Christine J. Catanzarite, Illinois State University; Rick Chapman, Des Moines Area Community College; Rick Clemons, Western Illinois University; Lois Cole, Mt. San Antonio College; David Crosby, Alcorn State University; Rita Csapó Sweete, University of Missouri–St. Louis; Ramona Curry, University of Illinois; Joan Dagle, Rhode Island College; Dr. Kathryn D'Alessandro, Jersey City State College; Mary Jayne Davis, Salt Lake Community College; Margarita De la Vega-Hurtado, University of Michigan, Ann Arbor; Larry R. Dennis, Clarion University; Carol M. Dole, Ursinus College; Gus Edwards, Arizona State University; John Ernst, Heartland College; Thomas L. Erskine, Salisbury State University; Jim Everett, Mississippi College; Patty Felkner, Cosumnes River College; Peter Feng, University of Delaware; Jody Flynn, Owensboro Community College; Mike Frank, Bentley College; Arthur M. Fried, Plymouth State College; Don Fredericksen, Cornell University; Keya Ganguly, Carnegie Mellon University; Dr. Joseph E. Gelsi, Central Methodist College; Jerry Girton, Riverland Community College; Joseph A. Gomez, North Carolina State University; John M. Gourlie, Quinnipiac College; William J. Hagerty, Xavier University; Mickey Hall, Volunteer State Community College; James Hallemann, Oakland Community College; Ken Harrow, Michigan State University; Rolland L. Heiss, Spokane Community College; Thomas Hemmetier, Beaver College; Bruce Hinricks, Century College; Tim Hirsch, University of Wisconsin–Eau Claire; Allan Hirsch, Central Connecticut State University; Rosemary Horowitz, Appalachian State University; Sandra Hybels, Lock Haven University; Frank E. Jackson, Lander University; Susan Jhirad, North Shore Community College; Kimberlie A. Johnson, Seminole Community College;

Edward T. Jones, York College of Pennsylvania; Leandro Katz, William Paterson College; Thomas K. Kegel, Oakland Community College; Harry Keyishian, Fairleigh Dickinson University; Les Keyser, College of Staten Island; Helmut Kremling, Ohio Wesleyan University; Al LaValley, Dartmouth College; Don S. Lawson, Lander University; Carol S. Layne, Jefferson Community College; Paul Lazarus, University of Miami; Peter Lev, Towson State University; Susan E. Linville, University of Colorado, Denver; Dr. Cathleen Londino, Keans College of New Jersey; Frances Lozano, Gavilan College; Jean D. Lynch, Villanova University; Karen B. Mann, Western Illinois University; Walter McCallum, Santa Rosa Junior College; James McGonigle, Madison Area Technical College; Marilyn Middendorf, Embry Riddle Aeronautical University; Joseph Milicia, University of Wisconsin, Sheboygan; Mark S. Miller, Pikes Peak Community College; Mary Alice Molgard, College of Saint Rose; James Morrison, North Carolina State University; Charles Musser, Yale University; Barry H. Novick, College of New Jersey; Kevin O'Brien, University of Nevada, Las Vegas; Jan Ostrow, College of the Redwoods; Richard Peacock, Palomar College; Richard Pearce, Wheaton College; Ruth Perlmutter, University of the Arts; David Popowski, Mankato State University; Joyce Porter, Moraine Valley Community College; Maria Pramaggiore, North Carolina State University; Cynthia Prochaska, Mt. San Antonio College; Leonard Quart, College of Staten Island; Clay Randolph, Oklahoma City Community College; Maurice Rapf, Dartmouth College; Jere Real, Lynchburg College; Gary Reynolds, Minneapolis Community & Technical College; David Robinson, Winona State University; James Rupport, University of Alaska, Fairbanks; Jaime Sanchez, Volunteer State Community College; Kristine Samuelson, Stanford University; Richard Schwartz, Florida International University; Richard Sears, Berea College; Eli Segal, Governors State University; Dr. Rick Shale, Youngstown State University; Craig Shurtleff, Illinois Central College; Charles L. P. Silev, Iowa State University; Joseph Evans Slate, University of Texas, Austin; Thomas J. Slater, Indiana University of Pennsylvania; Claude Smith, Florida Community College at Jacksonville; Terry J. Steiner, Spokane Falls Community College; Kevin M. Stemmler, Clarion University; Ellen Strain, Georgia Institute of Technology; Judith A. Switzer, Bucks County Community College; Julie Tharp, University of Wisconsin, Marshfield; John Tibbetts, University of Kansas; Marie Travis, George Washington University; Robert Vales, Gannon University; Jonathan Walters, Norwich University; Shujen Wang, Westfield State College; Dr. Rosanne Wasserman, U.S. Merchant Marine Academy; J. R. Welsch, Western Illinois University; Tricia Welsch, Bowdoin College; Bernard Welt, the Corcoran School of Art; Robert D. West, Kent State University; Mary Beth Wilk, Des Moines Area Community College; and Gerald C. Wood, Carson-Newman College.

ADDITIONAL THANKS Karen Woodward, of the Department of Foreign Languages at the University of Wisconsin–Eau Claire, shared various printed sources on film, some of which were used for this edition. Megan Williams contributed to Chapters 5 and 10 of this edition; Vicki Whitaker contributed to an earlier version of Chapter 13.

Dennis DeNitto, City College of New York, provided advice and encouragement and generously made available more than a dozen frame enlargements. The photographs of models in Chapter 2 were taken by Jon Michael Terry of Jon Michael Terry Photography, Turlock, California. Prints for many of the frame enlargements were done by manager Tom Evans's skillful employees Steve Allingham, Angie Bowers, and Mindy Nyseth at the Snap Shot, Eau Claire, Wisconsin. At the Museum of Modern Art/Film Stills Archive, Terry Geesken and Mary Corliss again helped me secure many photographs used in the book.

Finally, I want to thank the many dedicated, hardworking, and skillful people at the New York office of Bedford/St. Martin's who helped with the production of the second edition. First and foremost, I wish to thank my developmental editors, Simon Glick, who worked briefly on the project during the initial stages, and Michael Bagnulo, who proved to be knowledgeable, enthusiastic, constructive, and diplomatic. Michael made a major difference. James Long helped with some research. Pat Ollague was project manager. Michael Weber, senior production editor, and Joe Ford, senior production supervisor, were attentive to details, coordinated the work, and saw that it got done carefully and on time. Lucy Krikorian, the art director, oversaw the art program and the text design. Rosemary Winfield, the copyeditor, helped clean up and clarify many details in the manuscript. Patricia Rossi was the sponsoring editor. As with the first edition, the publisher Charles Christensen strongly supported the project and committed many company resources to it.

ABOUT THE AUTHOR

William H. Phillips received his B.A. from Purdue University, his M.A. from Rutgers University, and his Ph.D. (in dramatic literature and film studies) from Indiana University. His postdoctoral studies in film include three sabbaticals to write and to do research at major film archives, libraries, and film distributors in the United States and Europe; participation in an eight-week National Endowment for the Humanities Summer Seminar for College Teachers on the history of film at Northwestern University; and attendance at the first (two-week) American Film Institute Center for Advanced Film Studies Symposium for College Film Teachers. He has also served as producer of readings of original short film scripts for live performance then rebroadcast on cable TV.

Phillips has taught introductory film courses at the University of Illinois, Urbana; Indiana University, South Bend; California State University, Stanislaus; and the University of Wisconsin–Eau Claire. His publications include the books *Analyzing Films* (1985), *Writing Short Scripts* (2nd ed., 1999), and *Writing Short Stories: The Most Practical Guide* (2002).

Brief Contents

Contents

FILM
AN INTRODUCTION

Introduction

NUDITY ISN'T THE ONLY THING that sells newspapers in Italy. So do movies. Just as articles on bank robberies often feature a spaghetti-western still of Clint Eastwood, reports on child prostitution are almost always accompanied by a still of Jodie Foster in *Taxi Driver*. Adult prostitution is illustrated with shots from *Pretty Woman*. A recent *Il Messaggero* article on research on tar-blocking filters in cigarettes was printed alongside the image of Sharon Stone in *Basic Instinct*, lighting a cigarette in the film's famous interrogation scene. (Stanley)

The lines at the movie theater stretch down the block. At the neighborhood video store, all the copies of the latest hit movie are rented out. As a group of people in a remote Cuban village see their first film, their faces radiate joy and wonder, and a short documentary Cuban film, "For the First Time," records the event. Immigrant children watch a movie and are captivated by it and united in pleasure (Figure I.1). A young American filmmaker born in Vietnam returns there to make a documentary and interviews former Vietnamese leaders, who ask her "a lot of questions about American film stars." In a scene from the 1988 Senegalese film *Saaraba* (meaning "Utopia") alienated youths in Dakar are seen in the foreground smoking drugs; in the background hangs a poster for *Apocalypse Now*. Audiences watching the 1995 Academy Award–winning documentary *Anne Frank Remembered* glimpse photos of movie stars on Anne Frank's bedroom wall (Figure I.2). At various times in history, Mickey Mouse, Charlie Chaplin, Rudolph Valentino, Marilyn Monroe, John Wayne, Arnold Schwarzenegger, and other stars have been more widely known throughout the world than presidents, popes, and athletes. These examples attest to the power and pervasiveness of film, especially American commercial cinema.

No one questions the entertainment value of movies: the proof is in the huge number of people who watch them. Many people, though, disagree about whether films have any additional value. To some viewers, movies'

FIGURE I.1 **The joy of movies** Immigrant children from different countries and ethnic groups are mesmerized by "The Immigrant," a 1917 silent film starring Charlie Chaplin. *Courtesy of Rebecca Cooney and New York Times Pictures*

1

FIGURE I.2 Photographs of movie stars
Anne Frank—a girl who with her family hid in a secret apartment in an Amsterdam house during the Nazi occupation—is the subject of the documentary film *Anne Frank Remembered* (1995). At several points in the film audiences see her bedroom wall, on which are hung photographs of movie stars (at the top of the image shown here)—yet another indication of the widespread influence of movies on modern lives. *Sony Pictures Classics*

preeminent ability and commercial proclivity to show sex and violence have made them seem unworthy of study. Movies have been dismissed as "ribbons of dreams" and Hollywood as a "dream factory." Nonetheless, films can be more than commercial entertainment, and studying them and the film medium has many benefits.

STUDYING FILMS AND THE FILM MEDIUM

Some people fear that studying films will spoil their enjoyment of them. But with guidance and a chance to reach their own conclusions, nearly all viewers find that studying films increases their enjoyment of them and often their appreciation of the effort and creativity involved in making them. Many people find, too, that they enjoy a wider variety of films for more different reasons than they did before studying films.

Film study helps viewers understand how different filmmakers have used the medium. It also reveals the medium's possibilities and limitations. For example, together *Citizen Kane*, *Pulp Fiction*, and the documentary film *Hearts of Darkness* suggest how complex and varied the structure of a nonchronological film story may be. The experimental "Un chien andalou" shows how a film may be used not to show a story or present facts but to suggest something of the bizarre, irrational, yet sometimes striking qualities of dreams.

Film study also helps viewers understand and appreciate the wide variety of films, including short films, documentary films, experimental films, and combinations of those three basic categories of films, not to mention various groupings of fictional films, such as Italian neorealism and French new wave. Film study also helps viewers understand the various genres of fictional films, such as western and science fiction; mixtures of genres, such as horror and western; and the indebtedness of later films to earlier ones. Studying films will help you understand familiar films in new ways. For example, examining the story of *Gladiator* can reveal how that popular film, like so many popular movies, celebrates individualism and the potential of one person to make a major difference in the course of events.

Viewers trained in film studies tend to notice more significant detail while viewing a film. They are more likely to appreciate the expressiveness of the lighting, composition, camera angles, camera distances from the subjects, and other filmmaking techniques.

Studying films can make you more aware of contexts that influence how a film turns out. As illustrated in this book, when and where a film is made and the sources it draws on influence what the film will be like. A film made in a dictatorial third world country, for example, will differ fundamentally from any film made in modern Japan. A science fiction film will be influenced by earlier science fiction films: it will accept many of the conventions or traditions of sci-fi films; it may reject others.

People who have studied films and the responses they bring forth tend to understand the films' meanings in more variety and depth and to be more aware of how and why others might interpret the same film differently. They are also more likely to be aware of how the viewer's situation—where and when the viewer lives, for example—influences his or her responses to a film.

Finally, films can help us understand different places, people, and cultures—whether in a foreign country or in an obscure region of one's own country. However, films, even documentary films, can never be accepted as objective accounts. The films' subjects must be considered in light of the film medium's inherent properties and the filmmakers' motives, methods, and skills. In the case of experimental films, the worlds glimpsed often exist only in the filmmakers' imaginations.

ABOUT THIS BOOK

Film: An Introduction, Second Edition, attempts to help its readers understand the film medium more completely: the medium's general characteristics, its possibilities, achievements, and limitations. Consequently, the book includes a wide array of films, some of which have received less than glowing reviews— if they were reviewed at all. The intention here, however, is not to include only critically acclaimed films or to evaluate films but to better understand them and the film medium itself. These issues are illustrated by the following e-mail exchange I had with a colleague who does not teach film courses:

COLLEAGUE: Did you really see *Natural Born Killers*? I guess that's one of the downsides of specializing in film—kind of like correcting tests if you're a teacher.

AUTHOR: I see a huge variety of films and enjoy nearly all of them in some way or other. I do not so much try to judge them by some aesthetic standards (after all, my background and assumptions may not be the same as yours) but to see them in some sort of context (for example, a creative variation of a genre). Or I may enjoy a film for its structure or its editing or something else. All films, on one level, are an exercise in and celebration of human creativity.

COLLEAGUE: True, but still . . . *Natural Born Killers*??? Which I haven't seen but have read a lot about.

AUTHOR: *Natural Born Killers* is worthwhile for me to know. In fact, I will be discussing it briefly in the second edition of my film book as a critique of a type of TV news reporting. Parts of the film also exemplify black humor. Then, too, Stone's movies are always well filmed and edited. *NBK* is certainly not to everyone's taste. For many viewers, it is probably Oliver Stone's least accessible film. But seen in different contexts, the film is at least interesting on a number of levels.

To help readers understand unfamiliar terminology, many terms are explained within the text or in the margin. That way readers may read any chapter out of order without interruptions for trips to the glossary. Because of this feature, many terms, such as *genre*, are defined in multiple chapters.

This book includes many other features for the beginning film student: sidebars consisting of interesting supplementary information; a summary of the major points of each chapter; annotated suggestions for further reading; an appendix on reading, thinking, researching, and writing about films; and an extensive chronology that can help readers see when certain events happened in relation to other events. The chronology may also be used to find a date, check a spelling, and double-check one's memory. More than five hundred frame enlargements and other photographs, most with extensive informative captions, are also included in this edition.

Occasionally, readers of film books complain that they do not understand the concepts being explained when they have not seen the films used as illustrations. To try to minimize that problem, I have often supplied a photograph, drawing, table, or detailed description when explaining a point. In several places a description of an entire film is set off in a sidebar or is available on the book's Web site. Again so that readers may understand the concepts discussed without having seen the film. If readers know those films well, they can skip the summaries and go directly to the discussions that follow.

Throughout the book, the titles of short films (those less than sixty minutes) are set off by quotation marks, and those of long films (sixty or more minutes) by italics.

CREDIT WHERE CREDIT IS DUE

As we discuss a film and our responses to it, to whom should we give credit? If the film required only modest resources to make it—as is the case with many experimental films—often one person deserves most or even all of the credit. But what of full-length movies? What one person could create one? To write, costume, direct, light, perform, film, edit, score, finance, and promote a movie is beyond the powers of one mortal. Nonetheless, many film reviewers and critics credit and blame a single person, usually the director.

In the case of a novel or painting, assigning responsibility to one person is reasonable enough. With films made by many people, however, it is often difficult to know which filmmaker contributed which aspect to the finished product, and in most cases it is difficult to believe that the director is responsible for the creativity of every aspect. For instance, did the writers, director, actors, or someone else rewrite crucial lines of dialogue? Did the writers, director, editors, actors, or producer insist that certain scenes be dropped? Examining the film usually yields no answers to these and many other questions about creative contributions, and reliable publications about such information are rare. To compound the problem, screen credits often inaccurately report who did what. Many questions about specific contributions to the finished film remain unanswerable.

For compactness and ease of identification, in this book films are often identified by director, but readers should remember that such usage does not mean the director alone is responsible for all the film's creativity. Consider *Psycho*, which was directed by Alfred Hitchcock and was first shown in 1960. A reading of the source novel and the script that describes the finished film reveals that author Robert Bloch and scriptwriter Joseph Stefano deserve partial credit for the shape and texture of the finished film. Many of the performers—especially Anthony Perkins, Vera Miles, and Martin Balsam—do more than adequate work. Bernard Herrmann's music contributes to every scene in which it is employed: view any section without it and its absence is pronounced. The title work by Saul Bass at the beginning and the end of the film is unusually imaginative and appropriate. Doubtless, Hitchcock deserves much credit for supervising and coordinating all those and other efforts. In addition, various filmmaking strategies that Hitchcock tended to favor reveal Hitchcock's influence on *Psycho*. Nonetheless, to think of *Psycho* as "Hitchcock's *Psycho*" glosses over the contributions of many others. (For details on the creation of this film, see Stephen Rebello's *Alfred Hitchcock and the Making of Psycho*.)

Sometimes when I see someone giving the director full credit or blame for a film that many people helped make, I am reminded of an account, apocryphal though it may be, of the American director Frank Capra and his frequent collaborator, scriptwriter Robert Riskin. In Richard Walter's version of the story, in a lengthy interview Capra expounded on "the Capra touch" but not once mentioned Riskin. After the interview appeared, Riskin sent Capra a manuscript with the note "Frank, let's see you put the Capra touch on this." Inside were all blank pages (4).

WORKS CITED

Rebello, Stephen. *Alfred Hitchcock and the Making of Psycho*. New York: December, 1990. Harper, 1991.

Stanley, Alessandra. "Getting Creative about the News." *New York Times on the Web*. 20 Feb. 2000. <http://www.nytimes.com/library/review/022000italy-newspapers-review.html>.

Walter, Richard. *Screenwriting: The Art, Craft and Business of Film and Television Writing*. New York: NAL, 1988.

Part One
THE EXPRESSIVENESS OF FILM TECHNIQUES

W HAT ARE THE CONSEQUENCES for viewers of the innumerable decisions filmmakers make while creating films? Some answers will be explored in this, the first and largest, part of the book.

Part One, The Expressiveness of Film Techniques, discusses what the settings, subjects, and composition may contribute to a film; how the film stock, lighting, and camera can be used to create certain effects; how the resulting footage might be edited and with what consequences; and what the sound track can contribute to viewers' experience of a film. It focuses on the impact of the many choices filmmakers make. Part One concludes with a new chapter showing how various techniques can be used in a film, in this case *The Third Man*, to contribute to an enjoyable and meaningful experience for viewers.

◄ In *Secrets & Lies* (1996), a woman (on the right) realizes that the woman on the left is her daughter, the result of a brief liaison. The entire scene consists of only two shots, the second one more than seven and a half minutes long. In this publicity still, which closely approximates a frame from the second shot, the two subjects are centered and are the same height in the image: they are the main objects of interest and are of equal importance. The camera distance and lens make the subjects large enough that viewers can see the many shifting, complex feelings suggested by the actors' expressive faces. The background, a restaurant, is slightly out of focus and empty. The subjects and setting are clearly and evenly illuminated. The scene conveys many contrasts: the two women are of different races, social classes, and temperaments. The woman on the left is dressed professionally, holds briefcase and papers, and does not smoke. The woman on the right is casually dressed, disheveled, and smokes. The woman on the left has an enunciation and accent of an educated person; the woman on the right does not. The woman on the left largely reins in her emotions; the woman on the right gets extremely emotional. Although the two subjects are quite unlike, they share and help communicate a complicated, difficult emotional situation. Change the arrangement of the subjects within the frame, background, camera distance, camera lens, clothing, lighting, editing, or actors, and the scene and the audience's response to it would be altered. *October Films*

7

To create a desired effect, a technique, such as lighting or camera lenses or camera angles, may be changed as the film progresses—for example, to give a sense of the walls and ceiling closing in on the characters. Usually such changes are gradual and imperceptible, especially in mainstream movies.

A particular technique, such as a camera angle, may have one effect in one part of a film and a different effect elsewhere in the same film or in a different film. Often, a low camera angle reinforces the sense that the subject is large, dominant, imposing, or powerful, but not always. Sometimes, for example, the filmmakers simply want viewers to notice the relationship of the subject in the foreground to a tall object in the background. Similarly, a high camera angle does not always make the subject seem small, vulnerable, or weak, although in many contexts it does. It depends on the contexts and on other techniques used at the same time.

Finally, several techniques used together create a particular effect. For example, in some desert shots in *Lawrence of Arabia*, viewers may be struck by how much the characters are engulfed by an inhospitable environment. But it's not just the camera distance and smallness of the subjects in the image that create that effect: the high angle diminishes the size of the subjects, the (hot) color is unvarying and inhospitable, and the focus is shallow, as if even close by there is nothing worth seeing. To illustrate the expressiveness of various cinematic techniques, the following chapters focus on them one at a time, but in films they never function in isolation.

CHAPTER 1

Mise en Scène

MISE EN SCÈNE—pronounced "meez ahn sen," with a nasalized second syllable—originally meant a director's staging of a play. Often in film studies the term refers to everything put before the camera in preparation for filming. As used in this book, **mise en scène** consists of the major aspects of filmmaking that are also components of staging a play: the settings; the subjects being filmed, usually actors or people as themselves; and the composition, the arrangement of the settings, lighting, and subjects. In French *mise en scène* means "staging." The phrase is used in the opening credits for some French films where English-language films would use "direction," as in "*Mise en scène de Luis Buñuel,*" meaning "Direction by Luis Buñuel." Although the **designer** and **cinematographer** are often deeply involved in matters of mise en scène, in large productions of fictional films the director usually makes the final decisions about mise en scène.

So expressive can mise en scène be that sometimes entire major **scenes** use only visuals to convey moods, characterizations, and meanings or implications. The opening scene of the western *Rio Bravo* (1959), for example, introduces the main character (the sheriff), an alcoholic who later proves to be his deputy, and a murdering antagonist—all in a wordless scene of two minutes and thirty-two seconds. Mise en scène can be so expressive that sometimes only a few carefully selected images can convey much of a film's story, moods, and meanings. In *Shall We Dance?* (1996), an office worker in modern-day Japan surreptitiously takes up dance lessons that lead to unexpected complications at work and even more so at home. Much of the film's story is conveyed by only the four images shown in Figure 1.1 on the next page.

Terms in **boldface** are defined in the Illustrated Glossary beginning on page 539.

designer or production designer: The person responsible for much of what is photographed in a movie, including architecture, locations, sets, costumes, makeup, and hairstyles.

cinematographer: The person responsible for the motion-picture photography during the making of a film.

scene: A section of a narrative film that gives the impression of continuous action taking place in continuous time and space.

SETTINGS

The **setting** is the place where filmed action occurs—either on a **set,** a constructed place used for filming (Figure 1.2), or on **location,** a real place that is not built expressly for the filmmakers (Figure 1.3). A film's setting—such as the wide-open spaces of a western or the cramped confines in a prison—can have tremendous impact on the viewer's experience and is often used to imply a time and place or to reveal or enhance style, character, mood, and meaning.

FIGURE 1.1 Mise en scène conveying a story

The settings, subjects, and compositions of carefully selected images reveal much of the story of *Shall We Dance?* (1996). (a) In the background an exhausted man is holding a briefcase yet dozing in a crowded commuter train after a day's work. (b) From the train, the man sees a lovely tall woman looking out the window of a dance studio. (c) He begins dance lessons at the dance studio where he had spotted the tall woman. (d) Eventually, the man dances gracefully and skillfully with the tall dance instructor. Of course, these few frame enlargements cannot convey the many (often amusing) complications in the man's life after he begins dance lessons, but the basics of the plot are clear from just the mise en scène of these four images. Frame enlargements. *Shôji Masui & Yuji Ogata; Miramax*

Types of Settings

Filmmakers have many options in selecting and creating settings. In recent years, settings for certain movies, especially science fiction and action films, have been created in a computer then eventually transferred to film. Usually, though, most of a film's scenes are **shot** on a set or on location. Many films combine **shots** made on a set with those made on location.

A setting may be the main subject of the scene, as in the famous set from *Intolerance* (1916, Figure 1.4 on p. 12). At the opposite extreme, the setting may draw no attention to itself: for example, it may be blank (**limbo**) or out of focus (Figure 1.5 on p. 12).

shot (verb): Filmed, as in "They shot the movie in seven weeks."

shot (noun): An uninterrupted strip of exposed motion-picture film or videotape.

FIGURE 1.2 **Early film set**
Interior of Georges Méliès's glassed-in film studio, one of the world's first sets, which was built in France in 1897. Many windows were necessary because early films were made without artificial light. The studio was used for preparations for filming—for instance, for painting scenery—and for filming Méliès's early, very short films. Méliès himself is seen on the left. *The Museum of Modern Art/Film Stills Archive*

FIGURE 1.3 **Filming on location**
For "Feeding (the) Baby" (1895) the Lumière Brothers of France took a camera outside and recorded brief actions as separate films, such as a train arriving at a station, workers leaving a factory, children digging for clams, and a family having a meal. The film illustrated here is one of the earliest home movies. Frame enlargement. *The Museum of Modern Art/Film Stills Archive*

FIGURE 1.4 **The setting as subject**
This set of Babylon for *Intolerance* (1916), directed by D. W. Griffith, is the largest, most elaborate set ever built for a U.S. movie. The towers were 165 feet high. The set serves as the main subject of this shot, filmed from the gondola of a balloon. Because *Intolerance* was a box office disaster, there was not enough money to tear down the set after filming, and for years its remains stood on the corner of Sunset and Hollywood Boulevards. *The Museum of Modern Art/Film Stills Archive*

FIGURE 1.5 **Limbo set**
An indistinct background, sometimes called a limbo or limbo set, sets off Gene Kelly and Cyd Charisse in one of the dance numbers from *Singin' in the Rain* (1952). With such a background, viewers have no choice but to give full attention to the two dancers. *Arthur Freed; Metro-Goldwyn-Mayer*

Besides limbo sets, two other main types of settings are used by filmmakers: realistic settings, as in that huge set for *Intolerance*, and nonrealistic settings, as in a scene from the musical *The Band Wagon* (1953, Figure 1.6).

Realistic settings are used in most movies to try to convince viewers that what they are seeing could exist—and thus to help viewers get caught up in the world and action of the film. In *Reversal of Fortune* (Figure 1.15a), for example, the sumptuous clothing, table and table settings, and room furnishings help convince the audience that the two main characters live in a world of wealth and privilege.

Sometimes settings are deliberately nonrealistic: they may be exaggerated or lack the right details to convince audiences that they closely represent the world they know. Nonrealistic settings may include unexpected colors. They may look misshapen or contain abstract shapes. Such settings may be enjoyed for their creativity or whimsy, as in *The Band Wagon*. They may be used to reveal the main character's state of mind, as in the classic German film *The Cabinet of Dr. Caligari* (1919, Figure 1.7). Nonrealistic settings also appear in many animated films, as in *Tim Burton's The Nightmare before Christmas* (1993, Figure 9.36 on p. 344), and in symbolic or allegorical stories, such as "Neighbours" (1952, Figure 9.37 on p. 345). In "Neighbours," a detailed, realistic setting would serve no purpose: the film focuses not on setting or the characters' relationship to it but on the symbolic significance of two neighbors' actions. Often filmmakers on a budget use nonrealistic sets because they may be cheaper and faster to construct than detailed realistic ones.

FIGURE 1.6 Nonrealistic set establishing a scene's location and mood
An imaginative, playful, childlike setting for "Triplets," a whimsical and satirical song and dance in *The Band Wagon* (1953). As in many musical numbers, the set is nonrealistic; the designers made no attempt to re-create a background that viewers would accept as true-to-life. None is needed. *Arthur Freed; Loew's Incorporated*

FIGURE 1.7 Nonrealistic sets reflecting a character's mental state
In the classic German film *The Cabinet of Dr. Caligari* (1919) viewers see a story told by an insane narrator, and the sets of his story are done in an expressionistic style complete with many irregular, unexpected shapes. In the scene represented here, as in many scenes in this film, part of the image was also blocked out, or masked. Frame enlargement. *Decla-Bioscop; The Museum of Modern Art/Circulating Film Library*

Functions of Settings

Above all, settings indicate place and time. When the action shifts to Cuba in *The Godfather Part II* (1974), we can see that the location has a warm, humid climate (a long shoreline, palm trees, men dressed in short-sleeve shirts and lightweight hats, most people dressed in white or light-colored clothes). From the variety of skin tones of the many people on the sidewalks and from the style of the uniforms of the police or military authorities, we can infer that the story has shifted to a country with a tropical climate, probably somewhere in the Caribbean. From the car Michael is riding in, a 1950s Chevrolet we see earlier in the movie, another 1950s car parked by the curb, and the ankle-length skirts on the women, many viewers can infer that it is the late 1950s or so. We scarcely need the sound track to reveal that the action shifts to Cuba.

In action movies set in nature or outer space, the filmmakers may dwell on the settings by using frequent shots of settings without people or with people seen only from a distance. They may use shots of the setting that do not advance the story or that last longer than necessary for **narrative** purposes. Such shots often stress the beauty, wonder, and vastness of nature (Plate 9 in Chapter 2). When a shot presents the subject with abundant space around it, the framing is called **loose framing** (Figure 1.8a). At the opposite

narrative: A series of unified consecutive events situated in one or more settings. A narrative may be fictional or factual or a blend of the two.

a)

b)

FIGURE 1.8 Loose framing and tight framing
Framing refers to how the subject is positioned within the frame. (a) In loose framing, the main subject of the shot has ample space and does not seem hemmed in by the edges of the frame and the background. Such is the case in this frame from the Chinese film *King of Masks* (1996). (b) In tight framing, there is little visible space around the main subject. As a consequence, the subject usually seems to be trapped or at least confined somewhat, as in this frame from *King of Masks*. Frame enlargements. *Wu Tianming; Goldwyn*

extreme, **tight framing** leaves little space around the subject. Such settings often convey a sense of confinement and stress (Figure 1.8b).

Settings are often used to help reveal what a character is like or to create or intensify moods. In the Iranian *Taste of Cherry* (1997), most of the film is given over to a middle-aged man, Badii, driving around Teheran and vicinity

FIGURE 1.9 Setting reflecting character
In *Frankenstein* (1931), Dr. Frankenstein's castle is made up of massive, roughly hewn stone blocks suggesting a fortress. The building's few small windows and relative absence of natural light reinforce the sense of Dr. Frankenstein's illegal and immoral deeds away from the light of the world. The steep, wet, and uneven stairs, which lead up to the laboratory, are dangerous and uninviting. The outer door is massive and contains a small, heavily barred window similar to the one seen here in the background. Frankenstein's workplace is a lot like a prison. The building is largely given over to its upstairs laboratory, with its opening to the sky and the lightning that vitalizes the corpse Dr. Frankenstein steals from a grave in the film's opening scene. Frankenstein's building contains nothing to beautify or soften the interiors: no plants, no artworks, no fabrics, just barren surfaces of stone blocks and the equipment Dr. Frankenstein needs in his obsessive work. With its shadows, odd angles in its corners and wooden beams, and irregularly shaped windows, the setting is strongly reminiscent of expressionism. The castle of *Frankenstein* is appropriate for a scientist who has twisted out of line in daring to play god and create life. *Carl Laemmle; Universal*

looking for someone to cover up his body if he commits suicide, which he intends to do. "Instead of talking about his suicidal feelings, Badii passes over and over through a hellish stretch of industrial debris, abandoned machinery, and brown, dry, or dying vegetation. The land itself looks ready to give up. It's an emblematic use of landscape . . . simultaneously a real landscape and a projection of Badii's mental state" (Erickson 53). Near the end of the Japanese film *Gate of Hell* (1953), the agitated setting mirrors the feelings of the samurai who intends to kill the husband of the woman with whom the samurai has become obsessed. The first, brief shot of the samurai's approach to the couple's house is of plants buffeted by wind. The next shot is of plants in the foreground blowing in a strong wind then the appearance of the samurai far in the background, waist high in vegetation. As he approaches the house (and camera), the wind agitates the plants that surround him. Toward the end of the shot he disappears off to the right of the **frame;** only the plants and the sky remain briefly in the background. In the next, very brief shot, a few plants blow in the wind. The message conveyed by the setting is that the samurai is like the wind: his agitated presence powerfully affects what is around him.

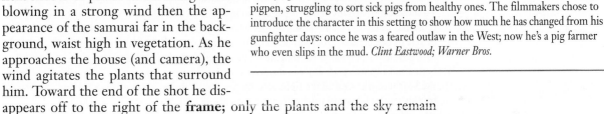

FIGURE 1.10 **Initial setting revealing character**
In *Unforgiven* (1992), viewers first see the Clint Eastwood character in a muddy pigpen, struggling to sort sick pigs from healthy ones. The filmmakers chose to introduce the character in this setting to show how much he has changed from his gunfighter days: once he was a feared outlaw in the West; now he's a pig farmer who even slips in the mud. *Clint Eastwood; Warner Bros.*

Where characters live or work, which objects surround them, and how they arrange those objects can also tell us much about the characters. The **expressionistic** castle of Dr. Frankenstein in *Frankenstein* (1931) seems entirely appropriate for its occupant (Figure 1.9) as does the setting in which viewers first see the main character in *Unforgiven* (1992, Figure 1.10). Settings can also be used throughout a film to mirror changes in situation and moods, as in *American Beauty* (1999, Figure 1.11 on the next page).

expressionism: A style of art, literature, drama, and film used to convey not external reality in a believable way but emotions in striking, stylized ways.

SUBJECTS

Like settings, subjects are crucial in understanding the expressiveness of mise en scène. In a fictional film, the subject is usually the film's characters. In a **documentary film,** real people are often a shot's main concern.

documentary film: A film whose representation of its subjects viewers are intended to accept primarily as factual.

a)   b)

FIGURE 1.11 Work and home settings revealing changing character
At the beginning of *American Beauty* (1999), the Kevin Spacey character, Lester Burnham, is a middle-aged man bored with his job and unengaged with his home life. He is cynical, lethargic, and unassuming. Appropriately, the film's settings reinforce the story and meanings. (a) The office of Lester's superior has desaturated colors, black objects, hard surfaces, contemporary furniture, and artificial light. There is lots of blank space on the wall opposite the boss's desk and evidently only one inconspicuous plant in the room. The only painting is abstract and in the same style as the office: simple, full of straight lines, and without vibrant colors. The desk is clear of clutter and family pictures. This man, who was hired to sniff out inefficiencies and suggest who should be laid off, has been in the position for only a month or so, and there is no sense that he has moved into his office. The setting suggests cold functionality, monotony, and sterility. There is more of the setting in the occupant than the occupant in the setting. (b) Behind the chair and unseen here is a remote-controlled toy vehicle that seemed to attack the feet of Lester's wife, suggesting Lester's rebellious return to childhood and its messy fun. Like his workplace, Lester's home is full of shades of gray or desaturated colors and perfectly kept expensive modern furniture. Here clutter has begun to appear in the previously immaculate room: Lester's bare feet on the coffee table, an open beer bottle, and a banana peel. Later in this scene, the wife is so concerned that Lester will spill beer on the $4,000 couch (seen on the right) that he gives up his attempting to seduce her and never again tries to approach her intimately. Frame enlargements. *Jinks/Cohen Production; DreamWorks*

Action and Appearance

We learn about people by observing their actions: dancing, marrying and divorcing, writing a novel. In movies, actions are usually the primary means of revealing characterization. Perhaps this is because films are superbly suited to single out actions, focus attention on them, and show them vividly and memorably. No one in *High Noon* (1952), for example, tells viewers that the town marshal lives by his principles and that his integrity and willpower are mightier than his fear. Those characteristics are shown by his direct actions, resolute movements, proud carriage, and worried face.

Often a character's cherished possessions suggest something about the owner. Cars are a favorite means of characterization: station wagons for family members, sports cars for independent singles, VWs for the unassuming, and Volvos for the cautious and middle-aged. As in the choice of actors, the choice of vehicle may surprise and amuse audiences because characters may drive vehicles audiences would not expect. An example is the Oldsmobile minivan that the John Travolta character, a Miami loan shark, drives and promotes in *Get Shorty* (1995).

We also learn about characters by their appearances, including physical characteristics, posture and gestures, clothing, makeup, and hairstyle. Charlie Chaplin's world-famous tramp outfit serves as an example (Figure 1.12). Clothing may serve many other functions. Costume may be used to contrast adversaries, as in the appearances of Obi-Wan Kenobi and Darth Vader (Figure 1.13), and even to hide a character's identity, as Darth Vader's costume illustrates. Sometimes contrasting clothing may be

FIGURE 1.12 Costume revealing character ▶
Charlie Chaplin in his now classic tramp outfit that he wore in many films, including here in *City Lights* (1931). At first glance, the character seems to be dressed as a gentleman: tie, hat, cane, jacket, vest, and carefully trimmed mustache. Closer inspection reveals, however, that the jacket is too tight, its sleeves too short, the trousers too loose. The cane is the flimsiest, cheapest one imaginable. His gloves are full of holes; his shoes are worn out and have holes. In some Chaplin films, including *City Lights*, the jacket elbows are patched or holey. He is not a wealthy gentleman though he tries to look like one. His is a constant but amusing battle to retain his sense of class and dignity. *Charles Chaplin; United Artists*

FIGURE 1.13 Contending costumes, contending characters
Opposing costumes reveal opposing characteristics in *Star Wars* (1977). The softness of Obi-Wan Kenobi's robe and hood (left) contrast with the heavier fabric and metallic helmet of Darth Vader. Obi-Wan Kenobi looks like a monk. Darth Vader looks militaristic, his helmet a blending of a helmet worn by German soldiers during World War II and one worn by warriors in the earlier Soviet film *Alexander Nevsky* (1938). Take away the light sabers and setting and one can almost imagine a monk confronting an armored knight. It looks as if Obi-Wan is poorly protected and at a disadvantage, but then the force is with him. *Gary Kurtz & George Lucas; Lucasfilm Ltd.*

FIGURE 1.14 Clothing setting off outsiders
In *My Cousin Vinny* (1992), an inexperienced New York lawyer and his flashy girlfriend come to small-town Alabama to defend some young men falsely accused of a crime. Throughout the film, the clothing of the New Yorkers contrasts amusingly with the usual wear of the locals. Here the two New Yorkers are seen in the Alabama courtroom, inappropriately attired for the occasion, so much so that the judge is offended and reprimands the lawyer. Frame enlargement. *Dale Launer & Paul Schiff; 20th Century–Fox*

used to mirror contrasting cultures, as in *My Cousin Vinny* (1992, Figure 1.14). Often a character's changing appearance reveals a change in situation and personality. In *Reversal of Fortune* (1990), for example, clothing mirrors Sunny's decline into misery and illness (Figure 1.15).

Appearance reveals character. It can also create character. As film scholar James Naremore explains:

Costumes serve as indicators of gender and social status, but they also shape bodies and behavior. . . . Who shall say how much the lumbering walk of Frankenstein's monster was created by Karloff and how much by a pair of weighted boots? We even have Chaplin's word that the Tramp grew out of the costume, not vice versa: "I had no idea of the character. But the moment I was dressed, the clothes and make-up made me feel the person he was." (88–89)

Appearance, including clothing, can be so expressive that a single image sometimes conveys the essence of a story. In *Star Wars* (1977), much of the story is conveyed by the contending forces, dressed radically differently and facing each other from opposing sides of the frame against a backdrop of high-tech danger (see Figure 1.13).

Characters and Acting

Characters are imaginary personages in a fictional story. They are often based in part on real people—as the main character in *Ed Wood* (1994) is based on the real movie director Ed Wood—or on a combination of traits from several people; but characters may be entirely imaginary, as are the characters in most action movies. In a fictional film, humans usually function as characters, but characters can be anything with some human features, such as a talking animal or visitors from outer space. Characters' actions and language—and sometimes their thoughts, dreams, and fantasies—are the main ways we viewers come to understand them and to get involved in the story. Depending on the needs of the story, characters may be round or flat. Round characters are complex, lifelike, multidimensional, sometimes surprising, and changeable. They tend to be the most important characters in a story. Flat characters are simple (stereotypical or minor), one-dimensional, and unchanging. They tend to play minor roles in a story, appearing in few scenes and rarely affecting the most significant actions. Narrative films tend to have only a few round characters because they have time to develop only a few characters in depth and most viewers find it confusing to keep track of more than a few major characters.

a)   b)

FIGURE 1.15 **Clothing reflecting changes in happiness and health**
(a) When Claus and Sunny first meet in *Reversal of Fortune* (1990), she is wearing a revealing dress that enhances her beauty and conveys her vitality. Frame enlargement. (b) After Sunny and her husband have lost their ardor for each other and her health is failing, she is miserable and never again wears revealing clothes or dresses in vibrant colors. No ruffles, no glamour, only plain, sexless, functional clothing. *Edward R. Pressman & Oliver Stone; Warner Bros.*

TYPES OF ACTORS

> Far from the movies not being an actor's medium, there's probably been no other artistic medium in this century whose appeal rests so strongly on the human presence, and in which the human image has occupied a place of such primacy and centrality. (Pechter 69)

In the earliest years of cinema, film acting was considered so disreputable that in the United States and elsewhere stage actors who appeared in movies would not let their names be publicized. How different is the situation today. Now American movie actors generally have more prestige, power, and wealth than anyone else involved in making a movie. The most popular actors can command many millions of dollars per movie. And by agreeing to do a particular film, a famous actor often ensures that it will be funded and made. Critics and film theorists have divided actors into various sometimes overlapping types, including stars, Method actors, character actors, and nonprofessional actors.

Some film industries—such as those of India, Brazil, France, and the United States—have film stars, famous performers who usually play a major if not the major role. Some American stars—such as Arnold Schwarzenegger and Sylvester Stallone—play a narrow range of characters but often generate widespread interest, command enormous salaries, and often guarantee a large box office, both in the United States and abroad. "Stardom seems more a state of being than a learned skill. . . . For a performer like Stallone . . . the ability to convey subtle shades of emotion, to enter personalities foreign to him, is essentially irrelevant. His skill is that of existing intensely on

a)

b)

FIGURE 1.16 Versatile acting

In *Tootsie* (1982) Dustin Hoffman plays a male actor who sometimes plays a female actor. Here Hoffman is seen as (a) Michael Dorsey, an actor, and (b) Dorothy Michaels, who is in fact Michael Dorsey made up like a "woman." With this film, Hoffman proved he was versatile enough to play two different yet related roles convincingly within the same film. Frame enlargements. *Sydney Pollack; Mirage; Columbia*

a)

b)

c)

FIGURE 1.17 One actor, one film, multiple roles

In *The Nutty Professor* (1996), Eddie Murphy plays (a) exercise guru Lance Perkins and all five members of the Klump family: (b) Papa Klump, (c) Ernie Klump, (d) Mama Klump, (e) Grandma Klump, and (f) Professor Sherman Klump. On the right in (f) is Rick Baker, a special effects makeup artist who won the first ever Academy Award for makeup for *An American Werewolf in*

screen, of communicating his uniqueness and inviting audiences to enjoy it and identify with it" (Kehr). With stardom comes prestige and power. A star's power may extend to the choice of the director and even to the script. Sometimes stars and their previous roles are so well known that scripts are written with them in mind or are rewritten to suit them better once they are signed up for a movie. Sometimes the stars' contracts give them the right to insist on script changes. Writer John Gregory Dunne details how Michelle Pfeiffer and Robert Redford—who both had script approval before and during the filming of *Up Close and Personal* (1996)—suggested or insisted on many changes in the script (132–75).

Dustin Hoffman (Figure 1.16), Robert De Niro, Tom Hanks, Marlon Brando, Al Pacino, Jack Nicholson, Peter Sellers, Alec Guinness, and others have been regarded as stars yet have played a wide range of roles, sometimes within the same film. In *Kind Hearts and Coronets* (1949), Alec Guinness plays eight brief roles, including a woman; and in *The Nutty Professor* (1996) and *The Nutty Professor II: The Klumps* (2000), Eddie Murphy (Figure 1.17) plays

d)

e)

f)

London (1981) and has also done work in *The Exorcist* (1973), *King Kong* (1976), *Star Wars* (1977), *Starman* (1984), *Gremlins 2: The New Batch* (1990), *Men in Black* (1997), *Mighty Joe Young* (1998), *Nutty Professor II: The Klumps* (2000), and *How the Grinch Stole Christmas* (2000). *Brian Grazer & Russell Simmons; Universal City Studios*

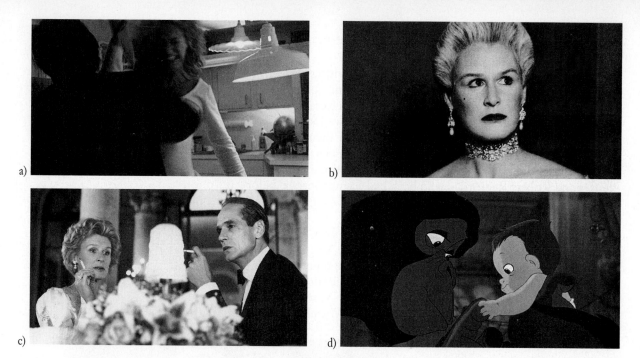

FIGURE 1.18 **The versatile Glenn Close**

(a) In *Fatal Attraction* (1987), Glenn Close plays a young woman who has a brief affair with a married man, becomes obsessed with him, and increasingly pursues him and disrupts his life. In the role, Close brings to life a huge range of emotions from seductive and sexy to calculating and vengeful to hateful and murderous. Here she is seen attacking her former lover with an intensity and credibility that might have alarmed even the actor seemingly under attack. Frame enlargement. (b) In *Dangerous Liaisons* (1988), Close plays an eighteenth-century aristocratic French woman who is calculating, manipulative, attractive, unscrupulous, and therefore very powerful. In the end, though, the one man she loves is killed in a duel. This photograph is of her very near the end of the film, ostracized by her society, which in her circumstances is arguably worse than death. (c) In *Reversal of Fortune* (1990), Close plays Sunny, an attractive, wealthy woman who marries Claus von Bülow. The film shows scenes from a variety of stages of her life: from young, vital unmarried woman to unhappy, unhealthy wife, listless, limping, and drug-dependent. Later still in her life, she is found in a coma, from which she never recovers. In all the many different stages of Sunny's life and in all the different moods, Close is completely credible. (d) In Disney's animated *Tarzan* (1999), Close plays the voice of a female ape who has recently lost her own baby then adopts the orphaned baby Tarzan even though her mate wants nothing to do with him. Close's role does not call for a wide range of emotion: mostly maternal feelings and the resultant concern, affection, love, and distress. Frame enlargement. (a) *Stanley R. Jaffe and Sherry Lansing; Paramount;* (b) *Lorimar Film Entertainment; NFH Limited Production; Warner Bros.;* (c) *Edward R. Pressman & Oliver Stone; Warner Bros.;* (d) *Bonnie Arnold and Christopher Chase; Walt Disney Pictures*

multiple roles, including all the members of the Klump family. Female stars—such as Vanessa Redgrave, Anjelica Huston, Jessica Lange, Meryl Streep, Maggie Smith, Faye Dunaway, and Glenn Close—have been no less versatile and accomplished though they rarely get a chance to play multiple roles in the same film (Figure 1.18). Versatile foreign stars include the French actor Gérard Depardieu and Gong Li of China (Figure 1.19).

FIGURE 1.19 **Chinese Star Gong Li in two diverse roles**
(a) Gong Li as an abused wife who takes a lover, has a son by him, then years later suffers misery from her own son in *Ju Dou* (1990) and (b) as an innocent university-educated young woman trapped into becoming the fourth concubine of a wealthy man in *Raise the Red Lantern* (1991). Gong Li has also played such diverse roles as a golden-hearted prostitute in *Farewell My Concubine* (1993) and, as Berenice Reynaud wrote, "an unglamorous, heavily pregnant, touchingly obstinate heroine" in *The Story of Qui Ju* (1992). She has also appeared in a comedy. (a) *Miramax*; (b) *Fu-Sheng Chiu; Orion*

Some actors (for stage and screen), such as Marlon Brando, Al Pacino, and Joanne Woodward, are **Method actors.** These performers were trained at the Actors Studio in New York, which was founded by Elia Kazan and two others in 1947 and later brought to prominence by Lee Strasberg. Before filming begins, the Method actor tries to figure out the character's biography and psychology and immerses herself or himself in the role (for example, by not sleeping enough if the actor needs to create an exhausted or distraught character). During filming, Method actors try to become the character and feel and act as the character would, in part by using people they know as models and by remembering situations from their own lives that evoke much the same emotion. Some Method actors, such as Robert De Niro, may also change their bodies drastically to look and feel the part (Figure 1.20).

Character actors specialize in more or less the same type of secondary roles. Recent examples of character actors are Lois Smith, Dan Hedaya, and Dennis Hopper. Hopper has often played antisocial or deranged characters (Figure 1.21). Actors such as Sydney Greenstreet, Peter Lorre, Harrison Ford, Gene Hackman, Morgan Freeman, and Kathy Bates began as character actors then with talent and luck became stars; but most character actors do not.

And then there are nonprofessional actors, people with no training or experience before the camera or theatrical audiences. Famed Soviet director Sergei Eisenstein preferred nonprofessional actors for ideological reasons: the

a)   b)

FIGURE 1.20 **Method acting**
In *Raging Bull* (1980) Robert De Niro as Jake La Motta in his fighting days and as Jake La Motta after his fighting days are over. To play the role of the aging prize fighter turned night club owner, Method actor De Niro put on more than fifty pounds. *Robert Chartoff & Irwin Winkler; United Artists*

Communist masses, not individuals, were the main subjects of his films; Eisenstein also believed that nonprofessional actors could best represent the types of working-class men and women and their oppressors, such as capitalists, Russian Orthodox priests, and tsarist military forces. With nonprofessional actors, directors do not have to worry about audiences being distracted by the actors' previous roles or their activities in their private lives. For reasons of novelty and greater authenticity, some filmmakers use at least some nonprofessional actors. Sometimes they have no choice. Films such as *Salt of the Earth* (1954) and many films made in countries with widespread poverty may use few or no trained film actors because none are available locally and the production lacks the money to bring them in. Sometimes nonprofessional actors are so awkward and self-conscious, as in the low-budget *Night of the Living Dead* (1968), that they are distracting, even unintentionally laughable, unless the film becomes a cult classic whose acting limitations have become

a)

b)

c)

d)

FIGURE 1.21 **A character actor**

(a) Dennis Hopper as a drug-dealing and drug-consuming hippie cyclist in *Easy Rider* (1969) (b) Hopper as a freelance photographer into drugs and his own mental world in *Apocalypse Now* (1979). (c) In *Blue Velvet* (1986), Hopper as a sadistic, deranged, gas-inhaling, kidnapping lowlife whose mood ranges all the way from angry to furious. (d) In *Waterworld* (1995) Dennis Hopper as the witty aquatic gang leader with a shaved head, pirate-like eye-patch, and codpiece. He is ironically called Deacon.

In addition to his roles illustrated here, Hopper has played the town drunk in *Hoosiers* (1986), a drug-crazed recluse in *River's Edge* (1987), a Vietnam marine veteran turned double-crossing hit man in *Red Rock West* (1994), a vengeful terrorist in *Speed* (1994), and in *Jesus' Son* (1999) a cameo as a rehab patient who had been shot in the mouth by an ex-wife. In all these and other roles he is so compelling that many viewers automatically expect his characters to be unstable, unreliable, menacing, and perhaps into drugs or alcohol. (a) *Peter Fonda; Raybert Productions; Columbia;* (b) *Francis Ford Coppola; Omni Zoetrope Studios, United Artists;* (c) *Fred Caruso; De Laurentiis Entertainment Group;* (d) *Kevin Costner; Universal*

FIGURE 1.22 **Hitchcock cameo** In *Strangers on a Train* (1951), as in other films he directed since 1926, early in the film Hitchcock makes a brief, silent appearance that has no impact on the story. Frame enlargement. *Alfred Hitchcock; Warner Bros. The Museum of Modern Art/Film Stills Archive*

part of the film's appeal. But some directors, such as Vittorio De Sica of Italy, are especially adroit at casting nonprofessional actors and eliciting effective performances.

A **cameo** is a small part usually limited to one scene and often unbilled. Though cameos are usually played by famous actors, they may also be played by famous people playing themselves or by insiders in the film community— a type of cinematic in-joke. Often cameos are little unexpected treats for viewers, who enjoy spotting the cameo. Perhaps the best-known cameos in cinema were done by film director Alfred Hitchcock, who put himself in *The Lodger* (1926) and every film he directed after it. As an actor who appears early in his films for only seconds and says nothing, Hitchcock contributed little to the movies he made. But his cameos are playful and enjoyable tests of viewers' powers of observation and a challenge to Hitchcock's inventiveness, since he did not want to make the same type of appearance twice (Figure 1.22).

CASTING

Once an actor becomes strongly associated with certain behavior outside the movies, for many viewers the actor in a film becomes more than the character. Sometimes those extra qualities supplement a role. Thus John Wayne, who was well known for his conservative political beliefs, was cast in many conservative and patriotic roles. Conversely, Jane Fonda, who was well known for her liberal political views, has often played liberal characters. To make a character even more unappealing than the script does, filmmakers sometimes choose an actor who is well known for playing offensive roles. In *Contempt* (*Le Mépris*, 1963) the part of the arrogant and pushy American film **producer** is played by Jack Palance, who was well known for his portrayal of unsavory characters in such earlier films as the western *Shane* (1953).

Filmmakers sometimes cast against type to catch viewers off guard. One of the best examples is the casting of Henry Fonda in a 1969 Italian ("spaghetti") western:

producer: A person in charge of the business and administrative aspects of making a film

a)

b)

c)

FIGURE 1.23 **Casting against type**
(a) Child killer: Henry Fonda in *Once Upon a Time in the West* (1968), a striking example of casting against type. (b) Earlier in his career Fonda played the low-key, trustworthy, and honorable Marshal Wyatt Earp in *My Darling Clementine* (1946) (c) In *12 Angry Men* (1957), Fonda played a dignified, intelligent, fair-minded jury member whose actions ensure that justice is served. Frame enlargement. (a) *Paramount; Rafran; San Marco. The Museum of Modern Art/Film Stills Archive*; (b) *Samuel G. Engel; 20th Century–Fox*; (c) *Henry Fonda & Reginald Rose; United Artists*

In Sergio Leone's *Once Upon a Time in the West* [1968], a homesteader and his two children are spreading a picnic in their front yard. This frontier idyll is shattered by the materialization of five menacing figures, who kill the family in cold blood. The sense of violation is exacerbated by the familiar, reassuring smile on the face of the leader of these merciless specters [Figure 1.23a]. It's the smile of young Abe Lincoln, Tom Joad, Wyatt Earp [Figure 1.23b], [a fair-minded juror (Figure 1.23c)], and Mister Roberts, a smile which for four decades in American movies has reflected the honesty, moral integrity, and egalitarian values synonymous with its owner—Henry Fonda.

By casting him as an almost abstract personification of evil . . . , Leone dramatically reversed the prevailing image of Fonda, at once complicating and commenting on our responses to that image. (Morris 220)

Casting against type is chancy. Some viewers want an actor to play the same type of role repeatedly and may reject the actor in the new role. But as

27

FIGURE 1.24 **Two stars cast against type**
Before *Mad Dog and Glory* (1992) Bill Murray (left) had played various amusing laid-back characters, and Robert De Niro had often played urban criminals. In *Mad Dog and Glory* they switch roles. Murray plays a Chicago hood who goes to a psychoanalyst and wants to be a stand-up comedian, but he also enslaves others and sanctions murders. De Niro plays a sensitive, mild-mannered police photographer ironically called "Mad Dog" by his coworkers. *Barbara De Fina & Martin Scorsese; Universal City Studios*

is illustrated by the casting of Fonda in *Once Upon a Time in the West*, casting against type can be effective. It can make viewers entertain new ideas: in this case, perhaps to be jolted into the realization that someone who looks virtuous and has a good reputation may in fact be evil. Casting against type may also intrigue viewers into checking out a film or video to see if the actors can succeed in the challenge they have undertaken (Figure 1.24).

In some animated films and some documentaries, actors use only their voices. In those cases, actors may also be cast against type. Usually, though, actors' voices are used as one might expect. In *Toy Story* (1995) and *Toy Story 2* (1999), Don Rickles, who is known for his insulting grouchiness, supplies the voice of the caustic, cynical Mr. Potato Head, and Wallace Shawn, who has played uncertain and insecure characters, supplies the voice of the unassertive (Tyrannosaurus) Rex. In *The Lion King* (1994) little Simba says to his malevolent uncle Scar, "You're so weird." In reply Scar, played by Jeremy Irons, says, "You have no idea." Scar's response echoes one of the most famous lines from one of Iron's earlier films, *Reversal of Fortune*. In *The Lion King*, Jeremy Iron's voice conjures forth the ironic, evil, duplicitous, weary characters he has played, whereas the deep, masculine, confident, commanding voice of James Earl Jones as the lion king evokes the mostly admirable characters from earlier in his career (Figure 1.25). In Ken Burns's nine-part documentary film *Baseball* (1994), offscreen Gregory Peck—who has played a variety of well-known movie heroes—reads letters or statements by admirable men, such as the 1919 Chicago White Sox manager, who was unaware that eight of his players were involved in throwing the World Series; elsewhere in the baseball documentary, Peck reads a passage from the Old

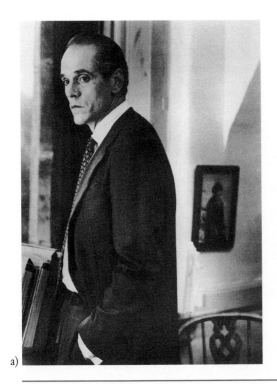

a)

b)

FIGURE 1.25 Earlier roles, earlier voices
(a) Jeremy Irons as Dr. Claus von Bülow, a man charged with trying to murder his wife in *Reversal of Fortune* (1990). Irons has had many roles but is perhaps most widely remembered for his role in *Reversal of Fortune* and as complex twin gynecologists in David Cronenberg's *Dead Ringers* (1988). (b) James Earl Jones as an African American U.S. senator who becomes president of the United States in *The Man* (1972). In plays, TV, and films, Jones has brought a seriousness and dignity to the many admirable characters he has played, including a professional prize fighter in *The Great White Hope* (1970), actor Paul Robeson, writer Alex Haley, a writer in *Field of Dreams* (1989), and a South African backwoods minister in *Cry, the Beloved Country* (1995). (a) *Edward R. Pressman & Oliver Stone; Warner Bros.*; (b) *Lee Rich; Lorimar Television; Paramount*

Testament. In contrast, mostly unrecognizable actors were chosen to read the statements of "Shoeless" Joe Jackson, who was involved in the 1919 scandal, and the parts of other men the film represents partially negatively, such as Ty Cobb.

PROCESS AND PERFORMANCE

A good part for an actor begins with an effective script and shrewd casting. Without a well-written part, usually an actor can achieve little. Often a successful screen performance also owes much to the casting. Many film directors, including Martin Scorsese and Robert Altman, say that if a movie is cast well, the acting will largely take care of itself. As Altman has said, "Once I get a film cast, 85% of my creative work is finished, and the actors really kind of take over. . . . I have to be there because they would all be fighting with each other if I weren't."

Unlike stage actors, movie actors in big productions do their scenes piecemeal, usually out of order, and with long waits between shots. Because filming is so time-consuming and costly, usually all the scenes at one setting are filmed together; then the crew moves to another setting and films all the scenes that take place there. Over many days, actors enact snippets here and

FIGURE 1.26 Understated comic acting
In *Mr. and Mrs. Bridge* (1990) with Joanne Woodward and Paul Newman, Newman's and Woodward's body languages and facial expressions subtly convey their doubts about the painting before them. *Ismail Merchant; Miramax*

snippets there. Unlike stage actors, film actors must be able to focus and deliver an appropriate performance after much waiting for the right weather, the right lighting, the right something or other. Often they have to maintain energy and focus through many **takes** (or versions) of the same shot.

Sometimes actors improvise during filming: they say spontaneously what they think their characters would say under the circumstances. Although many directors allow no improvisation, in some films directed by Robert Altman, Mike Leigh, Rainer Werner Fassbinder, and Martin Scorsese, improvisation plays a major role.[1] Those directors believe that what is improvised by an actor who is immersed in the character and the scene is likely to be truer to the character and situation than what has been imagined by the writer beforehand.

The actor's best allies are usually a skillful scriptwriter and a director who sets the contexts and establishes the moods for each scene. As is discussed in Chapter 3, the film actor can also be helped by an editor who se-

---

[1]Some critics would add John Cassavetes to this list of directors, but as Todd Berliner demonstrates, "John Cassavetes' dialogue comes so close to real speech that it often sounds peculiar, like ad-libbing. Many people think Cassavetes films are, in fact, ad-libbed, but they are not. . . . For all his later films, Cassavetes wrote complete scripts, and, although he and the actors changed the script in rehearsals, they rarely improvised on camera" (7).

lects the best take of each shot, shortens an ineffective shot, or **cuts** to a **re-action shot** during a lapse in the performance. Music can also cover weak moments in a performance. In films with many action scenes and frequent brief shots, the writer, director, and editor—not the actor—may be the main creators of a performance.

Usually an effective performance seduces viewers into believing in the character and helps keep them involved in the story. However, there is no one type of effective performance: what works depends on the film's **style** and to some extent on the viewers' culture. Droll, understated comedy—such as that found in *Mr. and Mrs. Bridge* (1990, Figure 1.26)—calls for re-strained acting. Many films, including many comic films, work best if the acting is exaggerated. Film acting should be judged not by one absolute standard but in light of the kind of film it is in.

Judging a performance is difficult after only one viewing. A second viewing, a comparison of a script and the performance, or a viewing of other films with the same actor can help viewers see the successes and failures of what is usually meant to be inconspicuous—the actor's art.

COMPOSITION: THE USES OF SPACE

Composition is the third and final major aspect of mise en scène. Composition refers to how lighting and subjects are arranged in relation to each other and to the sides of the frame. Before filming each shot, filmmakers may consider the following questions: What shape should the image be? When should empty space be used? Should the arrangement of subjects on the sides of the frame or in the foreground and background be used to convey a meaning or mood? Should the width and depth of the image be used expressively within the same shot? Should the objects of main interest within the frame balance each other or not? In this section we examine some of the consequences of answers to those and related questions.

Shape of Projected Image

The **aspect ratio** indicates the shape of an image, specifically the relationship of the image's width to its height. Thus an aspect ratio of 4:3 means that the image is wider than it is tall by a factor of four to three. Throughout film history the screen has nearly always been rectangular, but at different times the projected image has been relatively wider than at other times. From about 1910 to the early 1950s, most films were shown in the **standard aspect ratio:** approximately 4:3 or 1.33:1 (Figure 1.27a). Since the 1950s, wider formats have dominated in theatrical showings (Figure 1.27b–e). Figure 1.28 illustrates how **wide-screen films** can be made and later projected by using an **anamorphic lens,** which compresses the image onto the film during filming then expands the image back to its original width during projection.

cut: To sever or splice film while editing.

reaction shot: A shot, usually of a face, that shows someone or occasionally an animal reacting to an event.

style: The way subjects are presented in a text, such as a film. Styles for films or parts of films include farce, black comedy, fantasy, realism, abstract, magic realism, and parody.

wide-screen film: Any film with an aspect ratio noticeably greater than 1.33:1 (a shape wider than that of an analog TV screen).

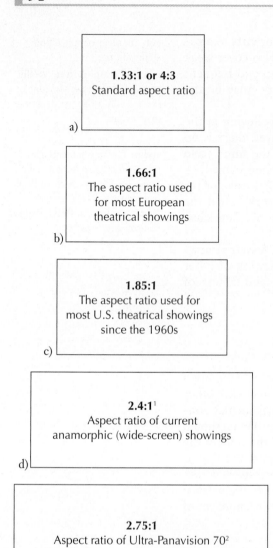

a)
1.33:1 or 4:3
Standard aspect ratio

b)
1.66:1
The aspect ratio used
for most European
theatrical showings

c)
1.85:1
The aspect ratio used for
most U.S. theatrical showings
since the 1960s

d)
2.4:1[1]
Aspect ratio of current
anamorphic (wide-screen) showings

e)
2.75:1
Aspect ratio of Ultra-Panavision 70[2]

FIGURE 1.27 Five frequently used aspect ratios
Movies have been shown in different rectangular shapes.
Here are five of the most often used ones. They are drawn
to scale; they are all the same height.

[1]Since about 1970, anamorphic showings of 35 mm films
should be at 2.4:1 and not, as is usually reported, 2.35:1.

[2]Anamorphic process used off and on in the 1950s and 1960s in
such films as *Ben-Hur* (1959), *It's a Mad Mad Mad Mad
World* (1963), and *The Greatest Story Ever Told* (1965).

As wide-screen formats became commonplace in the
1950s to counter the growing popularity of TV, some
skeptics claimed that the wider images would be suitable
only for wide subjects, such as snakes and funeral proces-
sions! But filmmakers learned how to use the wide space
effectively, as in *The Graduate* (1967) and in the Italian film
(The) Red Desert (1964). At various points in *(The) Red Desert*,
loose framing is used, and the characters are appropriately scattered across the wide frame at various distances
from one another and from the camera (Figure 1.29).

Although few filmmakers change the aspect ratio or
shape of the image during filming, they can do so. More
filmmakers did it in the silent era than since. A frame enlargement from *The Cabinet of Dr. Caligari* (see Figure
1.7) illustrates another way to change the shape of an image: parts of the image have been obscured by a process
called **masking** to create an **iris shot,** here a diamond-
shaped image. Other filmmakers change the shape of the
image by simply illuminating only part of what is being
filmed. As the frame enlargement from *Caligari* shows,
obscuring part of the image directs viewers' attention to
the visible subject.

Because films have been made in a variety of rectangular shapes and the TV screen is a fixed shape, in videotape versions of movies and in films broadcast on analog
TV, often the sides of the original image are lopped off
(Figure 1.28d). In extreme cases—films intended for theatrical presentation in a 2.75:1 aspect ratio, such as *Ben-
Hur* (1959, Figure 11.16c on p. 370) and *It's a Mad Mad
Mad Mad World* (1963, Figure 1.27e)—less than half of
the original image remains when the film is viewed in the
standard aspect ratio.

A **scanned print** is a version made in the standard aspect ratio from an original anamorphic film. In making a
scanned print, a technician—not the film's editor or director—decides which part of the complete anamorphic
image to show at each moment of the film or video. Often in scanned prints the camera seems to glide sideways
during a shot. To trained viewers, however, these horizontal movements are distracting, since they rarely occur
when and how camera movements do during filming.

For some years now, filmmakers have known that
their films will be shown in theaters and on television and
have composed their images so that no important details
are beyond the standard aspect ratio frame (Figure 1.30).

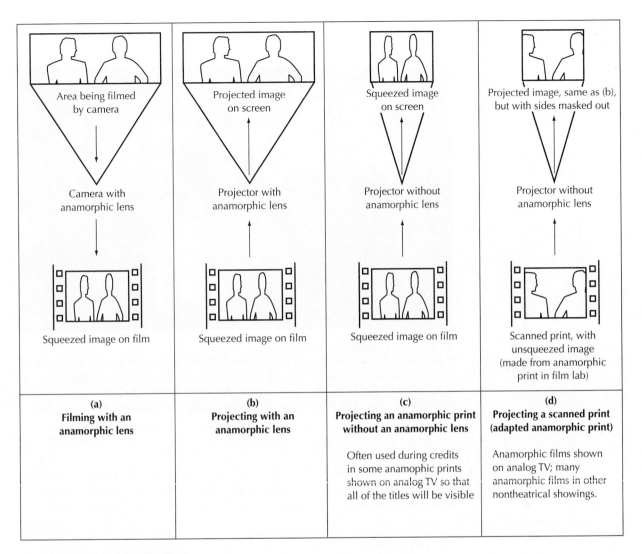

(a)	(b)	(c)	(d)
Area being filmed by camera	Projected image on screen	Squeezed image on screen	Projected image, same as (b), but with sides masked out
Camera with anamorphic lens	Projector with anamorphic lens	Projector without anamorphic lens	Projector without anamorphic lens
Squeezed image on film	Squeezed image on film	Squeezed image on film	Scanned print, with unsqueezed image (made from anamorphic print in film lab)
Filming with an anamorphic lens	**Projecting with an anamorphic lens**	**Projecting an anamorphic print without an anamorphic lens**	**Projecting a scanned print (adapted anamorphic print)**
		Often used during credits in some anamophic prints shown on analog TV so that all of the titles will be visible	Anamorphic films shown on analog TV; many anamorphic films in other nontheatrical showings.

FIGURE 1.28 **The anamorphic lens**
An anamorphic lens can be used to compress a wide filmed image onto the film in the camera.
Another anamorphic lens can be attached to a movie projector to unsqueeze the image during
projection. These images are not to scale.

Some videotapes include a message that the image has been "formatted
to fit your screen" or some similar message. But for a film originally released
in a wide-screen format (for example, a film in **CinemaScope** or any other
process with *scope* as part of its name), the full image will be visible only in a
videotape, laser disc, or DVD in the **letterbox format** (Figure 1.31). Some
videotapes of foreign-language films in the letterbox format include subtitles
in the darkened area under the images so that viewers can see the original
images in their entirety and read distinct subtitles.

CinemaScope: A wide-screen
process introduced in 1953 made
possible by filming and projecting with an anamorphic lens.

3 3

FIGURE 1.29 **Composition and meaning**
Composition can convey major meanings in a story. With the characters at different distances from the camera and spread across the image, this composition from *(The) Red Desert* (1964) reinforces the sense of the characters' alienation from each other, which is one of the film's main meanings. Frame enlargement. *Film Duemila; Cinematografica. The Museum of Modern Art/Film Stills Archive*

When considering the shape of an image on the screen, consider whether you are seeing the whole picture. If not, what you say about composition will probably not be true to the film as it was intended to be seen.

Empty Space

Empty space is often used to convey a sense of loss as in the Japanese film *Ugetsu* (*Monogatari*) (1953, Figure 1.32). Another film that uses empty space to suggest the feeling of loss is *Fargo* (1996), in which a husband arrives home and finds that his wife has been kidnapped, as he had arranged. The reality of what the husband has set in motion, however, is quickly and visually conveyed largely by empty space (things being badly out of order also contributes to the effect) (Figure 1.33).

Like everything else in a film, empty space has no inherent meaning: its impact depends on context. Empty space is not always used in a negative context. It often reinforces a sense of power and freedom, as in countless scenes of flying airplanes, or a sense of energy and free-spiritedness, as in enormous vistas in many a western and scenes of the open road (Figure 1.34).

1.33:1   1.85:1

FIGURE 1.30 Showing wide-screen films since the 1960s
Many theatrical films since the 1960s have been shot without an anamorphic lens with theaters
and analog television in mind and can be shown in 1.85:1 in theaters (inner rectangle) or 1.33:1
elsewhere (outer rectangle). As illustrated by this frame from *Schindler's List*, the visual information blocked out at the top and bottom of the wide-screen version is of no importance. Frame
enlargement. *Steven Spielberg, Gerald R. Molen, and Branko Lustig; Universal*

4

3   2.2:1   1.33:1

FIGURE 1.31 The letterbox format
The letterbox format is used to retain the original wide-screen aspect ratio (or a close approxima-
tion of it) when the film is shown on TV or a video monitor, as here in *2001: A Space Odyssey* (1968).
Letterbox images are more or less in the shape of a business envelope. Usually, the blacked-out
bottom and top parts of the image are the same size, though occasionally only the bottom part of
the screen is blacked out, which leaves more space for subtitles. Frame enlargement. *Stanley Kubrick;
Metro-Goldwyn-Mayer*

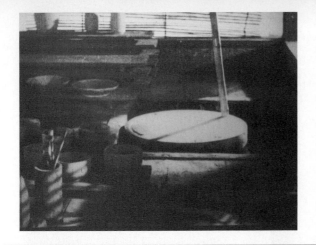

FIGURE 1.32 Empty space to convey a sense of loss
This frame from a shot late in *Ugetsu* (1953) parallels an earlier shot of the same composition with the potter's wife powering the wheel used to help make pottery. Coming late in the film, after the wife's murder in the civil war, this empty image suggests that the home is now drained of movement and life. Because of its composition and context in the film, the image here is poignant. A different camera angle or camera distance, a different framing, and the shot would not have been as effective. Frame enlargement. *Masaichi Nagata; Daiei Motion Pictures*

a)

b)

c)

d)

FIGURE 1.33 Empty space suggesting disruption of order
Four shots from three consecutive scenes in *Fargo* (1996) in which the husband returns home and discovers that his wife has been kidnapped. (a) In the first scene, as in an earlier happier scene, the husband enters through the front door. (b) and (c) In the second scene, taken from inside an upstairs bathroom in which one of the kidnappers had found the wife, we see no one, no life, no movement, just a mess, including an empty shower curtain rod seen from the husband's point of view. (d) In the third scene, downstairs again, viewers see the crumpled shower curtain then the TV that the wife had been watching when the two kidnappers broke into the house. Now the TV shows no picture—not because it would likely lack a signal at that time of day and not because one of the kidnappers somehow disrupted the signal input but because the empty screen contributes to the lifeless feeling of the scene: it's a dramatically appropriate detail. Frame enlargements. *Ethan Coen; PolyGram Film Productions*

If we see largely empty space in a shot, followed by something intruding abruptly, the results can be startling. For example, in *The Shining* (1980) we see a locked bathroom door, then an ax cutting through it, then the Jack Nicholson character, who is trying to get to his wife to murder her. Suddenly, he bursts into his wife's space—and the viewer's world (Figure 1.35).

FIGURE 1.34 Empty space to convey freedom
In *Wish You Were Here* (1987), the empty space and loose framing of this shot help convey a sense of freedom of movement and freedom from social convention. In a British town of the early 1950s— the place and time of the film's story—women were discouraged from displaying their bodies, but the young woman here defiantly does so. *Sarah Radclyffe; Zenith; Film Four; Atlantic Entertainment Group*

FIGURE 1.35 Violating space
In *The Shining* (1980), Jack Nicholson plays a crazed man intent on murdering his wife and child. As shown here, the Nicholson character's sudden breakthrough into the wife's and the viewer's space is startling and threatening. *Robert Fryer & Stanley Kubrick; Warner Bros.*

Mise en Scène or Editing?

For each scene, filmmakers decide how much to rely on mise en scène—settings, subjects, and composition—and how much to rely on edited shots, connected pieces of film each of which shows a fragment of action, time, and space.

In one scene in *Citizen Kane*, Charles Foster Kane, a wealthy newspaper publisher, and his wife, Emily, have gone to the residence of Kane's mistress, Susan, where they are met by Susan and a crooked politician (Gettys). During the scene Gettys tries to pressure Kane into withdrawing from the governor's race against him or face public exposure of Kane's affair with Susan. Early in the scene, one shot lasting 117 seconds contains the following compositions and major movements:

1. At the beginning of the shot, Kane is near the left of the frame facing Emily, who is on the right of the frame.

2. Susan joins Kane on the left (the camera pivots slightly to the left to accommodate her), and the three characters are positioned much as they are in the figure, although in the film Kane is closer to Susan than to Emily.

3. Kane turns away from the two women and starts to walk toward the background. As he walks, the camera pivots slightly to the right to follow him, excluding Susan from the frame, and Emily pivots and looks toward the background, where Kane joins Gettys. Emily is in the left foreground; the two men are in the background.

4. Gettys walks forward while staying on the right of the frame. Kane remains in the background, in the center of the frame between Emily on the left and Gettys on the right. For the rest of the shot Gettys and Emily remain in the foreground and on opposite sides of the frame.

5. Susan rushes into the frame from the left and joins Kane in the background, center.

6. Susan steps forward a few steps; Kane remains in the background.

7. Susan takes another step forward; Kane remains in the background.

8. Toward the end of the shot, Emily, Susan, and Gettys, all in the foreground, turn their heads and look toward Kane, who remains in the background (they await his response to Gettys's blackmail attempt).

Much is going on in this lengthy shot, both in groupings of characters (shifting alignments and confrontations) and in dramatic impact (who commands attention, who has power, who does not). For example, the shot begins with Kane between his wife and mistress, though closer to his mistress than his wife, and with the blackmailer out of the frame, in fact waiting in a dark part of the room. The shot ends with Kane in the center of the frame, facing his wife, mistress, and blackmailer in the foreground. By his own choice he is physically and emotionally alone. In spite of his wife's practical advice and his mistress's emotional appeals, he is determined that only he will make the decision he is about to announce.

Instead of using one shot and various movements and shifting compositions within it, director Orson Welles could have used a series of shots, edited after filming. With apologies to the memory of Orson Welles and to editor Robert Wise, here is one way the action could have been filmed as five shots:

Shot 1. Kane is near the left of the frame facing Emily, who is on the right of the frame. Susan joins Kane on the left (the camera pivots slightly to the left

to accommodate her), and the three characters are positioned much as they are in the figure, with Kane closer to Susan than to Emily. Kane turns away from the two women and starts to walk toward the background.

Shot 2. Kane arrives in the background where he joins Gettys. Emily is positioned on the left side of the frame in the foreground. After a while, Gettys begins walking toward Emily (and the camera).

Shot 3. Gettys joins Emily in the foreground, but on the opposite side of the frame. Kane can be seen in the background in the center of the frame.

Shot 4. Kane is seen in medium long shot as Susan rushes into the frame from the left and joins him. Later Susan begins to step forward.

Shot 5. As Susan finishes stepping forward, Emily can be seen in the left foreground and Gettys in the right foreground; Kane remains in the background. Susan takes another step forward. Toward the end of the shot, Emily, Susan, and Gettys turn their heads and look toward Kane, who remains in the background (they await his decision).

Many directors and editors would also include at least one reaction shot, a shot showing someone reacting to what is being said or done. The hypothetical edited version breaks up the continuity of space and time, gives less emphasis to the compositions, and in consequence gives somewhat more weight to the dialogue.

Mise en scène or editing? Anyone shooting and editing film or videotape faces the choice repeatedly.

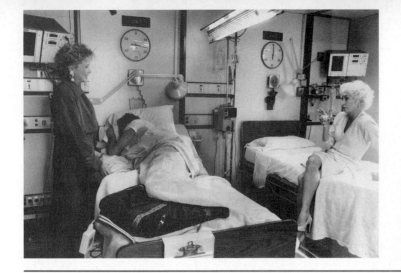

FIGURE 1.36 **Framing to display contending forces**
An often-used composition, illustrated by a shot from *The Grifters* (1990): two opposing forces on opposite sides of the frame, with the object of contention between them. *Robert A. Harris & Martin Scorsese; Cineplex Odeon Films Production; Miramax*

a)

b)

FIGURE 1.37 **Split screen serving different functions**
Until near the end of Abel Gance's *Napoléon* (1927), only the middle screen of three side-by-side screens is used. During the concluding approximately eighteen minutes, three projectors and all three screens are used. (a) Viewers sometimes see one vast subject spilling over into all three screens. Here Napoleon looks at his encamped troops. (b) At occasional points late in *Napoléon*, one image is projected on the center screen, and a different image is projected on the right and left screens. Sometimes the outer screens are mirror images of each other, as here. At other times, the outer screens are identical. Frame enlargements. *Images Film Archive. The Museum of Modern Art/Film Stills Archive*

Taking Sides

The width of the film image may also be used expressively. Films often show two people on opposite sides of the frame to suggest their alienation from each other. Late in *Raging Bull* (1980), the Jake La Motta character spots his brother Joey, from whom he has been estranged for years. Joey glances at Jake and walks away without a word. As Jake follows Joey, the camera moves parallel to them, and all the while we see Joey near the left edge of the frame and Jake near the right edge. The composition—the two on opposite sides of the frame, Joey keeping his back to his brother—conveys the emotional distance Joey wants to maintain. As in many films and staged plays, *The Grifters* (1990) often shows two opposing forces on opposite sides of the frame, with the subject of their conflict between them (Figure 1.36).

Occasionally filmmakers use split-screen **techniques** to show two or more images simultaneously on the same screen. *Napoléon* (1927) occasionally divides one standard aspect ratio screen image into three tall rectangles and early in the film divides the screen space into nine equal small rectangles, each one showing a different action. A split-screen effect may also be achieved by using separate films projected onto separate screens placed side by side, as in the ending of *Napoléon* (Figure 1.37). Often in *Napoléon*, multiple images allow the simultaneous viewing of events that are presumably happening at the same time.

A split screen may also contribute to a situation's suspense. In *Run Lola Run* (1998) the split screen shows time running out as Lola tries to reach her lover Manni before he foolishly tries to commit a holdup in broad daylight (Figure 1.38). In *The Grifters* the split screen emphasizes the characters' similarities (Figure 1.39).

The split-screen technique may be used for many different purposes within a film. The documentary *Woodstock* (1970) uses many variations of split screen—for example, to show action and simultaneous reactions; to show actions and someone commenting on them; to show different actions occurring simultaneously; and to show simultaneous views (different distances and angles) of the same subject, usually musical performers. In *Woodstock* the extensive use of two or three simultaneous images also suggests that although the film runs nearly four hours, the events were too widespread and significant to be conveyed by one mere image at a time, even wide-screen images.

technique: Any aspect of filmmaking, such as the choices of sets, lighting, sound effects, music, and editing.

FIGURE 1.38 Split screen intensifying suspense
In *Run Lola Run* (1998) Lola is trying desperately to reach her boyfriend Manni before he attempts to rob a grocery story when the clock's minute hand reaches 12. The split screen intensifies the tension of the situation as the two major characters briefly share the frame with a clock whose hand is quickly approaching a fateful moment. This example illustrates how split screen can be used as an alternative to editing—here, for example, instead of separate shots of Lola, Manni, and the clock. Frame enlargement. *Stefan Arndt; Sony Pictures Classic*

FIGURE 1.39 Split screen suggesting similarities and competition
Early in *The Grifters* (1990) the main characters, who are all grifters or con artists, appear on the same screen split vertically into three areas: mother, son, and son's lover. The three characters stop almost simultaneously, turn, and look around carefully before turning back and continuing with their work: the mother to enter a racetrack and cheat her mob boss out of some winnings, the son to enter a bar where he cons two men, and the son's lover to enter a jewelry store where she tries to con the jeweler. Filming the three characters in the same position (and having all three wear sunglasses) suggests that they have much in common. Here the young man is positioned between the two women, who will soon be in fierce competition for him. Frame enlargement. *Robert A. Harris & Martin Scorsese; Cineplex Odeon Films Production; Miramax*

FIGURE 1.40 Window and reflected looker
A window and carefully chosen camera angle and lighting are used in this shot from *Schindler's List* (1993) to show simultaneously Schindler looking at his factory workers and the workers he sees. If the filmmakers had instead used two shots to convey much the same information—a shot of Schindler looking and a shot of what he sees—they would have had to determine how much time to give to each shot, and the effect would have been much different. Frame enlargement. *Steven Spielberg, Gerald R. Molen, and Branko Lustig; Universal*

An effect similar to split screen can be achieved without using multiple separate images or editing by showing a reflection of someone looking through a window on one side of the frame and, on the other side, what that person is looking at (Figure 1.40).

Shots involving a window, a looker, and a subject looked at are also used in *The Godfather Part II* (1974) and *The Silence of the Lambs* (1991); in those films, however, the reflection is not of the looker but of what he or she sees (Figures 1.41 and 1.42). It's also possible to show the looker and what is looked at in basically the same position within the frame (Figure 1.43) and to show a camera lens within the projected image that reflects what someone looking through the camera can see (Figure 1.44).

In using a shot of a reflection off glass, filmmakers show simultaneously a person and what he or she looks at. They maintain continuity of action, time, and space rather than divide the information into a shot of the person looking and a shot of what is looked at. In other words, they choose to communicate the information by the composition of a single shot, not by the editing of two or more shots.

Foreground and Background

How filmmakers position people and objects in the background and how they situate them in the foreground are options that influence what the images communicate. The background of an action may go unnoticed because it is obscurely lit or out of focus or because subjects in the foreground draw so much of the viewers' attention. However, in some contexts, such as when a dangerous character is lurking nearby, a dark or out-of-focus background may command viewers' attention. Often the background is in focus, and details there affect

FIGURE 1.41 Window and reflected subject looked at
In this publicity still for *The Godfather Part II* (1974), viewers see the subject through the window and, elsewhere on the window, a reflection of what the subject sees. The filmmakers could have shown the boy followed by a point-of-view shot of what he sees. Instead they chose to present all the visual information in this one shot, which maintains continuity of action, space, and time. *Francis Ford Coppola; The Coppola Company, Paramount*

FIGURE 1.42 Window and reflected subject behind the looker
This publicity still for *The Silence of the Lambs* (1991) shows the character on the right looking and the character she is looking at reflected off a glass or plastic barrier separating them. *Edward Saxon & Kenneth Utt; Orion*

FIGURE 1.43 Reflection of looker superimposed on subject looked at
This photo from *My Darling Clementine* (1946) illustrates a reflection used to show the looker's face superimposed on what he sees. Doc Holliday, who is seriously ill and getting worse, drinks a shot of whiskey, looks at his medical certificate, says his own name scornfully ("Doctor John Holliday"), then throws the whiskey glass and breaks the glass protecting the certificate. Frame enlargement. *Samuel G. Engel; 20th Century–Fox*

FIGURE 1.44 **Looker and reflective surface revealing object looked at**
In *Chinatown* (1974) a detective takes photographs of a man and a young woman, and viewers see the detective at work and the object of his camera all within the same frame. As with the earlier examples of looker and object looked at within the same frame, this shot in *Chinatown* conveys much information quickly and economically and without editing: a shot of the detective then a shot of the man and young woman, or vice versa. Frame enlargement *Robert Evans; Long Road Productions, Paramount*

how viewers respond to something in the foreground, or details in the foreground may influence how viewers react to something in the background.

A filmmaker may use **rack focus**: changing the focus during a shot (usually rapidly) from foreground to background or vice versa. Rack focus directs viewers' attention to the relationship of foreground and background or to the action of a different subject. Often this shift in focus is done during a dramatic moment or while the primary subject of the shot is moving, or both, so that viewers do not notice the change in focus (Figure 1.45). In *Fatal Attraction* (1987), the Michael Douglas character, who is being stalked by a former lover, has driven into his driveway. For a few moments he listens to part of a taped message from his stalker. He gets out of the car and reaches across the driver's side to get his briefcase. Then, as he reaches in the car for a rabbit cage and the cage momentarily crosses the screen, rack focus is used quickly and unobtrusively, and the previously out-of-focus background is replaced with a focused image of the stalker's black car. Like the use of reflections on glass discussed in the previous section, rack focus maintains continuity of action, space, and time, and is an alternative to editing.

Foreground and background elements can show the importance of something in the background to the subject in the foreground, as in *The General* (1926, Figure 1.46). Another example of background subjects reveal-

a)   b)

FIGURE 1.45 **Rack focus**
In this shot from *Cruel Intentions* (1999) rack focus is used to shift the focus from the background subject to a foreground subject during the shot. As in many examples of rack focus, simultaneous camera movement helps disguise the change in focus within the shot. (a) Early in the shot, the man is in sharp focus in the background and the woman is in soft focus in the foreground. (b) As the camera pans toward the right, the camera operator shifts the focus from the background to the woman in the foreground. Frame enlargements. *Bruce Mellon; Columbia*

ing the values of a subject in the foreground is seen in *Do the Right Thing* (1989, Figure 1.47).

Sometimes viewers can see something significant in the background that a character in the foreground is unaware of. Such is the case in a scene in *Local Hero* (1983). The citizens of a small Scottish village have been meeting in a church but do not want the main character in the foreground to know about it. As the main character talks to his assistant in the foreground, viewers can see the villagers scampering out of the church in the distant background.

The foreground may comment on the background (Figures 1.48 and 1.49). Sometimes filmmakers film *through* a foreground object, but viewers are so interested in the main subject in the background that they may not notice the object in the foreground or consider how it relates to the subject in the background. For example, when filmmakers impose something with bars (a door, a window, a headboard) in the foreground, often the suggestion is of entrapment or imprisonment for the subject in the background. An example occurs in *Wish You Were Here* (1987). Lynda—an insecure teenage woman involved with Eric, a much older man—goes to live with Eric after her father learns of the affair. Eric calls her to his bed where he has stretched out. As she approaches the bed and sits on the edge of it, the camera moves so that it looks through the bars of the headboard at the two figures. The image suggests that being there with Eric is or will be a prison for Lynda.

Occasionally, both width and depth are used expressively within the same shot. In *The Bicycle Thief* (1948; also

FIGURE 1.46 Background conveying something about subject in foreground This photograph is Johnnie's gift to his sweetheart early in Buster Keaton's *The General* (1926). Overemphasizing the background at the expense of the human subject in the foreground effectively—and amusingly—demonstrates the extreme importance of the train to Johnnie. Frame enlargement. *Joseph M. Schenck; United Artists*

FIGURE 1.47 Expressiveness of background elements In *Do the Right Thing* (1989), part of a setting often seen in the background reveals the values of the Italian American owner of the pizzeria seen here in the foreground. Although his clientele is mostly African American, he hangs photos of only Italian Americans thus conveying a message of exclusiveness not inclusiveness. *Spike Lee & Monty Ross; Forty Acres And A Mule Filmworks; Universal*

FIGURE 1.48 Foreground affecting a shot's mood
Early in the last shot of *Annie Hall* (1977), the foreground contains empty tables and hard surfaces: no people, no plants, no soft textures. In the background, Alvy and Annie kiss good-bye for the last time, ending their relationship. The filmmakers could easily have filmed outside, with no objects between subjects and camera, but the mood of the shot is more effective—conveying a lonely or empty feeling—with Alvy and Annie's parting framed by a barren foreground. Frame enlargement. *Charles H. Joffe & Jack Rollins; United Artists*

FIGURE 1.49 Foreground, background, and in between
In this shot from *Pleasantville* (1998) a mother in the foreground holds a plate stacked high with breakfast food; more stacks of breakfast foods fill up the table in the background, and the relaxed father reads the paper a little behind the table. The composition quickly and amusingly suggests that the breakfasts seen in some 1950s TV shows were huge and completely natural to the characters of the time. Frame enlargement. *Jon Kilik, Gary Ross, & Steven Soderbergh; New Line Cinema*

new wave (cinema): A diverse group of French fictional films made in the late 1950s and early 1960s in reaction to the carefully scripted products of the French film industry and as explorations of more current subjects sometimes rendered with untraditional techniques.

known as *Bicycle Thieves*), when a boy is angry at his father, he is seen in the background and on the opposite side of the frame from the father (Figure 1.50).

Symmetrical and Asymmetrical Compositions

In symmetrical compositions with only one major subject, the subject is seen in the approximate center of the frame (Figure 1.51). In symmetrical compositions with two subjects, both may be in the center of the frame (Figure 1.52), although typically they are on the opposite sides of the frame, or both may be near the center (Figure 1.53). Even an extremely complicated composition may still be symmetrical (Figure 1.54).

In asymmetrical compositions, major subjects are not offset or balanced by other subjects elsewhere in the frame. An expressive asymmetrical composition occurs at the end of the French **new wave** film *Shoot the Piano Player* (1960). By the penultimate scene, Charlie, the main character, has lost the woman he loves. In the last shot of the film, Charlie is on the extreme left side of the wide-screen frame; on the right side is a plain wall. Charlie appears alone and out of balance—and he is. (This effect is lost if the film is not seen in its original wide-screen aspect ratio.) A film may use asymmetrical compositions more than only occasionally. *L'avventura* (1960) uses them repeatedly, including in the film's last shot, an image of the two main characters off to the left of the wide-screen frame (Figure 1.55). In *L'avventura*, typically the setting on one side of the frame offsets character(s) on the opposite side; this composition suggests the importance of the film's settings—which have little movement, vegetation, or life—and reinforces the sense that some human element is missing in the characters' lives.

FIGURE 1.50 Width and depth used expressively
After the father slaps his son in the Italian neorealist classic *The Bicycle Thief* (1948), the sulking boy keeps his physical and emotional distance. Their estrangement is suggested by the framing: they are on opposite sides of the frame and the boy is deep in the background. Frame enlargement. *Vittorio De Sica; PDS-ENIC*

FIGURE 1.51 Symmetrical composition with one subject
In a symmetrical composition from *The World of Apu* (1958), the single subject appears in the middle of the frame with nothing in focus around his head to draw the viewer's attention. Frame enlargement. *Satyajit Ray; Edward Harrison*

FIGURE 1.52 Symmetrical composition with one subject on top of another
This symmetrical composition from early in *Blowup* (1966) shows two subjects, one on top of the other, in the center of the frame, as a fashion photographer photographs a model. Frame enlargement. *Carlo Ponti; Metro-Goldwyn-Mayer*

FIGURE 1.53 Symmetrical composition with two subjects near each other
A symmetrical composition from *Personal Best* (1982) shows two subjects side by side near the center of the frame. They are close and in harmony. *Robert Towne; Warner Bros.*

FIGURE 1.54 Symmetrical composition with multiple subjects
In this image from *Cabaret* (1972) characters on the right balance characters on the left, and characters in the foreground are offset by characters in the background. The image, though filled with subjects, could scarcely be more symmetrical. *Cy Feuer; Allied Artists–ABC Pictures*

FIGURE 1.55 Asymmetrical composition
The director or *L'avventura* (*The Adventure*) (1960), Michelangelo Antonioni, often positioned human subjects on one side of the wide frame without corresponding human subjects on the opposite side of the frame. The resultant feeling is that things are out of balance. Frame enlargement. *Produzione Cinematografiche Europee and Société Cinématographique Lyre*

Occasionally tight framing is used until someone abruptly intrudes into the image. For example, a hand may quickly emerge from offscreen and grab a character, as often happens in eerie, frightening scenes (memorably in *Night of the Living Dead*). Sometimes this technique is used to frighten a character and viewers, but then both quickly realize that the intruder is not a threat. In *Fatal Attraction*, the Michael Douglas character is seen near an edge of the frame, listening to a menacing tape from his former lover; then his wife's hands quickly enter the frame to give his shoulders a massage. He and the viewers jump then are relieved, and perhaps viewers are a little amused.

MISE EN SCÈNE AND THE WORLD OUTSIDE THE FRAME

Sometimes filmmakers use settings, subjects, and composition to comment on the world outside the frame—for example, to express a political viewpoint or promote a product. Mise en scène can also be used amusingly to imitate human behavior outside the film, including another film, or to pay tribute to another film.

Filmmakers may use an image to express political ideas that relate to the story yet promote the filmmakers' political views (Figure 1.56).

Mise en scène can also be used to promote products or services. Moviemakers often make agreements with companies to display their products or services in exchange for money or, much more often, goods, services (such as air-

FIGURE 1.56 **Using mise en scène to promote a political viewpoint** In more than one shot of *Do the Right Thing* (1989), the graffiti in the background includes the slogan "Dump Koch." At the time of the film's making, Ed Koch was running for reelection as mayor of New York. The graffiti is credible in the story because many New York African Americans believed that Koch had failed to deal with racial strife effectively. The graffiti also allows director Spike Lee to express his own political views, at least indirectly. Before and during the making of *Do the Right Thing*, Lee openly opposed Koch's reelection. *Spike Lee & Monty Ross; Forty Acres And A Mule Filmworks; Universal*

line tickets or hotel accommodations), or promotion of the movie. Sometimes the products and services shown are cited in the film's end credits ("The Producers Wish to Thank Stanley Furniture, . . . Coca-Cola, . . . Black Death Vodka, Folgers Coffee, . . . American Tobacco"), but often they are not. So widespread has **product placement** become that some large companies pay specialists to arrange for placements in movies. An example of a film using mise en scène to promote products is *Wayne's World* (1992, Figure 1.57). In *Stand by Me*—released by Columbia Pictures in 1986 when Coca-Cola still owned controlling shares of Columbia—an early scene includes sixteen shots with an empty Coke bottle in the background. After a brief flashback to a different location, the scene resumes, and that Coke bottle can be seen in twenty-three more shots; in a few shots, the bottle on the left of the frame balances the human subject on the right. Movies may also plug a business. *Contact* (1997), released by Warner Bros., features Cable News

FIGURE 1.57 Egregious and deliberately amusing product placement
One scene in *Wayne's World* (1992) amusingly shows five name-brand products in a row, including Garth suddenly dressed in Reebok shoes, Reebok jogging suit, and a hat with "Reebok" emblazoned under the brim and above it. Here Wayne flaunts the Pizza Hut logo as he declares that he would never do a product placement. Frame enlargement. *Lorne Michaels; Paramount*

FIGURE 1.58 Using mise en scène to promote a product humorously
In *The Flintstones* (1994), various products are both adapted to prehistoric times in amusing ways yet promoted. For example, characters appear before a Liz Claybone store, a parody, or amusing imitation, of today's Liz Claiborne stores that sell women's clothing. Here, viewers see that sales are climbing at an early Roc Donald's. Frame enlargement. *Bruce Cohen; Universal City Studios and Amblin Entertainment*

Network (CNN) repeatedly. That's no accident. At the time *Contact* was being made, both Warner Bros. and CNN were owned by Time Warner. In multicorporate businesses, one branch often promotes another.

Product placements can be creative and amusing as in *The Flintstones* (1994, Figure 1.58). They may be subtle and go unnoticed by many viewers. The documentary film *The Big One* (1998) focuses on a book tour and many side trips that satirist and filmmaker Michael Moore takes in hopes of questioning CEOs about corporate downsizing and sending jobs abroad even though their companies have been making huge profits. Moore gives considerable screen time to his visits to bookstores to give talks and to the long lines of people waiting for him to sign their copies of his book. There's also a shot of his book as number one on the *New York Times* list of best sellers. The message: his book is important (and so is Michael Moore). One could argue that promoting his book and the messages it must contain indirectly supports the other main message of the film: the pain suffered by workers who are victims of corporate downsizing. But it could be argued that the emphasis on his book's popularity is also a self-promoting product placement. Regardless of Moore's motives, in *The Big One* Moore's book functions as a pervasive product placement.

Some filmmakers sometimes consciously conceal product identity to avoid possible lawsuits. If a movie shows someone committing a crime, filmmakers are usually careful not to associate the crime with a commercial product. That is why viewers will not see a character listen to a particular heavy metal number or drink a famous whiskey then go out and murder someone.

Mise en scène can also be used to parody someone or something. A **parody** is an amusing imitation of human behavior or of a **text** (such as a book or film), part of a text, or texts. For example, the mise en scène of a shot inside Han Solo's spaceship in *Star Wars* is amusingly re-created in many later parodies, such as the 1987 movie *Spaceballs* (Figure 6.14a and c on p. 212). Mise en scène can also be used to pay an **homage,** a tribute to an earlier text (such as a film) or part of one. For instance, some shots of the main character in the French new wave film *Breathless* (1959) re-create mannerisms that Humphrey Bogart used in his films (Figure 7.30a and b on p. 250).

text: Something that people produce or modify to communicate meaning.

SUMMARY

In this and other publications, the term *mise en scène*, which is originally a theatrical term, signifies the major aspects filmmaking shares with staging a play. It refers to the selection of setting, subjects, and composition of each shot. Normally, in complex film productions the director makes final decisions about mise en scène.

Settings

- A setting is the place where filmed action occurs. It is either a set, which has been built for use in the film, or a location, which is any place other than a film studio that is used for filming.

- A setting can be the main subject of a shot or scene. Depending on the needs of the scene, settings may be limbo (indistinct), realistic, or non-realistic.

- Settings often reveal the time and place of a scene, create or intensify moods, and help reveal what people (in a documentary film) or characters (in a fictional film) are like. Throughout a film, changes in the settings can also mirror changes in situations and moods.

Subjects

- In films, fictional characters or real people are the usual subjects, and their actions and appearances help reveal their nature.

- Performers may be stars, Method actors, character actors, or nonprofessional actors. There is some overlap among these categories: a star, for example, may also be a Method actor. Depending on the desired results, actors may be cast by type or against type.

- Usually film actors must perform their scenes out of order, in brief segments, and often after long waits.

- Effective performances may depend on the script, casting, direction, editing, and music. There is no one type of effective performance: what is judged effective depends in part on the viewers' culture and the film's style—its manner of presenting its subject.

Composition

- Filmmakers, especially cinematographers and directors, decide the shape of the overall image. They also decide how to use the space within an image: when and how to use empty space and what will be conveyed by the arrangement of significant objects on the sides of the frame, in the foreground, or in the background. Filmmakers also decide if compositions are to be symmetrical or asymmetrical.

- Composition influences what viewers see positioned in relationship to the subject and how the subject is situated within the frame; what information is revealed to viewers that the characters do not know; and what viewers learn about the characters' personalities or situations.

- Many films are seen in an aspect ratio (or shape) other than the one the filmmakers intended, and the compositions and the meanings and moods they help convey are thus altered, sometimes severely.

Mise en Scène and the World outside the Frame

- Mise en scène can be used to promote a political viewpoint or commercial product (the latter practice is called "product placement").

- Mise en scène can be used to parody human behavior or a text (such as a film). It can also be used to pay homage to an earlier text or part of one.

WORKS CITED

Altman, Robert, quoted in Scarlet Cheng, "It's All in the Acting." *Los Angeles Times* 8 April 1999. Originally (but no longer) accessible at <http://www.calendarlive.com/HOME/CALENDARLIVE/CALENDAR/t000031433.html>.

Berliner, Todd. "Hollywood Movie Dialogue and the 'Real Realism' of John Cassavetes." *Film Quarterly* 52.3 (Spring 1999): 2–16.

Dunne, John Gregory. *Monster: Living off the Big Screen.* New York: Random House, 1997.

Erickson, Steve. *"Taste of Cherry."* *Film Quarterly* 52.3 (Spring 1999): 52–54.

Kehr, Dave. "Big Stars in Little Movies." *New York Times on the Web.* 12 Sept. 1999. <http://www.nytimes.com/library/arts/091299ns-small-films.html>.

Morris, George. "Henry Fonda." *The National Society of Film Critics on the Movie Star.* Ed. Elisabeth Weis. New York: Penguin, 1981.

Naremore, James. *Acting in the Cinema.* Berkeley: U of California P, 1988.

Pechter, William S. "Cagney vs. Allen vs. Brooks: On the Indispensability of the Performer." *The National Society of Film Critics on the Movie Star.* Ed. Elisabeth Weis. New York: Penguin, 1981.

Reynaud, Berenice. "Gong Li and the Glamour of the Chinese Star." *Sight and Sound* Aug. 1993: 12–15.

FOR FURTHER READING

Affron, Charles, and Mirella Jona Affron. *Sets in Motion: Art Direction and Film Narrative.* New Brunswick, NJ: Rutgers UP, 1995. On the status of art direction in cinema and how set design can function in narrative films, with interpretations of many specific sets and films.

Bruzzi, Stella. *Undressing Cinema: Clothing and Identity in the Movies.* London: Routledge, 1997. Citing detailed examples from a variety of popular films, Bruzzi demonstrates how clothes are key elements in the construction of cinematic gender, identity, sexuality, and desire. The chapters are divided into three groups: dressing up, gender, and beyond gender.

By Design: Interviews with Film Production Designers. Ed. Vincent LoBrutto. Westport, CT: Praeger, 1992. Interviews with twenty film production designers; the book includes a glossary and a bibliography with many annotated entries.

Carringer, Robert L. *The Making of Citizen Kane.* Rev. and updated. Berkeley: U of California P, 1996. An in-depth examination that includes a chapter on the art director. Many black-and-white illustrations.

Dyer, Richard. *Stars.* 2nd ed. London: British Film Institute, 1998. Discusses stars in terms of social phenomenon, images, and signs and includes Dyer's detailed interpretations of such stars as Marlon Brando, Bette Davis, Jane Fonda, Marilyn Monroe, and John Wayne.

Garnett, Tay. *Directing: Learn from the Masters.* Lanham, MD: Scarecrow, 1996. Directors such as Scorsese, Spielberg, Malle, Fellini, and Truffaut discuss their decisions in making films.

Heisner, Beverly. *Production Design in the Contemporary American Film: A Critical Study of 23 Movies and Their Designers.* Jefferson, NC: McFarland, 1997. American films from the 1980s and 1990s are discussed under five headings: realistic films set in the present day, stylized films set in the present day, period films, period films that move through several decades, and science fiction and fantasy films.

Lumet, Sidney. *Making Movies.* New York: Knopf, 1995. On filmmaking by a famous American director. Chapter 6 is on art direction and clothes.

Making Visible the Invisible: An Anthology of Original Essays on Film Acting. Ed. Carole Zucker. Metuchen, NJ: Scarecrow, 1990. The essays in Part 1 deal "with film acting in a historical and generic context." The articles in Part 2 "concentrate on case studies of individual actors, or on a director's work with actors."

Michaels, Lloyd. *The Phantom of the Cinema: Character in Modern Film.* Albany: State U of New York P, 1998. Focuses on the representation of character in film and includes discussion of a variety of films with elusive and ambiguous main characters.

Miller, Mark Crispin. "Advertising: End of Story." *Seeing through Movies.* Ed. Mark Crispin Miller. New York: Pantheon, 1990. 186–246. A detailed discussion of product placement, sometimes called "product plugging."

Sennett, Robert S. *Setting the Scene: The Great Hollywood Art Directors.* New York: Abrams, 1994. Includes chapters on art direction in the silent film, the Hollywood musical, classic horror films, science fiction, and the western. Each chapter focuses on a few (usually famous) movies. Many photographs and sketches.

Tashiro, C. S. *Pretty Pictures: Production Design and the History Film.* Austin: U of Texas P, 1998. Shows how production design can support or contradict a film's story or exist in its own parallel realm of meaning.

Thomson, David. *A Biographical Dictionary of Film.* 3rd ed. New York: Knopf, 1994. Short essays on directors, producers, and especially actors.

CHAPTER 2

Cinematography

W HAT MOVIES DO IS MAKE PERCEPTION EASIER. The darkened theater cuts out the claims of peripheral vision. The large images on the screen open up the perceived world for analysis . . . and allow [viewers] to see details simply not available in ordinary experience. Because film makers can further assist perception by careful lighting, lens choice, and camera placement, and can guide expectations and discriminations in a thousand more subtle ways, they can radically enhance the efficiency of seeing. . . . And, in a sense, the film maker can make the viewer more intelligent perceptually, at least while the film is running. Movies use perception in ways that make being "perceptive" remarkably easy. That is one reason why they are so involving. (Eidsvik 21, 23)

In the previous chapter we saw how **setting,** subjects, and **composition**— all essential components of staged plays—can function in a film. In this closely related chapter, we explore some of the cinematic aspects of filming, such as some of the many ways the film stock, lighting, camera lenses, camera distances and angles, and camera movement affect the finished images. We take up these topics in a temporal order: the film stock that is put into the camera; some of the ways the camera itself may be manipulated during filming; and, after filming is completed, how the cinematography may be corrected or supplemented digitally. Cinematography strongly influences how viewers respond to the finished film: it helps convey the subject matter in expressive ways and powerfully shapes the viewers' emotional responses and the meanings viewers detect in films.

FILM STOCK

Film stock is unexposed and unprocessed motion-picture film. It is made up of two basic components (Figure 2.1). The clear, flexible base resembles the **leader** on microfilm—the clear or opaque piece of film that is threaded into a microfilm reader. On top of the base is a very thin gelatin coating called the **emulsion,** which contains millions of tiny light-sensitive **grains.** When

Terms in **boldface** are defined in the Illustrated Glossary beginning on page 539.

setting: The place where filmed action occurs. It is either a set, which has been built for use in a film, or a location, which is any place other than one built for use in a movie.

composition: The arrangement of settings and subjects (usually people and objects) within the frame.

grain: One of the many tiny light-sensitive particles embedded in gelatin that is attached to a clear, flexible film base (celluloid). After the film is exposed to light and developed, many grains make up a film's finished images.

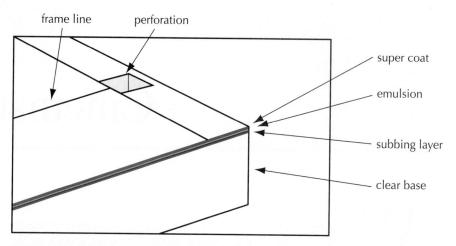

FIGURE 2.1 **Film's components (not to scale)**
A piece of film consists of a clear base, which constitutes most of the film's overall thickness, and the emulsion, which consists of a very thin layer of gelatin in which are suspended the tiny light-sensitive crystals that make up the image after exposure to light. The emulsion is attached to the base by a clear adhesive called the *subbing layer*. A super coat on top of the emulsion protects it against scratching. Most film also has an antihalation backing (not shown) to prevent light reflection back through the base that would cause a blurred effect (halation) around the bright part of an image, as with bright oncoming headlights. (Adapted from Malkiewicz 50.)

scene: A section of a narrative film that gives the impression of continuous action taking place in continuous time and space.

documentary film: A film whose representation of its subjects viewers are intended to accept primarily as factual.

footage: A length of exposed motion-picture film.

exposed to light then chemically developed, the emulsion is the part of the film that holds the image. It is also what has been scratched when you see continuous unwanted vertical lines in a projected movie.

The film stock influences the film's finished look, including its sharpness of detail, range of light and shadow, and quality of color. Cinematographers try to select film stocks that give the finished film an appropriate look. In preparing to film *Eve's Bayou* (1997), a family drama set in Louisiana in 1962, the cinematographer did extensive location scouting, shot hundreds of stills at various locations, and studied photographs of the period and place to be re-created in the movie. Later she chose different film stocks to achieve different effects. One stock was used for day interiors, one for day exteriors, one for night exteriors, and yet another for a character's "vision" **scene**s ("Newcomers . . ."). Many **documentary film**s combine older documentary **footage** with more recent footage shot on a different film stock. *Hearts of Darkness: A Filmmaker's Apocalypse* (1991), for example, combines footage shot during the making of *Apocalypse Now* with footage of interviews shot on a different film stock decades later. The different film stocks help viewers differentiate between the reactions of cast and crew then and their later recollections of the same events.

With the commercial viability of digital videotape in recent years, some cinematographers film parts of the movie on a particular film stock and shoot other parts using digital video, which is later transferred to film. Examples include Errol Morris's documentary *Fast, Cheap & Out of Control* (1997) and the German fictional film *Run Lola Run* (1998). For various reasons, including costs and ease of use, other filmmakers film entirely on digital tape, edit the material with computers, then transfer the results to film for theatrical showings.

Gauge

Film stocks are available in various **gauges** or widths (Figure 2.2). The most common width used for filming and projecting movies in commercial theaters is 35 millimeter (mm), though occasionally movies are filmed in 16 mm then blown up and copied onto 35 mm film. Increasingly, films such as *Time Code* (2000) are shot mostly or entirely on digital video and transferred to 35 mm for theatrical showings. Occasionally movies are shot on 65 mm stock and copied to 70 mm film for showings, though few movie theaters have the equipment to show 70 mm films. Generally, the wider the film gauge, the sharper the projected images (the laboratory work is also a determinant) because a wider gauge permits a larger frame, which requires less magnification to fill a screen. So a 35 mm print of a movie is less grainy than a 16 mm print of the same film (if both are seen on the same screen and projected from the same distance). Although both prints have the same density of particles or grain in the film emulsion, the area of the 35 mm frame is much greater than that of the 16 mm frame (Figure 2.2), and to fill up the screen the 16 mm film needs to be magnified much more than the 35 mm print. With the increased magnification comes increased graininess, just as when you hold a piece of processed film up to a light and look at it through a magnifying glass, you will see more of the grain than if you look at it with the naked eye.

Speed

The quality of an image also depends on the speed of the film stock, its sensitivity to light. **Slow film stock,** which often requires considerably more light than **fast film stock,** produces fine grain and a detailed, nuanced image. Often slow film stocks are used for musicals filmed on **sets** and for other films in which detailed images are important and the lighting can be carefully controlled during filming (Figure 2.3 on p. 59).

set: A constructed setting where action is filmed, it can be indoors or outdoors.

Fast film stock requires less light than slow film stocks. Often it is used in documentaries, especially when lighting options are limited, and in fictional films hoping to capture a documentary look (Figure 2.4). Fast film stock is also used in fictional film scenes with little available lighting, such as night scenes. In older films, fast film stock produces graininess. However, today's

FIGURE 2.2 Four film formats (actual size)

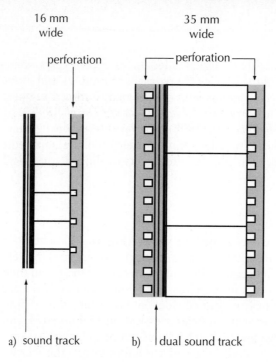

16 mm wide

35 mm wide

perforation

perforation

a) sound track

b) dual sound track

(a) 16 mm wide. Occasionally used by small commercial theaters, TV stations, industry, military, and schools and universities. Usually the aspect ratio of the projected image is 1.33:1. Other formats in 16 mm include anamorphic (squeezed) prints with an aspect ratio of 2.4:1 when projected with an anamorphic lens.

(b) 35 mm wide. Used in most commercial theaters, sometimes for major TV showings, and showings at some large universities. When projected, the screen image may have an aspect ratio of 1.33:1; 1.66:1 for many European theatrical showings; 1.85:1 for most U.S. nonanamorphic theatrical showings; or 2.4:1 for anamorphic showings. On films with digital sound, the digital information is located on the edges of the film or squeezed between the sprocket holes—or both. This placement can free up space for the individual frames and make possible somewhat improved image quality.

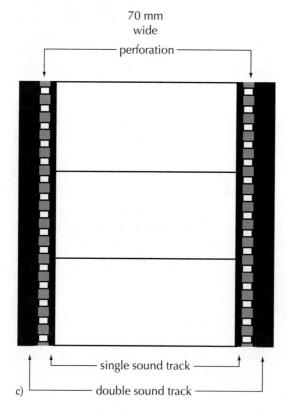

70 mm wide

perforation

c) single sound track
double sound track

(c) 70 mm wide, nonanamorphic (unsqueezed) image. Used only in selected large theaters. Aspect ratio: 2.2:1. In the United States and western Europe, films shown in 70 mm usually are shot on 35 mm and blown up or are filmed in 65 mm and printed on 70 mm stock. Here six sound tracks are included, depicted by the four dark stripes.

FIGURE 2.2 **(continued)**   70 mm
high

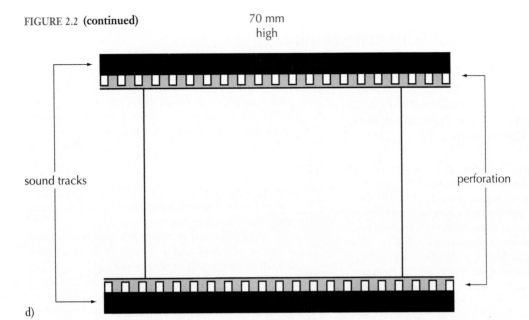

sound tracks   perforation

d)

(d) 15 perforation/70 mm format. Used by Imax. Filmed and projected by running the film horizontally through the camera and projector. The space for each frame is about ten times larger than the area of the 35 mm frame. The projector aspect ratio is 1.43:1.

FIGURE 2.3 **Fine-grain image**
This fine-grain photograph of Jennifer Lopez was taken when she was starring in *Selena* (1997). In moviemaking, fine-grain images may be achieved by the use of slow film stock and controlled lighting. Fine-grain images tend to be associated with controlled, perhaps studio, conditions, recent work, and professional quality. Such images may also help nurture the impression that a film was made on a set, not on location. *Moctesuma Esparza and Robert Katz; Warner Bros.*

Filmmakers Talk about Cinematography

The documentary film *Visions of Light* (1992) includes excerpts from interviews of many cinematographers and other filmmakers. All of the following quotations are from cinematographers, except for that of Robert Wise.

In the beginning all there was was a guy with a camera. There were no directors. . . . There was a guy and a camera, and he would shoot these subjects, and the subject may be twenty seconds long of a train coming at you, whatever it is. Then actors were brought in and because the cameramen were basically photographers and weren't that facile with performers, usually one of the performers directed the performers, so right in the very beginning you saw that there was the division of duties.　　　　—Stephen H. Burum

A great DP [director of photography] adds to the material that already exists and really works to understand the subject matter and the language of the director they're working with.　　　—Lisa Rinzler

I think visually. I think of how if you turned off the sound track, anybody would stick around and figure out what was going on.　　　　　—Conrad Hall

Notice the beautiful jobs that were done on [actress] Marlene Dietrich where . . . if you light a set at 100 foot candles, she would be at 110, 15 foot candles. She would have just a little bit more light on her than anybody else so she would pop out amongst the crowd.　　　　　　—William A. Fraker

By having the deep focus, he [cinematographer Gregg Toland] was able to give Orson [Welles] a lot more leeway on how he moved his actors and staged the scenes and freed him up. I think that was a tremendous contribution that Gregg gave to the film [*Citizen Kane*].
　　　　　　—Robert Wise

With [cinematographer John] Alton and the people in film noir they were not afraid of the dark, and in fact they were willing to sketch things just very very very slightly to see how you could use dark, not as negative space, but as the most important element in the scene.
　　　　　—Allen Daviau

You see some of the scenes [from *Touch of Evil*, 1958], and you realize how much hand-holding [camera work] was done in the film, but it's extremely seamless. That film in particular was an inspiration to all of us because it was a textbook of what you could do. It was shot on a small budget in a short time, mostly on locations, and . . . you had almost simultaneously the breakout in France of the new wave. You had Orson Welles doing a new wave film in a Hollywood studio. And I think it has continued to be an inspiration to a lot of filmmakers.　　　　—Allen Daviau

The films of the French new wave . . . captured a sense of life . . . by loosening up the camera and moving with it. . . . They would not think anything about picking up the camera and running with it. It had almost a documentary feel, and so that sort of quality about it would draw you into the film in the way that I think a more static camera would not.
　　　　　—Caleb Deschanel

The director is going to be the author of the performances of the film, the story of the film. The cinematographer is the author of the use of light in the film and how that contributes to the story.

　　　　　—Ernest Dickerson

Suddenly you're aware of the fact that things are not exactly as they seem. In other words, you create a representation of it, and lots of times that representation is more emotional than it is real.
　　　　　—Caleb Deschanel

60

FIGURE 2.4 **Rough grain or grainy image**
Grainy images may be achieved with older fast film stock or by other means and tend to be associated with amateur filmmaking, newsreels, old footage, and old documentary films. Sometimes,
as in parts of *Citizen Kane* and *Forrest Gump*, grainy images are deliberately created to support the
illusion of old footage. In *Pi* (1998), film stock that produces very high contrast and depending on
the light either washed-out, overly dark, or grainy images gives a documentary feeling to this film
about the lifestyle and work of an eccentric, brilliant loner mathematician. Note especially here
the grainy texture of the subject's right cheek, chin, and neck and on the door in the background.
Eric Watson; Artisan Entertainment

fast film stocks—and **fast lenses,** which transmit light efficiently—can produce remarkably detailed results even when shot with low levels of lighting.

Film processing can also affect graininess. Some filmmakers ask the laboratory to make the processed film grainier to create or enhance certain effects. This may be done, for example, to depict harsh living conditions.

Color

> It's funny how the colours of the real world only seem really real when you viddy
> [see] them on a [movie] screen.   —Narrator of *A Clockwork Orange*
> (1971 film)

As early as 1896, some films had color. Some black-and-white films were
hand-colored (each frame was painted with different colors using small
brushes, sometimes in assembly-line fashion). Other early films, including
many major **feature films** of the 1910s and 1920s, were **tinted:** whole scenes

feature film: A fictional film
that is at least sixty minutes
long.

sequence: A series of related consecutive scenes, perceived as a major unit of a narrative film.
flashback: A shot or a few shots, a brief scene, or (rarely) a sequence that interrupts a narrative to show earlier events.
negative: Unexposed film stock used to record negative images.

or groups of related scenes were dyed a color, and the same color was used for similar scenes or **sequences** throughout the film. Thus battle scenes might be tinted red and night scenes blue. Different tints could also indicate **flashbacks** or fantasies, as in the classic French film *Napoléon* (1927). By 1932, Technicolor combined three **negatives,** each sensitive to red, green, or blue, and in 1935, the first three-color Technicolor feature film was produced. Initially, color was used in ways that might surprise modern viewers: "In the 1930s and 1940s, . . . [Hollywood] decreed that colour should be reserved for certain genres that in themselves were not particularly realistic— stylized and spectacle genres (musicals, fantasy, epics)" (Hayward 70). But by the early 1950s, to counter the growing popularity of black-and-white television, more and more movies were made in color, and color was well on its way to becoming the usual way of showing celluloid lives.

Unfortunately, when you study film color, you cannot be certain you are seeing the shades and intensities that the filmmakers intended. Prints of color films, including those for theatrical release, may vary in quality because most are mass-produced. Eastman color films, especially those made for many years after 1949, usually turn reddish with age. Many color photographs available for study are not from the finished film and do not convey the film's colors very accurately.

There are also special considerations to be aware of when discussing the significance of color. Color may be used in so many ways that it is important not to overgeneralize. As with discussions of all cinematic **techniques,** discussion of color is most useful when it is considered in context, including where the color is used in the film and how the color is used in conjunction with other filmmaking techniques. It is also important to remember that color associations vary from culture to culture. For example, in pre-Communist China, yellow is often associated with the emperor, and saffron (orange-yellow) with Buddhist robes.

Saturated color, which is intense and vivid, has been used in countless contexts, such as to render the heat and tension of a setting, to show powerful emotions, and to represent violent actions. Saturated color may be used throughout an image as in *Princess Mononoke* (1997, Plate 1), or it may be employed in only part of the image to draw attention to one part of it, as in *La vie est belle* (1987, Plate 2). (The color plates follow p. 72.)

Desaturated color is muted, dull, and pale. Filmmakers may use it to suggest a lack of energy or the draining of life, as throughout Werner Herzog's *Nosferatu, the Vampyre* (1979) and in the late scenes of *Terms of Endearment* (1983), where the Debra Winger character is losing her bout with cancer. Desaturated color is used throughout nearly all of Antonioni's *(The) Red Desert* (1964), which focuses on an emotionally tormented woman's struggle to find some connection, comfort, and reassurance in most of the film's major settings: a run-down shack on a pier, plain contemporary interiors void of plant life, and life-suffocating industrial exteriors rendered in muted colors and grays (some parts of exteriors were painted gray). The desaturated color

technique: Any aspect of filmmaking, such as the choice of sets, lighting, sound effects, music, and editing.

in the Robert Altman western *McCabe and Mrs. Miller* (1971) has two purposes: Altman wanted the film to have the look of old, faded color photographs, and the desaturated color is appropriate to the story, which is set in a damp, cold environment and ends in death for one of the two main characters. Desaturated color may establish and reinforce certain moods throughout a film, as in Tim Burton's *Sleepy Hollow* (1999, Plate 3). Other films use desaturated color in only one of its **plotlines.** Much of *The Thirteenth Floor* (1999) is set in the present, but the scenes set in the 1937 Los Angeles region have muted colors (Plate 4).

A color image may display a limited spectrum of color, as throughout *Sleepy Hollow*, where nearly everything is a dull green, brown, black, or a shade of gray (Plate 5). Conversely and more typically, a wide range of color is used in a film (Plate 6).

Filmmakers may return repeatedly to a particular color or two throughout a film. *American Beauty* (1999) relies heavily on shades of gray—for example, in the main family's clothing, home interiors, and vehicles—and reds, including all the many red roses in the front yard and in the main character's fantasies about a teenage girl (Plates 7 and 8).

Colors are sometimes classified as "warm" or "cool." In most Western societies, warm colors (reds, oranges, and yellows) tend to be thought of as hot, dangerous, lively, and assertive and tend to stand forward in paintings and photographs. People trying to be sexy or feeling sexy may drive red sports cars, and women in Western cultures who want to emphasize their sex appeal (or sexual availability) have long been known to use red to draw attention to themselves. In Western cultures, the association of red with sexuality is at least as old as the "scarlet women" of the Bible. Warm colors may be used in countless other contexts—for example, to draw attention to nature's beauty (Plate 9).

Colors on the other side of the spectrum (greens, blues, and violets) are often characterized as "cool." In Europe and the United States, these colors tend to be associated with safety, reason, control, relaxation, and sometimes sadness or melancholy. Green traffic lights and blue or green hospital interiors are supposed to calm and reassure. In *Reversal of Fortune* (1990), blue light is used in all the scenes with Sunny von Bülow in a coma. The room, her bedding, and her skin are all bluish. In those scenes, the blue suggests cold and lack of vitality, the opposite of a lively, passionate red. In the scenes in which windows are open and it's zero degrees outside, and in a night scene in the von Bülows' bedroom after they have argued and turned out the light, blue adds to the sense of coldness. Blue is used in many other ways in our lives. In the United States, for example, dark blue has long been worn with business suits, perhaps to downplay the clothing and body and to suggest restrained emotions. Cool colors can also emphasize the desolation and malevolence of a damaged environment, as in the brief views of the lifeless earth in *The Matrix* (1998, Plate 10).

Films may use mostly cool colors in the early scenes and increasingly use warm colors as the film progresses. Conversely, films such as *The Iron Giant* (1999, Plates 11 and 12) initially use mainly warm colors then use cool colors.

plotline: A narrative or series of related events usually involving only a few characters or people and capable of functioning on its own as a story. Short films tend to have one plotline, but many feature films combine two or more.

In Western cultures, white—which is not, strictly speaking, a color—is often associated with innocence and purity, as in white wedding dresses. White may also imply lack of emotion or subdued emotions, as in men's white dress shirts and the white interiors and clothing used extensively in George Lucas's first feature film, *THX 1138*, which is set in a repressive futuristic society (1971, Plate 13).

Black, which is strictly speaking also not a color, is often associated with death or evil, as in black hats on countless cowboy gunslingers; the black charioteer costume and black horses of the Roman tribune in *Ben-Hur* (1959); the black bra Janet Leigh has changed into when she decides to steal $40,000 in *Psycho* (1960); black capes on all those movie Draculas; Darth Vader's helmet, face piece, and clothing; and the darkness enveloping characters in danger, as in *The Blair Witch Project* (1999, Plate 14). Black is used in many situations, so it is important not to overgeneralize. For example, in Europe, the United States, Latin America, and Japan—though not in China—black is the preferred color for mourning. In some formal contexts, black clothing can seem stately and elegant, at least to those raised in Western societies.

From the early days of cinema, filmmakers have occasionally combined color shots and black-and-white shots in the same film. The most famous example is *The Wizard of Oz* (1939), which renders Dorothy's ordinary life in Kansas in black and white and her adventures in Oz in color. *Schindler's List* reverses the situation: the opening and closing are in color and are set in the present, whereas, with the exception of a red coat on a little girl, the body of the film is in black and white and is set in the past. Alternating between color and black and white throughout a film may draw attention to the practice. Such alterations are used in the documentary *Madonna Truth or Dare* (1991), where most of the concert footage is in color and the off-stage action in black and white; in *JFK* (1991), where most of the flashbacks are in black and white; and in *The Hurricane* (1999), where black and white is used for past boxing matches (Figure 6.3 on p. 189) and other background events, such as demonstrations in the boxer's behalf. With the increased sophistication of computer programs, filmmakers can now render parts of an image in color and other parts in black and white. In *Pleasantville* (1998) two teens from the 1990s are trapped in a black-and-white 1950s television series. As the two teens introduce the complexities of the 1990s world into the stereotypical, idealized, black-and-white vision of small-town life, gradually the **mise en scène** gains in color (Plates 15 and 16).

As in many aspects of filmmaking, filmmakers often use colors intuitively, simply because they seem right. As cinematographer Allen Daviau has said of cinematographers in general, "We do some things that we don't even realize we're doing until we see the film put together. And we did them out of instinct." And as in other aspects of moviemaking, colors in films are often more true-to-movies than true-to-life. Many viewers know, for example, that real blood in movies wouldn't look real enough (or exciting enough?), so various substitutes have been used in filming.

mise en scène ("meez ahn sen," with a nasalized second syllable): An image's setting, subject (usually people or characters), and composition (the arrangement of setting and subjects within the frame).

LIGHTING

Light [is] the paintbrush of the cinematographer. (Turner 96)

Filmmakers often spend an enormous amount of time and money lighting their subjects. They do so because lighting can convey meaning and mood in subtle yet significant ways. The importance of lighting is evident in our lives: on sunny days, people are more likely to be cheerful; on cloudy days, people tend to feel subdued. Studies show that some people in northern climates are subject to severe depression in winter if they receive too little light. The importance of lighting in filming is suggested by the word *photography*, which literally means "writing with light."

Hard light tends to show people in unflattering ways—for example, by creating shadows in the eye sockets—so it may reveal characters or people as plain or even unattractive (Figure 2.5). Two excellent sources of hard light are a focused spotlight and bright (midday) sunlight, when the sun functions as an intense spotlight.

Soft light reflects off at least one object before it illuminates the subject. An excellent (and free) source of soft lighting is available during the so-called magic hour of each day. According to cinematographer Nestor Almendros, the best of the magic hour light is available for only twenty to twenty-five minutes after sunset (in the middle latitudes, with fewer minutes near the equator and more minutes near earth's poles). Sunlight at dawn is an equally useful source of soft light. Before dawn and briefly after sunset, the sky itself becomes a broad source of soft light. Soft lighting tends to have the opposite effects of hard lighting. It fills facial wrinkles and makes people look younger; it makes young people look even more attractive (Figure 2.6). Typically, cinematographers use soft light to present subjects in an appealing way, as in romantic films, or to make actors look their most youthful or most attractive, as in many Hollywood studio films of the 1930s and 1940s.

FIGURE 2.5 Hard lighting
The subject is illuminated by one direct, bright (spot) light. Hard light produces bright illumination; reveals many details, including imperfections in the subject; and creates shadows with sharp edges. *Model: Kimberlee Stewart; photographer: Jon Michael Terry*

FIGURE 2.6 Soft lighting
Soft light produces the appearance of smoother surfaces than hard light does by softening borders between light and shadow. If there are shadows, they will be faint. *Model: Kimberlee Stewart; photographer: Jon Michael Terry*

FIGURE 2.7 Backlighting
The model was illuminated by one light from behind. Often backlighting makes the subject seem threatening because viewers cannot interpret the subject's mood or perhaps discern the subject's identity. *Model: Kimberlee Stewart; photographer: Jon Michael Terry*

FIGURE 2.8 Top lighting
The model was illuminated by a single light from above. Top lighting used by itself is not flattering. Here the hair looks lighter than it is; a slight imperfection on the model's right cheek is visible; and she has shadows under her eyes. *Model: Kimberlee Stewart; photographer: Jon Michael Terry*

FIGURE 2.9 Bottom lighting
The model was illuminated by a single light from below. Like top lighting, bottom lighting is unflattering to the skin. Often bottom lighting also adds a touch of menace; it is often used to enhance a frightening mood, as in many horror films. *Model: Kimberlee Stewart; photographer: Jon Michael Terry*

Direction and Intensity of Light

The direction of light on a subject is another expressive option for filmmakers. Some ways to light a subject by using sources from different directions are illustrated in Figures 2.7 to 2.12. In all these examples, the model is the same and so is her makeup. The camera distance, lens, and angle are unchanged. But notice what different images a change in the direction of the lighting produces, what different moods and meanings. (You can usually detect the directions and intensities of the light sources by looking at the subject's eyes. **Catchlight,** a reflection of the light sources, is visible for all bright light that reaches the eyes.)

For filming on a set, often at least three lights are used for each major subject: the **key light,** or main light; **fill light,** a soft light used to fill in unlit areas of the subject; and a **backlight** (Figure 2.13). For filming, the key light is usually the first light set, or it may be handheld and moved around during a shot to keep the main subject illuminated appropriately. A key light and a fill light ensure adequate and fairly even illumination with few or no shadows on the subject. The backlight, often from above or below the subject, high-

FIGURE 2.10 Side lighting
Here the model is lit by one light from the side. Side lighting creates many shadows on the face, including prominent shadows under the eyes. It may be used to suggest someone with a divided personality or someone feeling contradictory emotions. *Model: Kimberlee Stewart; photographer: Jon Michael Terry*

FIGURE 2.11 Main, frontal lighting
The model was lit by a single light in front of her and a little to the right of the camera. This lighting presents the subject in an attractive way, though not quite as much so as main or key and fill lighting together. *Model: Kimberlee Stewart; photographer: Jon Michael Terry*

FIGURE 2.12 Key light and fill light
A combination of key light and fill light presents the subject's skin in the most appealing way. Here the slight imperfection on the model's cheek is less noticeable, and the right side of her face appears to be a little smoother than in the photo made with only main, frontal lighting (Figure 2.11). *Model: Kimberlee Stewart; photographer: Jon Michael Terry*

FIGURE 2.13 Three-point lighting
From the catchlight in Joel Grey's eyes in this publicity still for *Cabaret* (1972), we can see that the key light is to the right of the camera; a small fill light comes from slightly to the left and a little lower than the key light. Soft backlight is reflected off the back wall, but there is enough of it to highlight Grey's left shoulder a little and to set him off from the neutral background. *Cy Feuer; Allied Artists–ABC Pictures*

FIGURE 2.14 Low-key lighting
A shot with low-key lighting is mainly dark, often with areas of deep dark tones. By using little or no frontal fill lighting, the filmmakers can immerse parts of the image in shadows, as is seen here in this frame from *Touch of Evil* (1958) of the film's complex main character played by Orson Welles. Low-key lighting often adds a dramatic or mysterious effect, as in many detective and crime films and in many horror films. Frame enlargement. *Albert Zugsmith; Universal*

lights at least some of its edges, such as the hair or shoulders, and helps set the subject off from the background to give a sense of depth. Lighting the main subjects and parts of a set is complicated and often requires more than three light sources.

One of the most fundamental decisions filmmakers make is how much light to shine on the objects within the frame. **Low-key lighting,** in which the subject is lit by very low levels of illumination and much of the image is bathed in darkness, may be the choice if the filmmakers want to create a dramatic or mysterious effect (Figure 2.14). At the opposite extreme, with **high-key lighting** the main subject is flooded with light, and nearly all parts of the frame are illuminated (Figure 2.15b).

It's not unusual to light different characters differently within the same scene, as director Leni Riefenstahl did: "I always made sure the men, actors or not, were lit differently from the women. They were lit from the side so their features stood out. . . .

a)

b)

FIGURE 2.15 A star lit two ways: soft lighting and hard high-key lighting
(a) Soft lighting softens lines around the eyes and enhances Robert Redford's looks in *Butch Cassidy and the Sundance Kid* (1969). (b) The bright, hard lighting often used on Redford in *All the President's Men* (1976) does not soften facial lines and enhance his looks. In this movie he plays an investigative reporter, and lighting that glamorizes him would be inappropriate. Frame enlargement. (a) *John Foreman; 20th Century–Fox*; (b) *Wildwood Enterprises; Warner Bros.*

With a young woman, who must look beautiful, you need a very soft light from the front. No side-lighting at all, so no facial lines or flaws are visible."

Lighting can support the type of character an actor plays. As film scholar Richard Dyer points out, in *Butch Cassidy and the Sundance Kid* (1969) the lighting tends to glamorize the tongue-in-cheek, romantic character played by Robert Redford (Figure 2.15a). Conversely, in *All the President's Men* (1976) Redford plays a no-nonsense investigative reporter and is often lit by hard, bright lighting that does not conceal skin imperfections (Figure 2.15b).

Shadows

Figure 2.16 illustrates how light and shadows can emphasize and deemphasize parts of an image and thereby create moods and meanings. Light and shadows are also used to draw attention to part of an image in a scene late in *Schindler's List*. Oskar Schindler has arrived at the Auschwitz concentration camp to try to save a large group of Jewish women from extermination. For

a)

b)

FIGURE 2.16 **Expressive use of shadows**
(a) In *Citizen Kane* (1941), Charles Foster Kane signs his "Declaration of Principles" for a newspaper he has recently taken over as Jed Leland (left) and Mr. Bernstein (right) look on. Kane's face is in shadows, which undercuts this supposedly noble moment. Later in the film we learn that Kane abandons these principles. The lighting on and the position of Bernstein remind us that Bernstein was a witness to this event, too. (This scene is part of Bernstein's version of events). Frame enlargement. (b) A publicity still of approximately the same shot is less expressive because Welles's face is turned more toward the camera and is not obscured by shadows. This posed still fails to capture the irony of the moment: Kane's face in the dark as he makes a show of declaring his declaration of principles and signing them. The publicity still also does not capture Leland's admiration as successfully and sheds too much light on Bernstein, whereas, given the moment, most of the attention should be on Kane. *Orson Welles; RKO General Pictures*

FIGURE 2.17 Shapes of shadows
In *Blackmail* (1929) the main character has killed a man in self-defense. Late in the film, she has decided to surrender to the police. In this frame, the shadows of prison bars on and behind her suggest her possible fate. Frame enlargement. *BIP; The Museum of Modern Art/Circulating Film Library*

FIGURE 2.18 Shadows to obscure the identity of a subject
The lighting in this scene of *Psycho* (1960) helps hide the identity of the attacker and make the attacker seem even more frightening. This effect is intensified by the low angle of the shot and a knife that seems as long as the attacker's forearm. Frame enlargement. *Alfred Hitchcock; Universal*

FIGURE 2.19 Shadows, unusual lighting, unusual situation
Near the end of the Senegalese film *Saaraba* (1988), the subject shown here believes that he has reached *saaraba* (a mythical place without life's misery and uncertainties, or utopia). In the eleven-second shot represented here, the subject is driving a motorcycle at night, but the image was made indoors with the subject lit by three carefully positioned spotlights—one from each side and one from the back—and by one faint fill light. *Courtesy of California Newsreel, San Francisco*

a)   b)

FIGURE 2.20 Darkness and light in the *Godfather* films
Gordon Willis did the cinematography for the *Godfather* trilogy. Beginning with the opening
sequence, *The Godfather* (1972) often alternates between violent or dangerous actions in the dark
and (generally) safer events that take place in the light. (a) Here as in other films Willis has photographed, the lighting is minimal. In this scene a corrupt police captain arrives on the scene in darkness. In many scenes in *The Godfather*, dangerous people, including the godfather himself, are often
only partially visible, and the characters' eyes are obscured by darkness or seem to peer out of it.
For dangerous, powerful men—whose minds are difficult to read—the darkness seems appropriate.
(b) Many other scenes in *The Godfather* are filmed outdoors or in bright light, often of happy family
occasions, as in this photo of the family after the daughter's wedding. Frame enlargements. *The
Coppola Company; Paramount*

much of one scene in which he bribes a Nazi officer, the top half of the officer's
face is in shadows. It's as if he wears a mask, which is appropriate because he
is like an outlaw hiding in the dark. The shape of shadows can also be used
expressively, as in an early Hitchcock film *Blackmail* (1929, Figure 2.17).

In the 1960 *Psycho* and many other films, shadows are used to heighten
mystery and suspense (Figure 2.18). When used in combination with other
lighting, however, shadows can have a different effect (Figure 2.19).

Shadows and other areas of darkness can be central to an entire film or
even series of films. Cinematographer Gordon Willis lit the *Godfather* films
as darkly as he dared—and darker than most other cinematographers would
have dared. In *The Godfather* trilogy, many actors playing criminals are lit
primarily from above, and frequently we cannot see their eyes, only dark
sockets. That makes them hard to "read" or interpret, unnatural, and a little
frightening. Given the dark and evil doings, the many dark scenes throughout the three *Godfather* films are appropriate (Figure 2.20).

Other Uses of Light

A film's opposing settings may be lit differently. In *All the President's Men*, the
newsrooms where the journalists work so hard trying to shed light on the
perpetrators of the Watergate break-in during Nixon's presidency are lit

with bright, hard, white light that precludes shadows. In contrast, the parking garages where viewers glimpse the Watergate burglars and the unidentified informer are dark and shadowy. In *Desperately Seeking Susan* (1985), the suburban housewife's world is lit in soft light, whereas the punk world of the character played by Madonna is darker and more shadowed (Salt 288).

Filmmakers may change the lighting during a film to create or reinforce particular effects. As the main character of *American Beauty* starts to loosen up and enjoy life, the illumination on and around him gradually increases. Lighting can also be changed throughout a film to indicate both changes in mood and the film's most general meaning. Some films begin in the dark and end in the dark (*Citizen Kane*). Some films begin in the light until the mood and scenes tend to turn dark, and the films end in darkness (*I Am a Fugitive from a Chain Gang*, 1932). And some films begin in the dark but end in the light (*Jaws*, 1975).

THE CAMERA

To film, cinematographers need film stock, light, and a camera. What lens or lenses are used on the camera and the location of the camera relative to the subject are crucial determinants of the final images and thus their impact on viewers.

Lenses and Focus

Images are filmed with three types of lenses: the **wide-angle lens,** the **normal lens,** and the **telephoto lens.** Each type of lens has different properties and creates different images (Figures 2.21–2.23). Often all three are used at different times within the same film.

Striking uses of the wide-angle lens and the extreme wide-angle, or **fisheye lens,** occur near the end of *Seconds* (1966, Figure 2.24). In other films, the wide-angle lens has also been used to suggest that something is not right. Near the end of *Murder on the Orient Express* (1974), the detective tells the assembled suspects about parts of earlier testimony; as he does so, snippets of interviews with the same suspects and a brief shot of a woman walking away are repeated from earlier in the film, but now we see that activity through a wide-angle lens. Again, a technique may be modified as the film's story progresses. For example, the lens used to film an important character may be changed as the story develops. In *Crossfire* (1947), an anti-Semitic character is seen early in film through a normal 50 mm lens. As the story progressed, the director used shorter and shorter lenses. "Eventually in the last third of the picture . . . everything I shot with him was with a 25 [mm wide-angle lens]. . . . That slight subliminal distortion . . . made him a different kind of a character" (Dmytryk).

PLATE 1 **Saturated color throughout a frame**
In the Japanese movie *Princess Mononoke* (1997), people intent on industrializing the wilderness
threaten nature. Warriors of the iron foundry's boss have been firing guns that seem to shoot fire.
Next, viewers see one of their targets, a boar running in a blazing forest. The saturated warm colors
connoting the intensity of the fire and the ferocity of the situation permeate the image. Frame enlargement. *Studio Ghibli; Miramax*

PLATE 2 **Saturated color in part of frame**
The bright colors of the woman's dress
(plus her girth and gesture) draw attention
to her, even though she is at the extreme
right side of the frame. (The colors in this
photograph are close to those of the film,
but in the film the woman's dress and the
standing man's white clothing are not quite
as bright.) This is an outtake or, more likely,
a posed publicity still for *La vie est belle*
(Zaire [now Congo], 1987). *Courtesy of
California Newsreel, San Francisco*

PLATE 3 **Desaturated colors throughout a film**
In *Sleepy Hollow* (1999), the colors are drained of intensity. Nearly all of the colors are desaturated: dull, drab, faint, grayish. Except for the face of the main female character, even the actors' faces are pallid. Other elements of the images contribute to the overall mood and effect. There are lots of clouds and fog. The sun never shines. Nothing is in bloom; the trees are bare. It's cold, gloomy, and colorless. How appropriate for a land assaulted by a headless horseman intent on beheading those who still live. Frame enlargement. *Mandalay Picture; Paramount*

PLATE 4 **Desaturated colors, selective use**
Most of *The Thirteenth Floor* (1999), a science fiction–murder mystery–romance, takes place in a 1937 Los Angeles or a 1990s L.A. Unlike the other scenes, the usually stylish 1937 scenes, such as the one represented here, are always rendered in desaturated colors. Especially prominent in the 1937 scenes are subdued shades of brown, which are reminiscent of 1930s color postcards. Frame enlargement. *Centropolis Entertainment; Columbia*

PLATE 5 Limited spectrum of colors throughout a film
Throughout *Sleepy Hollow* (1999), only a few colors are used: mainly muted greens, dull metallic
blue, drab browns, lots of various shades of gray, and black. Nearly everyone wears clothing of the
same nondescript colors. Frame enlargement. *Mandalay Picture; Paramount*

PLATE 6 Wide spectrum of colors throughout a film
Like nearly all color films professionally made, *Smoke Signals* (1998) uses a film stock that allows a
full range of colors throughout the movie. In this frame, the many shadings of color in the woman's
dress, her skin tones, her hair, and the indistinct background exhibit a range of colors believably.
Frame enlargement. *Larry Estes & Scott M. Rosenfelt; Miramax*

PLATES 7 and 8 Dominant colors throughout a film

Plate 7: In *American Beauty* (1999), initially Lester Burnham lives in a gray world. Except for his daughter's room, the rooms in his home are decorated mostly in shades of gray. The first time we see all three family members, one morning as they go to the van, all three are dressed in grays. Both their Mercedes van and their car are gray. In the scene represented here, Lester's pajamas, the bedding, lamp, and back wall are all gray or some desaturated nondescript color. At this point, Lester's everyday life is drab and joyless, so all the engulfing grays are appropriate. Plate 8: The red roses, which are seen throughout the front yard at the beginning of the film, decorate most of the rooms in the house, which has a prominent bright red front door. One photo in the house of the family during younger, happier times, shows the wife dressed in red. After the wife begins having an affair, she dresses in red. As seen here, in Lester's fantasies red roses enfold or emanate from the young woman's bare skin. Lester buys a flaming red 1970 Pontiac Firebird, a throwback to his younger, happier days. Even the light above his weight bench in the garage is red. Finally Lester ends up on the kitchen floor in a pool of dark red. The colors chosen for the film—especially the many grays and reds—mirror and reinforce the character moods and transformations. Frame enlargements. *Jinks/Cohen; DreamWorks Pictures*

PLATE 9 Warm colors, nature's beauty
This frame from the western *Posse*, like so many shots in westerns and so many other films, momentarily and wordlessly draws attention to the environment's beauty, here a desert at sunset. In the context of this shot, the warm colors also reinforce the sense of heat and dryness. This shot is followed by a shot of the sun setting and a cactus in the right foreground, all still bathed in the same warm colors. Frame enlargement. *PolyGram Filmed Entertainment; Gramercy Pictures*

PLATE 10 Cold colors, nature's malevolence
In *The Matrix* (1998) "the world as it exists today" (seen here) is the result of twenty-first-century warfare between humankind and a race of advanced machines spawned by artificial intelligence. What remains of earth are the types of ruins seen here, drained almost entirely of color, mostly shades of gray though with a faint tint of green. Frame enlargement. *Joel Silver; Warner Bros.*

PLATES 11 and 12 **Warm colors then cold colors in a film**
The Iron Giant (1999) is set in autumnal rural Maine. Plate 11: In the first part of the film, warm,
fall colors (shades of yellow, red, and orange) are used for the day scenes. (As is usually the case in
movies, blues are used for night scenes.) Plate 12: The last part of the film, which takes place after
the first snowfall and is focused on the American military attacking the extraterrestrial creature,
takes place in an environment of whites and grays. The military actions are associated with snow,
cold, cloudy skies, white, and grays. Frame enlargements. *Allison Abbate; Warner Bros.*

PLATE 13 **Extensive use of white**
THX 1138 (1971) is set in a futuristic society that attempts to suppress emotion. Except for the robot police that are dressed in black and wear rigid silvery metallic masks, people are dressed entirely in white and all the interiors are white. People and their residences are not individualized by the colors they live in, and all the feelings colors suggest and evoke are absent. *Lawrence Sturhahn; Warner Bros.*

PLATE 14 **Extensive use of black**
As in countless films that aim to frighten audiences, *The Blair Witch Project* (1999) sets many scenes at night and lets darkness and unidentifiable sounds work on the viewer's imagination. In the scene represented here, the leader of the student filmmakers is running in the dark, panting and screaming in confusion and fear. Blackness, and the possible dangers it might hide, engulfs both setting and characters, so that neither participants nor viewers can know where they are and what (or who) is nearby. Frame enlargement. *Haxan Entertainment; Artisan Entertainment*

PLATES 15 and 16 **Black-and-white and color within the same frame**
In *Pleasantville* (1998), the black-and-white world of the 1950s TV series that the two 1990s teens
become trapped in gradually gains in color. Plate 15: First, colors begin to appear on or near those
who experience strong emotion—at first in the film, sexual desire. Later, colors are visible in
paintings reproduced in a library book, which in turn are the inspiration for the soda shop owner's
first paintings. Instead of the traditional Christmas scenes he always painted on his store windows,
he has painted a cubist Santa Claus! Plate 16: Here, the man is painting from his imagination and
from his memory of a Paul Cézanne still life he had seen in the library book (not from real subjects); later still his models are real, full-colored subjects. The suggestion is that art and the world
can inspire artists to bring creativity, self-expression, and vibrant feeling into colorless lives.
Frame enlargements. *A Larger Than Life Production; New Line Cinema*

Three Types of Lenses
(camera distance from subjects is unchanged)

FIGURE 2.21 Wide-angle lens (here a 28 mm lens on a 35 mm camera)

- The wide-angle lens may be used to emphasize distances between subjects or between subjects and setting because it causes all planes to appear farther away from the camera and from each other than is the case with a normal lens.
- Deep focus: all planes are in sharp focus.
- Compared to a normal lens, as in Figure 2.22, more of the image's four sides are visible.
- With extreme wide-angle lenses or with the subject close to the camera, there is much distortion or curvature of objects, especially near the edges of the image, as in Figure 2.24b. This is sometimes called *wide-angle distortion*.
- Movements toward or away from the camera seem speeded up. *Models: Kimberlee Stewart and Carlos Espinola; photographer: Jon Michael Terry*

FIGURE 2.22 Normal lens (approximately 50 mm lens for a 35 mm camera)

At most distances, this lens causes minimal distortion of image and movement. As its name implies, the normal lens creates images close to what the normal human eye would see in the same circumstances. *Models: Kimberlee Stewart and Carlos Espinola; photographer: Jon Michael Terry*

FIGURE 2.23 Telephoto lens (in this case, 200 mm)

- All planes appear closer to the camera and to each other than is the case with a normal lens (Figure 2.22).
- Shallow focus: only some of the planes very close to each other are in focus.
- Less of the image's sides is visible than is the case with a normal lens.
- Movements toward or away from the camera seem slowed down. *Models: Kimberlee Stewart and Carlos Espinola; photographer: Jon Michael Terry*

The normal lens is used most often in films because it most closely approximates the reality people see with their own eyes, and most films attempt to present the illusion of reality.

The telephoto lens has been used in many films to depict someone moving toward the camera laboriously slowly, as when the Dustin Hoffman character runs to prevent a wedding late in *The Graduate* (1967). Or it can compress a long row of signs, to seemingly crowd them together, as if to suggest the dense forest of signs in modern life. The telephoto lens is used similarly in several opening shots in *Short Cuts* (1993). Helicopters flying toward the camera are spraying Los Angeles with insecticide, but because they are shot with a telephoto lens, they look bunched up and slowed down. It's one of the film's first views of Los Angeles life and a striking image that viewers are unlikely to ignore.

Choice of lens, the lens **aperture** or opening, and film stock largely determine the **depth of field,** or the distance from foreground to background in which all objects are in focus. In **deep focus,**[1] which is achieved by using a wide-angle lens or small lens aperture or both, much or all of the depth of the image is in sharp focus. In low illumination, fast lenses and fast film stock also help achieve deep focus. Film theorist André Bazin argued that deep-focus scenes consisting of long takes are more open to interpretation than heavily edited scenes. Certainly deep-focus shots of long duration can let viewers experience clear images for lengthy segments of uninterrupted time. Deep-focus scenes may be less manipulative than edited footage. Viewers may be freer to look at the details in the frame and select those that seem significant, though in deep-focus and other shots filmmakers can guide viewers' attention through lighting, focus, camera placement, and composition (see the feature on *Citizen Kane* on pp. 38–39). Unarguably, deep focus does give filmmakers more opportunities to use foreground-background interplay expressively (see Figure 1.46 on p. 45).

When filmmakers use **shallow focus**—for example, by using a telephoto lens or a large lens aperture in low light—usually either the foreground or the background will be in sharp focus, and viewers' attention is directed to the subject(s) in sharp focus (see Figure 2.23). Depending on the context, unfocused subjects may be ambiguous, disturbing, threatening (see Figure 1.42 on p. 43), or some other effect. Subjects may be out of focus because the director chose to focus on something else within the frame or because the lighting, film stock, and lenses available when the film was made precluded deeper focus.

---

[1]*Deep focus* is a term used by many film critics and scholars. For the same situation, filmmakers are more likely to use the phrase *great depth of field. Deep focus* can be confused with *depth of focus,* which refers to the distance between the camera lens and the film in the camera in which the image remains in acceptable focus.

Yet another option for cinematographers—and one that is rarely used—is to use an **anamorphic lens** for only a few shots within a nonanamorphic film. Films are shot with either a flat (or spherical) lens—which does not squeeze the sides of the image onto the film in the camera —or, less often, an anamorphic lens— which squeezes the horizontal aspect of a wide image onto a normally shaped film frame. On rare occasions, filmmakers use an anamorphic lens within a film otherwise shot with flat lenses. Such shots make everything look tall and thin and may easily suggest that something is not right or is out of balance. In *Crooklyn* (1994) and *Summer of Sam* (1999), Spike Lee occasionally uses the anamorphic lens to increase the sense of the characters' and viewers' disorientation. The anamorphic lens is also used in a scene well into the 1997 version of *Lolita* to show Humbert Humbert and what he sees during an attack of hysteria after he learns that Lolita is seeing another man.

An image's resolution and mood may also be changed by using a **diffuser**— material such as a nylon stocking, frosted glass, spun glass, wire mesh, gelatin, or silk—placed in front of the camera lens or a light source to soften the image's resolution. Figure 2.25 illustrates how diffusers soften facial lines, sometimes to obscure aging and to glamorize, sometimes to lend a more spiritual or ethereal, less material look.

Camera Distances

Camera distance helps determine what details will be noticeable in the frame, what details will be excluded, and how large the subject will appear.

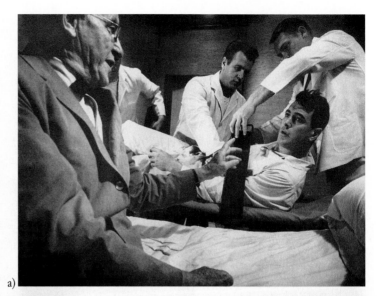

a)

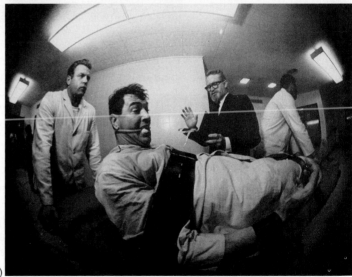

b)

FIGURE 2.24 **Wide-angle and extreme wide-angle lenses**
(a) In *Seconds* (1966), the Rock Hudson character is seen through a wide-angle lens as he is unexpectedly being strapped onto a gurney to be wheeled into an operating room and surgically killed. (b) When the character realizes what is happening to him but it is too late to do anything about it, he is filmed through an extreme wide-angle, or fisheye, lens. The effect is chilling and unforgettable. *Edward Lewis; Paramount*

FIGURE 2.25 Some functions of diffusers
A diffuser is a material placed over a light source or camera lens to soften the image. (a) The diffuser used here softens the image. Depending on the context, such a diffuser may glamorize, lend a more spiritual or ethereal look, obscure aging, or result in a combination of these consequences. (b) Heavy diffusion creates an even softer look. *Model: Eva L. Santos-Phillips; photographer: Jon Michael Terry*

a) b)

Figures 2.26 to 2.31 illustrate six camera distances and the terms usually used to describe them. (In the last three photographs, a longer lens was used so the photographer would not intrude into the model's space.)

When a film begins or when it shifts to a new setting, filmmakers often use an extreme long shot to present an **establishing shot,** a view of the surroundings. Once viewers are oriented, the camera normally moves in closer to the subject.

An extreme long shot or a long shot may create or enhance a humorous situation, perhaps because at that distance viewers cannot see the pain, discomfort, awkwardness, or embarrassment involved. The famous early film star and director Charlie Chaplin reputedly said, in effect, close-up for tragedy, long shot for comedy, and his own movies repeatedly illustrate that practice, as do many later movies (Figure 2.32).

Often a particular camera distance is chosen for surprising reasons. Ang Lee, the director of *Sense and Sensibility* (1995), used no close-ups during the movie's opening ten to fifteen minutes because the thirty-five-year-old lead actor was older than the source novel indicated, and Lee wanted the audience to accept her in the part before he used close shots. At other times, an extreme long shot or a long shot can distance viewers from a painful sight. In *Wish You Were Here* (1987), a teen, Lynda, feels unloved, so she seeks male attention in various ways, including displaying herself publicly and accepting as a sex partner her father's friend Eric, a man in his fifties who often belittles her. After her father discovers that Lynda has been having sex with Eric and

Camera Distances

FIGURE 2.26 **Extreme long shot**
If a person is the subject, the entire body will be visible (if not obstructed by some intervening object) but very small in the frame, and much of the surroundings will be visible. This camera distance is often used to show the layout and expanse of a setting. *Model: Carlos Espinola; photographer: Jon Michael Terry*

FIGURE 2.27 **Long shot**
Usually the subject is seen in its entirety, and much of its surroundings is visible. This camera distance has many possible uses—for example, to stress how small a human subject is in relationship to its environment. *Model: Carlos Espinola; photographer: Jon Michael Terry*

FIGURE 2.28 **Medium shot**
This camera distance tends to give equal importance to a subject and its surroundings. When the subject is a person, the medium shot usually shows the body from the knees or waist up. *Model: Carlos Espinola; photographer: Jon Michael Terry*

FIGURE 2.29 Medium close-up
The subject fills most of the height of the frame. When the subject is a person, the medium close-up usually reveals the head and shoulders. *Model: Kimberlee Stewart; photographer: Jon Michael Terry*

FIGURE 2.30 Close-up
The subject fills the height of the frame, and the shot reveals little or none of the surroundings. When the subject is a person, the close-up normally reveals all or nearly all of the head. *Model: Kimberlee Stewart; photographer: Jon Michael Terry*

FIGURE 2.31 Extreme close-up
The subject or, frequently, part of the subject completely fills up the frame and thus looks very large to the viewer. If the subject is someone's face, only part of it is visible. This camera distance is used to show the texture of a subject or part of a subject. With this camera distance typically none of the background is visible. *Model: Kimberlee Stewart; photographer: Jon Michael Terry*

FIGURE 2.32 **Extreme long shot to create humor**
In *Smoke Signals* (1998), twice viewers see a van at an Idaho country crossroad as we hear the radio traffic report. During the opening credits, this is the July 4, 1976, traffic report: "Big truck just went by. [pause] Now it's gone." Later, the radio announcer informs listeners that the "KRES traffic van [has been] broken down at the crossroads since 1972." The traffic reporter then gives the traffic report for the reservation: "Ain't no traffic, really." The amusing imitations of big-city traffic reports coupled with the extreme long shots revealing nothing for vast distances contribute to the humor of the shots. Frame enlargement. *Larry Estes & Scott M. Rosenfelt; Mirama*

FIGURE 2.33 **Extreme long shot to reveal character and environment**
A frame enlargement showing Kyuzo, the master swordsman in *The Seven Samurai* (1954), as seen in an extreme long shot. Kyuzo practices, in part for the art of it, alone in the woods, and even from this distance we can detect his focus, power, and gracefulness. The extreme long shot is also effective for showing the relationship of the subject to the environment. The camera is far enough back that viewers can see all of the swordsman's body yet see much of the surroundings—the trees, the rain, the stream that runs before his feet and toward the viewers. The extreme long shot here might also suggest that we viewers (and the film's characters) cannot get close to Kyuzo; he is a loner. Frame enlargement. *Sijiro Motoki; Toho Productions*

evidently kicks her out of the house, she goes to Eric's. Soon in a medium shot we see Eric start to unbutton her blouse; then she starts crying. He responds, "Come on. . . . What's all the fuss." She says, "Hold me, please; just hold me," but he doesn't. He keeps undressing her during most of the rest of the shot and the following medium close-up shot. In a second medium close-up shot, he talks to her briefly. Then in a long shot, we see him over her and still undressing her. Here the long shot prevents the viewer from spying too long or too closely at Lynda's emotional pain. The long shot also discourages viewers who find her sexually attractive from enjoying seeing her being further exposed. To some extent, it protects her from further (viewer) intrusion.

The long shot or extreme long shot requires viewers to be especially attentive to what is happening. Such a shot may also have emotional rewards. For instance, a long shot or extreme long shot may suggest that viewers cannot get close to or entirely understand someone (Figure 2.33).

Changing Perspective

FIGURE 2.34 Wide-angle lens (28 mm) at 8 feet 10 inches
This photograph was made by positioning the camera closer to the human subjects than in the comparable photograph made with a normal lens (Figure 2.35). Here the camera angle seems to be a slight high angle, and the bench seat on the left seems elongated. This camera distance and lens could be used to stress the depth of the background, to show more of the sides, or to emphasize the distance of the subjects from the background. *Models: Kimberlee Stewart and Carlos Espinola; photographer: Jon Michael Terry*

FIGURE 2.35 Normal lens (50 mm) at 15 feet 6 inches
This photograph closely mirrors the distances and relationships the human eye sees. *Models: Kimberlee Stewart and Carlos Espinola; photographer: Jon Michael Terry*

FIGURE 2.36 Telephoto lens (200 mm) at 62 feet
This photograph was made by moving the camera back from its position for Figure 2.35 and using a telephoto lens. Here the background seems much closer and more out of focus. The camera angle is not as high as in Figures 2.34 and 2.35, and the bench on the left now seems somewhat shorter. (To see how the camera angle seems to change, look again at the three photographs and note the angles from which the camera seems to view the cement area under the picnic table.) *Models: Kimberlee Stewart and Carlos Espinola; photographer: Jon Michael Terry*

For close-ups, the camera can be positioned near a performer's face, or, much more often, a telephoto lens will be used so the camera does not have to get close to the performer. Close-ups and medium close-ups may show the many nuances and complexities of human feeling. Directors especially fascinated with the nuances of emotions, such as the famed Swedish director Ingmar Bergman, may often use lengthy close-ups and **extreme close-up**s of faces. The usefulness of close shots to reveal emotions and character or personality cannot be overestimated. In his book *Kinesics and Context*, Ray Birdwhistell claims that the human face is capable of "some 250,000 different expressions" (8).

Perspective

By changing the camera lens and the camera distance at the same time, film-makers can change **perspective:** the relative size and apparent depth of objects in the image. Figures 2.34 to 2.36 illustrate three ways that filmmakers can use perspective.

In these three photographs the main subjects are approximately the same size in the frame and appear in about the same position within the frame. But everything else changes when camera distance and lens are modified together. By changing the lens and the distance together, cinematographers can emphasize or deemphasize certain areas of the image. They can change the relationships of people and objects in the frame to convey the information and the moods they intend. Often viewers cannot tell the distance of the camera from the subject or the type of lens used unless they know the subject and its setting well enough to detect distortion in their presentation.

Filmmakers often change perspective from shot to shot, but occasionally they change perspective within a shot by **dollying** forward or backward as they simultaneously use a **zoom lens**—a lens that can be changed smoothly toward the wide-angle range or telephoto range while the camera is filming. Depending on the movement of the dolly holding the camera and the simultaneous changes in the focal length of the camera lens, the background can be made to seem to recede or to move forward as the main subject remains the same size and in approximately the same position within the frame. In a shot in *Quiz Show* (1994), the camera dollies forward as the camera lens **zooms** out (changes from telephoto to wide angle). As a consequence, the back of the actor's head and shoulders remains largely unmoving in about the same position within the frame as the background seems to recede and come into sharper focus and more of the width of the background comes into view (Figure 2.37).

Another change in perspective during a shot occurs in *GoodFellas* (1990), but with the opposite camera movement and opposite simultaneous type of zooming. Late in the film Jimmy is meeting Henry in a restaurant. Jimmy is about to try to betray Henry and send him to his death. They sit on opposite sides of the frame, with a large window between them. As they talk, the camera

dolly: To film while the camera is mounted on a moving dolly or wheeled platform.

zoom lens: A camera lens with variable focal lengths; thus it can be adjusted by degrees during a shot so that the size of the subject and the area being filmed change.

a)   b)   c)   d)

FIGURE 2.37
Changing perspective during a shot
More than halfway into *Quiz Show* (1994) occurs an unusual shot that is slightly more than four seconds long. As the camera dollies forward toward Professor Charles Van Doren, a zoom lens zooms out (here is changed from telephoto to wide angle). The net result is that Van Doren, seen from behind his head and shoulders, stays in basically the same position within the frame as the background recedes. The four frame enlargements, which represent approximately one-second intervals, illustrate the changes that occur in the background. As the background recedes, more of its sides are visible and the background comes more sharply into focus. The shot creates an odd sensation for the viewer. It may also reinforce the sense of the stress the man is under as he struggles to come up with the correct answer to a quiz question. To some viewers the shot may suggests that his world is about to change, for in a moment he gives an incorrect answer and is dethroned as the champion of the popular 1950s TV quiz show, *The $64,000 Question*. Frame enlargements. *Hollywood Pictures; Buena Vista Pictures*

track: To film while the camera is being moved around.

tracks backward as it zooms in, going from normal to telephoto. The two men stay the same size and in the same positions within the frame, but the background becomes larger and its planes become more compressed: for example, the car parked across the street seems progressively closer to the large sign advertising sandwiches behind it. Viewers may not notice the change in the perspective, but it is eerie, unsettling, and effective. Perhaps the shot suggests that Jimmy's attempt to betray his friend is unnatural and unexpected.

These rapid but fluid changes in perspective within shots from *Quiz Show* and *GoodFellas* affect the subjects and their relation to the setting in disturbing ways. They also briefly disorient viewers, in part because the changes are unexpected. Although these changes in perspective last only a few seconds, they are so rarely used in films that they may momentarily draw viewers' attention to them.

Angles and Point-of-View Shots

Another important technique that filmmakers can use to determine the expressiveness of images is the angle from which they film the subject. Figures 2.38 to 2.41 illustrate four basic camera positions: **bird's-eye view, high angle, eye-level angle,** and **low angle.** The camera may be placed at any angle above or below those indicated in the figures.

In a **Dutch angle** shot the subject appears to be on a slanted surface. It is often used to disorient viewers or make them ill at ease. As a **point-of-view shot,** the Dutch angle may suggest a character's confused state of mind. The Dutch angle is used in many scenes in *The Third Man* (1949), *Do the Right Thing*, and *Natural Born Killers* (1994). It is also used in the early scenes of *Bagdad Café* (1988) to suggest unhappy personal relationships (Figure 2.42).

Camera Angles

FIGURE 2.38 Bird's-eye view
This bird's-eye shot in *The Hurricane* (1999) shows how small the prison cell of professional boxer Rubin Carter is, how much he is hemmed in, and how small and helpless he seems when viewed from above and at some distance. For a bird's-eye view, the camera is often mounted on a crane. The bird's-eye view is used at the conclusion of a moving crane shot from the original *Psycho* (Figure 6.12a on p. 210). A moving bird's-eye view is also used memorably late in *Taxi Driver* (1976) when viewers look down on the aftermath of a violent scene; the camera movement makes the shot even more disturbing than the usual bird's-eye view. In all three instances, the effect is disorienting, perhaps even dizzying, since viewers look straight down on the subject. Most filmmakers avoid the bird's-eye view, probably because it can attract attention to itself and be distracting. Frame enlargement. *Beacon; Universal*

FIGURE 2.39 High angle
In this shot from *Shakespeare in Love* (1998), Shakespeare playing Romeo appears at Juliet's balcony. From this angle, he seems somewhat small and a little helpless. High angles make the subject appear smaller and in some contexts shut off from the surroundings (sometimes all that is visible of the background is a floor or the ground). In other contexts, the subject seen from a high angle appears vulnerable. Frame enlargement. *Bedford Falls Productions, Universal Pictures, & Miramax; Miramax*

In point-of-view shots (often called *p.o.v. shots*), the camera films a subject from the approximate position of a character, a real person (in a documentary), or occasionally an animal. Such camera placements contribute to the viewer's sense of identification with the looking subject and of participation in the ac-

a)

b)

FIGURE 2.40 **Eye-level shots**
(a) An eye-level angle—such as this one of Chef from *South Park: Bigger, Longer & Uncut* (1999)—creates the effect of the audience being on the same level as the subject. Viewers neither look up to the subject nor look down at the subject. Frame enlargement. (b) The height of the camera may depend on the filmmaker and the culture in which the film is made. In films directed by Yasujiro Ozu of Japan, such as *Tokyo Story* (1953), eye-level shots are often taken with the camera approximately two feet above the ground when the subjects are sitting on the ground. In eye-level shots for films from Western societies, the camera is normally positioned five to six feet above the ground for standing subjects and three to four feet for sitting subjects. If Ozu had followed that practice, the results would have been a high angle, with the camera tilted down toward the subjects sitting on the floor. (a) *Comedy Central; Warner Bros.* and *Paramount;* (b) *Shochiku. The Museum of Modern Art/Film Stills Archive*

FIGURE 2.41 **Low angle**
In low angles, as in this publicity still for the Japanese film *Himatsuri*, or *Fire Festival* (1984), the surroundings are often minimized, with a lot of sky or ceiling in the background. The subject seems more prominent and, in some contexts, dominating or intimidating. Low angles are often used, as here, in shots emphasizing a person's physique. *Courtesy of Kino International, New York City*

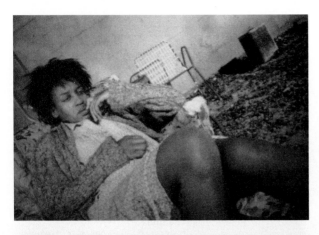

FIGURE 2.42 **Dutch angle**
Dutch angles are used early in *Bagdad Café* (1988) after a woman quarrels with her man and he leaves her. This image reinforces the sense that things are now out of order in the woman's life. Frame enlargement. *Zev Braun; New Yorker Films*

FIGURE 2.43 **Point-of-view shot**
In this point-of-view shot from within a coffin in *Vampyr* (1932), viewers see a vampire with a lighted candle looking down into the coffin. Later the coffin is carried outside, and viewers see the outside surroundings from within the coffin. Frame enlargement. *Julian West* & *Carl Theodora Dreyer; Filmproduktion Paris-Berlin*

FIGURE 2.44 **Sustained point of view**
Lady in the Lake (1946) was an experiment with sustained point of view: viewers see events from the main character's point of view, except for an occasional shot of a mirror showing the main character, detective Philip Marlowe. Here Marlowe is about to get slugged and knocked out. This frame is somewhat blurred because the subject is moving so rapidly. Frame enlargement. *George Haight; MGM*

tion. In *Vampyr* (1932), the main character hallucinates that he is in a coffin with a small glass window. He thinks he looks up and sees (and viewers feel as if they are seeing) what it looks like from inside a coffin (Figure 2.43). In parts of more modern films, such as the two murders in the 1960 *Psycho*, periodically throughout *Halloween* (1978), and late in *The Silence of the Lambs* (1991), viewers are frequently put into the uncomfortable position of seeing horrendous events through the eyes of a killer. On a less threatening note, in *Toy Story* (1995) and *Toy Story 2* (1999), viewers are often allowed to see impending dangers, such as a large menacing dog, from the same point of view as one of the toy characters. In 1946, a rare attempt was made to present an entire film from the point of view of a single character in *Lady in the Lake* (Figure 2.44).

FIGURE 2.45 **Panning**
For this shot for *Little Fauss and Big Halsy* (1970), two camera operators (left) pivot their cameras sideways on top of a tripod to follow the speeding motorcycles. At the same time, a camera operator on the crane films onrushing action. *Brad Dexter & Albert S. Ruddy; Paramount*

Much more often in films, the camera is placed outside the action, in an objective camera shot, and the audience is more spectator than participant.[2]

Moving Camera

The camera may be moved during filming without moving it around in space because a camera operator can **tilt** a camera up and down and pan from side to side. Tilting is a camera movement achieved during filming when a camera operator pivots the camera down to up or up to down while the camera is attached to a stationary base or is handheld. It is often used to reveal a subject by degrees, frequently with a surprising or humorous conclusion. In **panning,** the camera is handheld or mounted on a tripod and pivoted sideways, as the two camera operators on the ground are doing in Figure 2.45. Panning is often used to show the vastness of a location, such as a sea, plain, mountain range, or outer space. As film scholar Ira Konigsberg points out, it may also "guide the audience's attention to a significant action or point of interest, . . . follow the movement across the landscape of a character or vehicle [as in Figure 2.45], and . . . convey a subjective view of what a character sees when turning his or her head to follow an action" (284). Rarely, as in Woody Allen's *Husbands and Wives* (1992), a 360-degree (circular) panning shot is used to show the surroundings on all sides of the camera, though that practice usually draws attention from the subject to the technique itself.

---

[2]For helpful explanations of lighting, color, camera angles, and camera lenses selected to support the films he directed, see Sidney Lumet's discussion in Chapter 5, "The Camera: Your Best Friend," in his *Making Movies* (1995).

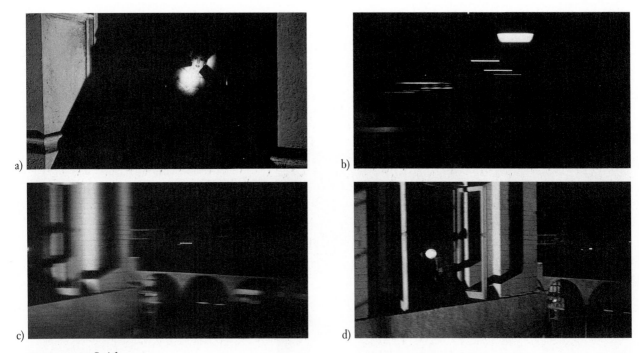

FIGURE 2.46 Swish pan
In *Touch of Evil* (1958) the Janet Leigh character enters her darkened hotel room and is immediately illuminated by a small light (a). A swish pan from right to left (b and c) ends with a clear view of the source of the light: a flashlight from a room across the way (d). Frame enlargements. *Albert Zugsmith; Universal*

Panning too quickly causes blurred footage; such a result is called a **swish pan** (Figure 2.46). It is seldom used in commercial films. In *Schindler's List*, swish pans done with an unsteady handheld camera intensify the chaos when Nazis roughly sort naked prisoners. Swish pans may also be point-of-view shots. Late in *The Wild Bunch* (1969), Angel, a member of the wild bunch, is upset when he realizes he is now under the control of a Mexican general. From Angel's point of view, we see some laughing Mexicans then after a swish pan other people laughing at him. After a very brief shot of Angel, we see another point-of-view swish pan in the opposite direction and more laughter at his expense. The point-of-view swish pans help convey his frustration and disorientation.

It is also possible to move the camera through space while filming. In the early years of cinema, however, filmmakers simply plopped down a camera before the subject, aimed it, and started turning the hand crank. The first films were extremely short, often only a minute or so. Later, the camera was still so bulky it had to be mounted on a sturdy tripod (Figure 2.47) and could be moved along with its subject only by placing the camera in some type of

FIGURE 2.47 Early cinematography
The early American cinematographer Billy Bitzer hand-cranking a large and bulky Biograph camera as he films some of the U.S. Army Field Artillery in approximately 1905. Later, Bitzer worked closely with D. W. Griffith for sixteen years and filmed such classics as *The Birth of a Nation*, *Intolerance*, and *Broken Blossoms*. *The Museum of Modern Art/Film Stills Archive*

FIGURE 2.48 The dolly
Two dollies used in filming *Boomerang* (1992). The dolly on the left supports a seated Steadicam operator; the one on the right a light source, power pack, and reflective screen used to soften the effects of hard outdoor light. Dollies allow the filmmakers to move lights and camera smoothly from place to place on a smooth surface. *Brian Grazer* & *Warrington Hudlin; Paramount*

moving vehicle, such as the back of a flatbed. By the 1920s, however, various filmmakers had learned other ways to film while moving the camera. In a striking shot from *Napoléon*, the camera was mounted at the base of a huge swing device suspended from a very high ceiling, and the camera filmed a crowded room below as it swung back and forth over the room. Almost as notable are the concluding two shots of *The Crowd* (1928), which were taken from a camera above the film's central family and receding from it, showing the family more and more engulfed by a crowd at a theater. However, in the early years of synchronized sound on phonograph records or on the film itself (late 1920s), moving the camera during filming largely halted because the sound from the camera was being picked up by the sound recording equipment. But gradually inventors developed camera shields (blimps and barneys) to muffle sound, and filmmakers learned how to record sound effectively while moving the camera. Since the early 1930s, camera movement during shots has again become commonplace. For example, as the camera is filming, it may glide about by tracking (being moving on tracks) or dollying (Figure 2.48). Such camera shots should not be confused with shots made with a stationary camera with a zoom lens. In zooming, the camera appears to move in or away from a flat surface, whereas in dollying or tracking, the camera is moved through space and viewers get some sense of contour and depth.

With a crane, a camera may be positioned at a particular location in the air or moved smoothly through the air (see Figure 2.45 on p. 86). A crane makes possible otherwise impossible camera angles and distances. Crane shots may be unobtrusively slow, gracefully slow, or rapid and disorienting; depending on the contexts, the effect can be soothing, exhilarating, or threatening. They may create or heighten many different effects (Figure 2.49).

a)   b)

FIGURE 2.49 **Filming from a crane**
In *High Noon* (1952), the town marshal—who knows he is soon to confront four armed men intent on killing him—is seen in a close-up revealing his worry and fear. The next shot begins as a medium shot; then immediately (a) the camera begins moving backward and (b) continues moving backward and upward, stopping when it shows him in an extreme long shot even more distant from him than the image seen in (b). During this crane shot, viewers see the marshal wipe sweat from his brow, turn away from the camera, and walk away alone toward a deadly showdown. Rather than show the action of this thirty-second crane shot in two or more shots—for example, a medium shot followed by a high-angle, extreme long shot—the director chose to preserve continuity of space, time, and action. Frame enlargements. *Stanley Kramer Productions; United Artists*

FIGURE 2.50 The Steadicam
This device for stabilizing moving handheld camera shots was first used in feature film production in the mid-1970s. Depicted here is a Steadicam Video SK with video monitor and Sony Hi-8 video camera below. A 35 mm movie camera is even larger and heavier than the video camera shown here. Operating a Steadicam expertly takes training and practice because it initially upsets the operator's sense of balance, especially when moving. It can also be tricky to maneuver in the wind, and achieving smooth starts and stops with one can be difficult. *"Steadicam" is a registered trademark of Cinema Products Corp., Los Angeles.*

The **Steadicam**—a device consisting of a lightweight frame, torsion arm, movie camera, and small TV monitor—is another piece of equipment that allows the camera operator to move around smoothly while filming (Figure 2.50). Using a Steadicam has many advantages: "Visually, the Steadicam duplicates many benefits of handheld shooting without the lack of stability in the latter practice; indeed, to the crew, it can provide speed, flexibility, mobility, and responsiveness. And, of course, it can also energize the film with visual dynamism" (Geuens 12).

The Steadicam can be used in long, continuous shots, such as in a celebrated shot from *GoodFellas*. In this shot, Henry gives money to a car attendant across the street from the Copacabana nightclub; then Henry and Karen walk across the street, cut through a line of people waiting to get into the club, go in a side entrance and down some stairs, and walk through corridors and the kitchen to the nightclub itself. There a special table is set up for them, and Henry is greeted by men at nearby tables. Henry and Karen sit; they receive a complimentary bottle of wine from men at another table and talk a little; then Henry and Karen watch the beginning of a comedian's routine. For a little more than three uninterrupted minutes, the use of a Steadicam allows viewers to see and to some extent experience the deference, attention, and favors that Henry enjoys as a mobster.

A Steadicam is also used effectively near the end of *The Shining* (1980). As the ax-wielding main character chases his son through a large, snow-covered outdoor maze, hoping to catch him and murder him, the Steadicam follows the pursued then the pursuer without making viewers nauseous. In *Reversal of Fortune* (1990), a Steadicam is used in the scenes narrated by the comatose Sunny. As the director of the film explains, the Steadicam "has a floating quality; it doesn't go straight from one point to another. It is not shaky, but it's floating. I said . . . that quality . . . can turn to my advantage here—whenever Sunny is narrating, having the camera float around the room like the soul of Sunny, or Sunny having an out of body experience" (Schroeder 6).

Camera movement may be used in countless ways. It is often used so viewers can follow along with a moving subject, as in the Steadicam shot from *GoodFellas* described earlier. Sometimes camera movement is used to show the subject from a very different angle, as when the camera moves to below Norman Bates's chin as the detective in the original *Psycho* questions him. Occasionally, camera movement is used to prevent the audience from learning information, as when a crane shot is used to position the camera

FIGURE 2.51 Camera movement to reveal subjects, setting, and mood
Four photographs approximating the opening tracking shot of *A Clockwork Orange* (1971). (a) The film begins with a close-up of the main character, Alex. Frame enlargement. (b) After a few moments the camera begins to dolly backward slowly, revealing Alex and the other drugged gang members, with Alex's feet propped atop one of two interlocking tables in the form of nude women. (c) As the camera continues tracking backward, viewers can see an attendant in the background to the far right and the first of the nude statues on pedestals. As the camera continues its backward movement, viewers see more and more of the setting, including more tables, more statues on pedestals, other immobile (and drugged) patrons on the sides of this futuristic bar, and the names of the liquid drugs available: Moloko (Milk) Plus and three others. (d) Toward the end of the shot, in the foreground viewers can see two more immobile attendants. Finally the camera stops moving, and during the last second or two of the shot the image looks much like this one, except a longer lens was used for this publicity still than in the movie so everything here looks slightly more compressed than in the movie. *Stanley Kubrick; Warner Bros.*

overhead immediately before Norman carries his mother down the stairs in both versions of *Psycho* (Figure 6.12 on p. 210).

Camera movement may allow viewers to see a subject more clearly. Moving the camera forward may create or intensify tension (what will we see next?) or slowly introduce viewers to the setting of the story, as in the beginnings of *West Side Story* (1961) and countless other films. Conversely, camera movement away from the subject can reveal more and more of a setting, as in the concluding two shots of *The Crowd* mentioned earlier and the opening shot of *A Clockwork Orange*. During this ninety-two-second shot, the camera reveals the main character in close-up (Figure 2.51a), pulls back to show his

FIGURE 2.52 **Tracking backward to reveal surprising information**
Sometimes a shot shows viewers its subject, then the camera moves backward and viewers see on the side of the frame someone watching the action they had recently seen, as is done in *Reservoir Dogs* (1992) seconds after the action depicted here. *Lawrence Bender; Miramax*

collaborators in crime (Figure 2.51b), then shows a major setting where the patrons are all drugged into immobility and where women are seen as sex objects to display and demean (Figure 2.51c and d). Sometimes camera movement backward reveals someone watching what viewers have been watching (Figure 2.52). Moving the camera back may give a sense of release or conclusion, as in the shots used for the endings of *The Shawshank Redemption* (1994), *Hilary and Jackie* (1998), and *Dr. T and the Women* (2000). A similar effect results when film stories end with the main characters walking away from the camera, as in the lengthy final crane shot of *Chinatown* (1974).

Camera movement without a Steadicam can disorient, confuse, or even sicken viewers, as in *The Insider* (1999) and *Dr. Strangelove: Or, How I Learned to Stop Worrying and Love the Bomb* (1963). Immediately after a guided missile hits a bomber in *Dr. Strangelove*, the camera jars around vigorously and erratically and viewers feel momentarily at a loss. The erratic camera movement seen throughout *The Blair Witch Project*—which was intended to convince viewers that they were seeing amateur camera work—was so disorienting some viewers experienced "extreme nausea." Filming with a handheld camera while moving through a crowd usually results in footage that might make viewers feel something like the movement and excitement of crowd scenes.

Camera movement can also help control *when* during a shot viewers learn certain information. In *National Lampoon's Vacation* (1983), a shot begins with children asleep in the backseat of a moving car at night. The shot continues with the camera panning to the front seat, where the mother is also asleep; then the camera continues its movement and we learn that the driver, the father, is also deep in sleep! Because of the context and camera movement, it's a hilarious moment.

DIGITAL CINEMATOGRAPHY

In postproduction—that is, after a film has been shot—computers are increasingly being used to create or manipulate film images. Any image, just as any written language, can be scanned into a computer then changed in many ways. Computers can be used to composite (or combine) two or more images.

They can also be used to **morph** images—to change their shape—so that
we can see a character's body change or even see a character morph into a
different character (Figure 2.53).

Computers can also be used to remove or cover up objects from images. An article in a major journal on cinematography cites several specific
examples:

> They can eliminate scratches and remove objects which don't belong in period
> films. In one recent Western, bloodstains were removed from a character's shirt
> to make it acceptable for use in a trailer. In another PG-rated film, a brief
> bathing suit bottom was extended to cover some of an actress' exposed body . . .
> with the aid of 'electronic paint.' In *Wrestling with Ernest Hemingway* [1993], an

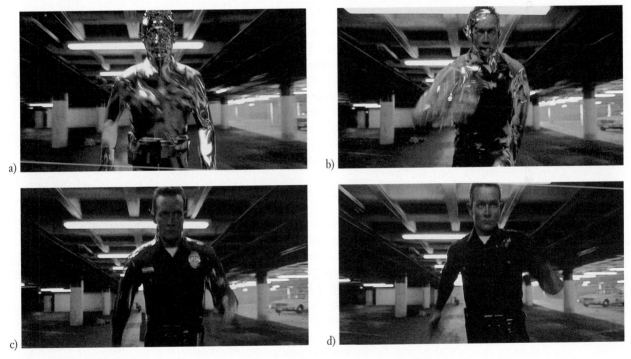

a)

b)

c)

d)

FIGURE 2.53 **Morphing**

In morphing, filmed frames are scanned into a computer. Then the parts of the image that are to
change are marked manually and transformed in stages by a sophisticated computer program. The
images are then transferred to film stock and incorporated into the finished film. Morphing was
used in many shots during postproduction of *Terminator 2: Judgment Day* (1991). An example is
the shot represented here that shows the running, evil cyborg (a) transform into a man dressed as
a police officer (b–d). Frame enlargements. *James Cameron; TriStar*

actor was clearly breathing after he was supposed to be dead. The image was fixed by scanning the film into digital format, literally erasing parts of frames where the actor's shirt was moving or breathing, and replacing it with cloned images from frames where the shirt was still. (Fisher 101)

After Brandon Lee was killed in an accident with three days of filming left in making *The Crow* (1994), for a few scenes a computer was used to move the image of his character to new settings. Now filmmakers with a large budget can use special effects during filming, as in *Wild Wild West* (1999), then clean up the images in the computer—for example, remove wires that supported actors as they were moved through the air.

Digital work allows filmmakers to correct mistakes that would be even more costly or impossible to correct (for example, perhaps the actor has moved on to another job and cannot return to reshoot an indispensable botched shot or scene). Like animation, computer work makes possible extensive manipulation of the film's images and makes visible what was previously impossible to show. For example, for one scene in *In the Line of Fire* (1993), footage of President and Mrs. Bush getting out of the presidential airplane was scanned into a computer, and their faces were replaced with the faces of the movie's characters. Digital cinematography, however, is not without its limitations. Some people think it still too often looks a little fake; then, too, it remains enormously costly and time-consuming. Even films known for their digital creativity—such as *Jurassic Park* (1993) and *The Lost World: Jurassic Park* (1997)—continue to combine digital visual effects with shots made by filming models (life-size or miniature), robots, **animatronics,** and the like.

animatronic: A puppet likeness of a human, creature, or animal whose movements are directed by electronic, mechanical, or radio-controlled devices.

Because of costs and visual quality, filming and projecting theatrical film as film, not video or digital images, seem likely for at least a few more years. It also seems certain that transferring parts of a film to a computer, manipulating the digitized visuals, then transferring the visuals back to film will grow in importance in large commercial films. Probably some combination of video and digital equipment will eventually replace traditional cinematography, but the history of film technology shows that technological advances alone do not bring about radical changes in filmmaking and film exhibition. At least for big-budget movies, profits for those involved in the production and distribution of moving images and sounds and the tastes of the viewing and paying public are also potent determinants.

SUMMARY

Cinematography involves the choice and manipulation of film stock, lighting, and cameras. Some of the main issues in cinematography are film grain, color, lenses, camera distance and angle from the subject, and camera movement.

Film Stock

- Film stock, which is unexposed and unprocessed motion-picture film, influences the film's finished look, including its sharpness of detail, range of light and shadow, and quality of color. Sometimes cinematographers use different film stocks in different parts of the same film to heighten certain effects.

- Generally, the wider the film gauge, the larger the film frames and the sharper the projected images.

- Slow film stock, which requires more light than fast film stock, can produce a detailed, nuanced image. In older films, fast film stock usually produces more graininess than slow film stocks.

- Color associations vary from culture to culture, and a color's impact depends on context—where and how the color is used. In most Western societies, warm colors (reds, oranges, and yellows) tend to be thought of as hot, dangerous, lively, and assertive. Greens, blues, and violets are generally characterized as cool. In Europe and the United States, these colors tend to be associated with safety, reason, control, relaxation, and sometimes sadness or melancholy.

- Color may be saturated (intense, vivid) or desaturated (muted, dull, pale).

Lighting

- Hard lighting comes directly from a source, whereas soft light comes from an indirect source. Hard lighting is bright and harsh and creates unflattering images. Soft lighting is flattering because it tends to fill in imperfections in the subject's surface and obliterate or lessen sharp lines and shadows.

- Low-key lighting involves little illumination on the subject and often reinforces a dramatic or mysterious effect. High-key lighting entails bright illumination of the subject and may create or enhance a cheerful mood.

- The direction of light reaching the subject can change an image's moods and meanings.

- Like light, shadows can be used expressively in countless ways—for example, to create a mysterious or threatening environment.

The Camera

- During filming, one of three types of lenses is used: wide-angle, normal, or telephoto. Often all three are used at different times within the same film. Each type of lens has different properties and creates different images.

- Choice of lens, aperture (or opening), and film stock largely determine the depth of field, or distance in front of the camera in which all objects are in focus.

- Diffusers may be placed in front of a light source or in front of a camera lens to soften lines, to glamorize, or to lend a more spiritual or ethereal look.

- Camera distance helps determine what details will be noticeable, what objects will be excluded from the frame, and how large the subject will appear within the frame.

- By changing the camera lens and the camera distance between shots or during a shot, filmmakers can change perspective: the relative size and apparent depth of objects in the photographic image.

- The angle from which the subject is filmed influences the expressiveness of the images. There are four basic camera angles—bird's view, high angle, eye-level angle, and low angle—and countless angles in between.

- In point-of-view (p.o.v.) shots, the camera films a subject from the approximate position of someone in the film. Such camera placements contribute to the viewer's identification with one of the subjects and sense of participation in the action.

- A motion-picture camera may remain in one place during filming as it is pivoted up or down (tilting) or rotated sideways (panning), or it may be moved through space.

- Panning too quickly causes blurred footage: such a result is called a swish pan.

- Ways to move the camera around during filming include dollying, tracking, using a crane, and employing a Steadicam. Like other aspects of cinematography, camera movement can be used in countless expressive ways.

Digital Cinematography

- Film images can be scanned into a computer, changed there, then transferred back to film. Such computer manipulation can correct errors or change the images in ways impossible or more troublesome and costly to do with film alone.

WORKS CITED

Almendros, Nestor (cinematographer). Interview. *Visions of Light* (documentary film). 1992.

Bazin, André. "The Evolution of the Language of Cinema." *What Is Cinema?* Ed. and trans. Hugh Gray. Vol. 1. Berkeley: U of California P, 1967.

Birdwhistell, Ray. *Kinesics and Context: Essays on Body Motion Communication*. Philadelphia: U of Pennsylvania P, 1970.

Daviau, Allen (cinematographer). Interview. *Visions of Light* (documentary film). 1992.

Dmytryk, Edward. Interview. *Hollywood: The Golden Years, Episode 5: Dark Victory*. BBC Television and RKO Pictures. 1987.

Dyer, Richard. *Stars*. 2nd ed. London: British Film Institutes, 1998.

Eidsvik, Charles. *Cineliteracy: Film among the Arts*. New York: Random, 1978.

Fisher, Bob. "Looking Forward to the Future of Film." *American Cinematographer* Aug. 1994: 98–104.

Geuens, Jean-Pierre. "Visuality and Power: The Work of the Steadicam." *Film Quarterly* 47.2 (Winter 1993–94): 8–17.

Hayward, Susan. *Cinema Studies: The Key Concepts*. 2nd ed. London: Routledge, 2000.

Konigsberg, Ira. *The Complete Film Dictionary*. 2nd ed. New York: Penguin, 1997.

Lumet, Sidney. *Making Movies*. New York: Knopf, 1995.

Malkiewicz, Kris. *Cinematography: A Guide for Film Makers and Film Teachers*. 2nd ed. Englewood Cliffs, NJ: Prentice, 1989.

"Newcomers, director Kasi Lemmons and Amy Vincent, Set *Eve's Bayou* in the Spiritual and Geographic Heart of Louisiana." Originally (but no longer) accessible at *American Cinematographer* Nov. 1997 <http://www.cinematographer.com/magazine/nov97/bayou/pg1.htm>.

Riefenstahl, Leni (filmmaker). Interview. *The Wonderful, Horrible Life of Leni Riefenstahl* (documentary film). 1993.

Salt, Barry. *Film Style and Technology: History and Analysis*. 2nd ed. London: Starword, 1992.

Schroeder, Barbet. "Justice, Irony, and Reversal of Fortune: An Interview with Barbet Schroeder." By Robert Sklar. *Cineaste* 18.2 (1991): 4+.

Turner, George. "A Tradition of Innovation." *American Cinematographer* Aug. 1994: 93–96.

FOR FURTHER READING

Alton, John. *Painting with Light*. 1949. Berkeley: U of California P, 1995. Alton, an accomplished cinematographer, explains the duties of the cinematographer and how lighting, camera techniques, and choice of location determine the visual mood of films. This edition includes new introductory material and a filmography.

Coe, Brian. *The History of Movie Photography*. New York: Zoetrope; London: Ash and Grant, 1981. A short history of evolving filmmaking equipment and processes. Many photographs, some in color.

Eyman, Scott. *Five American Cinematographers*. Metuchen, NJ: Scarecrow, 1987. Interviews with Karl Struss, Joseph Ruttenberg, James Wong Howe, Linwood Dunn, and William H. Clothier.

LoBrutto, Vincent. *Principal Photography: Interviews with Feature Film Cinematographers*. Westport, CT: Praeger, 1999. In-depth interviews with thirteen cinematographers; each interview is preceded by a short biography and a selected filmography. The book concludes with a glossary, bibliography, and index.

Lowell, Ross. *Matters of Light and Depth: Creating Memorable Images for Video, Film and Stills through Lighting*. Philadelphia: Broad Street Books, 1992. The book's subtitle accurately describes its subject.

Neale, Steven. *Cinema and Technology: Image, Sound, Colour*. London: Macmillan, 1985. Includes detailed descriptions and corresponding photographs of the various color processes.

Rogers, Pauline. *Contemporary Cinematographers on Their Art*. Boston: Focal, 1998. Thirteen interviews cover such topics as preproduction, special effects, aerial photography, and second unit. Often the cinematographers tell how popular shots were lit and filmed.

CHAPTER 3

Editing

T HE CLICHÉ ABOUT SCULPTURE, that the sculptor finds the statue which is waiting in the stone, applies equally to editing; the editor finds the film which is waiting hidden in the material. (Priestly 273)

In general, how do film editors work? After the many labeled strips of film have been developed, the film editor or editors—often in the later stages of the work, in cooperation with the director—select the best version, or best **take,** of each shot for the finished film. Often the editor shortens the shot; sometimes the editor divides a shot and inserts another shot or part of it (a **cutaway shot**) into the middle of the split shot. Often the editor consults a **master shot,** which records an entire scene, usually in a **long shot.** Sometimes parts of the master shot are used in the **final cut** of the scene; occasionally the master shot is used in its entirety. All of this work is usually done on an editing machine (Figure 3.1).

Terms in **boldface** are defined in the Illustrated Glossary beginning on page 539.

cutaway shot: A shot that briefly interrupts the visual presentation of a subject to show something else.

long shot: Shot in which the subject is seen in its entirety, and much of its surroundings are visible.

final cut: The last version of an edited film.

FIGURE 3.1 **An early flatbed editing table** Acclaimed Soviet filmmaker Sergei Eisenstein (1898–1948) works at an editing table with takes of 35 mm film. In the background, light behind frosted glass illuminates the film strips that hang before it. *Courtesy Herbert Marshall Archives, Center for Soviet and East European Studies, Southern Illinois University*

It's often said that an impressive performance is made in the cutting (or editing) room. The editor can make an actor look effective by selecting only the best takes and by cutting to a reaction shot if an actor even momentarily lapses out of character. The editor can also make the writer or writers look better, especially by dropping unnecessary dialogue and by ensuring an appropriate pace to the dialogue and action. Editors can make everyone involved in the film look better by cutting the tedious and extraneous. In a movie, viewers never see, for example, all the filmed reactions of someone in the film watching some important action. We should be grateful. As Hitchcock is reputed to have said, "Drama is life with the dull parts left out."

For a **feature film,** the editing process, which is often called "cutting the film," may take months and may require the efforts of two or more editors or an editor and assistants. Editing is so time-consuming that it's no wonder that for a feature film the job usually consumes months and can consume years. Although they faced extreme situations, the editors of *Crimson Tide* (1995) fashioned a 113-minute film out of 148 hours of **footage.** Documentary filmmakers often spend enormous amounts of time editing a film, too. Leni Riefenstahl had so much footage while making the **documentary film** *Olympia* (1936) that it took her ten weeks of ten-hour days just to view all the **dailies** (the prints made from a day's filming) then nearly two years to edit the film into its final version of more than three and a half hours (Riefenstahl). *Point of Order* (1963), a ninety-seven-minute documentary about the 1954 Army-McCarthy hearings, was fashioned during a three-year period from 188 hours of footage. Frederick Wiseman's *Belfast, Maine* (2000), which documents everyday life in a small coastal town, is 245 minutes long and is the result of 110 hours of filming and fourteen months of long days of editing. Even if the film is edited on computers, the process is as demanding and extremely time-consuming.

In large productions editors typically work within the boundaries set by the script and the footage the director has had shot. Nonetheless, by selecting shots and arranging, doubling, and shortening them, editors can expand or compress an action, promote **continuity** or lack of it, affect the film's pace and moods, and intensify viewer reactions. Sometimes editing can even salvage an otherwise mediocre film.

In this chapter, we examine how viewer responses can be affected by how the pieces of film are selected and combined. We consider how editing can be used (1) to promote continuity or disruptions; (2) to superimpose images; (3) to juxtapose images to make a point or to support a feeling or mood, intensify the viewer's reactions, or show parallel events; and (4) to affect the viewer's sense of pace, compress or expand time, and convey an enormous amount of information in a brief time. The chapter concludes with a brief discussion of how computers may be used in editing.

feature film: A fictional film that is at least sixty minutes long.

footage: A length of exposed motion-picture film, as in "they did not shoot enough footage."

documentary film: A film whose representation of its subjects viewers are intended to accept primarily as factual.

continuity (editing): Film editing that maintains a sense of uninterrupted time and action and continuous setting within each scene of a narrative film.

EARLY FILM EDITING

> In the first decades of this century, the film editor simply projected the uncut film, made notes, and then returned to a room equipped only with a bench, a pair of scissors, a magnifying glass, and the knowledge that the distance from the tip of his nose to the fingers of his outstretched arm represented about three seconds. (Murch 75)

In the first motion pictures, from the 1890s, filmmakers positioned the camera and filmed until the short **reel** of film ran out. That was it: one shot (see Figure 3.2). Later, the process of editing was limited to deciding the shots to include in the finished film and their order. Georges Méliès's early films, such as "Cinderella" (1900) and "A Trip to the Moon" (1902), were longer than previous films and consisted of a succession of scenes, each made up of one shot and showing continuous limited action in one place (see pp. 102–03). Film stories evolved further with the development of some scenes consisting of multiple shots.

reel: A metal or plastic spool to hold film.

In "The Life of an American Fireman" (1902) and "The Great Train Robbery" (1903), Edwin S. Porter tried more daring editing strategies, such as suggesting actions occurring at two places at the same time and combining others' footage with footage he filmed. However, Porter's innovation was surpassed by the techniques used by D. W. Griffith. In his short films from 1908 to 1913 and his first features, Griffith proved to be one of cinema's most innovative and adept editors. Griffith's controversial *The Birth of a Nation* (1915) has more than thirteen hundred shots of widely varying length, and parts of the film—such as the Civil War battles and the assassination of President Lincoln—are edited in a manner today's audiences still find engaging.

Some later Russian filmmakers—especially Lev Kuleshov, Dziga Vertov, Vsevolod I. Pudovkin, and Sergei Eisenstein—were much impressed with Griffith's editing (it is said that Pudovkin had planned to become a chemist until he saw Griffith's ambitious 1916 film *Intolerance*). These filmmakers studied some of Griffith's films closely and discussed or wrote about the art, craft, and theory of film editing. These four were part of a group of Soviet filmmakers who experimented with editing, and though they developed somewhat different editing **styles,** they promoted what

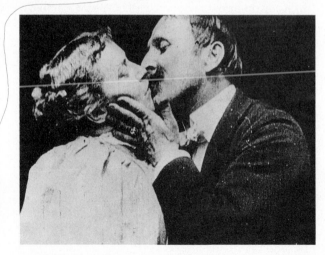

FIGURE 3.2 **Early film without editing**
The first films consisted of one shot. Technology did not yet permit editing. This frame shows two actors engaging in the first known screen kiss in the very brief, one-shot film "The Kiss" (1896). Frame enlargement. *Edison; The Museum of Modern Art/Film Stills Archive*

Editing of "A Trip to the Moon"

This 1902 silent French film runs about fourteen minutes and consists of fifteen scenes. Each scene is made up of only one shot. (The roman numerals in the following outline indicate one way to divide the story into sequences.)

I. EARTH

1. Astronomers' Club: a gathering of men dressed as medieval wizards. Five female attendants bring in telescopes, which they give to men in the front row. Their leader arrives. The telescopes change into stools, and the men sit. The leader draws on a blackboard and leads the animated discussion. The leader and five others change clothes and leave.

2. Factory: workers constructing a rocket. The six men arrive, inspect the rocket, and leave.

3. Rooftop of the factory: the six explorers arrive and gesture toward the industrial scene with its smoking chimneys and a cannon barrel being cast.

4. Launch site on a rooftop: the six explorers arrive and get into the rocket; the hatch is closed; the female assistants push the rocket into the giant cannon and wave to the audience with their hats.

5. Launch site, another view of the cannon: uniformed man with female attendants, brief ceremony with the French flag. The rocket is launched (Figure a), and the onlookers wave good-byes.

II. FLIGHT

6. Space: long shot of moon. The rocket approaches the "man in the moon," who is hit in the eye by the rocket (Figure b)

III. MOON

7. Lunar surface: the rocket lands, the six explorers emerge from it, and the rocket disappears. The earth rises; the explorers bed down; their dreams: a comet, stars of a dipper, other astronomical sights. It snows, so the explorers get up and descend into the moon.

8. Interior of moon (Méliès's 1903 catalog calls it a giant mushroom grotto): the leader's umbrella is transformed into a mushroom then starts to grow rapidly. Moon creatures (Méliès's catalog uses the French word for inhabitants of the moon, *Selenites*) arrive, are hit by the earth leader, and vanish in puffs of smoke. Other Selenites arrive and overpower the explorers.

9. Throne room of Selenite leader: the earthlings brought in. The earth leader tosses the moon leader to the floor where he explodes and disappears in a puff of smoke. The earthlings rush off.

10. Elsewhere on lunar landscape: the chase and further explosions, smoke puffs, and disappearing Selenites.

11. Rocket perched over the edge of precipice; all but the leader are inside. Nearby, he hits a Selenite (who disappears in a puff of smoke), closes the rocket hatch, and climbs down the rope suspended from the front of rocket. A moon creature clings to base of rocket as it falls (Figure c). Other Selenites arrive at edge of precipice and gesture after the departing rocket.

a)

b)

c)

IV. RETURN TRIP

12. Space above ocean: the leader of the explorers, the rocket, and the moon creature are all falling.

V. HOME

13. Ocean: the rocket approaches the ocean and hits it.

14. Bottom of ocean: the rocket hits the bottom and floats upward.

15. Off a port: a ship tows the rocket toward land.

Early editing
As in other early fictional films, throughout "A Trip to the Moon" (1902), the camera is unmoving; the action plays itself out before it; then a new shot and scene begin. (a) In one of the film's fifteen scenes, a huge canon is fired, launching the rocket. (b) In the next scene, the rocket expedition from earth lands whimsically in the eye of the man in the moon. (c) On the moon, a moon creature clings to the base of the rocket as it starts to fall. Frame enlargements. *Georges Méliès; The Museum of Modern Art/Circulating Film Library*

came to be called "Soviet montage" or simply **montage**. Such editing does not so much promote the invisible continuity of a story, strongly favored in **classical Hollywood cinema**; instead, it attempts to suggest **meanings** from the dynamic juxtaposition of many carefully selected details. As film theorist and scholar J. Dudley Andrew explains, Eisenstein

classical Hollywood cinema: Films that show one or more distinct characters facing a succession of problems while trying to reach their goal or goals; these films tend to hide the manner of their making by using continuity editing and other unobtrusive filmmaking techniques.

meaning: An observation or general statement about a subject.

> was appalled at how inefficient and dull most cinema was, especially cinema which sought to give its audience the impression of reality. Reality, he felt, speaks very obscurely, if at all. It is up to the filmmaker to rip reality apart and rebuild it into a system capable of generating the greatest possible emotional effects. (69)

Soviet montage is illustrated in *Strike* (1924), in which Eisenstein uses a visual metaphor to express the terrible situation of strikers in a capitalist society by cutting from shots of the striking workers and their families being attacked by police to shots of farm animals being slaughtered. Another example of Soviet montage occurs in Eisenstein's (*Battleship*) *Potemkin* (1925) after the tsar's troops and mounted Cossacks have attacked unarmed civilians in 1905 Odessa, Russia. In retaliation, the guns on the *Potemkin* have fired at the headquarters of the generals, and shells are starting to land. Then a sleeping stone lion seems to spring to life (Figure 3.3). The

FIGURE 3.3 **Editing to suggest ideas**
In the classic Soviet film (*Battleship*) *Potemkin* (1925), the editing of three consecutive shots makes a stone lion appear to come to life. The editing is used both to suggest a reaction to an event (the battleship's beginning to fire shells) and to suggest an idea (the *Potemkin* is so powerful that it brings stone to life). Frame enlargements. *Goskino; The Museum of Modern Art/Circulating Film Library*

three consecutive shots suggest that the *Potemkin*'s guns are so powerful that they rouse even a stone lion, or perhaps suggest that the Russian civilians (represented by the lion) are coming to life and will fight back; or perhaps these three shots suggest both meanings. The shots do not help develop the story; they do not even show any damage from the bombardment. Instead, they express an idea somewhat obtrusively (probably many viewers will be impressed and distracted by the editing of the three shots). Ever since the films of Griffith and those of the later Soviet masters Pudovkin and Eisenstein, the expressiveness and power of editing have been beyond dispute.

BUILDING BLOCKS

In constructing films that show stories, editors select shots to fabricate scenes and **sequences.** They connect shots in various ways, and most often they edit to create maximum continuity, an unobtrusive style of editing that helps viewers to follow the characters and action.

Shots, Scenes, Sequences

A **shot** is an uninterrupted strip of exposed motion-picture film or videotape made up of at least one **frame,** an individual image on the strip of film (Figure 3.4). A shot presents a subject, perhaps even a blank screen, during an uninterrupted segment of time. Typically, a feature film consists of hundreds of shots, sometimes more than a thousand. The original, uncensored version of *(Battleship) Potemkin* (1925) owned by the Museum of Modern Art in New York—which runs 72 minutes when projected at the silent speed of 18 frames per second—has 1,346 shots. *Toy Story* (1995), which is

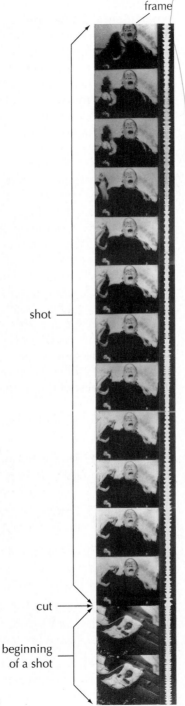

frame

shot

cut

beginning of a shot

FIGURE 3.4 **Frames, shot, and cut** The top twelve frames constitute a complete shot, and the bottom two the beginning of a new shot. The shots were spliced during editing of *(Battleship) Potemkin* (1925). When the film is projected at twenty-four frames per second, the top shot will last a half second. Frame enlargements. *Goskino; The Museum of Modern Art/Circulating Film Library*

experimental film: A film that rejects the conventions of mainstream movies and explores the possibilities of the film medium itself.

narrative: A series of unified consecutive events situated in one or more settings. A narrative may be fictional or factual or a blend of the two.

77½ minutes long, has 1,623 shots (Grignon). At the opposite extreme, some **experimental films** consist of a single, often very lengthy, shot. Andy Warhol's *Empire* (1964), which is seemingly a single shot of a view of the Empire State Building and runs for hours, is an example of this sort of film.

A **scene** is a section of a **narrative** film that gives the impression of continuous action taking place during continuous time and in continuous space. A scene seems to have unity, but editors often delete tedious or unnecessary footage in such a way that viewers will not notice. For example, we may not see every step a character presumably takes in moving within a scene. A scene may consist of one shot and usually consists of two or more related shots, but on rare occasions a shot is used to convey multiple scenes, as in the more than eight-minute opening shot of *The Player* (1992). At various times during that first shot, the camera moves closer to certain groups of characters so we can see them interact then moves to different characters elsewhere nearby (Table 3.1). In the opening of *The Player*, as in the famous opening of *Touch of Evil* (1958), there is not a scene consisting of the usual shot or shots but a shot consisting of scenes.

Sequence lacks a universal meaning: filmmakers, critics, and scholars often assign it different meanings. And comparison of several published outlines of sequences for the same film reveals different "sequences." It is most useful to think of a sequence as a group of related consecutive scenes, although what unifies the scenes is not universally agreed on.

To illustrate shot, scene, and sequence, I will describe the first two shots of the restored 1989 version of *Lawrence of Arabia*, which constitute the first scene and the rest of the scenes in the first sequence.

> Sequence 1 (in England):
>
> Scene 1:
>
>> Shot 1: On the left side of the **wide-screen** frame Lawrence fusses with a motorcycle as the opening credits roll in the center and on the right of the frame.
>>
>> Shot 2: Lawrence starts the motorcycle, gets on it, and drives away until he is out of sight.
>
> Scene 2 (consisting of twenty-three shots): As he rides quickly, even recklessly, up a hill, two bicyclists appear on his side of the road. He swerves and rides off the road.
>
> Scene 3 (consisting of two shots): After Lawrence's funeral in St. Paul's Cathedral and before a bust of Lawrence, Colonel Brighton and a cleric exchange brief and somewhat opposing views of Lawrence.
>
> Scene 4 (consisting of four shots): Outside St. Paul's Cathedral, four people are questioned about who Lawrence was; they are evasive, claim to have not known him well, or point out contradictory qualities.

wide-screen film: Any film with an aspect ration noticeably greater than 1.33:1 (a shape wider than that of an analog TV screen).

TABLE 3.1
The Opening Shot of *The Player*

SCENE NUMBER AND ACTION

1. A woman in Joel Levison's office takes a brief call from Larry Levy, then hangs up. Another woman scolds her, then sends her hurrying off for the day's trade papers.

2. Griffin drives into a parking space and gets out of his Range Rover. He is accosted by Adam Simon, who begins pitching a story for a possible movie. Griffin tells him to run the idea by Bonnie Sherow.

3. A man in a suit and another man who makes deliveries on a bicycle discuss tracking shots in movies.

4. Outside Griffin's office, we see through a window a man in a cap (Buck Henry) make a pitch for *The Graduate, Part Two*.

5. Adam Simon and Bonnie Sherow emerge from the same building; he is pitching his story to her. The delivery man on a bike has had an accident. Bonnie tries to help him.

6. A man in a Porsche briefly flirts with a young woman then asks where Joel Levison's office is. We learn that Levison is the studio head.

7. Another man is giving a studio tour to a group of Japanese people.

8. Bonnie, still pursued by Adam Simon, tells him to write down his story for her.

9. Joel Levison arrives in a large Mercedes immediately after the young woman of scene 1 arrives back and gives the papers to the other secretary.

10. Two men and a woman emerge from the building and talk about rumored upcoming changes at the studio, including the possibility that Griffin may be replaced.

11. In his office, Griffin hears two women make a story pitch.

12. The delivery man of scenes 3 and 5 mistakenly thinks that a man looking for Griffin Mill is the director Martin Scorsese.

13. The man in the suit from scene 3 and the man who made the pitch for *The Graduate, Part Two*, discuss editing and tracking shots in movies.

14. While crossing the parking lot, Bonnie scolds her assistant for meeting with a writer.

15. The man from scene 12 makes a movie pitch to Griffin.

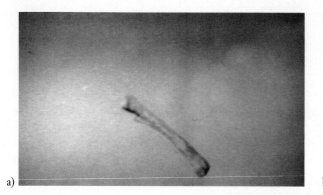
a)

b)

FIGURE 3.5 **Match cut of similar forms**

In *2001: A Space Odyssey* (1968), a shot of a bone is followed by a shot of an orbiting spacecraft. The transition suggests that both the bone, which minutes before had been used as a weapon, and the orbiting spacecraft are weapons. When projected, the film gives the appearance of the bone becoming the orbiting spacecraft, and viewers do not notice that the angles of the two objects do not match. Frame enlargements. *Metro-Goldwyn-Mayer*

a)

b)

FIGURE 3.6 **Match cut of form and movement**

In the German film *M* (1931), (a) the head of Berlin's underworld begins a sweeping motion with his arm, and (b) the movement is picked up and completed by a match cut to the chief of police at a different meeting. The suggestion is continuity and similarity between the groups: both have the same goal—to catch a child murderer and restore order to their disrupted routines. Frame enlargements. *Nero Films; The Museum of Modern Art/Circulating Film Library*

The first sequence of *Lawrence of Arabia* thus is made up of four scenes, and those four scenes consist of thirty-one shots. The next sequence begins in Egypt.

Narrative films stitch scenes together; if a film follows the traditions of classical Hollywood cinema, the scenes are usually combined in an unnoticeable manner. Feature narrative films vary enormously in the number of scenes, but a hundred or more is common.

Transitions

Shots may be joined in many ways. The most common method is to splice, or connect, the end of one shot to the beginning of the next. This transition is called a **cut** (or straight cut) (see Figure 3.4) because pieces of film are cut and spliced together. In narrative films, normally only cuts are used within a scene.

A **match cut** (sometimes called a form cut) maintains continuity between two shots by matching objects with similar or identical shapes or similar movements or both similar shapes and similar movements. One of the best-known examples of a match cut is from *2001: A Space Odyssey* (1968), in which a bone slowly tumbling end over end in the air is replaced by an orbiting spacecraft with a similar shape (Figure 3.5). A match cut in which the second shot continues a movement begun in the previous shot is found in *M* (1931, Figure 3.6).

A **jump cut** is a discontinuous transition between shots. For example, one shot shows a woman running on a beach toward the water, and the next shot shows her running away from the water. A jump cut is sometimes used to surprise or disorient viewers (see Figure 3.14b and c on pp. 118–19). It may also occur if the film print or video has missing footage.

The **fade-out, fade-in** can provide a short but meaningful pause between scenes or sequences. Normally in a fade-out, fade-in, an image is gradually transformed into a darkened frame; then the next shot changes from a darkened frame into an illuminated one. However, many variations are possible. Early in *The Discreet Charm of the Bourgeoisie* (1972), a shot (and scene) ends with the camera **zooming** in as the image goes out of focus; the next shot (and scene) begins out of focus then quickly comes into focus. The transition functions much like the more traditional fade-out, fade-in. If a fade-out, fade-in is done slowly, it can serve as a leisurely transition; if done rapidly, it is less noticeable or not noticeable at all. Perhaps because of the current popularity of fast pacing in films, in recent movies this transition is used far less often than it used to be.

In a **lap dissolve** or dissolve, one shot fades from view as the next shot fades into view then replaces it (Figure 3.7). This transition between shots has been used in many ways for example, to introduce and conclude a cutaway that shows what a character is thinking. In Buster Keaton's *Our Hospitality* (1923), the Keaton character looks straight ahead, then a rapid lap dissolve

zoom (in): To use a zoom lens to cause the image of the subject to increase in size as the area being filmed seems to decrease.

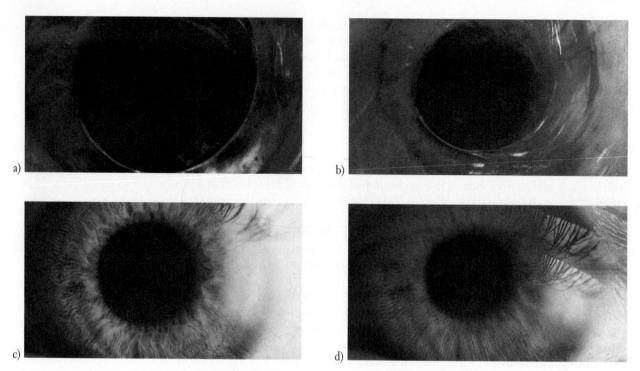

a)

b)

c)

d)

FIGURE 3.7 **Lap dissolve**
In *Psycho*, the 1998 remake, as in the 1960 original, a shot of a shower drain fades out as a shot of a dead woman's eye fades in, momentarily overlapping the first shot before replacing it. (a) The shot of the drain is (b and c) gradually replaced by the image of the woman's eye until (d) it is entirely replaced. In a few seconds, the lap dissolve allows the filmmakers to point out the visual similarity of a human eye to a drain. Because the woman is dead, the lap dissolve can also be interpreted as showing that the eye is now as inert and unchanging as the drain. Additionally, this lap dissolve slows the pace momentarily so the reality of the woman's murder can sink in for the viewers. Frame enlargements. *Imagine Entertainment; Universal*

setting: The place where filmed action occurs.

introduces a brief shot showing what he is thinking about, and a second rapid lap dissolve returns to the shot of him looking straight ahead. Usually filmmakers have used the lap dissolve to suggest a change of **setting,** the passage of time, or both. Lap dissolves may be rapid and nearly imperceptible or slow and quite noticeable, creating a momentary superimposition of two images, sometimes suggesting similarities or even symbolic meaning (see Figure 3.7). Dissolves between scenes have long been commonplace. Dissolves *within* a scene were occasionally used in early cinema (Figure 3.8). Now they are rare, although they are used in the scene in *Election* (1999) where the Reese Witherspoon character rips down rival candidates' posters from a high school corridor's walls.

a)

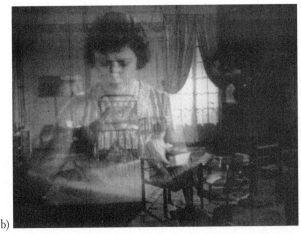

b)

c)

FIGURE 3.8 Lap dissolve within a scene
Although lap dissolves are now rarely used within scenes, earlier films—as in this example from the experimental film classic "Un chien andalou" (1928)—occasionally used them. Frame enlargements. *The Museum of Modern Art/Circulating Film Library*

A **wipe** seems to push one shot off the screen as it replaces it with the next shot (Figure 3.9). This transition, which comes in many variations, has been popular in science fiction, **serials,** and action movies, but it has also been used in such diverse films as *It Happened One Night* (1934), *The Maltese Falcon* (1941), *The Seven Samurai* (1954), *Ed Wood* (1994), and *Battlefield Earth* (2000). Yet other examples are found in the opening and closing credits of some Pink Panther movies, where an animated pink panther seems to help push off one shot as it is replaced with the next shot.

The six transitions discussed thus far are summarized in Table 3.2.

Many other transitions are used less often than these six. The others can be thought of as combination transitions. In many films from the silent era

serial: From the 1910s until the early 1950s, a low-budget action film divided into chapters or installments, one of which was shown each week in downtown and neighborhood movie theaters.

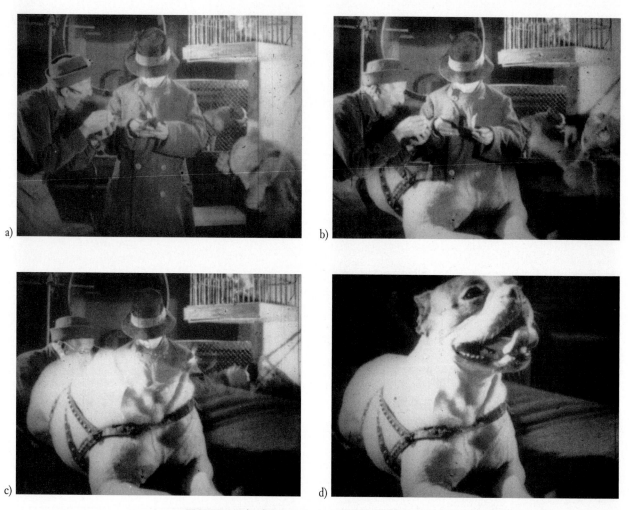

FIGURE 3.9 **A wipe**
In *Strike* (1924), a wipe is used between two scenes when (a) the image of two men is replaced
with (b to d) the image of a dog. Wipes may move across the frame from any direction: from below (as here), from above, from one of the sides, even on a diagonal. Frame enlargements. *The
Museum of Modern Art/Circulating Film Library*

and some sound films that try to evoke the silent era, an iris-in or iris-out
may connect scenes. In the **iris-in,** a widening opening reveals more and
more of the next shot until it is more visible (Figure 3.10). In an **iris-out,** the
image is closed out by a constricting shape, usually a circle.

In some films, a dark object approaches the camera and concludes a
scene. In *Beauty and the Beast*, directed by Jean Cocteau (1946), a man and his

TABLE 3.2
Six Frequently Used Transitions between Shots

Cut	The end of the first shot is attached to the beginning of the second shot. The most often used of all transitions, it creates an instantaneous change in one or more of the following: angle, distance, subject (Figure 3.4).
Match or form cut	The shape or movement of a subject in the beginning of the second shot matches or is very similar to a subject's form or movement at the end of the previous shot. (Figures 3.5 and 3.6).
Jump cut	A transition in which the viewer perceives the second shot as abruptly discontinuous with the first shot. (Figures 3.14b and c).
Fade-out, fade-in	The first shot fades to darkness (normally black); then the second shot fades in (by degrees goes from darkness to illuminated image).
Lap dissolve or dissolve	The first shot fades out as the second shot fades in, overlaps the first, then replaces it entirely. (Figures 3.7 and 3.8).
Wipe	The first shot seems to be pushed off the screen by the next shot. Not a common transition, but not rare either. For a "wipe chart" illustrating 120 types of wipes, see Roy Huss and Norman Silverstein, *The Film Experience* (New York: Dell, 1968), 60. Examples they give include beginning with a small part of the second shot in one area of the frame then expanding the smaller area until it displaces the original, larger one. As Huss and Silverstein also explain, "a second image 'wipes' . . . a first from the screen . . . in several directional and formal ways: horizontally, vertically, diagonally, in the shape of a fan, like the movement of the hands of a clock, with a 'flip' (the frame revolves 360 degrees)" (59). (Figure 3.9).

horse are lost in a foggy forest. The man passes close by the camera; then his black horse approaches so close to the camera that its flank completely darkens the screen and ends the scene. After a rapid fade-in, viewers see a new setting. This transition is like a wipe to black then fade-in.

Easy Rider (1969) uses a series of quick cuts to bridge two scenes. Viewers see the last part of a scene's last shot, the beginning of the next

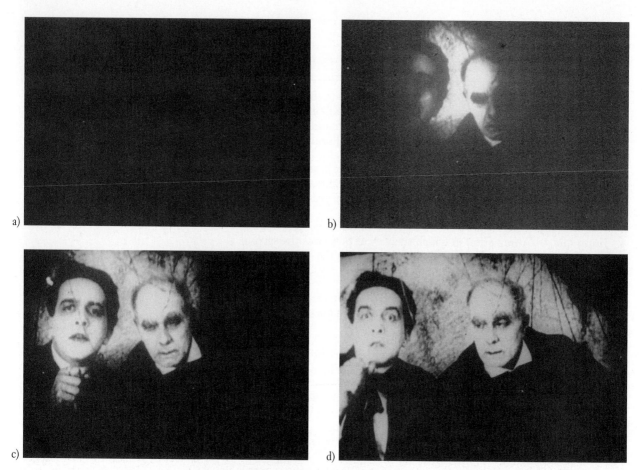

FIGURE 3.10 Iris-in

Four frame enlargements from early in *The Cabinet of Dr. Caligari* (1919) illustrate an iris-in: a transition between shots in which the image is gradually exposed by a widening opening, usually a circle. (a) The shot begins with four black frames then (b and c) reveals more and more of the image by means of an irregularly shaped opening. (d) As is common in *Caligari*, part of the image remains in the dark (is masked). Frame enlargements. *Decla-Bioscop; The Museum of Modern Art/ Circulating Film Library*

scene, the last part of the previous shot, the first part of the next scene again, and the same repetition two more times—all this consuming little more than a second before the second scene is finally allowed to play itself out. If 1 stands for several frames at the end of a scene and 2 for several frames at the beginning of the next scene, the transition between the two scenes would be represented like this: 1 2 1 2 1 2 1 2.

CONTINUITY EDITING

In narrative films and certainly in classical Hollywood cinema, **continuity editing** is normally used. Shots seem to follow one another unobtrusively, and viewers always know where the subjects of a shot are in relation to other subjects and in relation to the setting. Continuity editing allows the omission of minor details within scenes yet maintains the illusion of completeness. Continuity may be achieved in various ways. For example, **eyeline matches** may be used, in which a subject looks at something **offscreen,** and the next shot shows what was being looked at from approximately the point of view of the subject (Figure 3.11). Continuity is also maintained within scenes if all shots show the subjects from one side of an imaginary straight line drawn between them. This is sometimes referred to as the 180-degree system.

A scene from *Life Is Beautiful* (1998) illustrates various ways continuity can be maintained within a scene (Figure 3.12). Throughout the scene the viewer sees the actor on his left side or from behind him but not on his right side (the 180-degree system). Shot/reverse shot is another way to promote continuity. A shot from over the first person's shoulder or to the side of it shows the face of a second person; in the next shot the camera is behind or to the side of the second person, and we now see the first person's face (Figures 3.12c and d). During both shots, the background remains the same or is consistent with the previous shot. Shot/reverse shot is often used for scenes with dialogue. Continuity editing is also achieved by cutting on action: one shot ends during a subject's movement, and the next shot, usually from a different

a)   b)

FIGURE 3.11 **Eyeline match**
In the Iranian film *The White Balloon* (1995), (a) the main character points off-frame. (b) Then from her point of view, the camera sees what she sees: a fish she is eager to buy. Such eyeline matches are one way filmmakers maintain continuity from shot to shot within a scene. Frame enlargements. *C.M.I.*

a)

b)

c)

d)

FIGURE 3.12 Continuity editing within a scene
The scene from *Life Is Beautiful* (1998) represented here runs twenty-nine seconds and consists of eight shots:

1. The man rounds a corner riding a bicycle in a hurry: an angry man is chasing him (a).
2. A line of schoolchildren and a woman to the left of them are walking toward the nearby piazza.
3. The man on the bike reacts with alarm because the children and the woman inadvertently block his path.
4. The man runs into the woman (b) and falls on top of her.
5. Her reaction when she sees who it is (c) (they had met briefly earlier when he broke her fall from a barn)
6. His reaction to her (d)
7. He helps her up (e), says good-bye, and runs off (he is still concerned that the man who had been chasing him might catch up with him).
8. Her reaction to his abrupt departure

In this scene from *Life Is Beautiful*, all shots of the man are from his left side or from behind him, so viewers always know where he is in relationship to his surroundings. Applying the 180-degree system, the camera operator filmed the subjects from one side of an imaginary line drawn between the scene's main subjects: the man and the woman. Occasionally, as in (b), the camera is positioned *on* or a little beyond that imaginary line. If shots in a scene are filmed from the other side of that imaginary

e)

line—if, for example, we suddenly saw the man's right side—the relationship of the subjects to each other and to the setting shifts abruptly and perhaps confusingly. Here and in countless movie scenes, matching action also supports continuity: for example, the action seen in (c) seems to be continuous with the beginning the following shot. To promote continuity, the scene also uses an eyeline match: shots 3 and 4 show the man looking with alarm then what he is looking at. Here, as in nearly all edited scenes, the continuity of space, time, and action or the illusion of them is maintained. Actually, in many movie scenes, fragments of time and action are unobtrusively deleted. Because of continuity editing, however, the action seems to flow from shot to shot smoothly and clearly yet concisely. Frame enlargements. *Cecchi Gori Group; Miramax*

distance or angle, continues or concludes the action (Figures 3.12d and e). In such instances, sometimes dead time (some of the middle part of the movement) may be omitted, yet continuity is maintained because the same subject moves in a consistent and seemingly uninterrupted way. Eyeline matches are also used in the scene, as when the man on the bicycle looks offscreen to the left and the next shot shows what he is looking at: the schoolchildren and the woman.

Continuity editing is the usual way narrative films are edited, though some filmmakers choose to ignore continuity from time to time, and other filmmakers—such as the French actor and director Jacques Tati and the Japanese director Yasujiro Ozu—often reject the conventions of continuity editing.

IMAGE ON IMAGE AND IMAGE AFTER IMAGE

Editors can combine two or more images into the same image—although it's usually hard for viewers to distinguish more than two images at the same time—or they can juxtapose images in expressive ways.

superimposition: Two or more images photographed or printed on top of each other.

Superimpositions

Occasionally editors **superimpose** images during a lap dissolve. The lap dissolve near the end of *Psycho* (1960) fleetingly juxtaposes three images (Figure 3.13). If a dissolve is slow enough—or even halts briefly midway, as is done on rare occasions—viewers are more likely to notice the superimposed images.

Near the beginning of *The Wild Bunch* (1969) occurs a complex example of combined images within a lap dissolve. Children in a western town are burning scorpions and ants. A slow lap dissolve combines images of the burning insects with images of many townspeople and railroad employees who had recently been shot in the cross fire between bounty hunters hired by the railroad and the wild bunch. During the dissolve from the children to the scene of carnage, viewers hear the giggles of the children burning the insects mingled with some crying and the moans of the injured people. The combination of images and sounds suggests that people can be like helpless scorpions and ants, painfully destroyed by powerful forces indifferent to their wellbeing. The blending of images also undercuts any notion of youthful innocence: the children who enjoy destroying insect life may grow up and destroy human life, as did the bounty hunters and the wild bunch.

FIGURE 3.13 **Superimposition of three images**
In a few frames near the conclusion of *Psycho* (1960), viewers may notice that three images are superimposed briefly: Norman from the shoulders up, a skull, and Marion's car being pulled from the swamp by a chain. In a 35 mm version of the film that is in good condition or a laser disc or DVD version viewed on a high-resolution monitor, viewers may notice the images and consider their significance. (Viewers are unlikely to notice them on a videotape version.) The brief triple superimposition suggests that underneath Norman is his mother and that Norman is, in at least one sense, already dead. The superimposed images also suggest that Norman, his mother, and death are a swamp and that Norman embodies death and destruction. A psychoanalytical critic might see the swamp as the vast, untamed id near the human heart. Frame enlargement. *Alfred Hitchcock; Universal*

a)   b)

e)   f)

Expressive Juxtapositions

Even in films that use continuity editing extensively, filmmakers sometimes want to surprise, amuse, or confuse and may follow a shot with one viewers don't expect.

Occasionally the unexpected shot appears after a brief lap dissolve. In *Citizen Kane* (1941), immediately after Kane marries Susan, his second wife, he has decided she'll have a career as an opera singer. As the newlyweds are about to be driven off, Susan tells the reporters around the car that if necessary, Kane will build her an opera house. Kane shouts, "That won't be necessary." After a rapid lap dissolve, the next shot is a large newspaper headline reading "Kane Builds Opera House." The effect is surprising and amusing; the combination of shots also shows that Kane's judgment can be faulty.

Sometimes filmmakers use jump cuts to confuse or disorient viewers, as in several scenes in the classic French **new wave** film *Breathless* (1959, Figure 3.14). Editing can also be used to surprise or amuse viewers (Figure 3.15).

(French) new wave (cinema): A diverse group of French fictional films made in the late 1950s and early 1960s in reaction to the carefully scripted products of the French film industry and as explorations of more current subjects sometimes rendered with untraditional techniques.

c)

d)

g)

FIGURE 3.14 **Jump cuts to create discontinuity**

In one scene in Jean-Luc Godard's *Breathless* (1959), a man driving a car pulls off a country road to elude two pursuing motorcycle police officers; one of the officers pulls off the same road; and the man shoots the officer and runs away. To viewers reared on continuity editing, the scene sometimes seems discontinuous or jerky, as if the camera were sometimes in the wrong position or as if shots or parts of shots had been left out. The last seven shots of the scene illustrate three areas of confusion for viewers. Shots (a) and (b) are taken from one side of an imaginary line between the two subjects, with the man facing left; but shots (c–e) are inexplicably filmed from the other side of the line, and the man is now facing right. The scene is not edited using the 180-degree system. Where the police officer is when he gets shot (f) is also puzzling: he is certainly not on the path leading from the road, shown in shot (a). Finally, the relation of the last shot (g) to the preceding shots is unclear: viewers cannot know where the man is and how far he is from the shot police officer. Perhaps (g) is a new scene consisting of one shot. Although the seven shots are elliptical and confusing in some of their details, one could make a case that the main action is clear and that the discontinuous editing is appropriate for the action shown: a sudden, unplanned murder. Frame enlargements. *SNC; New Yorker Films*

a)

b)

FIGURE 3.15 **Editing creating humorous surprises**
Since editing allows filmmakers to change from one image to another instantaneously, filmmakers may insert an unexpected shot and surprise a character or the viewer, or both. In *Inventing the Abbotts* (1997), Doug, a high school boy, sees a girl he is attracted to at the school library. To get a better view of her legs, he drops his pencil to the floor then stoops to retrieve it. The girl is aware of his goal and allows him to look briefly. Doug gazes (a); then when he looks again, she has inserted a penciled greeting between her legs (b). Viewers are surprised and amused. Startled, the boy starts to spring up and bumps his head, which amuses her—and amuses the viewers again. Frame enlargements. *20th Century–Fox*

filmic: Characteristic of the film medium or appropriate to it.

Editors often join two shots to illustrate similarities. Near the end of *The Wild Bunch*, after the final shootout, we see a shot of perched vultures; then two shots later a shot of gleeful bounty hunters swooping down on the dead to strip them of valuables, as birds—vultures?—fly across the frame in the foreground and a vulture is visible briefly in the background, then a shot of a vulture perched on a dead man. The juxtaposition of shots constitutes a none-too-subtle **filmic** metaphor suggesting that the bounty hunters are vultures.

Less obvious yet still damning by association are some of the accompanying shots of Miss Michigan in the satirical documentary *Roger & Me* (1989). We first see Miss Michigan riding in a car on which is affixed a sign for a Chevrolet dealer during a parade in Flint, Michigan, immediately after a shot of a man scooping up horse dung from the parade route. Later a man speaking of the poor labor conditions in Flint concludes that some people know what is going on and some don't; the next shot is of Miss Michigan. Later still, we see brief footage of the 1988 Miss USA pageant and learn that Miss Michigan won the national title; the next shot is a match cut of a man in Flint knocking on a door to evict people from their housing, presumably because they are out of work and behind in the rent. Because of the selection and arrangement of the shots (and because of how Miss Michigan responds to director Michael Moore's unexpected questions), she comes across as someone who cares not about labor and living conditions in Flint but only about winning the national title. Consecutive shots may serve yet other purposes. Consecutive wordless shots, for example, may subtly suggest the predicament that characters are in (Figure 3.16).

a)

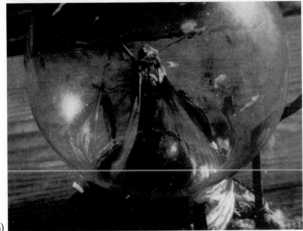

b)

c)

FIGURE 3.16 **Consecutive shots suggesting characters' situation** *Woman in the Dunes* (1964) begins with a city man collecting samples of insects in a remote setting near a sea. Some local men tell him that he has missed the last bus back into town and invite him to stay overnight with a woman in a shack in a sandpit. Soon the man realizes that the villagers and the woman intend for him to live with her and help her. Later the man catches the woman off guard and ties up her hands and feet, but he fails to escape from the pit. The three shots represented here come from the beginning of a scene. (a) A bird's-eye view shows the two of them sleeping (she is still bound hand and foot). (b) The next shot shows a trapped insect trying to escape its glass prison. (c) The third shot is of sand falling down cliffs of sand, presumably nearby. Shot (a) shows that the couple is exhausted (they are motionless and she sleeps even though her hands and feet are bound). Shot (b) suggests that though the man has tied up the woman, they are trapped, as is the insect the man had collected. Shot (c), of falling sand, reminds viewers that sand continues to fall and endanger the shack (viewers earlier had learned that the woman has to shovel sand or it will overwhelm her shack). In a mere seventeen seconds, the three wordless shots convey that the man and woman are tired, trapped, and in danger. Frame enlargements. *Pathe Contemporary Films Release*

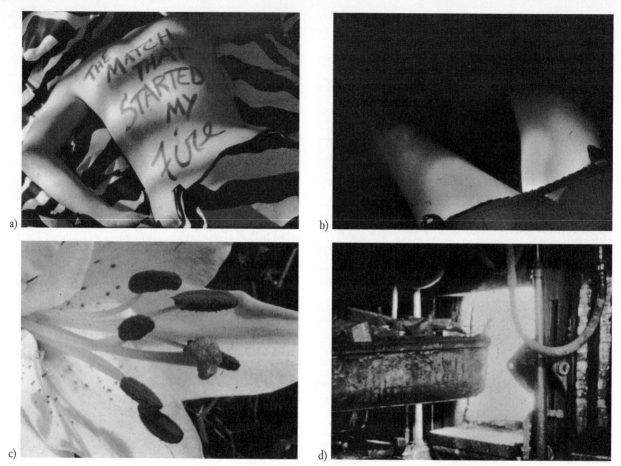

FIGURE 3.17 Consecutive shots creating meaning in a nonnarrative documentary
Three consecutive images from the nonnarrative documentary film "The Match That Started My Fire" (1991) illustrate how the selection and arrangement of shots can create meaning beyond what the shots convey individually. In the film various women describe their first awareness of their sexual feelings as viewers see a wide variety of images, some created for this film (b and c), some selected from existing footage (d). The three consecutive images shown here (b–d)—of a woman's bare legs illuminated in the dark, an open flower, and a mechanism pushing a load into a blazing furnace—suggest various facets of a woman's sexuality. Frame enlargements. *Cathy C. Cook; Women Make Movies, New York*

In nonnarrative films, the juxtaposition of shots may also be as expressive as in fictional films (Figures 3.17 and 3.18).

Action and Reaction

How viewers react to a movie is often intensified by how subjects in the film react. In virtually all narrative films (fictional and documentary), many scenes show actions and other people's reactions, and those **reaction shots** tend to intensify viewer's responses. Humorous scenes are usually

a)

b)

c)

FIGURE 3.18 Consecutive shots creating a visual poem in a nonnarrative experimental film

In a shot from the experimental film "Un chien andalou" (1928), (a) a man begins to fall forward, presumably mortally wounded. In the next shot (b and c), now in the countryside, as he continues to fall, his hands brush the bare back of a seated woman; then the woman's image fades away. The two shots show that dying can figuratively be like momentarily brushing the bare back of a woman who quickly fades away and leaves the beauty of nature. The juxtaposition of shots suggests the fragility and beauty of life as human life ebbs away. Frame enlargements. *The Museum of Modern Art/Circulating Film Library*

funnier because someone is shown to be bewildered, stunned, or in some way made uncomfortable. Horrifying scenes can be more frightening because of shots of characters reacting to scary sights or sounds. Suspenseful athletic contests, as in the **narrative documentary** *Hoop Dreams* (1994), are even more involving because of how individuals in the crowd are shown reacting to events. Images of anguish can be more gripping if interspersed with reaction shots, as in *The Bicycle Thief* (1948, Figure 3.19). Reaction shots that follow action shots can be used in a limitless variety of situations.

narrative documentary: A film that presents mainly a factual narrative or story.

123

a)

b)

c)

FIGURE 3.19 Action, then reaction
Two consecutive shots show an action and reaction in the last scene of the Italian neorealist film *The Bicycle Thief* (1948). The boy has recently seen a crowd chasing, catching, and reviling his father, who in desperation tried to steal a bicycle so he would not lose his recently acquired job. (a) First viewers see the father's emotional pain and (b and c) the boy looking up to see his father's anguish and taking his hand. The reaction shot of the boy shows his anguish and empathy and intensifies viewers' response to his and his father's plight. Frame enlargements. *PDS-ENIC*

Not that action followed by reaction is the editor's only choice. Sometimes we viewers see a reaction then what caused it (Figure 3.20). Filmmakers may dwell on reaction shots rather than on the subject being reacted to and let viewers' imaginations supply the rest. An amusing example occurs in *There's Something about Mary* (1998, Figure 3.21).

Parallel Editing

In **parallel editing,** or cross-cutting, the film shifts back and forth between two or more subjects or lines of action, often suggesting that the actions are occurring simultaneously and are related but sometimes depicting events from different times. Parallel editing that suggests simultaneous events is used in an early sequence in the classic German film *M* (Figure 3.22).

Parallel editing is occasionally used throughout a movie to suggest two or more simultaneous **plotlines** and to generate suspense, as in *Dr. Strangelove:*

plotline: A narrative or series of related events usually involving only a few characters or people and capable of functioning on its own as a story.

a)   b)

FIGURE 3.20 Reaction, then action
(a) In *Antz* (1998), the main character, an ant named Z, looks at something off-frame. (b) The next shot shows viewers what Z is alarmed about: Princess Bala stuck in gum on the bottom of a shoe of someone walking. Frame enlargements. *PDI; DreamWorks Pictures*

a)   b)

c)   d)

FIGURE 3.21 Reaction to implied action
These four frames represent four consecutive shots from *There's Something about Mary* (1998). (a) Mary looks on. (b) The young man (Ted) helps Mary's brother get positioned in the batting cage. (c) A shot from the point of view of the boy in the batting cage shows a baseball whizzing forward. (d) Mary and Ted react with alarm and concern. By implication, the ball hit the boy and knocked him down. Here the editing shifts the emphasis from the boy getting hit (which could be alarming to viewers) to the reaction of the two witnesses (which is amusing since viewers do not see the boy's pain). For a situation to be humorous, it usually has to be placed in a context where there is not too much pain to someone whom viewers care about. Frame enlargements. *Farrelly Bros.; 20th Century–Fox*

FIGURE 3.22 Parallel editing to suggest simultaneous events
In the German film *M* (1931), before the shots shown here, a young
girl, Elsie, leaves school and plays with a ball. Viewers learn that
a child murderer is on the loose and see Elsie being greeted by a
stranger who buys her a balloon. Elsie's mother waits for her daughter
and frets that she is late. (a) As the mother calls out Elsie's name,
we viewers see an empty stairwell in the building where Elsie and
her mother live, (b) an empty attic, presumably in their building,
and (c) Elsie's empty chair and table setting. The three parallel shots
suggest concisely, even eloquently, that at that moment Elsie is not
on the stairs, in the attic, or at the table. (The three shots being void
of life and tinged with darkness are disquieting, too.) The next two
shots resume the flow of action and confirm our suspicion that Elsie
has come to harm: (d) the ball she played with earlier rolls into view
and stops, and (e) the balloon the man had bought her floats up and
briefly gets caught in wires before being carried away by the wind.
The little movement in the last two shots ends in disturbing stillness.
Frame enlargements. *Nero Films; The Museum of Modern Art/
Circulating Film Library*

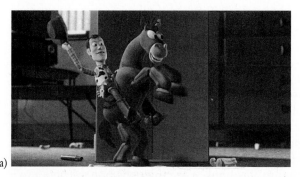

a)   b)

FIGURE 3.23 **Parallel editing of two plotlines**
Approximately half of *Toy Story 2* (1999) employs parallel editing of two plotlines: (a) Woody with his horse from his earlier career and (b) Woody's friends on the way to rescue him (here four of Woody's friends are in a toy car looking for Woody in the kidnapper's toy store). Frame enlargements. *Pixar; Walt Disney Pictures*

Or, How I Learned to Stop Worrying and Love the Bomb (1963). Except for that film's expository prologue, its doomsday device finale, and its third sequence, which is located in undisclosed residential quarters, all the film's sequences occur at one of three locations: a U.S. Air Force base where General Jack D. Ripper takes it upon himself to order a group of U.S. bombers to attack Soviet targets; an American bomber containing a crew trying to reach a target in the Soviet Union; and the Pentagon War Room, where the U.S. president and his advisers, the Soviet ambassador, and, via phone, the Soviet premier try to avert catastrophe. Although viewers get the sense of time moving forward as the film progresses, the parallel editing suggests that some of the events happen simultaneously.

Often parallel editing shows someone being menaced while someone else is on the way to help. Early in the twentieth century, D. W. Griffith perfected this technique and often used it in his films. It is still commonplace in movies, as in *Toy Story 2* (1999), which incorporates parallel editing of two plotlines during approximately half of the film (Figure 3.23). Parallel editing may also be used to show one subject trying to achieve a goal as another subject tries to overcome various problems and prevent the first subject from achieving the goal. A memorable example occurs near the end of Hitchcock's *Strangers on a Train* (1951), where extensive and suspenseful parallel editing shows one character on his way to plant incriminating evidence at a murder site as another character tries to overcome various problems and arrive there before him.

Parallel editing can show a contrast. In *A Fish Called Wanda* (1988), it is used amusingly to contrast a bored married couple getting ready for bed with a young unmarried couple fully attending to each other as they undress and have sex. In the documentary film "The Heck with Hollywood!" (1991), which is about the difficulties of marketing one's own low-budget film, parallel editing is briefly used to contrast the views of an independent filmmaker with those of her distributor.

Parallel editing can also highlight a similarity. Throughout *M*, parallel editing shows that the police, organized beggars, and organized crime in a German city of the early 1930s are all trying to capture a child murderer. Griffith also used parallel editing throughout *Intolerance* to present four stories illustrating intolerance in four eras and places.

As we see so many times in this book, a technique is not restricted to a certain type of film. Parallel editing can also be used in films that tell no story, as in the nonnarrative documentary *Titicut Follies* (1967, Figure 3.24).

PACE AND TIME

Pace is the viewer's sense of a film's material (such as succeeding events in a narrative film or information in a documentary film) being presented rapidly or slowly. Although it is a highly subjective experience and is influenced by many aspects of the film, a film's pace can help keep viewers involved or alienate them.

Fast and Slow Cutting

A shot may be as brief as one frame, but when it is, few viewers see its content. At the opposite extreme, as Hitchcock demonstrated in *Rope* (1948), a shot may run for as long as the reel of film in the camera. Shots in feature films typically range from several seconds to about twenty seconds. **Fast cutting** refers to consecutive shots of brief duration—say, a few seconds or less. **Slow cutting** refers to consecutive shots of long duration or editing dominated by long-lasting shots. Because again so much depends upon context, it's difficult to set a number here, but an average shot length (ASL) of fifteen or more seconds will seem slow to many viewers in Western cultures.

Fast cutting may impart energy to its subjects. It is also an effective way to convey a lot of information in a brief time, as in many **trailers** shown on TV, in movie theaters, and at the beginning of many videotaped movies. Makers of music videos and other filmmakers often use fast cutting to intensify a sense of confusion or loss of control or to add urgency or energy. It's no accident, for example, that the opera montage in *Citizen Kane* uses fast cutting throughout. During that section of the story, Susan is under unbearable pressure, and the fast cutting reflects the fact that events seem to gallop out of her control.

trailer: A brief compilation film made to advertise a movie or a video release.

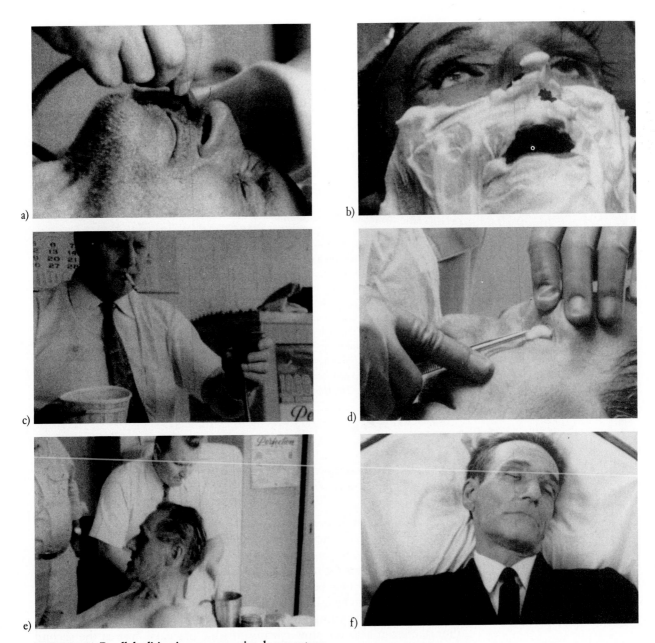

FIGURE 3.24 Parallel editing in a nonnarrative documentary

Parallel editing is not restricted to narrative films. It may be used to compare and contrast any two subjects from different places or different times. In *Titicut Follies* (1967), Frederick Wiseman's first film, shots of a man being force-fed by a psychologist in a mental hospital (left column, top to bottom) are alternated with shots of the corpse of the same man being prepared for display before his burial (right column). In his subsequent films, instead of using parallel editing, Wiseman nearly always presents long, uninterrupted shots of the subjects and gives viewers greater freedom in interpreting relationships and meaning. Frame enlargements. *Zipporah Films*

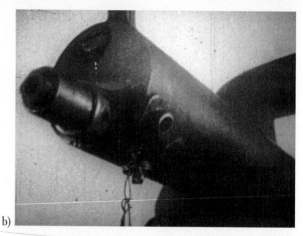

a) b)

FIGURE 3.25 Fast cutting and a regular rhythm
Early in *October* (1928), which was codirected and edited by Sergei Eisenstein, two frames of a soldier firing a machine gun are alternated with two frames of the gun being fired. This extremely rapid alternation between the soldier and gun, soldier and gun, soldier and gun, sets up a regular rhythm, as if the man is relentless, as if he is a machine or part of one, or as if the weapon consists of the man plus the gun. Through editing, the man and the gun become one. To recapture some of the experience of seeing these two alternating images in the film, look at the first frame only long enough to see its subject (much less than a second); then do the same with the second frame; then allotting the same fraction of a second to each image, look back and forth, back and forth, and so on. Frame enlargements. *The Museum of Modern Art/Circulating Film Library*

For some descriptions of the opera montage in *Citizen Kane*, see the Web site for this book: <http://www.bedfordstmartins.com/phillips-film>.

Fast cutting is sometimes used to show images flashing through someone's mind during a crisis, as when late in *Spanking the Monkey* (1994) the main character has jumped from a high cliff and is plunging toward water. Fast cutting is frequently used for fights, climaxes to races, and montages summarizing past events. Editing may be not only fast but also regular (Figure 3.25).

Slow cutting can be used to establish a subdued mood before fast cutting injects energy. Slow cutting may also be used in scenes of calm or reflection. Filmmakers can also use slow cutting to slow the pace, just as the second movement of a symphony or concerto typically does.

Too much of any technique—fast cutting or slow—causes viewers to lose interest, so editing is used to vary a film's pace. Like poets writing in meter, filmmakers can establish a more or less regular rhythm, then maintain it, or work expressive variations on it. In the last sequence of the classic Soviet film (*Battleship*) *Potemkin*, for example, the battleship *Potemkin* is steaming along. The cutting is brisk but by no means hurried or frantic. After possible rival ships are spotted and the men called to their battle stations, the cutting becomes faster and faster until it is clear there will be no battle after all; then the pace of the editing slows. Technique reinforces mood.[1]

Studies of editing show that since the mid-1970s, movies have had a much shorter average shot length than in earlier decades. Film scholar Barry Salt reports that from 1976 to 1987, the average shot length of a large sample of movies was about 8.4 seconds (296). Of course, some shots are twenty-five or even many more seconds, but there are also many stretches of fast cutting. Why there is so much fast cutting in recent movies, TV, and music videos in Western cultures is not easy to determine. Perhaps modern viewers absorb the meaning of a shot more quickly. Perhaps we are visually jaded and need more of a kick. If a narrative is poor, editors may dazzle viewers with exciting editing techniques, according to Michael Hoggan, a past president of American Cinema Editors. Or perhaps the fast cutting reflects the fast pace most people feel is an inescapable part of their lives. Maybe it's a combination of these or other causes. Music videos with their fast cutting and jump cuts bombard viewers with such an overload of information that it is often impossible to discern in them any coherence or meaning, and for many viewers this lack of coherence and meaning is characteristic of contemporary life.

Condensing Time and Stretching It: Montage and Other Editing Techniques

In classical Hollywood cinema—but not in fictional films of the Japanese director Yasujiro Ozu and Danish director Carl Theodor Dreyer, in some experimental films, and in some documentary films—one of the main goals of editing is to eliminate dead time, any footage that does not contribute to the desired effects. The sense of dead time, however, depends on who is doing the viewing, and shots that were engaging in former eras often seem uneventful to viewers of a later generation. For example, the many shots in classic western films of cowboys riding and riding on and on are dead time to so many of today's young viewers. One of the most effective means of cutting dead time and showing viewers much information quickly is a montage, or a "quick impressionistic sequence of . . . images, usually linked by dissolves, superimpositions or wipes, and used to convey passages of time, changes of place, or any other scenes of transition" (Reisz and Millar 112). One of the most famous montages in cinema is from *Citizen Kane*, the montage of breakfasts experienced

---

[1]David Mayer's detailed cutting continuity script for (*Battleship*) *Potemkin* includes the number of frames for each shot in the film. The descriptions reveal that as the men on the *Potemkin* prepare for possible battle, many shots are only a second or two long or even less than a second (calculated at sixteen frames per second, which many experts believe is the speed that best approximates the original showings). After it is clear that no confrontation will occur after all, the average shot length tends to increase (208–52).

a)   b)

FIGURE 3.26 The breakfast montage in *Citizen Kane* (1941)
(a) At the beginning of the sequence Charles Kane and his first wife are close to and attentive to
each other; by stages they become alienated; (b) at the end they are far apart, reading rival papers.
In slightly more than two minutes, this montage shows their growing alienation and failing marriage. Frame enlargements. *Orson Welles; RKO General Pictures*

title card: A card or thin sheet
of clear plastic on which is
written or printed information
included in a film.

by Kane and his first wife. In twenty-seven brief shots (plus brief blurry transitions that look like swish pans but are not) lasting altogether only 133 seconds,
the filmmakers show the couple's deteriorating marriage (Figure 3.26).[2]

Another use of a montage—this one without lap dissolves—occurs in
Raging Bull (1980). One scene ends with the boxer Jake La Motta soaking his
fist in a bucket of ice water. Then we see a **title card** announcing a La Motta
fight, a few brief stills from the fight, and snippets from home movies. The
same pattern is repeated during which six fights are accounted for; Jake and
Vicki date, marry, indulge in horseplay beside and in a swimming pool, and
begin a family, and Jake's brother Joey marries and begins a family. In two
minutes thirty-five seconds, the story jumps ahead more than three years,
from January 14, 1944, to sometime after a March 14, 1947, fight. This
montage shows Jake's work and personal life and Joey's personal life all going
well, but the filmmakers chose to skim through those events.

Montages usually consist of many brief shots, often connected by lap
dissolves, but a montage can be as simple as a few shots without lap dissolves.
In *Hook* (1991), we see three consecutive shots from behind a seated Wendy.
Each shot ends with Wendy turning around and revealing that she is older; this
simple montage represents an expanse of forty or so years in a matter of seconds.

[2]For a detailed description of the breakfast montage in *Citizen Kane*, including ten frame enlargements and an analysis of the sequence, see Reisz and Millar 115–21.

Montages are not the only way editors have of condensing time. Sometimes editors provide much information by a succession of relatively brief shots, as in the ending of *Breaking Away* (1979). The film presents the story of four unemployed young men living in a university town; they have graduated from high school but have not yet found their places in life. The most important of the four is Dave Stoller, whose father runs a used car lot and disapproves of Dave's zealous imitation of professional Italian bicycle racers and his attempts to emulate everything Italian. The four young men are harassed by university students and decide to prove themselves by entering the annual university team bicycle race, which they win in a close race against thirty-three fraternity teams.

After the race, the film has three more scenes, which seem to take place at the beginning of the following fall semester:

Scene (two shots, twelve seconds)

1. Used car lot, Mr. Stoller leaving on a bike; his pregnant wife is talking about a car to an interested couple, though we do not hear her.

2. On a bike, Mr. Stoller leaves the Cutter Cars lot and rides into street.

Scene (three shots, nineteen seconds)

3. On campus: a young French woman asks Dave where the "office of the bursar" is.

4. After hesitating, he replies, "You must mean the Bursar's Office."

5. She agrees and smiles.

Scene, the film's last (three shots, twenty-two seconds)

6. Dave and the French woman biking; Dave tells her he was thinking about studying French and talks to her about the major French bicycle race.

7. Dave continues to talk to the French woman; then Mr. Stoller, riding a bike from the opposite direction, passes Dave and the woman and calls out to Dave. Dave replies hello in French.

8. Mr. Stoller's startled reaction.

Without these last three scenes, the film would end after the bicycle race as a working-class success story, with four sons of limestone cutters as victors, working-class brothers united (one of the four young men and his police officer brother), and Dave and his parents reconciled. But the last three scenes, as in so many American movies, quickly shift emphasis from social class to individual psychology.

The last scene suggests that Dave may be about to take on a new role—that of would-be cosmopolitan student studying French, rather than Italian. He's still an adolescent trying out roles. The Stollers also assume new roles, probably too many in too short a time to be believable if we think about the situation. Mr. Stoller has changed the name of the car lot from Campus Cars to Cutter Cars, suggesting that he will henceforth seek the town market and that the victory by the four young men has renewed his social class pride. The father has imitated the son and taken up bicycle riding. For the first time in the film, he allows his wife to help with the work at the car lot. Finally, the Stollers are going to start a new family. Mr. Stoller is more relaxed, more accepting of his son, more willing to accept his own limitations (his wife's helping at the car lot). His calling out to Dave in the last scene reminds viewers of an earlier scene in which he snubbed Dave in public—when Dave was deep into his Italian period. The last two shots being of Dave (and the French woman) and Mr. Stoller is as it should be: throughout the film, Dave acts; Mr. Stoller reacts. In these last eight shots, viewers are swept along on a rapid river of images until the final one without noticing that all these changes in the lives of the Stollers are depicted in so brief a time. All this and more is conveyed by only eight shots, in fifty-three seconds of carefully edited film.

Editors nearly always try to condense time. But a few films—for the most part outside the classical Hollywood cinema—occasionally and briefly expand time, allowing more time to show an action than the action itself would take. Eisenstein used this technique in several of his films. In *October* (1928), he often stretched out an action slightly by including shots that repeat part of a movement, as in the toppling of a statue of a former tsar: one shot ends with the statue well on its way to the ground; the next shot begins with the statue not as far from the ground; the shot after that does the same thing. Three somewhat overlapping shots are used to show one brief action. Later in the film we see parts of the raising of a drawbridge more than once. Two other famous examples of expanded time are from Eisenstein's (*Battleship*) *Potemkin*. In one scene, an angry sailor breaks a plate, but the footage has been edited so that we see parts of the sailor's arm movement twice, from above first his left shoulder then his right.[3] Later in the film, parts of the famous massacre of civilians on the Odessa steps is edited so that the running time is longer than the **story time.** Because of the surprising **structure** of the classic film "An Occurrence at Owl Creek Bridge" (1962), the film's running time (twenty-eight minutes) is longer than its story time (slightly more than ten minutes).

Occasionally other films include brief instances of expanded time, as in three shots from *Shoot the Piano Player* (1960, Figure 3.27). Another example of expanded time occurs near the end of *A Little Princess* (1995). When

story time: The amount of time covered in a film's narrative or story.

structure: The selection and arrangement of the parts of a whole. In a narrative film, "structure" can be thought of as the selection and arrangement of scenes or sequences.

---

[3]For frame enlargements for each of the sixty-one frames making up the eight key shots in this scene, see Mayer 23–30. For Mayer's analysis of these shots, see 13–14, 15.

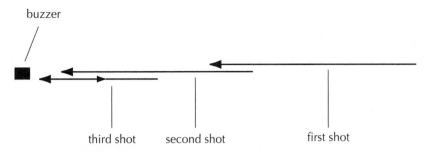

buzzer

third shot   second shot   first shot

FIGURE 3.27 **Expanding film time**
Three shots from *Shoot the Piano Player* (1960) overlap slightly and thus expand time a little. The shots show a character raise an arm and reach out toward a doorbell, hesitate briefly before touching it, then begin to withdraw his hand. The filmmakers could have shown this movement in one shot. Instead, they chose to present it in three shots that overlap slightly: at the beginning of the second and third shots the finger is slightly farther away from the doorbell than it was at the end of the preceding shot. By expanding time, the filmmakers emphasize the character's hesitancy.

Lavinia, the girl who had always disliked Sara, the main character, finally hugs her, the action is shown in three brief shots. The first ends as Lavinia's arms begin to encircle Sara's shoulders. The second, which is less than a half second, repeats the encircling action. The third begins with the same encircling and continues as Lavinia hugs Sara and Sara hugs her back. The effect is to prolong the action slightly and thus give it somewhat greater emphasis than normal.

(Although it is not a matter of editing, time can also be expanded when the camera films at a faster rate than the film is projected, as when an explosion is filmed at three hundred frames per second but is projected at twenty-four: an explosion that would normally last approximately a quarter of a second will last about three seconds.)

For a sample description and analysis that illustrates the expressiveness and impact of editing, see pp. 136–37.

DIGITAL EDITING

As with other aspects of filmmaking, computers increasingly are being used in editing. Shots may be scanned into a computer, where they can be edited. Once film footage has been transferred to digital format, the digital version may be integrated with special effects or even sent long distances electronically. When the computer editing is finished, the digital information is transferred back to film for theatrical showings.

Already some films such as *Time Code* (2000) have been shot entirely on digital video cameras and transferred to 35 mm film for showings in theaters.

The Expressiveness of Editing (and Other Techniques): An Excerpt from *High Noon*

In the 1952 western *High Noon*, Will Kane, the town marshal of Hadleyville, has learned that Frank Miller, a man Kane helped convict years ago, is on the noon train to Hadleyville. There he will be joined by three men; then the four men plan to kill Kane. For various reasons, the townspeople do not rally behind Marshal Kane. During the 11:55 to noon section of the film, viewers see the following sixteen scenes (each scene is divided into its shots):

Scene 1: Kane's Office

1. Kane looks at the boy as the boy (who had volunteered to help Kane in the coming show-down) leaves. Kane turns and glances at the clock on the wall (it reads 11:55); then he starts to sit down.

2. Kane sits at desk, takes a pistol from the drawer, checks the hammer of its firing mechanism, tucks it between his belt and his abdomen, opens a box of bullets, and dumps them into his hand.

Scene 2: Train station

3. Near the train tracks, all three members of the Miller gang check to make certain their gun cylinders move freely and are full of bullets.

Scene 3: Kane's office

4. Kane takes out a sheet of paper and begins to write.

5. He writes at the top of the sheet: "Last Will and Testament."

6. He looks up from his writing.

7. As the music begins, the camera tilts up from a swinging clock pendulum to reveal it's 11:58.

8. Kane looks down from the clock and resumes writing his will.

Scene 4: Train station

9. The three members of the Miller gang are by the railroad tracks.

10. The empty railroad tracks.*

Scene 5: Inside a church

11. Congregation at prayer.

12. In pew, Joe Henderson, a town leader, looks straight ahead.

13. Ezra, a man who urged the townspeople to stand by Kane during a debate that took place in the church, looks down.

Scene 6: Ramirez Saloon

14. At bar, men smoke, wait, and look at each other.

15. A man with a dark eye patch gazes at his drink as he sits alone at a corner table.

16. The bartender, who is behind the bar, looks tense.

Scene 7: Kane's office

17. The swinging clock pendulum.

18. Kane writing.

Scene 8: Town street

19. View of deserted town street.

20. Another section of deserted town street.

---

*According to Leonard J. Leff, shots 10 to 31 last 3.2 seconds each (159).

Scene 9: Outside train station
21. View of empty train tracks (nearly the same shot as shot 10)
22. The three Miller men (presumably looking down the train tracks)

Scene 10: Above town street
23. On a second-floor verandah, two old townsmen watch and wait.

Scene 11: Fuller house
24. Sam Fuller and his wife look at one another briefly then look down (and the wife also turns away slightly).

Scene 12: Martin's place
25. Martin, the former sheriff, looks offscreen.

Scene 13: Mrs. Ramirez's residence
26. Mrs. Ramirez, Kane's former lover, waiting.

27. Mrs. Kane waiting.

Scene 14: Kane's office
28. Clock reads 11:59.

29. The swinging pendulum

Scene 15: Train station
30. The three Miller men looking straight ahead.

Scene 16: Kane's office
31. Kane writing.

32. The camera tilts up from the swinging pendulum and reveals that it is 12:00.

This excerpt uses parallel editing to show three major kinds of information:

- How Kane prepares for the coming showdown; he gets out his pistol and bullets and writes his will.
- What Miller's men do; they check their guns and wait for the arrival of the noon train.
- How the townspeople do nothing to help Kane as they wait for the arrival of Frank Miller.

The editing here illustrates the enormous amount of simultaneous information edited film can convey. In little more than two minutes we viewers see what characters are doing in nine settings. And the film shows what is occurring at different places at about the same time by rapidly cutting between Kane in his office, Miller's three men at the train station, and residents of Hadleyville in different parts of town. As the shots of the empty streets reveal, Kane's potential allies do nothing but wait indoors in safety.

Shots of brief duration are used within and between the scenes, but there is little movement within each shot. Indeed, many shots look like still photographs. It's as though the townspeople are frozen in inaction. People do little but wait, think, and feel (or try not to feel). And they do so alone. Many shots show only one individual. In shots of groups, there is little interaction, little community. Together the brief shots, regular rhythm of the editing, and inaction within the shots reinforce the sense that the people of Hadleyville are frozen in nervous, isolated paralysis as simultaneously a momentous showdown moves steadily and inevitably toward them. All this—and more—the editing and other filmmaking techniques help us see and experience.

Filming with digital video cameras has several major advantages, including the ease with which the content of digital videotape can be copied to a computer and edited there. As digital filming supersedes the older technology, digital editing is sure to grow more widespread. Regardless of these and other editing advances, however, what will count for viewers then, as now, is the skill with which the final creation is edited and the impact from the way the shots are chosen and arranged.

SUMMARY

Editing involves decisions about which shots to include, the most effective take of each shot, the arrangement and duration of shots, and the transitions between them. Editing can strongly affect viewer responses. It can be used (1) to promote continuity or disruptions; (2) to superimpose images; (3) to juxtapose shots to make a point, support a feeling or mood, intensify the viewer's reactions, or show parallel subjects or events; and (4) to affect the viewer's sense of pace, compress or expand time, and convey an enormous amount of information in a brief time.

Early Film Editing

- The first films of the 1890s consisted of one shot or a series of one-shot scenes.
- By the time of *The Birth of a Nation* (1915), editing was used to maintain continuity while telling complex stories.
- In the 1920s, the editing of some Soviet filmmakers conveyed a story and promoted ideas by the juxtaposition of shots.

Building Blocks

- The shot is the most basic unit of editing. It is a piece of continuous film or videotape depicting an uninterrupted action or an immobile subject during an uninterrupted passage of time.
- A scene is a section of a narrative film that gives the impression of continuous action taking place during continuous time and in continuous space. A scene usually consists of one or more shots.
- A sequence is a series of related consecutive scenes that are perceived as a major unit of a narrative film.
- Editors can use one or more of many possible transitions between shots, such as a cut, lap dissolve, or wipe. Depending on conventions and con-

text, editing transitions can be used to convey or reinforce information or moods. For example, often a lap dissolve indicates that the next scene takes place at a later time or different location—or both.

Continuity Editing

- Continuity editing, which is used in most narrative films, maintains a sense of clear and continuous action and continuous setting within each scene.

- Continuity editing is achieved in filming and editing by making sure viewers will instantly understand the connection between shots and the relationship of subjects to other subjects and subjects to the setting.

Image on Image and Image after Image

- A momentary superimposition of two or more images is possible in a lap dissolve, as in the ending of the 1960 *Psycho*.

- Consecutive shots can stress differences or similarities. They may also be used to surprise, amuse, confuse, or disorient viewers.

- Reaction shots often intensify viewers' responses. Usually a reaction shot follows an action shot, but it may precede one, or it may occur alone with the action not shown but only implied.

- Parallel editing can be used to achieve various ends, including to give a sense of simultaneous events, contrast two or more actions or viewpoints, or create suspense about whether one subject will achieve a goal before another subject does.

Pace and Time

- Usually fast cutting is used to impart energy and excitement; slow cutting may be used to slow the pace or reinforce a sense of calm.

- A succession of shots of equal length may suggest inevitability, relentlessness, boredom, or some other condition.

- Shifting the rhythm of the editing can change viewers' emotional responses, as in the excerpt analyzed from near the end of (*Battleship*) *Potemkin*.

- Montage compresses an enormous amount of information, including story time, into a short time, as in the montage of Susan's opera career in *Citizen Kane*.

- Editing usually condenses time (for example, by cutting dead time), but it can expand time—for instance, by showing fragments of an action more than once.

Digital Editing

■ Computers increasingly are being used as part of the editing process. Images are scanned into computers, edited there, and transferred back to film for theatrical showings.

WORKS CITED

Andrew, J. Dudley. *The Major Film Theories: An Introduction*. New York: Oxford UP, 1976.

Grignon, Rex. Address. "The Making of Toy Story." Monterey, CA, Conf. Center. 10 Apr. 1996.

Hoggan, Michael, president, American Cinema Editors. Telephone interview. July 1994.

Huss, Roy, and Norman Silverstein. *The Film Experience: Elements of Motion Picture Art*. New York: Dell, 1968.

Leff, Leonard. *Film Plots: Scene-by-Scene Narrative Outlines for Feature Film Study*. Vol. 1. Ann Arbor: Pierian, 1983.

Mayer, David. *Sergei M. Eisenstein's* Potemkin: *A Shot-by-Shot Presentation*. New York: Grossman, 1972.

Murch, Walter. *In the Blink of an Eye: A Perspective on Film Editing*. Los Angeles: Silman-James, 1995.

Priestly, Tom (film editor). Quoted in Ralph Rosenblum and Robert Karen, *When the Shooting Stops . . . the Cutting Begins: A Film Editor's Story*. New York: Viking, 1979.

Reisz, Karel, and Gavin Millar. *The Technique of Film Editing*. Enlarged ed. New York: Hastings, 1968.

Riefenstahl, Leni (filmmaker). Interview. *The Wonderful, Horrible Life of Leni Riefenstahl* (documentary film). 1993.

Salt, Barry. *Film Style and Technology: History and Analysis*. 2nd ed. London: Starword, 1992.

FOR FURTHER READING

Balmuth, Bernard. *Introduction to Film Editing*. Boston: Focal, 1989. An introduction for someone who wants to edit film.

Oldham, Gabriella. *First Cut: Conversations with Film Editors*. Berkeley: U of California P, 1992. Interviews with twenty-three award-winning editors, including editors of documentary films.

Selected Takes: Film Editors on Editing. Ed. Vincent LoBrutto. Westport, CT: Praeger, 1991. Interviews with twenty-one film editors plus a glossary and a bibliography.

CHAPTER 4

Sound

Dᴜʀɪɴɢ ᴛʜᴇ 1986 Aᴄᴀᴅᴇᴍʏ Aᴡᴀʀᴅꜱ ᴄᴇʀᴇᴍᴏɴʏ, a clip from *Chariots of Fire* (1981) was shown of young men running on a beach accompanied by the sounds of feet splashing in water. Although the sound track may have been true-to-life, it was uneventful. Then the same **footage** was shown with the film's famous title music. The effect was so different that viewers felt as if they were seeing different footage. The runners gained the grace of dancers, and the action became special, more than life. It illustrated the importance of sound to the creation of vibrant cinema.

In movies, sounds usually seem lifelike. However, as with visuals, what seems true-to-life is an illusion. If you study sound in movies, you will notice that sounds we would normally hear are often omitted or replaced by music. Listen carefully and repeatedly to the sound that accompanies one character punching another, and you will notice that it is not entirely credible. In movies we do not question such sounds (yet another movie **convention**). What are a few of the many ways that film sounds are created, how are film sounds used, and, most important, how do they affect viewers? This chapter gives some answers to those questions by examining some specific uses of a sound track's four major components, possible sound transitions, and general uses of sound in **narrative** films.

EARLY FILM SOUND

Sound has always been a part of film viewing. Even during showings of the first short films in the 1890s, music was usually played to cover the sounds of the audiences and projectors and to reinforce mood and support **continuity.** Later in film history, the theater management also supplied sound effects. As is demonstrated repeatedly in *Monty Python and the Holy Grail* (1975), people could beat half coconut shells against a hard surface or against each other to make sounds like horses' hooves. Large pieces of sandpaper might be rubbed

Terms in **boldface** are defined in the Illustrated Glossary beginning on page 539.

footage: A length of exposed motion-picture film.

convention: In films and other texts, a frequently used technique or content that audiences accept as natural or typical.

narrative: A series of unified consecutive events situated in one or more settings. A narrative may be fictional or factual or a blend of the two.

continuity (editing): Film editing that maintains a sense of uninterrupted time and action and continuous setting within each scene of a narrative film.

FIGURE 4.1 **Allefex sound effects machine**

This machine was first marketed in Britain in 1909. Film historian David Robinson writes that the Allefex "was capable of producing upwards of fifty sound effects from storm noises, bird-song, and barking dogs to gun-fire, escaping steam and the rattle of pots and pans" (159). Historian Brian Coe includes a quotation that explains how some of the sounds were made: "The shot of a gun is imitated by striking a drum on the top of the machine, on which a chain mat has been placed. . . . Running water, rain, hail and the sound of rolling waves are obtained by turning a handle, which rotates a ribbed wooden cylinder against a board set at an angle from the top of which hang a number of chains. . . . The puffing of an engine is made by revolving a cylinder with projections against a steel brush. . . . Pendant tubes serve to produce the effects of church bells, fire alarm, ship's bell, and similar noises; the sound of trotting horses is caused by revolving a shaft carrying three tappets which lift up inverted cups . . . ; the cry of the baby is emitted by the dexterous manipulation of plug-hole and bellows" (91–92). *British Film Institute Stills, Posters and Designs*

FIGURE 4.2 **Vitaphone projection system**

In the late 1920s, the Vitaphone system was used in the United States during filming and projecting. This projection room has a 35 mm projector and attached record player. There were several drawbacks to the Vitaphone system that doomed it to a short life: the records could be played only twenty or so times before they became worn, and it was hard to keep the record always synchronized with the image being projected. The next development in movie sound technology, a sound track on the edge of the film itself, soon replaced the Vitaphone system. *The Museum of Modern Art/Film Stills Archive*

together to sound like a running river; a flexible strip could be stuck into spinning bicycle spokes to simulate the sound of an early airplane engine. Some theaters even had a sound effects machine with a whistle, bell, horn, chains, drum, and sheet metal for thunder. "Silent" films were rarely silent (Figure 4.1).

By the late 1920s, some sound films were shown using the Vitaphone system, a large phonograph disc synchronized with the projector (Figure 4.2). Warner Bros. created a sensation with this system in *The Jazz Singer* (1927), which was basically a silent film with synchronized musical numbers and a little ad-libbed dialogue. In 1928, Warner Bros. used the system in *The Lights of New York*, the first all-dialogue motion picture. In the same year, two rival and not entirely compatible sound-on-film systems were used on **feature films,** and the days of Vitaphone were numbered. With a sound-on-film system, the projector displays the image on the screen as it simultaneously converts the optical information in the sound track into electrical information. That electrical information is amplified and sent to the theater speakers. (Figure 2.2 on p. 58 illustrates where optical and the later magnetic sound tracks may be located on film.) Since 1928, if theaters have adequate sound equipment, audiences can hear the **vocals** (dialogue and other sounds made by the human voice), sound effects, music, and silence the way the filmmakers intended.

feature film: A fictional film that is at least sixty minutes long.

In the late 1920s and early 1930s, such directors as René Clair, Ernst Lubitsch, Rouben Mamoulian, Alfred Hitchcock, and Walt Disney experimented with film sound and discovered new uses for it. In later years, Orson Welles, Robert Altman, George Lucas, Walter Murch, and other filmmakers experimented with film sound and made major advances in its use. Today, with sophisticated filmmakers and advanced equipment including computer programs to create, store, manipulate, and blend sounds, cinematic sound is more varied and more expressive than ever.

COMPONENTS OF THE SOUND TRACK AND THEIR USES

Dialogue is usually dominant and intellectual, music is usually supportive and emotional, sound effects are usually information. Their uses, however, are not inflexible. Sometimes dialogue is nonintellectual and aesthetic, sometimes music is **symbolic,** and on occasion sound effects may serve any of those functions. Any of these elements may be dominant or recessive according to the sharpness or softness of the sound and the relationship of the sound to the image. (Murch 298)

symbol: Anything perceptible that has significance or meaning beyond its usual meaning or function.

Filmmakers can include vocals, sound effects, music, and silence in the sound track. In this section, we consider some of their choices and the consequences.

Vocals

Most sound films since 1930 include dialogue and other vocals. Movies such as *Swimming to Cambodia* (1987), *When Harry Met Sally* (1989), and *The Designated Mourner* (1997) have a dense mix of words, and dialogue or monologues cascade and swirl throughout them. These and other films may use overlapping dialogue. Viewers cannot make out all the words, but they hear most of them and sense the busy, chaotic atmosphere that overlapping dialogue can help create. In films using overlapping dialogue characters speak without being entirely heard by those they speak at, and flash floods of words may be indicative of the characters' nervousness, isolation, or unconscious attempts to mask their painful situations. Many films directed by Howard Hawks—such as *Bringing Up Baby* (1938) and *His Girl Friday* (1940)—and several films directed by Orson Welles—perhaps most notably *Citizen Kane* (1941), *The Magnificent Ambersons* (1942), and *Touch of Evil* (1958)—use extensive overlapping dialogue. Some films directed by Robert Altman—such as *McCabe and Mrs. Miller* (1971), *California Split* (1974), *Nashville* (1975), *The Player* (1992), and *Dr. T and the Women* (2000)—also use extensive overlapping dialogue.

Overlapping dialogue may also be used in a brief section of a film, as in *Saving Private Ryan* (1998). At the beginning of one **scene**, many typists are busy typing letters. Soon we begin to hear fragments of letters read by different male voices (presumably the commanding officers). The first voice begins, "Dear Mr. Brian Boyd: No doubt by now you have received full information about the untimely death of your son; however, there are some personal details . . ." and is overwhelmed and replaced by another male voice reading another fragment of a letter. The voices are always cut off in midsentence. The images of many typists busily typing and the continuous typing sounds and overlapping and interrupted dialogue suggest how many letters had to be sent, how many men were lost in the battles of World War II, and how enormous was the number of families devastated by the loss of their sons, brothers, and husbands. Overlapping dialogue is also used in a brief section of the **documentary film** "Personal Belongings" (1996): viewers hear many fragments of news reports about anti-Semitism and ethnic fighting in Central and Eastern Europe. During approximately thirty-two seconds, seven or eight **sound dissolves** and extensive overlapping dialogue convey the rapidly escalating strife. At the beginning of *Contact* (1997), as we viewers see the receding earth, planets, and galaxies, we hear overlapping snippets of music and speech from U.S. TV and radio, generally representing earlier and earlier moments in time and suggesting that the earth has been proclaiming its life to the universe ever since the first radio transmission near the beginning of the twentieth century (see the feature on p. 146).

Often in a theater or in our home viewing environment we hear dialogue more distinctly than we could in a similar situation in real life (another

scene: A section of a narrative film that gives the impression of continuous action taking place in continuous time and space.

documentary film: A film whose representation of its subjects viewers are intended to accept primarily as factual.

sound dissolve: A transition in which a sound begins to fade out as the next sound fades in and overlaps the first sound before replacing it.

movie convention). Usually dialogue in movies is louder and often more distinct than it would be in actuality. In a scene from *A Fish Called Wanda* (1988), for instance, viewers hear a couple arguing but not shouting even though they at first seem to be at least a city block away from the camera; as they approach, their voices become only slightly louder.

Vocals may also be deliberately distorted. In several scenes in *Nick of Time* (1995), what is being said to the main character is distorted. The effect is analogous to a visual **point-of-view shot:** viewers hear as the distracted character presumably does.

Dialogue is invaluable for revealing a character's ideas, goals, and dreams, though often it does so more concisely, obliquely, and revealingly than conversation in life. Consider the following dialogue from *Betrayal* (1983). Robert and his wife, Emma, are on holiday. Robert has discovered a letter at the American Express office addressed to Emma and recognized the handwriting as that of his friend, Jerry. The next day Robert tells Emma there was a letter for her at American Express. After a while she says she got it and it was from Jerry. Shortly after that, their dialogue in the film runs as follows:

> ROBERT: What do you think of Jerry as a letter writer? [pause] You're trembling. Are you cold?
>
> EMMA: No.
>
> ROBERT: He used to write to me at one time. Long letters about Ford Madox Ford. I used to write to him, too, come to think of it. Long letters about, ooh, W. B. Yeats, I suppose. That was the time when we were both editors of poetry magazines. Him at Cambridge, me at Oxford. Did you know that? We were bright young men and close friends. Well, we still are close friends. All that was long before I met you. Long before he met you. I've been trying to remember when I introduced him to you. I simply can't remember. I take it I did introduce him to you. Yes. But when? Can you remember?
>
> EMMA: No.
>
> ROBERT: You can't?
>
> EMMA: No.
>
> ROBERT: How odd. [pause] He wasn't best man at our wedding, was he?
>
> EMMA: You know he was.
>
> ROBERT: Aah, yes. Well, that's probably when I introduced him to you. [pause] Was there any message for me in his letter? [pause] I mean in the line of business. To do with the world of publishing. Has he discovered any new and original talent? He's quite talented at uncovering talent, ole Jerry.
>
> EMMA: [pause] No message.
>
> ROBERT: No message? [pause] Not even his love?
>
> EMMA: [pause] We're lovers.
>
> ROBERT: Ah, yes. I thought it might be something like that, something along those lines. . . .

point-of-view shot: Camera placement at the approximate position of a character or person (or occasionally an animal) that gives a view similar to what that creature would see.

Opening Sound Track for *Contact* (1997)

As images of the receding earth, solar system, and galaxies are seen, the following sounds can be heard:

Loud, indistinct, overlapping music
Song: "Be There" by All for One
Song: "Doot, doot, doot . . ."
Song by Hootie and the Blowfish
1997 song: "I Wanna be there when you're (gonna be there)" from "Wanna Be" by the Spice Girls
Song: "God shuffled his feet" by Crash Test Dummies
Song: "You wanna get with me, you gotta . . ."
Song: "Clearly, I've never been there, but it feels like . . ."
Song: "Broken Wings" by Mr. Mister
1986, announcer at launch of Challenger space shuttle: "situation obviously a major malfunction"
Music for *Dallas* TV show

. . .

1979 (music), "Funkytown" by Lipps, Inc.

. . .

Music: "Boogie Oogy"
Music: "Sometimes you feel like a nut" commercial theme for Almond Joy
Song by The Trammps
Sounds of asteroids in space [these are the only sounds not originating from earth]
1973, President Nixon: "your President's a crook. Well, I'm not a crook."
Song: "Got to Give It Up" by Marvin Gaye
1969, Neil Armstrong on the moon: "for man. One giant leap for man . . ."
Song: commercial theme for Coca-Cola
1968, announcer: "Robert Kennedy was shot in that ballroom."
Song: ". . . golden hair"
Song: whistled theme for *The Andy Griffith Show* TV Show
1963, Martin Luther King Jr.: "God almighty, we are free at last."

Music theme from *The Twilight Zone* TV show
1963, announcer: "A sniper has fired at President Kennedy."
Song: "Teeny Yellow Polka Dot Bikini"
Song: "Mr. Postman"
1961, President Kennedy's inauguration: "Ask not what you . . ."
1958: Dean Martin singing "Volare"
1954 (?) Army-McCarthy hearings: "Communist Party or have you ever been a member of the Communist Party?"
1951, General Douglas McArthur (addressing U.S. Congress): "Old soldiers never die . . ."
Song: ". . . my lucky . . ."
Lone Ranger shouting "Hi ho Silver." Gunshots.
Dance music played by a big band
1942 (?) Edward R. Murrow broadcasting from England (?): "something before never experienced"
Dec. 7, 1941, President Franklin D. Roosevelt: "1941, a date that will live in infamy"
1940(?): Hilter speech and crowd response
1939 song: "Somewhere over the Rainbow"
1939, announcer: "and we continue this evening's final edition of our *Maxwell House Good News of 1939*."
Walter Winchell radio broadcast: "Good evening, Mr. and Mrs. America and all our ships at sea. Let's go to press."
Song: "We're in the Money"
Announcer: "lurks in the hearts of men" from *The Shadow* radio program
Man singing
1933: President Roosevelt's inauguration: "The only thing we have to fear is fear itself."
Early instrumental jazz music heard on radio
1920 (?), announcer of an early radio broadcast: "Let us know if this broadcast is reaching you. Please drop us a card."
1900 (?): Morse code (ends at two minutes seven seconds from beginning of film)
Silence

This passage reveals Harold Pinter's skill in creating characters that say one thing when they feel and think something else. In this passage, Robert also does not say directly what is important to him. Evidently he suspects his wife has been unfaithful, but he does not come right out and say so. Part of the time, he feigns forgetfulness: "He wasn't best man at our wedding, was he?" Part of the time, Robert muses about the past and brings up the points that Jerry is an old and dear friend, that he has known Jerry in fact longer than he has known Emma, that he introduced Jerry and Emma, and that Jerry was best man in their wedding.

By not coming right out and saying what he fears, Robert is able to hold Emma in painful suspense about whether he suspects her affair. Like many other Pinter characters, Robert knows when to pause for effect. Often he asks a difficult question and pauses; Emma doesn't reply, so Robert continues. Emma is soon put on the defensive. She gives short answers (less chance of a slipup there). Reread all of Emma's responses. None is longer than four words! Toward the end of this exchange, she pauses before she replies. Careful. Careful. But at last, Emma admits, "We're lovers." Perhaps she thinks that Robert will at least stop his cat and mouse game.

After Robert hears Emma's admission, he again does not say what is bothering him, how painful for him Emma's words are: "Ah, yes. I thought it might be something like that, something along those lines." Elsewhere in the film we see how painful his wife's affair is for Robert, but he never comes out and says so directly. Like Jerry and Emma, most believable characters, and most people for that matter, Robert often says one thing when he means another. And he never comes right out and says what is most important to him. We viewers must watch and listen and figure that out for ourselves. That way we stay involved with the characters.

Sometimes word choices and accents provide clues about a character's background: country or region of origin, ethnic group, occupation. Tone, volume, speed, and rhythm of speech also reveal what a character is like. So infinitely expressive is the human voice that the words "You had better go" can be threatening, pleading, sad, indifferent, questioning, ironic, amusing, matter-of-fact, or something else. Perhaps second only to an expressive face, a trained voice can convey countless shades of emotion.

Many movies, however, use limited or no vocals because given the settings or goals of the film, few or none are needed. In *Quest for Fire* (1981), which is set eighty thousand years ago, the hominids use an assortment of grunts, pants, screams, and so forth, but the film has no intelligible dialogue, only imaginary prehistoric languages that are not translated and are only vaguely understandable. The first and fourth parts of *2001: A Space Odyssey* (1968) are without intelligible dialogue, and only 43 of the film's 141 minutes contain dialogue. Other feature films employing little dialogue are *Blood Wedding* (1981)—which consists of backstage preparations, a brief warm-up session, and a flamenco version of most of Federico Garcia Lorca's famous play of the same title—and *Sidewalk Stories* (1989), which has no dialogue during its 97 minutes except for a few lines near the end that are not integral to the story. Some short films also use little or no dialogue. The films' images, music, and perhaps sound effects convey story, meanings, and moods. "The String Bean" (1962) uses no vocals, and they are used only occasionally and briefly in the classic French film "The Red Balloon" (1955).

Often films begin without words, though they use music: the opening scenes reveal the **setting,** major character(s), and mood without the help of the human voice. Many movie scenes with sound are without the human voice, and many movies use dialogue less than half the time. As scriptwriting books and scriptwriting teachers typically advocate, many filmmakers use dialogue only to reveal important information that cannot be conveyed visually.

Sound Effects

Sound effects specialists tend to use sound effects highly selectively. In life we hear, but usually ignore, insignificant and potentially distracting sounds, such as an airplane overhead or a beeping digital watch. In cinema, such sounds are usually omitted from a sound track, and the sound effects that are included tend to be inconspicuous because they are usually played at low volume and along with music or dialogue or both.

Sound effects are often used to help create a sense of a **location,** and they can make a place seem more lifelike than it is (Figure 4.3). Sound effects can also make viewers feel more involved. In *Das Boot,* or *The Boat* (1981; expanded and reissued with eight-channel digital sound in 1997), when the German submarine is trying to evade detection deep below the surface, viewers hear sheet metal groaning and bolts popping from pressure they were not designed to withstand.

Effects are often used to intensify a mood. Sometimes a sound effect, such as a beating heart, intensifies the mood of the moment even though we wouldn't hear such a sound outside the movies—yet another movie convention. Throughout most of *The Blair Witch Project* (1999), strange, unidentifiable sounds emanating from the dark woods contribute to the tension in the characters lost in the woods and in the viewers in the audience. In the theater or out, a sound from an unknown source—in the basement, in the attic, outside the window, under the bed—may frighten us. We are rattled by the unknown, so films often use sound from beyond the lighted **frame,** in the darkness. Even if we know the source of the sound, such as a tree limb brushing against a window, hearing a sound and not seeing its source leaves much to the imagination. We have paid to be moved, and filmmakers try to oblige us.

Another example of sound effects used to support a mood comes from *The Godfather* (1972). After Michael prevents an attack on his hospitalized father, a corrupt police captain and his men arrive at the hospital entrance.

setting: The place where filmed action occurs.

location: Any place other than a film studio that is used for filming.

During the men's arrival and their confrontation with Michael, we viewers hear thunder three times: first as Michael pushes another man away and as police officers grab Michael, second as the police captain gets out of his car and approaches Michael, and third as we see the police captain's reaction after slugging Michael. We hear this thunder, though we may not much notice it, as we see the police in action. The thunder underscores the power of the police, especially the captain. In many other films, thunder often accompanies danger and violence. Its use is a bit of a cliché.

Sound effects are often used to enhance humorous or light moments. Early in Jacques Tati's *Mr. Hulot's Holiday* (1953), the sputtering and backfiring as Hulot drives his shaky, thirty-year-old car, which is not much bigger than a bathtub, are amusing in themselves, and the

FIGURE 4.3 **Sound used to fill out a set**
In *Citizen Kane* (1941), sound sometimes adds to the verisimilitude of a set. The budget for *Citizen Kane* was limited, and the set shown here was flimsy and incomplete (that's also a reason little or no lighting was often used in parts of the image). The set alone could not have nurtured the right sounds for the scene, but the reverberations in the sound track help mightily to convey the size, emptiness, and sterility of Kane's and Susan's lives in their huge Florida retreat. Frame enlargement. *Orson Welles; RKO General Pictures*

scenes in which they appear are funnier because of them. Sound effects from an unexpected source can create a humorous effect. In *Bowfinger* (1999), as the Eddie Murphy character is walking in a darkened parking garage, he hears the sounds of a woman's high heel shoes. Because he cannot see the source for the sound, he is puzzled and concerned. Soon viewers see the source: high heels on a dog's front paws.

Sound effects can be used just as effectively to intensify a sad or melancholy occasion. In the last shot of a documentary film about a much admired Italian actor, *Marcello Mastroianni . . . I Remember* (1999), Mastroianni, who died before the film was released, is off to one side of the frame, concluding his comments about the brevity of life while looking off frame; then the sound of wind is heard before the final fade-out and continues into the end credits. The subtle suggestion is of desolation, loneliness, and perhaps cold and death.

Another use of sound effects is to conceal an action. In *Chinatown* (1974), Jake, the detective, goes to the hall of records to investigate recent land sales. After he finds the page he wants, he lines up a ruler against the page and coughs loudly as he rips out part of the page. When Jake coughs, the clerk looks up but does not hear the ripping sound and resumes his work.

Near the end of *Fatal Attraction* (1987), Alex, a woman obsessed with a married man with whom she had a brief affair, has slipped into the man's home and attacks the man's wife with a knife in an upstairs bathroom. Meanwhile, the whistling teakettle in the kitchen masks the wife's screams—and prolongs and intensifies the suspense: will the husband learn of the danger soon enough to save his wife? The moment the husband takes the kettle off the stove and it stops whistling, he hears the screams and springs into action.

Like light and shadow, sound effects often add to a film in significant yet inconspicuous ways. In many of the examples discussed above—the timely confluence of thunder and police in *The Godfather* and the amusing sound of the sputtering old car in *Mr. Hulot's Holiday*—the effects are not true-to-life. Only occasionally, however, are the effects so untrue-to-life as to draw attention to themselves, especially during a first or even second listening.

Sound effects specialists often use sound sources that viewers are unaware of. Frank Serafine said that the 1983 TV movie *The Day After* used a blend of animal screams processed so viewers would not recognize the sources to indicate the sound of a nuclear explosion. Ironically, sounds that are faithful to their sources sometimes do not seem "real," so moviemakers substitute or add sounds, sometimes provided by a **Foley artist,** a person who creates and records sound effects as he or she watches the action in a film projected on a screen (Figure 4.4). The Foley artist may decide that the sounds of footsteps on dirt that were recorded during filming don't sound right and may substitute the sound of walking on coffee grounds on cement. To simulate the sounds of walking in grass, a Foley artist may take tape from a cassette, crumple it, then walk on it in synchronization with the film's action. For the sounds of insects in *A Bug's Life* (1998), the sound engineer mixed such sounds as the cracking open of uncooked crabs and various World War II bombers in flight (Rydstrom).

A sound specialist may speed up or slow down the original recorded sound in digital format. At least as early as 1938, sounds were played backward to create new sounds. In that year Loren L. Ryder—the eventual winner of six Academy Awards in sound—recorded a pig's squeal and played it backward as the sound of an ice avalanche. Similarly, a suction sound may be made by running the sound of an explosion backward.

Sound effects may be recorded during filming, added later from a library of sound clips, made up from existing sounds combined with new manipulated sounds, or recorded on location for later use (Figure 4.5). Other sound effects are more complicated to make. For the sounds of the giant creature's "voice" in *Godzilla* (1998), six sound specialists worked on blending sounds from a rare two-CD set of Godzilla sound effects plus metal grinding and metal stressing sounds and modified animal cries (from bears, walruses, sea elephants, and a hawk) ("Making Godzilla Roar").

Sometimes synthetic sounds are created and blended. Other times, especially in action movies (such as in the *Godzilla* example described above),

FIGURE 4.4 A Foley artist at work
Here a Foley artist clomps around in high heels on a hard surface in synchronization with the image projected before him (partially visible in the background) as someone else records the sound for later inclusion in the film's sound track. *Brian Vancho, Foley artist; Sound One Corp., New York*

FIGURE 4.5 Recording sounds in nature
In *Blow Out* (1981), the John Travolta character is a sound effects specialist who records and mixes sounds for movie sound tracks. Here he is shown with a microphone recording sounds of the night for storage on magnetic tape. *George Litto; Filmways Pictures*

animal sounds—such as a monkey screaming, a pig squealing, a lion roaring, or an elephant trumpeting—are distorted or used as is and blended with other sounds because many sound experts believe that animal sounds or variations of them can affect listeners more powerfully than human-made sounds. *Top Gun* (1986) includes many sounds of jet airplanes, but the recording of their sounds could not capture the excitement of the original

151

noise, so animal sounds and human screams were blended in. In this and other uses of sound, the effect can be subliminal: viewers are unaware of why they respond as they do.

Music

> Music can extend the emotional and psychological range of characters and envelop and involve audiences in ways nothing else in movies can.
>
> —Cecelia Hall

Music is infinitely flexible. It can be played in different keys, at different volumes, at different tempos, by different instruments, and by different combinations of instruments.

Music can serve countless functions, such as mirroring a film's central conflict while intensifying it, as in *The Omen* (1976). That film shows the story of an American family, the Thorns: Robert, an American ambassador, his wife, Kathy, and their son, Damien. They make a lovely family, except for one problem: Damien is the son of the devil. The movie shows what happens as the parents come to realize the nature of their son. In brief, the story is another variation of the battle of evil versus good. Jerry Goldsmith created two types of music for the movie: what I call "demonic music" and "Kathy and Robert's music." The contrasting types of music mirror the evil versus good theme. The demonic music is sometimes dissonant and electronic. More often, it is represented by many low male voices accompanied by relentless and pronounced rhythms. The low male voices are effective because masculine voices are usually felt to be more threatening than feminine ones. (When people—especially males?—feel hostile, they often automatically use their lowest, most threatening voice.) In contrast, Kathy and Robert's music is much more melodic and more varied to fit different moods. Unlike the demonic music, Kathy and Robert's music is never loud and threatening, never persistently rhythmical, and never electronic. It is usually played on a piano or stringed instruments. As Kathy and Robert's prospects grow more gloomy, though, their motif is played briefly and in minor keys: it's still beautiful but less prominent and sadder.

Throughout the film the two kinds of music war with each other. Sometimes they battle within the same scene. By the end of the film, the demonic music triumphs over Kathy and Robert's music—within the scene and in the film as a whole—just as Damien and evil triumph over Kathy and Robert and those who tried to help them.[1]

---

[1]Another example of the use of two competing types of music to reinforce the film's central conflict is Quincy Jones's score for *The Pawnbroker* (1965), the making of which is described by the film's director, Sidney Lumet, in his *Making Movies* (175–77).

One use of music is to tag an important object that viewers will meet again much later in the film. In *Antz* (1998), the first mention of the monolith (a Central Park water fountain) is accompanied by a specific musical motif. Later in the film, when viewers see the water fountain for the first time, the same music is heard.

Film music can help establish the place or time period of the story. In *Tom Jones* (1963), the lively harpsichord music helps establish the time of the narrative because the harpsichord was popular in the eighteenth century. In many movies, such as *American Graffiti* (1973), *Stand by Me* (1986), and *The Ice Storm* (1997), popular music establishes when the story takes place.

Often music suggests what a character feels. In *My Life as a Dog* (1985), as a girl plays a recorder with other students in front of a class, she sees another girl pass a note to the boy they both like and unintentionally starts playing badly. In the first scene of *The Purple Rose of Cairo* (1984), a young woman looks at a poster for a romantic adventure movie as viewers hear Fred Astaire singing. The woman's expression and the music show that she is lost in romantic thoughts, until her daydreaming and the music are abruptly cut off by the sound of a letter from the marquee crashing onto the sidewalk behind her. As in many films, music and an expressive face convey emotional nuances that words cannot.

As in *The Omen*, a musical motif may be played in different ways at different times to help convey something about a character. In *Citizen Kane*, Bernard Herrmann's music suggests how Kane feels at the six times his own song is heard. The first time it is played, Kane is near the height of his power and happiness. He has recently bought the staff of a rival newspaper, and a party has been arranged to celebrate the occasion. During the party a band plays Kane's song loudly, briskly, and in a major key. After his affair with a young woman becomes known and he loses the election for governor, his song is played softly, slowly, and in a minor key. It is so subdued that many viewers do not notice it, though it adds to the melancholy of the scene. (The visuals of these two scenes also reinforce this contrast: at the party the screen is alive with movement. The scene after the election defeat contains only two people—Leland and a man who is sweeping the sidewalk outside Kane's election headquarters—and their movements are lethargic, as if Leland and the worker were sapped of energy and hope.)

Another example of music played different ways at different times to reveal a character or situation occurs in *The War of the Roses* (1989). The song "Only You" is heard three times. The first time we hear it, Barbara Rose is watching and listening to the song on TV. The song is undistorted, but it is accompanied by her husband's snoring. Love has flown. Later in the scene Barbara tells Oliver she wants a divorce. The second playing occurs after Barbara has led Oliver to believe that she has killed his beloved dog and used it to make the pâté Oliver has been savoring. In a fury, Oliver spits out the remaining pâté, overturns the table, and chases Barbara up the stairs. As he

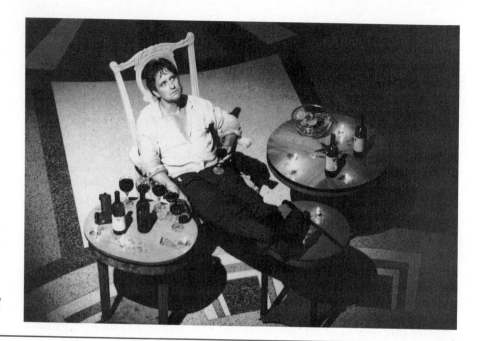

FIGURE 4.6 **Music to express a changed situation**
The Michael Douglas character uses a collection of partially full wineglasses to play part of "Only You" to his estranged wife in *The War of the Roses* (1989). "Only You" is heard three times in the film, each time more discordant than the last. *James L. Brooks and Arnon Milchan; 20th Century–Fox*

grabs at her and she kicks him down the stairs, "Only You" is played briefly, faintly, and in a minor key, accompanied by a sustained bass note (pedal point). The song is distorted and used ironically: it accompanies Oliver's attempts to hurt Barbara and her forceful rejection of him. The song is an appropriate choice because Oliver is obsessed with Barbara and wants only her, although she has declared she wants out of the marriage. The third time we hear the song, a drunken Oliver sings the first three notes as he tries to accompany himself with music he makes by dipping a finger in wine and running it along the rims of partially full wineglasses (Figure 4.6). Again, how the music is played is appropriate. Oliver's mood is no longer loving, and he's no longer entirely in control of himself, so the song is crudely rendered: he sings somewhat drunkenly and off-key, and the wineglass notes are only crude approximations.

Sometimes a musical motif is associated with a character or group of characters, and the music is played the same way every time it accompanies the character or group. In *The Seven Samurai* (1954), the samurai who is an outsider has his own (jazzy) melody, and the other six samurai have their own group melody.

Music is often used to intensify an emotional effect. In *Jaws* (1975), a relentless, strongly rhythmical, and accelerating bass melody accompanies the shark attack on a boy. As the shark approaches its victim, the music is played more loudly and more quickly, suggesting the shark's power and acceleration. Once viewers have heard the shark theme and associated it with the shark, the mere melody sets their nerves on edge because music and viewers' imaginations are a powerful combination.

Filmmakers sometimes use music—knowingly or not—to distract viewers from a weak part of the script or to enhance a performance. *The Omen* illustrates both uses. Certain details about the film's **plot** may trouble viewers, but the music is so effective it helps involve viewers and keep them from dwelling on narrative weaknesses. Though the acting in *The Omen* is generally convincing, as in many films the music enhances the performances. Billie Whitelaw is exactly right as the frightening, evil governess, but she is often accompanied by a fiendishly able assistant: the demonic music. Gregory Peck is also well cast and is convincing as the American ambassador, but in the scene where he learns of his wife's death, he is convincing only up to a point. As Peck buries his head in his hands in grief, the slow, melancholy strings and woodwinds increase in volume and build on the emotion he began.

> **plot:** The structure (selection and arrangement) of a narrative's events.

In other films, the music is not as integral as in *The Omen*. Inappropriate or intrusive music can distract viewers—and insult them and the actors. As film composer Thomas Newman said, "I just don't want the actors to be angry with me. They've put all this work into the scene, come up with all these subtle moves and gestures to communicate what they're trying to get across, so the last thing they want is that the music just explodes all over the place. How insulting is that to the actors? It's like you're saying to the audience, 'You're not sure what they're doing? Okay, let *me* tell you what they're doing!'" (Edwards). Then, too, films may use music to disguise shortcomings. The saying that cooks cover their mistakes with mayonnaise and physicians bury theirs should perhaps be joined by: filmmakers drown out weaknesses with (loud, insistent, overwrought) music.

More than ever, movies help sell recorded music. *Waiting to Exhale* (1995), *Batman Forever* (1995), *Evita* (1996), and *Space Jam* (1996) are examples of movies that helped make their music into huge successes. In turn, the music sales and music videos—sometimes with clips from the films—created more interest in the movies. As never before, movies have a symbiotic relationship with tapes and CDs. The composer or performer may also be a factor in selecting music for a movie. Names such as Elton John, Whitney Houston, and Jennifer Lopez generate interest not only in the movie but also in future music sales. In other words, in some movies, the music may be emphasized so that another division of the corporate conglomerate that made the film can sell tapes and CDs based on it.

At its most effective, music—which draws from the same creative well as poetry—helps elicit feelings and moods that are difficult or impossible to explain in prose. As Irwin Edman has written:

> But just because music cannot be specific it can render with voluminousness and depths the general atmosphere or aura of emotion. It can suggest love, though no love in particular; worship or despair, though it does not say who is worshiped

or what is the cause of the despair. Into the same music, therefore, a hundred different listeners will pour their own specific histories and desires. . . . Words are too brittle and chiseled, life too rigid and conventional to exhaust all the infinity of human emotional response. The infinite sinuousness, nuance, and complexity of music enable it to speak in a thousand different accents to a thousand different listeners, and to say with noncommittal and moving intimacy what no language would acknowledge or express and what no situations in life could completely exhaust or make possible. (116–17)

Silence

Filmmakers may use silence realistically. In *2001*, some scenes in outer space are aptly silent because it lacks air to carry sound waves. In the opening battle scenes of *Saving Private Ryan*, silence can plausibly indicate the loss of hearing due to injury and perhaps the nightmarish quality of intense, deadly warfare. Silence may also be used more symbolically.

From time to time, silence has been employed during dream scenes in sound films, as in Bergman's *Wild Strawberries* (1957) and Hallström's *My Life as a Dog*. The effect is unsettling and, if carried on for long, distancing.

Filmmakers have often used silence to suggest dying or death. In *2001*, as astronaut Frank Poole goes outside the spaceship, we hear Poole's breathing and the hiss of pressurized air. After the space pod has presumably cut Poole's air tube, all sounds stop as Poole struggles with his air tube and tumbles lifelessly through space. These deadly silent scenes outside the spacecraft are alternated with scenes containing **ambient sound** as the other astronaut, Dave Bowman, tries to help. Later when Bowman explodes the pod door of the spacecraft and is catapulted into the vacuum of the emergency air lock, at first we hear nothing. Then he pulls a switch that starts to close the spaceship's outer door and send air surging into the entry chamber, returning him and us listeners to the normal world of glorious sound. Silence can also be used to underscore the profound difference between life and death. One section of the documentary film *Titicut Follies* (1967) cuts back and forth between an asylum inmate being force fed and shots of his body being prepared for display before burial (see Figure 3.24 on p. 129). The shots of his being force fed include the usual sounds; the shots of his corpse are silent. A similar use of silence occurs in *The Body Snatcher* (1945). A singing woman walks into the darkness in the background of the frame and is followed by a slow-moving horse-drawn carriage. For eight to ten seconds after the woman and carriage disappear into the darkness, her voice remains strong and clear; then her singing stops abruptly in midsong. The rest is silence. The suggestion created by the interruption of the sound—and the engulfing darkness of much of the frame—is that she has been murdered.

As with any other technique, silence can be used in countless ways in countless contexts. Sometimes silence can be effective when words would be inadequate. A long silence occurs near the end of *Shall We Dance?* (1996) as

ambient sound: The pervading sound atmosphere of a place that people tend not to notice.

the dance instructor slowly approaches her former student to ask him to dance before a large group. At that moment, pace and emotion are best served in silence.

More generally, silence can function as a pause in music or poetry does: as a break in the natural rhythm of life, a change that can be unsettling and make us eager, even nervous, to return to the sounds of life.

For an illustration of how the different components of a sound track can function within a movie excerpt, see the feature on pp. 160–62.

ADDITIONAL USES OF SOUND

As has been suggested, vocals, sound effects, music, and silence may be used in countless creative ways within a film. Sound may also be used as a transition to foster continuity or promote discontinuity. In narrative films, sound may be used from an on-screen source or offscreen, as part of the story or not.

Transitions

One way sound designers direct viewer attention and promote continuity or discontinuity is by the type of sound transition they use between shots. Sound may be used to connect shots in many ways. Figures 4.7 to 4.11 illustrate five frequently used sound transitions.

Often the sound ends with the visuals of one shot and is replaced by new sound at the beginning of the next shot. The sound ending one shot may be similar to the sound beginning the next shot (this transition is comparable to a visual **match cut**). Sometimes the sound of the first shot is quite unlike the sound beginning the next shot (something like a **jump cut**) (Figure 4.7).

During a sound dissolve, the first sound begins to fade out as the next sound fades in and overlaps the first sound before replacing it (Figure 4.8). Sound dissolves may be used to shift sound and mood gradually from one shot to the next and to promote continuity. Continuity may also be promoted when a continuous sound is used between multiple shots, sometimes between only two shots (Figure 4.9). On rare occasions, the sound from the following shot occurs at the ending of the preceding shot (Figure 4.10). Sometimes the same sound is used to connect three or more shots (Figure 4.11). If only music is used between scenes, the transition is often called a **bridge.**

Depending on their similarity or difference, the sounds between shots contribute to continuity or disruption. Usually, in **classical Hollywood cinema** the new sound in the new shot is different but not noticeably so, and continuity is supported. Nonetheless, as with the editing of images, occasionally a discontinuous transition is used to surprise, amuse, or confuse viewers.

match cut: A transition between two shots in which an object or movement (or both) at the end of one shot closely resembles (or is identical to) an object or movement (or both) at the beginning of the next shot.

jump cut: A transition between shots that causes a jarring or even shocking shift in space, time, or action.

classical Hollywood cinema: Films that show one or more distinct characters facing a succession of problems while trying to reach their goal or goals; these films tend to hide the manner of their making by using continuity editing and other unobtrusive filmmaking techniques.

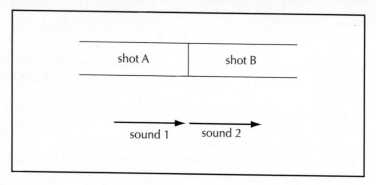

FIGURE 4.7 **Sound ends with a shot then a new shot and new sound begin**

A frequent sound transition between shots is for the first shot and its accompanying sound to end; then a new shot and its new sound begins. This transition can be used to promote continuity between shots or discontinuity.

If the sound of the first shot is even vaguely like the sound in the following shot, the transition seems continuous. An example of a similar linking sound occurs in *Local Hero* (1983). A shot at an office ends with a woman office worker responding to the main character's request for a date: she simply says no. The next shot, in the main character's apartment, begins with him on the phone saying, "No, it's not. It's Mac." Although the speaker and tone of voice are different, the linking word no is the same.

If the sound of the earlier shot does not match the sound of the next shot, the transition is discontinuous, even startling. One shot late in *Citizen Kane* ends with the butler saying that he knew how to handle Kane, "like that time his wife left him." The next shot begins with a cockatoo shrieking and flying away. The result: surprise and discontinuity.

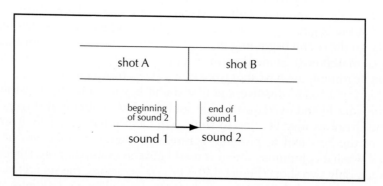

FIGURE 4.8 **A sound dissolve**

In a sound dissolve the sound accompanying a shot fades out as the sound from the following shot fades in, momentarily overlapping it then replacing it. At the end of *Betrayal* (1983), a man and woman are about to begin an affair. As Jerry takes Emma's hand, the party music is replaced by more melancholy music in a sound dissolve: the next music gets louder, momentarily coexists with the party music, then replaces it and becomes louder still. The mood shifts gradually from festive to subdued. With the freeze frame of Robert's and Emma's hands, the shot and narrative end, and a new musical theme announces the beginning of the end credits and continues to the end of the film.

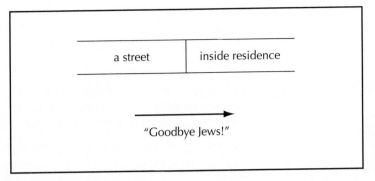

FIGURE 4.9 **The sound from one shot continues into the next shot**
Fairly often, the sound from the ending of one shot carries over, perhaps diminished in volume, into the following shot. In *Schindler's List* (1993), a girl's hateful shouts of "Goodbye Jews!" in a shot in the street are heard three times at lower volume at the beginning of the next shot, which takes place inside a well-furnished residence that Schindler is taking over from a Jewish family.

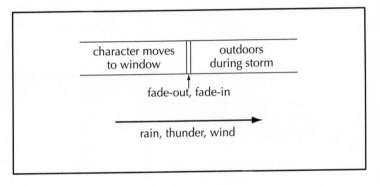

FIGURE 4.10 **The sound for the second shot begins before the shot does**
As a shot nears its conclusion, viewers may hear the sound from the following shot before they see its visuals. Early in *The War of the Roses* (1989), the sounds of rain, thunder, and wind can be heard. The wind sounds continue loudly during a brief visual fade-out, fade-in. In the next shot, which takes place in a different setting, it is a stormy day and the sounds of rain and thunder can be heard. Similar sounds are used at the end of the earlier shot, during the brief transition, and at the beginning of the next shot to promote continuity.

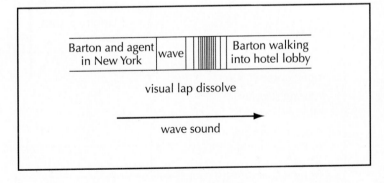

FIGURE 4.11 **A sound used to connect multiple shots**
In *Barton Fink* (1991), sound is used to connect three shots: from near the end of one shot, throughout a second brief shot, and into the beginning of a third shot. Slightly before the end of a shot in New York, viewers can hear the sound of an ocean wave. In the next shot, viewers see and hear a wave hitting a rock close to the shore. As the shot fades out visually and the next shot fades in, overlapping it then replacing it, the sound of the ocean decreases but continues briefly into the beginning of the following shot, in which Barton is walking in a deserted Los Angeles hotel lobby. In this excerpt, the sound of a wave helps viewers quickly understand the story's transition from New York to Hollywood.

Vocals, Sound Effects, and Music in an Excerpt from *Psycho* (1960)

An excerpt from *Psycho* illustrates some major ways filmmakers can use the sound track.

In a motel where she is staying, Marion Crane steps into a shower bath. Viewers hear the shower curtain being pulled, Marion sighing, soap being unwrapped, and water running. At first, there is no music (see figure). The sound of the water continues as we see through the shower curtain the indistinct image of someone coming toward Marion (and seemingly toward the audience). As that person pulls the shower curtain aside and begins to attack Marion with a large knife, the sound of water disappears from the sound track. At the beginning of the attack, we hear Marion's screams and, more loudly, a slashing sound and Bernard Herrmann's pulsating music. During the attack the loudest sounds are the pulsating extreme high notes played by an orchestra of string instruments. After the attack is well under way, the sound of the running water gradually reemerges, and briefly and simultaneously we hear screams, slashing sounds, music, and running water. (When the film was first released in 1960, some viewers also heard the audience's screams.)

After the attacker leaves and Marion is losing consciousness, the screams stop, and bass strings play loudly and slowly but still

rhythmically. As she reaches for the shower curtain and holds on to it momentarily, the music slows and decreases in volume, while the sound of the water

Sound in *Psycho*, before, during, and after Marion's shower

From the time Marion steps into the shower until she half falls out of it, about 106 seconds elapse. During this time, what happens is so riveting and upsetting that few viewers notice the sound track. However, this chart shows that it is not only the visuals and editing that make this part of *Psycho* effective and memorable.

Visuals	Vocals
Marion steps into shower tub.	
	Marion sighs.
Marion begins shower.	
Approaching person seen indistinctly through shower curtain.	
Shower curtain pulled aside.	
Person stabs Marion.	
	Marion screams and pants.
Attacker seen going out bathroom door.	
Marion slowly slips downward.	
Marion holds on to shower curtain.	
Marion falls forward over edge of tub to floor.	

gets louder. The music stops, and, while popping the shower curtain hooks in succession, Marion falls forward in death.

As is usually the case in films, in this scene from *Psycho* sound effects—only six in all—are used selectively. The first sounds are neither unusual nor particularly expressive. The soft tone and regular rhythm of the running water, for example, seem uneventful: all sounds normal. Once the attack begins, however, the sound of splashing water is not dramatic enough; instead we hear the sounds of Marion screaming and panting, music, and a knife supposedly slashing flesh. After the attacker leaves and Marion falls, the sounds of the shower curtain being pulled free and of her falling forcefully to the floor suggest life rushing from her body.

If we listen to this part of the film several times, we begin to notice that some of the sound effects don't sound as they would in life. When Marion unwraps the new bar of soap, for example, the paper sounds more crinkly and louder than any actual soap wrapper. And the running water in the shower doesn't sound like water running in a shower. It sounds nearly the same as the heavy rain Marion drove in while arriving at the motel. But the sound of the water in the shower also includes a sound like that of a liquid being sloshed around in a large container. The sound of the knife stabbing Marion is probably different from and more noticeable than that sound in life. One of my students said it sounded as if someone were slicing cabbage with a knife. Another said it sounded as if someone were chipping away on a block of ice with an ice pick.

The sound effects in this 106-second excerpt illustrate a commonplace in movies: what we see and hear normally seems true-to-life—which can be a source of cinema's enormous

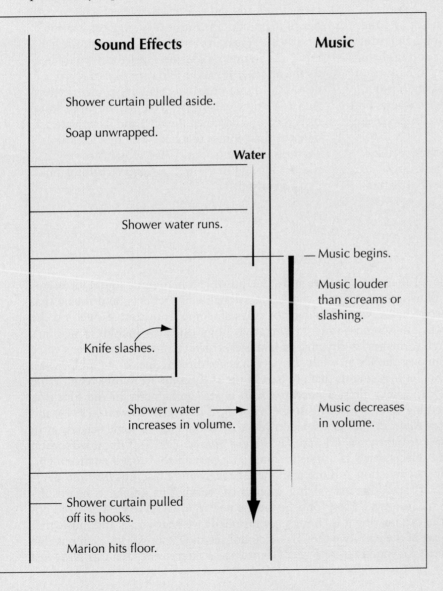

Sound Effects

Music

Shower curtain pulled aside.

Soap unwrapped.

Water

Shower water runs.

— Music begins.

Music louder than screams or slashing.

Knife slashes.

Shower water increases in volume.

Music decreases in volume.

Shower curtain pulled off its hooks.

Marion hits floor.

power—but under close examination is revealed to be artificial. In most popular movies such deceptions are to be expected. Audiences are meant to believe in what they see and hear and to stay caught up in what happens before them, but the techniques used are often truer of movies than of life.

Notice two sound effects *not* supplied in this section of *Psycho*: when the attacker pulls the shower curtain aside, we do not hear it slide on the rod, though we did earlier when Marion got into the tub. What is more effective is the loud, pulsating music that accompanies the shower curtain being pulled aside. The other significant sound not supplied is noise coming from the attacker, but the high-pitched music during the attack suggests both the attacker's violent and sexual frenzy and Marion's (and the viewers') panic.

Music is not used before the attack. Unlike countless film scenes, this excerpt lacks music to establish a mood or create suspense. But as the attack begins, Bernard Herrmann's music intensifies the audience's shock. During the attack, the music is louder than any other sound. The people mixing the sounds could have relied more on the screams or the slashing sounds, or both, but they chose to emphasize the music. During the attack, the loud, piercing string music sounds like bird cries (perhaps many viewers hear bird cries in the music because images of birds and references to them appear earlier in the film). The music also suggests Marion's heartbeat. When the attack begins, the music is rapid and frantic, as Marion's heartbeat would be. As the attacker leaves and Marion slips toward death, the music slows but retains a regular rhythm. And as Marion loses her grip on life, the music loses its jagged up and down melody, and its volume or force then comes to a halt. The melodies and rhythms of life fade out. What remain are only a silent body and the sound of water streaming on indifferently.

Uses of Sound in Narrative Films

Table 4.1 illustrates sources and some possible functions of sound for narrative films. In most films, vocals, occasional sound effects, and music that someone hums, whistles, sings, or plays all come from sources seen on the screen. On-screen sound in narrative films can also include a person's thoughts, memories, dreams, or fantasies, conveyed by the character's voice played over the action while the person is not directly speaking (Table 4.1A).

Sometimes sounds that are part of the story come from offscreen (Table 4.1B). In a few films, a **narrator** who is also a character in the film says something about a scene he or she is not in, as in *Double Indemnity* (1944) and *Citizen Kane*, or makes a few introductory comments in some scenes, as in *Menace II Society* (1993) and *The Virgin Suicides* (1999). Often, **offscreen** sound effects, such as ambient sound, are part of the story's environment. They may function as more than mere background noise. In *American Graffiti*, Curt and John are talking when a car revving its engine is heard offscreen. Curt says, "Hey, John. Someone new in town." We viewers need not see the car; hearing it is enough. Occasionally we hear vocals and music that are part of the narrative though we do not see their sources. It's even possible to hear the sounds of one scene as we see a later scene. Late in *Nelly and*

narrator: A character, person, or unidentifiable voice in a film that provides commentary continuously or intermittently.

162

Monsieur Arnaud (1995), we hear Arnaud's voice on a telephone imploring Nelly to come to him as we see her hurrying along a sidewalk in response to his call.

Occasionally—as in *Ferris Bueller's Day Off* (1986), *Just Another Girl on the I.R.T.* (1992), *Double Happiness* (1995), and *High Fidelity* (2000)—a character looks at the camera and says something that is not part of the story (Table 4.1C). Another example of a sound that is not integral to the story yet whose source is visible on-screen occurs in *Blazing Saddles* (1974, Figure 4.12). In classical Hollywood cinema, however, viewers rarely hear a sound that is not part of the story as they see its source.

Sounds that are not part of the narrative are more typically used off-screen (Table 4.1D). An example of this film convention is music that creates

TABLE 4.1
Some Sources of Sound in Narrative Films

	ON-SCREEN SOUND	OFFSCREEN SOUND
	A	B
▪ PART OF THE STORY (Sound derives from someone or something that is part of the story)	▪ INTERNAL Vocals to convey thoughts, memories, dreams, or fantasies ▪ EXTERNAL Vocals Sound effects Music	▪ VOCALS Sound effects Music
	C	D
▪ NOT PART OF THE STORY (Sound derives from a source outside the story)	EXAMPLES ▪ Someone looks at the camera and says something that is not part of the story or something that comments on the story ▪ The source of background music is visible, as in a scene in *Blazing Saddles* (Figure 4.12)	EXAMPLES ▪ Music that is not part of the story but serves some function in conveying it, for example, by heightening a mood ▪ Vocals, often narration, by someone who is not in the story

FIGURE 4.12 Visible source of background music
As in many movies directed by Mel Brooks, *Blazing Saddles* (1974) sometimes makes viewers aware of movie conventions by presenting something unconventionally. Immediately before this point of *Blazing Saddles*, the main character is riding along on a horse as high-society big-band swing music plays in the background. Then the man rides up to the music's source: Count Basie and his band! *Warner Bros.*

a)

b)

FIGURE 4.13 A sound from a surprising source
In *The 39 Steps* (1935), directed by Alfred Hitchcock, (a) a cleaning woman has discovered a body with a knife sticking out its back and opens her mouth to scream. (b) In the next shot, viewers see and hear a loud onrushing train. Photo (a) is of the last frame of the shot; photo (b) is a frame from a half-second or so into the next shot. Frame enlargements. *Gaumont British. The Museum of Modern Art/Film Stills Archive*

or reinforces a mood. For example, the screeching violins in both the 1960 and 1998 versions of *Psycho* tend to frighten viewers. Of course, the string section is not part of the story: viewers have no sense of a string orchestra holding a timely rehearsal in the Bates Motel. Another example of offscreen sound that is not part of the story is **narration** by someone outside the story, as in *Tom Jones*, *The Age of Innocence* (1993), and the opening of *Dr. Strangelove: Or, How I Learned to Stop Worrying and Love the Bomb* (1963).

Most often sounds are synchronized with their sources, as when spoken words match lip movements. But filmmakers may use **asynchronous sound**— a sound from a source on-screen that precedes or follows its source. And movie sounds usually sound like what we expect from their sources: a scream, for example, usually emanates from a frightened or an upset person. In Hitchcock's *The 39 Steps* (1935), though, the sound of a loud, onrushing train seems to emanate from a woman's mouth (Figure 4.13).

Today surround sound (360-degree sound) is available in theaters equipped with both projectors capable of reading multiple sound tracks on the film and speakers in front of, on the sides of, and behind the audience. For such showings, sound can be used in new, more flexible ways. For example, viewers can hear the corresponding sounds as something seemingly approaches the audience and goes over or beside it. An airplane can be shown firing a machine gun as it approaches viewers, flies over them, and a split second after it is beyond the viewers' peripheral vision a booming explosion can be heard behind them. Nobody is going to remain uninvolved through that.

No aspect of film is so taken for granted as the sound track. Perhaps part of the reason we disregard sound is that even if we want to discuss it, we have a paltry vocabulary to do so. English and many other languages have many more words for visuals than for sounds, so to describe a sound we must often compare it to other, well-known sounds.

Viewers are seldom meant to notice the shadings of a trained voice, sound effects, music, and silence, but an effective sound track helps involve us in the film and amplifies our responses to it. Like **designers,** cinematographers, and editors, sound designers can direct viewers' attention and powerfully influence how audiences respond. In movies usually the results seem true-to-life—and they are in spirit—but they are also true to cinema, its illusions and its artistry.

narration: Commentary in a film about a subject in the film or some other topic, usually from someone offscreen.

designer or **production designer:** The person responsible for much of what is photographed in a movie, including architecture, locations, sets, costumes, makeup, and hairstyles.

SUMMARY

The chapter briefly explains a few of the many ways that film sounds have been created. More important, it explores some specific uses of a sound track's four major components, possible sound transitions, and general uses of sound in narrative films.

Vocals

- Vocals consist of dialogue and other sounds of the human voice.

- Overlapping dialogue can create or reinforce a sense of nervousness, stress, and isolation.

- Vocals, such as Darth Vader's voice, may be distorted for effect.

- Dialogue is invaluable for revealing a character's ideas, goals, and dreams, though often it does so more concisely, obliquely, and revealingly than conversation in life.

- Although vocals can be extremely expressive, many films rely heavily on visuals and use only limited vocals.

Sound Effects

- Sound effects are sounds other than vocals and music.

- Some of the many possible uses of sound effects are to help create a sense of a location, intensify a mood, enhance a humorous situation, or conceal an action.

- Sound effects specialists have many options in manipulating sounds, such as playing them backward, playing them faster or slower than they were recorded, constructing them, and blending them.

Music

- Music can be played in countless ways, including in different keys, at different volumes, in varying tempos, and by different instruments.

- Film music may mirror a film's central conflict, direct viewers' attention, establish place and time, suggest what a character feels or an animal is like, cover weak acting, and be used in many other ways.

- In large-budget movies, sometimes the film music is selected with an eye to future recorded music sales.

Silence

- Possible uses of silence in films include during dreams, to suggest dying or death, or to interrupt the regular rhythm of life's sounds.

Transitions

- There are many possible ways to use sound between shots, such as to have the sound of the first shot end as the shot does.

- Sound transitions between shots are used to reinforce continuity or contribute to discontinuity.

Sources of Sound

- Sound in narrative films may come from on-screen or offscreen and may derive from a source in the story or outside the story.

WORKS CITED

Coe, Brian. *The History of Movie Photography*. New York: Zoetrope, 1981.

Edman, Irwin. *Arts and the Man: A Short Introduction to Aesthetics*. New York: Norton, 1939.

Edwards, Mark. "Moving Sounds for Moving Pictures." *The Times* (U.K.) 23 Apr. 2000. Accessible at <http://www.the-times.co.uk> by searching Back Issues.

Hall, Cecelia (executive sound director, Paramount Pictures). Telephone interview. 5 Aug. 1994.

Lumet, Sidney. *Making Movies*. New York: Knopf, 1995.

"Making Godzilla Roar." *Morning Edition*. National Public Radio. 20 May 1998. With an audio player, one may hear the report at <http://www.npr.org/ramfiles/980520.me.16.ram>.

Murch, Walter. "The Sound Designer." *Working Cinema: Learning from the Masters*. Ed. Roy Paul Madsen. Belmont, CA: Wadsworth, 1990.

Robinson, David. *The History of World Cinema*. New York: Stein, 1973.

Rydstrom, Gary. Audio Commentary. *A Bug's Life: Deluxe Edition* (DVD), 1999.

Serafine, Frank. "Audio Cinemagic." Lecture delivered at the Art Institute of Chicago. 27 Apr. 1985.

FOR FURTHER READING

Brown, Royal S. *Overtones and Undertones: Reading Film Music*. Berkeley: U of California P, 1994. The book focuses "on how the interaction between a film and its score influences our response to cinematic situations." Includes interviews with eight major film composers, including Miklós Rózsa, Bernard Herrmann, and Maurice Jarre. An appendix contains an outline of what to listen for and consider about a film score.

Film Score: The Art and Craft of Movie Music. Ed. Tony Thomas. Burbank, CA: Riverwood P, 1991. Includes a list of film scores for each composer featured.

Film Sound: Theory and Practice. Ed. Elisabeth Weis and John Belton. New York: Columbia UP, 1985. Part I, History, Technology, and Aesthetics; Part II, Theory; Part III, Practice.

Gorbman, Claudia. *Unheard Melodies: Narrative Film Music.* Bloomington: Indiana UP, 1987. A work of theory on and analysis of the possible functions of music in fictional films.

Kalinak, Kathryn. *Settling the Score: Music and the Classical Hollywood Film.* Madison: U of Wisconsin P, 1992. History, theory, and analysis of music in classical Hollywood cinema plus an extensive bibliography.

MacDonald, Laurence E. *The Invisible Art of Film Music: A Comprehensive History.* New York: Ardsley House, 1998. A history of film music, from the birth of films until 1997. Includes a bibliography, filmography, and three indexes.

Sound-on-Film: Interviews with Creators of Film Sound. Ed. Vincent LoBrutto. Westport: Praeger, 1994. Includes glossary, filmographies, and bibliography.

Sample student essays exploring the expressiveness of film techniques in individual films can be found on the Web site for this book at <http://www.bedfordstmartins.com/phillips-film>.

A sample analysis of the expressiveness of film techniques in one film is found in the following chapter.

CHAPTER 5

Expressive Film Techniques in *The Third Man*

*T*HE THIRD MAN, which was filmed mostly in post–World War II Vienna, was released in Britain in 1949. The film was written by Graham Greene, directed by Carol Reed, and produced by the American David Selznick and the British Michael Korda. On its release in Britain and later in the United States, the film was an immediate success. It won the Grand Prix at the Cannes Film Festival, a British Academy Award for Best Film, and an American Academy Award for the best black-and-white cinematography. The film is still highly esteemed. In 1999, the British Film Institute conducted a poll to determine the best British films ever made. Producers, directors, writers, actors, technicians, academics, exhibitors, distributors, executives, and critics throughout the United Kingdom voted *The Third Man* as the top British film of all time.

Vienna, the setting of *The Third Man*, suffered massively toward the end of World War II. "In the last months of the war Vienna would be bombed by the Americans, besieged by the Russians and shelled by the retreating Germans. The statistics reveal what its peculiar fate—to be stuck in the middle— meant in practice. More than 8,000 buildings were completely destroyed, and another 40,000 damaged. . . . 270,000 people were made homeless. Not even the dead were allowed to rest in peace: 536 bombs fell on the Central Cemetery, where Harry Lime [one of the main characters in *The Third Man*] would be buried" (Drazin 14). World War II ended in 1945, with the Americans, Russians, British, and French as victorious allies. Soon afterward, tensions between the Russians and the other allies mounted, and the political uncertainty of the cold war began. In 1948 Communists gained control of the government of Czechoslovakia, one of Austria's neighbors; the Soviets blockaded western access to Berlin; the United States began flying in supplies; and the belief was widespread that war between the United States and the Soviet Union was imminent. Vienna of the late 1940s was divided into occupied zones (British, American, French, and Russian). The city had extensive enduring damage from bombings, many refugees, food shortages, a thriving black market, and many spies.

FIGURE 5.1 Filming on location
Many shots for *The Third Man* (1949) were filmed in the actual large, complex sewer system under Vienna. These cool, dark, and damp settings required hard bright lighting, especially to create the kinds of sharp-edged shadows seen both here on the right wall and throughout the film's many night scenes. *Larry Edmunds Cinema & Theatre*

FIGURE 5.2 Music in *The Third Man*
Anton Karas playing the zither on a tabletop. The five strings closest to him are for melody. The other strings are for harmony. *Larry Edmunds Cinema & Theatre*

The Third Man was one of the few films of its day to be filmed mostly on location (some scenes were shot in England), and most scenes were shot at night or in dark conditions (Figure 5.1). The filming in Vienna began in October 1948 and lasted for seven weeks. Filming in England ran from late December 1948 to late March 1949.

The film's music was arranged and played on the zither by Anton Karas. For some months after the film's release, the "Third Man Theme" was high on the popular music charts of both Britain and the United States. The zither, an ancient stringed instrument, is held in the lap or set on a table and strummed or plucked with a pick or fingers (Figure 5.2). It is widely played in western Austria and Bavaria. In the 1940s, few feature films used a solo instrument as the only source of music, but Reed insisted on its use in the film.

DESCRIPTION

If you have not seen *The Third Man* recently or will not be seeing it, please read the following description at least twice.

During the opening montage, a narrator explains the situation in war-scarred Vienna as footage of the occupied city is shown (Figures 5.3–5.4).[1] In *The Third Man* Holly Martins (played by Joseph Cotten) who is an American writer of pulp western fiction, arrives in Vienna to do "publicity work for some kind of charity" that his friend Harry Lime (Orson Welles) is running. Shortly after Martins arrives, he learns that Lime had recently been hit by a car and killed. Martins arrives at the cemetery at the end of

---

[1]In the British version, director Carol Reed narrates slightly different lines than Joseph Cotten does in the American version. The two versions, British and American, are quite similar in all other respects. When the film was first screened, it was shown in a 93-minute version, and occasionally that version is still shown instead of the 104-minute one.

a)   b)

FIGURE 5.3 **Consecutive shots revealing contradictory aspects of the setting**
The Third Man (1949) begins with a montage showing conditions in postwar Vienna. (a) Early in
the montage, a shot of Beethoven's statue is seen. (b) The next shot shows two black-marketeers.
The two shots quickly illustrate contradictory aspects of Vienna in the late 1940s: a city of both
culture and crime. Frame enlargements. *London Film Productions. Library of Congress.*

FIGURE 5.4 **Damaged setting**
Last shot of the opening montage, before Martins's train arrives
at the station. Note the extensive, snow-covered bombing
damage in the foreground and the two scavengers. In the background is the large ferris wheel that will be the setting for an
important scene late in the film. Frame enlargement. *London
Film Productions. Library of Congress.*

FIGURE 5.5 **Setting, mood, and meaning**
Late in the film's last shot, Anna walks past Holly Martins,
thereby rejecting him. Notice the gray sky, the leaf falling above
Anna's head, and the many fallen leaves, a reminder that it is
autumn, the dying time of the year. Frame enlargement. *London
Film Productions. Library of Congress.*

Lime's funeral. Soon he is suspicious about the circumstances of Lime's death and stays on in Vienna to try to solve the mystery. In three eventful days, Martins meets Lime's girlfriend, Anna, and Lime's associates: Kurtz, Dr. Winkel, and Popescu. He also keeps meeting up with Major Calloway (Trevor Howard), a British officer in charge of the military police in the British section of occupied Vienna, because Calloway is trying to gather evidence about Lime's associates who were involved with him in criminal activities. The second night Martins is in Vienna, he unexpectedly sees Lime alive after all, but Lime runs away and disappears. Major Calloway finally convinces Martins that Lime had sold diluted penicillin that caused injury and death for many, including children. Because Martins both is repulsed by what Lime has done and wants to help Anna escape repatriation by Russian authorities, he finally agrees to help lure Lime into the open so authorities may capture him. Lime arrives at the café where the meeting is to take place, quickly grasps the situation, nearly shoots Martins, but runs away as Calloway's assistant, Sergeant Paine, arrives. During a chase through the sewers of Vienna, Lime shoots and kills Sergeant Paine, and Calloway shoots Lime. Martins comes face to face with the trapped and injured Lime and, after a pause and a slight nod from Lime, shoots him. After a second funeral for Lime, Anna rejects Martins.

> For a more detailed description of the plot of *The Third Man*, see the Web site for this book at <http://www.bedfordstmartins.com/phillips-film>.

There is neither space nor need for the following analysis to be comprehensive. Instead the techniques discussed in the four chapters of Part One are used to illustrate some of the many ways in which they contribute to the impact of *The Third Man*.

MISE EN SCÈNE

The following section illustrates some of the many ways in which settings, subjects, and composition contribute to the expressiveness of *The Third Man*.

Settings

Before World War II, Vienna stood as a symbol of high art and classicism. It was once home to Johann Strauss and to Beethoven, whose statue is glimpsed early in the film dusted with snow (Figure 5.3a). Postwar Vienna was a changed city:

> We see . . . the blue Danube but a dead body floats in it, and all we hear about it later is that the sewers empty into it. . . . The Prater [amusement park] . . . is a

scene of devastation, and the Riesenrad [large ferris wheel], site of amorous moments, is now a meeting place for a killer and a vantage point for his cynical philosophy; the General Hospital, home of the famous Vienna Medical school, is a last home of dying children; once luxurious Palaces of the nobility are now rental apartments with peeling plaster. . . . And the charming Viennese? Hard faces full of misery, fear, and suspicion. And the beautiful women of Vienna? The only real beauty is a foreigner [the Italian who plays Anna]. (Jarka 254)

In the late 1940s, Vienna was also beset with the corruption and deceit of the postwar black market (Figure 5.3b).

Throughout the film, the settings are cold and damp; people wear coats and hats, and sometimes their breath is visible. Most of the film is dark because so much of it was filmed at night or in the sewers. Since it is autumn, trees are largely leafless (Figure 5.5 on p. 171). And in nearly every exterior scene, the bombed ruins of Vienna are visible in the corners or background of the image (Figure 5.4). The film inundates the spectator with images combining Vienna's culture and beauty with its destroyed buildings. The entranceway to Anna's apartment building has classical arches on the outside but piles of bricks and rubble on the inside. Sometimes the film combines images of damage with darkness. Lime makes his third and final entry into the story atop a badly damaged building. In the next shot, he is seen amid the rough remains of one of the building's walls to the left of him, the jagged remains to the top of another wall underfoot and to the right, and deep blackness in most of the right side of the frame. Lime is associated with destruction and darkness.

Subjects

As the similarity between their first names suggests, Harry Lime and Holly Martins are by no means opposites. Both are attracted to the same woman. Both men are disruptive and destructive Americans—Lime deliberately so, Martins inadvertently. Both are responsible for the deaths of others, and their fates are intertwined. Only Paine's timely arrival prevents Lime from shooting Martins, and Martins shoots Lime in the film's most ambiguous scene (Figure 5.6). The viewer cannot know if Martins kills Lime to save him from the authorities, to punish him for his uncaring maiming and murdering of children and others, if he kills him because Lime subtly seems to invite him to end his misery, or if because of a combination of motives. One may interpret Lime as the American business operator willing to use and sacrifice others to achieve security and a profit and Martins's actions throughout the film as an indictment of American naïve, well-meaning interference in international affairs (Figure 5.7).

Clothing is also used to support characterization, perhaps especially Lime's fondness for black: shoes, slacks, coat, muffler or scarf, and hat. Of course, as a night creature, he would be safest entirely in inky black, but there

FIGURE 5.6 Setting, subject, and composition
In the last image of Lime, he is trapped and cornered in a darkened sewer, and he is positioned somewhat off-center in the frame. The setting and composition help convey the subject's abysmal situation and desperation. Frame enlargement. *London Film Productions. Library of Congress.*

FIGURE 5.7 Martins's rushing forward carelessly
As Martins arrives at Lime's building, he walks under a ladder, an action that has long been considered bad luck—and indeed Holly Martins is about to undergo a series of mostly unpleasant adventures. It also shows that he is reckless: it can be dangerous to walk under ladders without checking what is above. As the film later shows, Holly Martins often rushes into situations without adequately weighing the dangers involved.

The filmmakers could easily have moved the ladder or filmed the scene from another angle and thus kept the ladder out of the frame or far off to the side. Or they could have drawn more attention to it, for example by having Martins look at it or hesitate briefly before walking under it. But they filmed and edited the scene as they did, probably hoping most viewers would notice the ladder and appreciate its significance. This scene illustrates one of the paradoxes of Western art: less may be more. Frame enlargement. *London Film Productions. Library of Congress.*

FIGURE 5.8 A point-of-view Dutch-angle shot
Here is what Martins sees on his arrival at the Cultural Reeducation Section, where members are eager to hear his speech about the crisis of faith in the modern novel. Martins knows nothing about the topic and has been so caught up in trying to clear his friend's name that he arrives unexpectedly and totally unprepared. No wonder that from Martins's point of view the situation looks off balance. Frame enlargement. *London Film Productions. Library of Congress.*

is an obvious symbolic appropriateness to his clothing choices, as there is in the mixture of black, grays, and white that the complex and conflicted Martins wears. Clothing is also used to show Lime's continuing impact on Anna. She sleeps in his pajamas. In one scene, Lime's monogram, HL, is briefly visible on the pajama top Anna wears.

Cotten had worked in Welles's *Citizen Kane* (1941) as Kane's journalist friend who refuses to betray his principles by writing a dishonest review. Orson Welles's impact on audiences when *The Third Man* was originally shown was also affected by his earlier roles. Welles memorably depicted much of the complexity of the American male as the title character in *Citizen Kane*. In the title role in *Macbeth* (1948), he played a traitorous usurper eventually brought low by the forces for order and lawful succession. Lime is not only evil but also charismatic. Throughout the film, Anna remains unconditionally loyal to him. It is possible to interpret Martins's act of shooting Lime as an example of this same sense of loyalty. Lime has also exerted a spell over many viewers who years after seeing the film remember best Harry Lime and think of Orson Welles as the film's star.

Composition

Dutch angles are used extensively in the film—some critics believe excessively—and the overall sense of the film's many compositions is of people and things being askew (Figure 5.8).

The filmmakers also use foreground and background interplay and the sides of the image expressively. When Martins is whisked away in the speeding taxi and he and viewers fear that he is being driven to his death, three shots show the driver looking forward in the foreground, vertical bars and a glass barrier immediately behind him, and behind bars the hapless Martins, seemingly imprisoned—as indeed he is for the duration of the ride. Perhaps the film's most expressive composition is one of its most famous—the film's last shot (see Figure 5.5). As Martins waits off to the left of the frame, Anna walks forward. Perhaps she will fill that huge empty space in the middle of the frame. Instead, she walks forward, eyes straight ahead, past Martins then off the frame to the right, and viewers are left to experience the empty space and the empty leaf-strewn road that runs into an unknown background. The film ends, as it so often returned to, an image out of balance as far as its human subject is concerned.

CINEMATOGRAPHY

The Third Man uses a wide variety of cinematographic techniques, all of which contribute to the film's impact. Below we look at a few examples of the lighting and camera work.

Lighting

Lighting and the lack of it are two of the most expressive techniques used in *The Third Man*. In more than one sense, it is a very dark film (best seen as a film or DVD or laser disc but not a videotape). Perhaps the most famous example of the film's use of lighting occurs when Martins first sees Lime in the darkened doorway. After Martins approaches the doorway, a neighbor above turns on a light, and Martins glimpses Lime smiling slightly sardonically (Figure 5.9). The camera is positioned slightly below Lime's eye level and accentuates the shadows out of which Lime briefly materializes.

At the beginning of the film when Martins arrives at the Vienna train station and at Harry Lime's apartment building, it is light although not cheerfully bright. Most of the rest of the film takes place at night or in the mostly dark underground sewers, and the film's images tend to be tinged or immersed in blackness. Appropriately, the film's last scene, at the cemetery again, takes place during the day. As in the film's beginning, the lighting is not bright and cheerful but soft and subdued. In the film's last shot, Anna's long faint shadow suggests that it is late afternoon, the dying part of the day. Although images of death permeate the scene (for example, tombstones in the background of nearly every shot), the light (and absence of Dutch angles) suggest that a greater degree of normalcy has returned after Lime's death.

Often in the film viewers see a character's larger-than-life distorted moving shadow on an exterior wall. The effect can be a little eerie. Sometimes we see the shadow before we see its source, most notably the ominous shadow of a balloon man who appears shortly before Lime's final emergence (Figure 5.10). At other times, character and viewers see only the shadow, not its source, as when Martins spots Lime, who quickly runs away. As Martins brings Calloway and Paine toward the square where Lime had vanished, he explains that he followed Lime's shadow until he disappeared. In the chase in the sewer, viewers also sometimes see only the large distorted shadows of men without seeing their sources.

Camera

Even the first-time viewer of the film will notice that the settings are often filmed in Dutch angles (Figure 5.8). This technique is first used when Martins talks to the porter in the stairwell of the building where Lime lived. The porter is seen against a background that seems to slant downward to the left, whereas Martins is seen against a background that seems to be angled downward to the right. The contrasting shots of the porter and Martins are the first of many in the film showing the characters off balance relative to their environment, to each other, and to viewers.

As is demonstrated in Chapter 2, camera angle and distance can be powerful expressive options, and so they are in *The Third Man*. For example, when Kurtz, Winkel, and Popescu meet the fourth man on the bridge, the fourth man's identity is obscured by an extreme long shot and a high-angle, extreme long shot. Camera angles and distances can also increase or decrease the size, status, power, or importance of the human figure. In the scene where Martins is suspected of murdering the porter, an extreme low-angle close-up of a man's head invests him with both size and dominance and conveys some sense of his danger to Martins. On the other hand, both a high-angle, extreme long shot from the ferris wheel of the antlike people below and a high-angle, extreme long shot of Martins pacing outside the military police headquarters reduce the subjects not only in size but also in importance or power.

FIGURE 5.9 **Bright but not hard lighting dispelling some darkness**
A light, supposedly from above, inadvertently exposes Lime, who has been hiding in a darkened doorway. Lime is a creature of darkness, brought forth from the shadows only unwillingly. Frame enlargement. *London Film Productions. Library of Congress.*

EDITING

The film uses continuity editing: shot follows shot in a clear, efficient manner, as in the scene where the taxi driver races Martins to the meeting. Occasionally, though, a shot does not occur where viewers might expect. Consider the scene where Martins goes to visit Dr. Winkel. Martins stands alone in a street, looking at the building. In the next shot and scene, we do not see him outside Dr. Winkel's door or entering Winkel's apartment or already inside the apartment. Instead, we see a knife slicing a cooked chicken as the doorbell rings (announcing Martins's arrival). Another example of editing helping to confound the viewer's expectations occurs in the sequence in which Martins is being rushed to the Cultural Reeducation Section meeting. Film conventions about speeding cars and abductions have conditioned us how to read this scene; thus, experienced movie viewers suspect that something terrible is finally going to happen to the intrusive and bumbling Martins. As the taxi speeds through the Viennese streets, the pace quickens, and the fast cutting between shots showing the helpless and alarmed Martins, shots of the speeding taxi, and shots of the bewildered bystanders can alarm viewers and make

FIGURE 5.10 **A shadow used to alarm and mislead**
A larger-than-life shadow, one of many in this very dark film, here at a suspenseful moment when the military authorities are expecting Lime's arrival at a café. The source of the shadow, though, is an old balloon man. Frame enlargement. *London Film Productions. Library of Congress.*

them even a little dizzy. When Martins is dropped by the door leading into the meeting hall where he is to deliver a lecture, the audience realizes that it has been misled, in part by editing usually used in movie abduction scenes.

Reaction shots are used in varied, expressive ways. The scene where Martins discovers that the porter has been murdered includes five reaction shots of people on the sidewalk who suspect Martins of the murder. An earlier scene ends disturbingly with a reaction shot without showing what the porter is reacting to (Figure 5.11 on p. 178). The same strategy of using reac-

FIGURE 5.11 A reaction shot but not a shot of what is being reacted to
A brief scene in which the porter agrees to meet with Martins that night ends with this reaction shot. Although viewers never see who or what the porter is seeing, the implication here and especially later in the film is that he is seeing someone who has come to murder him. Frame enlargement. *London Film Productions. Library of Congress.*

FIGURE 5.12 Repeated reaction shots but no shots of what is being reacted to
In the children's ward of a hospital, Martins, accompanied by Calloway, sees the results of Lime's diluted penicillin. Throughout the scene, viewers see six shots of Martins's reactions to the children in the hospital beds but never see what he sees. Those horrors are left to the viewers' imaginations. Frame enlargement. *London Film Productions. Library of Congress.*

tion shots without showing what is being reacted to is used repeatedly in the scene of Calloway and Martins's visit to the children's ward of a hospital (Figure 5.12). In both scenes, the impact can be greater on viewers because their imaginations can conjure up fearful images.

Fast cutting serves different functions in *The Third Man*. The film begins with a montage supplying an enormous amount of information about postwar Vienna, including two consecutive but discontinuous brief shots illustrating contradictory aspects of the occupied city (Figure 5.3). Later in the film, the montage of evidence about Lime's criminal activities demonstrates how much information can be conveyed in thirty or so seconds of skillfully edited film. That montage also incorporates a brief shot showing the devastating impact the information is having on Martins. Fast cutting is also used in the wild taxi ride and early in the sewer chase. The film even includes an example of expanded time. After Martins sees Lime illuminated briefly in the doorway, he begins to cross the street but stops abruptly and backs up a bit as a car speeds in front of him. In the next shot, from a different angle, the car is farther back than it was at the conclusion of the previous shot, and Martins has to wait again briefly as the car again speeds in front of him. There is a slight repetition of part of the movement (the car's and Martins's), a slight expansion of time, so that Lime's escape seems a little more plausible (just barely).

SOUND

Sometimes sound is used in the film to confuse both characters and viewers. An example occurs in the sewer sequence when Lime stands immobilized before several archways because he cannot match sound to image. Because of the many echoes, in much of the sewer sequence sound obscures who is where doing what. Sound is also used to mystify, mislead, then surprise when Martins runs away from two thugs and enters a darkened room and hears an unidentifiable sound. It sounds something like a baby or something else until it squawks and the light reveals the parrot.

Sound is also often used to establish a situation immediately. Martins's opening to his "speech" to the Cultural Reeducation Section is curt yet oh so revealing. His "well" followed immediately by his clearing of his throat are faint, trailing off, revealing more than a little uncertainty and embarrassment. After one word and that additional vocal, we viewers know his "speech" will be a disaster. Sound is also used to help advance the plot. The meowing of Anna's cat directs Martins's attention to the darkened doorway and in turn to Lime. No cat sound, no discovery of Lime.

Music, too, is used expressively. The musical theme associated with Lime is first played after the completion of his first funeral service. The same theme is used many times thereafter. A fragment of it, played slowly and at low volume, is heard as Martins looks at Anna from offstage and tells her that he was a friend of Harry Lime. The theme accompanies each major appearance of Lime. It is heard after the sudden illumination of Lime in the darkened doorway but only until the car drives by. A fragment of it, played slowly and with trills, is heard as Martins enters the empty square where Lime has disappeared and for the rest of the brief scene. We hear the melody in the scene where the coffin is dug up, as if to mislead viewers into expecting Lime's body in the coffin. Shortly after the coffin is opened and Calloway and Paine see that it contains the body of the missing orderly, Joseph Hobbin, the music quickly fades out; it is no longer useful to the scene. As Martins waits for Lime near the ferris wheel and as Lime arrives, walking vigorously and seeming jovial, Lime's melody is played loudly and briskly. When Lime appears atop the damaged building before his night meeting with Martins, his musical theme announces his arrival before we see him close enough to see for certain who it is. As Lime opens the door to the café and hears Anna berating Martins, his entry is not surprisingly accompanied by his musical theme. The theme is played softly and slowly along with indistinct voices of the men in the tunnels during the last three shots of the final scene between Lime and Martins, as Lime is losing his vitality and Martins is in anguish about whether to shoot his friend. After we hear the gunshot, the music stops abruptly. The theme is heard a last time immediately after the conclusion of Lime's second funeral, again played at low volume and slowly. It is heard until the jeep Calloway is driving passes Anna, a final reminder of the man, drained of his life. Throughout the film the musical theme announces Lime's appearances and elsewhere suggests the level of his energy or mood and his impact on events. It might even be regarded as his life spirit.

As these highly selective examples of the expressiveness of film techniques illustrate, *The Third Man* is an accomplished example of the ways that mise en scène, cinematography, editing, and sound can help reveal and support a film's settings, subjects, moods, and meanings. The expressiveness of the film's techniques helps re-create the settings vividly and memorably and helps bring to life characters and story widely esteemed for their complexity, subtlety, entertainment value, and enduring appeal.

WORKS CITED

Drazin, Charles. *In Search of* The Third Man. London: Methuen, 1999.
Jarka, Horst. "*The Third Man* and Vienna: From Gray to Evergreen." *Modern Austrian Literature* 32.3 (1999): 253–70.

Part Two
THE VARIETY
OF FILMS

Now that we have studied the expressiveness of film techniques, we consider completed films. Part Two discusses the sources, types, and other characteristics of the live-action fictional film and the alternatives to it: documentary, experimental, hybrid, and animated films.

There are many reasons to consider the broad diversity of film. Considering the sources, type, and other characteristics of a film can help us relate it to other films and understand it more clearly. Examining a variety of films also helps us understand the film medium more fully: the properties, techniques, forms, and purposes of different films. Understanding that the film medium is far more inclusive and diverse than what is found on the screens of the nearest multiplex, in the neighboring video store, on movie channels, and in music videos helps us avoid simplifying and overgeneralizing about the film medium. A film, for example, does not always last 80 to 180 minutes, tell a story, and reassure viewers of their values; indeed, a film does not even necessarily aspire to coherence,

◄ *Witchcraft through the Ages* (*Häxan*)—which was directed by Benjamin Christensen and made in Sweden in 1922—illustrates how varied a film can be and how problematic it can be to classify one. *Witchcraft through the Ages* combines elements of narrative and nonnarrative documentary with experimental film and of realism with surrealism as it re-creates and illustrates a variety of historical and contemporary manifestations of witchcraft and witch hunting. The film abounds with information for students of witchcraft and memorable expressive images for students of film. Seen here is one of the film's most famous and most striking images: a re-creation of part of a witches' Sabbath as the lascivious bearded Satan leans over a woman who is reaching up to embrace him and surrender herself to him. *Svensk Filmindustri. The Museum of Modern Art/Film Stills Archive*

completeness, and popularity. As the following chapters demonstrate, film is and has been much more. Part Two concludes by applying the concepts of Chapters 6 to 9 to one film, the narrative documentary *Hearts of Darkness: A Filmmaker's Apocalypse,* thus demonstrating some of the many ways the material of Part Two may help viewers better understand a film and the film medium.

CHAPTER 6

Sources for Fictional Films

U SUALLY, A FICTIONAL FILM IS BASED ON A SCRIPT. The script may be an original story, but often it is based on historical events, a fictional work (usually a novel), a play, a TV show or series, or other films. In this chapter we will focus on some of the most frequent sources for fictional films and on the process of transforming sources into films. In doing so, we come to understand the film medium more completely—to understand, for example, some strengths and limitations of a film and its sources.

Terms in **boldface** are defined in the Illustrated Glossary beginning on page 539.

SCRIPTS AND STORYBOARDS

Each script, regardless of its source, may appear in different versions. The **screenplay** is the earliest version, written before filming begins and describing or supplying the **settings,** action, dialogue, and structure. A **shooting script** is the version of the script used during filming. It includes changes made in the screenplay; it usually breaks the **scenes** into **shots;** and it normally includes instructions on camera placement and use. The third general type of script, the **cutting continuity (script),** is not a source for a film but a description of the finished film.[1]

setting: The place where filmed action occurs.

scene: A section of a narrative film that gives the impression of continuous action taking place in continuous time and space.

shot: An uninterrupted strip of exposed motion-picture film or videotape that presents a subject, perhaps even a blank screen, during an uninterrupted segment of time.

---

[1] A cutting continuity script serves different functions from a screenplay or a shooting script. It indicates each setting and describes major events and any dialogue. It may include descriptions of camera distances, camera angles, camera movements, transitions between scenes, and indications of where music is heard.

This type of script, with its detailed description of the finished film, can refresh the viewer's memory of the film and reveal details and patterns not noticed in seeing the film. Cutting continuity scripts usually provide more complete, accurate, and legible translations for foreign language films than are given in the film subtitles.

No version of a script, however, can re-create the experience of watching a film. Cutting continuity scripts may include some subjective interpretation and cannot convey the editing, sounds, moving images, and environment of theater and audience that contribute to the experience of seeing a film. Most viewers find that reading any type of script before seeing a film is tedious because the script itself is neither literary nor cinematic. Many scripts, too, are carelessly published and abound in factual errors.

Scripts

Table 6.1 illustrates the elements of a film that are usually the responsibility of the screenwriter and those that are the contributions of others. In large productions, how closely the scriptwriter's wishes are followed depends on arrangements with the **producer,** director, and perhaps actors. Usually all other aspects of a film—such as camera angles and transitions between shots—are the domain of the other filmmakers such as the cinematographer and editor, usually under the guidance of the director. We cannot know the scriptwriters' exact contributions to a film with a large production company because so many people involved—especially the producer, director, actors, and editors—may rewrite or edit parts of the script or insist on changes in it. In large, complicated productions, one or more "script doctors" may be hired to rewrite the script, sometimes again and again, and they often go uncredited.

Comparison of a screenplay or shooting script with the finished film sometimes reveals the different contributions of the writer(s) and others, especially the director. We can see these relative contributions by comparing a scene from a script for *The Third Man* (1949) with the comparable section of

producer: A person in charge of the business and administrative aspects of making a film.

TABLE 6.1
Creative Territories for Making Fictional Films

THE WRITER'S TERRITORY	TERRITORY OF PRODUCTION PERSONNEL
▪ SETTINGS: where and when the action takes place and something about what the settings look like	▪ CASTING AND PERFORMANCE: people, animals, or creatures selected to play the roles; behavior, gestures, tone of voice
▪ SUBJECTS: the characters' actions and dialogues	▪ CINEMATOGRAPHY AND MISE EN SCÈNE: camera distances, angles, lenses, lighting, composition, and so forth
▪ STRUCTURE: the selection and arrangement of dialogue (if any) and actions	▪ EDITING: length and arrangement of shots; transitions between shots[a]
▪ MEANINGS: stated in the story or more often implied by it; what the film explains about its subjects in general terms or, more often, shows about them	▪ MUSIC AND MOST SOUND EFFECTS[a]

Source: Adapted from Phillips.

[a]Occasionally directions for editing transitions, music, and sound effects that were indicated by the writer are followed by the production personnel.

the finished film. In the film Holly Martins has come to Vienna to work for an old friend, Harry Lime. Martins learns that Lime has been involved in stealing penicillin, diluting it, and selling it at an enormous profit. Late in the film Calloway, a British officer trying to enlist Martins's aid in trapping Lime, has brought Martins to a children's hospital. Here is how the shooting script describes what happens:

123. CHILDREN'S HOSPITAL (NIGHT):

As they [Calloway and Martins] *come through the doors, a nurse passes and Martins realizes he has been shanghai-ed, but it is too late to do anything.*

CALLOWAY: I want to take a look in No. 3 Ward.

NURSE: That's all right, Colonel Calloway.

CALLOWAY (*to Martins*): You've been in on this story so much, you ought to see the end of it.

124. CHILDREN'S WARD (NIGHT):

He pushes open a door and, with a friendly hand, propels Martins down the ward, talking as he goes in a cheerful, professional, apparently heartless way. We take a rapid view of the six small beds, but we do not see the occupants, only the effect of horror on Martins's face.

CALLOWAY: This is the biggest children's hospital in Vienna—very efficient place. In this ward we have six examples—you can't really call them children now, can you?—of the use of the Lime penicillin in meningitis. . . . Here in this bed is a particularly fascinating—example, if you are interested in the medical history of morons . . . now here. . . .

Martins has seen as much as he can stand.

MARTINS: For pete's [*sic*] sake, stop talking. Will you do me a favour and turn it off?

As they continue their walk past the small beds, dissolve. (123–24)

This version of the script is written in scenes, the **master-scene format,** which indicates the scene number, the setting, and the segment of the day (such as day, night, dawn, noon, late afternoon). The scriptwriter describes the action briefly and supplies all the dialogue but does not indicate how the dialogue is to be delivered. The writer knew that well-written dialogue usually suggests its delivery and that the director and actors would probably have ignored overly specific directives.

Now here is my description, including all the dialogue, of the comparable part of the finished film. It's only one scene, which runs about fifty-eight seconds.

Martins and Calloway enter a large ward of a hospital. As they walk past beds and Martins looks into them, Calloway tells Martins, "This is the biggest children's

hospital in Vienna. All the kids in here are the result of Lime's penicillin racket."
Calloway moves away from Martins and talks to a nurse (unheard) as Martins
walks on slowly, still looking into each bed. Martins stops at the foot of one bed
and looks into it; Calloway joins him and says, "It had meningitis. They gave it
some of Lime's penicillin. Terrible pity, isn't it?" Calloway then walks away from
Martins, and Martins turns away and walks a few steps (we do not see Calloway
and Martins together again during the scene). Nurses tend the **offscreen** children: taking temperatures, giving oxygen, marking a chart, tossing aside a teddy
bear (presumably the child who had it won't need it anymore).

The scene in the film is generally true to the script and takes its cue from
the script not to show the children, only Martins's reactions to them. But the
film has many differences from the script. Two scenes in the shooting script
have become one scene in the film—a wise decision because the earlier of
the two written scenes adds little to the story. The film also has far less dialogue (34 words versus 103) and relies more on the visuals, especially the expressions on Martins's face, which we see in six of the scene's fifteen shots. In
the film scene, Martins says nothing. In the film, too, Calloway is subtler. He
does not push Martins along and talk so much; instead he brings Martins
into the ward and lets the sights of the place work on Martins, while the director lets the images of Martins work on viewers. In the film viewers can infer
how extensive is the evil that Lime's actions have spawned. The film also por-
trays a large ward full of Lime's victims; the script indicates victims in only
six beds. The film shows many nurses busy tending the children; the script
says nothing about the nurses' work. When we compare screenplays or
shooting scripts with the corresponding films, we find that, as in the case of
The Third Man, the film is usually more concise, less reliant on dialogue, and
more visual.

Although we cannot say with certainty who is responsible for all the
changes in this part of *The Third Man*, we can see roughly what the scriptwriter, Graham Greene, wrote and the final filmed product. Director Carol
Reed probably deserves much credit for the changes from the script, which
compress the action and present the information and moods more visually
and more subtly.

Storyboards

A **storyboard** is a series of drawings (or occasionally photographs) of each
shot (or sometimes part of a shot) of a planned film or video story, usually accompanied by brief descriptions or notes (Figure 6.1). Storyboards are the
visual equivalent of a rough draft of a written story. They allow filmmakers
to see how the finished film might look before the laborious and costly
processes of filming and editing begin. Storyboards are useful for deciding how

FIGURE 6.1 Sample storyboards

Storyboards are the visual equivalent of an outline for a story. Each panel represents an intended shot or part of a shot. Here are the last few storyboards for Hitchcock's *North by Northwest* (1959). The first two storyboards represent the film's penultimate shot and show that the camera begins close to the two subjects then pulls back to reveal the surprising setting, the upper berth of a train compartment. The final shot is of the train speeding into a darkened tunnel. Storyboards are not binding on filmmakers; they are simply visual explorations of a film's possible shots. Hitchcock, however, worked out all of a movie's shots before filming began and rarely deviated from his plans once shooting was under way. *MGM. The Museum of Modern Art/Film Stills Archive*

to divide the script into shots, determining how to arrange the shots (a sort of preediting), and deciding camera placement.

In animation, storyboarding is crucial because creating each frame of an animated film is usually especially time-consuming and expensive. Typically, once the storyboard for an animated film has been worked out in detail and the voices cast and recorded, the creation of individual frames begins.

INDIVIDUAL SOURCES

The history of cinema shows that just about any human subject can become the source of a fictional film. Possible, but infrequent, sources include non-fiction magazine articles (*Pushing Tin*, 1999, and *Isn't She Great*, 2000), video games (*Mortal Kombat*, 1995), comic books (*X-Men*, 2000), comic strips (the Peanuts films), series of short animated movies (*South Park: Bigger, Longer and Uncut*, 1999), musical albums (*Pink Floyd the Wall*, 1982), and operas (*Carmen*, many times). Although fictional films can have other sources, five of the most frequent ones are history, fiction, plays, TV, and other films. As we will see illustrated in this chapter's last section, often there is a series of sources, and even films based on one major source inevitably have been influenced by additional sources.

The filmmakers' adaptations of their sources may be loose (perhaps the adaptation retains only a few major aspects of the original—for example, only the title and a character or a few scenes). An adaptation may be faithful (it follows the story of the original and captures its mood or spirit but with some changes). An adaptation may be literal (as nearly as possible a transla-tion from the sources). Literal adaptations are rare but most likely to happen when plays are adapted into films. Which type of adaptation is "best" is sub-ject to debate. Some advocate literal adaptations, assuming that re-creating the original as closely as possible is most important. At the opposite extreme, those who support loose adaptations argue that effective films, whatever their sources, are most important.

History

Many fictional films, such as *Stand and Deliver* (1987) and *The Hurricane* (1999), are based on historical events. Often single historical events are the source for multiple, highly distinct film interpretations, as in the case of the sinking of the *Titanic*—*Saved from the Titanic* (1912), *Titanic* (1943), *Titanic* (1953), *A Night to Remember* (1958), and *Titanic* (1997). Usually movies based on his-torical events must attract large audiences to recoup the fortunes needed to make and market them. Consequently, filmmakers do not typically aim to teach their audiences traditional written historical accounts because they tend to be unengaging as movies and therefore unprofitable. When a film deals with news or history, filmmakers usually omit, add, or change details to make the film more entertaining or to imply different **meanings,** or both. For centuries novelists and playwrights, including Shakespeare, have done the same. (For a sample of the debate about the issues involved in one movie's interpretation of history, see pp. 192–94.)

Typically, fictional films based on history blend fiction and fact through-out. One example is *Stand and Deliver*, the story of a real Latino high school math teacher, Jaime Escalante, and one of his largely Latino classes. The film shows various barriers to learning in the students' lives, the methods the

meaning: An observation or general statement about a subject.

teacher uses, and the students' hard work. All this is presented in such a way that viewers are led to believe that the account is factual. In spirit, yes; in some details, no. For example, in the film the entire class seems to have to retake a test because authorities at a national testing service suspected cheating, but in fact only fourteen of the eighteen students had to take the test again. The film shows the students having only one day to review for the second test. In actuality, the second test was administered several months later. Yet another example: as in nearly all fictional films, the movie character is livelier and more engaging than the real person (Figure 6.2).

The makers of *The Hurricane* (1999)—which shows the story of Rubin (Hurricane) Carter, a successful boxer imprisoned for a triple murder but eventually freed—take great pains to make the film look historically accurate (Figure 6.3). The story is based on historical events about which there is disagreement. Before and after the film's opening in December 1999, reporters and attorneys involved in the original case painted a very different picture of the Carter case than the movie does.[2] The changes made seem to be the usual ones for movies based on history. Thus, for example, nine Canadians living on a commune become three Canadians doing some sort of work to end injustices in society. The detectives, prosecutors, witnesses, judges, and juries whose work led to two convictions of Carter become one racist police officer and two suspect witnesses. A trial and conviction, nine months of liberty for Carter and John

[2]For example, a former newspaper reporter who covered the case is highly critical of the movie's accuracy and has established a Web site (<http://www.graphicwitness.com/carter>) with links to many newspaper articles about the case.

FIGURE 6.2 **Actor and subject**
Actor Edward James Olmos (left) as Jaime Escalante in *Stand and Deliver* (1987), with the real high school math teacher Jaime Escalante. Comparison of clips of the celluloid Escalante teaching with documentary footage of the real Escalante teaching illustrates that, as in most movies based on real people, the movie character seems more lively and engaging than the actual person. *American Playhouse; Warner Bros.*

FIGURE 6.3 **Re-creating the look of an earlier time and place**
Like other commercial films based on historical events, the images in *The Hurricane* (1999) look authentic. Here actor Denzel Washington and others reenact a celebration after one of Rubin (Hurricane) Carter's boxing victories. The scene was filmed in black-and-white, as photographs of the time would have been, and everything else about the image looks true to the story's time and place. Frame enlargement. *Beacon; Universal*

Artis (the other man arrested for the triple murder), a second trial, and a second conviction become one brief courtroom sentencing in the movie. In the film Artis becomes a minor character while the young Lesra Martin, who worked with the Canadians on Carter's behalf, plays a major role.

Some actual events after Carter's second release from prison are at odds with the movie's concluding explanations about the main characters' fates. After his release from prison, Carter married one of the Canadians but eventually became disillusioned with her and the others of the commune and evidently remains aliened from them all. The film informs viewers before the movie's closing credits only that "Terry, Sam, and Lisa returned to Canada. Rubin Carter joined them there and makes his home in Toronto. He is the Executive Director of the Association in Defence of the Wrongly Convicted."

Like so many other movies based on historical events, *The Hurricane* illustrates all of the following points made by historian Robert Brent Toplin:

> Filmmakers must attend to the demands of drama and the challenges of working with incomplete evidence. In creating historical dramas they almost always need to collapse several historical figures into a few central characters to make a story understandable. Often they are pressed to simplify complex causes so that audiences will comprehend their movies' principal messages and not lose interest, and the dramatic medium often leads them to attribute changes in history to the actions of dynamic individuals rather than to impersonal forces. Cinematic historians often lack detailed evidence about situations in the past, so they invent dialogue and suggest impressions about the emotions and motivations of historic figures. Also, they suggest **closure** on a story, revealing few doubts, questions, or considerations of alternative possibilities. (10)

closure: A sense of resolution or completion at the end of a narrative.

A fictional film based on historical events always fictionalizes the material to a greater or lesser extent.

Some filmmakers and film distributors downplay the fictional elements of movies based on history—for example, by burying the disclaimer (if there is one) at the end of the film when only a few viewers remain in the theater. (Such disclaimers may be unreadable on home videotape versions.) In theatrical showings, both *Gladiator* (2000) and *The Hurricane* end with disclaimers that are on screen only a few seconds. Here is the disclaimer for *The Hurricane:* "While this picture is based upon a true story, some characters have been composited or invented, and a number of incidents fictionalized." "Some" and "a number of" conceal the extensiveness and nature of the changes made. After the prolonged, intense controversy about the historical accuracy of *The Hurricane* when it was released in theaters, the video and DVD releases carry the disclaimer at the beginning and ending. Filmmakers may even go so far as to hide their fiction by presenting a statement as factual. *Fargo* (1996) begins as follows:

THIS IS A TRUE STORY.
The events depicted in this film took place in Minnesota in 1987.
At the request of the survivors, the names have been changed.
Out of respect for the dead, the rest has been told exactly as it occurred.

Some reviewers of *Fargo* were skeptical of the above claim, and an investigation by the *Minneapolis Star Tribune* failed to unearth any case like the one the movie depicts. A film may even imply at its conclusion that it has been factual though it has not. The 1994 Russian-French film *Burnt by the Sun* has an epilogue explaining the fates of the main characters, but the film's director and cowriter, Nikita Mikhalkov, said "he added the epilogue for dramatic effect and invented the characters himself" (Stanley B1).

Other fictional filmmakers enhance their films' semblance of actuality by including **documentary**-like material. *Schindler's List* (1993) includes **title cards** about what actually happened, and the main body of the movie concludes with documentary footage of Schindler Jews and their relatives honoring Schindler by placing stones on his grave. *JFK* (1991) begins with documentary footage of President Eisenhower warning of the powers of the military-industrial complex and includes frequent excerpts from historical films and TV newscasts. *Apollo 13* (1995) uses old TV clips, interviews, subtitles conveying factual information, and (concluding) narration to enhance the appearance of factuality.

With a fictional film based on historical events, let the buyer beware: such a movie should be regarded primarily as a fictionalized entertainment nearly always with a greater focus on enjoyable storytelling than the written accounts regarded as historical. In both *Stand and Deliver* and *The Hurricane*, for example, as in so many American movies, the two major goals of the films are to entertain audiences and to give hope that individuals or small groups who work hard and persistently can eventually triumph over society's flaws.

> Many historical sources for films are cited in the first column of the chronology for 1895 to 2000 (see pp. 487–529).

documentary film: A film whose representation of its subjects viewers are intended to accept primarily as factual.

title card: A card or thin sheet of clear plastic on which is written or printed information included in a film.

Fiction

According to critic and theorist Dudley Andrew, "well over half of all commercial films have come from literary originals" (98). To see some of the changes made when fiction is adapted into a film and to see what each medium is capable of, we look at a passage of fiction and the corresponding section of a film based on the fiction. The passage is from the end of Chapter 12 of *The Woman in the Dunes* (1964), Kobo Abé's Japanese novel about a man trapped in a large sand pit with a woman who lives there in a shack.

JFK: Fact and Fiction

Someone assassinated President John F. Kennedy in Dallas, Texas, on November 22, 1963, and shortly afterward his accused murderer was himself murdered while in custody. Soon a flood of theories as to who was behind the two murders surged forth. The Warren Commission, appointed by President Lyndon B. Johnson, investigated the matter at length and issued a report that failed to gain widespread acceptance. To this day, many people remain uncertain about the causes of Kennedy's death. Oliver Stone's *JFK* (1991) presents one theory about the Kennedy assassination, but it is very much a minority view, one to which few or no published historians subscribe. Even before Stone's film came out in December 1991, controversy about its merits broke out around the United States. Following are excerpts from the wide-ranging debate.

The following are excerpts from a seven-page statement by Jack Valenti, the president and chief executive of the Motion Picture Association of America and a former top aide to President Johnson, as reported in the national edition of the *New York Times* on 2 April 1992:

> Does any sane human being truly believe that President Johnson, the Warren Commission members, law-enforcement officers, C.I.A., F.B.I., assorted thugs, weirdos, Frisbee throwers, all conspired together as plotters in Garrison's wacky sighting? And then for almost 29 years nothing leaked? But you have to believe it if you think well of any part of this accusatory lunacy.
>
> In scene after scene Mr. Stone plasters together the half true and the totally false and from that he manufactures the plausible. No wonder that many young people, gripped by the movie, leave the theater convinced they have been witness to the truth.
>
> In much the same way, young German boys and girls in 1941 were mesmerized by Leni Riefenstahl's *Triumph of the Will*, in which Adolf Hitler was depicted as a newborn God. Both *J.F.K.* and *Triumph of the Will*

are equally a propaganda masterpiece and equally a hoax. Mr. Stone and Leni Riefenstahl have another genetic linkage: neither of them carried a disclaimer on their film that its contents were mostly pure fiction.

This op-ed piece in the 7 March 1992 national edition of the *New York Times* was written by David W. Belin, a former counsel to the Warren Commission:

> What far right-wing extremists tried to persuade a majority of Americans to believe in the 1960's with their "Impeach Earl Warren" billboards, Hollywood has been able to achieve in the 1990's in its impeachment of the integrity of a great Chief Justice.
>
> Earl Warren is not the only victim. The Kennedy assassination is called a "coup d'etat," a "public execution" by elements of the C.I.A. and the Department of Defense, while President Lyndon B. Johnson is called an accessory after the fact—in other words, a murderer.
>
> When the film not only alleges conspiracy but names the guilty parties, it goes beyond just artistic license and entertainment. It crosses the threshold of slander and character assassination—a 1990's version of McCarthyism.

A letter from John Roberts in the 18 August 2000 issue of the *Chronicle of Higher Education* included the following:

> In his [Stone's] preposterous film *JFK*, the only unassailable fact presented in the movie is that Kennedy is dead. The numerous threads of Mr. Stone's paranoid conspiracy theories can be held together only by his creating out of whole cloth a person who did not exist (Donald Sutherland's character) who breathlessly tells the hero (Kevin Costner) that "Yes, this assassination was a coup!" All of it was done to keep Kennedy from doing something he never intended to do in the first place—namely, get out of Vietnam. . . . Kennedy understood the logic of the cold war, the danger of

He's a District Attorney.

He will risk his life, the lives of his family, everything he holds dear
for the one thing he holds sacred . . . the truth.

KEVIN COSTNER

AN OLIVER STONE FILM

JFK

The Story that Won't Go Away

Poster for *JFK* (1991)
From this poster, potential viewers learn that the film will focus on one man's difficult and
dangerous task in pursuing a noble goal, a frequent subject in popular American movies.
Because of the placement and size of the lettering, certain groups of words receive more
prominence than others. The largest lettering and the boldface is for *JFK* (the movie's name);
the next largest lettering is for Kevin Costner (the name of the popular actor playing the
main role). Also prominent is lettering is for *The Story that Won't Go Away* (a reminder that
the causes of the Kennedy assassination are still much in dispute).

   As the movie *JFK* does, the visuals on the right side of the poster combine fiction and
fact—an image of the actor playing the main role combined with fragments of three historical images: a photograph of part of the motorcade shortly after President Kennedy had
been shot; a newspaper headline announcing Kennedy's assassination; and a photo of the
accused assassin, Lee Harvey Oswald, holding a rifle. *Warner Bros.*

authoritarianism, and the threat
of passivity in the face of real
oppression. Keep in mind, this
is the man who wrote *Why
England Slept*. He was not into
appeasement.

   Mr. Stone seems to think
that this is a minor triviality.
But it cuts to the core of his
and others' conspiracy theories
about the case. And without
evidence to support the asser-
tion that Kennedy was killed
because he wanted to pull out
of Vietnam, the conspiracy evap-
orates into thin air, whence Mr.
Stone seems to have pulled it in
the first place.

As film critic Roger Ebert,
writing in the 20 December
1991 Chicago *Sun-Times*, saw it:

Stone's film is hypnotically
watchable. Leaving aside all of
its drama and emotion, it is a
masterpiece of film assembly.
The writing, the editing, the
music, the photography, are all
used here in a film of enormous
complexity, to weave a persuasive
tapestry out of an overwhelming
mountain of evidence and testimony. Film students will examine
this film in wonder in the years
to come, astonished at how much
information it contains, how
many characters, how many
interlocking flashbacks, what
skillful interweaving of documentary and fictional footage.
The film hurtles for 188 minutes
through a sea of information
and conjecture, and never falters
and never confuses us. . . .

193

The achievement of the film is not that it answers the mystery of the Kennedy assassination, because it does not, or even that it vindicates Garrison, who is seen here as a man often whistling in the dark. Its achievement is that it tries to marshal the anger which ever since 1963 has been gnawing away on some dark shelf of the national psyche. John F. Kennedy was murdered. Lee Harvey Oswald could not have acted alone. Who acted with him? Who knew?

David Ansen, one of the film critics for *Newsweek*, wrote in the 23 December 1991 issue:

> By turning Jim Garrison—a troubling, shoot-from-the-hip prosecutor whose credibility has been seriously questioned—into a mild-mannered, four-square Mr. Clean, Stone is asking for trouble. *JFK's* Garrison is perhaps best viewed more as a movie convention than as a real man. Stone has always required a hero to worship, and he turns the D.A. into his own alter ego, a true believer tenaciously seeking higher truth. He equally idealizes Kennedy, seen as a shining symbol of hope and change, dedicated to pulling out of Vietnam and to ending the cold war.
>
> But it is possible to remain skeptical of *JFK's* Edenic notions of its heroes and still find this movie a remarkable, necessary provocation. Real political discourse has all but vanished from Hollywood filmmaking; above and beyond whether Stone's take on the assassination is right his film is a powerful, radical vision of America's drift toward covert government. What other filmmaker is even thinking about the uses and abuses of power?

Finally, historian Robert A. Rosenstone wrote in his 1995 book *Visions of the Past: The Challenge of Film to Our Idea of History* (123–24):

JFK, despite the many documentary-type elements that it contains, belongs to what is certainly the most popular type of film, the Hollywood—or mainstream—drama. This sort of film is marked, as cinema scholars have shown, by a number of characteristics, the chief being its desire to make us believe that what we see in the theater is true. To this end, the mainstream film utilizes a specific sort of film language, a self-effacing, seamless language of shot, editing, and sound designed to make the screen seem no more than a window onto unmediated "reality."

Along with "realism," four other elements are crucial to an understanding [of] the mainstream historical film:

- Hollywood history is delivered in a story with beginning, middle, and end—a story that has a moral message, and one that is usually embodied in a progressive view of history.
- The story is closed, completed, and ultimately, simple. Alternative versions of the past are not shown; the *Rashomon* approach is never used in such works.
- History is a story of individuals—usually heroic individuals who do unusual things for the good of others, if not all humankind (ultimately, the audience).
- Historical issues are personalized, emotionalized, and dramatized—for film appeals to our feelings as a way of adding to our knowledge or affecting our beliefs.

Such elements go a long way toward explaining the shape of *JFK*. The story is not that of President Kennedy but of Jim Garrison, the heroic, embattled, uncorruptible investigator who wishes to make sense of JFK's assassination and its apparent coverup, not just for himself but for his country and its traditions—that is, for the audience, for us.

The woman sidled up to him. Her knees pressed against his hips. A stagnant smell of sun-heated water, coming from her mouth, nose, ears, armpits, her whole body, began to pervade the room around him. Slowly, hesitantly, she began to run her searing fingers up and down his spine. His body stiffened.

Suddenly the fingers circled around to his side. The man let out a shriek. "You're tickling!"

The woman laughed. She seemed to be teasing him, or else she was shy. It was too sudden; he could not pass judgment on the spur of the moment. What, really, was her intention? Had she done it on purpose or had her fingers slipped unintentionally? Until just a few minutes ago she had been blinking her eyes with all her might, trying to wake up. On the first night, too, he recalled, she had laughed in that strange voice when she had jabbed him in the side as she passed by. He wondered whether she meant anything in particular by such conduct.

Perhaps she did not really believe in his pretended illness and was testing her suspicions. That was a possibility. He couldn't relax his guard. Her charms were like some meat-eating plant, purposely equipped with the smell of sweet honey. First she would sow the seeds of scandal by bringing him to an act of passion, and then the chains of blackmail would bind him hand and foot. (90–91)

The comparable section of the film version runs about forty-five seconds and consists of the conclusion of one shot and three additional shots. The following is my description; dialogue is from the film's subtitles, not the published script.

Shot 1. . . . *At the end of this lengthy shot, the woman, carrying a pan of water and a rag, approaches the man—who is lying on his back, naked from the waist up—and kneels beside him.*

WOMAN: How do you feel?

Shot 2. *The man turns his head slightly away from her and groans.*

MAN: Not too bad.
WOMAN: I'll wipe you down.

As she turns him on his side, he lets out more groans. The camera moves slightly to the left, and we see and hear her rinse and wring the rag in the metal pan; the camera moves right and we see her begin to wipe the man's back with the damp rag (Figure 6.4 on p. 196). She turns the rag over.

Shot 3. *We see part of the man's back and side. The camera follows the woman's hand as she slowly wipes near his side. With a finger, she thumps or tickles his side.*

Shot 4. *As we see the man's head and shoulders, he giggles then quickly turns his head back toward the woman.*

MAN (*angry and loud*): Stop it!

With a serious look on his face, he lowers his head and faces forward again.

WOMAN (*unseen*): It hurts?
MAN (*still serious*): Yes!

FIGURE 6.4 Fiction into film
In *Woman in the Dunes* (1964), the woman wipes down the injured man. Unlike fiction, films allow viewers to quickly see such actions in all their nuances and complexity. *Pathe Contemporary Films Release*

Obviously, there are many differences between the experience of reading the passage and seeing and hearing the corresponding section of the film. Some of the differences result from choices of the filmmakers. For example, the filmmakers chose to have the man laugh, then catch himself and become brusque, whereas in the book the man shrieks and the woman laughs. Although filmmakers typically prune the dialogue they adapt from fiction, the filmmakers of *Woman in the Dunes* chose to supply slightly more dialogue than is in the novel.[3]

Many differences between the passage in Abé's novel and the corresponding section of the film, however, result from differences in the two media. The novel gives many of the man's thoughts, including a memory, but to render these mental states in a film might confuse viewers. Look again at the last two paragraphs reprinted from the book. How can film accurately convey what those words do? Without words, how can a filmmaker convey the simile and the two implied metaphors in the sentences "Her charms were like some meat-eating plant, purposely equipped with the smell of sweet honey. First she would sow the seeds of scandal by bringing him to an act of passion, and then the chains of blackmail would bind him hand and foot"? The figurative language cannot be entirely converted into visual images and sounds, including music. Similarly, neither images nor sounds can convey well the experiences of smell, taste, and feeling. Thus, "A stagnant smell of sun-heated water, coming from her mouth, nose, ears, armpits, her whole body, began to pervade the room around him" cannot be converted into film.

Other differences between the passage and the film result from the capabilities of film. In forty-five seconds, the film gives viewers an excellent sense of place, shape, volume, textures, and sounds. For example, we can see the forms and sizes of the man and woman; we can see the texture of the man's skin; we hear his groans and the tone of voice of the man and woman. Most of these details are not rendered in the comparable passage of fiction. To do so would require enormous space and slow the story to a crawl, and even then

[3]The title of the English translation of the novel is *The Woman in the Dunes*. The title of the English translation of the film is *Woman in the Dunes*.

the images in the reader's mind would be less precise than the images and sounds of the film. The movie camera can select actions and render them with clarity and force (as in the second shot where the camera moves left, then right); it can capture movements and gestures and their significance (such as the man's spontaneous laugh, followed by a quick suppression of it). Film can convincingly show places, real and imaginary. It can juxtapose images more quickly than the blink of an eye. It can present visual details such as faces, the viewing of which, as scientist and educator David Attenborough has said, is itself extremely expressive:

> Letting others know how you feel is a basic part of communication. No creature in the world does so more eloquently than man, and no organ is more visually expressive than his face. Even in repose the human face sends a message and one that we tend to take for granted. Each face proclaims individual identity. In teams, recognition of other members is of great importance. A hunting dog in a pack proclaims its identity by its own personal smell. Primates, with their reduced sense of smell but their very acute vision, do it by the infinite variety of their faces. We have more separate muscles in our faces than any other animal. So we can move it in a variety of ways that no other animal can equal, and not only convey mood but send precise signals. By the expression on our face we can call people and send them away, ask questions and return answers without a word being spoken.

Film can also capture well the nuances of sound and music. Prose is hard pressed to compete with cinema in presenting what can be seen and heard and in making us feel that we are at a particular place.

Fictional films that are based on novels or short stories rarely re-create the source fiction in its entirety. In film stories, passages of characters' thoughts, descriptions of characters' backgrounds, analysis by the author, and a more or less consistent point of view or means of perception are uncommon. The order of scenes may also be changed. Especially in popular movies, the ending of the source novel is often changed to a happier, more crowd-pleasing conclusion (Figure 6.5). Nor does the fictional film usually re-create all the characters and action of a novel. *Greed*—the 1925 American film

JONIK
USA   "In the book she dies."

FIGURE 6.5

Copyright 1989 by John Jonik, from Movies Movies Movies: An Entertainment of Great Film Cartoons, *edited by S. Gross.*

event: In a narrative or story, either an *action* by a character or person or a *happening* (a change brought about by a force other than a person or character).

plot: The structure (selection and arrangement) of a narrative's events.

classic, which is a literal adaptation of the novel *McTeague*—attempted to do so, but the initial version reportedly ran nine and a half hours. Such a length was quickly judged too long to be marketable because it could be screened only in two or three lengthy showings, whereas a two-hour film can be shown several times a day and thus can generate more revenue. Soon *Greed* was edited down to about two hours. Even *Tom Jones* (1963), which critics have praised for capturing the structure, **events,** and moods of the very long, complicated source novel, omits characters and events.

Reading fiction and seeing a film are different experiences because each medium has its own techniques, potential, and limitations. Perhaps the basic difference between fiction and film is that fiction requires its audience to visualize and subvocalize from words on the page or computer monitor, whereas film presents images and sounds directly. People who enjoyed a novel are rarely satisfied with a film made from it because, in part, they visualize the characters and events as they read, and the film presents different visuals and sounds. Then, too, sometimes readers are disappointed that film adaptations do not include all of the novel's characters or **plot.**

Fiction and film are distinct media, with their own strengths and weaknesses. It is misleading to judge a film by how closely it re-creates the novel one visualizes while reading. Instead, the film is something related yet new and separate, a creative expression in a different medium with its own resources and techniques. Likewise, whenever a novel or play is based on a film, it is unfair and misleading to evaluate the later work in another medium by how well it re-creates the source film. If one takes the view that a derivative creative fictional work should be judged by its fidelity to its source(s), then, for example, many of Shakespeare's plays, such as *Macbeth* and *Richard III*, would be judged deficient: they are not reliable history but make for effective theater.

Instead of evaluating a film by comparing it to its source, it is more helpful to compare the film version to other, similar films (and to compare the fiction with other, similar fiction). However, a close comparison of a film and its fictional source can be instructive, revealing what creative decisions were made during the transformation and what the two forms share and what is distinct to each.

For a sample student essay about a fictional work transferred into a film, see the Web site for this book at <http://www.bedfordstmartins.com/phillips-film>.

Plays

In the early years of cinema, many fictional films imitated plays closely. After all, plays had been around the Western world for more than two thousand years, and in the 1890s people on both sides of the footlights had a good sense of what a play was and wasn't. For this reason, many early films look

FIGURE 6.6 **Early film actors with theatrical backgrounds** In the 1912 *Queen Elizabeth*, Sarah Bernhardt, one of the most famous actors of her era, played her part with broad stylized gestures because actors of the day used such gestures extensively so they could be seen in large theaters. Film actors with a background in theater had not yet learned to restrain their acting style for the movies. Frame enlargement. *The Museum of Modern Art/Film Stills Archive*

like awkwardly filmed theater (Figure 6.6). Gradually, though, film found what it could be and developed beyond filmed theater. Today, the two forms are still cousins but are not as close as they were in film's first few decades.

Basically, plays are the more verbal medium. If you listen to a recording of a play, you will notice that much of its moods and meanings are communicated by the lines of dialogue and their delivery. So expressive is the human voice that a trained actor can convey a world of information and feeling by pauses, volume, timbre, timing, and pronunciation.

Films, in contrast, tend to be more visual. Several times I have begun a film course by turning off the volume of the projector or TV monitors and showing students the beginning of a British film few of them have seen. Before I show the clip, I give the students a list of questions to consider, such as Who is the main character? What does he or she seem to want? What does that character's personality seem to be like? Where and when does the story take place? I show the film clip twice; after each showing, I ask students to jot notes in answer to my questions and about anything else they noticed in the clip. Then I collect and read the responses aloud. The results: students generally come close to what the film is showing—and without the sounds of the film, with only its moving pictures. Films can convey so much information visually that the acclaimed 1924 silent German film *The Last Laugh* includes readable words only four times. If you examine many movies—for example, *2001: A Space Odyssey* (1968) and Jane Campion's *The Piano* (1993)— you will notice that many scenes have little or no dialogue or sign language. If you watch a foreign-language film with inadequate subtitles—and do not allow yourself to be distracted with thoughts about how annoying it is not to know all that is being said—you will notice how much you understand from the film's visuals.

Some would argue that the essence of a play is at least one actor acting and reacting. Actors also interact with the audience. Experienced theater actors attest to how much an alert, responsive, and supportive audience contributes to their performance. Live acting differs markedly from the rehearsed, edited, larger-than-life performances shown from different distances and angles on the movie screen. The live actor is more nearly what we see in our lives outside the theater, someone who might even occasionally seem to look us in the eye, someone who makes imperfect delivery or has all-too-human movements. In small theaters where the audience is close up, live acting also seems more intimate.

Because of these basic differences between plays and films, certain changes tend to be made when a play is transformed into a film. Most filmmakers want to make a film, not simply record a performance of a play. A film version of a play tends to locate some of the scenes outdoors. This process is called "opening up" the play. With more scenes, it's not unusual for a film to have more characters than its source. The film derived from a play often prunes the play's dialogue and relies more on the visuals, music, and **sound effects.** And as we watch a film, we seem to get to sit in many seats and view the action from many distances and angles.

In staging a play, directors, actors, costumers, set designers, and others decide what words and actions to include, how to show the action and deliver the dialogue, how to costume the characters, and what the lighting and settings will be like. In the stage directions printed with their plays, some playwrights include details about how the plays should be staged. Other writers, such as Shakespeare, supply few such directions (perhaps in Shakespeare's case in part because he himself did not prepare his own plays for publication).

When a play is filmed, filmmakers make many of the same decisions that people staging a play do—about the selection of dialogue and actions, lighting, costuming, settings, and the like. Filmmakers have many additional concerns, such as camera distances and angles, editing, and nearly always a more complex mixture of **vocals,** sound effects, and music than is found in a staged play.

To see some of the differences between a play and one of its film adaptations, consider Shakespeare's *Richard III*, which was a play (probably first published in 1597) before it was a film (the version discussed below is the 1995 production with Ian McKellen) (Table 6.2 on pp. 202–3). That is the usual but not inevitable order of creation.

In its fundamentals, the film adaptation remains faithful to the original play. The film's opening, for example, retains most of the play's dialogue; the personalities of the major characters are unchanged, and the focus stays on a

sound effect: A sound in film other than vocals or music.

vocal: Any sound made with the human voice, including speech, grunts, whimpers, screams, and countless other sounds.

FIGURE 6.7 Main determinant of actions, consequences, and meanings
As in most Shakespearean film adaptations, in the 1995 version of *Richard III*, many changes were made between the play and film. The focus of the film, however, remains on Richard—his charm and political skills but also his utter ruthlessness (even to those who support him), his overreaching, and his fall from power—and finally, as in other Shakespearean dramas, including *Hamlet*, the restoration of political order. Like many other major British actors, Ian McKellen has an extensive background in theater, including Shakespearean productions and the lead role in *Richard III*. (Notice in this photo of McKellen, the hard, mainly overhead lighting does not glamorize him in any way and leaves his eyes largely in the dark. Lighting supports characterization and mood.) *Lisa Katselas Paré and Stephen Bayly; United Artists*

disgruntled Richard setting in motion schemes to harm others while advancing himself into a position of power (Figure 6.7).

Here, as in most plays transformed into films, there are many differences. As is usually the case when a play is compared with its corresponding film, the 1995 film version of *Richard III* has many more scenes. The film shows actions only mentioned in the play—the murders of the Prince of Wales and his father, the king. The film also has more settings than the play. In Shakespeare's play the entire first scene takes place on a London street. The opening of the McKellen *Richard* takes place in King Henry VI's field headquarters, on a London street, in the palace, at an airport, back at the palace, and near a docked boat. The film not only changes the setting of the play's opening soliloquy from a London street but also presents the soliloquy in two settings: before a large party and in a men's rest room. In the film, objects in the settings (car, airplane, palace,

TABLE 6.2
Richard III, **Scene 1 of the Play and the First 14 Scenes of the 1995 Film**

[ ] = Dialogue deleted for the film.   Boldface = Dialogue added in the film.   { } =Additional information.

THE PLAY (first scene),
Act 1, Scene 1
London. A street.

Enter Richard, Duke of Gloucester, solus.

GLO. Now is the winter of our discontent
Made glorious summer by this sun of York,
And all the clouds that lowered upon our house
In the deep bosom of the ocean buried.
Now are our brows bound with victorious wreaths,
Our bruisèd arms hung up for monuments,
Our stern alarums changed to merry meetings,
Our dreadful marches to delightful measures.
Grim-visaged war hath smoothed his wrinkled front,
And now, instead of mounting barbèd steeds
To fright the souls of fearful adversaries,
He capers nimbly in a lady's chamber
To the lascivious pleasing of a lute.
But I, that am not shaped for sportive tricks,
Nor made to court an amorous looking-glass;
I, that am rudely stamped, [and want love's majesty
To strut before a wanton ambling nymph;
I, that am curtailed of this fair proportion,
Cheated of feature by dissembling nature,]
Deformed, unfinished, sent before my time
Into this breathing world, scarce half made up,
And that so lamely and unfashionable
That dogs bark at me as I halt by them—
Why, I, in this weak piping time of peace,
Have no delight to pass away the time,
Unless to spy my shadow in the sun
And descant on mine own deformity.
And therefore since I cannot prove a lover,
[To entertain these fair well-spoken days,]
I am determinèd to prove a villain
And hate the idle pleasures of these days.
Plots have I laid, [inductions dangerous,
By drunken prophecies, libels, and dreams,]
To set my brother Clarence and the King
In deadly hate the one against the other,
[And if King Edward be as true and just

THE FILM
(first 14 scenes, 11 minutes, 34 seconds)

1. Field headquarters of King Henry VI's army at Tewkesbury. Richard kills the Prince of Wales and the prince's father, King Henry VI. Only dialogue in the scene: Son: **Goodnight, your Majesty.** King: **"Goodnight, son."** Son: **"Father."**

2. Richard is driven in an escorted car in London.

3. At the palace, young prince Edward playfully tries to avoid being dried after his bath.

4. Nurse to King Edward IV: **"Your Majesty."** She gives him his medicine.

5. Clarence finishes developing some photos, grabs his coat and camera, and rushes off.

6. At the airport, Rivers gets off a plane and gives a stewardess his card.

7. Richard's motorcade arrives at the palace, and Richard gets out.

8. Richard addresses the Duchess of York as **"Mother,"** but she and her granddaughter, the young Elizabeth, pass by Richard without a word.

9. Clarence sets the camera timer and takes the York family photo. {Up to this point, the film has supplied information on three titles cards and two superimposed title cards.}

10. At a party the Yorks throw to celebrate their victory over King Henry VI and the House of Lancaster, King Edward IV dances with his queen, Elizabeth. Richmond asks the young Elizabeth to dance. Buckingham and Richard greet each other warmly.

11. Outside, Rivers, the queen's brother, arrives by car; he gets out of the car and walks up the steps toward the party.

12. The queen dances with young Edward, her son and the heir to the throne. Rivers greets various people and dances with the queen and his young nephew Edward. Clarence is led away by several men. Richard steps up to the microphone and begins to speak {8 minutes, 47 seconds into the film}:

Now is the winter of our discontent
Made glorious summer by this sun of York,
And all the clouds that lowered upon our house
In the deep bosom of the ocean buried.

THE PLAY (continued)

As I am subtle, false, and treacherous,
This day should Clarence closely be mewed up,
About a prophecy, which says that G
of Edward's heirs the murderer shall be.
Dive, thoughts, down to my soul—here Clarence
   comes.]

Clarence enters, under guard. He is being taken as a prisoner to the Tower. Richard acts surprised and vows to help him.

After Clarence is led away, Richard, alone, reveals he plans to have Clarence killed.

Lord Hastings, who has recently been released from imprisonment in the Tower himself, tells Richard that King Edward IV is very ill.

Alone again, Richard reveals more about his plans for Clarence and how Richard for tactical reasons plans to marry Lady Anne, whose husband and father-in-law (King Henry VI) Richard himself had killed.

THE FILM (continued)

Now are our brows bound with victorious wreaths,
Our bruisèd arms hung up for monuments,
Our stern alarums changed to merry meetings,
Our dreadful marches to delightful measures.
Grim-visaged war hath smoothed his wrinkled front,
And now, instead of mounting barbèd steeds
To fright the souls of fearful adversaries,
He 13. {Richard enters men's room} capers nimbly in a lady's
   chamber
To the lascivious pleasing of a lute.
But I, that am not shaped for sportive tricks,
Nor made to court an amorous looking-glass;
I, that am rudely stamped, [and want love's majesty
To strut before a wanton ambling nymph;
I, that am curtailed of this fair proportion,

Cheated of feature by dissembling nature,]
Deformed, {flushes urinal} unfinished, sent before my time
Into this breathing world, scarce half made up,
And that so lamely and unfashionable
That dogs bark at me as I halt by them—
Why, I, in this weak piping time of peace,
Have no delight to pass away the time,
Unless to espy my shadow in the sun
And descant on mine own deformity.
Why I can smile and murder while I smile
And wet my cheeks with artificial tears
And frame my face to all occasions.
And therefore since I cannot prove a lover,
[To entertain these fair well-spoken days,]
I am determinèd to prove a villain
And hate the idle pleasures of these days.
Plots have I laid {Richard leaves men's room} [inductions
   dangerous,
By drunken prophecies, libels, and dreams,]

14. {above a pier leading to a boat and some distance from it}
To set my brothers Clarence and [the] King **Edward**
In deadly hate the one against the other.
[And if King Edward be as true and just
As I am subtle, false, and treacherous,
This day should Clarence closely be mewed up,
About a prophecy, which says that G
Of Edward's heirs the murderer shall be.
Dive, thoughts, down to my soul—here Clarence comes.]

clothes) show the York family's wealth and power. Viewers may also notice that the uniforms and banners resemble those used by the Nazis, suggesting that York-ruled England is a fascist state. Unlike the play, the film uses five brief title cards to supply basic information about settings and situations. The film also has less dialogue than the play. During its first eight minutes forty-seven seconds, only nine spoken words are heard (not counting the lyrics the woman sings at the party). Of the forty-one lines of the play's first soliloquy, only thirty are used in the film plus three lines inserted from Act 3, Scene 2 of Shakespeare's *Henry VI, Part 3* (see the three consecutive lines in boldface in Table 6.2). Throughout the film, as in nearly all films based on plays, the film relies more heavily on visuals than does the play.

Shakespeare's plays have been a deep and enduring well for films. The stories remain of interest to viewers. The insight into human behavior is matched by perhaps only a few other writers in the history of Western literature. The language—though often difficult for modern audiences and in places obscure even to scholars who have dedicated their lives to its study— is often striking, apt, and memorable.

As we saw with the example of the McKellen *Richard III* in Table 6.2, in transferring a play to the screen, filmmakers often take major liberties— especially in the case of Shakespeare. Period, settings, costumes, and props may all be added or altered. Lines are nearly always pruned. The actors' gestures may suggest possible new interpretations. Consider the 2000 film *Hamlet*. The period is shifted from Denmark in approximately 1600 to New York City in 2000. Instead of a castle at Elsinore, scenes are set in the Hotel Elsinore, which is a high-rise luxury hotel presumably near Times Square; a laundromat; a diner; and the Guggenheim Museum. In the action videos section in the neighborhood Blockbuster, Hamlet delivers part of his "to be or not to be" soliloquy. Instead of traveling to England in a boat, Hamlet is transported via a jet. Costumes are not period clothing but what today's New Yorkers would wear. Props include a plethora of the latest electronic gadgets, a pistol to supplement fencing foils, and a briefly glimpsed little rubber duck Ophelia returns to Hamlet along with his love letters. King Claudius is now a dapper new CEO of the Denmark Corp., although he is as smooth and treacherous as ever. Hamlet is an aspiring film/videomaker whose mousetrap to test the conscience of the king is not a play within the play but a film within the film. In this as in other *Hamlet*s, not only lines are pruned; characters are dropped, and whole scenes eliminated. The performances also work to add new or at least unusual interpretive possibilities. The Laertes of this first filmic *Hamlet* in the new century, for example, seems to have a stronger than brotherly attachment to his sister Ophelia. She seems more emotionally pained and more prone to serious instability than in many earlier productions. Gertrude seems to sense that the cup of wine Claudius offers Hamlet is poisoned and drinks from it anyway. The results are another *Hamlet:* same basic plot, same language—in what remains of Shakespeare's lines—but a *Hamlet* that the makers of the film doubtless hoped would attract and engage a new generation.

There are exceptions to the above generalizations about films and plays. Some films—*My Dinner with André* (1981), for example—have much in common with traditional plays: few scenes, much dialogue, and limited visuals. And some recent plays have much in common with films—scores of short scenes, many settings, and sparse dialogue.[4]

Television

Traffic (2000)—which was based closely on a British TV miniseries called *Traffik* and was a huge commercial and critical success—is a forceful reminder that TV shows can serve as sources for films. Television has long been a source for movies, especially since the box office success of *The Addams Family* (1991). Since then, U.S. studios have made a slew of old TV shows into movies, including *The Fugitive* (1993), *The Beverly Hillbillies* (1993), *The Flintstones* (1994), *Mission Impossible* (1996), *South Park: Bigger, Longer and Uncut* (1999), *Mission Impossible 2* (2000), *Charlie's Angels* (2000), and many others that were not box office or critical successes, such as *Lost in Space* (1998). TV has been a frequent source for the characters and plots of movies and the writers, actors, and directors who bring them to life on the big screen. Perhaps almost as often, TV borrows from films. It is a two-way street with heavy traffic. The mutual dependence of one medium on the other has become so commonplace that knowledge of the relationship of the two media deepens one's understanding of both.

The TV medium has also been a frequent subject for films. Commercial television's proclivity to present a sanitized and artificial world was a subject of several late 1990s films. In *Pleasantville* (1998), David wishes that his life were more like the TV series *Pleasantville*, a re-creation of 1950s sitcoms

---

[4]In recent decades films increasingly influence plays, both in the writing and the staging. Sometimes films are discussed or alluded to, as in *The Baltimore Waltz* (1990), a play that refers to the films *The Third Man* (1949); *Dr. Strangelove: Or, How I Learned to Stop Worrying and Love the Bomb* (1963); and *Wuthering Heights* (1939). Plays may also be structured as a film typically is. In general, more and more recent plays consist of many more brief scenes than before the arrival of cinema. *The Baltimore Waltz*, for example, has thirty scenes during its approximately eighty minutes of playing time. A. R. Gurney's *The Dining Room* (1982) has eighteen scenes (and nearly sixty characters) and a playing time of about ninety minutes. Often, staging is influenced by films. A 1996 production of *Four Dogs and a Bone* added video versions of imaginary film footage made during a day's work.

Films have also been modified and staged as musical plays. Examples are *Little Shop of Horrors*, which was a 1960 film, then a musical play, and finally a more lavish 1986 film; *Sunset Boulevard; Big; Victor/Victoria;* the MGM musicals *Singin' in the Rain, Meet Me in St. Louis*, and *Seven Brides for Seven Brothers;* and the Disney hits *The Little Mermaid, Beauty and the Beast*, and *The Lion King*. Occasionally plays are based on a movie topic or type, such as *Action Movie: The Play—The Director's Cut*, a 1998 parody of action movies.

such as *(The Adventures of) Ozzie and Harriet* (1952–66) and *Leave It to Beaver* (1957–63). Because David's family life and social life are frustrating, he is attracted to the stable and comforting lives he sees on the show. In this fictional world, it's always 72 degrees and sunny, divorce is nonexistent, there is no conflict, Mom is always home to make dinner and cookies, and one of the prettiest girls in school is eager to date David. Nevertheless, when he and his sister become trapped in the TV show as two black-and-white characters, David slowly realizes that the sanitized world of Pleasantville is artificial and constricting. While this fifties TV world is safe, it also precludes opportunity for individualism, creativity, and deeply felt emotions. Like the widely held view of the 1950s as a decade, Pleasantville is colorless and is characterized by a restricted range of options. *The Truman Show* (1998) provides much the same image of TV shows. The movie focuses on a character who eventually realizes his life in an idealized small town is controlled by a television producer and that his entire life is being broadcast for the benefit of a huge television audience. As in Disneyland, which itself is a creation of the 1950s, *Pleasantville* and *The Truman Show* present a safe, sanitized, reassuring world—at least initially.

By implication, George Lucas's early film *THX 1138* (1971) criticizes TV because it is used throughout a repressive futuristic society to help monitor and sedate the masses. Movies often **satirize** other aspects of television, as in *Network* (1976), which shows the extremes to which an unpopular TV network will go to achieve higher ratings. The satire of tabloid TV coverage found in Oliver Stone's *Natural Born Killers* (1994) is similar though more biting (Figure 6.8). In that film, Robert Downey Jr. plays Wayne Gale, the host of a sensational TV tabloid show, *American Maniacs*, who will do anything to get a story. The film satirizes the American public's love affair with violence—especially when it is largely used against authorities—by showing how ratings-hungry journalists turn two killers into international celebrities. Gale's behavior reveals the extremes to which a reporter will go to get spectacular ratings based on sensational news. The film also shows how smug such a journalist can become: he loses control of himself, gets caught up in a prison escape and fires at prison guards, then assumes he is safe because he holds the TV camera.

Two other sources for films, though rarely the main sources, are TV commercials and music videos. Commentator Maria Demopoulos points out that directors of music videos seek "to translate into film the ethos characteristic of the young demographic of the music: rebellion, defiance, individuality, teen angst. Music videos, by design, reflect a youth-driven agenda, distinguished by impermanence and disposability" (36). Often, these are the same subjects and outlook of teen movies.

Demopoulos also points out that the techniques and ideas of TV commercials and music videos have influenced filmmakers and vice versa:

satire: A representation of human behavior that has as its aim the humorous criticism of the behavior shown.

The techniques and ideas behind these short formats have crossed over to **feature films.** Commercials and music videos have long served as a testing ground for visual styles migrating upward, and at the same time have spawned a new generation of directors. . . . Still, the influence flows both ways. Much of the raw material mined for music videos and commercials derives from films in the first place. The video-as-movie-adventure-epic, for instance, dates back to MTV's infancy with Duran Duran's video "Hungry Like the Wolf" ([directed by] Russell Mulcahy, [19]82). (35)

feature (film): A fictional film that is at least sixty minutes long.

Commentators concur that the two short TV formats have influenced moviemaking most notably in editing. It seems likely that viewing both TV commercials, including movie **trailers,** and music videos has conditioned a new generation of viewers to process a succession of images more quickly. Because so many viewers have seen so many TV commercials and music videos, filmmakers can rely less on continuity editing and more on editing by association, intuition, or accident, as in sections of *Natural Born Killers*.

trailer: A brief compilation film shown in movie theaters, before some videotaped movies, or on TV to advertise a movie or a video release.

For its part, TV has often borrowed from film. Television parodies of movies or parts of movies have a long history in the United States, going all the way back to TV's birth and providing subjects for performers like Milton Berle, Sid Caesar, Imogene Coca, Carol Burnett, and the show *Saturday Night Live*. A Thanksgiving episode of *South Park* (1997; Episode 109, "Starvin' Marvin") provides another instance of TV borrowing from film. In that episode, an attack by vengeful turkeys is made even more amusing because it parodies the epic battle scenes in *Braveheart* (1995). Over the years, various popular movies, such as *M*A*S*H* (1970) and *Buffy the Vampire Slayer* (1992), have also led to TV series.

The relationship of the two media is sometimes more complex than adaptation. The successful transformation of the *Star Trek* TV series into six films furnishes an example of this mutual dependence. The first Star Trek movie, *Star Trek: The Motion Picture* (1979), reunited the television cast from the *Enterprise*; it was followed by five sequels and inspired a new television series. In the second TV series, crew members can walk onto the "holograph deck" of the *Enterprise* and enter simulated environments that are often inspired by films or are informed by film aesthetics.

FIGURE 6.8 TV as source and subject for a film
In the scene from *Natural Born Killers* (1994) represented here, the main male character is finally caught by police officers, who give him a savage, prolonged beating as TV crews cover the event. The scene is reminiscent of the widely publicized TV broadcasts of the beating police officers gave Rodney King in Los Angeles. *Natural Born Killers* shows the story of two murderous lovers and their victims, most prominently law enforcement officers, prison guards, a prison warden (indirectly), and a TV tabloid journalist. A police officer/author who murders a prostitute, the warden who is twisted by hatred of the murdering couple, and the TV host of *American Maniacs* are also satirized, the TV tabloid journalist most of all for his self-promotion, thin veneer of self-control, pride, and pandering to the worst in human nature. The frequent music, garish saturated colors bathing entire scenes, fast cutting, occasional lack of continuity within scenes, inclusion of images from the couple's minds within scenes of the couple, and the frequent use of Dutch angles all contribute to the hallucinatory or nightmarish quality of the film, which at times looks and sounds like a music video. Frame enlargement. *Regency; Warner Bros.*

Although television and film now provide innumerable sources for each other, they have not always coexisted amicably. When television appeared on the American national scene in force during the 1950s, its arrival coincided with a time when Hollywood was floundering. During the war years of 1941 to 1945 and the postwar years from 1946 to 1948, Hollywood experienced its most profitable period. Until 1948, weekly attendance was measured at ninety million people, a number that was five times the number in the mid-1990s (Cook 442). This wartime boom for the movie industry, however, slowed in the late forties and early fifties as television viewing grew. By 1949, movie attendance dropped from ninety million to seventy million. In the same year there were one million television sets in the United States. By 1951, the number had climbed to ten million, and by 1959, it had reached fifty million (Cook 459). For some years, television and film competed intensely for the same audience. Hollywood's initial reaction was to refuse to interact with television or even acknowledge its existence. Members of the Motion Picture Association of America would not lease or sell their films for broadcast until 1956, and many film studios refused to allow their stars to appear on television (Cook 459). Gradually and haltingly, movie studios got into TV production, and media conglomerates included movie and TV production components under one corporate umbrella. Today, TV and film have grown more comfortable with—or at least more resigned to—their marriage, though flashes of envy and condescension remain.

For more information on the development of TV and other mass media, see the third column of the chronology for 1895–2000 (pp. 487–529).

FIGURE 6.9 A serial
From the teens of the twentieth century to the early 1950s, serials were shown in weekly installments in movie theaters. They featured extensive action, danger, and romance often in exotic settings, most of which are evident in this publicity still for one of the fifteen chapters of the Republic serial *Nyoka and the Tigermen* (1942).

Other Films

I'm often asked by younger filmmakers why do I need to look at old movies. . . . I'm always looking for something or someone that I can learn from. I tell the younger filmmakers and young students: do it like painters used to do, what painters do. Study the old masters. Enrich your palette. Expand the canvas. There is always so much more to learn. —Martin Scorsese

A film is one of many possible kinds of **texts.** A text is something that people produce or modify to communicate meaning, such as a film, photograph, painting, newspaper article, and T-shirt with a message. Some theorists refer to the relationship of one text to another as **intertextual,** a term that literally means between texts. Films are intertextual—they use earlier texts, including written history, fiction, plays, and other films—in an immense variety of creative ways. The *Star Wars* movies and *Indiana Jones* movies borrow their frequent cliff-hanging action and exotic locations from earlier serials (Figure 6.9). In *What's Up, Tiger Lily?* (1966) Woody Allen took a Japanese movie, deleted the original sound track, and added a sound track that tells a different story. *Babe: Pig in the City* (1998) includes frequent references to other texts as amusing, enjoyable rewards for informed adult viewers (Figure 6.10). In both her personality and her manner of speaking, the pink poodle is reminiscent of a major character in *A Streetcar Named Desire*, both the play and first film adaptation of it. Intertextuality in films may take many forms, including allusion, remake, parody, homage (or tribute), sequel, or prequel.

Filmmakers often make an allusion or passing reference to earlier texts. Occasionally, they make allusions to their own earlier films. In two scenes in *The Sure Thing* (1985), directed by Rob Reiner, a poster for *This Is Spinal Tap* (1984), also directed by Reiner, is visible briefly in the background. In a scene in *Spaceballs* (1987), which was produced and directed by Mel Brooks, various videotapes on a spaceship's shelf are for films directed by Brooks! In *American Graffiti* (1973) director George Lucas makes a sly allusion to an earlier film directed by the film's co-producer (Figure 6.11).

In a remake, the original film is re-created but usually updated: changes are made in the hope that the remake will seem more appealing to current audiences. Remakes are attractive to producers because the original film usually made a lot of money and some of the public will remember it favorably and be curious to see a more modern version of it. For economic reasons, then, remakes have been plentiful in Hollywood (Figure 6.12). Sometimes foreign films are remade as American films. At other times, American films are remade abroad with alterations meant to appeal to foreign audiences. The classic comedy *It Happened One Night* (1934) has twice been remade in India as *Chori Chori* (1956) and *Dil Hai Ke Manta Nahin* (1991) but with changes:

> Whenever a Hollywood film is remade in India it has to be recast in the Indian mould, that is, emotions have to be overstated, song, dances and spectacle have to be added, family relationships have to be introduced if they do not exist in the

FIGURE 6.10 Intertextuality as a bonus
Intertextuality may be subtle, as in *Babe: Pig in the City* (1998). In his manner of speaking and low, gravelly voice, the pit bull sounds like a movie gangster. Critic Christopher Kelly points out a connection between the representation of one of the dogs and *The Godfather* (1972): "the pit bull . . . sounds like Vito Corleone's long-lost pet" (42). In a speech recalling the making-an-offer-that-he-couldn't-refuse story in *The Godfather*, after Babe saves the pit bull's life, the dog steps forward and addresses the other animals: "I'd like to offer up a solution that I feel confident you'll all respond to. Whatever the pig says goes. Anyone hostile to the notion?" Such intertexuality is a source of amusement and pleasure for viewers with a broad knowledge of American culture but will pass unnoticed by those unfamiliar with the earlier texts. Frame enlargement. *A Kennedy Miller Film; Universal*

intertextuality: The relation of one text (such as a film) to another (such as a journalistic article, play, or another film). Intertextuality includes such forms as translation, citation, imitation, and extension.

FIGURE 6.11 An allusion to a friend's earlier work
George Lucas directed *American Graffiti* (1973); his friend Francis
Coppola co-produced it. Well into the film and on a background
movie marquee, the attentive viewer can briefly spot *Dementia 13*,
the title of an early Coppola film. If *American Graffiti* is not seen in
letterbox format, the title on the marquee is excluded from the image.
Frame enlargement. *Francis Coppola and Gary Kurtz; Universal*

original, traditional moral values such as dharma (duty)
must be reiterated and female chastity must be eulogised.
Only then will the film find success at the box office.
(Kasbekar 412)

If you examine one of the reference books,
CD-ROMs, or Web sites that describes and evalu-
ates thousands of films, you may be surprised by
how many hundreds and hundreds of them are remakes. A later film with the same title, however,
does not guarantee that it is a remake because
many titles are reused for a different story (both
film stories and titles get recycled, but not necessarily together).

A film may remake an earlier film or part of
it, either as a parody or homage. A **parody** is an
imitation intended for comic effect. In a parody
viewers who know the subject being parodied
recognize similarities yet see amusing differences.

a)   b)

FIGURE 6.12 A literal remake
(a) A frame from the 1960 *Psycho* shows a bird's-eye view of the detective at the top of the stairs as
he goes to investigate the Bates home. (b) A frame from the comparable shot in the 1998 remake,
also called *Psycho*. Here, as throughout the remake, the mise en scène, camera work, editing, and
sound track all closely re-create the original film.

Usually remakes are made to capitalize on an earlier film's popularity. Typically, the remake
updates the language, settings, camera work, sound track, and plot in hopes of attracting new and
usually mostly young audiences. New and more recognizable actors are employed, and if the original was in black and white, color is usually used instead, as it was in the 1998 *Psycho*. The remake
of *Psycho* proves that a literal remake will not necessarily attract large audiences.

Typically, remakes vary widely from the originals, sometimes so much so that viewers who
know an earlier film feel misled by the title (if the same title is used again) and the promise of an
updated presentation. Frame enlargements. *Universal*

In *Analyze This* (1999), the Billy Crystal character, a psychiatrist, has a dream that parodies shot by shot the scene in *The Godfather* where two men attempt to assassinate the godfather as he is buying oranges from a street vendor, and his youngest son Fredo fumbles his chance to protect his father. Re-creating the approximate look of a film or part of it is not the only way to parody earlier films. Parody may also result from re-creating highly selected excerpts from the original story, as in "The Fifteen Minute Hamlet" (1996), which reenacts snippets of the original play (and delivers the lines at maximum speed). For example, as Laertes is dying, he is cut off in midsentence and instead of the original "Exchange forgiveness with me noble Hamlet" we hear "Exchange forgiveness with me noble Ham."

FIGURE 6.13 **Parody of a film type and parts of other films**
Scary Movie (2000) parodies the *Scream* and *I Know What You Did Last Summer* type of horror film. It also often imitates parts of other famous movies. Here, as in *The Matrix* (1999), a character bends over backward to avoid an onrushing projectile aimed at him. He evades the plate but suffers a sharp back pain in doing so. Note the similarities and differences between this image and that of Figure 7.25a (p. 245). Frame enlargement. *Dimension Films*

A feature film may consist of parodies of a general film type and many parodic references to other films. *Spy Hard* (1996), a parody of James Bond movies, includes brief parodies of *Speed* (1994), *True Lies* (1994), *Pulp Fiction* (1994), *Sister Act* (1992), *Home Alone* (1990), and other movies. *Scary Movie* (2000) parodies the various *Scream* and *What You Did Last Summer* movies and parts of *The Exorcist* (1973), *The Blair Witch Project* (1999), *The Sixth Sense* (1999), *The Matrix* (1999), *The Usual Suspects* (1995), and others (Figure 6.13). A single movie is rarely the main subject of a later parody, although the original *Star Wars* (1977) was the main subject for the parodies "Hardware Wars" and Mel Brooks's *Spaceballs* (Figure 6.14).

Films that parody a film **genre** or group of movies include *The Rocky Horror Picture Show* (1975), mainly a musical parody of classic horror movies like *Frankenstein* (1931), (Figure 6.15); *Blazing Saddles* (1974), a parody of western films (see Figure 7.21 on p. 242); and "The Dove" (or "De Duva"), a 1968 film parody of several earnest films by the Swedish director Ingmar Bergman. The more unamusing the original subject being parodied is and the better the viewer knows it, the more amusing the parody might be. Thus, to those who know well the early films directed by Bergman, "The Dove" is especially amusing. The Swedish of the original films becomes the mock Swedish of "The Dove," as when Death says, "All dem peoples bin feelin my presenska zooner or latska," the English subtitle reads, "Yes, all mankind feels my presence eventually." And "He must've morten in da blacka" is translated as "He must have died at night."

Other films are parodies of documentary films. At first, these **mock documentary** films seem to be factual and to follow the conventions of documentary filmmaking, such as the use of interviews, subtitles, and handheld

genre ("ZHAHN ruh"): A commonly recognized group of fictional films that share settings, subjects, or events (and sometimes techniques) and that change over time.

a)

b)

c)

FIGURE 6.14 **Parodies of a film or films**
Star Wars (1977) is parodied by "Hardware Wars" (1978). *Star Wars* and other science fiction movies are parodied by *Spaceballs* (1987). (a) In this widely distributed image for *Star Wars* (left to right): Chewbacca, Luke Skywalker, Obi-Wan Kenobi, and Han Solo in Solo's Millennium Falcon. (b) The image from "Hardware Wars," with its low-budget setting (here a stripped-down "space vehicle" sporting dangling dice in the window), includes dim actors and a spaced-out or nauseous Cookie Monster: left to right: Wookie Monster, Fluke Starbucker, Augie "Ben" Doggie, and Ham Salad. (c) Late in *Spaceballs* occurs this image of the inside of a recreational vehicle space craft (from left to right): Barf (who's half man, half dog, and his own best friend), Dot Matrix (a protective female robot with the voice of Joan Rivers), Princess Vespa (the endangered damsel), and Lone Starr (the heroic pilot).

How marvelous the powers of the human mind: while watching both "Hardware Wars" and *Spaceballs* many viewers immediately recognize similarities to *Star Wars* and laugh at the differences. The compositions are the same, the setting roughly the same, but the characters are amusingly different. Parodies of the various *Star Wars* films—even of the inspiration for the original *Star Wars* ("George Lucas in Love," 2000)—have been extremely popular on the Web. (a) *Lucasfilm Ltd.*; (b) *Michael Wiese; Pyramid Film and Video, Santa Monica, Cal.*; (c) *Mel Brooks; MGM*

camera shots. Mock documentaries do not mock documentaries; they imitate them in playful, humorous ways. They are amusing fictional imitations using documentary filmmaking techniques. *This Is Spinal Tap* is purportedly a documentary about an inept, aging heavy-metal band, and *Fear of a Black Hat* (1994) is supposedly a documentary film about the endless problems confronted by a rap group, including troubles with various recording companies, rivalries with other rap groups, and losing their managers to gunfire—six of them in a row! (Figure 6.16). *Best in Show* (2000) uses interviews and subtitles to impart an initial documentary feel to an otherwise completely fictional and wryly satirical story of dog shows and especially dog owners and trainers.

a)

FIGURE 6.15 A parody of a film genre
The Rocky Horror Picture Show (1975) is a parody mostly of horror films, especially various Frankenstein movies. (a) The Dr. Frankenstein–type character (center) is the "scientist" Dr. Frank N. Furter, a homosexual transvestite from the distant planet of Transylvania. His assistant, Riff Raff (left), at first looks and acts like Dr. Frankenstein's hunchback assistant of the 1931 *Frankenstein*. (b) Near the end of *The Rocky Horror Picture Show*, Riff Raff dresses (at least from the hips up) and acts as if he stepped out of a 1930s low-budget sci-fi Flash Gordon serial or movie. *20th Century–Fox*

b)

FIGURE 6.16 A parody of a film type: the mock documentary
Fear of a Black Hat (1994) imitates documentaries in amusing ways. Its subject is an imaginary rap group. The film uses (and sometimes exaggerates) the techniques of cinéma-vérité, such as handheld camera work, interviews, and surprising, supposedly even embarrassing developments for the film's subjects. Here the "documentary filmmaker" interviews the straight-faced members of the group, from left to right: Tasty Taste, Tone Def, and Ice Cold. If viewers quickly figure out that the film is a parody of the documentary, they can enjoy its creativity, playfulness, and humor. *ITC Entertainment Group*

FIGURE 6.17   Documentary or mock documentary?
In *20 Dates* (1998), the main subject, Myles, is on a date with Christian, who called herself a feminist ballerina. After he points out to her that a hidden movie camera has been photographing their date, Myles says "her reaction was disappointing—and surprisingly violent." In the next scene, viewers learn she had attacked him, necessitating twenty stitches in his hand, and was suing him for invasion of her civil rights (the second of his dates to file a lawsuit). Is *20 Dates* a documentary or an amusing mock documentary where a lot goes wrong for the main subject? Frame enlargement. *Phoenician Films; Fox Searchlight Pictures*

Occasionally, it is difficult to be certain if a film is a documentary or a mock documentary (Figure 6.17). Many reviewers interpreted *20 Dates* (1998) as a documentary with perhaps a few staged scenes. Other viewers, however, see the film as a mock documentary. Certainly by the end of the film no viewer can say with certainty which parts are factual (if any) and which are fictional. However, so many things go wrong for Myles and the film has such a tidy happy ending (Myles succeeds in both his work and his love life), that the entire film or most of it may be a mock documentary or amusing fiction disguised as a documentary. In general, reviewers who interpreted the film as a documentary judged it negatively, whereas those who saw the film as a "mock doc" and were amused by it valued it more highly.

Unlike a parody, an **homage** is a tribute to an earlier text, a part of one, or a maker of texts. It may be a brief reference to or an affectionate re-creation of parts of an earlier film. An example occurs near the end of *Play It Again, Sam* (1972), which more or less re-creates part of the ending of *Casablanca* (1942).

a)    b)

FIGURE 6.18   Homage to a film's setting
(a) Parts of the opening setting of *A Clockwork Orange* (1971)—a place where people congregate and drink—are closely imitated in (b) a night spot in *Trainspotting* (1996), especially the style of lettering of the words on the back wall. *Trainspotting* also focuses on the subjects of the earlier film: alienated youths, disrupted homes, drugs, sex, and violence. (b) Frame enlargement.
(a) *Polaris; Warner Bros.* (b) *Channel Four Films, A Figment Film; Miramax Films*

a)   b)

FIGURE 6.19 **A film and its prequel**
(a) The Sundance Kid (left) and Butch Cassidy in *Butch Cassidy and the Sundance Kid* (1969).
(b) The youthful Sundance Kid (left) and Butch Cassidy in the prequel *Butch and Sundance: The Early Days* (1979). *20th Century–Fox*

Homages may be verbal or visual or—as the example from *Play It Again, Sam* illustrates—both. A good example of a visual homage is found in *Trainspotting*. In one scene the setting is strikingly similar to a setting in a famous earlier film (Figure 6.18). Perhaps the films of Alfred Hitchcock have elicited the most homages. A British Film Institute booklet lists twenty selected homages to Hitchcock in such films as *High Anxiety* (1977), *Basic Instinct* (1992), and *Twelve Monkeys* (1995) (*Hitchcock* 14).

Another source for a movie is a sequel. If a film is popular and contains enough unresolved events and if later filmmakers see ways to continue the story and develop it, they may make a sequel. If the ending of a popular fictional film seems too final (the main character dies, for example), a sequel based on one of the main characters' offspring may be made, as in *Son of Kong* (1933). Since 1997, the death of a protagonist no longer precludes a sequel. Thanks to cloning, the main character of the *Alien* movies was reconstructed from leftovers before the plot of *Alien Resurrection* (1997) begins.

Occasionally a movie is the inspiration for a **prequel:** a popular movie is followed by a movie depicting some of the characters from the original film at earlier stages of their lives. *Butch Cassidy and the Sundance Kid* appeared in 1969; in 1979, *Butch and Sundance: The Early Days* came out (Figure 6.19). It's also possible but rare for a film to be both a prequel and a sequel, as in the case of *The Godfather Part II* (1974), which has related events involving the same characters that precede and follow the story of *The Godfather* (1972). It is

TABLE 6.3
A Highly Selective Chronology of a Story's Versions

Clarissa (The History of Clarissa Harlowe), 1747 English novel of letters by Samuel Richardson

Julie (Julie, ou la nouvelle Héloïse), 1761 French novel of letters by Jean-Jacques Rousseau

Les liaisons dangereuses, 1782 French novel by Choderlos de Laclos consisting of 175 letters by about a dozen characters.

(French revolution, 1789–99)

According to Milos Forman, the director of *Valmont*, there were several stage adaptations of *Les liaisons dangereuses* in the nineteenth century and at least three stage adaptations in the twentieth century.

Les liaisons dangereuses, 1961 French black-and-white modern-dress film adaptation set in Paris and a Swiss ski resort, with Jeanne Moreau and Gerard Philipe as the two main characters who are married to each other and aware of each other's seductions. Directed by Roger Vadim (106 minutes)

Les liaisons dangereuses, 1985 British period play by Christopher Hampton, based fairly closely on the source novel with two former lovers still warily attracted to each other scheming with and against each other as he seduces a very young woman and a pious married woman. The play enjoyed critical and commercial success in London then New York.

Dangerous Liaisons, 1988 American and British period film in color with Glenn Close and John Malkovich as former lovers. Direction by Stephen Frears and screenplay by Christopher Hampton, based closely on Hampton's own play, which in turn was "adapted from the novel" by Choderlos de Laclos. Compared with the play *Les liaisons dangereuses*, this film version captures more of the epistolary quality of the original novel by dramatizing some brief scenes that are only recounted in the play. (120 minutes)

Valmont, 1989 French/U.S. period film with updated language, filmed in color on location in France with extensive attention to visual details. Stars: Annette Bening and Colin Firth; screenplay: Jean-Claude Carrière and Milos Forman; and direction: Forman. The film is based loosely on the French novel: the endings of the novel and film, for example, differ widely. Compared with other adaptations, *Valmont* also devotes much more time to the fifteen-year-old Cecile, her innocence and social education. (137 minutes)

Cruel Intentions, 1999 American film in color with Sarah Michelle Gellar and Ryan Phillippe as stepbrother and stepsister. The stepbrother seduces a willing young virgin and eventually an unwilling young virgin with whom he soon falls in love. Directed and scripted by Roger Kumble. Modern-dress version with young cast and characters set in New York City. The film's credits include the following: "Script suggested by the novel *Les liaisons dangereuses*." (97 minutes)

Note: Unavoidably, this table simplifies. For example, a later creative work will not be shaped equally by all previous influences, and later works are typically also influenced by sources outside the lineage represented here.

also possible to make chronologically related films in succession—such as *Star Wars*, *The Empire Strikes Back* (1980), and *Return of the Jedi* (1983)—then chronologically related prequels: *Star Wars: Episode I—The Phantom Menace* (1999) and its two successors.

MULTIPLE SOURCES

Although most fictional films derive mainly from history, a novel, a novella, a short story, a play, a TV show or series, or previous films, films inevitably have a more complicated ancestry. Such is the case with *Cabaret* (1972). A story—"Sally Bowles" in the 1939 book *Goodbye to Berlin* by Christopher Isherwood—was the basis for the play *I Am a Camera*, which was filmed in 1955 then made into a Broadway musical, called *Cabaret*, in 1966. The film version of *Cabaret*, with Liza Minnelli and Joel Grey, appeared in 1972. *Music of the Heart* (1999) is based on the 1996 documentary film *Small Wonders*, which in turn was based on a published essay.

Even when a film seems to have one main source, lesser influences are at work. The film *Dangerous Liaisons* (1988), with a screenplay by Christopher Hampton, is based on Hampton's 1985 play *Les liaisons dangereuses*, but that play in turn was based on the 1782 French novel of the same title, which had many other sources itself, including two earlier epistolary novels (Duyfhuizen 46 and 47; see Table 6.3). Another influence on the 1782 French novel is the story of Don Juan in its many variations, including the popular 1665 Molière play, *Dom Juan ou le festin de Pierre*.

Other factors further complicate the matter of sources. Consider the hypothetical example of a film based mainly on a novel. Perhaps the scriptwriter and director of the film had seen a production of a play that is based on the novel. Maybe the director saw an earlier TV movie version of the novel and was deeply impressed by the mise en scène including some of the details in the acting. Maybe something that both the scriptwriter and one of the actors in the film read about one of the earlier adaptations, such as the earlier TV movie version, influenced them as they worked on their film. In interviews, filmmakers often tell of being impressed by a technique or detail in one film and later using it while making an unrelated movie. In practice, although a film may be based primarily on one main source or on an adaptation of the original source, it is also the product of the scriptwriters', directors', and actors' previous experiences. Sources for a creative work are varied and not always easily identifiable by audience or artist. After all, successful creative people spend most of their time and energy creating (and revising)—not introspecting about their sources. Then, too, few are probably aware of the full range and interdependence of their sources, their intertextuality.

Texts do not emerge out of only a single human imagination or a team of people working on the same creative project during the same time: texts are always intertextual, always related to other texts. Awareness of some of the countless connections between works of the human imagination will help you avoid such oversimplifications as the following from a college newspaper article about an upcoming production of the 1985 play by Christopher Hampton: "The 1999 movie *Cruel Intentions* was based on the [1985 Hampton] play." That statement and the entire article made no mention of the main source, the original French novel, let alone the many other intermediate versions of the story between the source novel and *Cruel Intentions* (Table 6.3).[5]

SUMMARY

Fictional films may be based on a script, which may be an original story but often is not. Frequently, a script is based on historical events, a fictional work (usually a novel), a play, a TV show or series, or other films. Texts, including fictional films, do not emerge out of only a single human imagination or a team of people working on the same creative project during the same time: they are always intertextual, always influenced by other texts.

Scripts and Storyboards

- Typically the scriptwriter indicates the settings, subjects (action and dialogue), and structure of a fictional film and directly or indirectly many of its meanings.

- Comparing a screenplay or shooting script with the finished film seldom reveals who contributed exactly what, but typically the film is more concise, less reliant on dialogue, and more visual than the script.

- Storyboards are a series of drawings or photographs of each shot or part of a shot for a planned film or video story. They help filmmakers visualize how the story might look and might work as a story before filming and editing begin.

---

[5]Sometimes art is an important source for films. At various times in film history, painters and other visual artists have been especially prominent in making films. Two such periods were the 1920s in Europe and the 1950s and 1960s in the United States (pop art). Filmmakers have also long learned from painters, especially in the use of lighting, composition, color, and grain. Such filmmakers as Martin Scorsese in *The Last Temptation of Christ* (1988), Stanley Kubrick in *Barry Lyndon* (1975), Tony Richardson in *Tom Jones* (1963), Derek Jarman in *Caravaggio* (1986), Peter Greenaway in *The Cook, the Thief, His Wife and Her Lover* (1989), and Carlos Saura in *Goya in Bordeaux* (1999) have all imitated particular painters and sometimes specific paintings. In recent years, some filmmakers have made artworks, including temporary museum exhibitions involving two or more arts (installation art), and increasingly museums of modern or contemporary art include film or video art combined with other media.

Individual Sources

Nearly any subject can become the source of a fictional film, but five of the most frequently used sources are history, fiction, plays, television, and other films.

HISTORY

- Fictional movies based on history omit, change, or fabricate some of the events.

- In spite of the advertising claims and the documentary qualities of an historical movie itself, commercial fictional films based on history, such as *The Hurricane*, tend to give priority to drama and entertainment, not the accepted written historical accounts.

FICTION

- Novels, short stories, and novellas are well suited to render a character's mental activity. Other strengths of fiction include descriptions of characters' backgrounds, analysis by the author, figurative language, and a more or less consistent point of view or means of perception.

- Film is adept at presenting sights and sounds. It can also show the nuances of faces and the infinite flexibility and expressiveness of movement. It can render the human voice and music in much of their fullness. And through editing, it can condense the time needed to present significant events and transport viewers through time and space instantaneously.

- People who admire a novel are usually disappointed with a film adaptation of it because as they read the novel, they visualize it and later usually find the filmmakers' visualization inadequate. Then, too, a novel is usually too long and involved for a complete rendition on the screen; consequently parts of it are omitted.

- A film based on a fictional source should be understood and evaluated as a film, not as adapted fiction.

PLAYS

- Plays, in general, are a verbal medium; films, a visual one. Plays filmed with minimal variations in the camera work and editing tend to be disappointing as films because they do not take advantage of film's capabilities.

- Fundamentally, plays rely on the give-and-take of audience and live performer, whereas films rely on the audience's responses to controlled moving images and usually a sound track.

TELEVISION

- Although initially American TV and film were in fierce competition and their makers refused to cooperate with each other, now the two media are intertwined and often borrow actors, writers, directors, characters, stories, and techniques from each other.

- Often film and TV represent each other critically, even satirically. Sometimes they parody each other.

OTHER FILMS

- Films are often based, at least in part, on earlier films.

- A movie or part of one may include allusions or references to earlier films. A movie may be a remake, an amusing remake (parody), or a respectful remake of parts of an earlier film (homage).

- A movie may also be a sequel or, far less commonly, a prequel.

Multiple Sources

- A text is something that people produce or modify to communicate meaning. Texts do not emerge out of only a single human imagination or a team of people working on the same project during the same time: they are always intertextual, always related to earlier texts.

- Even when a film seems to have one main source, other influences are at work.

WORKS CITED

Abé, Kobo. *The Woman in the Dunes*. Trans. E. Dale Saunders. New York: Knopf, 1964.

Andrew, Dudley. *Concepts in Film Theory*. New York: Oxford UP, 1984.

Attenborough, David. "The Compulsive Communicators." *Life on Earth*. Program 13. BBC Bristol. 1979. (The wording is from the television program, not the book based on the series.)

The Citizen Kane Book: Raising Kane, by Pauline Kael. The Shooting Script, by Herman J. Mankiewicz and Orson Welles, and the Cutting Continuity of the Completed Film. Boston: Little, Brown, 1971.

Cook, David A. *A History of Narrative Film*. 3rd ed. New York: Norton, 1996.

Demopoulos, Maria. "Blink of an Eye: Filmmaking in the Age of Bullet Time." *Film Comment* 36. 3 (May/June 2000): 34–39.

Duyfhuizen, Bernard. *Narratives of Transmission*. Rutherford, NJ: Fairleigh Dickinson UP, 1992.

Hitchcock. Ed. Nick James. London: British Film Institute, 1999.

Kasbekar, Asha. "An Introduction to Indian Cinema." *An Introduction to Film Studies.* 2nd ed. Ed. Jill Nelmes. London: Routledge, 1999.

Kelly, Christopher. "Toys in the Attic: The Unsung Pleasures (and Terrors) of *Babe: Pig in the City* and *Small Soldiers*." *Film Quarterly* 53. 4 (Summer 2000): 41–46.

Phillips, William H. *Writing Short Scripts.* 2nd ed. Syracuse: Syracuse UP, 1999.

Scorsese, Martin (filmmaker). Commentary. "The Director as Smuggler." *A Personal Journey with Martin Scorsese through American Movies* (documentary film). 1995.

Stanley, Alessandra. "Surviving and Disturbing in Moscow." *New York Times* 21 Mar. 1995, natl. ed.: B1+.

Toplin, Robert Brent. *History by Hollywood: The Use and Abuse of the American Past.* Urbana: U of Illinois P, 1996.

The Third Man: *A Film by Graham Greene and Carol Reed.* New York: Simon, 1968.

FOR FURTHER READING

Armes, Roy. *Action and Image: Dramatic Structure in Cinema.* Manchester: Manchester UP, 1994. The first of the book's three parts, Film as Drama, consists of four chapters: Readings and Viewings, Showing and Telling, Text and Performance, and Stage and Screen.

Atkins, Robert. *ArtSpeak: A Guide to Contemporary Ideas, Movements, and Buzzwords, 1945 to the Present.* 2nd ed. New York: Abbeville, 1997. Short entries on terms used in art, including some terms used in film studies. Includes a timeline of major world events and major events in art from 1945 to 1996 (9-36).

Based on a True Story: Latin American History at the Movies. Ed. Donald F. Stevens. Wilmington, DE: SR Books, 1997. Various essays on how films have represented Latin America from the late fifteenth century to the present.

Bluestone, George. *Novels into Film: The Metamorphosis of Fiction into Cinema.* Baltimore: Johns Hopkins UP, 1957. Includes a chapter titled "The Limits of the Novel and the Limits of the Film" plus chapters on six films adapted from famous novels.

Custen, George F. *Bio/Pics: How Hollywood Constructed Public History.* New Brunswick, NJ: Rutgers UP, 1992. Using a sample of over 100 biographical films from 1927 to 1960, Custen argues that Hollywood created a virtually monochromatic view of history that was systematically distorted in regard to race, gender, nationality, and profession.

Film Adaptation. Ed. James Naremore. New Brunswick, NJ: Rutgers UP, 2000. An investigation of how cinema transforms stories from other sources, such as literature and history, into films. Contributors examine the process of adaptation in both theory and practice, discussing a wide variety of films.

Manvell, Roger. *Theater and Film: A Comparative Study of the Two Forms of Dramatic Art, and of the Problems of Adaptation of Stage Plays into Films.* Rutherford, NJ: Fairleigh Dickinson UP, 1979. Part I: Stage Play and Screenplay: Forms and Principles; Part II: Examples of Adaptation from Stage to Screen. Appendix C: Select List of Dramatists Whose Plays Have Been Filmed.

Revisioning History: Film and the Construction of a New Past. Ed. Robert A. Rosenstone. Princeton: Princeton UP, 1995. Theoretical issues about films based on history.

Rosenstone, Robert A. *Visions of the Past: The Challenge of Film to Our Idea of History.* Cambridge: Harvard UP, 1995. Argues that history is a mode of thinking that can use "elements other than the written word" and that history can be done through films.

Tibbetts, John C., and James M. Welsh. *Novels into Film: The Encyclopedia of Movies Adapted from Books.* New York: Checkmark Books, 1999. More than 120 entries, each describing a novel and one or more of its film adaptations. Each entry concludes with a brief references section.

CHAPTER 7
Types of Fictional Films

FICTIONAL FILMS ARE NUMEROUS, POPULAR, AND ENDURING. Perhaps that is why critics and scholars often try to classify them (Figure 7.1). Seeing similarities and patterns helps viewers place a film in context and understand it more completely. Considering some of the types of fictional films also helps viewers understand the properties and potentials of the film medium.

Documentary, experimental, and **hybrid films** are major alternatives to fictional films, but those groupings of films are so large that they are treated in a separate chapter. Here we will examine a few of the most frequently used ways to group fictional films: classical Hollywood cinema (throughout the world the most popular and influential type of fictional film), Italian neorealist cinema, French new wave cinema, and independent films.[1] Although various groupings of films are discussed in this chapter and

Terms in **boldface** are defined in the Illustrated Glossary beginning on page 539.

documentary film: A film whose representation of its subjects viewers are intended to accept primarily as factual.

experimental film: A film that rejects the conventions of mainstream movies and explores the possibilities of the film medium itself.

hybrid film: A film that is not exclusively fictional, documentary, or experimental but instead shares characteristics of two or all three of the major film types.

NON SEQUITUR   by WILEY

©1999 Wiley Miller / Dist. by Universal Press Syndicate

FIGURE 7.1

---

[1]Because space in an introductory book and time in an introductory film course are severely restricted, the coverage in this chapter is limited largely to films and cultures that are most likely to be familiar to American students.

Chapter 9, it is important to remember that filmmakers are not ruled by formulas or books. They may be influenced by such matters as intuition, creativity, cinematic traditions, demographic patterns (such as the percentage of teens who attend movies), and box office potential. As a consequence and increasingly so in recent years, some films are not exclusively one type.

CLASSICAL HOLLYWOOD CINEMA

> The film experience resembles a fun house attraction, a wild ride, the itinerary of which has been calculated in advance but is unknown to the spectator. By spurts and stops, twists and roller coaster plunges, we are taken through a dark passage, alert and anxious, yet confident we shall return satisfied and unharmed. (Andrew 144)

Film scholars have explored many ways of grouping fictional films. David Bordwell, Janet Staiger, and Kristin Thompson studied representative American films across the years to see if they could discover recurrent stylistic **conventions** (3). In their influential book *The Classical Hollywood Cinema: Film Style and Mode of Production to 1960* and elsewhere, Bordwell, Staiger, and Thompson argue that most American **feature films**—and indeed most movies worldwide—share certain qualities that will be explained below.

Characteristics of Classical Hollywood Cinema

According to Bordwell, Staiger, and Thompson (1–84), **classical Hollywood cinema** tends to have the following characteristics:

1. The story is mainly set in a present, external world and is largely seen from outside the action, although **point-of-view shots,** memories, fantasies, dreams, or other mental states are sometimes included.

2. The film focuses on one character or a few distinct individuals.

3. The main characters have a goal or a few goals.

4. In trying to attain their goals, the main characters must confront antagonists or a series of problems.

5. The film has **closure**—a sense of resolution or completion at the end of a **narrative**—and often the main characters succeed in reaching their goals (happy endings).

6. The emphasis is on clear causes and effects of actions: what **events** happen and why are clear and unambiguous.

7. The film uses unobtrusive filmmaking **techniques.**

---

convention: In films and other texts, a frequently used technique or content that audiences accept as natural or typical.

feature film: A fictional film that is at least sixty minutes long.

point-of-view shot: Camera placement at the approximate position of a character or person (or occasionally an animal) that gives a view similar to what that creature would see.

narrative: A series of unified consecutive events situated in one or more settings.

event: In a narrative or story, either an *action* by a character or person or a *happening* (a change brought about by a force other than a person or character).

a) b)

FIGURE 7.2 **Classical Hollywood cinema: two examples**
So pervasive is classical Hollywood cinema that most fictional films, including foreign films and animated stories, exhibit its characteristics. (a) The Chinese film *Not One Less* (1999) and (b) the animated feature *Antz* (1998) are examples. Both stories are set in the present world and are largely seen from outside the action. Both movies show only a few distinct characters and focus on one character. In *Not One Less*, the young girl has been hired to keep order in a small, rural school and to deter students from dropping out. In pursuing her goals the girl faces a series of problems. In *Antz*, a male ant called Zee has two goals: to win the princess and later to thwart the mass extermination of the ant colony. In pursuing his goals, Zee confronts a succession of problems. Both films have closure: they leave no major unanswered questions and no uncertainty as to what happened and why. Like most movies of the classical Hollywood cinema, the endings are happy for those in the audience they intend to please. Finally, both *Not One Less* and *Antz* avoid distracting filmmaking techniques. (a) Frame enlargement. *Columbia Pictures Film Production Asia; Sony;* (b) Frame enlargement. *PDI; DreamWorks Pictures*

Bordwell, Staiger, and Thompson argue that in American films of recent decades, "the classical paradigm continues to flourish, partly by absorbing current topics of interest and partly by perpetuating seventy-year-old assumptions about what a film is and does" (372). They also point out that many foreign films exemplify the traits of classical Hollywood cinema. Recent examples are *Shall We Dance?* (1996) from Japan and *Not One Less* (1999) from China (Figure 7.2a).

So pervasive are the basic story components of classical Hollywood cinema that they also shape animated films that show a story. *Antz* (1998) is the story of a male ant seeking to win a society's most highly prized female while in the end attempting to save his society from a deadly outside threat. Throughout the story, the protagonist confronts a series of impediments, but the story ends with closure and a happy ending as the main character, who was initially full of self-doubts, achieves his goals and gains his society's adulation (Figure 7.2b).

So widely seen is classical Hollywood cinema that it has influenced virtually all narrative films: filmmakers either imitate characteristics of classical Hollywood cinema or purposely ignore its conventions.

FIGURE 7.3 **Dispelling stereotypes**
Although traditional westerns helped perpetuate demeaning stereotypes about American Indians, later westerns and non-westerns such as *Smoke Signals* (1998) present a different picture. The first feature-length movie made by and about American Indians, *Smoke Signals* repeatedly undercuts the stereotype that Native Americans lack humor (with or without a satirical bite). Here Thomas, on the left, and Victor are talking to two Indian women who gave them a ride:

FIRST WOMAN: Ain't you guys got your passports?
THOMAS: Passports?
FIRST WOMAN (with mock seriousness): Yah. You're leaving the rez and going to a whole different country, cousin.
THOMAS (seriously): But it's the United States.
SECOND WOMAN: Damn right it is. That's as foreign as it gets. Hope you two got your vaccinations.
(The women laugh.)

Frame enlargement. *Larry Estes & Scott M. Rosenfelt; Miramax*

setting: The place where filmed action occurs.

Film Genres: Related Films

What genre does is recognize that the audience [watches] any one film within a context of other films, both those they have personally seen and those they have heard about or seen represented in other media outlets. . . . In general, the function of genre is to make films comprehensible and more or less familiar. (Turner 97)

Action, war, western, comedy, science fiction, horror, mystery/suspense, drama, family, and children. Sound familiar? These major categories are commonly used for ease of marketing in video stores. Many other films are seen as part of a group, including adaptations of literature (for example, movies based on the novels of Jane Austen or the plays of Shakespeare), road movies, urban comedies, and ethnic films. Filmmakers, film critics, film scholars, and film viewers all think of films in terms of categories, although for different reasons.

Most films of the classical Hollywood cinema are **genre** films or members of a widely recognized group of films. Exactly what constitutes a film genre (or type) and which films belong to it are subject to much debate. For our purposes we can think of film genres as commonly recognized groups of fictional films—such as the western, musical, romantic comedy, detective, gangster, science fiction, horror, and war—that share settings, subjects, or events (and sometimes techniques) and that evolve. The criteria for one genre, however, differ from those for another genre, and different critics and scholars define particular genres in somewhat different ways. Westerns, for example, tend to share the same basic conflict (civilization versus the wilderness) and usually the same **setting** (sparsely settled regions west of the Mississippi River, in northern Mexico, or in the Canadian Rockies. Detective films all share the same basic story: the uncovering of causes (who did what when).

Filmmakers and experienced film viewers share a sense of what constitutes a particular genre at a particular time and place. Filmmakers can follow the traditions of the genre and thus reassure audiences; reject the genre's conventions and thereby amuse, shock, or disturb viewers; or in some ways reassure audiences but in other ways reject some of the genre conventions. Genres evolve because social attitudes change. Many westerns before World War II depicted Native Americans in negative ways that encouraged European Americans to continue to think of themselves as superior. An example can be seen in the comedy western *My Little Chickadee* with W. C. Fields and Mae West (1940), which consistently depicts American Indians in stereotypical ways and as the butt of tired jokes. But later westerns such as *Little Big Man* (1970) and *Dances with Wolves* (1990) show Native Americans in a far more sympathetic light, in fact sometimes more favorably than they do the European American settlers. Even more recently, the first feature movie made by and about Native Americans, *Smoke Signals* (1998), does much to dispel stereotypes about American Indians—for example, that they are stoic and humorless (Figure 7.3). Makers of genre films cannot help be influenced by previous films of the same genre. They either imitate earlier films, reject the genre's fundamentals, or follow the genre in some ways and change it in others. Let's consider two of the most enduring genres: the western and film noir.

THE WESTERN

As early as "The Great Train Robbery" (1903), many viewers have enjoyed western films (Figure 7.4). Westerns have proven so popular that they have been made in many countries, including Italy, Mexico, Spain, and East Germany. "Between 1965 and 1983, the East German studio . . . produced 14 westerns. **Shot** on **location** in Yugoslavia, Czechoslovakia, Romania, Bulgaria, the Soviet Union, and Cuba, and usually starring a hulking former

shot (verb): Filmed.

FIGURE 7.4 **An early western** "The Great Train Robbery" (1903)—which Charles Musser claims was "the most commercially successful film of the pre-nickelodeon era, perhaps of any film prior to *The Birth of a Nation* (1915)" (18)—includes what was to become the basic story of many western films: a threat to civilization in the West (outlaws committing a crime) and the eventual reestablishment of order (outlaws getting killed and the stolen goods regained). Frame enlargement. *Edison; The Museum of Modern Art/Film Stills Archive*

FIGURE 7.5 **Generic western**
Early in *Red River* (1948) viewers learn that men have returned
from the Civil War and found their Texas "homes gone," their
"cattle scattered," and their "land stolen by carpetbaggers."
There's no money and no work for cowboys because there's
no market for beef. Ranchers are "roasting grain and calling
it coffee." One cowboy reports he has seen "a man try to swap
a steer for half a sack of flour." A strong-willed man, played by
John Wayne, organizes and leads the first-ever huge cattle drive
to a northern rail connection, though his growing tyranny, bad
weather, weak or rebellious followers, and hostile Indians create major obstacles along the way. In the film's championing
of the settlement of the West by English-speaking men in the
face of a series of adversities, *Red River* is a generic western.
The film also includes an attractive, spunky young woman
typical of earlier films directed by Howard Hawks and a father–
adopted son relationship that grows increasingly strained until
a showdown in the dust (shown here) and readjustment of power.
Frame enlargement. *Howard Hawks; Monterey Productions; United
Artists*

physical-education instructor . . . , these so-called *In-
dianerfilme* are as clumsy and predictable as many of
Hollywood's cowboy films. There is one notable dis-
tinction: in East German westerns, the American Indians are always the good guys" (Shulman), fighting
"'wars of liberation against the capitalists'" (Barton
Byg, quoted in Ingalls).

Typically the setting of a western film is the
United States plains, the Rockies, the Northwest, the
Southwest, northern Mexico, or perhaps the Canadian Rockies, and usually some shots linger on the
vastness, openness, beauty, or menace of the terrain.
The usual focus of westerns is people who stand for
law and order, for settling and taming the West (often territories before they become states), and for
bringing to the wild the civilization of the eastern
United States or Europe (often women serve this last
role). The transformations so often celebrated in
westerns can be seen in excerpts from two western
films: in *Bend of the River* (1952) a settler says, "We'll
use the trees that nature has given us. Cut a clearing
in the wilderness. We'll put in roads. . . . Then we'll
build our homes. . . . There'll be a meeting house, a
church. We'll have a school. Then we'll put down
seedlings," and near the end of *The Man Who Shot
Liberty Valance* (1962) the main woman character says
of the area now settled, "It was once a wilderness.
Now it's a garden." To achieve the western's goals,
those who represent civilization usually have showdowns and shootouts with one or more of the following: Native Americans, Mexicans, and the men who
wear black hats. Makers of westerns work variations,
slight or major, on the generic western.

A good example of a film that fits into the parameters of the generic western is *Shane* (1953). The film
is situated in the western United States and focuses
on the attempts of a small community of settlers—families that grow gar-
dens and raise pigs, chickens, and dairy cows—to resist a greedy and powerful cattle baron who finally hires one of those lean, mean men wearing a
black hat. Ultimately the settlers prevail: the hired gun and his employer are
killed in the final showdown and shootout, and the unhired gun who defends
the community (Shane) is self-exiled presumably because he knows that
henceforth he will be in the way of family and community. Another generic
western was directed by Howard Hawks: *Red River* (1948, Figure 7.5).

Sometimes viewers enjoy having their expectations gratified by a conventional genre film. Other times viewers enjoy seeing major variations on a genre. Since about 1950, most westerns have been revisionist: they ignore or challenge the fundamental traditions of the western film. Films may be revisionist because the times change and the films reflect those changes or because the filmmakers deliberately reject major conventions of the genre. For some films, such as Robert Altman's *McCabe and Mrs. Miller* (1971), both causes of revisionism are at work. Fifties revisionist westerns include *Broken Arrow* (1950), which depicts Native Americans at least as sympathetically as the European settlers; *High Noon* (1952), which attacks the cowardly group behavior of townspeople afraid of or sympathetic to those in black hats; and *The Searchers* (1956), which shows the human cost of pursuing vengeance long-term (Figure 7.6).

The early sixties also saw various revisionist westerns. John Ford's *Two Rode Together* (1961) may at first look generic, but the town lacks community; the settlers seeking their relatives long lost to Comanches are largely misguided or delusional; the soldiers lack the camaraderie of earlier Ford westerns. In addition, the soldiers and their wives are intolerant of an outsider, and the two central figures, a civilian and a military man, fall short of the usual western heroes (the civilian, a marshal preoccupied with money, especially so). In short, the "civilization" the European Americans are trying to bring to the wilderness is more than a little suspect. *The Man Who Shot Liberty Valance* also exhibits major creative variations of the western. Here the agent of civilization is a man of the law, in this case a lawyer who doubles as a teacher of English and civics, but like *Shane*, the film shows that without the power conferred by skill

FIGURE 7.6 **A 1950s revisionist western**
The Searchers (1956), directed by John Ford from a script by Frank Nugent, begins in 1868 with Ethan Edwards (on the right) arriving at his brother's ranch in Texas. Here we see Ethan shortly after the reunion with his brother, nephew, two nieces, and sister-in-law, Martha. Ethan proves to be a complex hero, unlike any seen in westerns before and few since. He has many of the typical western hero's qualities—including knowledge of a Native Indian culture, skill with guns and horses, bravery, self-sacrifice, and perseverance. Such details as the tender way Martha hangs up Ethan's coat hint that the two share deep though undefined feelings: he seems worthy of an admirable woman's love. However, Ethan becomes consumed by vengeance and doomed to remain an outsider. The film's memorable last shot shows him with his mission finally accomplished but ignored by a family and outside the door leading into a home from which he turns and walks away. Then that door closes on his image in the windy wilderness, and darkness fills the screen. In *The Searchers* the main agent of European American civilization is flawed and without a place in an enclave in the wild, without a place to hang his coat or have it hung. *C. V. Whitney; Warner Bros.*

in using a gun, the agent of law and order is helpless in the face of a bullying murderer (Figure 7.7 on p. 230). *The Man Who Shot Liberty Valance* also shows that legend masks the truth, in this case of the real hero's bravery and integrity. From late in 1963 to the end of the sixties, the United States experienced massive domestic upheaval: political and racial assassinations; an increasingly unpopular war in Vietnam; civil rights unrest, violence, and demonstrations; and growing demonstrations against the war. Many viewers of the late 1960s who had become disillusioned with government and others

FIGURE 7.7 Skill and power protecting law and order from violence and disorder
The mise en scène of this publicity still for *The Man Who Shot Liberty Valance* (1962) captures much of the film: between the gunslinger on the left, Liberty Valance, and the civil man skillful in the use of force is the new and evidently only lawyer in town, who's been robbed and reduced temporarily to working in a saloon. The men in the background are uninvolved because Liberty has already intimidated them. *John Ford Productions and Paramount*

FIGURE 7.8 Western showing the end of an era
The Wild Bunch (1969), which is set in 1913, begins and ends with prolonged and elevated levels of violence never before seen in a western. This publicity still represents action near the end of the film when four of the wild bunch are on their way to try to free a Mexican colleague regardless of the considerable danger to themselves. "While early modern Westerns tended to deal with stories from the period of pioneering and the beginning of settlement, Westerns of the 60s and 70s more often centered around the end of the West, the passing of its heroic and mythical age and its entry into the modern world of cities and technology. . . . By the time of *The Wild Bunch* . . . [director Sam] Peckinpah's aging bandits confronted a modern world of machinery [including machine guns and automobiles], militarism and social revolution which destroyed them" (Cawelti 7). *Phil Feldman; Warner Bros.*

FIGURE 7.9 **Revisionist representation of western settings** Unlike most earlier westerns, *McCabe and Mrs. Miller* (1971), which was filmed on location, teems with the messiness of life. Even the film's weather is untraditional for westerns: except for a few shots, it is persistently gloomy and the color is desaturated throughout. At the beginning of the story, the air is so cold and drizzly that McCabe wears a huge animal coat to try to stay warm and dry. Later there is lots of mud, rain, gray skies, fallen snow, light snowing, and near the end heavy snowing. Throughout most of the exterior scenes, there is also an unfriendly howling wind, which is loudest at the film's end. *David Foster & Mitchell Brower; Warner Bros.*

in power identified with the violent outlaws of *The Wild Bunch* (1969) who try to adjust and cope during the sunset of an era (Figure 7.8).

Like a number of late 1960s American movies, *McCabe and Mrs. Miller* implies criticism of the power structure. The film has an inhospitable, rough-hewn setting rarely seen in western films (Figure 7.9) and two central characters who are not settlers bringing the usual socially acceptable goods or services to the untamed West. Mrs. Miller is a practical, intelligent opium-smoking prostitute and madam who has goals and a clear sense of how to achieve them. McCabe is a card shark–businessman–pimp who ignores Mrs. Miller's sound advice, lacks the confidence and power he initially seems to have, and is too naïve to see when to cut a deal with those with power. Near the end of the film the townspeople are more concerned with saving the burning church, which they had ignored and will likely continue to ignore, than with helping McCabe in his deadly confrontation with three murderous thugs sent by an acquisitive corporation. As scholar John H. Lenihan points out, the film implies that "the future of America lay not with the individual but with the corrupt and indomitable corporation" (164).

In the 1980s and into the 1990s, some critics were writing about the death of the western. Then came *Unforgiven* (1992), which set off a wave of revisionist westerns. The setting and subject of *Unforgiven* make it instantly recognizable as a western, but for those who have seen many westerns, the film has many surprises. The major antagonist is not a Native American, a

a)   b)

FIGURE 7.10 A feminist revisionist western
In *The Ballad of Little Jo* (1993), (a) Josephine Monaghan is first seen dressed much as she is here, carrying a suitcase and protecting her head from the sun with a parasol. Viewers eventually learn that she has had a baby out of wedlock and been exiled by her family. (b) In the West, men menace her—she is nearly raped—so to avoid further danger and abuse, Josephine becomes Jo by inflicting a scar on her cheek, dressing as a man, and gradually learning how to act as one. Unlike most westerns, *The Ballad of Little Jo* shows both the limited options available to nineteenth-century American women and the civilizing influences that a woman doing men's work could bring to the wild West. *PolyGram Filmed Entertainment; Fine Line Features*

Mexican, or an evil cowboy but the sheriff himself; he's so brutal the towns-people are both embarrassed and afraid when he starts (literally) kicking someone around. The film's killings, which are committed in the name of justice, are based on rumor and dubious moral grounds and are messy, ex-cruciating, and in one instance protracted. Perhaps most surprisingly, the hero is not a macho cowboy. He is an aging pig farmer aching to forget his past and to be left alone and longing for his deceased wife, who helped him give up alcohol and helped civilize him. Furthermore, the hero has a nagging conscience: he regrets murders he committed years before.

FIGURE 7.11 **An African American revisionist western**
Posse (1993)—which focuses on five African Americans and one European American—gives a
contemporary African American perspective on a group rarely seen in mainstream westerns, even
in recent years. In *Posse*, blacks do not face opposition from the usual western antagonists, such as
native American Indians, Mexicans, or an assortment of obvious outlaws. Instead, they have to
contend with the white power structure. The posse's major antagonists are two European Americans:
a cruel, corrupt army officer and his motley band of Spanish-American War veterans eager to steal
war booty from the "posse" while exacting revenge and a racist, greedy, power-hungry sheriff and
his followers who years earlier had killed blacks with impunity. It is not clear if the white sheriff
and his followers constitute the local version of the KKK or if that is a separate group, but the KKK
is also a threat. Another problem for the African American community is that the black marshal of
an all-black town has naively struck an illegal business deal with the racist white sheriff and fails to
oppose him when the sheriff treats blacks unjustly. *PolyGram Filmed Entertainment; Gramercy Pictures*

Other nineties westerns explored the possibilities of subjects usually
pushed to the sides or backgrounds of movie screens, such as single women,
African American males, and female prostitutes. *The Ballad of Little Jo* (1993)
shows the trials, triumphs, and civilizing effects (such as compassion) of a
woman in the man's world of 1870s Montana territory (Figure 7.10). Another western that focuses on a group usually on the periphery of westerns,
if included at all, is *Posse* (1993); most of its main characters are African
American (Figure 7.11). *Bad Girls* (1994) also focuses on characters normally
peripheral in the conventional western (Figure 7.12 on p. 234). Yet another

FIGURE 7.12 **Taming the wild West**
Throughout *Bad Girls* (1994) the four major women characters fight back against any injustice. Initially, they are prostitutes wronged by men's laws, but when provoked they outsmart, outride, and outshoot the men. Early in the film one of them catches up with a runaway horse-drawn carriage, jumps into it, and reins it to a halt. Among their many accomplishments as a group are rescuing one of their own from being hanged, killing four armed outlaws, and evading two detectives on their trail. While they are at it, two of them also win the love of two attractive young men. In their own fashion, they help tame the West. *Ruddy Morgan Productions; 20th Century–Fox*

a)

b)

FIGURE 7.13 **Prominent love lives in a revisionist western**
Most of *The Hi-Lo Country* (1998) is set in New Mexico shortly after World War II ended. Traditional western elements remain, but the West and the western are changing. *The Hi-Lo Country* sometimes looks and acts like the familiar western. (a) Viewers see many shots of cowboys on horses tending cattle. There also are scenes in a bar, where much whiskey drinking, dramatic poker games, and the usual fistfights transpire. The cowboys look much as viewers have seen them in countless westerns. The story includes a greedy cattle baron, the big guy nobody much likes, and others who oppose him and are determined to make a living the old way, on desolate land in a difficult climate.

On the other hand, at times *The Hi-Lo County* does not look much like a western. Motorized vehicles—jeeps, trucks, and cars, enclosed and convertibles—go racing around stirring up the plentiful dust. Some of the pistols are of twentieth-century vintage. Most of all, the film spends a lot of time on relationships. (b) Two young men who are best friends are powerfully attracted to a married woman. The two men are so close that some viewers will wonder if they have stronger feelings for each other than either one has for the married woman. (The film also includes a more traditional female role, a sensible Latina who's devoted to one of the two men.) Frame enlargements. *De Fina-Cappa & PolyGram Filmed Entertainment; Gramercy*

option available to makers of western films is to blend elements of the old western with elements of the new West (Figure 7.13).

In recent years, critics yet again revived talk about the death of the western. *Shanghai Noon* (2000) is set in the nineteenth-century American West—at least for most of its story—but it is not so much a western as a combination of genres (kung fu and western with a lot of broad comedy). Whether the western is now largely corralled, only time will tell, though Christmas of 2000 finally saw the release of *All the Pretty Horses*, which shows two young cowboys, soon accompanied by a third youth, heading to Mexico to seek a continuation of the cowboy life fast fading as unprofitable from 1949 west Texas.

FILM NOIR

> This large body of films, flourishing in America in the period 1941–58 [from *The Maltese Falcon* to *Touch of Evil*], generally focuses on urban crime and corruption, and on sudden upwellings of violence in a culture whose fabric seems to be unraveling. Because of these typical concerns, the film noir seems fundamentally about violations: vice, corruption, unrestrained desire, and, most fundamental of all, abrogation of the American dream's most basic promises—of hope, prosperity, and safety from persecution. (Telotte 2)

Film noir ("film nwahr") is a partial translation of *cinéma noir* (black or dark cinema), a term first used by some French critics to describe a group of American films made during and after World War II. Different critics and scholars define the term differently and use such terminology as genre, "subgenre of the crime thriller or gangster movie," movement, "quasigeneric category," "fluid concept," mode, mood, **style,** visual style, or "stylistic and narrative tendency." But here and in other sources, film noir stands for a film genre whose films tend to have frequent **scenes** with dark, shadowy (**low-key**) **lighting** (often including shots with shadows made by open venetian blinds, as in Figure 7.20a and many night scenes (Figure 7.14). Other characteristics of film noir are urban settings and characters who are motivated by selfishness, greed, cruelty, and ambition and are willing to lie, frame, double-cross, and kill or have killed (Figure 7.15). Often films noirs are fatalistic, and the main characters seem doomed to fail. *Detour* (1945), for example, includes such lines as "Until then, I'd done things my way, but from then on something else stepped in and shunted me off to a different destination than the one I had picked for myself" and "That's life. Whichever way you turn, Fate sticks out a foot to trip you." Films noirs tend to exhibit embittered or cynical moods and to be compressed and convoluted, as in *Double Indemnity* (1944), which begins and ends in the present and has five **flashbacks,** and *Out of the Past* (1947), which also includes flashbacks.

Because these films were made when the American production code was strongly enforced (see pp. 378–79), characters who go astray are eventually

style: The way subjects are presented in a text, such as a film.

scene: A section of a narrative film that gives the impression of continuous action taking place in continuous time and space.

low-key lighting: Lighting with predominant dark tones, often deep dark tones.

FIGURE 7.14 Film noir lighting and darkness
This still closely approximates the last shot of *The Big Combo* (1955), cinematography by John Alton, who later wrote a book on cinematography, *Painting with Light*. In his introduction to a reprinting of that book, Todd McCarthy writes, "In fashioning the nocturnal world inhabited by noir's desperate characters, Alton was ever consistent and imaginative in forging his signature, illuminating scenes with single lamps, slanted and fragmented beams and pools of light, all separated by intense darkness in which the source of all fear could fester and finally thrive. . . . Often, the light would just manage to catch the rim of a hat, the edge of a gun, the smoke from a cigarette. Actors' faces, normally the object of any cameraman's most ardent attention, were often invisible or obscured, with characters from *T-Men* to, perhaps most memorably, *The Big Combo* playing out their fates in silhouette against a witheringly blank, impassive background. . . . [In *The Big Combo*] Alton pushed his impulse toward severe black-and-white contrasts and silhouetting of characters to the limit. . . . And the final shot, with the figures of a man and woman outlined . . . against a foggy nightscape and illuminated by a single beacon [beyond the fog and midway between the man's head and the woman's], makes one of the quintessentially anti-sentimental noir statements about the place of humanity in the existential void" (x, xxix). *Sidney Harmon; Allied Artists*

punished. By the end of *Murder, My Sweet* (1944), for example, the three who commit murder have murdered each other; by the end of *The Lady from Shanghai* (1948), the three lethal characters have also killed each other. Near the end of *Force of Evil* (1948), the three major criminal characters confront one another in a dark room; two are shot; then the third calls the police and says he'll be turning himself in.

Often films noirs feature a femme fatale, invariably an attractive, young, worldly woman who thinks and acts quickly and is verbally adroit, manipulative, evasive, sexy, dangerous, perhaps even lethal, especially to men who succumb to her wiles and charms—and many do (Figure 7.16). In *The Lady from Shanghai* the femme fatale is a Circe who figuratively enchains her husband's business partner and nearly lures the film's central character to his doom (Figure 7.17 on p. 238). In *Criss Cross* (1949) the self-centered and monetary motives of the femme fatale are hidden from both the viewers and the main character—a gullible young man who had trouble living with her but thinks he cannot live without her—until it is too late (Figure 7.18). In *Out of the Past*, the femme fatale is so dangerous that when another woman character says of her, "She can't be all bad. No one is," the Robert Mitchum character, who is no innocent yet succumbs to her more than once, replies, "Well, she comes the closest."

The changing role of women in American society influenced film noir. During World War II women were urged to take over factory jobs traditionally held by men, and millions did. After the war, the men returned and displaced the women workers, often unceremoniously. The self-sufficiency many women showed during the war doubtless threatened many men, perhaps including those involved in making films noirs: "A large number of the postwar noir thrillers are concerned to some

a) b)

FIGURE 7.15 **Film noir classic**
Some critics regard *Touch of Evil* (1958) as the last of the classic films noirs. The film has all the
characteristics of film noir, including (a) many scenes with dark, shadowy (low-key) lighting (here
a man and his shadow follow another man and his shadow) and (b) as the central character a police
detective (on the left) who's shrewd, driven, complex, and flawed. Frame enlargements. *Albert
Zugsmith; Universal*

FIGURE 7.16 **A femme fatale**
Like most femmes fatales in films noirs, Kathie, the Jane
Greer character in *Out of the Past* (1947), is young, worldly,
attractive, calculating, resourceful, and charming when need
be, and she gets her way with men, including Jeff, the Robert
Mitchum character. As Nicholas Christopher points out, the
other major female character in the film is "antiseptic, static,
sexually repressed, socially rather dull, she lives with her
parents and works as a schoolteacher; she wants to marry and
have kids and never leave her hometown. Should we be surprised that when reunited with Kathie, who is freewheeling,
worldly, intellectually (if criminally) active, dangerous, and
highly sexed, Jeff finds it so easy to fall back under her spell?"
(198–99) *Warren Duff; RKO General Pictures*

a)

b)

c)

FIGURE 7.17 **Various faces of a femme fatale**
Rita Hayworth as the femme fatale in *The Lady from Shanghai* (1948). (a) She is on a boat deck singing, and her song lures the main male character up to the deck; she's a Circe. (b) The background reminds viewers she doesn't obey laws. (c) By the end of the film, she has pulled a gun on her husband and is ready to kill him in a fun house full of mirrors. She does, but the film was released in 1948 and was subject to the production code, so she does not go unpunished. Frame enlargements. *Orson Welles; Columbia*

FIGURE 7.18 **Femme fatale motivated by self-interest**
In *Criss Cross* (1949), the main male character, Steve, does not see how dangerous his former wife is (here, as first seen in the film, dancing). Eventually he and the audience learn her major motivation: self-interest. Near the end of the film as she is packing up the money he stole for her during an armored-car robbery and preparing to leave a badly injured Steve, she tells him, "You have to watch out for yourself. That's the way it is. . . . What do you want me to do? Throw away all this money? You always have to do what's best for yourself." Frame enlargement. *Michel Kraike; Universal International*

degree with the problems represented by women who seek satisfaction and self-definition outside the traditional contexts of marriage and family" (Krutnik 61). Preeminent in this group of women characters are those femmes fatales (see the feature on p. 240).

Films noirs can be understood as in part a reaction against the brightly lit studio entertainment films of the 1930s. The look of films noirs was also influenced by German and Austrian immigrant filmmakers attuned to **expressionistic** lighting and **mise en scène.** Then, too, it is likely that the urban painting of such American artists as Edward Hopper influenced the look of film noir. "When Abraham Polonsky, the director of *Force of Evil,* was dissatisfied with the look his cinematographer . . . was getting, he took him to an exhibition of Hopper's paintings at a Greenwich Village gallery and said, 'This is how I want the picture to look.' And it did: full of black windows, looming shadows, and rich pools of light pouring from recessed doorways and steep stairwells" (Christopher 15).

The detective fiction of such writers as Raymond Chandler, Dashiell Hammett, and James M. Cain was a major influence and provided sources for some of the major scripts. Films noirs reject the nationalistic films of World War II and reflect the unsettled postwar times, the disorientation and lack of clear identity many experienced after surviving the severe economic depression of the 1930s and the massive casualties, genocide, torture, and atomic clouds of World War II. In *Crossfire* (1947), a civilian explains to a despondent G.I. his theories about Americans struggling to adjust to life after the all-consuming war:

> For four years now we've been focusing our mind on, on one little peanut (as *he picks up a peanut*), the win-the-war peanut. That was all. Get it over. Eat that peanut. (*The man eats the peanut.*) All at once, no peanut. Now we start looking at each other again. We don't know what we're supposed to do. We don't know what's supposed to happen. We're too used to fightin'. But we just don't know what to fight. You can feel the tension in the air. A whole lot of fightin' and hate that doesn't know where to go.

Many film scholars see the 1941 version of *The Maltese Falcon* as the first film noir, and although that film has most of the characteristics outlined here, it is not nearly as dark and shadowed as many later films noirs. In addition, as critic and scholar Foster Hirsch points out, various earlier films have elements of film noir (12–13). Undisputed major films noirs include *Double Indemnity; Murder, My Sweet; Detour; The Big Sleep* (1946); *Out of the Past; The Lady from Shanghai; Force of Evil; Criss Cross; The Big Combo* (1955); and *Touch of Evil.*

Many later American color films are film noir or have been influenced by it—such as *Chinatown* (1974, Figure 7.19 on p. 241); *Body Heat* (1981); *Pulp Fiction* (1994); *Fargo* (1996); *Devil in a Blue Dress* (1995); and *L.A. Confidential*

expressionism: A style of art, literature, drama, and film used to convey not external reality in a believable way but emotions in a striking, stylized ways.

mise en scène: An image's setting, subject (usually people or characters), and composition (the arrangement of setting and subjects within the frame).

A Femme Fatale in Action

The following excerpt is from the screenplay for the classic film noir *Double Indemnity* (1944), screenplay by Billy Wilder and Raymond Chandler, which in turn is based on the novel by James M. Cain. (The following screenplay excerpt is reprinted in Raymond Chandler's *Later Novels and Other Writings*, 1995.) The movie follows the excerpt closely but not slavishly, pruning words and lines and changing a few words. Nonetheless, the situation of the excerpt and corresponding section of the film is classic film noir: a man, who is eager and gullible, is outmatched by an attractive, dangerous woman unhappy in her marriage. She is a *femme* who in more than one sense is *fatale*.

The doorbell rings. Neff goes to the door and opens it, revealing Phyllis standing there.

PHYLLIS: Hello. (*As Neff just looks at her in amazement.*) You forgot your hat this afternoon. (*She has nothing in her hands but her bag.*)

NEFF: Did I? (*He looks down at her hands.*)

PHYLLIS: Don't you want me to bring it in?

NEFF: Sure. Put it on the chair. (*She comes in. He closes the door.*) How did you know where I live?

PHYLLIS: It's in the phone book. (*Neff switches on the standing lamp.*) It's raining.

NEFF: So it is. Peel off your coat and sit down. (*She starts to take off her coat.*) Your husband out?

PHYLLIS: Long Beach. They're spudding in a new well. He phoned he'd be late. About nine-thirty. (*He takes her coat and lays it across the back of a chair.*) It's about time you said you're glad to see me.

NEFF: I knew you wouldn't leave it like that.

PHYLLIS: Like what?

NEFF: Like it was this afternoon.

PHYLLIS: I must have said something that gave you a terribly wrong impression. You must surely see that. You must never think anything like that about me, Walter.

NEFF: Okay.

PHYLLIS: It's not okay. Not if you don't believe me.

NEFF: What do you want me to do?

PHYLLIS: I want you to be nice to me. Like the first time you came to the house.

NEFF: It can't be like the first time. Something has happened.

PHYLLIS: I know it has. It's happened to us.

NEFF: That's what I mean.

Phyllis has moved over to the window. She stares out through the wet windowpane.

NEFF: What's the matter now?

PHYLLIS: I feel as if he was watching me. Not that he cares about me. Not any more. But he keeps me on a leash. So tight I can't breathe. I'm scared.

NEFF: What of? He's in Long Beach, isn't he?

PHYLLIS: I oughtn't to have come.

NEFF: Maybe you oughtn't.

PHYLLIS: You want me to go?

NEFF: If you want to.

PHYLLIS: Right now?

NEFF: Sure. Right now.

By this time, he has hold of her wrists. He draws her to him slowly and kisses her. Her arms tighten around him. After a moment he pulls his head back, still holding her close.—Then they break away from each other, and she puts her head on his shoulder.

NEFF: I'm crazy about you, baby.

PHYLLIS: I'm crazy about you, Walter.

NEFF: That perfume on your hair. What's the name of it?

PHYLLIS: I don't know. I bought it down at Ensenada.

NEFF: We ought to have some of that pink wine to go with it. The kind that bubbles. But all I have is bourbon.

PHYLLIS: Bourbon is fine, Walter.

FIGURE 7.19 **A night scene in a modern film noir**
Detective Jake Gittes (left) is about to get his nose cut by two thugs hired to guard secrets in the night. In its night scenes filled with mystery, danger, and violence and in its lying, duplicitous, and murderous antagonists, *Chinatown* (1974) is a film noir not in black and white but color. Like so many films noirs, it also includes interiors with the shadows of venetian blinds against the walls. Frame enlargement. *Long Road Productions; Paramount*

a)

b)

FIGURE 7.20 **Continuing popularity of film noir**
Throughout the 1990s, many films noirs continued to be made. By anyone's definition of the term, *L.A. Confidential* (1997) is film noir or, more precisely, film noir in color. (a) As in many films noirs, in *L.A. Confidential* light and shadows from partially opened venetian blinds illuminate several interior scenes. Here a meeting of Los Angeles police detectives has been called to announce the discovery of multiple murders, including the killing of a recently discharged police detective. (b) A beautiful, mysterious woman (here a high-class prostitute) also plays a prominent role in the story. Part of the continuing appeal of films noirs in the 1990s is that they reinforce the widespread public perception that those in authority, perhaps especially the police, are not to be trusted because they act as if they are above the law. Frame enlargements. *Regency; Warner Bros.*

(1997, Figure 7.20). Some French films—such as *Breathless* (1959); *Shoot the Piano Player* (1960); and *Alphaville* (1965)—have also been labeled film noir or influenced by it. Critics also speak of certain British crime films as Brit noir. An example is a British-Irish-German-French co-production, *Croupier* (1998)—a twisted tale set in a nocturnal city. The story includes crime, intrigue, lies, betrayal, and a beautiful, worldly, mysterious, duplicitous, and

FIGURE 7.21   A parody of westerns
The bad (and dense) guys rein up to pay a toll for the Governor William J. Le Petomane Thruway. Here, as elsewhere in *Blazing Saddles* (1974), the subjects (cowboys) and settings (wild West) are those of the traditional western, but such actions as building a railroad, saving a town from corruption, and brawling in a saloon are exaggerated and mocked. As illustrated here, often *Blazing Saddles* also knowingly includes details from twentieth-century life. *Crossbow; Warner Bros.*

potentially dangerous woman. Writing in 1998, Hirsch summarizes noir's subjects, evolution, and enduring appeal:

> The private-investigation quest; crimes of passion and profit; stories involving masquerade, amnesia, split identity, and double and triple crosses continue to be the genre's abiding concerns. . . . Noir endures, but, inevitably, not in the same way as forty and fifty years ago. Like any genre that survives, it has had to adapt; and as a set of narrative patterns, a repertoire of images, a nucleus of character types, it has proven remarkably elastic. Against the odds, and after several premature obituaries, noir is a mainstay of commercial narrative filmmaking. (14, 320)

Film noir, then, is not restricted to one period (1941–1958) or to one country (the United States). It is not a movement restricted to a place and time but a genre that has been adapted to different times and places and has continuing appeal.

Occasionally a film is a **parody** of a genre—an amusing imitation of traditional films in the genre. Examples of parodies of westerns are Paul Bartel's *Lust in the Dust* (1985) and Mel Brooks's *Blazing Saddles* (1974, Figure 7.21). Westerns have been parodied elsewhere. In one, a supremely poised ("cool") fighter for hire arrives in a town torn by two greedy, violent, warring factions. Amused by the shortcomings of both groups, he plays one off against the other. In fact, he partially orchestrates their eventual mutual destruction (though greatly outnumbered, he also kills some on his own) then strides away. The story re-creates many elements of the western, such as *High Noon* and *Shane*, but much of its characterization and action is rendered humorously, even **satirically.** The country and film: Japan and *Yojimbo* (*The Bodyguard*) (1961).[2]

satire: A representation of human behavior that has as its aim the humorous criticism of the behavior shown.

[2] For a comparison and contrast of *Yojimbo* and *High Noon*, see Alan P. Barr, "Exquisite Comedy and the Dimensions of Heroism, Akira Kurosawa's *Yojimbo*" *Massachusetts Review* 16 (1975): 158–68. *Yojimbo* was remade in Italy as the first of the so-called spaghetti westerns, Sergio Leone's *A Fistful of Dollars* (1964), and in the United States as a story of an outsider and two rival groups of gangsters in a Prohibition-era Texas town in *Last Man Standing* (1996) starring Bruce Willis.

FIGURE 7.22 **Sci-fi western: science fiction setting, western story**
Outland (1981) is set in the future on a moon of Jupiter, but the story closely mirrors that of the classic western *High Noon. The Ladd Company; Warner Bros.*

Many filmmakers combine elements of two or more genres. *Westworld* (1973) and *Outland* (1981, Figure 7.22) combine science fiction and the western. Elements of horror films are combined with those of westerns in *Curse of the Undead* (1959) and *Billy the Kid vs. Dracula* (1965, Figure 7.23). The French new wave film *Shoot the Piano Player* mixes crime, romance, and slapstick comedy. *Alien* (1979) and its sequels combine horror and science fiction (Figure 7.24), as do some films written and directed by David Cronenberg, including *eXistenZ* (1999). *Blade Runner* (1982, revised and rereleased

FIGURE 7.23 **A vampire western**
In this publicity still for *Billy the Kid vs. Dracula* (1965), a vampire in western clothes and in a western setting menaces a beautiful woman. "The text [is] endowed with a strong degree of logical coherence, largely through a kind of process of condensation, whereby elements common to both genres [horror and western] . . . receive heavy emphasis. A key site of such condensation is the film's lead player, [John] Carradine, being an iconographic figure for both the horror and western genres, having played both numerous poverty-row vampires and numerous western character roles. . . . His nineteenth-century costume, the horse-drawn carriages he often travels in, and the cave-turned-silver mine he sleeps in all seem appropriate to both the western and the horror film" (Knee 145). *Circle Productions; Embassy Pictures*

243

FIGURE 7.24 **Horror stories in science fiction settings**
As so often happens in the *Alien* movies, in *Alien³* (1992) people cut off from others are destroyed by a swift, voracious, and unrelenting monster. Here the Sigourney Weaver character is once again in mortal danger from an alien, but she survives this encounter halfway into *Alien³* because of a surprising condition viewers learn about later. Like the other *Alien* movies, *Alien³* combines the horror film components of shadows, disturbing sounds, unsettling music, and a lurking monster with a futuristic science fiction setting. *20th Century-Fox*

in 1991) combines visual and story elements of film noir, characters typical of a horror film (a Dr. Frankenstein type and his dangerous yet finally pitiable creation), and a decayed futuristic science fiction setting. *The Matrix* can also be seen as a combination of elements from three genres (Figure 7.25). Director Jim Jarmusch has called his own *Ghost Dog: The Way of the Samurai* (2000) a gangster samurai hip-hop eastern western. Although a blending of genres can be inventive, refreshing, and fun, sometimes these combined genre films yield outrageous results, as in *Plan 9 from Outer Space* (1959, Figure 11.14 on p. 369), which mixes "science fiction" and "horror" with its story of aliens resurrecting the dead.

Genres are subject to swings in popularity. The western, for example, was out of favor in the 1980s, and not a few film critics proclaimed the "death of the western." After *Unforgiven* appeared in 1992 and was a major critical and commercial success, the genre revived vigorously for several years. Another genre subject to changing fortunes is the musical. Since the 1960s, movie musicals have been scarce, and some critics have lamented the "death of the musical." However, the Disney animated musicals of recent years, music videos, *South Park: Bigger, Longer and Uncut* (1999), *Moulin Rouge* (2001), and a few others are evidence that the genre is far from moribund.

FIGURE 7.25 **Sci-fi, action, kung fu movie**
The Matrix (1999) blends elements of science fiction, action, and kung fu movies. (a) Neo, the Keanu Reeves character, tries to dodge bullets that he and we viewers can more or less see, an image one might expect in a science fiction movie. (b) The Laurence Fishburne character leaps out of a building on the right as Neo, who is tethered to a helicopter, jumps toward him. Such exciting actions are not of this world but of the world of action movies. (c) The Carrie-Anne Moss character does a somewhat slow-motion cartwheel off a wall (on the left) as bullets and stone chips fly all around her. Many acrobatic movements here and elsewhere are reminiscent of kung fu movies. The filmmakers had seen many Hong Kong action movies, and the major cast members were trained for months with a system of wires used to support them. Frame enlargements. *Joel Silver; Warner Bros.*

OTHER CINEMAS

There are many influential groups of fictional films other than classical Hollywood cinema, but space and limited accessibility to certain groups of films allow us to consider only a few of them: the two movements of Italian neorealist cinema and French new wave cinema plus European and American independent cinemas.

Critics and scholars sometimes group films into movements—related films, typically from the same country and usually made during a period of a few years. Two widely studied film movements are Italian neorealist cinema and French new wave cinema.

Italian Neorealist Cinema

> Along with [Luchino] Visconti, such other directors as Roberto Rossellini and Vittorio De Sica strove to create a film art of authenticity. . . . Feeling that reality could better be conveyed through created situations than through the direct recording of actual events, they employed a synthesis of documentary and studio techniques, merging actual situations with a scripted story line. The essentials of neorealist films were the use of nonprofessional actors, authentic settings, naturalistic lighting, simple direction, and natural dialogue. (Phillips 686)

In *The Bicycle Thief* (a.k.a. *Bicycle Thieves*, 1948), a long-term unemployed family man, finally gets a job pasting up movie posters but soon loses his bicycle to a thief and accomplices then faces the loss of his job if he cannot retrieve the bicycle by Monday morning. Most of the film is devoted to showing the man and his young son searching for the bicycle in various parts of Rome and the conditions under which different people live. *The Bicycle Thief* exhibits the characteristics of Italian **neorealism:** heavy but not exclusive use of nonprofessional actors (in the three major roles), mostly unaltered location settings, and a chronological story. The film uses little or no supplemental lighting (Figure 7.26), few **close-ups,** and generally unobtrusive filmmaking techniques (even its **wipes** are about as inconspicuous as an editor could make them). Its dialogue is natural, not rhetorical, and includes a range of dialects.

close-up: An image in which the subject fills most of the frame and little of the surroundings is shown.

wipe: A transition between shots, usually between scenes, in which it appears that one shot is pushed off the screen by the next shot.

> For an outline of the scenes of *The Bicycle Thief*, see the Web site for this book: <http://www.bedfordstmartins.com/phillips-film>.

In addition to *The Bicycle Thief*, other important neorealist films include *Open City* (1945), *Shoeshine* (1946), and *Umberto D* (1952). *Open City* shows Catholics (especially a humane and compassionate priest), Communists, and others working together to resist the brutal Nazi occupation of Rome and exposes the myth of German superiority. A year later, *Shoeshine* showed two boys, who are best friends, trying to survive in the streets of Nazi-occupied Rome but getting into trouble and suffering arrest, prison, reform school, and mutual betrayal. *Umberto D* is the story of an old pensioner increasingly distraught because he is behind in his payments to his wealthy, uncaring landlady; he is comforted only by his dog and to a lesser extent by his landlady's young, pregnant, unmarried servant (Figure 7.27).

The characters in neorealist films are ordinary and believable but are not probed for their psychological complexities. Instead, the focus is on characters caught up in the difficult conditions of Italy during and after World War II, such as poverty and unemployment. Generally these films failed to make money in Italy because audiences found them depressing, an affront to national pride, and not diverting enough. They fared better at foreign box offices, especially in the United States.

The movement began in Italy during World War II and largely died out there by the early 1950s. It was a product of the economic and social conditions of its times. In part, neorealism was also a reaction to prewar and wartime Italian cinema that often presented idealized images of fascist Italy, studio-made comedies, and costume histories.

Neorealism did not set out mainly to be an alternative to classical Hollywood cinema; indeed, in its clear linear plots and unobtrusive filmmaking

FIGURE 7.26 **The Italian neorealist film** *The Bicycle Thief* **(1948)** This photograph illustrates how Italian neorealistic filmmakers use real people, actual locations, and little or no supplemental lighting. The seated woman is an untrained actor playing the part of a fortune teller. Like other neorealist films, *The Bicycle Thief* deals with ordinary, believable characters—often played by nonactors—caught up in difficult social and economic conditions. The main character and his son (the actors playing those two central characters are seen on the right side of the photograph) have come to see the fortune teller in hopes she can give the man information that will help him regain the stolen bicycle he needs to retain his desperately needed, recently acquired job. *PDS-ENIC; The Museum of Modern Art/Film Stills Archive*

FIGURE 7.27 **The Italian neorealist film** *Umberto D* **(1952)** In *Umberto D*, a childless retired civil servant is struggling to live in Rome on his limited pension. Added to his problems is a callous landlady intent on getting him out of the room, seen here after she has had it torn up during the man's absence in preparation for major renovations. Also seen here are the man's only two reliable friends: a kind young woman who works for the landlady and the man's dog, which plays a major role in the story. Like *The Bicycle Thief*, *Umberto D* exhibits the characteristics of Italian neorealist films: mostly nonprofessional actors (the man playing Umberto was a university professor without previous acting experience), location filming, and a chronological story. The film uses few close-ups and generally unobtrusive filmmaking techniques (although its music is sometimes prominent). The everyday people in the story are in no way glamorized or idealized. Like *The Bicycle Thief*, *Umberto D* shows believable characters trying to cope with difficult social and economic circumstances. But the film shows even more. As scholar and author Roy Armes concludes, the film operates "as social study and meditation on solitude, as a critique of bourgeois rapacity [the landlady] and a defence of bourgeois dignity [the old pensioner], as stark tragedy and warmly human story" (*Patterns* 163). *Rizzoli-De Sica-Amato; The Museum of Modern Art/Film Stills Archive*

FIGURE 7.28 American neorealist-like film
Salt of the Earth (1954) shows zinc miners in New Mexico striking to gain a safe and fair deal from the callous big business mine owners, who control the district attorney, the sheriff, and the sheriff's deputies. First, the men, mostly Mexican Americans, go on strike. When their efforts seem to be at a dead end, gradually the women become involved in the strike. Eventually, some of the women leaders are arrested illegally and jailed, including the film's narrator and main character, seen here in jail giving up her baby to its father (on the left) so he can see that it gets its formula.
    Like Italian neorealist films, *Salt of the Earth* was shot on location on a low budget. Except for the woman shown here, a Mexican cinematic star, and a few other professionals (including the actor who plays the sheriff, on the right), the large cast is nonprofessional. Like Italian neorealist films, *Salt of the Earth* uses mostly unobtrusive filmmaking techniques, blends fact and fiction, and focuses on the difficult social and economic conditions under which poor workers try to survive with some dignity. The film is unlike neorealism in its overt messages, its use of a narrator who explains many of the story's important points, and its hopeful ending. It is no accident that the film's central character is named "Esperanza," which means hope. *Paul Jarrico; Independent Productions Corp. and The International Union of Mine, Mill and Smelter Workers; The Museum of Modern Art/Film Stills Archive*

techniques, neorealism parallels it. However, in its frequent use of nonprofessional actors, unadorned location settings, simplified lighting, natural dialogue, concern for the social and economic problems of everyday people, and credible unhappy endings, neorealism was an alternative to the studio-made classical Hollywood cinema of its time. Neorealist films were also a strong influence on some later films —such as the early films directed by acclaimed Italian directors Federico Fellini and Michelangelo Antonioni, French new wave directors (see below), the Bengali filmmaker Satyajit Ray, and some American directors working after World War II, such as Nicholas Ray, Elia Kazan, Jules Dassin, Joseph Losey, Robert Rossen, and Edward Dmytryk (Cook 438). Various other films—such as *Salt of the Earth* (1954), which shows poor zinc miners and their families trying to cope during a prolonged labor strike—have strong resemblances to Italian neorealist films (Figure 7.28). Since the 1950s, students of Italian neorealist films have come to see their artifice more clearly. Nonetheless, the stories and contexts of neorealist films continue to fascinate and involve film students and film scholars.

French New Wave Cinema

New wave films were a diverse group of French fictional films made in the late 1950s and early 1960s as a reaction to the carefully scripted products of the French film industry and as explorations of more current subjects sometimes rendered with untraditional techniques.

> The New Wave—however we define it—captures the surface texture of French life in a fresh way, if only because the low budgets with which most young directors work initially necessitate a certain contemporary flavour lacking in the 1951–57 period, when the characteristic works were . . . period reconstructions. The newcomers had no money to build elaborate **sets,** pay for costumes or employ star names: they shot on location, with reduced crews and fresh young performers. But this contemporary flavour was not accompanied by any real social or political concern. . . . The post-1958 feature film industry . . . remains essentially a Parisian cinema, dealing with

set: A constructed setting where action is filmed; it can be indoors or outdoors.

middle-class problems in middle-class terms, and above all concerned with the "eternal" issues of human emotions and relationships. (Armes, *French* 169, 170)

The films of the new wave were made by such directors as François Truffaut, Jean-Luc Godard, Claude Chabrol, and, to a lesser extent, Eric Rohmer and Jacques Rivette.[3] Most new wave directors had watched many films at the Cinémathèque Française (French national film archive) and various film clubs and had written about films and the film medium in the journal *Cahiers du cinéma*. In their writings they advocated that directors should have control over all creative stages of production and criticized traditional French films, especially those of the preceding decade. Before the new wave, French movies—as typified by the famous 1945 film *Children of Paradise*—tended to be period pieces and more literary than **filmic** (Figure 7.29). New wave directors argued that such films gave too much control to writers at the expense of directors.

New wave films are often imbued with a knowledge of earlier films, especially American genre films, and even more so are marked by unpredictable plot developments and the independent spirit of their directors. Jeanne Moreau, whose independent and openly sexual characters embody quintessential qualities of new wave films, said that the new wave way of making films freed up actors:

In other films I made . . . the lighting was so complicated. There were shadows on one side and another light on the other side, so, really, when you are in close-ups you are in a corset. It was impossible to move. That's what the new wave was about, that absolute freedom. The light was made in such a way that you could move and do whatever you wanted, like in real life.

FIGURE 7.29 **French film before the new wave**
In the theatrical and literate *Children of Paradise* (*Les enfants du paradis*) (1945), one of the main characters is a mime (top, right). As a costume film and period piece that was shaped more by the script than the direction, *Children of Paradise* was the type of film the French new wave directors rebelled against in their publications and their filmmaking. *S. N. Pathé Cinéma*

filmic: Characteristic of the film medium or appropriate to it.

---

[3]As Susan Hayward points out in her *Cinema Studies: The Key Concepts* (2nd ed., 2000), Agnès Varda's 1954 film *La pointe courte* is a forerunner of French new wave cinema (146).

a)

b)

c)

FIGURE 7.30 **Homages to another actor and to an earlier transition in film**
In the French film *Breathless* (1959), the main character, Michel, sometimes pays homage to American actor Humphrey Bogart. For example, in various scenes Michel runs his thumb across his lips and back as Bogart did in many films. In the last three shots of the scene represented here viewers see (a) a lobby card (photograph advertising a movie) of Bogart and (b) a shot of Michel rubbing his thumb across his lips. (c) The scene ends with another homage: an iris-out, a popular transition between scenes in silent films. Frame enlargements. *SNC; New Yorker Films*

cinéma-vérité: A type and style of documentary filmmaking developed in France during the early 1960s, the aim of which was to capture events as they happened.

fast film stock: Film stock that requires relatively little light for capturing images.

cutaway: A shot that briefly interrupts the visual presentation of a subject to show something else.

Like a type of documentary filmmaking evolving in France at about the same time (**cinéma-vérité**), new wave films were set in the present or recent past and were often shot on location with portable handheld cameras and sound equipment, **faster film stock,** and new more portable lighting equipment. Sometimes they include surprising or whimsical moments, perhaps the product of improvisation while filming.

New wave cinema may also include **homages** or tributes to earlier films or parts of them (Figure 7.30). Another homage results when visual details from the two main characters in Charlie Chaplin's *The Kid* (1921) are seen briefly in the appearance of the main woman character of *Jules and Jim* (1961, Figure 7.31).

New wave films abound in editing rarely used in classical Hollywood cinema. Sometimes the results are surprising and whimsical. In *Shoot the Piano Player*, a gangster says to a boy he is kidnapping, "I swear it on my old lady's head. May she die if I lie." In a **cutaway,** a woman old enough to be his mother moves her hand toward her chest, falls down backward, and briefly kicks her legs straight up in the air. In the next scene, the boy says, "Then I believe you," and the gangster replies, "Didn't I tell you so?" And the film resumes its story. *Breathless* sometimes uses **jump cuts,** as in the scene where Michel shoots the motorcycle police officer; as edited, the scene is a little disorienting and confusing (see Figure 3.14 on pp. 118–19). Jump cuts are also used in a later scene where Michel and Patricia are talking in a moving car and between shots the background changes in inexplicable ways. There is continuity in the conversation in the foreground (continuity of action and time) but discontinuity of settings in the background. In *The 400 Blows* (1959), two boys emerge from a movie theater and start running; then their movement blends into a blurred horizontal image (**swish pan**) that ends by blending with the boys arriving at another movie theater. In one brief scene

jump cut: A transition between shots that causes a jarring or even shocking shift in space, time, or action.

swish pan: The blurred images that result from pivoting a movie camera horizontally too rapidly during filming.

FIGURE 7.31 **A source and a French new wave homage**
(a) The two main characters in *The Kid* (1921): Charlie Chaplin as the tramp and Jackie Coogan as the abandoned boy the tramp is raising. (b) An homage from one filmmaker (François Truffaut) to another (Chaplin): in this publicity still we see Jeanne Moreau as she appears in a brief section of Truffaut's *Jules and Jim* (1961): her shoes and mustache are reminiscent of Charlie Chaplin's in *The Kid*; her cap and sweater are like the boy's. (a) *Charlie Chaplin; First National;* (b) *Marcel Berbert; Les Films du Carrosse*

of *Shoot the Piano Player,* Charlie and Léna are in bed; as she talks to him, five times the scene alternates with even briefer shots of them together in bed at some other time. Quite unconventionally, each of these five cutaway shots is preceded and followed by a rapid **lap dissolve:** as the first shot fades out, the next shot fades in, momentarily overlapping it.

FIGURE 7.32 **Self-reflexiveness**
In *Shirley Valentine* (1989), the title character sometimes interrupts the story to look at the camera and tell viewers what is on her mind. As she looks toward the camera, she may speak out loud, or, if someone else is present, viewers may hear her thoughts. Her comments to the audience are usually about the characters and situations in the film's story, but they may be about a filmic convention. At one point as she and a man are having sex on a sailboat and orchestral music plays loudly, she looks at the camera and says, "Oh, my God. Where did that orchestra come from?" Self-reflexiveness is sometimes used in films that are alternatives to the classical Hollywood cinema. *Lewis Gilbert; Paramount*

European Independent Films

Neorealism and new wave cinema are not the only European alternatives to classical Hollywood cinema. Various films since the 1960s directed by European directors working outside of the commercial mainstream—such as Jean-Luc Godard and François Truffaut (throughout their careers, not merely during their earlier new wave years), Ingmar Bergman, Federico Fellini, Michelangelo Antonioni, and Luis Buñuel—are also alternatives to classical Hollywood cinema. Sometimes these films are called "art cinema," but it is more descriptive to refer to them as "European independent films." Perhaps the easiest way to begin considering these films is to compare and contrast their features with the features of classical Hollywood cinema (see the list on p. 224).

1. Their characters' memories, fantasies, dreams, and other mental states are rendered much more often than in classical Hollywood cinema. Such films are more likely to be fragmented, more likely to shift quickly and without explanation between different states of consciousness.

2. As in classical Hollywood cinema, the films focus on one character or on only a few distinct characters.

3. Often the main characters' goals are unclear or shifting. Often the characters are ambivalent and hard to figure out (as in most films directed by Antonioni).

4. The main characters confront various antagonists or a series of problems, but the antagonists and problems are not always as evident (for example, as obviously evil) or as singular as in classical Hollywood cinema.

5. Often the films lack closure and have unresolved **plotlines,** and the protagonists do not succeed in reaching a goal (the endings are more likely to be true-to-life than the endings of most commercial American movies of the time).

6. The emphasis is not as emphatically on clear causes and effects of actions; ambiguity may be pervasive; and sometimes the narratives are **episodic:** scenes could be shifted without changing the film substantially, as in films directed and co-written by Jacques Tati.

7. As in classical Hollywood cinema, filmmaking techniques tend to be unobtrusive, but European independent films are more likely to have authorial **narration,** as in some films directed by Truffaut or Godard.

European independent films have additional features:

8. They are more likely than classical Hollywood films to be **self-reflexive.** They are more likely to be in part about the film medium or filmmaking or to interrupt the viewers' involvement to draw attention to themselves as films. *Tom Jones* (1963) is full of amusing self-reflexive touches, as when Tom takes off his hat and places it in front of the camera so viewers cannot gawk at a woman who has lost most of her blouse. In *Shirley Valentine* (1989), the title character sometimes interrupts what she is doing and looks at the camera and speaks her thoughts (Figure 7.32). *Persona* (1966) is another highly self-reflexive film: on one level, it is about the nature of film and film presentation. At one point, for example, the story is interrupted with a **title card** reading "One moment please while we change **reels,**" and after a **fade-out,** we see briefly only blackness and hear silence before a rapid **fade-in** introduces the next scene.

9. European independent films are likely to stress relationships between people and to have a **pace** and intensity that approximate those of normal human experience, whereas the films of classical Hollywood cinema are more likely to emphasize physical action and to have a pace and intensity exceeding normal experience.

10. The European independent cinema is more likely to be explicit about sexuality, whereas classical Hollywood cinema is more likely to be explicit about violence.

11. Finally, films directed by independent European directors are much less likely to be genre films than are the films of classical Hollywood cinema. *Run Lola Run* (1998), for example, is not recognizable as a western, musical, science fiction film, horror film, or any other genre. Often European independent films are more identifiable by director. Thus viewers who have seen films directed by Antonioni will have certain expectations about an Antonioni film they are about to see.

The Italian film *8½* (1963)—which was directed by Federico Fellini and is partly autobiographical (Fellini himself had completed eight films before directing *8½*)—exemplifies European independent cinema. It focuses on the

narration: Commentary in a film about a subject in the film or some other topic, usually from someone offscreen.

self-reflexive: Characteristic of a text, such as a novel or film, to refer to or comment on itself or its medium.

fade-out: Optical effect in which the image changes by degrees from illumination to darkness (usually black).

fade-in: Optical effect in which the image changes by degrees from darkness (usually black) to illumination.

story of Guido, an exhausted movie director besieged with doubts and fears about the film he is trying to complete and beset with problems with his wife and his mistress, his producer and actors, and the press (Figure 7.33).

For an outline of the sequences of *8½*, see the Web site for this book: <http://www.bedfordstmartins.com/phillips-film>.

8½ exhibits all of the characteristics of the European independent film.

1. Memories, fantasies, and dreams are rendered much more often than in classical Hollywood cinema, so much so that the film is fragmented and shifts quickly between different states of consciousness. Sometimes viewers initially believe that certain events are "real" but soon realize that they are dreams or fantasies or memories. At other times, viewers cannot be sure that certain scenes are dreams, fantasies, or memories or a combination of them or tell exactly when a dream, fantasy, or memory begins.

2. As in classical Hollywood cinema, the focus is on one character: Guido, the film director and his problems, but he is surrounded by a larger group (family and colleagues) than is usually found in a film of the classical Hollywood cinema.

3. Like the situation of the main characters in classical Hollywood cinema, Guido's professional goal is clear: to finish the current film successfully. But his goals for his personal life are unclear: does he want to be reconciled to his wife or continue with his mistress and wife, or is he uncertain about what he wants of both of them? He can be hard to figure out because he is uncertain himself exactly what he wants and how to go about achieving it. For much of the story, he avoids making decisions and taking action, though he is surrounded by many who ask him or urge him to do so.

4. The main character confronts numerous problems, though no one problem seems dominant. He is plagued by doubts and uncertainties more than by any opposing person. Certainly there is no obvious major adversary to overcome as in many movies of the classical Hollywood cinema. His problems are intellectual, psychological, and spiritual—not physical.

5. Unlike most films of the classical Hollywood cinema, the film lacks unambiguous closure, and different viewers will interpret Guido's final richly symbolic fantasy differently.

6. The main parts of the plot—from Guido's taking the cure at a spa as he tries to finish a film until he seems to abandon the film project—is told

chronologically though with large gaps of time in the story. Often the main story is interrupted for a fantasy or dream or memory and resumes at a later time and place that viewers could not have anticipated.

7. Like most films of the classical Hollywood cinema, *8½* uses techniques that do not call attention to themselves.

8. *8½* is much more self-reflexive than films of the classical Hollywood cinema: much of the film is about the creative process and the complexities and difficulties of completing a film successfully, such as reconciling the many people competing for the director's attention and giving the film **structure** and meaning.

9. *8½* stresses relationships between people and has a pace and intensity that approximate those of normal human experience (in terms of physical action, not much happens during the film's four-day story time), unlike many films of classical Hollywood cinema, which are more likely to emphasize physical action and to have a pace and intensity exceeding normal experience.

10. *8½* is not explicit about sexuality but is more openly sexual than American movies of the time (before the U.S. rating code was instituted in 1968), and the film contains no violence.

11. Like other films made by the European independent filmmakers, *8½* is not a member of any film genre. First-time viewers of *8½*, however, might approach the film with expectations created by previous experience of other films directed by Fellini. His film tend to have certain recurrent characteristics.

Although few films have all the characteristics outlined here, all European independent films have many of them.

FIGURE 7.33 **European independent film**
Guido, the main character of *8½* (1963), is a film director who often evades the many problems in his personal and professional lives by escaping into fantasies and memories. After his wife berates him as a liar, he retreats into two fantasies: his wife and mistress getting along fabulously and a fantasy where nearly all the major women in his life are part of his own personal harem. After the women in his harem temporarily rebel, he takes up a whip (seen here) and quickly restores an order pleasing and reassuring to himself—but then it is *his* fantasy. The frequent transitions from present-tense reality to fantasy or dream or memory is a characteristic more common in European independent films of the 1960s than in films of the classical Hollywood cinema. *Angelo Rizzoli; Kino International*

American Independent Cinema

In theory, American independent films are made without Hollywood studio support or creative control. In reality, ever since the huge box office successes of some independent films, independent production or distribution companies, such as October Films, are sometimes under the influence of their big studio owners. Independent films are made all over the United States, not only in southern California. An example is *Just Another Girl on the I.R.T.* (1992), which is a candid film about a bright seventeen-year-old African American living in Brooklyn who plans to go to college but gets pregnant. The movie concludes with a title card reading "A Film Hollywood Dared Not Do." In recent years some American independent films have later been distributed by major studios, such as Warner Bros., MCA/Universal, Paramount, MGM/United Artists, Buena Vista (Disney), and TriStar/Columbia. Some independent films—such as *Pulp Fiction* and *Four Weddings and a Funeral* (1994)—may be distributed by and sometimes partially financed by "such quasi-independents as Miramax, Gramercy and Fine Line, which are owned by large companies but operate with a high degree of freedom and flexibility" (Weinraub B2).

So varied are American independent films that it is extremely difficult to generalize about their subjects and techniques, as we can about neorealist films, new wave cinema, and European independent films. Usually American independent films are made without costly directors, writers, and stars (or with stars willing to work for a relatively small salary, a percentage of the profits, or both). Many beginning directors of independent films are so hard pressed for funds that they tap a variety of sources, including family and friends. Often, they also run up a series of credit card debts and seek funding from various grants. Thanks to the increased versatility and affordability of computer programs for making and editing moving images and the expansion of Web sites for downloading films, especially **short films,** more filmmaking options and outlets to market films have been opening up to independent filmmakers. With lower budgets, independent films need not draw huge crowds to turn a profit, and the filmmakers are freer to take on a controversial subject or a subject of limited interest, so independent films tend to be more varied, less formulaic, and more individualistic than films of the classical Hollywood cinema. They are more likely, for instance, to deal with a controversial subject without showing audiences what they want to see and to include an unhappy ending if the story has been building toward it.

Independent films such as *Night of the Living Dead* (1968), *Blood Simple* (1984, revised and rereleased in 2000), *She's Gotta Have It* (1985), *Daughters of the Dust* (1991), *Reservoir Dogs* (1992), and *El Mariachi* (1993) have won awards and often secured a distributor at one of the major film festivals such

short film: Variously defined, but usually regarded as a film of less than sixty minutes.

as Cannes, New York, or Sundance.[4] Many independent films garner excellent reviews and critics' awards, like those given by the National Society of Film Critics, a group of critics who write for major U.S. newspapers and magazines.

Independent filmmakers have two major cooperating organizations: the Association of Independent Video and Filmmakers (AIVF) and Independent Feature Project (IFP). Both groups foster independent filmmakers and promote the independent film. Each organization also publishes a magazine: AIVF publishes *The Independent Film & Video Monthly* and IFP publishes *Filmmaker*. Each March since 1986, members of Independent Feature Project/ West, one of four branches of IFP, have gained publicity for independent films by giving Independent Spirit Awards. Best feature awards for 1990–2000 have gone (in order) to *The Grifters, Rambling Rose, The Player, Short Cuts, Pulp Fiction, Leaving Las Vegas, Fargo, The Apostle, Gods and Monsters, Election,* and *Crouching Tiger, Hidden Dragon.*

Two cable channels devoted solely to the independent film—the Independent Film Channel (since 1995) and the Sundance Channel (since 1996)—have also been important in promoting independent films, including fictional shorts and documentaries, from countries throughout the world.

Classical Hollywood cinema is so much a part of the world most of us were born into and grew up in that many viewers do not easily adapt to other cinemas; initially other films seem odd and perhaps too demanding. But in seeing more of these films and learning about them, many viewers come to enjoy and appreciate them and to broaden their understanding of the possibilities and achievements of the film medium.

SUMMARY

Most fictional films, including foreign films and animated stories, exhibit the major characteristics of classical Hollywood cinema. Alternatives to classical Hollywood cinema include Italian neorealist cinema, French new wave cinema, and European and American independent films from the 1960s to the present.

---

[4]In addition to promoting independent films during its annual festival, the Sundance Institute "holds producer conferences and screenwriting workshops and provides cash grants for filmmakers throughout Latin America, helping to nurture their native film industries and to discover new talent. . . . There are many . . . examples ranging from documentaries to feature films from Cuba, Mexico, Argentina, Brazil and Uruguay that have been made with the support of the Sundance Institute" (Muñoz).

Classical Hollywood Cinema

- Throughout the world, classical Hollywood cinema has been the most influential group of fictional films in history.

- Such films show one or more individualized characters with clear goals who face a series of problems in reaching them; these films stress continuity and the clear causes and effects of actions; and they tend to use unobtrusive filmmaking techniques.

- A film genre is a commonly recognized group of fictional films that share settings, subjects, or events (and sometimes techniques) and that change over time. Two widely studied film genres are the western and film noir. Traditionally the western features civilization versus the wilderness and is set west of the Mississippi River, in northern Mexico, or in the Canadian Rockies. Films noirs include scenes with low illumination, convoluted plots, and complex, flawed characters caught up in crime.

- A genre film may be traditional or revisionist. Most westerns made since about 1950, for example, are revisionist and vary widely from the traditional western.

- Occasionally a film is a parody of a genre. A film may also be a combination of two or more genres, such as horror and science fiction or, far less frequently, western and horror.

Other Cinemas

- Other fictional films—such as those of (Italian) neorealism, (French) new wave cinema, the European independent cinema since the 1960s, and many American independent films since the 1960s—offer alternatives to classical Hollywood cinema.

- Neorealism was a film movement in Italy during and after World War II. Neorealist films, which are a mixture of scripted and actual situations, are located for the most part in real settings and show ordinary and believable characters caught up in difficult social and economic conditions, such as poverty and unemployment. The endings of neorealist films tend to be unhappy. Other characteristics are the heavy reliance on nonprofessional actors and the use of available or simple lighting and natural dialogue.

- New wave films were a diverse group of French fictional films made in the late 1950s and early 1960s in reaction to the carefully scripted products of the French film industry and as explorations of more current subjects sometimes rendered with untraditional filmmaking techniques.

- Films directed by such Europeans as Ingmar Bergman, Federico Fellini, Michelangelo Antonioni, and Luis Buñuel since the 1960s are also alternatives to classical Hollywood cinema. These films are likely to have a pace and intensity that approximate those of normal human experience. Compared to the films of the classical Hollywood cinema, they are more likely to be explicit about sexuality than violence, are less likely to belong to a genre, and are more likely to be self-reflexive.

- American independent fictional films since the late 1960s are made all over the United States, not just in southern California, have lower budgets than their Hollywood counterparts, and are largely free of Hollywood studio creative control, so they tend to be more varied and less formulaic than the movies of classical Hollywood cinema.

WORKS CITED

Andrew, Dudley. *Concepts in Film Theory*. New York: Oxford UP, 1984.

Armes, Roy. *French Cinema*. New York: Oxford UP, 1985.

———. *Patterns of Realism: A Study of Italian Neo-Realist Cinema*. Cranbury, NJ: Barnes, 1971.

Bordwell, David, Janet Staiger, and Kristin Thompson. *The Classical Hollywood Cinema: Film Style and Mode of Production to 1960*. New York: Columbia UP, 1985.

Cawelti, John. "(Post)Modern Westerns." *Paradoxa* 4.9 (1998): 3–28.

Christopher, Nicholas. *Somewhere in the Night: Film Noir and the American City*. New York: Holt, 1998.

Cook, David. *A History of Narrative Film*. 3rd ed. New York: Norton, 1996.

Hirsch, Foster. *Detours and Lost Highways: A Map of Neo-Noir*. New York: Limelight, 1999.

Ingalls, Zoë. "Notes from Academe." *Chronicle of Higher Education* 12 Nov. 1999: B2.

Knee, Adam. "The Compound Genre Film: *Billy the Kid versus Dracula* Meets *The Harvey Girls*." *Intertextuality in Literature and Film: Selected Papers from the 13th Florida State University Conference on Literature and Film*. Ed. Elaine D. Cancalon and Antoine Spacagna. Gainesville: UP of Florida, 1994. 141–56.

Krutnik, Frank. *In a Lonely Street: Film Noir, Genre, Masculinity*. New York: Routledge, 1991.

Lenihan, John H. *Showdown: Confronting Modern America in the Western Film*. Urbana: U of Illinois P, 1980.

McCarthy, Todd. Introduction. In John Alton, *Painting with Light*. Berkeley: U of California P, 1995.

Moreau, Jeanne. Interview. *Morning Edition*. National Public Radio. 11 Mar. 1994.

Muñoz, Lorenza. "Movie-Making without Borders." <www.latimes.com>. 22 Jan. 2000, Calendar Sec.

Musser, Charles. "The Innovators 1900–1910." *Sight and Sound* 9.3 (NS) March 1999: 16–18.

Phillips, William H. "Neorealist Cinema." *Benét's Reader's Encyclopedia*. 3rd ed. Ed. Katherine Baker Siepmann. New York: Harper, 1987.

Shulman, Ken. "From a Vanished Country, a Viewable Cold-War Archive." *New York Times* 26 Oct. 1997, Arts and Leisure Sec. *New York Times on the Web* at <http://www.nytimes.com>. Click on Archives.

Telotte, J. P. *Voices in the Dark: The Narrative Patterns of Film Noir*. Urbana: U of Illinois P, 1989.

Thompson, Kristin, and David Bordwell. *Film History: An Introduction*. New York: McGraw, 1994.

Turner, Graeme. *Film as Social Practice*. 3rd ed. London: Routledge, 1999.

Weinraub, Bernard. "In Sheer Quality, TV Is Elbowing Hollywood Aside." *New York Times* 14 Feb. 1995, natl. ed., B1+.

Wilder, Billy, and Raymond Chandler. "Double Indemnity." In *Raymond Chandler, Later Novels and Other Writings*. New York: Library of America, 1995.

FOR FURTHER READING

Altman, Rick. *Film/Genre*. Bloomington: Indiana UP, 1999. On the origins, evolution, and transformations of film genres and the role of audiences in shaping and defining genres.

Coyne, Michael. *The Crowded Prairie: American National Identity in the Hollywood Western*. London: Tauris, 1997. Close analysis of westerns as a source for exploring American concerns—such as miscegenation, dysfunctional family structures, McCarthyism, civil rights, Vietnam, and receding frontiers—during the period from 1939 to 1976.

Film Genre Reader II. Ed. Barry Keith Grant. Austin: U of Texas P, 1995. A wide variety of essays by a variety of film scholars. Includes bibliographic references.

Film Genre 2000: New Critical Essays. Ed. Wheeler Winston Dixon. Albany: State U of New York P, 2000. Essays by film scholars on American genres since 1990 and on the influences of new technologies and market forces on genre filmmaking.

Levy, Emanuel. *Cinema of Outsiders: The Rise of American Independent Film*. New York: New York UP, 1999. On the major cycles in the indie film movement from the late 1970s to 1999, including regional cinema, the New York school of film, African American, Asian American, gay and lesbian, and movies made by women.

Phillips, Patrick. "Genre, Star and Auteur—Critical Approaches to Hollywood Cinema." *An Introduction to Film Studies*. 2nd ed. Ed. Jill Nelmes. London: Routledge, 1999. 161–208. Uses Martin Scorsese's film *New York, New York* to explore issues in genre, star, and auteur.

Pierson, John. *Spike, Mike, Slackers and Dykes: A Guided Tour across a Decade of American Independent Cinema*. New York: Miramax/Hyperion, 1995. An introduction to American independent films from 1984 to 1994 by someone involved in their making and marketing. Appendix I lists all American independent features from late 1984 to 1993.

Spehner, Norbert. "Wanted! A Selective Roundup of Secondary Sources about the Western—Novel and Film." *Paradoxa* 4.9 (1998): 49–60. An unannotated bibliography.

CHAPTER 8

Narrative Components of Fictional Films

Bｙ **definition**, **narrative** always recounts one or more events. . . . It does not simply mirror what happens; it explores and devises what can happen. . . . Narrative can thus shed light on individual fate or group destiny, the unity of a self or the nature of a collectivity. . . . [B]y marking off distinct moments in time and setting up relations among them, by discovering meaningful designs in temporal series, by establishing an end already partly contained in the beginning and a beginning already partly containing the end, by exhibiting the meaning of time and/or providing it with meaning, narrative deciphers time and indicates how to decipher it. In sum, narrative illuminates temporality and humans as temporal beings. (Prince 60)

A few years after the first motion pictures were created in the 1890s, the new medium was used to present short, entertaining fictional stories. Fictional films became so popular that during the late 1910s, **feature films** became commonplace, drew large audiences, came to serve as an evening's or afternoon's major pastime, and supported a large and growing filmmaking industry. Since then, people have remained captivated by fictional films, in part because they are endlessly fascinated by the causes and consequences of human behavior. As part of the opening monologue of *Blood Simple* (1984) indicates, "nothing comes with a guaranty. I don't care if you're the Pope of Rome, the President of the United States, or Man of the Year. Something can all go wrong." Often fictional films show how neither the characters nor the audience can anticipate how things "can all go wrong." And as some stories show, developments can also be profound and far-reaching. In *A Simple Plan* (1998), movements by a wild animal and the decisions of three men result in unexpected complications, unanticipated grief. Near the beginning of the film, a fox runs across the path of a pickup truck with three men inside; the driver swerves to miss it, and the truck hits a tree. After the accident, the three men pursue the fox, which leads to their discovery of a downed plane with $4.4 million stuffed in a duffel bag. The decisions of the three very different men

Terms in **boldface** are defined in the Illustrated Glossary beginning on page 539.

feature film: A fictional film that is at least sixty minutes long.

FIGURE 8.1 Action leading to complications
Early in *A Simple Plan* (1998), three men find a small crashed airplane covered by snow in the woods. Inside the plane are a dead pilot and a duffel bag full of money. Soon the three decide what to do with the money, and that decision leads to complications and more complications and death for six characters. This shot, the last one in the crucial scene where the men decide to keep the money, is framed so that the crow looms large in the foreground, dwarfing the men (with a dog) and plane in the background. A little earlier, one of the characters had said of the crows in an offhand manner that later proves significant, "Those things are always waiting on something to die, so they can eat it." Frame enlargement. *Mutual Film Company; Paramount*

about what to do with the money lead to all sorts of complications no one could have anticipated (Figure 8.1).

Most people are so drawn to narratives or stories that when they are confronted by any type of **text** with no obvious story, they still try to find one. As film archivist and critic Robert Rosen wrote,

Film and painting . . . display intriguing points of convergence, among them the inescapability of narrativizing spectators. Even in the face of totally nonrepresentational works, viewers have a powerful urge to uncover or invent narrative—a basic need to normalize the challenge of the unfamiliar by situating it in a comfortably recognizable sequence of events. (252)

In this chapter we briefly consider what a narrative is and examine some major aspects of the fictional narrative, the fictional film.

NARRATIVES

text: Something that people produce or modify to communicate meaning.

meaning: An observation or general statement about a subject.

Unlike ordinary experience, which mixes the meaningful with the amorphous and random, a story's ingredients are selected for appropriateness to the story's intended effects, **meanings,** and structures. A story can therefore be almost free from redundancy, meaninglessness, and, especially, inexpressiveness. . . . Thus a story promises comprehensibility in a way that ordinary experience does not. (Eidsvik 61)

"Narratives" or stories are commonplace in every society. We all produce them, enjoy them, and often learn from them directly or indirectly, yet explanation of what precisely constitutes a narrative is a complex, contentious issue in critical theory. For our purposes, ***narrative*** can be defined as a series of unified **events** (happenings and actions) situated in one or more **settings.** The events may be arranged chronologically or nonchronologically and may be factual, fictional, or a blend of the two. Consider the main events of the seventeen-minute wordless fictional film "The String Bean" (1962):

setting: The place where filmed action occurs.

1. An old woman finds a discarded potted plant near her apartment building.

2. In her apartment, she discards the dead plant and takes a seed she took from a package and plants it in the pot.

3. In her apartment, the plant grows to only a certain size.

4. The woman transplants the plant in a park, where it thrives.

5. One day, she sees park caretakers uproot the plant and discard it. The woman takes pods from the discarded plant.

6. In her apartment she takes seeds from a pod, plants them, places the pot outside on the sill, and looks on as rain begins to fall on the pot.

This narrative shows selected, chronologically arranged events in the life of one character. Viewers can usually figure out the relationship of later events to earlier ones. To illustrate: between the major units of the narrative (or **sequences**) numbered 3 and 4, viewers can infer that the woman transplants the plant in the park because she hopes it will grow even larger and healthier outdoors.

If the film showed only sequences 1 to 5, it would still be a narrative, though one with an unhappy ending, both for the woman and for those in the audience who identify with her. If the film showed only sequences 1 to 3, there would still be a narrative, though to many viewers it would be unsatisfactory because it would lack complications and resolution of them.

A narrative's events are unified in some manner. The following describes three events (selected and adapted from a short film discussed later in this chapter), but they are not clearly related:

5. At a university, wary students accept flyers that Leon gives them and quickly discard them. Leon finds the discarded flyers.

4. At the *Los Angeles Times* building, Leon is unable to see his friend Keith to give him a copy of a news release.

1. In his basement apartment Leon, who is dressed as a priest, puts on a false mustache and leaves.

If a film showed only these sequences, viewers could detect no unity to the events and could make no sense of them. The film would lack a narrative.

Some films—such as many films directed by the French directors Jean-Luc Godard and Alain Resnais—make it difficult or impossible for viewers to perceive the unity of events. Other films—such as *Mr. Hulot's Holiday* (1953), *Nashville* (1975), *Short Cuts* (1993), and *Clerks* (1994)—are only loosely unified overall. Although individual **scenes** are unified and easy to follow, some scenes could be located elsewhere in the story with little consequence. Such films are said to have an **episodic plot**.[1]

sequence: A series of related consecutive scenes, perceived as a major unit of a narrative film, such as the Sicilian sequence in *The Godfather.*

scene: A section of a narrative film that gives the impression of continuous action taking place in continuous time and space.

---

[1]Technology has made it possible to shuffle and play a film's parts in a different order, especially on the Web. For example, "digital technology [was used] to shuffle audio and visual tracks, reassembling a different story on each viewing" of "City Hall 2.0" on the Web site The Bit Screen: Films Made for the Internet (Stables 5).

A fictional film is a narrative that shows imaginary events arranged in a unified and meaningful order. The events are selected and arranged (structure). They are presented over time (chronologically or not). In addition, the events are presented in one or more styles. The rest of this chapter explores how the fictional film may handle structure, time, and style.

STRUCTURE

Structure, which some scholars and theorists call *form*, refers to the parts of a text and their arrangement. In a fictional film, the selection and order of events help viewers comprehend the story and strongly influence how they respond. This section discusses the basic fictional structure (characters, goals, and conflicts); some functions of beginnings, middles, and endings; and the combination of different brief stories (plotlines) into a larger, more complex story.

Fictional films include at least one character (imaginary person in a narrative) that is usually based in part on characteristics of actual people. It is even possible to base a character almost entirely on an actual person. *Being John Malkovich* (1999) includes the character John Malkovich, who seems to be exactly like the real John Malkovich (except for a peculiar portal inside his head). Occasionally other subjects with human qualities—such as extraterrestrials, robots, zombies, animals, even abstract shapes—function as characters (Figure 8.2). Fictional films show imaginary events, although filmmakers often re-create some actual events, film them, and combine them with the completely fictional events. It is even possible, though rare, to combine fictional events with **footage** of actual (not re-created) events, as in some scenes late in *Medium Cool* (1969) where one character gets into the 1968 Chicago Democratic National Convention and another character is threatened by tear gas and rioting outside the convention hall. Similarly, the fictional *Chinese Box* (1998) includes actual action: parts of the ceremony of Hong Kong's transition from British to Chinese

footage: A length of exposed motion-picture film.

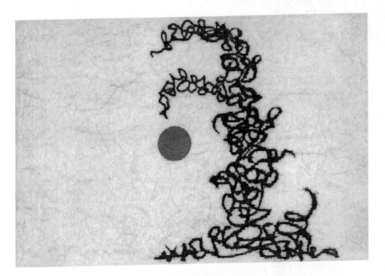

FIGURE 8.2 Shapes functioning as characters
Most fictional films include humans enacting characters, but occasionally a character is played by something with human qualities. "The Dot and the Line: A Romance in Lower Mathematics" (1965) shows the story of a love triangle with each of the characters represented by a shape. The story's three main characters are a dot and the two males contending for her: a line and an ever-changing squiggle. Seen here is the dot cavorting or dancing with her initial boyfriend. *Chuck Jones & Les Goldman; MGM; Turner Entertainment*

rule. The settings of narratives may be fictional, as in most science fiction stories, or they may be essentially factual, as in the Italian **neorealist** films or other movies filmed on largely unaltered **locations**.

Characters, Goals, Conflicts

Some generalizations about characters, goals, and conflicts apply to all fictional films regardless of length, but feature films and short films have some major differences. In this section we first consider the qualities of fictional films, regardless of length, and later turn our attention to how characters, goals, and conflicts tend to be handled in the short film.

FEATURE FILMS AND SHORT FILMS

A fictional narrative nearly always includes at least one character who wants something but has problems trying to obtain it. People are fascinated with characters who have trouble reaching their goals, in part because in such circumstances they learn about human nature or think they learn about how they might handle a similar situation. Perhaps viewers also sometimes enjoy seeing others have trouble. Whatever the motivations of viewers, they tend to be fascinated by how others try to overcome problems and how their efforts affect them and others around them.

Typically the main character's goals are not immediately apparent, though usually one major goal becomes clear early in the film or viewers lose interest. As a story progresses, sometimes a second goal emerges. In the French film *Ridicule* (1996), viewers soon learn that the main character, an engineer, wants the king's support for draining a swamp that breeds disease and kills the engineer's peasants. In pursuing that goal, the man goes to Versailles, where he meets two women: one young, attractive, and intelligent; the other older, more worldly, and more calculating. The story illustrates that pursuing a second goal (the young woman) may preclude achieving the first (Figure 8.3). Sometimes a story's main character fails to achieve either of two major goals. In *Citizen Kane* (1941), Charles Foster Kane has two major goals in his life. One is to win a woman's lasting love (his first wife leaves him after his affair becomes public; his second wife leaves him because of her isolation, her boredom, and his self-centeredness). Kane's other goal is to win the love of the populace, most noticeably by becoming governor. He fails to attain that goal, too.

In films with two or more major characters, usually the characters have different goals, at least initially; the result is conflict, with or without humor. Conflict largely without humor is prominent in many movies, including most war movies and westerns. Conflict with humor abounds in most romantic comedies, such as *It Happened One Night* (1934), *Bringing Up Baby* (1938), *My Best Friend's Wedding* (1997), and *Bridget Jones's Diary* (2001).

neorealism: As a film movement in Italy during and after World War II, neorealist films are a mixture of imaginary and factual occurrences usually located in real settings and showing ordinary and believable characters caught up in difficult social and economic conditions, such as poverty and unemployment.

location: Any place other than a film studio that is used for filming.

a)

b)

c)

FIGURE 8.3 Character, goals, conflicts Nearly all of *Ridicule* (1996) takes place in 1783 France at a time when wit was king and ridicule could kill. (a) The main character is an engineer who seeks royal support to clear swamps and thus eradicate a fatal disease. (b) In pursuing his goal, he meets and becomes entangled with a calculating, worldly woman of the king's court, who helps him gain the king's ear. (c) At about the same time, the engineer becomes attracted to Mathilde, an intelligent, individualistic woman. After many complications, the man abandons the woman of the court, who arranges his downfall so that he fails to attain his initial goal. A concluding title card informs viewers that twelve years later the engineer and Mathilde succeed in draining the swamps. Frame enlargements. *Miramax Zoë*

FIGURE 8.4 The three types of conflict
The three main human subjects of *Jaws* (1975) are (left to right) the chief of police (Brody), a veteran fisherman (Quint), and a marine-life specialist (Hooper). During the film each comes into conflict with each of the others. All three come into conflict with a great white shark. Early in the film Brody comes into conflict with townspeople, and the mayor and is in conflict with himself. In short, the film illustrates the three basic types of conflict in stories: people versus people, people versus nature, and one aspect of a character versus another aspect. *David Brown & Richard D. Zanuck; Universal*

In pursuing goals, conflict or problems are inevitable, in fiction as in life. In *Jaws* (1975), a huge killer shark is menacing people who venture into the waters off an island that caters to summer tourists. Throughout *Jaws* a major conflict is between people and the shark (people versus nature). But the film also shows many conflicts between people (Figure 8.4). There are conflicts between some townspeople and the island's chief of police, Brody; between the mayor and Brody; and between Mrs. Kintner, whose young son was killed by a shark, and Chief Brody. Also Brody is in conflict with himself: early in the film he allows his better judgment to be overruled, and he's feeling guilty about the consequences. At the film's end, however, presumably all the conflicts are resolved. The veteran fisherman Quint is destroyed by his shark adversary; soon afterward the shark is destroyed. Hooper and Brody paddle back to the beach. The townspeople and tourists are no longer in danger. *Jaws* exemplifies the three traditional types of conflict: people versus nature (for example, Quint and Hooper versus the shark), people versus people (the chief versus the mayor), and conflict within a character (Brody wants to accommodate the political leaders and businesspeople yet wants to protect townspeople and tourists against shark attacks). Often fictional stories take the form of two opposing characters or two opposing groups of characters (Figure 8.5).

In films of **classical Hollywood cinema,** regardless of their length, typically the main characters achieve all their major goals. If a feature film has only one major character, that character normally has more than one major goal. For example, in countless movies—such as *Rocky* (1976), *Top Gun* (1986), *The Mask* (1994), and *Mission: Impossible 2* (2000)—the central male character tries to succeed in love and work or some other major goal and does so. In many musicals, the main male character eventually wins the

classical Hollywood cinema:
Films that show one or more distinct characters facing a succession of problems while trying to reach their goal or goals; these films tend to hide the manner of their making by using continuity editing and other unobtrusive filmmaking techniques.

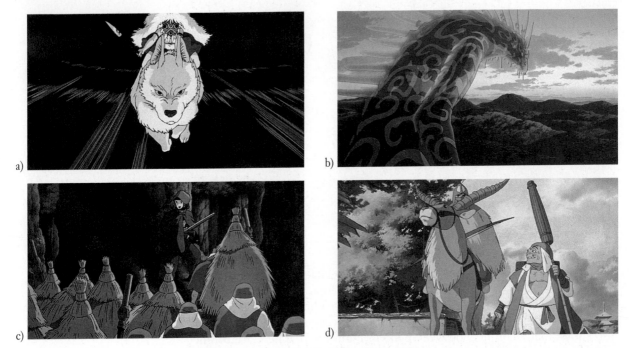

FIGURE 8.5 Two opposing forces in a fictional film
Hayao Miyazaki's animated Japanese feature *Princess Mononoke* (1997) shows a long, complicated story, but, as in many fictional tales, in *Princess Mononoke* basically two forces war with each other: those who seek to protect nature and those who seek to convert it for industrial uses. (a) Princess Mononoke, or San—a young woman here seen wearing a mask—has been raised by wolf gods and lives with them. She is allied with wild animals and (b) forest spirits to defend the natural environment. (c) The other major force—consisting of Lady Eboshi, her ironworkers, and her soldiers—intend to industrialize nature. (d) Jigo (right) is yet another threat to nature: he and his men intend to take the great forest spirit's head back to the emperor, who believes he would thus gain immortality. One major character belongs to neither warring group: Ashitaka (seen on the left), a brave young man who tries to mediate between the warring factions. Frame enlargements. *Studio Ghibli; Miramax*

woman of his dreams and is instrumental in the successful staging of a show or making of a movie. In most movies, especially the popular ones, the major characters don't just succeed; they succeed against enormous odds. In *Stand and Deliver* (1987), an overworked high school math teacher in an L.A. barrio wins the respect of his students, and they both overcome their various problems at home and work so diligently that they all pass the math advanced placement test twice, the second time after only a few days to study. *Music of the Heart* (1999) is yet another movie in which the main character—a violin teacher in an East Harlem elementary school—endures setback after setback, including, early on, a husband who abandons her and their two sons;

loss of income and resultant housing problems; resentment from fellow teachers and resistance from some parents; difficulties coping with her two sons, especially the older one who misses his father; a short-term boyfriend who is commitment impaired; and loss of her position and loss of funds for her violin program even after it becomes so successful that students have to enter a lottery for a chance at admittance. She even endures one parking ticket after another because she never gets a parking space at work! Early in the story, she decides in effect that she needs no social life and perseveres in her life with her two sons and her work. Her story inspires many viewers by showing that despite seemingly unending hurdles one person who works very hard can achieve both a dream she never dared dream and standing ovations.

SHORT FICTIONAL FILMS

From 1895 to about 1906, all fictional films were less than sixty minutes, the usual definition of the **short film.** Until the 1960s, short fictional films often accompanied a feature film in movie theater showings. Today, short films are seldom shown in theaters and are rarely available in video stores. They are shown at film festivals; by film societies, museums, and libraries; on some cable channels, including the Sundance Channel, the Independent Film Channel, and Turner Classic Movies; in various school and college courses; and on many Web sites. In addition, a series of collections of short films—called *Short 1, Short 2,* and so on—is available on DVD. Helping make a short film is usually required of filmmaking students. Sometimes their short films attract attention at film festivals and lead to funding for feature productions. At its best, a short fictional film is not a truncated feature but a flexible and expressive form in its own right. Like a short story, its brevity can be an advantage: for example, compared with a feature film, it may be more compressed, demanding, and subtle. And since its budget is far less than that for a feature, even for an **independent film,** typically its makers are under fewer financial pressures to conform to the usual Hollywood movie and are freer to be true to their vision. Let's examine briefly two sample short films.

independent film: Film made without support or input from the dominant, established film industry.

"Leon's Case" (1982), which is twenty-five minutes long, shows the often amusing story of the idealistic and sincere Leon Bernstein, who resides in 1980s Los Angeles but thinks of himself as "the last fugitive member of the [1960s] Village 8." Accordingly, he still thinks and acts as he did two decades earlier. In trying to publicize his opposition to the U.S. military-industrial complex, Leon Bernstein goes through the following steps:

1. In his basement apartment Leon, who is dressed as a priest, puts on a false mustache and leaves.

2. At the house of his two friends, Keith and Karen, Leon tells them of his plans and hides his manuscript about his life in the resistance. His two friends offer no direct support and sometimes ignore him.

3. At a duplicating shop, Leon gets copies made of a press release and of a flyer announcing a demonstration he plans to stage. The worker in the store, a former hippie, does not give Leon a "discount for the movement."

4. At the *Los Angeles Times* building, Leon is unable to see his friend Keith, who writes a real estate column, to give him a copy of a news release.

5. At a university, wary students accept Leon's flyers and quickly discard them. Leon finds the discarded flyers.

6. Leon has trouble getting in to see a lawyer he knows, and when he does, he learns the lawyer doesn't do resistance work anymore "'cause there's no resistance."

7. At a telephone booth, Leon calls the FBI to announce the demonstration the next day, but he learns that President Carter pardoned war resisters years ago.

8. Back at his apartment, Leon's friends give him a surprise party. He is uncomfortable and uncharacteristically speechless; his friends do not entirely support him in his cause.

9. The next day, Leon cuts his hair, puts on conventional clothing, goes to the Los Angeles Airport, presumably chains himself to a bomber on display there, gets arrested, and gets coverage on the local television news. Mission accomplished.

Like "Leon's Case," most short fictional films exhibit the characteristics of classical Hollywood cinema but have fewer major characters and fewer events. Most short fictional films have

1. One or two major characters, who usually do not change goals or personality during the film;

2. A brief story time, usually a few days or less;

3. One goal, which the main character usually does not state explicitly but which viewers can figure out early in the film;

4. One or more obstacles or conflicts in trying to reach the goal but none of them very time-consuming;

5. Success or failure in reaching the goal.

A minority of short fictional films rejects the conventions of the classical Hollywood cinema. A good example is "The Other Side," a ten-minute 1966 black-and-white film from Belgium. The film has no dialogue, no narration, and no music except during the opening credits and the final moments. The only sound effect is occasional machine-gun fire. "The Other Side" is a brief, complex, and somewhat ambiguous film that calls for multiple viewings, which are easier to manage with short films than with features. The film is a **symbolic** story about masses of people in an unidentified town who are forced to keep their hands against the walls of buildings as they move slowly sideways. Eventually, some try to rebel but are gunned down.

symbol: Anything perceptible that has significance or meaning beyond its usual meaning or function.

Conflict between characters is used in stories of classical Hollywood cinema to show what individual characters are like and to initiate and develop the plot. In "The Other Side" we see only one side of the conflict: we never learn about those suppressing the people in the street, nor do we know why they do so. The oppressors kill people one at a time and evidently kill no more than necessary to keep the others in line (literally and figuratively). The film shows that authorities shoot rebels. At the beginning of the film we cannot be sure, but they may also shoot nonrebels at random.

Unlike classical Hollywood cinema, "The Other Side" reveals little about individual characters. Certainly we learn nothing about the oppressed characters from dialogue—the film has none—and the film has no written language except the final "1966." "The Other Side" also lacks **close-ups** of faces, so viewers cannot infer what the characters are feeling. No one looks happy, yet no one looks angry either. In nearly all of the film, people move lethargically, like drugged inmates in an institution or animals in a zoo. The lack of emotion and interaction between characters are two of the film's most prominent features. The main character is not an individual or a few distinct characters, as in classical Hollywood cinema, but a group. The film focuses not on individual psychology but on political issues, force, and conformity.

close-up: An image in which the subject fills most of the frame and little of the surroundings is shown.

As in most short films of classical Hollywood cinema, the main characters—here a mass of people—have a single goal: freedom from oppression and conformity. Failing at that, they want to survive, even if that requires conformity, lack of interaction, and the absence of vitality. Unlike most films of classical Hollywood cinema, the characters fail to achieve their main goal, and the film ends as it began—except more bodies fill the street than in the beginning.[2]

Beginnings, Middles, and Endings

The beginning of a fictional film tends to establish where and when the story starts and to involve viewers. Many fictional films start with one or more shots of the setting before introducing the subjects. Soon after that, the story starts to get viewers anticipating and readjusting to developments as they unfold before their eyes.

Typically, a fictional film's beginning uses minimal **exposition** (information about events that supposedly transpired before the beginning of the

---

[2]Both the description and analysis of "Leon's Case" and "The Other Side" are adapted from Phillips.

FIGURE 8.6 A character's initially lacking something causes consequences Nanyuma (right) is the main character in *Finzan* (Mali, 1990). Early in the film Nanyuma's husband dies; soon her husband's brother, the village idiot, wants to marry her. In pursuing that goal, he sets in motion most of the film's complications. The story ends with the man not getting what he wants: the widow evades the consummation of her forced marriage but only by exiling herself and her young son from her village and chancing an uncertain future. *Courtesy of California Newsreel, San Francisco*

plot): more than a little of it, especially at the beginning of a story, tends to keep audiences uninvolved. Tellers of tales—whether in print, on the stage, or on the screen—typically use as little initial exposition as possible but feed their audiences tidbits of it when needed as the story progresses.

Usually beginnings introduce the major characters and allow viewers to infer their goals. The events of fictional films are so intertwined that often something missing in a character's life at the story's beginning largely determines the story's ending. Early in *Finzan* (*A Dance for the Heroes*) (1990), a man wants to force his late brother's widow to marry him (Figure 8.6). *Women on the Verge of a Nervous Breakdown* (1988) begins with the main character wanting to talk to her lover. Much of the film shows her trying to connect with him, but only in the penultimate scene does she succeed.

The middle section of fictional feature films typically includes a series of obstacles that prevent or delay the main characters from achieving their goals. In the long central section of *Schindler's List* (1993), for example, Schindler tries to thwart the Nazis and help save as many Jews as possible, but in pursuing his goals, he faces setbacks, dangers, and delays. In dealing with the impediments to reaching their goals, the central characters reveal their natures and the consequences of their actions for them and others. Consider the structure of *Unforgiven* (1992). The film begins with acts of injustice both by a cowboy who slashes a woman's face and by the sheriff who cavalierly acts as law officer, jury, and judge. The large middle section of the film shows who will avenge the injustice against the woman, how they will do so, and the consequences of their actions, for themselves and others. The middle section of a fictional film also tests the filmmakers' inventiveness and skill in creating satisfying surprise and suspense and in other ways keeping the audience involved with the story.

Narrative endings show the consequences of the major previous events. Filmmakers, however, sometimes tack on an ending that doesn't dovetail with the rest of the story. As one film critic explains,

Films can choose between two basic sensibilities. They can either show the way the world is, or they can show the way the world should be. . . . Movies that start as one and finish as the other invariably test either our sympathy or our intellect.

. . . *Wonder Boys* [implies] . . . in a saccharin epilogue that there's nothing more to maturity than mastering the virtues of the clean shave, the ribbed polo-neck and the personal laptop. . . . If only the film were true to the satirical prom-ise of its first half. Then Grady [the main character, a writer and professor] would be a howlingly mediocre writer who vows never to give up. (Macaulay)

Another example of an inconsistent ending occurs in *Schindler's List*. After Schindler has retrieved the Jewish women from the Auschwitz concen-tration camp, he seeks out his wife to be reconciled with her and presumably strays no more. Viewers learn that the armaments his factory builds are de-liberately flawed to sabotage the German war effort. He urges the rabbi who works for him to prepare for the Sabbath. Viewers learn that Schindler spent a lot of money sustaining his workers and bribing Reich officials. At the war's end, he credits his Jewish workers with saving themselves and persuades the armed camp guards to leave without harming the workers. Later, as the music swells, he breaks down as he says that he squandered money and should have saved even more Jews; then he is quietly and lovingly enfolded by many of those he did save. Earlier, the film showed Schindler as a complex, fascinat-ing man—exploitative, philandering, and callous, yet shrewd, self-confident, powerful, and somewhat inexplicable. The movie ends not with modulated chords but a single note, hero worship. The ending may be emotionally sat-isfying for many viewers—and understandable given the filmmakers' desire to honor Schindler—but it does not tie in with the film's earlier restraint and complexity, and as the film draws to an end, it tries too hard to make sure no one could miss Schindler's admirable qualities.

Sometimes a film ends improbably because the filmmakers responded to political or societal pressures. The Chinese film *Not One Less* (1999) shows both the inadequate conditions of a rural Chinese primary school and the brusque or uncaring attitude of nearly everyone the main character meets in a Chinese city. But as the film nears its end, it morphs into a fairy tale. The thirteen-year-old girl who takes over the teaching while the adult teacher is away is suddenly rewarded in highly unlikely ways: a TV broadcast helps her locate the boy she went to the city to retrieve; a TV crew drives the boy and her home, all the while recording the happy developments; and the village receives gifts and money to rebuild the school and refurnish it. A final **title card** informs viewers that a million Chinese children drop school for work each year, but the number is much higher. The happy ending and inaccurate final title cards were included because the director (Zhang Yimou) has had trouble with Chinese censorship in the past and feared the authorities would object to too unfavorable a representation of life in contemporary China (Figure 8.7).

title card: A card or thin sheet of clear plastic on which is written or printed information included in a film.

FIGURE 8.7 Ending shaped by the context of the production
Not One Less (1999) is the story of a resolute girl put in charge of a small rural Chinese primary school while the teacher is away for a month. The film shows the difficult conditions in which the children are taught—for example, a run-down schoolroom with only one piece of chalk per day, a pitted chalkboard, pitted walls, a leaky roof, no books, and an unqualified substitute teacher. Most of the story shows the conditions at the school and in a city in a credible way. To avoid censorship, however, the filmmakers showed that those in positions of power were eventually helpful and compassionate and included a completely happy ending. Frame enlargement. *Columbia Pictures Film Production Asia; Sony*

Films with **closure** end by showing the consequences of events viewers have become curious about. Closure supplies viewers with the sense of completion and answers that real life itself so often withholds. Films may also lack closure—that is, be open-ended: the fate of a significant character or person is uncertain or the causes or consequences of an important event unknowable. Generally, films of classical Hollywood cinema have a sense of completion because mainstream audiences tend to dislike inconclusive or puzzling endings. The endings of independent films, however, are more likely to be open. Examples are *The Crying Game* (1992) and *L.A. Confidential* (1997). At the end of *The Crying Game* viewers cannot know what Fergus and Dil's relationship will be. They can only review relevant events from the film and make an informed guess. In *L.A. Confidential*, the ending for one of the two main characters is open: viewers cannot know Ed Exley's fate. He has survived an attempt on his life and been awarded honors again. For now, the police chief and district attorney are using Exley to repair damage done to the image of the LAPD—and Exley knows it—but in the long run can he trust the police chief and the DA, especially now that his colleague, a powerful ally, is leaving for Arizona?

Plotlines

A **plotline** is a brief narrative—a series of related events, perhaps continuous—usually involving a few characters or people. A plotline can function as a complete short narrative, as it typically does in a short film. A feature film, however, often has two or more plotlines. When a film consists of two or more plotlines, often one plotline is given prominence (more of the film's total time). Plotlines may be combined in countless creative ways and, as we will see, serve many different functions.

To compress a wide-ranging story into an endurable movie, plotlines can be consecutive yet with large gaps of story time between them. *2001: A Space Odyssey* (1968) contains the consecutive but not continuous plotlines of four groups: man-apes, scientists, a computer and two astronauts, and the starchild. *Being Human* (1994) has five plotlines (set, for example, in cave times, ancient Rome, and the modern era) with vast gaps of time between them.

Multiple alternating plotlines can be used to show relationships between different time periods. *The Godfather Part II* (1974) and *Heat and Dust* (1983) alternate between a narrative primarily about one character and a story set years earlier about a relative. *Intolerance* (1916), directed by D. W. Griffith, alternates four stories, each set at a different place and historical period: Babylon in 539 B.C., Judea toward the end of Christ's life, France in 1572, and America early in the twentieth century. As might be expected from a film with so complicated a structure, many viewers see little unity in the film and are confused about its purpose.

A film can alternate between simultaneous plotlines to heighten suspense. *Dr. Strangelove: Or, How I Learned to Stop Worrying and Love the Bomb* (1963) has three major simultaneous plotlines: at a U.S. Air Force base where the paranoid General Jack D. Ripper has ordered U.S. bombers to attack the Soviet Union; on a U.S. bomber on its way to bomb a target in the Soviet Union; and in the Pentagon war room, where the U.S. president, military commanders, and Dr. Strangelove, the leading scientist, try to call back the plane and prevent the catastrophe.

To show various aspects of a large group, plotlines may also be numerous, chronological, simultaneous, and intersecting. *Short Cuts* includes nine pairs of major characters plus six other important characters, but the film has so many groupings of characters that one cannot say there are nine plotlines. Different critics of the film have detected "nine interlocking narratives," "approximately ten stories," or "a dozen stories." There are at least ten (Figure 8.8). The film's multiple plotlines are arranged chronologically or simultaneously—the viewer cannot tell which—and each couple interacts with at least one other major character. With so many characters and intersecting plotlines in something as fleeting and onrushing as a film, however, a viewer may sometimes lose track of who is who. There is also a danger that with so many events some may be implausible (one murder seems insufficiently motivated and its "cover-up" highly unlikely). Nonetheless, a story consisting of many intersecting plotlines can effectively present a panoramic view of a society. In *Short Cuts* as in *Nashville* (1975), *A Wedding* (1978), and *The Player* (1992), director Robert Altman and his collaborators are exploring how inclusive a narrative can be—both in terms of the number of

FIGURE 8.8 **A plotline that shares a character with another plotline**
Short Cuts (1993) shows the stories of nine pairs of characters. In addition, one member of one of the nine pairs (center) leaves his wife and goes on a fishing trip with two male friends. They have breakfast at a diner (seen here); they drive to a site, park, and hike; they set up camp, find a woman's body in the water, and decide what to do with the rest of their weekend. That is one plotline. Frame enlargement. *Cary Brokaw; Fine Line Features*

FIGURE 8.9 Multiple, simultaneous, and intersecting plotlines
Short Cuts (1993) has twenty-four major characters and many different groupings of them. For
example, (a) Howard Finnigan (a TV news commentator) and his wife, Ann, have a son Casey
who is hit by a car, walks home, falls asleep, lapses into a coma, and is treated in a hospital. Two
other characters are seen in the film only in relation to the Finnigans: (b) Mr. Bitkower, a baker
who as requested has made a special birthday cake for Casey, and (c) Howard's father, Paul, who
unexpectedly appears at the hospital after years of alienation from his son. Other characters have
lives in the film beyond their interactions with the Finnigans: (d) Doreen, a waitress, drives the
car that Casey darted in front of; (e) Ralph Wyman is the physician in charge of Casey's care; and
(f) Zoe is a disturbed cellist who lives next door to the Finnigans with her mother and is upset by
news of the boy's fate. Frame enlargements. *Cary Brokaw; Fine Line Features*

characters and the various combinations of plotlines—yet remain unified enough and comprehensible enough to be satisfying (Figure 8.9).

Director Mike Figgis has also experimented with how inclusive a narrative can be in *Time Code* (2000), which also consists of multiple, chronological, simultaneous, and intersecting plotlines that present a panoramic view of a group, in this case an assortment of small-time independent Hollywood movie-makers and others with ties to them. But the film uses no editing. Instead, it shows simultaneous, often converging, uninterrupted plotlines on four different sections of the screen (Figure 8.10). While viewing *Time Code*, the viewer's attention is often directed to the fragment of an event unspooling on one of the quadrants when its accompanying sound track becomes louder or more distinct. At other times, the viewer is less guided as to which quadrants to observe and for how long. (Each viewer in effect edits the film and constructs a somewhat different story.) With more than twenty characters to keep track of, so many visuals bombarding the viewer from four sources simultaneously, and sometimes more than one sound track competing for the viewer's attention, no viewer can completely reconstruct the plot from one viewing. *Time Code* invites multiple viewings. However, like viewers

FIGURE 8.10 **Four inter-connected plotlines shown simultaneously**

In *Time Code* (2000), occasionally action in one plotline intersects with action from another plotline, but usually viewers see four separate unedited plotlines simultaneously. Frame enlargement. *A Red Mullet Production; Screen Gems/Sony Pictures Entertainment Company*

a)

d)

b)

e)

c)

FIGURE 8.11 Multiple simultaneous plotlines
In *Night on Earth* (1992), each of the five uninterrupted and simultaneous plotlines involves a taxi driver and his or her fare, and the stories take place (in order) in (a) Los Angeles, (b) New York, (c) Paris, (d) Rome, and (e) Helsinki. In its use of simultaneous nonintersecting plotlines that are presented successively, the film's structure is rare, perhaps even one-of-a-kind. *Jim Jarmusch; Fine Line Features*

struggling with the four alternating plotlines of *Intolerance*, many viewers may find trying to figure out the story of *Time Code* too demanding and frustrating to give the film a second chance.

Plotlines may even be consecutive yet simultaneous because they occur in different time zones. Jim Jarmusch's *Night on Earth* (1992) has five consecutive brief plotlines, each set in one of four different time zones, but each begins at the same moment in time: 7:07 P.M. in Los Angeles, 10:07 P.M. in New York, 4:07 A.M. in Paris and Rome, and 5:07 A.M. in Helsinki. As a consequence, viewers are offered the rare opportunity to see what happens at the same moment of time at various places around the world (Figure 8.11).

Plotlines may be nonchronological and from many time periods yet for all but one of the major characters intersect at one time and place, as in *The Joy Luck Club* (1993), which has eight major plotlines: for four middle-aged women born in China and for the American-born grown daughter of each (Figure 8.12).

FIGURE 8.12 **Multiple interwoven plotlines**
The Joy Luck Club (1993) tells the stories of four Chinese mothers and the Chinese American daughter of each. The film illustrates how complex the combinations of multiple plotlines may be. In the months before the plot of *The Joy Luck Club* begins, Suyuan (on the left) has died, and Suyuan's middle-aged women friends (seen here) have written to China and located the two women who Suyuan had been forced to abandon as babies during a war in China. The movie begins with a going-away party for Suyuan's daughter June (the second woman from the left), who plans to leave for China the next day to meet her two half sisters. Most of the movie consists of flashbacks from the going-away party to each middle-aged woman's painful childhood or early adulthood in China, present-tense scenes from the party, and flashbacks to selected events from the lives of the four adult daughters. The film concludes with June's arrival in China and her meeting her two half sisters. Except for Suyuan, all the other seven major characters meet at one place and time, the going-away party. *Wayne Wang; Amy Tan; Ronald Bass; Patrick Markey; Buena Vista*

Ways to structure a narrative seem limitless. Plots may be extremely complicated yet entertaining and easy to follow, as in *Run Lola Run* (see the feature on pp. 282–83). That film begins and proceeds chronologically except for some brief flashbacks. Then from the time Lola begins to run, the story progresses chronologically (with three scattered brief flashforwards) to an ending. But the story begins again as Lola begins to run; this time with a different three brief flashforwards and a very different ending. The film is still not over. The story begins a third time as Lola begins to run yet again and includes a brief flashforward as the story races to its conclusion. As critic Stephen Holden writes, the film shows "how human destiny has everything to do with timing and the instant and endless chains of causality that ripple from a single chance encounter."

TIME

In fictional films there are three tenses: present, future, and past. Also to be considered is the matter of the time it takes to show a film and the time span represented by a story.

Present Time, Flashforwards, and Flashbacks

> "Movies should have a beginning, a middle, and an end," harrumphed French Film Maker Georges Franju at a symposium some years back. "Certainly," replied [film director] Jean-Luc Godard. "But not necessarily in that order." (Corliss)

Most makers of narrative films agree with Franju and arrange scenes chronologically. But the earliest scenes of a film's story may occur late in the film or even at its ending, and the latest scenes of some other story may occur early in the narrative, as in *Heavenly Creatures* (1994). As we will see, these and countless other temporal arrangements of scenes are possible because of flashbacks and flashforwards.

Only a few movies use chronological order with an occasional **flashforward.** *Easy Rider* (1969) is one of them. At one point the Peter Fonda character, Captain America, is in a brothel; he looks up past a small statue toward a plaque that reads "Death only closes a man's reputation and determines it as good or bad." Next we see from a helicopter a split-second shot of something burning off to the side of a country road. In the brothel, Captain America looks down, and the action resumes. Does the shot suggest he vaguely glimpses the future, or are viewers meant to see this as a glimpse of the future, or is the shot meant to make viewers a little uneasy because it doesn't fit in and make sense at the moment? Or does the shot function in two or more ways? Viewers cannot even recognize it as a flashforward unless they remember it as they see the end of the film, when Captain America is shot by a passing motorist and his motorcycle explodes into flames off to the side of a country road. Occasionally during the opening credits, a flashforward shows events that are repeated well into the film, as in *My Life as a Dog* (1985), *GoodFellas* (1990), *Go* (1999), and *American Beauty* (1999).

Although flashforwards are usually mainly visual, they may be auditory. Late in *Medium Cool* the car radio announces a serious car accident that we witness nearly fifty seconds later. According to the French scholar Marc Vernet, this **technique** was used in Alain Robbe-Grillet's *L'immortelle* (1962): "We hear the sound of an accident at the beginning of the film even though that crash will occur later in the film" (92).

Flashforwards "can only be recognized retrospectively" (Chatman 64) and are demanding of viewers. They can be confusing and frustrating if the events shown are too far into the future or the flashforwards are frequent or lengthy. Perhaps because flashforwards let viewers glimpse consequences they do not anticipate or are not yet even interested in, they are rarely used.

Flashbacks are much more common than flashforwards. Like flashforwards they are nearly always visual or visual and auditory, but they may be exclusively auditory. In *The Night Porter* (1974), the main character, who had gone fishing with another man, returns home and remembers the other man's voice seconds before the main character had pushed him into the water and let him drown.

Often a flashback briefly interrupts a chronological progression of events to show what influenced a character earlier. Flashbacks may also be used at the end of a film to reveal causes of previously puzzling events, as in *Exotica* (1994). Near the end of that film a flashback reveals how the discovery of a murdered girl affected an enigmatic young woman, and in the film's last two scenes a flashback to an even earlier time reveals more information about the enigmatic young woman's relationship to the troubled main male character. By withholding these revelations until the last scenes, which is what some theorists refer to as a "privileged" placement, the final scenes help clarify the whole. A flashback may also be used within a flashback as when viewers learn who indeed shot Liberty Valance in *The Man Who Shot Liberty Valance* (1962) and as when viewers see scenes that two twelve-year-old characters (Vern and later Gordie) recount or remember in *Stand by Me* (1986).

In some films—such as the Italian classic *8½* (1963) and the Japanese classic *Rashomon* (1950)—it is sometimes difficult, sometimes impossible, to know which events happened and which are dreams, fantasies, or lies. In *8½* a director tries to regain his creativity and confidence and finish a costly and complicated film while trying to cope with his wife, lover, producer, actors, and the press. That much of the narrative proceeds chronologically but with frequent scenes of the director's dreams, fantasies, or memories, although sometimes viewers cannot know which is which. In *Rashomon* viewers cannot

technique: Any aspect of filmmaking, such as the choice of sets, lighting, sound effects, music, and editing.

Structure of *Run Lola Run*

EXPOSITION (11 MIN., 51 SEC.)

Crowd seen in fast motion. Actors are highlighted briefly. Bank guard kicks soccer ball high up in air. Film's title formed by masses of people. Opening credits over animation of Lola running. Photo I.D.s of characters and cast. Establishing shots. Inside Lola's apartment, she answers phone call from a desperate Manni. In black-and-white flashbacks, we see how Lola's moped was stolen and learn she could not pick up Manni after his criminal transaction. We also learn Manni had to get on a subway train, on which he left a bag with the money he was to deliver to his criminal boss, Ronnie. Lola has twenty minutes to reach Manni with DM 100,000 (approximately $60,000). She runs by a room in which her mother is on the phone. On the nearby TV, we see a cartoon Lola running toward stairs and down them (See Figure a).

I (22 min., 26 sec.)	II (20 min., 15 sec.)	III (20 min., 57 sec.)
■ Cartoon Lola runs by cartoon dog on the stairs.	■ Cartoon boy on stairs trips cartoon Lola, and she tumbles down stairs.	■ Cartoon Lola jumps over cartoon dog on stairs.
■ On sidewalk, Lola brushes against a woman pushing a baby stroller.	■ Running outside, she limps for a while.	■ Lola does not brush against the woman with a baby stroller.
■ Flashforward photos: authorities take the woman's baby; she steals a baby.	■ She bumps against woman with the baby stroller.	■ Flashforward photos: the woman becomes a Jehovah's Witness.
■ Lola's father with his disgruntled mistress.	■ Flashforward photos: the woman wins a lottery.	■ On sidewalk, nuns do not part, so Lola runs into street and nearly hits cyclist.
■ On sidewalk, nuns part and allow Lola to run through their group.	■ On sidewalk, nuns part and allow Lola to run through their group.	■ Cyclist rides off and stops at a snack place; he offers to sell his cycle to the homeless man.
■ Nearby cyclist offers to sell Lola his bicycle.	■ Nearby cyclist offers to sell Lola his bicycle.	■ Lola runs into Mr. Meyer's car and ends up on its hood; the white car passes by. Lola runs off.
■ Flashforward photos: cyclist beaten up; courtship; marriage.	■ Flashforward photos: cyclist's unhappy fate.	■ Lola rounds a corner where we previously saw the homeless man walking with the bag of money.
■ Lola runs in front of Mr. Meyer's car.	■ Lola runs over hood of Mr. Meyer's car.	■ Homeless man cycling.
■ Meyer's car hits side of white car driving by.	■ Meyer's car hits side of white car driving by.	■ Lola's father learns that his mistress is pregnant and assumes the child is his. He hurriedly leaves his office as Lola runs toward his office.
■ Lola runs by the homeless man carrying Manni's bag of money.	■ Lola bumps into the homeless man carrying Manni's bag of money.	■ Lola's father gets in Meyer's car, and they drive off as Lola vainly shouts after them.
■ Mistress tells Lola's father that she is pregnant.	■ Lola runs by woman in bank hallway.	■ A blind woman by a phone booth helps Manni spot the homeless man who is cycling by. Manni chases him.
■ Lola runs by woman in bank hallway.	■ In Lola's father's office, mistress has already told Lola's father that she is pregnant but not by him. . . . Lola calls the mistress a stupid cow. Lola's dad slaps Lola; she wrecks part of his office as the frightened mistress looks on.	
■ Flashforward photos of that woman's tragic fate.		
■ Lola's dad escorts Lola out of the bank and tells her he is not her birth father.		

a)

b)

Run Lola Run (1998) consists of a prologue followed by three variations of the rest of the story. In the film, some actions are repeated, such as (a) the cartoon Lola beginning to run down the stairs. Other events transpire only once, such as (b) Lola intervening in her boyfriend's attempted robbery by hitting the security guard in the back of the head with a small bag of groceries. Frame enlargements. *Stefan Arndt; Sony Pictures Classic*

I (continued)

- Outside bank, Lola asks old woman the time of day.
- Red ambulance stops short of hitting large plate glass being carried across the street.
- Lola is a second too late, and Manni enters market and begins robbing it. Lola hits armed guard on back of head with a plastic bag of groceries (see figure b) and helps Manni with the robbery.
- Outside, they run as the song "What a Difference a Day Makes" is heard on soundtrack.
- Police stop Lola and Manni and accidentally shoot Lola.
- Her dying thoughts: she asks Manni many questions related to his feelings for her.

II (continued)

- In bank hallway, Lola shouts at woman.
- Lola takes bank guard's pistol and takes her father hostage.
- Flashforward photos for woman in bank hallway: romantic happiness with male bank colleague.
- Bank guard places his hand near his heart as if the stress were causing him pain as Lola robs the bank.
- Lola tosses the gun aside then leaves the bank. Outside, police push Lola aside, assuming that someone else is trying to rob the bank. She runs away.
- Red ambulance runs through large plate glass being carried across the street.
- Lola arrives in time to stop Manni from robbing market, but looking straight ahead at Lola, he walks in front of ambulance.
- Manni's dying thoughts: Lola will soon forget him and find another lover.

III (continued)

- The homeless man and Manni indirectly cause the car with Meyer and Lola's father to run into the white car after all. The man who stole Lola's moped runs into the back of the white car.
- Lola runs in front of a large truck and is nearly hit by it.
- She goes into a nearby casino and wins a lot of money.
- Manni pulls his gun on the homeless man on the cycle, gets back the bag of money, but gives homeless man the gun.
- After the red ambulance stops to avoid hitting the plate glass, Lola gets into the back of the ambulance. It contains the bank guard, who has a life-threatening heart problem. After Lola holds his hand, his heart recovers.
- At the intersection where she is supposed to meet Manni, Lola gets out of the ambulance.
- Down the block, Manni arrives in black car with Ronnie. All is OK between them.
- Manni kisses Lola briefly; then they walk away. Lola is carrying the sack of money. Freeze-frame. (75:48 total)

283

know which of the four quite different accounts of a man's death and events leading up to it is the most reliable and which are self-serving lies. Both *8½* and *Rashomon* question "the assumptions on which all conventional (Hollywood-style) film narrative is based, namely that the world is wholly decipherable, that people's motivations can be understood, that all events have clear causes and that the end of a fiction will offer us the chance to fuse all elements of the plot into a single coherent dramatic action" (Armes 103–04).

On rare occasions, a film is basically chronological but includes flashbacks and flashforwards, as in *Run Lola Run* (see the feature on pp. 282–83). *Don't Look Now* (1973) is also mostly chronological but sometimes uses flashbacks and occasional flashforwards. One memorable flashforward occurs when the main male character glimpses his wife on a passing boat with two other women, and all three are dressed in black. Near the film's ending viewers see some shots related to that earlier scene, but they are from the man's funeral procession in Venice. The flashforward earlier in the film reveals that the man is so psychic he could briefly see beyond his own life although he did not realize what he was seeing then. One movie narrative that jumps around in time extensively is *Slaughterhouse-Five* (1972). It uses many flashforwards and flashbacks, some of which are difficult to place in a chronological ordering of the events, but then its central character has become "unstuck in time."

Chronological Time and Nonchronological Time

Plot is the selection and arrangement of a story's events. **Fabula** is the mental reconstruction in chronological order of all the events in a nonchronological plot. Both a plot and its corresponding fabula contain the same events, but the nonchronological arrangement of events changes focus, mood, and viewer interest—sometimes considerably.

Like many earlier stories including *The Odyssey* by Homer, *Shoot the Piano Player* begins in the middle of the story, then flashes back to the main character's earlier life before resuming the story and finishing it (Figure 8.13). Such a structure has at least two advantages in *Shoot the Piano Player*. It allows the filmmakers to begin at an exciting and intriguing point: two men in a car are trying to run down a third man. After the film is well under way and viewers have become interested in the main character, the flashback helps them understand why he is so emotionally guarded.

The plot for *Pulp Fiction* (1994) includes many deviations from a straight chronology, and, unlike nearly all fictional films, it also includes repeated action and parallel action. In the film, Jules (the Samuel L. Jackson character) is prominent at both the beginning and ending. In the fabula, he does not appear in the last two major sections, though for many viewers he is probably the film's most complex and intriguing character. The nonchronological plot of *Pulp Fiction* makes possible a more exciting, more engaging first scene than a chronological arrangement of all the film's events: the beginning of a robbery versus two guys talking in a car. The nonchronological plot also re-

The Past   ---------------
                                  1

The Present   ---------------   ------------------------
                  2   3

2 Chino, one of Charlie Kohler's brothers, briefly eludes two fellow crooks (Ernest and Momo) and goes to Charlie for help. . . . After Léna and Charlie escape from Ernest and Momo, Léna takes Charlie to her apartment where he sees a poster of himself as Edouard Saroyan, a successful concert pianist.

1 Sometime earlier, Edouard is married to Théresa. Unknown to him, she has reluctantly slept with an impresario so that Edouard could become a famous concert pianist. After she commits suicide, Edouard gives up his career, changes his name, and becomes a piano player in a café.

3 Back in Léna's apartment, Léna and Charlie become lovers. After further complications Léna is killed by Ernest, and Charlie returns to his job playing a piano in the café.

FIGURE 8.13 **The plot and fabula of *Shoot the Piano Player* (1960)**
The plot = 2, 1, 3.
The fabula = 1, 2, 3.
Along with other movies, *Criss Cross*, a classic 1949 American film noir, has the same structure.

sults in a less upbeat ending: by the end of the film's plot, we know that for Vincent death lurks around the corner; at the end of the fabula, Butch picks up his girlfriend, and they drive off on a motorcycle. The plot's last scene also allows viewers to experience the unusual situation of learning what happens before and after the film's first scene. Because the plot includes two viewings of the action in the grill and of the apartment where men are killed, we viewers can more fully understand the context of actions we saw earlier and see the perspectives of different characters at the same place. For example, the first time the scene in the grill is shown, the film focuses entirely on Ringo and Honey Bunny; the second time, it focuses on them and on Vincent and especially Jules. Compared with the fabula, the plot of *Pulp Fiction* is much more demanding of the audience. However, for some viewers the film's complex structure is both a challenge and a pleasure, though the plot is so intricate that few viewers can completely reconstruct the fabula after only one viewing.

For a description of the plot and fabula of *Pulp Fiction*, see the Web site for this book: <http://www.bedfordstmartins.com/phillips-film>.

Citizen Kane's nonchronological plot also results in a very different film than a version of the events arranged chronologically (see the feature on pp. 288–90). The film's plot, for example, immediately shows Kane's decaying estate and his death; the fabula begins with Kane's childhood in Colorado, which is not as likely to engage audiences as much as the film's beginning does. The film begins in darkness, shadows, and Kane's isolation; the fabula begins in brighter lighting with the playful young Kane and his parents, although Kane is soon turned over to the banker as guardian. The plot follows Kane's death with a newsreel summarizing his life. No such summary is provided in the fabula. Early in the film, viewers hear Kane's dying word *Rosebud*, which many of them find intriguing; the fabula provides this puzzler much later. The plot makes possible different perspectives on some of the same events (such as Leland's account of Susan's opera career and her own account); the fabula shows those events only once. The nonchronological plot is more demanding of viewers than a chronological arrangement of events, and viewers need repeat showings to notice significant details that would be more apparent in a linear version of the story.

So strong is the human proclivity to try to sort through events and make sense of them (that's perhaps the main reason most people are endlessly fascinated by narratives) that for most viewers, attempting to construct fabulas is irresistible. But as demonstrated by *Slaughterhouse-Five*, *Jacob's Ladder* (1990), *Lost Highway* (1997), and occasional other movies, constructing the fabula may be problematic because different attentive and thoughtful viewers will disagree if certain events are present, past, or future events or are only imagined (fantasized or dreamed).

Running and Story Times

Running time is the amount of time it takes to see a film and includes opening and closing credits. Sometimes the credits accompany images of the film's subjects; sometimes they do not. Running times of features vary from one hour to nearly twenty-six hours for a TV series later shown in theaters (*Heimat II*, 1993) or seven hours for a film made for theatrical release (*Sátántangó*, 1993).[3]

Story time is the amount of time covered in a film's narrative or story. For example, if a film's earliest scene occurs on a Sunday and its latest scene takes place on the following Friday, the story time is six days.

---

[3]It is impossible to know which was the longest film for theatrical release because there are no surviving copies for many early films (there are no known copies of more than 70 percent of all feature films made before the 1920s and only about 50 percent of all American films made before 1950) and many films that have survived may be incomplete. Then, too, before the late 1920s, projectors did not run at the same speed. The French film *Travail* (1919) may have run eight hours. The 1925 *Les misérables* reputedly consisted of thirty-two 35 mm reels (each reel could be from thirteen to sixteen minutes long), so that movie might have run anywhere from seven to eight and a half hours.

From as early as some of the early short silent films by the Frenchman Georges Méliès, story time has nearly always been much longer than running time. The story time of the Chinese film *To Live* (1994) is approximately twenty-five years (from "the 1940s" to "the 1960s" then five or six more years); the running time is 129 minutes. The plot of *Women on the Verge of a Nervous Breakdown* begins one morning and ends approximately thirty-six hours later, on the evening of the following day; the film's running time is eighty-eight minutes.

In a few movies the story time is approximately the same as the running time. For example, the story time of *High Noon* is about 102 minutes (from about 10:30 to 12:12), and the film's running time is eighty-one and a half minutes. The story time of *Nick of Time* (1995) is about ninety-five minutes (from noon until at least five minutes after the attempted assassination at 1:30), but the running time, excluding the opening credits, is only about eighty minutes. *Nick of Time* keeps story and running times approximately equal by sometimes condensing story time, sometimes expanding it. For example, the opening events supposedly take 480 seconds, but actually only 143 seconds pass. Conversely, the events shown in the film from precisely 1:28 to exactly 1:30 take not 120 seconds but 327. For both *High Noon* and *Nick of Time* many critics and viewers have commented that their story times coincide with their running times. Almost. Examples of films in which running time and story time are identical are extremely rare, although, excluding its opening credits, *Time Code* is such a film.

On rare occasions a film's story time is less than its running time. *Night on Earth* consists of five plotlines set in four time zones, each beginning at the same moment in time and each having a story time of thirty-five minutes. The film's story time then is thirty-five minutes; its running time is 125 minutes. Another film with a story time less than its running time is "An Occurrence at Owl Creek Bridge" (1962), a story of a civilian facing being hanged from a railroad bridge during the American Civil War. The film's story time is slightly more than ten minutes; its running time is almost twenty-eight minutes.

Nearly all fictional films are imprecise about how much time supposedly elapses between scenes. "The String Bean" (discussed on pp. 262–63) shows an old woman finding a discarded plant, planting seeds, nurturing the new plant, finding it uprooted, then planting seeds from it, presumably to begin the cycle again. How much time passes between the time the woman first plants the seeds and one sprouts? How much time passes altogether in the film? What is the story time: one month, two months, three? This imprecision is not a weakness of the film but a characteristic of fictional films, which are generally less specific about their story time than fiction or published plays.

Filmmakers can present many events selected from a brief story time, as in *High Noon*, or relatively few events taken from a long story time, as in *2001*, which depicts highly selective events from 4 million B.C. to beyond our sense of time. Storytellers may even repeat the same block of story time and segments within it—for example, a twenty-four-hour period and various

The Plot and Fabula of *Citizen Kane*

PLOT OF *CITIZEN KANE*

I. At Xanadu (Charles Foster Kane's decaying, incomplete mountaintop retreat), Kane utters his last word, *Rosebud*, drops a glass paperweight from his hand, and dies.

II. At a screening room, a newsreel depicting key events in Kane's life (not in chronological order) is shown. Afterward, reporters discuss the newsreel and the possible significance of *Rosebud*. Rawlston directs reporter Thompson to discover the significance of the word.

III. At an Atlantic City nightclub, Thompson finds Kane's second wife, Susan Alexander Kane, drinking and unwilling to talk about Kane.

IV. The next day at the Thatcher Memorial Library in Philadelphia, Thompson reads (and the film enacts) portions of Thatcher's unpublished memoirs:

1. In 1871 (Colorado), young Charles's mother has come into wealth and signs papers allowing a bank to manage the Colorado Lode and act as the boy's guardian. Charles meets Thatcher, a banker and his new guardian.

2. Charles (presumably the following Christmas) receives a sled as a Christmas gift from Thatcher.

3. Christmastime, when Charles is nearly twenty-five and about to attain financial independence. He wants to take over a newspaper, the *New York Inquirer*.

4. Kane does so and defends the interests of the underprivileged.

5. He also promotes the Spanish-American War and argues with Thatcher about priorities in life.

6. Winter 1929: Because he did not invest and instead bought so many things, Kane gives up some control of some of his newspapers to Thatcher and his bank.

V. At Bernstein's office in New York City, Bernstein (Kane's personal manager) tells Thompson about Kane's background and his friend Leland:

1. First day at *Inquirer*, introductions and Kane moving into editor-in-chief Carter's office.

2. Kane establishes new newspaper policies. Carter quits/is fired. Kane declares his publishing principles.

3. *Inquirer*'s rapid, purchased growth.

4. Party to celebrate *Inquirer*'s success. Kane announces he's going abroad.

5. Kane has been amassing art treasures during his travels abroad and shipping them to New York. His welcome back by his employees; his engagement announcement and hasty departure with his fiancée, Emily, the U.S. president's niece.

VI. At a New York City hospital, Leland talks to Thompson about Kane's lack of convictions and recounts some events in Kane's life:

1. Emily and Kane's deteriorating marriage (montage). Leland talks briefly with Thompson about Kane's desire for love and his inability to give it.

2. On the street Kane meets Susan. The two in her room and in the parlor, where she "sings."

3. Leland gives a speech in support of Kane's candidacy for governor.

4. Conclusion of Kane's political speech to a large audience.

5. After the speech: Emily tells Kane that she is going to check on the source of a note she has received. Kane goes with her.

6. In the presence of Emily and Susan, Kane confronts his political rival Gettys, who tries to blackmail Kane into withdrawing from the governor's race. Kane refuses.

7. The Kane-Susan affair is reported in newspapers; Leland disillusioned.

8. . . . At Kane campaign headquarters, an intoxicated Leland (now drama critic) criticizes Kane and asks to be transferred to Chicago. Kane toasts to love on his own terms.

9. Kane marries Susan (and builds an opera house in Chicago).

10. Susan's disastrous opera debut in Chicago.

11. Chicago *Inquirer* office: . . . Leland drunk and passed out on top of a typewriter. While finishing Leland's negative review of Susan's performance, Kane fires Leland. Back in the present, Leland tells Thompson that Kane never finished anything.

VII. At the Atlantic City nightclub again, Thompson sees Susan. Now she talks:

1. During a singing lesson for Susan, Kane imposes his will on her and her singing coach.

2. Her Chicago opera debut and its poor reception.

3. Susan angry about Leland's review; Leland sends Kane the torn-up pieces of Kane's $25,000 severance check and the "Declaration of Principles," which Kane tears up.

4. Susan's disastrous opera career (montage).

5. Aftermath of her suicide attempt; . . . Kane finally relents and says she can give up her opera career.

6. Xanadu: Their isolation and pastimes, Susan's frustration.

7. On an elaborate picnic Kane and Susan quarrel, and he slaps her.

8. Susan is packing to leave Xanadu; Kane attempts to stop her but fails.

VIII. At Xanadu, Raymond, the butler, tells Thompson about *Rosebud:*

1. Susan leaves Kane.

2. Kane starts tearing up her room, stops when he sees Susan's glass paperweight, picks it up, looks briefly at the "snowy" object, whispers *Rosebud*, then carries the paperweight out of the room.

3. Kane walks past the opposing mirrors that reflect self, self, self.

IX. Back in the present, Thompson is not impressed by Raymond's explanation of *Rosebud*. Picture taking in Xanadu, taking inventory, and departures. Piles and piles of things. Rosebud is tossed into the flames. Outside, night: smoke coming out of chimney; a No Trespassing sign, a gate with *K* on top, and Xanadu with smoke coming out of chimney in background right.

FABULA OF *CITIZEN KANE*

In Colorado, Charles Foster Kane's mother has become wealthy and in 1871 puts her young son, Charles, under the guardianship of a banker (Thatcher) to oversee Kane's childhood and education. As a wealthy twenty-five-year-old man, Kane becomes interested in running a New York newspaper, and he buys his way to success as a newspaper tycoon. He uses the *New York Inquirer* to expose people who abuse power and to foment war with Spain. Kane travels widely abroad and amasses a huge collection of artworks.

He becomes engaged to Emily, the American president's niece, marries her, has a son with her (Junior), and eventually becomes alienated from her. He runs for governor but loses because his political rival exposes Kane's affair with Susan, a young woman who sells sheet music in a shop. Emily divorces him. Two weeks later, Kane marries Susan. In 1918, Emily dies in an auto accident with Junior. Kane has an opera house built in Chicago and pressures Susan into an opera career for which she is ill suited. Kane fires his friend Leland for writing the beginning of an honest though negative review of Susan's opera debut. Eventually, the stress of Susan's disastrous opera career results in her attempted suicide. Kane reluctantly agrees to let her abandon singing, and the two retreat to Xanadu, their vast estate in Florida, where Susan becomes desperately bored. Some years later she leaves Kane. His economic empire partially collapses; and some years after that he dies alone at Xanadu. His funeral is reported in the media around the world.

A newsreel describing Kane's life is screened. A reporter is assigned to try to discover the meaning of *Rosebud*, Kane's dying word, and in pursuing that goal reads portions of Thatcher's diary and interviews various people who knew Kane. Susan, Kane's second wife, initially refuses to be interviewed because she is so upset. Thompson succeeds in interviewing Bernstein, a friend and business associate; Leland, Kane's oldest friend who ended up alienated from him; Susan (the second time Thompson sees her); and Raymond, who is in charge at Xanadu. After Thompson receives limited information about *Rosebud* from Raymond, he and other reporters begin to leave Xanadu as various objects from Kane's huge collection of objects, including Rosebud, are being incinerated.

minutes within it—over and over, though with many variations in the events during each repetition of the time. That was done for parts of a day in *Groundhog Day* (1993). Repetition is also used in the three versions of the sequence of Lola running to save her boyfriend in *Run Lola Run*.

STYLE

socialist realism: A Soviet doctrine and style in force from the mid-1930s to the 1980s that decreed that all Soviet texts, including films, must promote communism and the working class and must be "realistic" (actually an idealized depiction of the working class) so as to be understandable to working people.

satire: A representation of human behavior that has as its aim the humorous criticism of the behavior shown.

Style is another one of those terms with different meanings to different critics and theorists. Here *style* refers to the way a text, such as a film, presents its subjects. Possible styles include farce, black comedy, fantasy, realism, abstract, magic realism, **socialist realism,** and parody. A style may be used in any kind of film. For example, a parody (an amusing imitation of human behavior or of a text, part of a text, or texts) may be used in any **genre** or type of fictional film. A western or horror film, for instance, may include a parody, or an entire film may be a parody. There is not space here to introduce all possible film styles, and some film styles, such as parody and socialist realism, are discussed elsewhere in the book. What follows illustrates only two of the most challenging styles for beginning film students: black comedy and magic realism.

Some writers, filmmakers, and other weavers of tales have tacitly asked viewers to consider the possible humor in subjects often considered off-limits for comedy, such as warfare, cannibalism, murder, death, and illness. Such a narrative style is usually called black humor or **black comedy.** Often black comedy is used in **satires.** After its first fifteen minutes or so, *Citizen Ruth*

FIGURE 8.14 Black humor within a serious situation
Initially, the opening scene of *Happiness* (1998) shows a serious subject
treated in the usual serious way. The story's first shot is of a concerned
young woman's face; then appears this man's anguished look. As the
scene develops, we viewers soon figure out that she has just told him
that she doesn't want to date him anymore. Later, he cries briefly and
blows his nose into his cloth napkin. Later still, he asks if she is sure,
and when she replies without hesitation that she is, he asks, "Is it
someone else?" and she responds without malice, "No. It's just you."
For many viewers, this part of the scene is unexpectedly humorous,
and sometimes in this film, viewers don't know whether they should
laugh or feel for the emotional pain being witnessed. As elsewhere in
Happiness, the first scene shows amusing moments in situations not
normally considered humorous. In black comedy, certain moments
may amuse some viewers but offend or shock others. Frame enlargement. *Good Machine/Killer Films; Good Machine International*

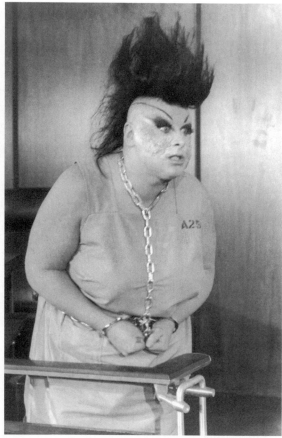

FIGURE 8.15 A black comedy that may amuse or offend
John Waters's *Female Trouble* (1974) shows the biography of
Dawn Davenport (played by Divine/Dave Lochary), a woman
who starts to go wrong in her high school days, especially after
her parents fail to give her "cha-cha heels" for Christmas and
she attacks them and overturns the Christmas tree on them.
Nearly everything that could go wrong in a woman's life goes
wrong in Dawn's. For example, she is raped and ends up with
an uncontrollable child, who years later is nearly raped by the
same man. After many complications, Dawn ends up standing
trial for kidnapping and multiple murders. (Her face is scarred
from one of her many unhappy experiences, when her former
husband's aunt threw acid at her.) For some viewers *Female
Trouble* is mostly offensive; to others it is fairly consistently
amusing. *Copyright 1974 by New Line Productions, Inc. All rights
reserved. Photo by Bruce Moore. Photo appears courtesy of New Line
Productions, Inc., New York City*

(1996) satirizes the extreme behavior of both anti-
abortion groups and abortion rights groups, daring
choices as the main subjects of a comedy. *Happiness*
(1998) also has flashes of black humor (Figure 8.14).

In plot summary, black comedies rarely sound
amusing because they often involve violence or death
or at least extreme emotional or physical pain. To
make them work, their makers must handle timing,
pace, and mood masterfully. Typically, black comedies
amuse some viewers and shock or offend others. In *Female Trouble* (1974), the main character has so many
problems—some of them outrageous or at least startling—that some viewers are offended, some are
amused, and still others are by turns offended and
amused (Figure 8.15). Comedy involves pain—such as
embarrassment, confusion, a fall—for someone else.

a)

b)

c)

FIGURE 8.16 Magic realism with far-reaching consequences
Like Water for Chocolate (1992) is set during the Mexican revolution in 1910. Most of its story is plausible or realistic. At times, however, the film includes magical events. For instance, a dish with rose petal sauce that Tita prepares inflames everyone who eats it except her married sister, (a) including the man she loves. (b) Gertrudis, Tita's other sister, is so aroused by the food that she rips open the clothing covering her breasts and moves her hand over them and suggestively underneath the dining table. Next, Gertrudis rushes outside to take a shower, during which the wooden shack enclosing the shower bursts into flames. Some distance away rebels are fighting federal troops. A Villista, or rebel, chief on horseback stops in the middle of the battle because he smells something in the air, and a narrator says that the rose smell that Gertrudis emitted "caused the Villista chief to seek out something unknown at an unspecified place." The man on the horse and Gertrudis are mysteriously drawn toward each other. When they meet, the man swoops her up onto his horse and (c) they ride away. In this example, the original incident of magic realism has far-reaching consequences because henceforth Gertrudis will live with the Villista chief. At other times, in this film and elsewhere, incidents of magic realism are far less consequential. Frame enlargements. *Alfonso Arau; Miramax*

Makers of black comedies dare to include more pain than some viewers are used to seeing in comedies. Depending on the filmmakers' skill in anticipating viewers' responses and on the viewers' backgrounds and tastes, black comedies may amuse or offend.

Another style used since World War II, mainly in fiction, is **magic realism,** improbable or impossible events in an otherwise plausible or realistic narrative. Most of *Erendira* (1982)—based on a script by a master of literary magic realism, the Colombian writer Gabriel García Márquez—is rendered in a realistic style. But the film also has many scenes incorporating magic realism. In one, the cruel grandmother consumes an enormous amount of rat poison mixed into a birthday cake and collapses onto her bed. After she starts to revive, the young man who had poisoned her observes, "Incredible! She's

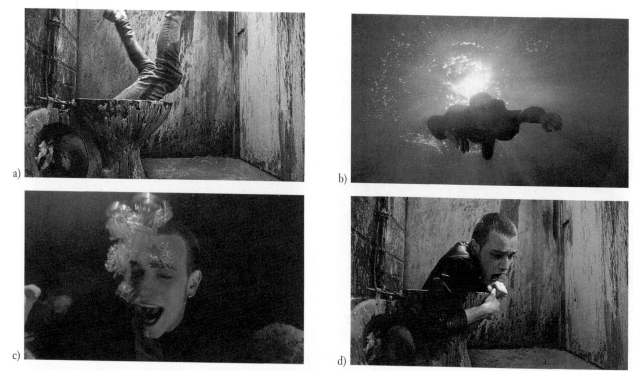

FIGURE 8.17 Magic realism as symbol
In *Trainspotting* (1996), a young man addicted to drugs has hidden two suppositories of illegal drugs in the back of his pants. Urgently, he goes to a public toilet. After relieving himself, he realizes the suppositories have fallen into the toilet. Then begins the magic realism: (a) he plunges into the toilet; (b) swims down through clear water to the bottom; (c) snatches up the two suppositories, turns to swim back up, and says something unintelligible. (d) He emerges from the toilet and spits out some water. These actions are impossible in actuality, but they symbolically and memorably show to what depths a person hooked on drugs might descend. Frame enlargements. *Channel Four Films, A Figment Film; Miramax Films*

tougher than an elephant! There was enough poison to kill a million rats!" The next morning, the grandmother wakes up, smiles, then says to her granddaughter Erendira, "God bless you, child. I hadn't slept that well since I was fifteen! I had a beautiful dream of love." The only ill effect from her previous night's dessert is that her hair is falling out, which seems to amuse her. The episode is unreal or magical (and in this case probably symbolic): no one could survive so huge a dosage of poison or would react with amusement as her hair falls out.

In the 1992 film *Like Water for Chocolate*, the scrumptious food that Tita prepares causes those who eat it to feel as Tita felt when she prepared it—for example, sad or lustful (Figure 8.16). Some of the film's magic realism is unrelated to food. At one point, while riding off in a horse-drawn carriage,

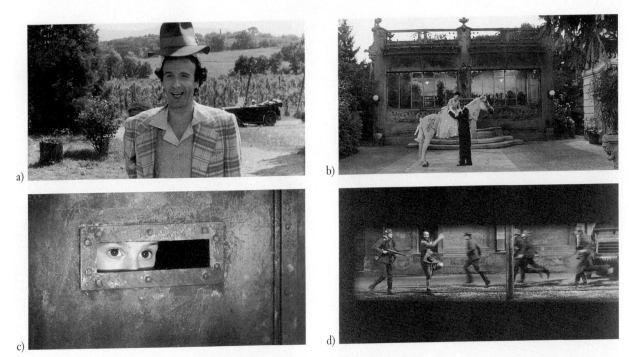

a)
b)
c)
d)

FIGURE 8.18 Shifting styles as a film progresses
(a) Initially, *Life Is Beautiful* (1998) is a romantic comedy set in 1939 Italy in which a man courts a woman. Gradually the political situation glimpsed in the background worsens and comes to the foreground. Frame (b), from near the end of the film's first half, combines romance and anti-Semitism: Guido has rescued the woman, Dora, from her stuffy fiancé, and they have ridden off on the horse of Guido's Jewish uncle, but the horse has been painted "Attention, Jewish horse." Later in Nazi Germany, where the family is imprisoned, the horrors of the Nazi camp are kept largely in the background, visually and aurally. (d) Visually, the camera is usually kept focused on Guido and his son in the foreground and by filming the Nazis in long and extreme long shots. The sound track is also used to mute the horrors of the concentration camp, most notably in two scenes. In one, for his son's benefit Guido "translates" the German guard's orders as if they were part of a game. In the other, to serenade Dora he plays part of an opera on a phonograph (the same opera he and Dora had heard when Guido courted her). The second part of the film is not black comedy: it does not treat the Nazi imprisonment itself as humorous. The second half is a muted, sorrowful, and occasionally amusing fable mainly about Guido's inventive attempts to guard his son from awareness of the horrors thrust on their family and secondarily his attempts to boost his wife's morale. (c–d) Guido, dressed as a woman, has been caught by a Nazi guard and is being marched off. Even then, Guido looks in the direction of his hidden son, winks at him, and exaggerates his walking to make the boy think that this development is also only part of a game. The boy chuckles as he sees his father for what is to be the last time. Within the film, the styles and moods shift gradually and subtly but eventually drastically. It's a demand the film makes of it audience that some viewers accept but others balk at. Frame enlargements. *Cecchi Gori Group; Miramax*

Tita trails a shawl nearly half as long as an American football field because of the enormous cold she has been feeling. Magic realism may be less prominent in a story than it is in *Erendira* and *Like Water for Chocolate*. In *Trainspotting* (1996), a film that is overwhelmingly gritty and realistic, one of the most memorable scenes is rendered as magic realism (Figure 8.17 on p. 293).

A film may use one style sporadically, as in *Fargo*, which mixes black comedy with unamusing realism. Or a fictional film may use two or more styles. At first, the Italian film *Life Is Beautiful* (1998) is a romantic comedy in which a man courts a woman amusingly and romantically. Later disquieting signs of Fascism and anti-Semitism begin to emerge. The last part of the film, which is set in a Nazi concentration camp, is more gritty and realistic, though flashes of romance and comedy survive (Figure 8.18).

Styles can strongly influence how viewers react to a film. If viewers refuse to go along with the magic realism of *Erendira* or *Like Water for Chocolate*, they will miss much of the pleasure of interacting with the film on its own terms. Likewise, if viewers beginning to watch the famous **experimental film** "Un chien andalou" (1928) expect the usual mixture of realism and fantasy so prevalent in Hollywood movies, they will remain uninvolved and disappointed. Viewers who quickly recognize that the film consists of a series of discontinuous scenes like the irrationality of dreams, are much more likely to become intrigued by the film and enjoy it. If audiences are watching a film that uses a particular style that they have not previously seen, such as magic realism, they need to figure out the film's style quickly and give the film a chance to do what it can do within the parameters it has set out for itself. If viewers know nothing about the film's style and cannot figure it out quickly or if they refuse to play along with a style they know about—for example, decline to be amused by a parody—they will sit glumly and hope for a different style and a different film, in vain.

> **experimental film:** A film that rejects the conventions of mainstream movies and explores the possibilities of the film medium itself.

SUMMARY

This chapter explains briefly what a narrative is then examines some major aspects of the fictional narrative, the fictional film: structure, time, and style.

Narratives

- A narrative—both in film and other texts—may be defined as a series of unified consecutive events (represented actions and happenings) situated in one or more settings.

- A narrative may be factual or fictional or a blend of the two. It may be chronological or nonchronological.

Structure

- A fictional film is a narrative film including at least one character (imaginary person) and largely imaginary events; its settings may be factual or imaginary.

- In fictional films usually the major characters have one or more goals but face problems in trying to reach them.

- Short fictional films typically have only one or two major characters that do not change much during the film's brief story time. The major characters of a short fictional film usually have a goal or goals (which are not explained but which viewers can figure out early in the film), have obstacles to overcome, and succeed or fail in reaching the goal.

- Typically, the beginning of a fictional film does not supply much exposition, although it usually establishes where and when the story starts. It also attempts to involve audiences in the story.

- Among other functions, the middle section shows how the central characters deal with problems that impede progress toward their goals and reveals how happenings and the characters' actions affect them and others.

- The ending of a fictional film usually shows the consequences of major previous events. In stories with closure, by the end of the narrative the consequences of previous major events are shown or clearly implied. Most films of classical Hollywood cinema have closure, but many other narrative films do not.

- A plotline is a brief narrative focused on a few characters or people that could function on its own as a separate (usually very brief) story. Typically, short films have only one plotline, whereas feature films have multiple plotlines.

- In feature films, many combinations of plotlines are possible. For example, they can be consecutive but with large gaps of story time between them; can alternate between different time periods; or can be chronological, simultaneous, and occasionally intersecting.

Time

- Flashforwards are used only occasionally in fictional films, usually to suggest a premonition or inevitability. Flashbacks are often used and can serve many different purposes, such as to show how a character's past influences the character or continues to trouble the character. On rare occasions, fictional films combine present-tense action with flashforwards and flashbacks.

- A fabula is the mental reconstruction in chronological order of all the events in a nonchronological plot. Although a nonchronological plot contains the same events as its corresponding fabula, the plot creates different emphases and causes different responses in viewers.

- How much time is represented in a fictional film (story time) is usually unspecified and difficult to determine very specifically, but story time nearly always far exceeds the film's running time.

Style

- A style is the way subjects are presented in a text, such as a film. A film may be rendered in one or more styles.

- If viewers know nothing about a film's style, such as black comedy, and cannot figure it out quickly, the film will probably not engage them. If viewers know about the film's style yet refuse to accept it—for example, they refuse to accept the story as black comedy—they will also likely fail to become engaged by the film.

WORKS CITED

Armes, Roy. *Action and Image: Dramatic Structure in Cinema*. Manchester: Manchester UP, 1994.

Chatman, Seymour. *Story and Discourse: Narrative Structure in Fiction and Film*. Ithaca: Cornell UP, 1978.

Corliss, Richard. Review of *Continental Divide*, directed by Michael Apted. *Time* 14 Sept. 1981: 90.

Eidsvik, Charles. *Cineliteracy: Film among the Arts*. New York: Random, 1978.

Holden, Stephen. "'Winter Sleepers': Against a Breathtaking Landscape, Young Adults Lacking in Vision." *New York Times on the Web*. 17 March 2000. <http://www.nytimes.com/library/film/031700winter-film-review.html>.

Macaulay, Sean. "Downmarket, Not Downbeat." *The Times* (U.K.), 28 Feb. 2000. <http://www.the-times.co.uk/news/pages/tim/2000/02/28/timartcin01001.html?999>.

Phillips, William H. *Writing Short Scripts*. Syracuse: Syracuse UP, 1991.

Prince, Gerald. *Dictionary of Narratology*. Lincoln: U of Nebraska P, 1987.

Rosen, Robert. "Notes on Painting and Film." *Art and Film since 1945: Hall of Mirrors*. Ed. Kerry Brougher. Los Angeles: Museum of Contemporary Art, 1996.

Stables, Kate. "Zap the Gerbil, Blend the Frog." *Sight and Sound* 10.1 (NS) (Jan. 2000): 5.

Vernet, Marc. "Cinema and Narration." *Aesthetics of Film*. Trans. and rev. Richard Neupert. Austin: U of Texas P, 1992.

FOR FURTHER READING

Hayward, Susan. *Cinema Studies: The Key Concepts*. 2nd ed. London: Routledge, 2000. Especially pertinent to the study of the fictional film are the entries *flashback, form/content, narrative, sequencing/sequence, setting,* and *space and time/spatial and temporal continuity*.

Phillips, William H. *Writing Short Scripts*. 2nd ed. Syracuse: Syracuse UP, 1999. Includes three unproduced scripts for short films, detailed descriptions of two award-winning short films, discussion of the general characteristics of the short script and short film, and partial credits and brief descriptions for many short films.

Stam, Robert, Robert Burgoyne, and Sandy Flitterman-Lewis. "Part III Film-Narratology." *New Vocabularies in Film Semiotics: Structuralism, Post-structuralism and Beyond*. London: Routledge, 1992. 69–122. Theoretical issues about narrative for the advanced student.

CHAPTER 9

Alternatives to Live-Action Fictional Films

I N THE PREVIOUS THREE CHAPTERS we considered the fictional film, which has overwhelmingly dominated viewer and critical attention almost since the birth of motion pictures. This chapter considers four alternatives to the live-action fictional film: documentary, experimental, hybrid, and animated films.

Terms in **boldface** are defined in the Illustrated Glossary beginning on page 539.

DOCUMENTARY FILMS

Documentaries, which are more or less films about reality, are actually not considered by most people to be real films, but Hollywood films, which usually have an extremely high fantasy quotient, are considered to be real.
—Ross McElwee's narration in his documentary *Six O'Clock News* (1997)

A **documentary film** represents its subjects in ways viewers are intended to accept not primarily as the product of someone's imagination but primarily as fact. Documentary filmmakers select what subjects to film and under what conditions; sometimes they stage or re-create situations; and they nearly always edit the resultant footage. Documentary films are sometimes referred to as *nonfiction films*. I prefer the older and more widely understood term *documentary films* because *nonfiction films* identifies this group of films not by what they are but what they are not (they are not fiction) and because *nonfiction film* suggests that this type of film is the opposite of fictional films, whereas these two major film types may have much in common. Documentary filmmakers may have various goals. They "(1) communicate insights, achieve beauty, and offer understanding . . . , or (2) improve social, political, or economic conditions" (Ellis 7). Other documentarians celebrate their subjects. Examples are most of the films directed by Les Blank, perhaps especially those focusing on music or food; a documentary about a famed Italian film actor, *Marcello Mastroianni . . . I Remember* (1999); and "A Great Day in Harlem" (1994), which pays tribute to many great American jazz musicians (Figure 9.1).

FIGURE 9.1 Documentary as celebration
On one level, "A Great Day in Harlem" (1994) celebrates this famous group photograph of fifty-seven of the most esteemed American jazz musicians and singers of the late 1950s as they stand before a Harlem brownstone. On another level, the film celebrates the music, individuality, creativity, and friendships of the musicians pictured here. Like so many documentaries, "A Great Day in Harlem" includes many interviews. Musicians in the group photo (plus a few of their children) talk about other musicians in the famous photo, and the emphasis is emphatically on the positive. No jealousy, pettiness, or bitterness is heard. Above all, the film is a celebration of people, their music, and a magical moment in time when these musical legends came together at the same time and place. Frame enlargement. *Jean Bach; Castle Hill Productions*

soft light: Light that somewhat obscures surface details and creates shadows that are soft-edged.

footage: A length of exposed motion-picture film.

title card: A card or thin sheet of clear plastic on which is written or printed information included in a film.

shot: An uninterrupted strip of exposed motion-picture film or videotape that presents a subject during an uninterrupted segment of time.

Sources

Documentary films can be about any subject—for example, human behavior, including human creativity or any aspect of history, animal behavior, plant life, or any other aspect of science. A documentary film may be about any combination of subjects as long as the representation is primarily factual or informative. In creating a documentary film, filmmakers may film new material, staged or unstaged. In re-creating subjects, they may try to capture the look and sounds of the original as closely as possible, or they may choose to stylize the representation in one or more ways, for example with **soft lighting** or different colors. They may use existing **footage** exclusively or incorporate existing footage with footage they **shot.** Their film may be made up exclusively of footage they shot. As we see below, they may use all types of sources for information beyond existing footage or footage they shot: fragments of radio or TV broadcasts, still photographs, audio recordings in any of their permutations, paintings, signs, maps, and many other sources. They often add narration, interviews, or **title cards**—or a combination of two or all three. They may add sound effects or music—or both. Typically, documentary filmmakers do a lot of editing: selecting their **shots** and arranging them into some sort of unified whole. The possible sources—and combinations of them—are endless, for human creativity knows no bounds.

As with fictional films, a documentary may be a remake or a sequel. Jill Godmilow's "What Farocki Taught" (1998) is a close remake of Harun Farocki's 1969 German documentary entitled "Inextinguishable Fire," which is about Dow Chemical's development of napalm B during the Vietnam War. The remake, which is in color and in English, re-creates the original black-and-white film shot-for-shot, often superimposing shots from the original (complete with subtitles) over newly staged sections. "What Farocki Taught" challenges spectators to question conventional approaches to documentary while enabling Farocki's original film to receive the American screening it was denied on release. Normally sequels are fictional films, but a documentary film may also be one. An example is "Pets or Meat: The Return to Flint" (1993)—Michael Moore's follow-up to his **satirical** documentary *Roger & Me* (1989)—which shows what happened to some of the people featured in the earlier film and even more sharply satirizes its subjects. Another sequel to a documentary is *Best Man* (1998); this follow-up to the award-winning *Best Boy* (1979) shows how the gentle, mentally impaired subject of the earlier film is faring nearly twenty years later.

satire: A representation of human behavior that has as its aim the humorous criticism of the behavior shown.

Nonnarrative and Narrative

Most documentary films tell no narrative or story. These **nonnarrative documentaries** include most scientific films, many TV documentaries on social conditions, industrial films (which present information about a company or industry), training films, promotional films, and many TV advertisements. Most nonnarrative documentary films either present a variety of information organized into categories or make an argument.

An example of a nonnarrative documentary film is *Fast, Cheap & Out of Control* (1997), which conveys a wide variety of information and suggests many possible **meanings** by alternating between four occupations and the thoughtful and articulate men who pursue them (Figure 9.2).

meaning: An observation or general statement about a subject.

Other nonnarrative documentary films make an argument, as in the very brief "Television, the Drug of the Nation" (1992). The phrase "Television, the drug of a nation, breeding ignorance and feeding radiation" is heard repeatedly in the film. The rap **narrator** also claims that TV is the reason so few Americans read books and the reason most people think "Central America means Kansas." The narrator adds, "A child watches fifteen hundred murders [on TV] before he's twelve years old, and then we wonder why we've created a Jason generation." The film's chaotic but mesmerizing visuals suggest that TV is dizzying, fragmented, and highly manipulative yet addictive and dangerous to one's health. "Television, the Drug of the Nation" conveys information but mainly makes an argument: (commercial) TV is detrimental to American life.

narrator: A character, person, or unidentifiable voice in a film that provides commentary continuously or intermittently.

Often a nonnarrative documentary film uses editing to praise or criticize; it may **cut** from one shot to the next to criticize, as is often done in *Hearts and Minds*, a 1974 film about U.S. involvement in the Vietnam War. At one point in the film an enraged high school football coach in a locker room shouts at and hits some of his players. Boys play part of a football game, and an injured player is shown in pain. And President Johnson (whom viewers may equate with the out-of-control coach) declares that the United States will win (the war in Vietnam). The next footage shows some of the chaos and destruction of a massive surprise counterattack, which abruptly casts into doubt when and how the Vietnam War would finally end. Elsewhere the film again uses editing to suggest guilt by association. At the conclusion of the film, editing is used to criticize. A shot of countless freshly

cut: Sever or splice film while editing.

a) b) c) d)

FIGURE 9.2 A nonnarrative documentary film with multiple subjects
Fast, Cheap & Out of Control (1997) alternates between four primary subjects, four occupations and the men who pursue them: (a) making robots shaped approximately as insects, (b) studying mole-rats, (c) taming wild animals, and (d) doing topiary gardening that features plants shaped like large animals. The film presents information about its four major subjects and ideas related to each of them yet implies meanings transcending its parts. Critic Richard Corliss wrote that the film "is a funny, thrilling tribute to people's urge to find play and profundity in the work they do." Karen Jaehne has written, "In the final sequence, we witness the lion tamer retiring and passing his baton to a kinder, gentler tamer who sticks her head in the lion's mouth. Then footage from *Darkest Africa* shows the lost city collapsing, a volcano spewing, and our hero [Clyde] Beatty scrambling for his life, before we return to the brave new world of a robot on lunar terrain, as the circus elephants depart. We see a storm looming over Green Animals, and George the gardener with his shears in his hand holding an umbrella against the raging elements. This bleak conclusion reminds us of the evanescence of human existence: not much survives. Creativity is our only consolation" (46). As commentator Peter Applebome sees it, "Mr. Morris's films . . . are about . . . epistemology—the nature of knowledge: what things are and what they seem to be, how people know what they think they know, and do they really know it or just think they know it?" (c–d) Frame enlargements. *Errol Morris; Sony Pictures Classics*

dug, empty Vietnamese graves accompanied by sounds of moaning and crying is followed by shots in the United States of marching soldiers, a flag-waving spectator, marching boys in military uniform, a formation of motorcycle police, and other shots of parades and demonstrations. The suggestion (though not evidence) is that pain and suffering in a foreign country is caused by a regimented, patriotic, and militaristic American society.

A small percentage of documentary films present a narrative or story. **Narrative documentary** films are largely true narratives: a series of unified

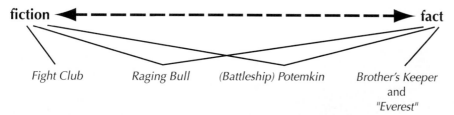

fiction ⟵ — — — — — — — — — — — — — ⟶ fact

| Fight Club | Raging Bull | (Battleship) Potemkin | Brother's Keeper and "Everest" |

FIGURE 9.3 **The narrative films continuum**
Some narrative films are completely fictional, but many blend fiction and fact. *Fight Club* (1999) is completely fictional: as we watch it, we recognize no character as being based on a famous person and no actions re-creating real occurrences. But *Raging Bull* (1980) is a fictional film that many viewers will recognize as partially factual: certain aspects of the celluloid Jake are the same as those of the real Jake La Motta, the famous boxer. Some narratives are more difficult to categorize. The Soviet classic (*Battleship*) *Potemkin* (1925) is a blend of fiction and fact, and though scholars usually categorize it as a fictional film, some consider it a narrative documentary. Even narrative documentary films are never entirely factual. For example, significant details might be omitted or the order of some events changed in editing. Narrative films that blend fiction and fact and have as their subjects recent news or history are sometimes called *docudramas*, especially if they were originally made for TV.

factual **events** in one or more settings. But as Figure 9.3 illustrates, many narratives combine fiction and fact and blend them in different proportions.

Like the fictional film, the narrative documentary often features someone with a goal or goals. In *The Farmer's Wife* (1999), a farmer and his wife work extremely hard to try to save their farm and save their marriage. In *Brother's Keeper* (1992) the main person, who has been accused of suffocating a brother suffering from ill health, wants to avoid being convicted (Figure 9.4).

event: In a narrative or story, either an *action* by a character or person or a *happening* (a change brought about by a force other than a person or character).

FIGURE 9.4 **A narrative documentary**
Seen here are three of the Ward brothers, who are featured in the narrative documentary *Brother's Keeper* (1992). As in most stories, the main person has a goal but has trouble reaching it. Delbert (on the right) wants to avoid conviction for the smothering death of one of his ill brothers, but impediments include Delbert's signed confession, damaging testimony given by another brother, and a prosecution tactic discovered before the trial. *Photo by Joe Berlinger; Courtesy of Creative Thinking International, New York City*

303

FIGURE 9.5 A secondary subject in a narrative documentary film
The problems in filming the fictional film *Fitzcarraldo* (1982) are the main subject of the narrative documentary *Burden of Dreams* (1982). One of the secondary subjects of *Burden of Dreams* is the lifestyles of the Amazon Indians, seen here, including how they bathe, wash clothes, weave, cook, and play games. *Photo by Maureen Gosling: Courtesy of Flower Films, El Cerrito, California*

Like fictional films, narrative documentaries may not present events chronologically. *The Gate of Heavenly Peace* (1995) focuses on the historical occurrences leading up to the 1989 military crackdown on student demonstrators in Tiananmen Square in China and its aftermath, but from time to time the film also includes historical background footage, some dating as far back as 1919. Viewers watching the film will have little trouble sorting through all the material and understanding it.

Narrative documentaries are never simply narratives. They also include supporting artifacts and informative language. Consider *Burden of Dreams* (1982), a film by Les Blank, which focuses on a story about what happened during the filming of the movie *Fitzcarraldo* (1982). Viewers can easily figure out the order of events in *Burden of Dreams* and see how they are connected. The scenes are even arranged chronologically, from November 1979 to November 1981. The film concentrates on the people making *Fitzcarraldo*, although occasionally the main story is interrupted for various details of life in the Amazonian jungle (such as the size, speed, and dexterity of ants) and, most of all, details about the lives of the natives of the region (Figure 9.5). The narrative is also punctuated with frequent interviews, especially with Werner Herzog, the director of *Fitzcarraldo*. Not that *Burden of Dreams* lacks unity, but like most narratives, whether fictional or documentary, it includes more than a story.

Like nonnarrative documentary films, narrative documentary films may use editing to criticize or praise a person or idea. Consider the opening of *Triumph of the Will* (1935). Leni Riefenstahl made the film to document and celebrate a huge Nazi party conference. It opens with aerial shots of clouds, church spires and the tops of other buildings, an airplane flying above a city, the shadow of the airplane speeding over the ground of the city below, and troops marching. On the ground, many shots of excited crowds alternate with the plane landing and pulling to a stop, followed by the emergence of Adolf Hitler, and Joseph Goebbels, the Nazi minister of propaganda. In the next **sequence,** shots alternate between the large and excited crowds on the sides of the streets and Hitler standing in a moving car and saluting with a

sequence: A series of related consecutive scenes, perceived as a major unit of a narrative film.

a)

b)

FIGURE 9.6 **Multiple plotlines in a narrative documentary** *Hoop Dreams* (1994) shows the stories of two inner-city young males who dream of playing in the National Basketball Association: Arthur Agee (a) and William Gates (b). The film captures parts of their lives from their days in junior high to the beginning of college. Although the two stories occasionally intersect (the two commuted to the same high school for a while, and their paths cross occasionally after one of them goes to a different school), basically this narrative documentary alternates between their two stories. *KTCA-TV & Kartemquin Films; Fine Line Features*

stiff arm. Thus in the film's opening scenes, Hitler is associated with power, speed, grace, the adoration of the masses, and perhaps even spirituality (those churches).

Narrative documentary films often have only one **plotline,** but like fictional films they may have two or more. *Hoop Dreams* (1994) has two plotlines, each about an inner-city youth who hopes to play in the National Basketball Association (Figure 9.6). "The Heck with Hollywood!" (1991) alternates the narratives of three groups of filmmakers trying to market their films outside the Hollywood network: a young man, a young woman, and three young men. Most of *Pumping Iron* (1976) consists of five plotlines: the background and training of two bodybuilders, then their competition for the

plotline: A narrative or series of related events usually involving only a few characters or people and capable of functioning on its own as a story.

a)

b)

FIGURE 9.7 **Narrative or nonnarrative documentary**
Nanook of the North (1922), a famous early documentary film, reveals important aspects of Inuit life, especially getting food and surviving a harsh environment. Through the film's various parts, viewers learn how Nanook, a Canadian Inuit, and his family could live: for example, by using a kayak, trading, spearing fish (a), hunting walrus, traveling, building an igloo, hunting seal, and preparing for a storm. The film's emphasis seems to be as much on presenting different types of information as in telling a story. (b) Director Robert Flaherty took many liberties with his subjects, including asking them to restage or modify their behavior or the world they live in. For example, Flaherty found that the igloos were too small and too dim for him to fit in his bulky 35 mm camera and tripod and to provide enough light to film, so he had the Inuits build a larger igloo without a top. (a) Frame enlargement. *Revillon Frères; The Museum of Modern Art/Circulating Film Library*

1975 Mr. Universe title, followed by the background, training, and competition of three men, including Arnold Schwarzenegger, for the 1975 Mr. Olympia title.

Occasionally it is difficult to categorize a documentary film as nonnarrative or narrative, as is the case with one of the first feature-length documentaries, *Nanook of the North* (1922, restored 1976; Figure 9.7a). There is little clear-cut unity to the film's sections (many could be switched without consequences for viewers), yet the Inuits' lives are presented more or less chronologically (from a summer to a winter). Although the film's skimpy story is loosely **structured** and the film presents information as much as it shows a story, many critics identify *Nanook* as a narrative.

Other Characteristics of Documentary Films

Whether narrative or not, a documentary film has most or all of the following characteristics: mediated reality, real people instead of actors, **location** shooting, artifacts and informative language, and use of a wide range of **techniques.**

structure: The selection and arrangement of the parts of a whole.

location: Any place other than a film studio that is used for filming.

technique: Any aspect of filmmaking, such as the choice of sets, lighting, sound effects, music, and editing.

MEDIATED REALITY

Documentary films are mediated reality: they are a selected, perhaps staged, and edited presentation of their subjects. A documentary film may *seem* to present reality objectively, but it cannot. Consider Frederick Wiseman's *Belfast, Maine* (1999), which has a **running time** of slightly over four hours and shows different aspects of life in and near the seacoast town of Belfast, Maine (such as a social worker picking lice out of a woman's hair and a high school English teacher lecturing on *Moby Dick*). The film has no narration, no interviews, no title cards, no music that does not derive from a source shown in the film. The opening title card does not cue viewers about the film to come. In plain lettering, it simply announces the title: Belfast, Maine.

At first glance, the filmmakers seem to have only selected the subjects, filmed them, then selected what footage to include. However, in constructing the film, the filmmakers made many significant decisions that influence the outcome of the film and how viewers respond to the film. For example, the filmmakers selected which subjects to film and which to ignore. They selected the time of year in which to film (autumn) and often the time of day (many shots were filmed in the morning hours or in the late afternoon, when the outdoors are bathed in flattering soft lighting). They decided how many shots would be of locations without people and which shots would be of rundown or even polluted areas and which would not. For each shot, they decided camera location, distance from subject, and lens. They decided how long to hold a shot, when to use a zoom lens (only very rarely in this film), when to move the camera during a shot (also rarely).

Later, the filmmakers decided which shots to include and their duration, the order of shots, and the transitions between them (one black screen of a few seconds, otherwise only **cuts**). During fourteen months of editing, 110 hours of footage was fashioned into a four-hour film. Probably during editing, whole sections that had been filmed were dropped. Often a section begins with one or two establishing shots, frequently including a building's identifying sign; sometimes an identifying sign is seen in a section's concluding shot. During the editing, decisions were also made about where to include reaction shots and how often, as during a lawyer's presentation to the Belfast city council. The filmmakers decided the order and duration of each major section and the **pacing** of the parts and of the whole film. In addition, they decided what sounds would be prominent (the many sounds of motorized vehicles, for example, remind viewers that even in this small town and surrounding area, motorized vehicles are an integral part of life.) The filmmakers also decided to occasionally use sound from a source before we viewers see the source and to carry over a sound from one location into the following one. Thus, even documentary films that might seem simply presentations of reality are actually complicated mediations of reality. They are not objective, indisputable truth. Rather, they are one group's selection, recording, manipulation, and presentation.

running time: The time that elapses when a film is projected.

cut: The most common transition between shots, made by splicing or joining the end of one shot to the beginning of the following shot.

pace: A viewer's sense of a subject (such as narrative developments or factual information) being presented rapidly or slowly.

Another example of the selectivity involved in making a documentary can be seen in *Marcello Mastroianni . . . I Remember.* The film focuses on the Italian actor's stage and film acting, a wide variety of his films, his travels and thoughts about various cities, and his work with different directors. Mastroianni himself supplies all the narration. The film includes no interviews with family, friends, or filmmaking colleagues, and there is little information about his adult personality. Unaddressed are such questions as was Mastroianni difficult to work with? Was he aloof in his personal life? Was he as modest and charming **offscreen** as in interviews and in his narration of the documentary? What was his identity when he was not making a movie? Was he ever married? Who was the mother of his daughter? Was he close to his daughter? The director and editor of the film, Mastroianni's companion of more than two decades, decided to focus on his films and filmmaking and largely avoid his personal life and any perspective other than his and hers.

Other documentarians make changes in a film's subject before filming it (Figure 9.7b). A similar situation arose in the filming of *Crumb* (1994). An interviewer on the Sundance Channel observed that a large wall cabinet full of 78 rpm records in director Terry Zwigoff's house looked a lot like Crumb's record cabinet in the film. Zwigoff responded, "We actually shot fake scenes in this room where he's [Crumb's] sitting here with, like, a drawing board and we moved this lamp that used to be in his house over here and this [indicating Zwigoff's record cabinet] is the background. We faked it for his house because we didn't want to drive back up there." Near the beginning of cinema, in "The Execution of Mary, Queen of Scots" (1895), the filmmakers substituted a dummy for the person enacting Queen Mary immediately before the beheading. Since then, countless documentary filmmakers have staged actions or re-created them or in other ways changed details about the way things were. Like fiction makers, for various reasons—including to save time and money or to show something judged important in an engaging way—documentary makers sometimes fudge the details.

Some filmmakers change the order of presentation through editing. A title card at the beginning of *Dead Birds* (1963), a film about the lifestyles of similar warring New Guinea tribes, states that the film

> is a true story composed from footage of actual events photographed. . . . No scene was directed and no role was created. The people in the film merely did what they had done before we came and, for those who are not dead, as they do now that we have left.

Yet the director Robert Gardner later wrote that the film has "compressions of time which exclude vast portions of actuality. There are events made parallel in time which occurred sequentially" (346–47).

offscreen: The area beyond the frame line, here meaning in life outside the movies.

REAL PEOPLE

When the subject is human behavior, the documentary film nearly always uses ordinary people, not actors. For example, *Hoop Dreams* features two real youths and their families. Only rarely do documentaries use actors. Charlie Sheen plays a judge in Emile De Antonio's *In the King of Prussia* (1983); actors reenact some minor roles in *The Thin Blue Line* (1988); and actors play all the roles in the many re-created scenes of *Thirty-Two Short Films about Glenn Gould* (1993).

LOCATION SHOOTING

Documentary films are usually filmed on location. Location shooting became common with the development of lighter and more mobile cameras and sound recording equipment in the late 1950s. Recent years have seen the development of digital equipment that is even more versatile and produces even better quality, and many documentaries are now shot on location with a lightweight digital video camera. More than ever it is possible for one or two people to go practically anywhere and film and record sound unobtrusively. Later if the opportunity for a theatrical release arises, the video can be transferred to 35 mm film, as was done for *Buena Vista Social Club* (1999), *The Original Kings of Comedy* (2000), and *Startup.com* (2001).

Occasionally documentary films are not filmed entirely on location. Les Blank told me that his "Gap-Toothed Women" (1987) was shot largely within his own studio instead of in the homes or workplaces of his subjects. Other exceptions: Errol Morris shot parts of *The Thin Blue Line* in New York City, not Texas, and he filmed the interviews for *A Brief History of Time* (1992) and *Fast, Cheap & Out of Control* in a studio.

ARTIFACTS AND INFORMATIVE LANGUAGE

Artifacts used in documentaries include photographs, objects a person has made or owned, newsreels or clips from movies, home movies, or TV shows. Sometimes only one type of artifact or a few types of artifacts are used in a documentary film. *The Atomic Café* (1982)—which is about the arrival of nuclear weapons and some of the subsequent U.S. government's responses—consists entirely of excerpts from commercial and government media. *Point of Order* (1963), by Emile De Antonio, is a ninety-seven-minute **compilation film** made mostly from 188 hours of TV footage of the 1954 Army-McCarthy hearings.

compilation film: A film made by editing together clips from other films.

Often a documentary film includes informative language: narration (or title cards or subtitles), interviews, signs, even headstones, or a combination of sources (Figure 9.8). The words of songs may also function as narration or commentary on the film's subjects, as they do throughout Les Blank's "Chulas Fronteras" (1976), a film about Chicano experiences and the centrality of

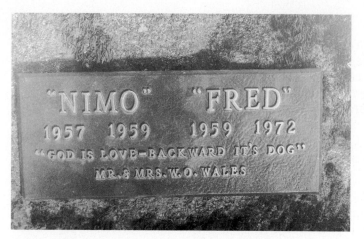

FIGURE 9.8 Informative language in a documentary film
Informative language used in documentary films may appear in various forms.
Here it is used in a pet cemetery on a headstone honoring departed dogs in
Errol Morris's first documentary film, *Gates of Heaven* (1978). *Errol Morris;
New Yorker Films*

FIGURE 9.9 Artifacts and language in a documentary film
"The Match That Started My Fire" (1991) by Cathy Cook includes supporting artifacts (including existing film clips) and informative language (off-
camera accounts by women). In the shot represented here, artifact is combined
with information language: a woman twirls around and around as a woman's
voice recounts how as a girl she would sometimes wear a certain type of skirt
to school and spin around and around for her pleasure and the boys'. *Photo by
Cathy Cook, dancer: Heidi Heistad; Women Make Movies, New York; Film-makers'
Cooperative, New York*

music in Chicano lives. Until the early
1960s, documentary films relied heavily
on all-knowing narrators, in part because
the equipment then available made it cumbersome to film and to record synchro-
nous sound on location. In the newsreels
shown in movie theaters until the early
1960s, an authoritative-sounding narrator
was used. Most recent documentary films
use interviews more often than narration
or use interviews alone, in part because of
the availability of more portable filmmaking equipment and in part because of the
widespread belief that no one person or
narrator can do justice to a subject's complexity. Some films, such as those directed
by Frederick Wiseman, use neither narration nor interviews. And a few—such as
*The Wonderful, Horrible Life of Leni Riefen-
stahl* (1993) and the *Up* series of documentaries, such as *42 Up* (1999)—use both.

Artifacts and informative language help
persuade viewers of the truthfulness of a
film's presentation. They may be incorporated into a film in countless creative ways.
In the third part of Ken Burns's *Baseball*
(1994), we see a photograph of the exterior
of a building, presumably where a grand
jury is meeting, then a photograph of a
man's face looking toward the camera. As
we see these photographs, we hear a gavel
banging, the usual sounds of people inside a
room, and voices of two actors reenacting a
prosecutor posing questions about the
throwing of the 1919 World Series and
Chicago White Sox player "Shoeless" Joe
Jackson responding to them. After the offscreen re-created testimony has finished,
we are allowed about four seconds to continue to scrutinize the photograph of Joe
Jackson in silence. Other documentaries
that include artifacts and informative language are represented in Figures 9.9 and
9.10.

FIGURE 9.10 **Multiple sources in a documentary film**
Carmen Miranda: Bananas Is My Business (1994) is a film directed by one Brazilian woman about one of her compatriots, Carmen Miranda, who was first a popular singer and movie star in Brazil and later a star in American musical movies and TV. The film shows Miranda initially closely identified with her Brazilian roots but eventually alienated from them by her transforming experiences with American media, which presented her progressively as exotic, stereotypical, and a self-parody and a subject of parody by others. She was torn between two different cultures; demoralized by depression, drugs, and an abusive marriage; and dead by 1955 at age forty-six.

To convey a broad range of information and perspectives, the film uses a wide range of sources. Artifacts shown include a Carmen Miranda paper doll, a Miranda puppet, small Miranda models, a self-portrait painting, many photos, and calendar pages for different days rapidly floating toward and past the camera. Other artifacts used to convey information and perspectives include reenactments of Miranda's death by a heart attack and of one of the documentary director's dreams, clips from movies including Miranda, clips that parody her, an excerpt from a trailer, home movies, and clips from a travelogue about Brazil, newsreels, and TV shows. Informative language used includes newspaper headlines, program notes, Miranda's handwriting, narration (by the director and others), interviews, an excerpt from a song, and a fragment of a radio broadcast to the people of Brazil. Amassing so many sources and such a wide range of them and editing the film were massive endeavors. *Helena Solberg and David Meyer; Women Make Movies, New York*

WIDE RANGE OF TECHNIQUES

As with fictional filmmaking and experimental filmmaking, technology influences techniques used in documentary filmmaking and the results achieved. Since the late 1990s, documentarians' much wider use of digital video has made possible fewer interruptions while filming and much longer **takes.** Some documentary filmmakers believe that fewer interruptions make it easier to win their subjects' trust and more often capture the essence of a situation because they no longer have to interrupt filming every ten minutes. In the late 1950s and early 1960s, development of 16 mm **fast film,** handheld 16 mm cameras with a **zoom lens,** and portable sound packs gave filmmakers much greater mobility and flexibility (Figure 9.11). In the United States, filmmakers using portable equipment developed **direct cinema,** a type of documentary filmmaking in which the film is shot on location with minimal planning. The aim of such films is not so much to prove a point but

take: A version of a shot.

fast film (stock): Film stock that requires relatively little light for capturing images.

zoom lens: A camera lens with variable focal lengths; thus it can be adjusted by degrees during a shot so that the size of the subject and the area being filmed change.

FIGURE 9.11 The portability of direct cinema equipment
To film the onstage and offstage action of a three-day outdoor concert attended by an estimated 400,000 people, one or two cameras would have been inadequate. Fortunately, by the time of the Woodstock concert in 1969, documentary filmmakers could use portable 16 mm cameras and lightweight, largely unobtrusive magnetic tape recorders. In this photograph can be seen two of the many cameras (left and extreme left) used in making the documentary *Woodstock* (1970). Some of the cameras were propped on the stage itself; some were mounted on tripods; some were handheld. *A Wadleigh-Maurice, Ltd. Production; Warner Bros.*

to explore a subject. An exchange between an interviewer for the film journal *Cineaste* and the filmmaker Frederick Wiseman, who is one of the main practitioners of direct cinema, highlights that purpose:

> CINEASTE: And your film [*Welfare*, 1975] doesn't generalize, at all. Nor does it attempt to suggest any possible solutions or answers. That stance characterizes all of your films.
> WISEMAN: That's right. I don't know the answers. I'm interested in the complexities and ambiguities of our experience. (Lucia 9)

Makers of direct cinema attempt to win their subjects' trust and to minimize interference with their lives; consequently, they often use the **long take** and the zoom lens so they may film their subjects from afar or close up without the camera distracting them. At about the same time as direct cinema emerged and using the same type of equipment, a similar type of documen-

long take: A shot of long duration. Not to be confused with **long shot.**

tary filmmaking, **cinéma-vérité,** developed in France, although during filming, French filmmakers were likely to ask questions of their subjects and talk with them, as in the later cinéma-vérité film *Divorce Iranian Style* (Figure 9.12).

Two examples of direct cinema are Wiseman's *Titicut Follies* (1967), which shows some of the activities of the inmates, staff, and volunteers at a Massachusetts mental hospital, and Michael Wadleigh's *Woodstock* (1970), which shows action on- and offstage at a huge open-air concert in upstate New York. These and other films of direct cinema often have technical imperfections: the camera operator sometimes does not refocus on a new subject as quickly as film viewers are used to seeing. The camera work might occasionally be wobbly; the dialogue might be indistinct; and at times the film might be too dark or too light. To some viewers these imperfections only strengthen the film's credibility. Viewers can imagine that the film is not a slick, manipulated presentation—as, for example, *Triumph of the Will* is—but more nearly a presentation of actions as they hap-

FIGURE 9.12 Documentarians as observers and participants
Although *Divorce Iranian Style* (1998) is mostly cinéma-vérité, occasional narration is used to fill gaps in the information that viewers need to follow the situations, including occasional questions from the filmmakers to their subjects. Late in the documentary, the filmmakers are unwittingly and briefly transformed from observers and recorders to participants when the divorce court judge turns to the filmmakers and asks if they saw the woman depicted here tear the judge's court order as her husband alleged. After the filmmakers reply that they did not, the judge rescinds his order that the woman be held in detention for a day, although she is still under order to turn over custody of her child, shown here, to her previous husband. *Kim Longinotto and Ziba Mir-Hosseini; Women Make Movies, New York.*

pened. Nonetheless, as we saw with *Belfast, Maine,* direct cinema entails its own, perhaps less obvious, manipulations. For instance, the camera operator chooses what to film and how to film it, and the editor chooses what shots to include and in what context.

At the other extreme, some documentary films look and sound as polished and professionally made as fictional films with a large budget. In *Brother's Keeper* it's not as if the filmmakers simply recorded one scene after another, cut some dead time, and presented the results. Far from it, as a look at the excerpt in Table 9.1 shows. In scene 1, the man says in effect that Delbert probably put his brother out of his misery as one would a sick cat. In the next scene, viewers see a Ward brother, then a dead cat: the second scene hints at the validity of the point expressed in the first. **Parallel editing** is used to contrast the state police's picture of Delbert with the one viewers see. In scenes 2, 4, 7, and 10, offscreen sound is used, the second and third times

parallel editing: Editing that alternates between two or more subjects, often suggesting that different events or occurrences are related to each other or are occurring simultaneously.

TABLE 9.1

Ten Consecutive Scenes from *Brother's Keeper*

SCENE NUMBER	LENGTH IN SECONDS	DESCRIPTION
1	28	A man in a truck says he now thinks Delbert probably did murder his brother Bill to put him out of his misery, "like you would a sick cat or something like that."
2	12	Voice of man from previous scene continues as he says of the four Ward brothers, "They've been damn good boys" and we see one of Delbert's brothers lying on the ground. Then we see a cat sniffing a dead cat.
3	24	An official (a subtitle earlier identified him as Captain Loszynski of the New York State Police) justifies the use of question and answer in interrogation.
4	7	Long shot of man unloading bales of hay from a conveyor belt as we hear a voice asking the beginning of a question: "Were you befuddled in any way on the 6th of June. . . ."
5	7	Close-up of Delbert. The off-frame voice finishes the question begun in scene 4, and Delbert answers no. In response to a follow-up question Delbert admits he doesn't know what *befuddled* means.
6	17	Another official (a subtitle earlier identified him as Investigator Cosnett) explains that Delbert understood his rights (when he was brought in for questioning).
7	4	Long shot of the man shown in scene 4 now covering bales of hay with a tarp as voice is heard asking a question.
8	17	Delbert answers the question from the previous scene. On request, he demonstrates on the man beside him (much earlier in the film identified in a subtitle as Harry Thurston/Friend) how officials said Delbert suffocated his brother.
9	20	Another official (identified in a subtitle as Investigator Killough) says Delbert has changed his story and that on the night of his interrogation Delbert put his hand over his own mouth to demonstrate "how he did it."
10	65	Shots of foggy farmland and Delbert as we hear the voice of Delbert and presumably the voice of the prosecutor asking whether Delbert understood what he was signing (his confession) and if he had been forced to sign it. Throughout this scene, music is heard, except just before the end when it quickly fades out.

fast cutting: Editing characterized by many brief shots.

swish pan: Blurred images that result from pivoting a movie camera horizontally too rapidly during filming.

from a questioner in the following scene. In the tenth scene, music adds to the mood, as do the many shots of farm life. Throughout the film the cinematography and editing are as accomplished as in many features.

Other documentary films demonstrate yet other techniques. *Unzipped* (1995) includes frequent wobbly handheld shots plus **fast cutting, swish pans,** and even **fast motion**—all of which contribute to an out-of-control, dizzying effect. *The Thin Blue Line* uses some extremely **high-angle** shots; **slow motion;** lighting and color that are dramatic rather than strictly functional (note the warm-colored light on and behind the prisoner being interviewed in prison); and imaginary and repeated re-creations filmed years after the actions depicted (Figure 9.13). The film also uses parallel editing; unexpected **cutaway shots;** movie clips, some only obliquely related to the subject at hand; and a striking score by Philip Glass. As Errol Morris, the director of *The Thin Blue Line*, acknowledged, his film **style** is the polar opposite of Frederick Wiseman's (Bates 17). Yet both styles strike audiences as credible.

The first and last moving images of Harvey Milk in *The Times of Harvey Milk* (1984) are in slow motion. In both cases, viewers see a man who was charismatic and full of energy rendered as graceful yet drained of his natural vitality. Allie Light's *Dialogues with Madwomen* (1994), which is about the experiences and perspectives of seven northern California women who have suffered from mental illness, consists largely of alternating interviews with the women. During each interview, we see brief clips related to what the speaker is describing. Sometimes these cutaway shots reenact what is being described, for example—children rummaging through trashcans in search of food. Such cutaways are sometimes redundant and too literal to evoke emotional truth. More often, however, the cutaways are **symbolic** and evocative. For example, at one point as we hear a woman explaining what a tyrant her father was, we see a man in a nondescript **setting** gesturing as if directing traffic and walking forward in slow motion. This cutaway is made even more unsettling because it is the **negative** of a black-and-white shot and the man's face looks light, indistinct, and inscrutable. (For an example of a negative image, see Figure 9.14a.)

Finally, like fictional and experimental films, documentary films may be **self-reflexive.** Brief sections of Ross McElwee's *Time Indefinite* (1993) include a darkened screen or the tail **leader** (after the reel of film in the camera had run out) or occasional humorous, deliberately wobbly handheld shots. One of the earliest and most famous (experimental) documentaries is re-

cutaway (shot): A shot that briefly interrupts the visual presentation of a subject to show something else.

negative: Excluding reversal film, film that has been exposed and processed.

self-reflexive: Characteristic of a text, such as a novel or film, to refer to or comment on itself or its medium.

FIGURE 9.13
Re-created scene in *The Thin Blue Line* (1988)
Here and elsewhere, the film uses re-creations to show different people's versions of the same event, the killing of a Dallas police officer. As director Errol Morris pointed out in a TV interview, it is up to viewers to decide which version of the murder is most probable. *BFI; Third Floor; American Playhouse*

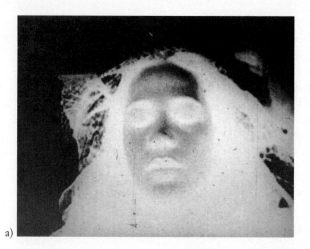
a)

b)

FIGURE 9.14 **A negative image and a positive image of it**
Only the concluding shots of Maya Deren's "Ritual in Transfigured Time" (1946) are negative images. (a) This frame is from the film's last shot and is of a woman as she sinks deeper and deeper into some water and presumably is dying. (b) This image, which does not appear in the finished film, is a positive print of the same negative. Frame enlargements. *Maya Deren; The Museum of Modern Art/Circulating Film Library*

plete with self-reflexive details, Dziga Vertov's *Man with a Movie Camera* (1929). The film includes many shots showing the major components of the film medium, both filmmaking and film exhibition (Figure 9.15).

Studying documentary films reveals that many share characteristics with fictional films. Often both are selectively filmed and edited versions of human behavior. Like fictional filmmakers, documentarians have countless options and enormous influence over the films they create. All documentary films purport to be factual. If their makers are scrupulous about details, well

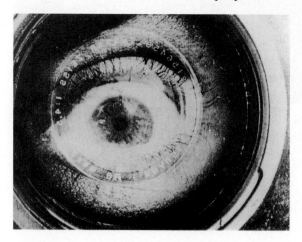

FIGURE 9.15 **Self-reflexiveness in a documentary**
This frame from the last shot of the famous experimental documentary *Man with a Movie Camera* (made in the Soviet Union in 1929) shows a camera lens, presumably the lens used to film *Man with a Movie Camera*. Here and throughout the film, viewers see various aspects of film-making and film exhibition: cameras, tripods, camera operator, lenses, editing table and editor, theater, audiences, projector, and a film being projected. To a degree perhaps unprecedented in documentary film, *Man with a Movie Camera* is self-reflexive. Frame enlargement. *VUFKU; Kino International; The Museum of Modern Art/Circulating Film Library*

informed, and fair-minded (for example, the film clips and interviews are representative of different viewpoints and are not taken out of context), viewers tend to trust them. Unless viewers lose faith in the credibility of the filmmakers or know of contradictory information from other sources, they accept such films as true or as a credible interpretation.

An original extensive interview with documentary filmmaker Errol Morris can be found on the Web site for this book: <http://www.bedfordstmartins .com/phillips-film>.

EXPERIMENTAL FILMS

> The experience [of studying experimental films] provides us with the opportunity (an opportunity much of our training has taught us to resist) to come to a clearer, more complete understanding of what the cinematic experience actually can be, and what—for all the pleasure and inspiration it may give us—the conventional movie experience is *not*. (MacDonald 2)

Scott MacDonald is a scholar of the experimental film; he and other scholars believe, as I do, that studying experimental films deepens one's understanding of the film medium. Indeed, as experimental filmmaker and theorist Edward Small demonstrates in his book *Direct Theory: Experimental Film/Video as Major Genre*, some experimental films are correctives to the generalizations of film theorists who focus exclusively on the fictional film.

The enormous variety of films often labeled *experimental* makes it difficult to define them. Films I consider as *experimental* have been referred to as *avant-garde, underground, personal,* or *independent*. All five terms reveal something of the nature of such films, while also hinting at the inadequacy of any one term. Whenever you encounter *experimental films* in this book, think of films that explore the possibilities of the film medium, may have been ahead of their times, and are out of the mainstream, heavy on self-expression, and largely free of the limitations placed on commercial movies.

Experimental Films versus Movies

Before we examine the experimental film in some detail, let's contrast experimental films with conventional movies. **Experimental films** explore the film medium—for example, the filmmakers may scratch or paint the film itself— and reject the **conventions** of mainstream films. Often a major impulse of experimental filmmakers is to rebel against what movies are and what they stand for. Experimental filmmaker, teacher, and author Stan Brakhage argues:

convention: In films and other texts, a frequently used technique or content that audiences accept as natural or typical.

> Everything we have been taught about art and the world itself separates us from a profound, true vision of the world. We are straitjacketed by myriad conventions

classical Hollywood cinema:
Films that show one or more distinct characters facing a succession of problems while trying to reach their goal or goals; these films tend to hide the manner of their making.

surrealism: A movement in 1920s and 1930s European art, drama, literature, and film in which an attempt was made to portray or interpret the workings of the subconscious mind as manifested in dreams.

that prevent us from really seeing our world. So it is with the filmmakers: the so-called rules of good filmmaking that are so carefully followed by commercial filmmakers prevent them from expressing all but the most trite reformulations of the same boy-meets-girl story. (Peterson 4)

Movies reflect or imply the dominant, usually unexamined fundamental beliefs of a society, its **ideology**—for example, its belief that hard work results in success and that one individual can make a difference in the outcome of major developments. Experimental films, however, tend to question the dominant ideology, including a society's political assumptions and sexual mores. Various experimental films of the 1960s—such as Kenneth Anger's "Scorpio Rising" (1963), "Blow Job" (1963), Barbara Rubin's "Christmas on Earth" (1963), Andy Warhol's "Couch" (made in 1964 but unreleased), and Carolee Schneemann's "Fuses" (1964–67)—represent sexuality explicitly (Figure 9.16). Since the sixties, even more experimental films deal openly with sexuality. Autobiographical films or visual diaries—by Carolee Schneemann, George Kuchar, Robert Huot, Stan Brakhage, and others—show what we never see in mainstream films: the everyday and the intimate. In separate films, George Kuchar and Robert Huot, for example, have shown themselves masturbating.

Experimental films contrast with movies in other ways. Experimental films are typically made by one person or a few people; commercial movies are the products of large groups of specialists. Experimental films can be made on a low budget with inexpensive equipment, such as super-8 film cameras or video cameras; commercial movies typically require large budgets and are often made with the latest equipment.

Experimental films deliberately frustrate expectations of viewers brought up on **classical Hollywood cinema.** They do not aim to please audiences in the usual ways and often aim to startle, if not shock. Characteristic of the experimental film is "Un chien andalou" (1928). In its dreamlike association of scenes, the film avoids the coherence of narrative (Figure 9.17). "Un chien andalou" runs only seventeen minutes and is the work mainly of two people, Luis Buñuel and cowriter (and artist) Salvador Dali. Buñuel later wrote, "This film has no intention of attracting nor pleasing the spectator; indeed, on the contrary, it attacks him, to the degree that he belongs to a society with which **surrealism** is at war" (30).

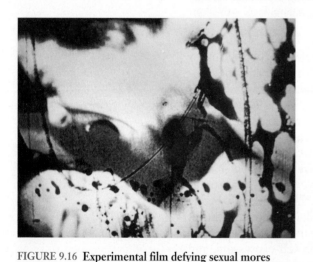

FIGURE 9.16 Experimental film defying sexual mores "Fuses" (1964–1967) shows filmmaker Carolee Schneemann and her lover enjoying each other sexually in ways unimaginable in commercial American movies before 1968. As film scholar Wheeler Winston Dixon has written, "this film . . . celebrates the beauty of the female and male body without shame or censorship, with a freedom at once casual and (to some viewers) terrifying" (141). In this frame, as elsewhere, the film uses techniques that momentarily obscure the brief but explicit views of lovemaking: markings from having been baked, deliberate scratches, out-of-focus shots, superimpositions, unexpected camera angles, fast cutting, and darkness and ambiguity. Frame enlargement. *Anthology Film Archives*

a)

b)

FIGURE 9.17 **Lack of continuity in an experimental film**
In "Un chien andalou" (1928), directed by Luis Buñuel, two frames from consecutive shots illustrate that the film often lacks the usual continuity of movies. (a) A character is about to throw something out an open window at night. (b) In the next shot viewers see what he threw in the previous shot falling toward the ground, but now it is day. Throughout, the film rejects narrative conventions and surprises or shocks viewers. Frame enlargements. *Luis Buñuel; The Museum of Modern Art/Circulating Film Library*

Sources and Subjects

Experimental filmmakers usually work independently of the usual sources for financing and distributing films. In the United States they are largely unrestricted by censorship or a ratings system and tend to be free of outside pressures on the shape and content of their finished films, especially if they make their films for showing on the Web. Experimental filmmakers are, of course, influenced by films they have seen and inevitably imitate them, reject them, use parts of an existing film, or even rework whole films.

Frequently experimental filmmakers use the most recent advances in filmmaking, or they apply advances in other forms of human expression to experimental films. For example, once **anamorphic lenses** were developed, some experimental filmmakers explored their use. As computer graphics emerged and evolved, experimental filmmakers explored their uses. Once video became less cumbersome and less costly (and **film stock** and developing film became more expensive), many artists and experimental filmmakers rushed to experiment with video's creative possibilities.

Other experimental filmmakers take a variety of footage—TV ads and old movie footage, for example—and reedit it to create compilation films that surprise, entertain, and often "take a critical stance toward the culture that supplies their imagery" (Peterson 11). Bruce Conner's first film, a

anamorphic lens: A lens that squeezes a wide image onto a film frame in the camera, making everything look tall and thin. On a projector, an anamorphic lens expands the image, returning it to its original wide shape.

film stock: Unexposed and unprocessed motion-picture film.

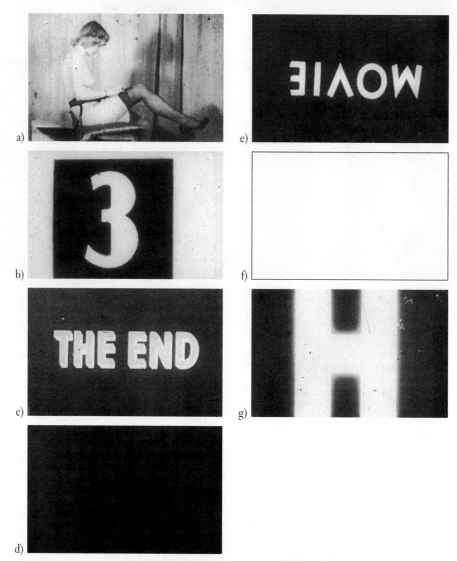

FIGURE 9.18 Sixteen shots from an experimental compilation film

Early in Bruce Conner's "A Movie" (1958) occur the following seven brief consecutive shots:
(a) A woman taking off a nylon stocking. (b) A frame from a section of academy leader, the numbered piece of opaque film that normally appears at the beginning of a reel to protect the film from damage and to help the projectionist know when the film is about to begin but used here by Conner after his film is under way. (c) The first but not last time the title card "The End" appears. (d) Some black frames. (e) Part of the film's title but here upside down. (f) One of four clear frames, which when projected results in a split second of bright white light. (g) An "H," which will be followed by "E," "A," and "D," letters that are also included in academy leaders.

The film announces that it will differ from classical Hollywood movies in many fundamental ways. No story is begun, let alone developed. In fact, it is difficult to see how the shots are related. Some of the apparatus of cinema—especially the academy leader—is shown rather than hidden from viewers as it normally is. Some images are inverted. Parts of the film are blank, either black or white. And parts of the film are placed out of order: for example, "The End" title card appears early in the film, though it does not appear at the conclusion.

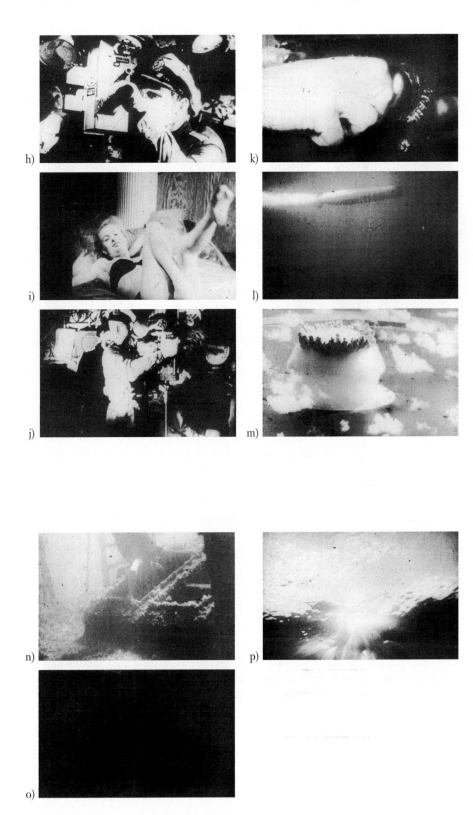

h)

i)

j)

k)

l)

m)

n)

o)

p)

Later in "A Movie" occur the following six shots (h–m): a submarine officer looking into periscope, a woman dressed in a bikini posing for the camera, the officer giving an order, a hand pushing a mechanism forward, a torpedo being fired from a submarine, and a nuclear explosion. Here the editing creates sexually playful or ominous results: the suggestion that the submarine's phallic-shaped projectile fired at the sexy woman results in a nuclear explosion.

The film ends with the following three shots (n–p): a scuba diver descends into an opening in a sunken ship, some black frames, and the surface of the water seen from below with shimmering sunlight on the surface. During these concluding shots, the music swells to a clear-cut conclusion, though the corresponding visuals convey no sense of unity or completion. There is not even a "The End" title card.

As these frame enlargements illustrate, "A Movie" lacks the usual continuity of "movies" and conveys no narrative. In fact, except for its violence and sex, occasional shots of exotic locales (East Asia and Africa), fast cutting, and jaunty music, "A Movie" has little in common with the usual entertaining feature films commonly referred to as "movies." The title of Conner's film is tinged with irony. Frame enlargements. *Bruce Conner; Anthology Film Archives*

FIGURE 9.19 Excerpts from existing films to create a new film In "Meeting Two Queens," shots from the movies of Greta Garbo (left) and shots from the movies of Marlene Dietrich (right) are combined to suggest that the two stars interact and eventually become lovers. The film is organized into a dozen or so silent-film style vignettes (a few include music), and each is preceded by a title card indicating the location or situation. Sample vignette titles are "The library," "The telephone," "The dialogue" (in which film superimpositions and split screens make it appear that the two actors interact with each other in the same frame), and "The alcove" (in which the editing makes it appear that the two stars face each other and begin to undress). Frame enlargement. *Cecilia Barriga; Women Make Movies, New York*

frame: A separate, individual photograph on a strip of motion-picture film.

mise en scène: An image's setting, subject (usually people or characters), and composition (the arrangement of setting and subjects within the frame).

twelve-minute work entitled "A Movie" (1958), includes disparate footage from "cowboy and Indian" and submarine adventure movies, newsreels, documentaries, so-called girlie movies (which feature nude or scantily dressed young women posing for the camera), various types of leader including black leader, and title cards (Figure 9.18). "A Movie" is the antithesis of classical Hollywood cinema. It "is a series of middles and connections, a film without a beginning, with titles and credits broken up and interspersed in the middle; rather than an ending, there is a respite—the film runs down, exhausted" (Mellencamp 192). In its incorporation of leader and its untraditional placement of title cards, "A Movie" is self-reflexive. And it continuously thwarts audience expectations. It includes "The End" title card early in the film and more than once but not at the end of the film; the opening title cards are repeated at various points in the film; and it uses rousing music to accompany many images of accidents and disasters (auto, motorcycle, and plane crashes; sinking ships; the dirigible *Hindenburg* on fire; the mushroom cloud of an atomic blast; falling bridges; and the like).

Another example of experimental filmmakers fashioning excerpts from films into a film with new situations and new meanings is Chilean video artist Cecilia Barriga's "Meeting Two Queens" (a.k.a. "Meeting of Two Queens," 1991, Figure 9.19).

Experimental filmmakers may take not only snippets from various existing films but also whole films, especially films no longer protected by copyright law, and fashion them into their own film. In "Keaton's Cops" (1991), Ken Jacobs shows only the bottom fourth or fifth of each **frame** of Buster Keaton's classic silent film "Cops" (1922). In Jacobs's version we can see a subject in its entirety only rarely—for example, when Keaton falls down. Throughout the film, viewers see many feet (and horses' hooves) but not facial expressions. Nevertheless, if one has seen Keaton's "Cops," even years earlier, one may follow the story in Jacobs's version fairly well; such is the expressiveness of **mise en scène** and movement that only a partial view evokes much of what happens in the whole of the film. A viewer who has never seen "Cops" might be more available to Jacobs's aim:

My intention is to interfere with narrative coherence and sense. To deny it, so as to release the mind for a while from story and the structuring of incident (compelling as it is in Keaton's masterly development). My filming, only showing the bottom fifth of Keaton's black-and-white screen-world, limits us to the periphery of story. Moves us, from the easy reading of an illustrated text, towards active seeing. Reduced information means we now must struggle to identify objects and places and, in particular, spaces. A broad tonal area remains flat, clings to the screen, until impacted upon by a recognizable object: Keaton smashes into it, and so it's a wall, diagonal to the screen . . . or a foot steps on it or a wheel rolls across it and it's a road! We become conscious of a painterly screen alive with many shapes in many tones, at the same time that we notice objects and activities (Keaton sets his comedy in some actual street traffic) normally kept from mind by the moviestar-centered moviestory.

Experimental filmmakers may use entire films in many other creative ways. For "Intolerance (Abridged)" (1971), Stan Lawder took D. W. Griffith's *Intolerance* (1916), which runs over two hours, and copied every twenty-sixth frame twice, thus reducing that film's running time by a factor of thirteen. In "Intolerance (Abridged)" most of the title cards are unreadable, but so expressive are the film's images that much of its story, structure, mise en scène, editing, and camera work flash through the onrush of images. At an opposite extreme, in 1993, video artist Douglas Gordon transformed Hitchcock's *Psycho* (1960) into *24 Hour Psycho*. He created the new film by projecting *Psycho* not at the usual twenty-four frames per second but at two frames per minute, thus stretching the film's running time from almost two hours to twenty-four hours. As a result, the film showing eliminates the sound track, movement within the images, and the sense of pace and other aspects of editing but makes possible greater viewer awareness of each frame's mise en scène and cinematography. In effect, Gordon transformed the movie into a long series of still photographs.

Like lyric poems, experimental films explore an immense variety of subjects usually avoided in narrative. One subject is shifting colored abstract forms created by painting directly onto clear film, as in Evelyn Lambart and Norman McLaren's "Begone Dull Care" (1949, Figure 9.20).

Another subject for experimental films is the scope and limitations of mental activities (Figure 9.21). An experimental film may also explore the scope of human perception and cognition, as in J. J. Murphy's "Print Generation" (1974). The film consists of 3,002 shots: fifty generations of sixty shots plus two title cards. A generation is a copy, so the second generation of a shot is not quite as distinct as the first, and the third generation is a copy of a copy and is even less clear. Before the fiftieth generation of a shot, its content is unrecognizable. (The same thing happens with a photocopy machine if you make a copy, then a copy of the copy, and so forth for a total of fifty generations.) The film begins with the forty-ninth generation of each of sixty shots; these images are a series of abstract patterns of indistinct lights against a reddish background, such as in Figure 9.22a. Gradually viewers figure out that the film is made up of many brief full-color shots of the same duration (one second each) and can discern more and more of the subjects of other shots until, near the middle of the film, almost all of the subjects are

FIGURE 9.20 **Making a film without using a camera**
The acclaimed Canadian filmmaker Norman McLaren paints on clear 35 mm film in making part of "Begone Dull Care" (1949), an abstract film with Oscar Peterson jazz. In that film the changing forms occasionally correspond to the music; for example, at one point as single notes are played, corresponding vertical white lines are added against the black background. *Norman McLaren and Evelyn Lambart; National Film Board of Canada*

recognizable (Figure 9.22b–h). However, it's impossible to see much of a connection between the sixty shots, so by somewhere near the film's middle, viewers conclude that the sixty shots do not constitute a story.

After a title card, "Print Generation/(A-WIND)/JJ Murphy/©1973–74," the images begin to degenerate, to return gradually to the abstract patterns seen at the film's beginning. The film ends with the fiftieth generation of each shot and a second title card, "Print Generation/(B-WIND)/JJ Murphy/©1973–74." Overall as the film progresses from abstract patterns to recognizable subjects and back to abstract patterns, an opposite action is happening on the sound track: sounds of ocean waves gradually become unrecognizable then after the middle title card again gradually become recognizable.

In experiencing "Print Generation," viewers constantly watch, listen, and think as they try to perceive the film's subjects, see a unity to the shots, make some meaning from the film's 3,002 shots. On one level, the film is

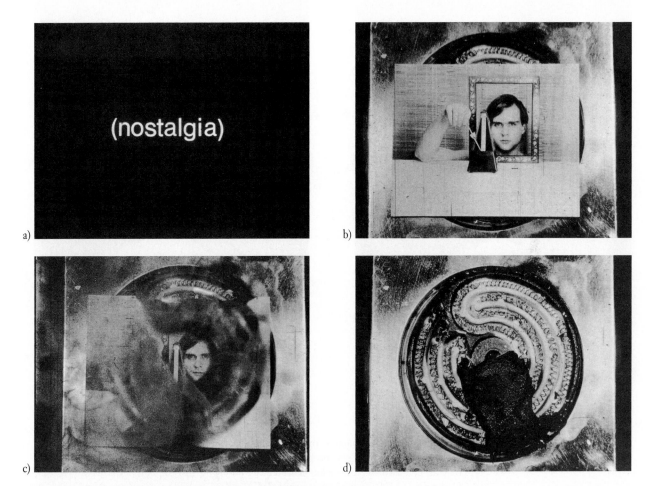

FIGURE 9.21 The limits of memory and other subjects
Hollis Frampton's experimental film "(nostalgia)" (1971) begins with (a) the title card and the simultaneous narration: "These are recollections of a dozen still photographs I made several years ago." Each of the following shots shows (b) a bird's-eye view of a photograph and (c) the photograph slowly catching fire on top of a hot plate and completely combusting as a narrator gives background and brief commentary about the *next* photograph viewers will see. After the narration accompanying each photo ends, in one to two minutes of silence we see (d) ashes slowly twisting on the hot plate. The film's last shot includes narration for a photo we viewers never get to see (even at the film's beginning) about which the narrator concludes, "What I believe I see recorded in that speck of film fills me with such fear, such utter dread and loathing, that I think I shall never dare to make another photograph. Here it is. Look at it. Do you see what I see?" Then the image goes black. The film is constructed to prevent viewers from experiencing synchronized image and sound throughout and suggests the difficulty of linking memory to the appropriate image, the transitory quality of images, and the impossibility of capturing and holding on to the past. Frame enlargements. *Hollis Frampton; Film-makers' Cooperative, New York*

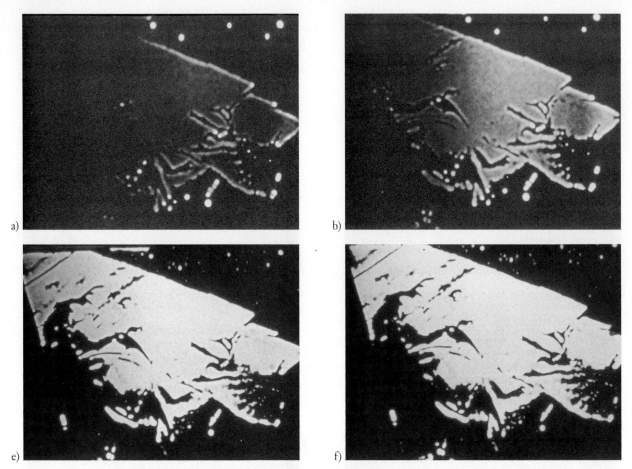

a)

b)

e)

f)

FIGURE 9.22 **Perception and cognition as subjects**
Eight spaced frame enlargements from different generations of the same one-second shot illustrate the gradual increased resolution of an image during the first half of J. J. Murphy's "Print Generation" (1974). Frame enlargements. *J. J. Murphy; Film-makers' Cooperative, New York*

emulsion: A clear gelatin substance containing a thin layer of tiny light-sensitive particles (grains) that make up a photographic image.

about the changes that occur to images as more and more generations are made from them: beneath recognizable film images are increasingly abstract patterns, and underneath a full-color film image is less and less color until only red remains (the bottom layer of color **emulsion**). "Print Generation" is also about the limitations of perception, visual and auditory, and cognition: as more and more distortion is introduced into the representation of the subjects, viewers are limited as to what they can perceive and understand. On the most general level, the film shows that from chaos, signs of life emerge and just as quickly return to chaos. Murphy could have structured the film so that it began with recognizable subjects that gradually decompose and later regenerate into the original images. Such a structure would have suggested a different, more upbeat meaning: life may decompose into unrecognizable parts and just as quickly regenerate itself.

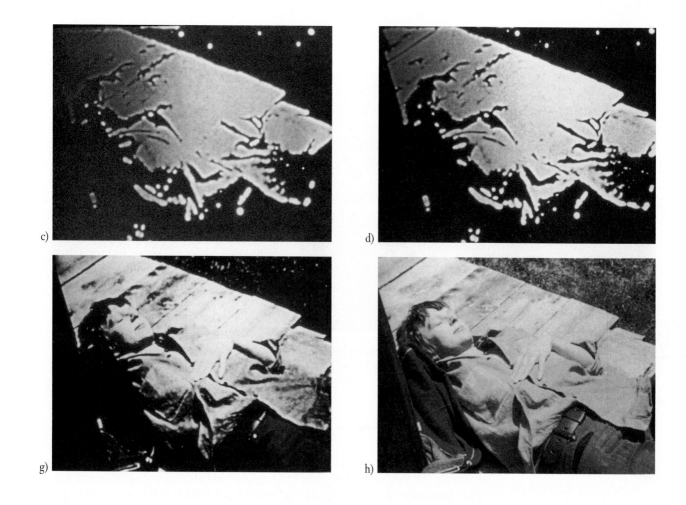

c)

d)

g)

h)

Filmmaking Techniques

Experimental filmmakers tend to use traditional techniques in new ways. As critic Patrick S. Smith points out, Andy Warhol's films from 1963 to 1968 use well-known **filmic** techniques in ways rarely used by mainstream films. During that period, Warhol's films feature an unmoving camera; shots sometimes thirty or more minutes long; strobe cuts (used only in the later films), which result in a few white frames and a loud "bloop" sound at the beginning of each shot; and arbitrary **zooming.** Warhol reportedly also welcomed accidents during filming; when one occurred, he would keep filming. Warhol's films "remove the viewer's psychological identification with the performers by means of various interruptions or sustained viewpoints, so that one may notice qualities normally obscured by the perceptions of everyday

filmic: Characteristic of the film medium or appropriate to it.

zoom: To use a zoom lens to cause the image of the subject to either increase in size as the area being filmed seems to decrease (zoom in) or to decrease in size as the area being filmed seems to increase (zoom out).

FIGURE 9.23 Untraditional filmmaking techniques, traditional subject
Using an optical printer to make multiple images of two dancers, "Pas de deux" (1968) combines music with the expressiveness of human movement during the ritual of male and female courtship. The setting is nil; form, movement, and music are all. *Norman McLaren; National Film Board of Canada*

optical printer: A device consisting of a camera and one or more projectors used to reproduce images or parts of images from already processed film.

existence or by the traditional condensations of narrative form" (Smith 150).

Experimental filmmakers tend to explore film techniques. They may superimpose a readable text over a moving image, present parts of the film upside down (Figure 9.18e), or use double or triple exposure. Experimental filmmakers may alter an exposed and processed film by scratching, painting, dyeing, or baking it. In some of her films Carolee Schneemann painted over and scratched the film after it had been used to record action. An entire film may be made without a camera: the film consists of images painted or scratched directly onto film or leader plus perhaps a sound track (Figure 9.20). For part of an untitled black-and-white film made by George Kuchar and a college film class, Kuchar gave each student actor "white eyebrows, lipstick, etc., on a face that was painted black." Then the footage of the black-faced actors was processed and the processed negative included with the rest of the finished film. "It all worked out OK except that their teeth appeared black whenever they smiled. This made for a rather horrifying and funny effect as we were shooting glamour shots of the rather attractive cast." In "Pas de Deux" (a.k.a. "Duo," 1968), Norman McLaren uses two dancers dressed in white against a black background and on a black floor, opposing lighting from each side of the frame, and frequent flowing multiple images made with an **optical printer.** In slow-motion dance the film shows the isolation, courtship, and union of male and female with novelty, grace, and feeling (Figure 9.23).

Other Characteristics of Experimental Films[1]

Most experimental films are less than thirty minutes long; some are only a few minutes or less. Bruce Conner's "Ten Second Film" (1965) is indeed ten seconds. Peter Kubelka's "Schwechater" (1958) is one minute long. Ann Marie Fleming's "New Shoes: (An Interview in Exactly 5 Minutes)" (1990) has precisely the running time it claims to have.

[1]In the following section I have used some of the same phrases as Edward Small did in his book *Direct Theory: Experimental Film/Video as Major Genre*, but I have added, combined, and renamed characteristics and supplied my own examples.

Usually experimental films use a minimum of language. This characteristic is in part a consequence of experimental filmmakers' affinity for mental images. Experimental films tend to avoid words in all their manifestations, such as signs, title cards, subtitles, narration, and dialogue or to use only indistinct words or puzzling fragments of sentences. Many experimental films avoid sound entirely although they were made when inclusion of a sound track was an option. For the most part, experimental filmmakers strongly favor imagery over language.

Experimental films rarely show stories. If one initially seems to do so, viewers soon realize they cannot find the unity that stories offer. The forty-five-minute film "Wavelength" (1967) initially seems to show a story, but viewers eventually realize it does not (Figure 9.24). "The long journey across

FIGURE 9.24 **Film events but no narrative**
"Wavelength" (1967) has only four brief actions: 1. At the beginning of the film two men carry in a bookcase accompanied by a woman who indicates where to leave it; the men set the bookcase down, and all three leave. 2. Later, two women enter the room and go to the far side, where one turns on a radio that plays part of a song and the other closes a window. Soon one woman leaves, and the other woman turns off the radio and leaves. 3. After a variety of breaking sounds and footsteps are heard from offscreen, a man slowly walks into the room and collapses. 4. Later a woman enters the frame, looks toward where the man had fallen, goes to the phone, and calls someone. The woman says that she thinks the man is dead, asks what to do, and asks the person on the other end of the phone to come over. She hangs up the phone and leaves. These limited actions are glimpsed during a mostly continuous zoom shot, from wide-angle to close-up of a photograph of waves on the back wall, but like nearly all actions in experimental films, they do not add up to a coherent story. *Michael Snow; The Museum of Modern Art/Film Stills Archive*

c)

d)

g)

h)

FIGURE 9.25 Lack of narrative in an experimental film

Alexander Hammid and Maya Deren's "Meshes of the Afternoon" (1943) focuses on one character and various events but lacks narrative continuity and coherence. These ten frame enlargements illustrate five consecutive but discontinuous shots. First shot (a–c): The woman (Deren herself) looks down and off-frame; the camera pans left, and viewers see what she was seeing: a knife and herself sleeping. Second shot (d): Now near a window, she looks down, perhaps at herself sleeping. Third shot (e–f): Outside and below, a woman—whom viewers had seen earlier dressed all in black and with a mirror instead of a face—rushes away, carrying a large plastic flower. Later in the shot, Deren runs after her. Fourth shot (g–h): The mysterious woman is in the distant background walking rapidly, rounding a corner, and going out of sight. Deren is running toward the mysterious woman but is even farther behind her than toward the end of the previous shot; Deren stops and walks off to the left of the frame. Fifth shot (i–j): Deren is again seen at the window; later in the shot she takes a key from her mouth. Like "Un chien andalou" (see Figure 9.17), "Meshes" seems dreamlike and ambiguously symbolic. Frame enlargements. *Maya Deren; Film-makers' Cooperative, New York* and *Women Makes Movies, New York*

FIGURE 9.26 Experimental film as antithesis to movies
Empire (1964)—an eight-hour experimental film by Andy Warhol consisting solely of a view of the Empire State Building as seen from the same position—is the antithesis of traditional films. It has no human subject, no perceptible variation in its subject, little noticeable movement from moment to moment, and no variation in filmmaking techniques. Furthermore, its pace is *so* slow it gives viewers extremely little information during its very lengthy duration, except that outdoor lighting changes gradually over time. Frame enlargement. *Andy Warhol Foundation*

the loft . . . deliver[s] the audience to the absolute nemesis of the conventional cinema: to a still photograph viewed in silence for several minutes" (MacDonald 36). Like "Un chien andalou," at first "Meshes of the Afternoon" seems to offer a narrative—we see the same character in consecutive scenes—but soon displays lack of continuity (Figure 9.25). Another experimental film that is the antithesis of traditional narrative motion pictures is *Blue* (1993), which was directed by Derek Jarman and is not to be confused with another film of the same title directed by Krzysztof Kieslowski. Jarman's film is not pictures in motion that convey a story but seventy-six minutes of unvarying solid blue light and a sound track that includes narration (both prosaic and poetic) and other voices, sound effects, and music.[2] Andy Warhol's *Empire* (1964), which consists of eight seemingly uninterrupted hours of a view of the Empire State Building from the same camera position, comes close to static images, too, especially in the short term (Figure 9.26).

Finally, experimental films often draw attention to themselves as films or to the film medium itself. As we have seen, both fictional and documentary films may be self-reflexive, but experimental films are even more likely to be so. For example, they may show the camera filming part of what will be included in the final version of the film or include a film's opening leader. They may show the parts of a projector as it is projecting a film. They may make motion-picture film itself the main subject of a film, as Owen Land did in "Film in which there appear sprocket holes, edge lettering, dirt particles, etc." (1965–66).

Film Apparatus and the Experimental Film

As a traditional film or video is made, the camera, film or videotape, lenses, and so on are used in fundamentally conventional ways. For example, ever since a sound track was included with the images on film itself in the late

[2]For the text of *Blue*, see Derek Jarman, *Blue: Text of a Film* (Woodstock, NY: Overlook Press, 1994).

1920s, the speed of the film being exposed is rarely changed during filming. When a conventional film or video is shown, its components—projector or video player, film or videotape, screen or monitor—also tend to be used in the usual ways. For example, traditionally the same lens is used throughout a showing. Many experimental films, though, change one or more of the basic components of making and exhibiting a film or video. A film is normally projected onto a flat, white, reflective, rectangular screen or wall, but it need not be so. During the opening night of the 1996 Los Angeles exhibition on the relationship of film and art since 1945, a film was projected onto a woman's bare chest, and throughout the exhibition different films were projected onto objects such as a bucket of milk and a spinning fan. In another part of the exhibit, a video projector suspended above an unmade bed projected a video image of a reclining man onto the bed. Table 9.2 on p. 334 lists the basic components of the film apparatuses and some conventional and unconventional ways in which filmmakers may use them.

Categories of Experimental Films

Experimental films have been categorized different ways by different scholars. Sometimes they are divided into "representational" and "abstract." In representational experimental films, the subjects are recognizable as people and real objects, as in "Un chien andalou" (Figure 9.17 on p. 319). In abstract experimental films, the subjects are unrecognizable, as in "Begone Dull Care" (Figure 9.20 on p. 324). In a more sophisticated classification, film theorist James Peterson divides American experimental films since World War II into three "open and flexible grouping[s]": poetic, minimal, and assemblage (especially compilations of footage) (10). Edward Small divides experimental film and video into five categories: European avant-garde, American avant-garde, American underground, expanded cinema, and minimalist-structuralist (81). So boundless is human imagination, however, that two or three or five categories often prove inadequate, and many experimental films elude clear-cut classification.

Experimental Films and Other Arts

Since the 1970s, some films or videos have been combined with other visual objects and arts and shown in museums, usually museums of modern or contemporary art. Such ensemble artworks are called **installation art.** An example is Jeff Wall's "Eviction Struggle" (1988), which combines a large fluorescent-lit transparency (about 13½ feet wide and 7½ feet tall) on one side of a gallery wall with nine close-up or medium close-up video excerpts of the same struggle and reactions to it on the other side of the wall (Figure 9.27 on p. 335). One version of the installation *Bordering on Fiction: Chantal Akerman's "D'est"* (1995) consisted of a showing of *D'est* (*From the East*, 1993), which is

TABLE 9.2

Film Apparatus and the Experimental Film: A Few of the Visual Possibilities*

APPARATUS	TRADITIONAL USES	EXPERIMENTAL USES
PRODUCTION		
▪ CAMERA	Filming at the same speed within each shot	Using distorting camera lens(es)
		Filming at variable speeds
		Filming, cranking back, and filming again to produce multiple exposures
▪ FILM	Recording consecutive fragments of space, time, or, most often, both on consecutive frames	Recording mostly clear frames, perhaps resulting in a strobe effect
		Painting
		Scratching
▪ EDITING	Coordinating multiple shots, usually through continuity editing	Rejecting editing by making a film consisting of one shot
		Avoiding continuity
		Making a compilation film, a film made up of clips from others films
EXHIBITION		
▪ PROJECTOR	Running at unvarying speed, usually 24 or 25 frames per second for modern sound film	Projecting the images upside down, backward, or both
		Causing multiple images, superimposed images, or both through multiple versions
	Using no distorting projector lens(es) other than possibly anamorphic	Projecting through some intervening substance, such as a full fish tank
▪ FINISHED FILM	Depicting consecutive fragments of time, action, or both within each shot through consecutive frames	Depicting discontinuous fragments of time, action, or both within each shot
▪ SCREEN	Using a flat or concave, white, reflective, rectangular, uniform surface for projected film	Using a person's body or an inanimate object, such as a shirt or milk jug, for projected film
▪ THEATER	Allowing audience members to be in full sight of other audience members	Shutting off audience members from each other by erecting panels between seats

*A comparable table could be made for video production and exhibition consisting of video camera, videotape, player, and monitor, or video camera, tape, player-projector, and screen.

a)

b)

FIGURE 9.27 Installation art: photography and video

Jeff Wall's installation "Eviction Struggle," which was made in British Columbia in 1988, has two sides. (a) On one side of an art gallery wall is a large still photograph showing two officers struggling with a man (to the right of the car parked at an angle to the sidewalk), a woman rushing from the direction of a house toward them, and various other people in the neighborhood watching the conflict. (b) The other side of "Eviction Struggle" consists of nine nineteen-inch video monitors showing brief close-up and medium close-up clips enacting some of the situations seen in the huge photograph. The three monitors on the left and the two monitors on the right side of the wall show people looking at the struggle. The four central monitors show, from left to right, an officer, the struggling man, another officer, and a woman running toward the men. By looking at the large image and then the nine video monitors (or vice versa), viewers can compare the expressiveness of the photograph's mise en scène with the expressiveness of video clips of the same subject. The nine monitors also allow viewers to function as editors in that they will select the order, duration, and repetition, if any, of the clips seen. The installation gives viewers the opportunity to compare and contrast two different representations of the same subject and to consider the expressiveness and limitations of still photography and video. *Collection: Ydessa Hendeles Art Foundation, Toronto*

Akerman's feature-length documentary, in one museum gallery, video clips from it on multiple monitors in the next gallery, and in a third gallery a single video monitor and the filmmaker's recorded voice from yet another source reading a passage in Hebrew from the Bible and a selection from her own writings about the film. "Viewed in its entirety, *Bordering on Fiction: Chantal Akerman's 'D'est'* engages in a deconstructive tour of the production process, working back from the completed feature film to the individual shot segments of which it is constructed and, in the end, back to language itself" (*Bordering* 9).

One of the biggest problems facing the student of experimental films is getting to see them, especially if one does not live near a museum of modern or contemporary art or near a large city offering a wide range of film showings. Video stores rarely carry them. (For that matter, some experimental filmmakers will not allow their films to be transferred to video.) To date, cable channels are of limited help, although the Sundance Channel and the Independent Film Channel sometimes show them. Some libraries have a few of the classic titles or may be able to get them for you through interlibrary loan. Some university film series show them from time to time. In video, both Facets Multimedia in Chicago and TLA Video in Philadelphia and New York have some titles or collections of short experimental films. Some titles are beginning to appear on DVD, including the DVD magazine of award-winning short films called "Short" (Short 1, Short 2, and so forth). On the Web, the first site to visit is Flicker at <http://www.hi-beam.net>. Included is a wide array of information about experimental films and filmmakers and many useful links, including some of film clips and short films. As Flicker's home page asserts, "Here you will find films and videos that transgress the boundaries of the traditional viewing experience, challenge notions of physical perception and provide cutting edge alternatives to the media information technocracy." In each January/February issue of recent years, *Film Comment*, a popular film journal available in large bookstores and many libraries, has been carrying an article about current developments in experimental or avant-garde film.

HYBRID FILMS

Most films are exclusively and unquestionably fiction or documentary or experimental. Viewers watching any of the *Star Wars*–related films, for example, never think of them as anything other than fiction. Some films, however, although clearly a member of one of the three types of films, blend aspects from at least one of the other two major types.

Combinations of experimental and documentary are unheard of in classical Hollywood cinema but appear from time to time in **independent films**

independent film: Film made without support or input from the dominant, established film industry.

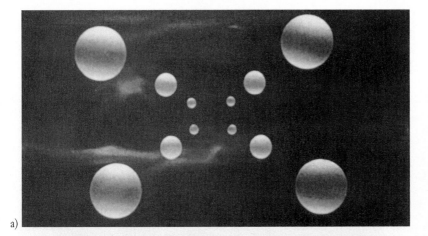

a)

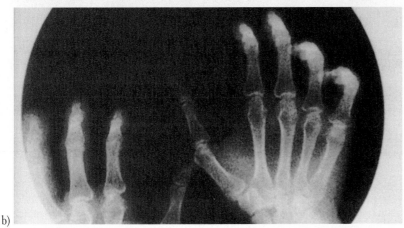

b)

FIGURE 9.28 **Hybrid film: experimental and documentary**
Thirty-Two Short Films about Glenn Gould (1993) is a documentary about the famous pianist, but the film sometimes looks like an experimental film. (a) One of its thirty-two films, "Gould Meets McLaren," is an animated experimental film by Norman McLaren and René Jodoin. The film begins by showing a white moving sphere divide into other moving spheres that move symmetrically. After the spheres divide into the maximum number and an animated butterfly briefly flits between some of them, the moving spheres quickly merge into one sphere again. "Gould Meets McLaren" is accompanied by a Bach fugue played on a piano (Girard and McKellar 117–19). (b) Another of the short films, "Diary of One Day," includes part of a Schoenberg suite for the piano as viewers see excerpts from Gould's health diary, many notations about his blood pressure readings, and motion-picture X-rays of a person's hands, arms, trunk, and head moving as if the person were playing a piano. In part, "Diary of One Day" is about human movement rendered in an untraditional, playful, and surprising manner (Girard and McKellar 147–52). Frame enlargements.
Canadian Broadcasting Corp.; Samuel Goldwyn

from various nations. Andy Warhol's *Sleep* (1963), which shows only a man sleeping for nearly five and a half hours, can be labeled experimental documentary. *Sleep* is a documentary film—it shows its subject factually—yet it is so unconventional as to be experimental (so long, so uneventful, so unvaried, so unengaging). In places, *Thirty-Two Short Films about Glenn Gould* is an experimental documentary (Figure 9.28). "You Take Care Now" (1989) by Ann Marie Fleming is an experimental narrative documentary. The film uses a blank screen, a wobbly camera that causes blurred images, repeated close-ups of a live bird's head surrounded by animated lines and patterns, the head of a man jumping up into the frame briefly and repeatedly (the camera is aimed above his head), an extreme close-up of a man's mouth as he presumably shouts curses as viewers hear a dog barking, snow on a TV screen, an out-of-focus night shot, and many other techniques to help convey the dis-

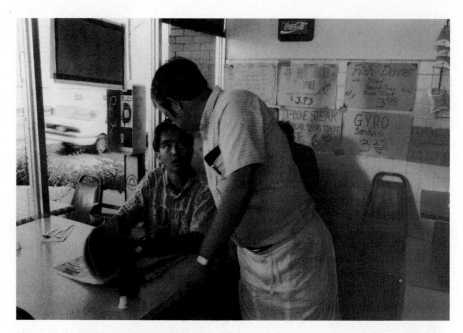

FIGURE 9.29 **A nonnarrative fake documentary**
While watching *Slacker* (1990), the viewer might initially think that the film is a documentary made
by a highly mobile camera crew that recorded a few subjects briefly (often a one-sided conversation
or monologue), moved on to a new small group of characters, and repeated this pattern throughout
the film. After a certain point, it is clear the film shows no coherent narrative, so the viewer might
conclude that the film is a nonnarrative documentary. As the film unspools even further, the
viewer might start to suspect that the film is not a documentary after all (for one thing, some
episodes seem too contrived to be entirely credible). The concluding credits include credits for
the "writer" (the same person as the producer and director) and for someone in charge of casting.
The film is a nonnarrative fake documentary.

Three of the film's ninety-six characters can be seen in this still. The seated young man, identified in the closing credits as "Happy-go-lucky guy," has entered a restaurant. There a paranoid
man seated behind him tells him, "Quit following me"; a stranger, who speaks continuously and
haltingly to herself, scolds him, "You should quit traumatizing women with sexual intercourse"; and
the cook, seen here in the center, treats him grumpily. As in the film's other episodes, the episode
represented here looks and sounds like part of a narrative documentary. But the film's episodes are
only loosely related (people out of the mainstream, the same twenty-four hours or so, and the same
city). Richard Linklater—the film's producer, writer, and director—is less interested in presenting
a story than in re-creating a society of mostly youthful outsiders, eccentrics, and loners in Austin,
Texas, at the end of the 1980s. *Richard Linklater; Orion Classics*

orientation and physical and psychological pain of being raped and on another occasion being hit by one car and run over by another. The film's female narrator recounts two brief, presumably factual stories and provides
whatever context and continuity the film has; the visuals show little of the
stories and instead create or reinforce moods.

A film may be a blend of fiction and documentary. As Figure 9.3 illustrates, occasional films, such as (*Battleship*) *Potemkin* (1925), may be classified as fiction or documentary because they have characteristics of both types. On rare occasions, a film may be either a **fake documentary** or a **mock documentary.** Both kinds of film are made with documentary techniques (such as interviews, handheld camera shots, subtitles), but they are not documentaries. As viewers watch a fake documentary, they see it as factual (sometimes the film's closing credits reveal that the film is not factual after all). A fake documentary does not necessarily show a fictional story (Figure 9.29). Most fake documentaries, however, do, as is the case with *The Blair Witch Project* (1999, Figure 9.30). As is explained in Chapter 5, a mock documentary is a fictional film that at first seems to be a documentary, but while watching it, most viewers quickly catch on that the film is fictional and is an extended joke.

Films, especially independent films, may also combine elements of fiction and experimental. *The Cabinet of Dr. Caligari* (1919) is a fictional film with both a mise en scène and a preoccupation with a disturbed mental state more often found in experimental films. Another fictional film incorporating experimental aspects is Bergman's *Persona* (1966, Figure 9.31). The film shows the fictional story of two women: a famous woman actor who has suddenly become mute and the nurse who comes to care for her. Parts of the film, however, include material extraneous to the **plot** and repetition rarely found in a fictional film: self-reflexive shots of motion-picture cameras, projectors, and 35 mm film that do not fit into the plot along with accusations by Alma as we see Elisabeth, followed by the same accusations by Elisabeth as we see Alma. *Persona* also includes a lengthy shot that begins badly out of focus and soon comes into focus.

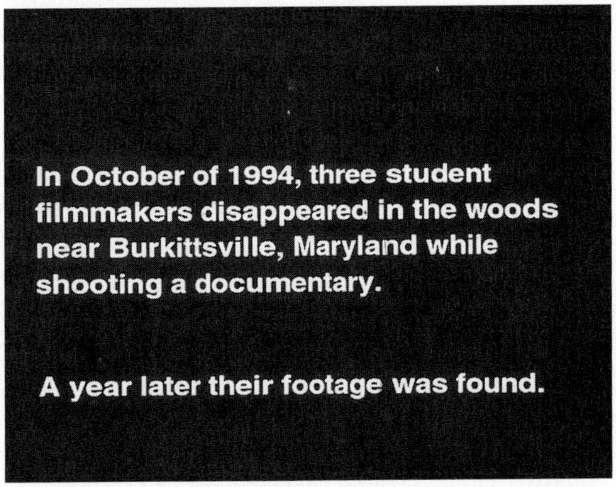

Occasionally a film outside classical Hollywood cinema exhibits characteristics of all three major types of films, as in *David Holzman's Diary* (1968). Initially, the film seems to be a narrative documentary with experimental aspects, such as the self-reflexive shots of the equipment used during filming and editing; shots of the dark screen accompanied by narration; a galloping succession of shots supposedly representing one frame from each shot of an evening's worth of TV; and a shot viewed through a **fisheye lens** looking down on the top of "David Holzman's" head (Figure 9.32). When the end credits reveal that the film was scripted and acted and is not factual, the viewer can understand that the film is fictional with documentary and experimental components.

plot: The structure (selection and arrangement) of a narrative's events.

fisheye lens: An extreme wide-angle lens that captures nearly 180 degrees of the area before the camera and causes much curvature of the image, especially near the edges.

In October of 1994, three student filmmakers disappeared in the woods near Burkittsville, Maryland while shooting a documentary.

A year later their footage was found.

FIGURE 9.30 **A narrative fake documentary**
One of the many ways that *The Blair Witch Project* (1999) gives the impression of factuality is its use of informative title cards, which are often used in films to convey factual information. In fact, *The Blair Witch Project* is the product of the imaginations and work of some film students at the University of Central Florida. Frame enlargement. *Haxan Entertainment; Artisan Entertainment*

FIGURE 9.31 **Hybrid film: experimental and fictional**
The two main characters of *Persona* (1966) are a nurse, Alma, (left), and her patient, Elisabeth, (right), a famous actor who suddenly has become mute and withdrawn. As this publicity still suggests, at times the two characters seem to change roles. At other times, as when a shot shows the halves of the two faces seemingly fused into one, they seem to blend into one another. In these and many other ways, *Persona* blends a fictional story and experimental filmmaking. *Ingmar Bergman; The Museum of Modern Art/Film Stills Archive*

black comedy: A narrative style that shows the humorous possibilities of subjects often considered off-limits to comedy, such as warfare, murder, death, and illness.

Critics and scholars sometimes disagree about how to classify a film. Some film specialists see *Female Trouble* (1974) and other early films directed by John Waters as experimental fiction, whereas others believe that they are fictional films done in a particular style, **black comedy** (see Figure 8.14 and Figure 8.15 on p. 291). Disagreements are inevitable because they involve judgment calls and sometimes different uses of terms, and different informed and thoughtful people will categorize some films differently. Filmmakers' imaginations and creativity outrun critics' and scholars' classifications.

ANIMATION

> Animation can redefine the everyday, subvert our accepted notions of reality and challenge the orthodox understanding of our existence. . . . Animation can defy the laws of gravity, challenge our perceived view of space and time, and endow lifeless things with dynamic and vibrant properties. (Wells 238)

Animation is not a type of film (as are fictional, documentary, and experimental films) or a combination of types of films (as is the hybrid film). Rather it is a technique for making a film or part of one.

a)

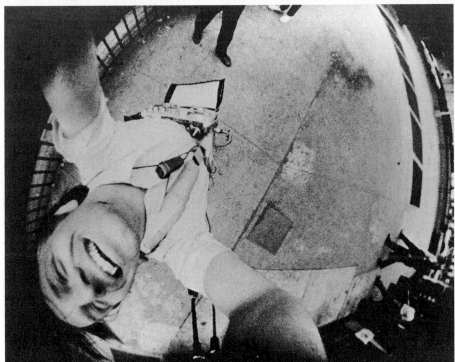

b)

FIGURE 9.32 **A hybrid of fiction, documentary, and experimental**
(a) This frame enlargement from late in *David Holzman's Diary* (1968) illustrates the film's occasional self-reflexiveness by showing most of the apparatus used to make the film: left to right, the main character's portable reel-to-reel audio tape recorder, rewinds and 16 mm reels, and a 16 mm editor/viewer, and above them and reflected in the mirror, a tripod holding a 16 mm camera. Elsewhere in the film, viewers see shots of the zoom lens presumably used in filming *David Holzman's Diary* and the portable tape recorder and the accompanying microphone. (b) A view through a fisheye lens of the main character seemingly dangling above sidewalks. In this frame he is about to reach up and turn off the camera. This and other shots are characteristic of experimental films; in fact, it's hard to see how this shot fits into the story of this hybrid film. Frame enlargements. *Jim McBride; Direct Cinema Ltd. The Museum of Modern Art/ Film Stills Archive*

FIGURE 9.33 Animation of flat (two-dimensional) subjects
The first Mickey Mouse was seen in "Steamboat Willie" (1928), an example of the animation of flat subjects. *Walt Disney; The Museum of Modern Art/Film Stills Archive*

FIGURE 9.34 Animation of plastic (three-dimensional) subjects
In the Wallace and Gromit short animated films, Wallace is "the daft, loquacious inventor and [Gromit is his] silent, long-suffering dog" (Canemaker). In this scene from "A Close Shave" (1995), Gromit and Wallace have discovered a hungry lamb in their kitchen. Worse yet, the lamb is gnawing on Gromit's bone. According to Rich Aardman of Aardman Animations (production company), the plasticine model of Wallace is about ten inches high, and the one for Gromit is approximately eight inches high. *Aardman; The Museum of Modern Art/Film Stills Archive*

To "animate" means to bring to life. Both flat (two-dimensional) and plastic (three-dimensional) subjects may be animated. Flat subjects include drawings (Figure 9.33); paintings;[3] photographs; paper cutouts with hinged and movable body parts; computer graphics images; and drawings, scratchings, or paint applied directly on the film itself (Figure 9.20). Plastic objects that may be animated include people in rigid poses, clay, and plasticine, a synthetic material used as a substitute for clay (Figure 9.34). In all cases, the inanimate is brought to life by showing the viewer a rapid succession of changing images of the same subject. If the subject changes only slightly from frame to frame and many frames are exposed per second, as in the Disney animated features, the projected movement will seem fluid. Conversely, if the subject is moved appreciably from frame to frame or is photographed at only six or five or even fewer different images per second, the movement may seem jerky. Animators may use only six or so frames per second because time or budget is severely limited. However, as in the case of Bill Plympton, they may create only six different drawings for a second of film because they choose to create moving images that twitch and wiggle, not move with life's fluidity.

In some computer-assisted animation, penciled drawings are scanned into the computer. Next, the computer is used to choose and assign colors to areas of the image, ink and paint the images, set the characters against a background, add "camera movements," match the image to the sound track, and transfer the finished product to either film or videotape. It is now also possible to do the animation completely within the computer and transfer the results to film. Another way to do animation without a camera is to scratch or paint

[3]Experimental animator Robert Breer paints on individual 4-by-6-inch cards. After he has completed a number of consecutive cards, he flips through them to see how that section will look and move. Once he is happy with the results, he photographs each finished frame.

onto the individual frames of film, or, as Stan Brakhage and others have done, to affix small objects to the film stock and copy the film (Figure 9.35).

The Web has become a major source for producing and viewing short animation in part because of the availability of an easy-to-use software program called Flash animation. Some of this animation is interactive: for example, the user can manipulate the mouse to change the direction of an animated character or control the story's pace. Much Web-based animation is clearly drawn and the sound is appropriate, but the animation is without fluid movement; the skin tones are flat and unvaried; and the faces restricted to a narrow range of emotion. Like the movie **serials** that used to be shown in weekly installments in neighborhood movie theaters, some animated stories on the Web are divided into episodes of a few minutes, each except the last ending in a dangerous or unresolved situation for the main character. Again, like some of the old serials, some Web series feature a (male or female) superhero triumphing over a series of assorted dangers. In spite of its technical limitations, the Web is proving to be a place for animators to develop their skills and perhaps attract attention and funding for more ambitious projects.

In the animation of plastic objects, stop-motion cinematography and one of its subcategories, pixillation, are two major techniques. In stop-motion cinematography, which was used in making such films as *Tim Burton's The Nightmare before Christmas* (1993), an object such as a puppet is filmed in a miniature setting, usually from the side, for a frame or two. Then the object's position is changed slightly, one or two more frames are filmed, and so on (Figure 9.36). **Pixillation** is rapid, jerky stop-motion cinematography that usually uses people in rigid poses as subjects and makes possible the appearance of new types of movement, such as a person sliding in circles across a level lawn while balanced on one foot, as in Norman McLaren's "Neighbours" (1952, Figure 9.37).

FIGURE 9.35 **Film made without a camera**
To make "Mothlight" (1963), a four-minute silent film, Stan Brakhage pasted pieces of moth wings, grass, seeds, leaves, and flowers on clear 16 mm film then copied the results. Frame enlargements. *Courtesy of Stan Brakhage*

a)　b)　c)　d)　e)　f)

FIGURE 9.36 Stop-motion animation

(a) Producer Tim Burton with some puppets used in making *Tim Burton's The Nightmare before Christmas* (1993). In the movie, each holiday has its own place and own set of characters. Jack, the leader of Halloween Town, discovers Christmas Town and tells the other Halloween Town residents about it. He thinks Christmas Town could be improved, so Halloween Town characters are dispatched to kidnap "Sandy Claws," and Jack as Santa Claus returns to Christmas Town on Christmas and leaves grotesque and frightening toys.

During filming, usually the puppets or parts of them and perhaps parts of the setting were moved slightly between exposures, and twenty-four separate images were exposed for each second of finished film. Figures (b–f) show five equally spaced frames from three seconds (seventy-two frames) of continuous film that reveal a young boy showing his parents a Christmas present left by a Halloween Town character. The parents react by shuddering. (In a later scene, we see that they are still passed out!) (b–f) Frame enlargements. *Tim Burton and Denise Di Novi; Walt Disney; Touchstone*

Animation may be used throughout fictional films, documentary films (though extended use of animation in documentaries is rare), and experimental films (frequently used). Occasionally—as in *Mary Poppins* (1964), *Jurassic Park* (1993), *Stuart Little* (1999), and *Osmosis Jones* (2001)—animation is joined with live action, thereby combining imaginary worlds with the world viewers know.

An animated film may be as accomplished in its visuals, sound track, and narrative as live-action fictional films. "T.R.A.N.S.I.T." (1997) exemplifies how subtle, sophisticated, and engaging a short animated film can be (see pp. 346–47). Although only twelve minutes long, the film shows the complicated story of a love triangle, an attempted murder, and two murders. The film's seven sequences are arranged in reverse chronological order, so viewers need to be particularly attentive to the film's plot to figure out the chronological arrangement of the events. So carefully made is the film that viewers are rewarded with each repeat viewing as the characterization and plot becomes clearer, as do subtleties in the filmmaking, such as the symbolism of the strawberries, selective use of red, and the appropriateness and expressiveness of the original music.

Animation can allow viewers to see and experience from a new perspective. In "The Fly" (1980), we see the countryside and the inside of a large country home entirely from the point of view of a fly. We see and hear and to some extent experience the flying and stopping, flying and stopping. Near the end, we also hear footsteps and the sounds of a person swatting at the fly and finally see through a blur a collection of mounted insects as the fly's life and the film end together.

Animation has many other advantages. Compared with live-action filming, animation provides filmmakers much greater control of mise en scène: they can easily control all aspects of settings, subjects, and composition.

FIGURE 9.37 **Pixillation**
Five consecutive frames from the experimental fictional film "Neighbours" (1952) illustrate pixillation, stop-motion animation that shows rapid, discontinuous or jerky movement. Here two neighbors are maneuvering for possession of a flower that has grown along the property line between them. Pixillation makes possible movements that are impossible in live action, such as a person gliding around a level lawn on one leg. Frame enlargements.
Natural Film Board of Canada; The Museum of Modern Art/Film Stills Archives

"T.R.A.N.S.I.T." (1997): A Description

a. Live action. Suitcase presumably floating. Opening title card superimposed. Travel labels on suitcase. Last label shown (in French): "SS L'Amerique du Sud."

1. Ship in ocean. Hole of ship: men stoking furnace. On deck: rich passengers passing their time (a). Newspaper headline: "Oil Tycoon Murdered in Egypt. Wall Street in Turmoil." Oscar (we learn his name at the end of the film) comes onto the deck. One arm is in a sling; his head is bandaged. He carries the heavy leather suitcase seen at the beginning of the film. All activities on deck stop momentarily. Oscar walks across a shuffleboard game in progress. From the back of the ship he throws the suitcase overboard. It floats away from the ship. Lap dissolve to the suitcase covered with travel labels.

2. Orient Express train (b). Night. Map: Venezia (Venice) → Verona → Milano. Emily (we learn her name at the end of the film) opens a train window and a suitcase with travel labels. She takes a red cloth from it and tosses it (and the gun inside it) out the window into water below. Oscar, with a bandaged head, is on a plane within sight of the train. The plane passes the train. Oscar waiting at Paris train station. Train arrives. He gets on, enters a compartment, seems to kill Emily, then sits with his head in his hands.

3. Venice. Large luxurious hotel. Emily and Oscar in bed. She has a black eye and bruised mouth (c). She gets up, gets a gun, and shoots at Oscar twice. Emily leaving hotel as a Charlie Chaplin movie being shown outside is finishing. Carrying the suitcase, she gets into a gondola. Oscar, bloodied, staggers out onto the balcony of the hotel room.

4. Egypt. Desert. Near pyramids area guide, Emily, and the tycoon. Emily ignores guide's gesture to help her down off her camel and instead accepts the tycoon's help. The guide is enraged. Tycoon starts to kiss Emily. Guide stabs tycoon with a knife and is revealed to be Oscar. He slaps Emily in the face (d). Using his own garment, Oscar covers up the tycoon. Emily has a black eye.

5. St. Tropez (France). Emily and Oscar picnic. She feeds him a strawberry and eats one herself. The juice bleeds down her chin. They kiss. Nearby a sports car is parked (e).

6. Baden Baden (Germany) resort. Men's steam room. Tycoon getting a massage. In casino, Oscar wins at roulette (f). Emily stands near tycoon and smiles in Oscar's direction. In Oscar's hotel room, Emily rubs fresh strawberries on his body and indicates her sexual availability. At dawn, she returns to the room where the tycoon is sleeping, kisses him lightly, and slips into her bed.

7. Emily and the tycoon drive through the countryside. City street: suitcase falls out of the back of the car (same one as in sequence 5). Oscar picks it up and hands it to Emily. She kisses a card advertising a hotel (where the couple will be staying) and gives it to Oscar. He's a handsome though unshaven butcher in a bloody apron and has a pregnant wife and two small children.

b. Live action with animated effects. The suitcase full of travel labels floating in the ocean and superimposed title cards about Emily Buckingham Parker, who was last seen boarding the Orient Express in Venice in 1928. A shark swims nearby then the suitcase sinks abruptly and a faint red (Emily's blood) briefly stains the sea. Title cards tell about Oscar Bleek's later successful new life in Argentina.

The plot = a, 1–7, b
The fabula = 7, 6, 5, 4, 3, 2, 1, a, b

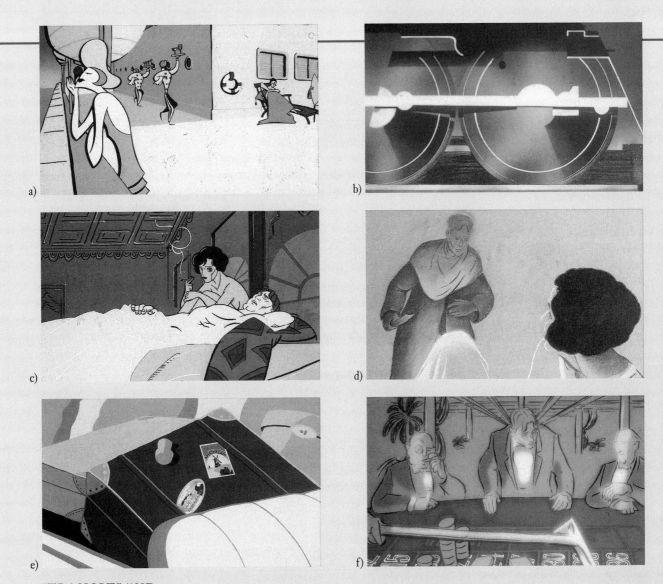

"T.R.A.N.S.I.T." (1997)

(a) A wealthy woman on the deck of a luxury ocean liner headed to South America. (b) Two of the wheels of the Orient Express as the train speeds along (toward Paris). (c) In a hotel room, a bruised Emily is smoking and thoughtful. (d) Oscar has knifed the tycoon and slapped Emily; here he is about to show her that he has a pistol tucked into his belt. (e) The cork from the champagne bottle Oscar had been holding hits the sports car parked nearby the picnicking Emily and Oscar. (f) In a casino at Baden Baden, Oscar has won large stakes. Frame enlargements. *Piet Kroon; Short 4: Seduction (DVD)*

See the Web site for the film at <http://www.awn.com/transit/index.htm>. (The section on "Story" is an inventive construction that does little to illuminate the film itself.)

morphing: The alteration of a film image by degrees by use of sophisticated computer software and multiple advanced computers.

designer or **production designer:** The person responsible for much of what is photographed in a movie, including architecture, locations, sets, costumes, makeup, and hairstyles.

As many scenes in Disney animated movies demonstrate—the death of Bambi's mother in *Bambi* (1942), the terror of the evil witch in *Sleeping Beauty* (1959), and the death of Mufasa in *The Lion King* (1994)—animation can also call forth strong emotional viewer responses, both from children and adults. Animation can create characters as memorable as people: for years throughout the world, Mickey Mouse was as popular as any movie star. (Perhaps as computer animation grows more and more powerful and subtle, one day animated stars will rival flesh-and-blood stars and even displace them.) And animation makes possible the impossible, such as a man metamorphosing (or **morphing**) into a beast and back into a man, dinosaurs roaming the earth sixty-five million years ago (*Dinosaur*, 2000), or remnants of the human race scattered about the universe because alien invaders destroyed Earth in the thirty-first century (*Titan A.E.*, 2000). No wonder animation so animates animators: they can play **designer,** casting director, director, and editor; they can show entire stories from otherwise impossible points of view; they can create life, set it in motion, act out what they wish, and decide the precise moment the life fades out or the image cuts to black.

SUMMARY

Although live-action fictional films have been by far the most popular films in the history of world cinema, there are other major types of films: documentary, experimental, and hybrid. Also to be considered is animation, which is not a type of film but a filmmaking technique.

Documentary Films

- Whether narrative or not, a documentary film represents its subjects in ways that viewers are intended to accept primarily as factual, not imaginary.

- Most documentary films present no narrative or story. The information in many nonnarrative documentary films is organized into groups or categories. Some nonnarrative documentary films attempt to praise or criticize a subject, as in *Hearts and Minds*.

- Narrative documentary films present a story that is largely factual, but like fictional films they are never simply a succession of related events— for example, they may also linger on settings or interrupt the narrative for interviews. They may also suggest praise or criticism.

- Documentary films—nonnarrative and narrative—always present a version of mediated reality: they are a selected, perhaps staged, and edited presentation of their subjects.

- Typically documentary films depict occurrences where they happened and use no actors.

- Documentary films usually include supporting artifacts—such as photographs or old film clips—and informative language, such as narration or interviews, or both.

- As *Titicut Follies* and *The Thin Blue Line* illustrate, documentarians use an enormous variety of film techniques. Some use basic techniques, whereas others experiment with a wide range of sounds and images in their films.

Experimental Films

- Because experimental films are so various, no one term—*experimental, underground, avant-garde, personal,* or *independent*—entirely captures their complexity and scope.

- Unlike commercial movies, experimental films often radically reject the conventions of earlier films and explore the possibilities of the film medium.

- Unlike commercial movies, experimental films tend to rebel against a society's ideology (the influential and usually unexamined underlying social and political beliefs of a society or social group).

- Experimental filmmakers often work alone and tend to be largely free of censorship.

- Experimental filmmakers may explore the use of recent technological advances in communications (such as personal computers and the Web), use existing films or parts of them in a changed form, or focus on other subjects rarely explored in fictional or documentary films, such as the limits of memory.

- Often experimental films use traditional filmmaking techniques in new ways, as in "Wavelength."

- Experimental films are usually brief, highly visual (and not very verbal), nonnarrative, and often self-reflexive.

- Often experimental filmmakers change one or more components of filmmaking and film exhibition—for example, by projecting a film onto a hanging shirt.

- Experimental films may be divided into representational and abstract; poetic, minimal, and assemblage; or in other ways. Because of their individuality and enormous variety, however, experimental films are especially difficult to define and classify.

- Installation art, which is usually displayed in museums of modern or contemporary art, often incorporates film or video into an ensemble or environment of arts and objects.

Hybrid Films

- Although most films are exclusively fictional, documentary, or experimental, some films are hybrids: they exhibit characteristics of more than one of the three basic types. For example, *The Cabinet of Dr. Caligari*, though mainly fictional, also has characteristics of experimental films, and Andy Warhol's *Sleep* is an experimental documentary.

Animation

- Animation is a technique that may be used in making any type of film. It may be of flat or plastic subjects.

- Animation affords filmmakers the greatest control over the mise en scène, allows viewers to see and experience from new perspectives, and often makes possible the otherwise impossible.

WORKS CITED

Applebome, Peter. "A Taste for the Eccentric, Marginal and Dangerous." *New York Times on the Web.* 26 Dec. 1999.

Bates, Peter. "Truth Not Guaranteed: An Interview with Errol Morris." *Cineaste* 17.1 (1989): 16–17.

Blank, Les, independent filmmaker. Telephone interview. April 1995.

Bordering on Fiction: Chantal Akerman's "D'est." Minneapolis: Walker Art Center, 1995.

Breer, Robert. Showing and Lecture. "Breer on Breer: The Films of Robert Breer." Walker Art Center, Minneapolis. 25 Feb. 2000.

Buñuel, Luis. "Notes on the Making of Un Chien Andalou." *Art in Cinema.* Ed. Frank Stauffacher. 1947. New York: Arno, 1968. 29–30.

Canemaker, John. "Chickens Fleeing on Feet Made of Clay." *New York Times on the Web.* 30 April 2000. <http://www.nytimes.com/library/film/043000sum-chicken.html>.

Corliss, Richard. "Take This Job and Love It." *Time* (27 Oct. 1997): 111.

Dixon, Wheeler Winston. *The Exploding Eye: A Re-Visionary History of 1960s American Experimental Cinema.* Albany: State U of New York P, 1997.

Ellis, Jack C. *The Documentary Idea: A Critical History of English-Language Documentary Film and Video.* Englewood Cliffs, NJ: Prentice, 1989.

Gardner, Robert. "Chronicles of the Human Experience: *Dead Birds.*" *Nonfiction Film Theory and Criticism.* Ed. Richard Meran Barsam. New York: Dutton, 1976. 342–48.

Girard, François, and Don McKellar. *Thirty-Two Short Films about Glenn Gould.* Toronto: Coach House Press, 1995. (screenplay)

Jacobs, Ken, independent filmmaker. Letter to the author. January 1998.

Jaehne, Karen. Review of *Fast, Cheap & Out of Control. Film Quarterly* 52.3 (Spring 1999): 43–47.

Kuchar, George, independent filmmaker and author. Letter to the author. January 1998.

Lucia, Cynthia. "Revisiting *High School*: An Interview with Frederick Wiseman." *Cineaste* 20.4 (Oct. 1994): 5–11.

MacDonald, Scott. *Avant-Garde Film: Motion Studies.* New York: Cambridge UP, 1993.

Mellencamp, Patricia. *Indiscretions: Avant-Garde Film, Video, and Feminism.* Bloomington: Indiana UP, 1990.

Peterson, James. *Dreams of Chaos, Visions of Order: Understanding the American Avant-Garde Cinema.* Detroit: Wayne State UP, 1994.

Small, Edward S. *Direct Theory: Experimental Film/Video as Major Genre.* Carbondale: Southern Illinois UP, 1994.

Smith, Patrick S. *Andy Warhol's Art and Films.* Ann Arbor, MI: UMI, 1986.

Wells, Paul. "Animation: Forms and Meanings." *An Introduction to Film Studies.* 2nd ed. Ed. Jill Nelmes. London: Routledge, 1999. 237–63.

FOR FURTHER READING

Barnouw, Erick. *Documentary: A History of the Non-Fiction Film.* 2nd rev. ed. New York: Oxford UP, 1993. A concise illustrated history plus an extensive bibliography.

Barsam, Richard M. *Nonfiction Film: A Critical History.* Rev. and expanded ed. Bloomington: Indiana UP, 1992. Part One (1820–1933): Foundations of the Nonfiction Film; Part Two (1933–1939): Documentary Films to Change the World; Part Three (1939–1945): Nonfiction Films for World War II; Part Four (1945–1960): Nonfiction Films after World War II; Part Five (1960–1985): Continuing Traditions and New Directions.

Bendazzi, Giannalberto. *Cartoons: One Hundred Years of Cinema Animation.* Bloomington: Indiana UP, 1994. A comprehensive and detailed history and critique of film animation. Includes ninety-five color plates and comprehensive indexes of names and titles.

Borowiec, Piotr. *Animated Short Films: A Critical Index to Theatrical Cartoons.* Lanham, MD: Scarecrow, 1998. Five sections: a brief history of animated short films, reviews of over 1,800 cartoons, director index, chronological index of cartoons from 1906 to 1997, and four- and five-star reviews.

Canyon Cinema Film/Video Catalog No. 8. San Francisco: Canyon Cinema, 2000. Descriptions of available films and videos. Especially valuable for information on the experimental.

Collecting Visible Evidence. Ed. by Jane M. Gaines and Michael Renov. Minneapolis: U of Minnesota P, 1999. Sixteen essays by various film scholars for the advanced introductory student.

Documenting the Documentary: Close Readings of Film and Video. Ed. Barry Keith Grant and Jeannette Sloniowski. Detroit: Wayne State UP, 1998. Essays by twenty-seven film scholars; each essay is focused on one or two major films.

Film-makers' Cooperative Catalogue No. 7 and *Film-makers' Cooperative Catalogue No. 7 Supplement*. New York: Film-makers' Cooperative, 1989, 1993. Descriptions of films and videos available through the co-op, arranged alphabetically by filmmaker. Especially valuable for information on the experimental.

James, David E. *Allegories of Cinema: American Film in the Sixties*. Princeton: Princeton UP, 1989. Survey of American experimental cinema of the 1960s and its various cultural contexts.

Jenkins, Bruce. "Explosion in a Film Factory: The Cinema of Bruce Conner." *2000 BC: The Bruce Conner Story Part II*. Minneapolis: Walker Art Center, 1999. 184–223. Background and analysis of the films; includes many frame enlargements, some in color.

MacDonald, Scott. *A Critical Cinema: Interviews with Independent Filmmakers*. Berkeley: U of California P, 1988. Introductory essay followed by a short essay on the life and films of each of seventeen experimental filmmakers and an interview with each.

———. *A Critical Cinema 2: Interviews with Independent Filmmakers*. Berkeley: U of California P, 1992. Fifteen more interviews plus three interviews each focusing on a film.

———. *A Critical Cinema 3: Interviews with Independent Filmmakers*. Berkeley: U of California P, 1997. Includes an overview for each interviewee, interviews with experimental filmmakers from many nations, film/videographies, and bibliographies.

———. *Screen Writings: Scripts and Texts by Independent Filmmakers*. Berkeley: U of California P, 1995. Includes introduction and a script for or a partial description of a wide variety of experimental films. Also includes nearly a hundred stills, most of them frame enlargements; distribution sources; and a bibliography.

Rees, A. L. *A History of Experimental Film and Video*. London: British Film Institute, 1999. A history of avant-garde film and video ranging from Cézanne and Dada, via Cocteau, Brakhage, and Le Grice, to the new wave of British video artists in the 1990s.

Rothman, William. *Documentary Film Classics*. Cambridge: Cambridge UP, 1997. Detailed analyses, supported with many frame enlargements, of some major documentary films, such as *Nanook of the North*, *Chronicle of a Summer*, and *Don't Look Back*.

Wells, Paul. *Understanding Animation*. New York: Routledge, 1998. Includes history and theory. Discusses such issues as representations of race and gender, "Disneyesque hyper-realism," and animation and audience research.

Other materials exploring sources, types, and other characteristics of films can be found on the Web site for this book: <http://www.bedfordstmartins.com/phillips-film>. Other applications of some of the material in Part Two can be found in Chapter 10.

Variety of Films and *Hearts of Darkness*

*H*EARTS OF DARKNESS: *A* FILMMAKER'S *A*POCALYPSE (1991) is a ninety-six-minute narrative documentary film written and directed by Fax Bahr with George Hickenlooper. The film shows some of the background and planning for the making of the movie *Apocalypse Now* (1979, expanded and reissued in 2001 as *Apocalypse Now Redux*) and many of the problems Francis Coppola and his crew confronted as they filmed his fictional Vietnam War epic in the Philippines (Figure 10.1a). One major source for *Hearts of Darkness* was excerpts from behind-the-scenes footage shot by Eleanor Coppola (Figure 10.1b). During filming, *Apocalypse Now* was beset by one problem

a)

b)

FIGURE 10.1 **The director of *Apocalypse Now* and the photographer of behind-the-scenes footage**
(a) Francis Coppola, seen here with a camera, decided that the story of *Apocalypse Now* (1979) should be filmed in the Philippines. (b) Eleanor Coppola, wife of the director, shot documentary footage on the making of *Apocalypse Now* that a decade or so later was incorporated into *Hearts of Darkness: A Filmmaker's Apocalypse* (1991). *Showtime Network*

after another and ended up requiring 238 days of principal photography, not the sixteen weeks originally planned. Like Les Blank's *Burden of Dreams* (1982), *Hearts of Darkness* belongs to that category of films about the making of another film. *Hearts of Darkness* received awards for editing (American Cinema Editors) and for best documentary film of the year (both International Documentary Association and National Board of Review). Critic Gene Siskel called it the best film of 1991. The film has received many positive reviews. In addition, it is often shown in university film courses.

DESCRIPTION

Because the story of *Hearts of Darkness* is complex and not always chronologically arranged, I have used an outline format instead of a description written in paragraphs. If you have not seen *Hearts of Darkness* recently or will not be seeing it, read the following description at least twice. Dates supplied in brackets are from a source outside *Hearts of Darkness*.

1. **Cannes Film Festival, [May] 1979**   Excerpt from Francis Coppola's press conference . . . film's title

2. **Flashback: Planning and Filming**
   a. Title card: In February 1976 Francis Coppola went to the Philippines to shoot *Apocalypse Now*.
   b. Orson Welles's 1939 plans to film Conrad's 1902 novella, *Heart of Darkness*.
   c. Getting started and getting focused: initially George Lucas to direct the John Milius script.
   d Casting session, Coppola with actors, November 1975.
   e. Marlon Brando agrees to play Kurtz.
   f. Coppola arriving in Philippines in February 1976.
   g. Construction of temple, one of the film's major sets.
   h. Filming of *Apocalypse Now* begins [March 1976] and quickly falls behind schedule.
   i. After the first week of filming, Coppola replaces actor Harvey Keitel with Martin Sheen, and scenes need to be reshot.
   j. On different days the Philippine military send different Filipino helicopter pilots to help in filming *Apocalypse Now*, causing delays and additional expense. The helicopters must return to fight rebels on some days.
   k. Problems in negotiating with Brando to allow Coppola additional time to rewrite the film's ending.
   l. Typhoon destroys sets, which are rebuilt; downtime in California [May–July, 1976].

m. Costly and time-consuming French plantation sequence shot; angry Coppola deletes it.

n. Coppola rewriting scenes.

o. Actor Sam Bottoms talks about heavy drug use by himself and others involved in the production.

p. Martin Sheen says that during filming he was confused about what his character was like.

q. During filming of the hotel room scene, Sheen intoxicated and extremely disturbed, August 3, 1976.

r. Sheen's heart attack, March 1, 1977; a healthy Sheen returns to location on April 19, 1977.

s. At set for Kurtz compound . . . Coppola tries to communicate with a spaced-out Dennis Hopper.

t. Celebration of two hundredth day of filming.

u. Brando and Coppola talk and talk about Brando's character; then Coppola films Brando day after day as Brando improvises, September [and October] 1976.

v. Coppola's despair about the quality of the film, especially about the ending.

w. Clips from the ending of *Apocalypse Now* cross-cut with Eleanor Coppola's footage of the same actions.

3. **Cannes and Afterward**

a. Subtitle: "2½ years later . . ." Coppola, his wife, and daughter arriving at Cannes Festival [May 1979].

b. Title cards inform that *Apocalypse Now* opened on August 19, 1979, and that the film eventually grossed more than $150 million, received three Golden Globe Awards and two Academy Awards, and shared the Cannes Palme D'Or prize.

c. Final excerpt from interview with Coppola about his hopes for the future of filmmaking.

SOURCES

Like many documentary films, *Hearts of Darkness* draws from a variety of sources. The film includes excerpts from sixty hours of footage of a casting session, developments on location in the Philippines, and the downtime at the Coppola estate in Napa, California—all shot by Coppola's wife Eleanor (French 100). As Figure 10.2 on p. 357 explains, *Hearts of Darkness* combines clips and outtakes from *Apocalypse Now*, excerpts from Eleanor Coppola's footage, interviews taken a decade or so after the release of *Apocalypse Now*, and various other sources.

Figure 10.3 illustrates some of the types of sources used to construct *Hearts of Darkness*.

a)

b)

Coppola Loses His Beard, 38 Pounds And Star Keitel

By JOSEPH McBRIDE

Harvey Keitel has been fired from the lead role in Francis Ford Coppola's "Apocalypse Now" in what Keitel's agent, Harry Ufland of ICM, says is a

c)

d)

e)

"Apocalypse Now" opened on August 19, 1979. It has since grossed more than 150 million dollars worldwide. The film went on to win three Golden Globe Awards, two Academy Awards and the Cannes Film Festival's Palme D'Or...

f)

FIGURE 10.2
Sources for *Apocalypse Now* and *Hearts of Darkness: A Filmmaker's Apocalypse*

fiction (Conrad's *Heart of Darkness*) + script (by John Milius) + narration (by Michael Herr) + storyboards + rewrites (by Coppola) + improvisations (by the actors) → ***Apocalypse Now***

Apocalypse Now (excerpts and outtakes) + Eleanor Coppola's 16 mm footage (many excerpts) + Eleanor Coppola's audio recordings of Francis Coppola (excerpts) + Orson Welles's 1938 radio broadcast (excerpts played at various times in the film) + narration by Eleanor Coppola + informative title cards + subtitles + TV programs excerpts + still images (such as of people, storyboards, drawings, and newspaper headlines) + postproduction interviews (excerpts) → ***Hearts of Darkness: A Filmmaker's Apocalypse***

The title *Hearts of Darkness* alludes to Joseph Conrad's novella *Heart of Darkness*, which is about someone pursuing a difficult goal and gradually being bogged down in a world that is not what it initially seemed to be. The same situation applies to the American involvement in the Vietnam War itself, to the making of *Apocalypse Now*, and to Coppola's own personal struggles in making the film. On the last point, remember that the subtitle of *Hearts of Darkness* is *A Filmmaker's Apocalypse*.

TYPE

Hearts of Darkness is a narrative documentary with a focus on the trials and triumphs of an individual. In many ways, *Hearts of Darkness* shows a classic story of one man facing tests of both character and nature as he tries to realize his vision. In its focus on a distinct individual with goals, a succession of problems in reaching the goals, closure, clear cause-and-effect relationships,

◄ FIGURE 10.3 **Some sources used in *Hearts of Darkness***
(a) Title card for *Hearts of Darkness* superimposed over a night image of fire and explosions associated with *Apocalypse Now*. (b) George Lucas years later being interviewed about his involvement in the early stages of planning *Apocalypse Now*. Lucas's interview is one of many with people involved in the planning or making of *Apocalypse Now*. (c) A newspaper headline indicating some of the early problems in the filming of *Apocalypse Now*. (d) As filmed by Eleanor Coppola, some of the extensive typhoon damage in the Philippines—a storm that set back the production even further. (e) A clip from near the end of *Apocalypse Now:* the Martin Sheen character rises slowly out of the water as lightning flashes. (f) The final title card indicating that *Apocalypse Now* was a success. Frame enlargements. *George Zaloom and Les Mayfield; New Yorker Films*

and unobtrusive filmmaking techniques, the film is in tune with classical Hollywood cinema. *Hearts of Darkness* is also an example of an independent film made outside the Hollywood system. The film was made on a low budget for the Showtime cable network and only later shown in theaters.

NARRATIVE COMPONENTS

Hearts of Darkness begins at the Cannes Film Festival in May 1979, soon flashes back to the large, mostly chronological, middle section, then returns briefly to the 1979 Cannes Film Festival and events after it. The film's structure can be represented as B, A, C, although the huge middle section is not always arranged chronologically.

Francis Coppola is the main person in the story of *Hearts of Darkness*, and his goal is transparent: to finish filming an effective story within a reasonable time and at an endurable cost. In attempting to achieve his goal, he is beset with problem after problem—after problem. Some of Coppola's troubles, it could be argued, were of his own making, such as too often trusting to chance developments.

Hearts of Darkness shows the three types of conflict: people versus people, people versus nature, and conflict within a person. The cast was one major source of conflict and adversity. After Coppola replaced Harvey Keitel with Martin Sheen, many scenes had to be reshot. Later, Sheen's heart attack created additional delays and expense. As with many U.S. soldiers late in the Vietnam War, some actors in *Apocalypse Now*, most conspicuously Dennis Hopper and Sam Bottoms, were consuming drugs copiously. Marlon Brando's slowness in getting into the role proved a formidable oblique conflict as well. For whatever reason, Brando was the only major actor in *Apocalypse Now* who did not give one of the postproduction interviews included in *Hearts of Darkness*.

Coppola was also forced to struggle with nature when a typhoon hit the Philippines and halted production. The American technology that Coppola brought to the Philippines was no match for the storm that destroyed sets and disrupted the production for two months. Both Sheen and Coppola suffered from conflict within themselves: Sheen during filming of the hotel room scene and Coppola, from time to time, as he despaired about being able to successfully finish the Herculean task involving himself and many others.

Hearts of Darkness has yet other narrative components. Like most successful stories, its beginning intrigues the audience, in this case by emphasizing that the production was plagued with problems. In the film's opening shots, at a Cannes Film Festival news conference, Coppola says,

> My film is not about Vietnam. It *is* Vietnam. It's what it was really like. It was crazy. And the way we made it was very much like the way the Americans were in Vietnam. We were in the jungle. There were too many of us. We had access to too much money, too much equipment, and little by little we went insane.

The film continues by supplying additional background information, including information about Coppola's despair about being able to conclude *Apocalypse Now* successfully. As the outline of the film shows (pp. 354–55), the large middle section presents a succession of problems for Coppola and his company, a string of setbacks that were vexing to them but are engaging to viewers of *Hearts of Darkness*. The ending of *Hearts of Darkness* has closure, a sense of wholeness and completion, implying that eventually the obstacles were overcome, and the film became a commercial and critical success.

Like some other narrative documentary films, such as *Hoop Dreams* (1994), *Hearts of Darkness* has two plotlines: Coppola facing problems while filming and, in less detail, Coppola facing personal problems (stress, collapse, depression, and suicidal impulses). Unlike Eleanor Coppola's book called *Notes*, which she wrote during the production of *Apocalypse Now*, *Hearts of Darkness* does not include information about Coppola's infidelity during the filming and the subsequent major though temporary disruption of his marriage (210–12).

Using a structure by no means rare in narrative documentaries, *Hearts of Darkness* presents its tale out of order. The film includes a huge flashback, the middle section, that is not arranged entirely chronologically. Which occurred earlier—the press conference at the beginning of the film or the Coppola family's arrival at Cannes near the end—is unclear. Like nearly all narratives, *Hearts of Darkness* is often vague about when certain actions occurred and how much time it took for some of them to transpire. In common with the treatment of time in nearly all narrative films, the film's story time (approximately four years) far exceeds its running time (ninety-six minutes). Finally, like nearly all documentaries, the dominant style of *Hearts of Darkness* is realism: the presentation of subjects in ways viewers are used to perceiving as true to life.

DOCUMENTARY ASPECTS

Documentaries are mediated reality: the selection and arrangement of information. As in the construction of many other documentaries, such as *Triumph of the Will* (1935) and *Carmen Miranda: Bananas Is My Business* (1994), *Hearts of Darkness* entailed an enormous amount of selecting and arranging. When the makers of *Hearts of Darkness* were selecting excerpts from earlier texts—such as clips from *Apocalypse Now* and from Eleanor Coppola's footage—they were presenting a mediated reality based on an earlier mediated reality.

Hearts of Darkness illustrates yet other recurrent features of the documentary film. It uses real people being themselves. The excerpts from Eleanor Coppola's footage show people doing what they do in their work and in their spare time, not (presumably) posing for her camera. Like so many other documentaries, *Hearts of Darkness* was filmed on location, where the subjects live and work, in this case mostly in the Philippines.

a)

b)

FIGURE 10.4 Editing to comment on a subject obliquely
(a) Filipino boys have been playing with a toy sailboat seen here immediately after it topples over.
(b) The next shot is of Coppola talking about building projects inevitably going over budget. The juxtaposition of images suggests that Coppola is like a boy with a toy that is not entirely under control and ends up in an accident. The juxtapositioning of the two shots is sly but expressive. Frame enlargements. *George Zaloom and Les Mayfield; New Yorker Films*

a)

b)

FIGURE 10.5 Interviewee in late 1970s and more than a decade later
(a) Dennis Hopper being interviewed during the making of *Apocalypse Now*. (b) The next shot is of Hopper being interviewed during the making of *Hearts of Darkness*. In the later interview he says that at the time of the filming of *Apocalypse Now* his acting career was "not in the greatest shape." Frame enlargements. *George Zaloom and Les Mayfield; New Yorker Films*

FIGURE 10.6 **Darkness and despair**
Coppola with darkened eyes, depressed and despairing during the late stages of trying to finish *Apocalypse Now* successfully. So anguished had he become that he had been considering what sickness he could contract to get himself off the hook or even how he could commit suicide. Frame enlargement. *George Zaloom and Les Mayfield; New Yorker Films*

    As is explained in Chapter 9, various documentary films—such as those by Frederick Wiseman and those of Errol Morris—use quite different filmmaking techniques. Sometimes within the same film, a wide variety of techniques are used. As a few examples will illustrate, *Hearts of Darkness* uses a fairly wide range of techniques. The film cuts from Filipino boys to Coppola himself to suggest a point (Figure 10.4). Editing is also used to show how much someone has changed when the film occasionally cuts between an actor then and now (Figure 10.5). Another particularly expressive example of filmmaking occurs when the camera moves in on one of Coppola's darkened eyes; after a fade-out and fade-in, the camera moves away from his eye, and viewers see Coppola holding a pistol to his head (Figure 10.6). Then, too, music original to *Hearts of Darkness* is occasionally used to support the film's many moods and meanings.

    Hearts of Darkness: A Filmmaker's Apocalypse illustrates some of the possibilities of both narratives and documentaries. The film engages audiences in its factual story: the trials and eventual triumph of an individual and his associates. Like other narrative documentaries, *Hearts of Darkness* also informs viewers and gives them the chance to ponder the unexpected, sometimes far-reaching consequences of actual decisions and actions.

WORKS CITED

Coppola, Eleanor. *Notes.* New York: Simon and Schuster, 1979.

French, Karl. *Karl French on* Apocalypse Now. New York: Bloomsbury, 1999.

Part Three
UNDERSTANDING FILMS

W<small>E HAVE CONSIDERED</small> the impact of various filmmaking techniques and the variety of films. Part Three considers some of the ways viewers can come to understand a film. In Chapter 11, we examine how knowledge of a film's contexts helps viewers understand a film more completely. The chapter explores how where and how a film is made, where it is seen, and who sees it all influence filmmakers and in turn their films and viewer responses to the films. Chapter 12 considers some of the many complex ways viewers think about a film. For example, as viewers see a film, they form expectations and hypotheses and readjust them as the film progresses. As viewers see a film and as they think about it afterward, they also usually try to make sense of it—to figure out its meanings. Viewers are sometimes told some meanings by the film itself, and they often make meanings by various ways, including explaining the general implications of the story or the significance of a symbol. Chapter 12 examines these and other issues, including some of the ways the formulations of meanings are influenced by the viewer's background and other circumstances. Chapter 13, the third and last chapter of Part Three, applies the concepts of Chapters 11 and 12 to one film, thus demonstrating some of the many ways an informed and thoughtful viewer may understand a film.

◀   If a film succeeds in capturing the viewers' interest, viewers react emotionally and mentally, including formulating and reformulating expectations and figuring out the film's general significance or meanings. As illustrated here in a scene from *The Accidental Tourist* (1988), usually film viewing is also communal. *Warner Bros.*

CHAPTER 11

Understanding Films through Contexts

CONTEXT IS WHAT PEOPLE USE to make sense of new information. An unfamiliar word can make sense in a sentence. An unfamiliar place can have meaning on a map. An isolated event can be significant in the context of history. Context turns information into knowledge. It's the difference between a warehouse and a museum. (Herz, "What Is Art?")

Terms in **boldface** are defined in the Illustrated Glossary beginning on page 539.

We have all heard of people who were upset that their statements were "taken out of context" and thus their meaning distorted and misunderstood. Conversely, any statement examined in its contexts is more likely to be understood. As this chapter illustrates, knowledge of the conditions that precede and surround the making of a film and the conditions under which the film is viewed—its contexts—helps viewers understand a film more completely. A film does not begin when the house lights dim and the projector begins to send dancing lights through the darkness or when we turn on the TV and pop a tape into the VCR. What has happened before a film was made and sometimes what is going on while the film is being made influence how the finished film begins, how it all unwinds, and how viewers respond to it.

Let's consider three examples of how knowledge of contexts can help the viewer better understand a film. Before you are shown a 1920s Soviet film in a course or a film series, someone may stand before the audience and explain the political climate in the Soviet Union at the time the film was made. As a result, when you watch the film, you understand why it focuses not on a few individuals but on large groups. Imagine that before you see *Fatal Attraction*, you learn that shortly before the film appeared in 1987, the AIDS epidemic had led to mass media warnings about the dangers of unprotected sex. You also learn that in the 1980s, growing numbers of American men felt threatened by successful, financially independent, career-minded, sexually active single women. When you see *Fatal Attraction*, you notice that the film shows horrible consequences after a married man has unprotected sex with a single career woman, and you notice that the movie's career woman is shown unsympathetically. You now understand how societal attitudes at the time of

FIGURE 11.1 Showing affection in a 1950s film from India
Kissing was not allowed in Indian films in the 1950s, so loving feelings had to be conveyed in other ways. In *The World of Apu* (1958) a new wife gives her husband a look that blends love and concern. Frame enlargement. *Satyajit Ray; Edward Harrison*

the film's making can influence its content. Finally, imagine that you see *The World of Apu*, a 1958 film from India, and think it curious that the young married couple never kiss, though they are clearly in love. Later you learn that censorship regulations for Indian films of that time prohibited kissing, so the couple's affection had to be conveyed by other means (Figure 11.1). In these and countless other situations, knowing something about when and under what conditions a film was made helps viewers better understand the film.

Both filmmakers and film exhibitors often consider how much of a film's context their audiences are likely to know. Most filmmakers assume that audiences know something about the context of the film's story. If audiences may not, filmmakers often include background information in the film itself. **Title cards** give

title card: A card or thin sheet of clear plastic on which is written or printed information included in a film.

tidbits of historical information throughout *Schindler's List* (1993). The opening two title cards in *Das Boot*, or *The Boat* (1981), inform viewers that "the battle for control of the Atlantic is turning against the Germans" as the story begins in the autumn of 1941 and that of the 40,000 German sailors who "served on U-boats during World War II, 30,000 never returned." Television channels that focus on old movies, such as Turner Classic Movies, also usually include a brief introduction to each film explaining at least a little of the film's contexts.

Once viewers understand that filmmakers work under forces that restrict how they can represent political, religious, or sexual subjects, viewers are less likely to misjudge how a film represents these three subjects. Viewers who know when and where a film was made and under what conditions are also more likely to notice when filmmakers follow conventions and when they depart from them. They are more likely to understand how the film's budget precludes certain options and how the available filmmaking technology and the audio and visual presentations of competing media and electronic entertainments may influence the film. In addition, they are more likely to be aware that where a film is seen and who sees it may influence viewer responses to the film. The influences at work can be schematized as follows:

contexts in which a film has been made
and   }→ filmmakers → film → viewer responses
contexts in which a film is seen

Viewers who see influences behind (and around) filmmakers can more clearly and more fully understand why a film is the way it is.

There are so many possible contexts for a film that it would take a sizable book to begin to explore them fully. The first part of this chapter—contexts in which a film has been made—introduces five types of contexts: society and politics, censorship, artistic conventions, financial constraints, and technological developments. Generally, these contexts are presented from the most abstract to the most concrete—from ideas, such as societal attitudes, to practical realities, such as money and filmmaking equipment. The second part of the chapter—contexts in which a film is seen (viewing environment and audience) can also influence filmmakers, the films they make, and viewer responses to the films.

CONTEXTS IN WHICH A FILM HAS BEEN MADE

Society and Politics

Human freedom of expression is relative: there are always limits to what filmmakers can show. Their freedom to express themselves is strongly affected by the dominant attitudes of the society in which they work and the society's political climate.

Societal attitudes may exert powerful influences on filmmakers. For example, dominant attitudes about homosexuality influence whether, when, and how homosexuals are portrayed in films. Because so many people disapproved of homosexuality (some heterosexual males violently so), from the birth of cinema in the 1890s until the production code went into effect in 1934, American movie gays were nearly always represented as laughable. After the production code placed restrictions on filmmakers (see pp. 378–79), from 1934 into the 1960s homosexual characters were seldom identified openly. In *The Maltese Falcon* (1941), for example, several characters are homosexual though the film does not make their homosexuality explicit (Figure 11.2). *Rebel without a Cause* (1955), *Tea and Sympathy* (1956), *Cat on a Hot Tin Roof* (1958), *Suddenly Last Summer* (1959), and many other American films refer to homosexuality only obliquely.

As attitudes in Western societies have changed, so has the representation of gays in films. In his book *The Celluloid Closet: Homosexuality in the Movies*, Vito Russo says that the first positive images of gays in commercial cinema appear in two 1961 British movies, *A Taste of*

FIGURE 11.2 **Advertising for a 1940s movie that hints at a character's homosexuality**
This photo for *The Maltese Falcon* (1941) approximates a few brief images from the movie itself and hints at the Peter Lorre character's homosexuality—the cane handle near his mouth—the explicit depiction or mention of which was forbidden by the U.S. production code then in effect. *Hal B. Wallis; Warner Bros.–First National*

FIGURE 11.3 **Gay stereotypes in a film**

The Boys in the Band (1970) includes eight gay or bisexual male characters. It is ambiguous whether the film's one heterosexual character is completely heterosexual. Although the film was the first widely distributed U.S. movie featuring gays, it also perpetuated gay stereotypes, especially the universality of gays' emotional misery. Near the end of the film, one character announces slowly, and in effect twice, "If we [homosexuals] could just learn not to hate ourselves quite so very much." *Mart Crowley; National General Pictures*

Honey and *Victim* (126–33). In *A Taste of Honey*, a sensitive homosexual friend cares for the main character, an unwed pregnant teenager. In *Victim*, a British movie star, Dirk Bogarde, plays a man who admits to his desire for another man; some of the film's "character portrayals are relatively sympathetic, given the era and social climate in which the film was made" (Jones 321–22). After the U.S. film industry abandoned the production code and instituted a rating system in 1968, more adult subjects, including homosexuality, began to appear on movie screens. *The Boys in the Band* (1970) was the first American commercial movie featuring a cast of gay characters (Figure 11.3). In *Dog Day Afternoon* (1975), Al Pacino was perhaps the first major movie star who had played only heterosexual characters to act the role of a bisexual, and he did so credibly and without inviting ridicule or condescension. The film also includes a persuasive performance by Chris Sarandon as the Pacino character's homosexual lover.

Even with the coming of the ratings system, more than a few movies trod well-worn paths and showed gays as miserable, depressed, suicidal, dangerous, or laughable. In *La cage aux folles* (1978), its sequels, and its remake as *The Birdcage* (1996), gay characters have pivotal roles, though they and the situations they end up in are stereotypical, amusing, and nonthreatening to heterosexual audiences. In many other films since the 1960s, however, gay characters are seen in less stereotypical, more complex roles, as in *Longtime Companion* (1990) and *Philadelphia* (1993). The huge commercial success of *The Crying Game* (1992) is a barometer of changing social tolerance in matters of sexual orientation (Figure 11.4). From then on, films with credible gay characters became commonplace in American cinema, and even societies that have attempted mightily to repress homosexuality, such as Castro's Cuba, brought forth an occasional film sympathetic to gays (Figure 11.5).

FIGURE 11.4 Tolerance of sexual preference
The Crying Game (1992), featuring an IRA volunteer (left) and a hairdresser, questions whether sexual preference is the only consideration in a close relationship. The film, which was a critical and popular success, treats its complex characters sympathetically in ways inconceivable in earlier eras. *Palace; Channel 4; Miramax*

FIGURE 11.5 Stereotypical yet complex and sympathetic gay character
The Cuban film *Strawberry and Chocolate* (1993) can be seen as mainly the story of a growing friendship in spite of the two men's many fundamental differences. The main character, Diego (left) is a gay photographer who is religious and critical of Cuban governmental policies. The other main character, named David (right), is a heterosexual though initially virginal university student from an impoverished village background who is not religious and basically supports the Castro government. Gradually, Diego teaches David a greater awareness of the power of the arts and increases his tolerance toward those who have been labeled as different. The film devotes much time to Diego's homosexuality though, since the film is a product of 1990s Cuba, no homosexual contact is shown. Often the actor playing Diego plays the part broadly and amusingly, with a full range of belongings, dress, tastes, gestures, and manners thought typical of gays. But because of some details in the script and the often-nuanced performance of the main actor, Diego can be subtle, amusing, engaging, complicated, and sympathetic. Furthermore, he is articulate, intelligent, talented, brave in speaking out for more tolerance and artistic diversity in Cuba, yet proudly Cuban as well. Frame enlargement. *Cuban Institute of the Arts and Film Industry; Robert Redford and Miramax Films*

a)

b)

c)

d)

As times change, so do representations of subjects, including stories that continue to speak to audiences and so get made and remade and remade. Consider the **celluloid** Tarzan, whose characters, story, and concerns vary according to time and place of production (Figure 11.6).

Because mainstream movies cost so much to make and market, if they are to turn a profit, they must appeal to the tastes and values of huge audiences. As was explained in Chapter 9, **experimental films** usually cost relatively little to make, so their makers need not draw large audiences and thus are much freer to express themselves without regard to popularity. Accordingly, the tastes and values of experimental films are often at odds with prevalent tastes and values

celluloid: Synonym for movie, as in "celluloid heroes."

experimental film: A film that rejects the conventions of mainstream movies and explores the possibilities of the film medium itself.

◄ FIGURE 11.6 **Different societies, different Tarzans**
(a) American Edgar Rice Burrough's novel *Tarzan of the Apes* (1912) was first adapted, in most
of its essentials, into an American film of the same title six years later. The first Tarzan movie
is set in what for 1918 American audiences must have been exotic locales and features plenty of
action, including attacks by a variety of wild animals. *Tarzan of the Apes* stars a boy playing Tarzan
at a youthful age then the portly Elmo Lincoln as the strong but not particularly graceful adult
Tarzan, who never swings through trees—perhaps for fear of cracking tree branches. Typical
of the film's racial insensitivity is the title card stating that before Jane, Tarzan had never seen a
woman, although earlier in the film viewers saw him looking at African women. The film consistently shows that Tarzan is much more at home with apes than with native Africans and reflects
the fear and distrust so many European Americans of the time felt about people with dark skins.
(b) *Tarzan: The Ape Man* (1932) stars former Olympic swimming champion Johnny Weissmuller
and Maureen O'Sullivan. This *Tarzan* gives no explanation how Tarzan happened to be living
in the jungle with wild animals. The film can be seen as Depression-era escapist fare featuring
exotic locales, lots of action, condescending stereotypes of Africa and Africans aplenty, a love
triangle of two men pursuing the same woman, a crowd-pleasing resolution, and little interest
in such issues as race, colonialism, imperialism, and identity. (c) *Greystoke: The Legend of Tarzan,
Lord of the Apes* (1984) was an international though largely British production. The story alternates between western Africa and Scotland, as it focuses on the loneliness and loss of being
caught between two worlds, two families: "lord of the apes" and earl of Greystoke. The film
also shows the artifice and shortcomings of civilized society, and "civilized" man's exploitation
of the African environment and callous treatment of its wildlife. Kenneth M. Cameron writes,
the film was "heavily weighted . . . toward environmental concern—the Green Party version
of Tarzan— . . . [and] examined the great apes, particularly, in far more detail and with far more
sympathy than other Tarzan pictures" (166). (d) Disney's *Tarzan* (1999) is curiously void of
Africans and, as so many Disney films do, exalts the glories of nature and the worth of an outsider. Here a handsome, athletic Tarzan moves through trees as youths do when they surf or
skateboard. Like the 1984 *Greystoke*, Disney's *Tarzan* also shows "civilized" men's cruelty and
their callous and exploitative treatment of animals. The film also deals with such subjects as
the outsider, family, assimilation, and identity—issues generally of more concern to the later
twentieth century than to early in the century when Tarzan came to light. Unlike *Greystoke* but
in keeping with the Disney tradition, the film is often amusing and concludes with romantic love
triumphant. (a) *The Museum of Modern Art/Film Stills Archive*; (b) *Bernard H. Hyman*; *MGM*;
(c) *Hugh Hudson and Stanley S. Canter*; *Warner Bros.*; (d) Frame enlargement. *Bonnie Arnold and
Christopher Chase*; *Walt Disney Pictures*

of their time. Often their makers create films to protest orthodox beliefs, values,
and behavior. Unlike the movies of the time, many of Andy Warhol's films include cross-dressing (*Screen Test 2*, 1965) and homosexuality (*My Hustler*, 1965).
Often his films show no story at all, as when he simply turned on the camera
and filmed the Empire State Building (*Empire*, 1964). Like so many experimental films, in subject matter his films defied the mores of the time.

Political developments—especially as reported in the mass media—influence what topics people are concerned about and how they think about
them. In turn, political concerns affect the choice of subjects represented in
many forms of human expression, including films.

Consider the situation in the United States shortly after the end of World War II, with the Soviet Union's rise in power. With heavy media coverage of those political developments, many Americans began to worry about Communist infiltration of American institutions. As part of its activities, in 1947 the House Committee on Un-American Activities (HUAC, as the committee was often imprecisely called) held hearings in Hollywood to investigate Communist infiltration of the film industry. Some filmmakers—either on the grounds that the committee's actions infringed on their constitutional rights or because they had been Communist Party members—refused to cooperate with the committee. Ten filmmakers, mostly screenwriters, dubbed the "Hollywood Ten," were eventually sentenced to prison for contempt of Congress. In 1951, HUAC held a second round of hearings on Communist influence in Hollywood, and more than three hundred Hollywood filmmakers either confessed to past membership in the Communist Party or were accused by witnesses of having been members. Until well into the 1960s, most of those people were blacklisted and could not find work in the American film industry.

The atmosphere of fear and distrust caused enormous upheaval in the industry. Some filmmakers found other work; some moved abroad to find film work; others worked in the American film industry under assumed names. Freedom of expression was curtailed for all who worked in the film industry at the time, not just for those who were accused of being Communists. Filmmakers shied away from controversial projects, especially those with political subjects. Some films commented indirectly on the political climate of the time. For example, some commentators see parallels between those who refused to cooperate with HUAC and the town marshal in the western *High Noon* (1952); both acted on their principles and refused to give in to intimidating forces. Some critics see parallels between *The Invasion of the Body Snatchers* (1956) and its times. The film shows a cautionary story about the gradual, unobtrusive invasion of alien life forms that take on the appearance of people but not their emotions then replace the people. To some critics, the film is symptomatic of the menace and passivity of the era.[1]

In every era, political climate influences the choice and representation of subjects. Another example is seen during the cold war period, from the late 1940s to the 1980s. Such American movies as *Red Dawn* (1984), which shows Soviets and Cubans invading a small Colorado town, and *Rambo: First Blood Part II* (1985) depict Soviets as untrustworthy and treacherous. *Rocky IV* (1985) also reflects the political mood through two boxing matches between representatives of the Soviet Union and the United States, and it is unsur-

---

[1]For an opposing interpretation of the causes and consequences of the HUAC investigations of Hollywood, see Jon Lewis, "'We Do Not Ask You to Condone This': How the Blacklist Saved Hollywood." *Cinema Journal* (Winter 2000): 3–30.

a)   b)

FIGURE 11.7 **The cold war in a boxing ring**
Rocky IV (1985) culminates in a boxing match between Rocky and his Goliath Soviet opponent, Ivan Drago. It's not giving away a surprise ending to reveal that Rocky prevails. He does so for a combination of reasons. In part, Rocky wins because *Rocky IV* is an American movie made during the cold war. Although the film is draped in national flags and the last image before the ending credits is of Rocky with a U.S. flag above him, Rocky's victory is also a victory for the old ways of doing things. (a) Rocky trains in nature with nature's objects (rocks, mountains, snow, logs) and simple country tools (sled, ax, block and tackle, rope, yoke, cart, and saw). (b) Drago uses all the most advanced computerized exercise equipment and is injected with drugs. Rocky is advised by a trainer with years of experience with professional boxing. Drago is trained by a cadre of state-employed scientists and a trainer with no professional experience in boxing. Other factors contribute to Rocky's victory. He keeps getting back up and going at Drago, and he is not burdened by arrogance. He also prays and he fights for others, including his late friend Apollo Creed. By the twelfth round, even the initially hostile Soviet crowd begins chanting "Rocky!" "Rocky!" "Rocky!" Of course, Rocky has earned the loving support of his wife and young son. (Are there any emotional buttons this film does not push?) Before the final round, a Soviet official berates Drago, who announces that he fights to win—for himself. Drago is then alone and on the doorstep of defeat. Frame enlargements. *Robert Chartoff and Irwin Winkler; United Artists*

prising which political system the movie champions (Figure 11.7). *Rocky IV* and other cold-war-era movies exalt Americans and encourage nationalism while denigrating the Soviet system. In contrast, since the increased cooperation between Russia and the United States in the 1990s and beyond, few such anti-Russian American movies have been forthcoming.

Censorship

Censorship is closely related to societal attitudes and political climate. From the beginning of cinema, some people have been concerned about the possible harm inflicted on *others* who see certain behavior, especially sex and violence, or who are exposed to certain ideas, particularly religious and political ones. Different societies address those concerns in different ways.

close-up: An image in which the subject fills most of the frame and little of the surroundings is shown.

Some societies forbid the making of certain films. Iranian movies, most of which are funded by the government, forbid criticism of the Iranian Islamic government and all religions. In Iranian films women must be shown in head scarf and long coat. Forbidden are **close-ups** of women, makeup, kissing, handholding, and eye contact between men and women. To ensure compliance with these and other guidelines, the government imposes multiple stages of censorship, beginning with the approval of the script.

In Vietnam, a censor is always present during filming, as one was during the filming of *Three Seasons* (1999). If the censor sees or hears anything questionable, the filmmakers must make changes on the spot or to come to an agreement with the official. In China, filmmakers are not supposed to make sexy films, films that criticize the government explicitly or implicitly, or depressing films with sad endings. If filmmakers shoot their film without first getting the script approved and a permit, they face the likelihood of a stiff fine and exclusion from the large Chinese market. *Xiu Xiu: The Sent Down Girl* (1998), which Joan Chen filmed on the sly in a remote western province, is a film suffering this fate, as is the more widely seen *Farewell My Concubine* (1993). Chinese control over movies is far reaching. *Postman* (1995)—which is not to be confused with the Italian film *Il Postino (The Postman)* of the same year or Kevin Costner's *The Postman* (1997)—touches on adultery, prostitution, homosexuality, and drug use. Even before its completion, director He Jianjun was banned from making further films.

Sometimes government authorities may halt a production, as was the fate of the Soviet filmmaker Sergei Eisenstein, who was forced both to abandon

a)   b)

FIGURE 11.8 **Early, local censorship**
(a) An 1897 American film, "Fatima's Dance," shows a woman dancing provocatively (shimmying and bumping), at least by the standards of the day. (b) Some exhibitors showed a censored version of "Fatima's Dance" with scratched emulsion obscuring the women's clothed breasts and legs. Frame enlargements. *The Museum of Modern Art/Film Stills Archive*

Bezhin Meadow in 1937 and to repudiate it publicly. Eisenstein ran into trouble with *Bezhin Meadow* and most of his later films because he did not follow the general guidelines of **socialist realism.** This Soviet doctrine and **style,** which were in force from the mid-1930s to the 1980s (until the Gorbachev era), decreed that all creative works—including music, artworks, and films—must promote socialism, communism, and thus the proletariat or working people. Soviet creative works were not to imply approval of Western ideas and lifestyles or even ambivalence toward them. Under socialist realism, creative works were supposed to be "realistic" (actually an idealized depiction of the working class) and readily accessible to mass audiences. Styles judged innovative or arty were taboo. Works that were judged to fall short of the standards of socialist realism were labeled "decadent," "bourgeois," "capitalistic," or "formalist"— and sometimes in the 1930s and 1940s Stalin himself made that judgment. At a minimum their makers were publicly rebuked. For fifty years socialist realism severely restricted both the subjects and styles of Soviet artists, not just such filmmakers as Sergei Eisenstein and Lev Kuleshov but also the composers Dmitri Shostakovich and Sergei Prokofiev, writer Isaak Babel, theater director Vsevolod Meyerhold, and many others. Unlike the United States, the Soviet Union, and many other countries, censored its own films because of their unflattering representation of the country.

In the United States, early films were sometimes censored by state or city boards (Figure 11.8). By the early 1930s, much of the American public found many popular American movies offensive. Some viewers seemed especially upset by violence and sex, whereas others swarmed to such popular gangster films as *Little Caesar* (1930), *The Public Enemy* (1931), and *Scarface* (1932) and films featuring unrepentant, sexually assertive women, especially those played by Mae West (Figure 11.9). Of West's impact scholar Ramona Curry writes:

> Unlike most other Hollywood movies of the 1930s, West's films do not suggest that morality or questions of taste dictate female sexual behavior. Instead, West's

FIGURE 11.9 Mae West's sexuality in pre–production code movies

In *I'm No Angel* (1933)—which was written by Mae West and included a youthful Cary Grant (seen here)—West wears her usual variety of revealing and often glamorous clothes. She plays a single woman who is quick-witted, resourceful, confident, attractive to many men, and nearly always fully in control of situations with men. Although she is skimpy with her displays of affection and usually turns away from the men's attempted embraces and kisses, she often looks at men directly (not obliquely), wears tight and revealing clothing, and sings suggestively as she gently sways her hips. Even today, the Mae West characters are sometimes still quoted for such well-timed witty double entendres as, "When I'm good, I'm very good, but when I'm bad, I'm better." By today's standards, the Mae West characters in her early 1930s movies are campy and suggestive, even quaintly so, not carnal, and certainly not as one Hearst newspaper editorial of the time proclaimed a "menace to . . . the American Family." To many 1930s U.S. audiences, she was sexual, assertive, unrepentant, and shocking, and her movies have been blamed as partially responsible for stricter enforcement of the production code. *William LeBaron; Paramount* films and star image present female sexual allure as a commodity that women themselves can control and benefit from. . . . West's movie image exposed contradictions in the well-established American capitalist practice of simultaneously exploiting and repressing female sexuality as a commodity under men's control. (28)

Rather than face government interference, in 1930 American film producers and distributors set up a written production code (see pp. 378–79), a self-regulatory system of acceptable speech and behavior in films. In 1934, the code was revised and from then on more strenuously enforced. Until 1968, all movies to be shown in the United States were supposed to be submitted to the Production Code Administration for a seal of approval. The production code restricted the explicit or attractive depiction of vast areas of human experience—such as illegal drugs, illicit sex (including homosexuality), scenes of passion, prostitution, miscegenation, childbirth, and obscene and profane speech. From 1934 to 1968, to earn the seal of approval American films had to be suitable for audiences of all ages, including young children. Some of the differences between films made before and after the code was enforced are evident in stills for *Gold Diggers of 1933* and *Gold Diggers of 1937* (Figure 11.10).

Enforcement of the code often undermined a story's plausibility or logic, resulting in incoherence. *The Big Sleep* (1946) is confusing because it omits nearly all references to the sex and drugs so prominent in the source novel by Raymond Chandler. As critic Frank Krutnik shows, enforcement of the code in a romantic scene involving the two main characters in *Out of the Past* (1947) could be confusing:

> The couple run through the rain to the beach-house, laughing like carefree young lovers. When they arrive there, Kathie dries his hair, and Jeff does the same for her. He kisses her on the back of the neck and then tosses away the towel, which knocks the lamp over. When the light goes out, there is a swirl of music, and the camera then **tracks** towards the door, which blows open in the wind. There is then a cut to the outside, with the camera continuing its forward-tracking. This leading away from the scene, together with the reprisal of the film's love-theme and the dousing of the light, suggests that Jeff and Kathie are making love. However, the film cuts back to the inside of the beach-house: Jeff closes the door, and Kathie takes a record off the gramophone. There is a marked, seemingly post-coital change in their attitudes. However, although the slow forward-tracking of the camera has implied that intercourse takes place, the cut back to the inside, and the continuity of Jeff shutting the door after it has blown open, suggest that there has been no time-lapse. Sex is thus both firmly suggested and disavowed. (246)

The code is also responsible for more than one implausible ending, such as in *Detour* (1945). That film was initially refused a seal of approval because it ended with the main character, who had inadvertently killed someone, free and walking along a road. To gain a seal, a short scene was appended: the police

track (verb): To film while the camera is being moved around.

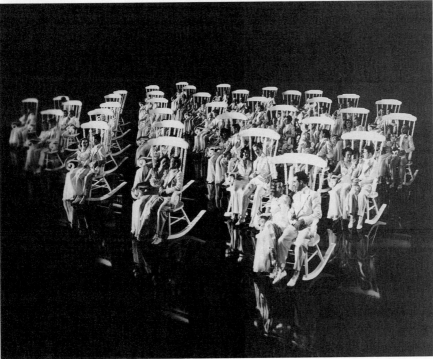

FIGURE 11.10 **Pre– and post–production code movies** (a) From the "Pettin' in the Park" musical number in *Gold Diggers of 1933* (1933). After the production code was applied to all movies from 1934 on, such glimpses of sexuality were forbidden on U.S. movie screens. (b) A few years after the production code was fully in effect, *Gold Diggers of 1937* (1936) depicts men and women as innocent (dressed in white), childlike (small in comparison to the chairs), and unerotic (covered up and sitting, not uncovered and lying down as in the 1933 film). The language of *Gold Diggers of 1937* is also less suggestive than that of *Gold Diggers of 1933*, and in the later film words such as "pettin'" or "petting" are nowhere to be heard. (a) *Jack L. Warner; Warner Bros.*; (b) *Hal B. Wallis; Warner Bros.–First National*

Excerpts from *The Production Code of the Motion Picture Producers and Directors of America, Inc.—1930–1934*

PREAMBLE

Motion picture producers recognize the high trust and confidence which have been placed in them by the people of the world and which have made motion pictures a universal form of entertainment.

They recognize their responsibility to the public because of this trust and because entertainment and art are important influences in the life of a nation.

Hence, though regarding motion pictures primarily as entertainment without any explicit purpose of teaching or propaganda, they know that the motion picture within its own field of entertainment may be directly responsible for spiritual or moral progress, for higher types of social life, and for much correct thinking. . . .

On their part, they ask from the public and from public leaders a sympathetic understanding of their purposes and problems and a spirit of co-operation that will allow them the freedom and opportunity necessary to bring the motion picture to a still higher level of wholesome entertainment for all the people.

GENERAL PRINCIPLES

1. No picture shall be produced which will lower the moral standards of those who see it. Hence the sympathy of the audience shall never be thrown to the side of crime, wrongdoing, evil or sin. . . .

    I. CRIMES AGAINST THE LAW

    These shall never be presented in such a way as to throw sympathy with the crime as against law and justice or to inspire others with a desire for imitation.

      1. Murder

        a) The technique of murder must be presented in a way that will not inspire imitation.

        b) Brutal killings are not to be presented in detail.

        c) Revenge in modern times shall not be justified. . . .

II. SEX

The sanctity of the institution of marriage and the home shall be upheld. Pictures shall not infer that low forms of sex relationship are the accepted or common thing.

    1. Adultery and illicit sex, sometimes necessary plot material, must not be explicitly treated or justified, or presented attractively.

    2. Scenes of passion

      a) These should not be introduced except where they are definitely essential to the plot.

      b) Excessive and lustful kissing, lustful embraces, suggestive postures and gestures are not to be shown.

      c) In general, passion should be treated in such manner as not to stimulate the lower and baser emotions.

    3. Seduction or rape

      a) These should never be more than suggested, and then only when essential for the plot. They must never be shown by explicit method.

      b) They are never the proper subject for comedy. . . .

    6. Miscegenation (sex relationship between the white and black races) is forbidden. . . .

III. VULGARITY

The treatment of low, disgusting, unpleasant, though not necessarily evil, subjects should be guided always by the dictates of good taste and a proper regard for the sensibilities of the audience.

IV. OBSCENITY

Obscenity in word, gesture, reference, song, joke, or by suggestion . . . is forbidden.

V. PROFANITY

Pointed profanity and every other profane or vulgar expression, however used, is forbidden.

No approval by the Production Code Administration shall be given to the use of words and phrases in motion pictures including, but not limited to, the following:

. . . broad (applied to a woman); . . . God, Lord, Jesus, Christ (unless used reverently); . . . fanny; fairy (in a vulgar sense); finger (the); . . . hot (applied to a woman); . . . louse; lousy; . . . nerts; nuts (except when meaning crazy); pansy; . . . slut (applied to a woman); S.O.B.; son-of-a; tart; . . . traveling salesman and farmer's daughter jokes; whore; damn. . . .

The Production Code Administration may take cognizance of the fact that the following words and phrases are obviously offensive to the patrons of motion pictures in the United States and more particularly to the patrons of motion pictures in foreign countries: Chink, Dago, Frog, Greaser, Hunkie, Kike, Nigger, Spig, Wop, Yid. . . .

VIII. RELIGION
   1. No film or episode may throw ridicule on any religious faith.
   2. Ministers of religion in their character as ministers of religion should not be used as comic characters or as villains. . . .

REASONS SUPPORTING PREAMBLE OF CODE

. . . The MORAL IMPORTANCE of entertainment is something which has been universally recognized. It enters intimately into the lives of men and women and affects them closely; it occupies their minds and affections during leisure hours; and ultimately touches the whole of their lives. A man may be judged by his standard of entertainment as easily as by the standard of his work. . . .

   3. D. The latitude given to film material cannot, in consequence, be as wide as the latitude given to book material. In addition:
      a) A book describes; a film vividly presents. One presents on a cold page; the other by apparently living people.
      b) A book reaches the mind through words merely; a film reaches the eyes and ears through the reproduction of actual events.

      c) The reaction of a reader to a book depends largely on the keenness of the reader's imagination; the reaction to a film depends on the vividness of presentation.
      Hence many things which might be described or presented in a book could not possibly be presented in a film. . . .

F. Everything possible in a play is not possible in a film:
   a) Because of the larger audience of the film, and its consequential mixed character. Psychologically, the larger the audience, the lower the moral mass resistance to suggestion.
   b) Because through light, enlargement of character, presentation, scenic emphasis, etc., the screen story is brought closer to the audience than the play.
   c) The enthusiasm for and interest in the film actors and actresses, developed beyond anything of the sort in history, makes the audience largely sympathetic toward the characters they portray and the stories in which they figure. Hence the audience is more ready to confuse actor and actress and the characters they portray, and it is most receptive of the emotions and ideals presented by their favorite stars.

G. Small communities, remote from sophistication and from the hardening process which often takes place in the ethical and moral standards of groups in larger cities, are easily and readily reached by any sort of film. . . .

In general, the mobility, popularity, accessibility, emotional appeal, vividness, straightforward presentation of fact in the film make for more intimate contact with a larger audience and for greater emotional appeal.

Hence the larger moral responsibilities of the motion pictures.

FIGURE 11.11 Sexual frankness in 1950s and 1960s European films
Some European films of the 1950s and 1960s were more candid in their depictions of sexuality than American films of the time and were shown without the
production code seal of approval in some, mostly big-city American theaters.
Here one of the two main characters of Ingmar Bergman's *The Silence* (1963) is
seen reacting as she masturbates, an act that is not shown in the film. Elsewhere,
the other main character sees a couple having sexual intercourse in the back of
a movie theater. In both instances, the depictions of sexuality would have been
inconceivable in American movies of the time because of the force of the production code. The inclusion of such scenes made these European films more
appealing to many American viewers and distributors and probably contributed
to the abandonment a few years later of the U.S. production code and adoption
of a ratings system that permitted more adult films for adult audiences. Frame
enlargement. *Allan Ekelund; Svensk Filmindustri; Embassy*

drive up, stop, pick up the man, and drive off, as he narrates, "Someday a car will stop to pick me up that I never thumbed. Yes. Fate or some mysterious force can put the finger on you or me for no good reason at all." In this case, the not so "mysterious force" was the production code.

As more and more films were re-leased without a seal in the 1950s and 1960s, it became harder and harder to enforce the code. As film historian and scholar Robert Sklar explains:

> The tendency in motion-picture pro-duction and exhibition had always been to get away with as much risqué and so-cially disreputable behavior as the vigi-lance of censors would allow and economic necessity dictated. For nearly two decades after 1934, the Production Code Administration had maintained stringent control over Hollywood pro-ductions, and rising box-office figures through 1946 seemed to confirm that clean family entertainment was the road to prosperity. But as families found their clean entertainment on the TV screen, there was a natural impulse in the movie trade to revert to shock and titillation. (294)

In 1953, the American film *The Moon Is Blue* was refused a seal because it treated seduction and adultery comically, and its distributor, United Artists, resigned from the producers association and released the film on its own without a seal. Later in the 1950s and in the 1960s, such European films as the French *And God Created Woman* (1956) were more candid sexually than American films and were shown without a seal of approval in art theaters in large cities throughout the United States (Figure 11.11).

Finally in 1968, the U.S. production code was replaced with a rating sys-tem loosely modeled on the British rating system. The American ratings have been modified several times since then. (For an explanation of the cur-rent American ratings, see Figure 11.12.) Studios that belong to the Motion Picture Association of America are required to submit finished films for a rating. **Independent film** companies, which operate outside Hollywood

What Everyone Should Know About The Movie Rating System.

GENERAL AUDIENCES

G

G GENERAL AUDIENCES
All Ages Admitted

Nothing that would offend parents for viewing by children.

PARENTAL GUIDANCE SUGGESTED

PG

PG PARENTAL GUIDANCE SUGGESTED
SOME MATERIAL MAY NOT BE SUITABLE FOR CHILDREN

Parents urged to give "parental guidance." May contain some material parents might not like for their young children.

PARENTS STRONGLY CAUTIONED

PG-13

PG-13 PARENTS STRONGLY CAUTIONED
Some Material May Be Inappropriate for Children Under 13

Parents are urged to be cautious. Some material may be inappropriate for pre-teenagers.

RESTRICTED

R

R RESTRICTED
UNDER 17 REQUIRES ACCOMPANYING PARENT OR ADULT GUARDIAN

Contains some adult material. Parents are urged to learn more about the film before taking their young children with them.

NO CHILDREN UNDER 17 ADMITTED

NC-17

NC-17 NO CHILDREN UNDER 17 ADMITTED

Patently adult. Children are not admitted.

FIGURE 11.12 **The current U.S. movie rating classifications** Before the latest change in the ratings system in 1990, both sexually explicit films and serious films unable to win an R rating were given an X, which meant that many theaters would not show them, many newspapers would not advertise them, and many video stores would not carry them. The NC-17 rating was devised for films that are made primarily to present their subjects with candor and not to stimulate sexual arousal. Since the inception of the NC-17 rating, the Motion Picture Association of America no longer assigns films an X rating. Few sexually explicit films were ever submitted for a rating, anyway. © *Motion Picture Association of America, Encino, Calif.*

control, are not. Advertisements and theaters are to display the rating so viewers will know what to expect, and theaters are supposed to exclude certain age groups from films with certain ratings. Although both the industry and public generally approve of the system, it is a source of persistent problems and persistent complaints. The ratings board continues to tend to be much harsher on films with sexual content than films with violence. Children under 17 are often admitted or find ways to get into R-rated films. And the NC-17 rating, which was intended to remove the pornographic stigma from frank but serious representations of sexual subjects, is a failure. Films released with the NC-17 rating are shut out of many theaters and advertising venues, and films so rated are often released by the distributor without a rating. Because of dissatisfaction with the rating system, from time to time alternatives to it emerge.[2]

In many countries, filmmakers often face pressures, perhaps contractual obligations, to delete parts of a film before its release so that the film can receive a more commercially viable rating (in the United States, an R rating). Commercial interests also impose limits on political views. Few Hollywood movies, for example, focus on Communist characters or ideas. In part because so many American newspapers will not carry ads for NC-17 films and, before them, X-rated movies, American distributors faced with the prospect of that rating sometimes release films as unrated, as was done with *Requiem for a Dream* (2000) and *Bully* (2001). American studios that release videotape versions may also face pressure from Blockbuster Video, with the commercial clout of its approximately five thousand U.S. outlets, to reedit films and omit some of the violence, sex, and obscene language because Blockbuster will not carry films rated NC-17 or X. Even after a film has been rated and released in the U.S. market, it may be subjected to inconspicuous forms of censorship. On cable, for example, Turner Classic Movies has shown altered versions. Even such unrated tame films as *L'avventura* (1960) and such PG-rated movies as *Tootsie* (1982) may be preceded with the announcement "This feature has been edited due to content."

Knowing something about the restrictions on filmmakers and film distributors helps viewers understand and judge films more accurately and fairly. Such knowledge may help one understand, for example, why *Detour* stumbles to its conclusion and why two films that share the same general subject and are only a few years apart are so different (see Figure 11.10).

---

[2]Since September 1995, an agency of the United States Catholic Conference has run a movie review line (800-311-4CCC) that provides brief reviews of films currently in theaters and a family video of the week. For six or so films each week, callers can hear explanations for the USCC's classification (A-1 = general patronage; A-2 = adults and adolescents; A-3 = adults; A-4 = adults only and with reservations; and O = morally offensive) and the Motion Picture Association of America rating for the same films. Callers also hear a brief description and evaluation of the film. Current brief movie reviews and an archive of USCC movie reviews are also available on the Web at <http://www.usccb.org/movies/index.htm>.

Artistic Conventions

Subject: FW: Things you learn at the movies:

- It does not matter if you are heavily outnumbered in a fight involving martial arts. Your enemies will wait patiently to attack you one by one by dancing around in a threatening manner until you have knocked out their predecessors.
- All beds have special L-shaped cover sheets that reach up to the armpit level on a woman but only to waist level on the man lying beside her.
- Once applied, lipstick will never rub off—even while scuba diving.
- In war it is impossible to die unless you make the mistake of showing someone a picture of your sweetheart back home.
- A man will show no pain while taking the most ferocious beating but will wince when a woman tries to clean his wounds.
- If staying in a haunted house, women should investigate any strange noises alone in their most revealing underwear.
- If you decide to start dancing in the street, everyone you meet will know all the steps. (from an uncredited list widely circulated on the Internet)

And as yet another cowboy dressed in black enters yet another saloon, the music changes from a major to a minor key, but we don't notice the shift because that's the way we've so often heard it done (Figure 11.13). Like the examples quoted above, this use of music in movies is a **convention**—a technique or content that audiences are used to and accept without question. Most movies are permeated with conventions. Consider dialogue, for example:

> Does anyone believe that when police show up at a bank heist, the criminals say coolly, "We got company"? And has a real police detective ever said to a reticent witness, "You and I are going downtown for a little chat"? At no point in my life has anyone used these words with me: "I hope so, Todd. I hope so." In fact, I hardly ever hear anyone use my name at all in conversation. It would sound peculiar, yet in movies it happens all the time, and it sounds perfectly natural. Movie dialogue obeys its own customs. We accept it according to the terms of the cinema, not of reality. (Berliner, 3)

These and many other cinematic conventions are traditional ways of making a film or including traditional content in it.

FAR SIDE

"Bad guy comin' in, Arnie! . . . Minor key!"

FIGURE 11.13 **A musical convention in movies**
The Far Side © 1992 Farworks, Inc. *Used by permission of Universal Press Syndicate. All rights reserved.*

iris shot: Shot in which part of the frame is masked or obscured, often leaving the remaining image in a circular or an oval shape.

new wave: A diverse group of French fictional films made in the late 1950s and early 1960s in reaction to the carefully scripted products of the French film industry and as explorations of more current subjects sometimes rendered with untraditional techniques.

genre: A commonly recognized group of fictional films that share settings, subjects, or events (and sometimes techniques) and that change over time.

slow motion: Motion in which the action depicted on the screen is slower than its real-life counterpart, as when people are seen running slowly.

Some conventions—such as showdowns and shootouts in western films and telephone conversations in which one speaker is shown but both are heard—endure for decades. If used too often or for too long, conventions may become boring or in other ways ineffective, as has happened with tremolo stringed instruments used to accompany suspenseful moments. Conventions may also fall out of favor but later be rediscovered. An example is the reintroduction of a variety of techniques, such as **iris shots,** by the directors of French **new wave** films. Another example is the reintroduction by *Star Wars* (1977) of **wipes**—a transition in which it appears that one image pushes off the preceding image as it replaces it (see Figure 3.9 on p. 112). Yet other conventions—such as the introduction of scenes of memories by an undulation of the image—simply disappear for long stretches of film history (and may be revived).

Often iconoclastic filmmakers draw attention to filmmaking conventions by flouting them. Mel Brooks is one such filmmaker. In *High Anxiety* (1977), for example, the camera moves toward French doors through which viewers can see people sitting at a formal dinner. The camera moves forward and forward until it loudly shatters a glass pane, and the dinner party stares at it; after a brief pause, the camera begins to retreat. In the last scene of the same film, the camera pulls back from its subjects rapidly, and viewers hear a camera operator warn, "We're going too fast. Were going to hit the wall." Almost instantaneously they do, noisily, and make a gaping hole in it. As the camera continues to retreat, the other man says, "Never mind. Keep moving back. Maybe no one will notice." Gliding exploratory camera work is a conventional technique most viewers take for granted. But most viewers have probably neither seen a camera operator have an accident nor considered when, how, and why camera movement is used.

A film may also be unconventional in its subjects. In the conventional western **genre,** for example, the protagonist is a European American male, and his antagonists are American Indians, Mexicans, or European American male outlaws. In American westerns since World War II, the protagonist may be female (*The Ballad of Little Jo,* 1993; *Bad Girls,* 1994), African American (*Posse,* 1993), or European American and Mexican outlaws (*The Wild Bunch,* 1969). On the other side, the antagonists may be European American males, as throughout Jim Jarmusch's *Dead Man* (1995). The antagonist may be a law enforcement officer (*Unforgiven,* 1992; *Posse*). European American outlaw antagonists may even be supported by the inaction of the townspeople (*High Noon*).

Some breaks with conventions—such as having an actor step out of character to speak directly to the audience—never catch on with other filmmakers, though this one was used throughout *High Fidelity* (2000). Other breaks with conventions seem odd initially but are imitated by other filmmakers and eventually become conventions themselves. One example is the use of **slow motion** to depict violence. When *Bonnie and Clyde* (1967) used it in a violent scene, many viewers commented on its use and found it distracting. But soon other movies, including those directed by Sam Peckinpah, followed the practice. It became widespread and, through repetition, now seems natural to many viewers. As in other arts, the unconventional can become conventional through repetition.

Unconventional filmmakers help us see that conventions are arbitrary: they do not have inevitable and unchanging meanings or significance. For instance, a **lap dissolve**—in which one image fades out as the next image fades in, momentarily overlaps it, and replaces it—does not have to mean "now the **setting** changes," though it usually does in films of recent decades. In films before the 1930s, lap dissolves are occasionally used within a scene (see Figure 3.8 on p. 111). Filmmaking practices take on widely understood meanings or associations through repeated use in similar contexts. For instance, if enough filmmakers use lap dissolves to suggest that the action now shifts to a new setting, viewers learn that meaning (similarly, we learn the meanings of most words by hearing or reading them in context, not by hearing or reading definitions).

setting: The place where filmed action occurs.

When we examine **filmic** conventions, we start to see how widespread, expressive, and influential they are. Conventions influence how a film is made and in turn how viewers respond. Conventions are like teachers and clergy: although most people take them for granted most of the time, they strongly influence succeeding generations.

filmic: Characteristic of the film medium or appropriate to it, such as parallel editing or the combination of editing and a full range of vocals, silence, and music.

Financial Constraints

> Lot of times just your schedule, your budget determines how you're going to do things. (Altman)

> Digital video has dramatically lowered the barriers to **feature film**-making. For aspiring film-makers who don't have $200,000 to shoot on 35 mm, or $50,000 for 16 mm, it's an affordable alternative. Instead of spending years searching for financing, film-makers can devote their time to improving the script, rehearsing the actors and shooting the best possible movie. When their film is finished, they can decide if it is good enough to launch their careers. If not, they can make another feature for a few thousand dollars, learning from their mistakes. . . . DV is shifting power from financiers to film-makers, who no longer need their money, permission or approval. (Broderick 7)

feature film: A fictional film that is at least sixty minutes long.

The budget for a film influences the choice of equipment, personnel available, settings, time that can be devoted to making the film, and promotion and distribution. Consider the situation of Terry Zwigoff, the director of the acclaimed **documentary** *Crumb* (1994), whose lack of money restricted what he could film and influenced how he filmed it:

documentary film: A film whose representation of its subjects viewers are intended to accept primarily as factual.

> I just didn't have any film to use. It was horrible. I'd be in this situation with great stuff happening, and I'd have to allot myself two rolls of film instead of ten. And it was also what forced me to prompt and to stage and to manipulate a lot of things—you just couldn't wait for them to happen naturally with that kind of budget. (Katz 38)

location: Any place other than a film studio that is used for filming.

Big feature films are terrifically expensive to make (see the feature on pp. 388–89). A movie with stars, special effects, lots of action filmed at foreign **locations,** and widespread advertisements requires a budget in the tens of millions of dollars, perhaps even more than $100 million. To attract enough viewers to earn back all the expenses and make a profit, such a movie has to be entertaining to huge audiences. In other words, once a big-budget deal is fashioned—for example, for *Pearl Harbor* (2001)—or the making of the film proves much more costly than it was budgeted for—as with *Titanic* (1997)—the filmmakers are under a lot of pressure to deliver a movie with some proven popular characteristics. Popular components are chases, fights, explosions, spectacular sights, romantic or sexual attraction and interaction, a youthful heartthrob, and a happy ending. Filmmakers responsible for making a movie with a big budget are also under pressure to avoid generally unpopular subjects, such as religion, and unconventional styles, such as **magic realism.**

magic realism: A style in which occasional improbable or impossible events are included in an otherwise realistic story.

Many movies are not just movies. They are mines for other products to be marketed by other components of the media conglomerate that includes the company that made or distributed the movies in the first place. Consider *Austin Powers: The Spy Who Shagged Me* (1999), which is distributed in the United States by New Line Cinema, which had been taken over by Ted Turner, who in turn agreed to a merger with Time Warner. The *Austin Powers* movies, in other words, are now the property of Time Warner. As one commentator explained shortly before the film's initial release,

Within weeks, Warner Brothers retail stores and Spenser Gifts stores across the country will roll out a plethora of merchandise from snazzy nightshirts to the Austin Powers Swedish Penis Enlarger ("the perfect gift for Dad on Father's Day!"). TBS and TNT, two cable networks owned by Time Warner, will feature wall-to-wall promotion of the movie. *Entertainment Weekly*, the glossy magazine owned by Time Warner, is set to have an Austin Powers cover.

Warner Records will release the soundtrack album, which includes a single, "Beautiful Stranger," by Madonna, whose label, Maverick Records, is also a Warner subsidiary. And by now,

FIGURE 11.14 Low budget, curious results
The budget for Ed Wood's *Plan 9 from Outer Space* (1959) was minimal. When actor Bela Lugosi died early in the filming, another actor was brought in to take over the part. Rather than reshoot Lugosi's scenes, director Ed Wood had the new actor cover his face, presumably so no one would notice Lugosi's absence! The results are laughable. *Edward D. Wood, Jr.; Reynolds Pictures, Inc.*

Warner Books has probably delivered to stores the first of its no doubt multiple printings of "The Austin Powers Encyclopedia."

There's more. The home video, due out in the fall [of 1999], will be sold by Time Warner's sales force; early next year there will be an animated series by HBO, a Time Warner subsidiary. . . .

There may also be a theme park tie-in with Six Flags Great Adventure, which was sold recently by Time Warner but retains a licensing agreement with the company. (Hass)

For an independent film without stars, special effects, and exotic locations, the budget will be far less—though raising money to produce it still tends to be very time-consuming and frustrating. With a smaller budget, the return need not be huge to cover all the expenses and turn a profit. Independent filmmakers—such as John Sayles, Jim Jarmusch, Charles Burnett, Ang Lee, Julie Dash, and Robert Rodriguez—are freer to fashion a film more to their liking, such as one with a controversial or offbeat subject or perhaps an ending that lacks **closure** or a happy fate for characters that viewers identify with. As illustrated in *Plan 9 from Outer Space* (1959), budgets may be so restricted, however, as to cause curious results (Figure 11.14).

closure: A sense of resolution or completion at the end of a narrative.

Budget Is Destiny?

As the following two hypothetical budgets by a Hollywood producer illustrate, different films result from different budgets. In this case, both planned films originate from the same source story that is set in the 1930s. The big-budget version has stars, a large budget for the script (scenario), a costly (and perhaps famous) director, a lengthy shooting schedule, period sets and costumes, and a sizable music budget. The small-budget version has no stars and a short shooting schedule and is set in the present (lacking the glamour of period sets and costumes). The big-budget version has a lot of money for advertising (not shown here: the "publicity/stills" entry is for only the unit publicist and still photographer). It generates attention to itself. The small-budget version needs a shrewd script, creative director, and enthusiastic reviews. Positive word of mouth would be a plus. Recognition at a major film festival and awards would probably help, too. In filmmaking, budget often is destiny.

Source for pp. 388–89: Art Linson, "The $75 Million Difference," *New York Times Magazine* 16 Nov. 1997: 88, 89. "Bills, Bills, Bills," *Los Angeles Calendar (on line)* 20 Dec 1998, lists "the typical costs associated with producing a major Hollywood studio movie," including "Sound equipment: $1,800 a week," "Ferrari Daytona: $850 to $1,000 a day," and "Rattlesnake: $400 a day." The article is available (by purchase) through the archives at <http://www.latimes.com>.

(BIG BUDGET)

APPOINTMENT IN SAMARRA

START DATE: February 2, 1998
FINISH DATE: May 12, 1998
LOCATION: Albany, NY
TOTAL DAYS: 70
5-day weeks/12-hour shoot/10-hour prep
HOLIDAYS: 2
POST: 22 weeks, Los Angeles

Story rights	$ 300,000
Scenario	1,727,250
Producer	2,740,308
Director	5,305,514
Principal cast costs	32,299,197
Misc. star costs	1,912,747
Julian English	20,000,000
Caroline English	4,000,000
Lute Fliegler	2,000,000
Froggy Ogden	500,000
Harry Reilly	500,000
Dr. English	1,000,000
Al Grecco	2,000,000
Mrs. Walker	250,000
Casting	136,450
Supporting cast	1,939,054
Stunts	317,850
Rehearsals	9,000
ATL travel and living	2,260,112
Total fringes	705,899
TOTAL ABOVE-THE-LINE	**47,604,184**
Extras	1,293,456
Production staff	1,268,019
Art department	925,672
Set construction	2,500,000
Grip/set operations	927,339
Camera	1,216,657
Production sound	262,875
Electrical/set lighting	974,143
Special effects	514,390
Creatures/mechanical FX	0
Set dressing	1,195,882

Animals/handlers	25,000
Wardrobe	2,016,205
Makeup/hair	451,264
Video playback and assist	150,283
Props	249,456
Action props/pic vehicles	929,000
Prod raw stock & lab	600,590
Second unit	250,000
Visual FX (and miniatures)	1,500,000
Tests	50,000
Transportation	1,808,354
Location and office expenses	2,139,335
BTL travel and living	2,085,078
Stage and backlot charges	272,100
Total fringes	3,236,200
TOTAL PRODUCTION EXPENSES	**26,841,298**
Picture editorial	693,221
Sound/music editorial	525,821
Postproduction sound	521,243
Postproduction film/lab	122,380
Stock picture footage	5,000
Music	1,500,000
Visual effects—postproduction	0
Titles/dissolves/wipes	100,000
Projection	45,615
Total fringes	207,966
TOTAL POSTPRODUCTION	**3,721,246**
Miscellaneous charges	194,100
Insurance	727,453
Publicity/stills	114,541
Total fringes	28,765
TOTAL OTHER EXPENSES	1,064,859
TOTAL BELOW-THE-LINE	**31,627,403**
Total above- and below-the-line	79,231,587
Completion bond: 3%	0
Contingency: 10%	0
GRAND TOTAL	**$79,231,587**

(SMALL BUDGET)

APPOINTMENT IN SAMARRA

START DATE: February 2, 1998
FINISH DATE: March 7, 1998
LOCATION: Suburban NYC
TOTAL DAYS: 30
6-day weeks/12-hour shoot/10-hour prep
HOLIDAYS: 0
POST: 18 weeks, NYC

Story rights	$ 50,000
Scenario	54,000
Producer	207,700
Director	116,950
Principal cast costs	239,600
Misc. star costs	1,750
Julian English	50,000
Caroline English	50,000
Lute Fliegler (per week)	5,000
Froggy Ogden (per week)	5,000
Harry Reilly (per week)	5,000
Dr. English (per week)	5,000
Al Grecco (per week)	5,000
Mrs. Walker (per week)	5,000
Casting	32,850
Supporting cast	109,619
Stunts	21,781
Rehearsals	1,000
ATL travel and living	36,880
Total fringes	41,554
TOTAL ABOVE-THE-LINE	**879,084**
Extras	135,637
Production staff	241,950
Art department	76,334
Set construction	15,000
Grip/set operations	126,834
Camera	115,689
Production sound	32,551
Electrical/set lighting	110,708
Special effects	78,086
Creatures/mechanical FX	0
Set dressing	132,673

Animals/handlers	0
Wardrobe	98,469
Makeup/hair	55,470
Video playback and assist	3,740
Props	57,815
Action props/pic vehicles	27,500
Prod raw stock & lab	139,065
Second unit	0
Visual FX (and miniatures)	50,000
Tests	2,500
Transportation	304,430
Location and office expenses	361,296
BTL travel and living	5,000
Stage and backlot charges	0
Total fringes	225,840
TOTAL PRODUCTION EXPENSES	**2,396,587**
Picture editorial	219,042
Sound/music editorial	119,040
Postproduction sound	193,490
Postproduction film/lab	61,550
Stock picture footage	0
Music	125,000
Visual effects—postproduction	0
Titles/dissolves/wipes	33,000
Projection	7,125
Total fringes	49,686
TOTAL POSTPRODUCTION	**807,933**
Miscellaneous charges	83,700
Insurance	63,404
Publicity/stills	25,700
Total fringes	3,432
TOTAL OTHER EXPENSES	176,236
TOTAL BELOW-THE-LINE	**3,380,756**
Total above- and below-the-line	4,259,840
Completion bond: 3%	127,795
Contingency: 10%	425,984
GRAND TOTAL	**$4,813,619**

For a short film or video on the Internet, the budget can be so small that many filmmakers can afford to shoot and edit until they get nearly exactly the results they want. Because makers of short films do not require a large audience, they have enormous freedom to express themselves on film.

Technological Developments

Although new technology makes possible effects that were previously impossible, advances in filmmaking technology are not without their costs and sometimes limitations. In the late 1920s and early 1930s, films began to be made with sound synchronized with the image, but because the microphones picked up the camera noise during filming, the cameras were placed in soundproof rooms and camera movement in dialogue scenes largely came to a halt (Figure 11.15). Such films tended to be unmoving and overwhelmed by dialogue.[3]

New technology can also affect the types of movies that get made. In the late 1920s, for example, the introduction of **film stock** that contained a sound track made possible the union of film and vaudeville, which was a type of musical comedy variety stage show:

> In the case of Hollywood this produced a new genre—the musical. However, it also put an end to other generic types, such as the gestural, slapstick comedy associated with Chaplin and Keaton. Conversely, it created a new type of comedy: the fast repartee comedy with snappy dialogue (as with the Marx Brothers and W. C. Fields) and screwball comedy—usually based on the "battle between the sexes." (Hayward 333)

Competition from other media may also spur the movie industry to develop technology that makes movies more appealing to consumers. For example, when box office revenues began to decline in the United States in the late 1940s with the growth of small-screen black-and-white television, the film industry countered with greater use of color films and a variety of other new technologies. One of the most spectacular was the Cinerama process introduced in 1952, which used three projectors and seven-**track** stereo sound

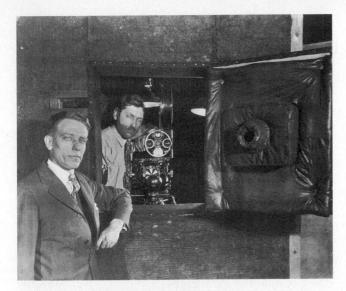

FIGURE 11.15 The coming of sound
In the late 1920s several films were made using the Vitaphone system, which involved recording sound onto a separate large photograph record during filming. To muffle the camera's sounds, the camera was entombed in a small soundproof room. Such an arrangement ended the mobility of the camera during shots. *The Museum of Modern Art/Film Stills Archive*

film stock: Unexposed and unprocessed motion-picture film.

track (noun): A film sound track, a narrow band on the film that contains recorded optical, magnetic, or digital sound.

---

[3]*Singin' in the Rain*—a 1952 American musical film whose narrative is set in the late 1920s—includes fairly accurate, humorous scenes demonstrating some of the problems of filming while recording sound on records and later synchronizing the records with the projected images.

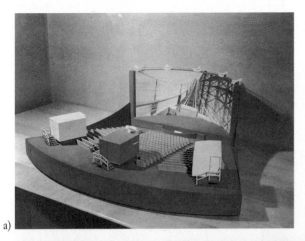

a)

b)

c)

FIGURE 11.16 Competing with the popular new medium, TV

During the 1950s, moviemakers and movie exhibitors introduced new technologies in filmmaking and film exhibition to try to lure customers away from their new, small, increasingly popular, black-and-white TV sets and back into movie theaters. Three of the technologies of the 1950s and 1960s are illustrated here. (a) Cinerama (a scale model) was a wide-screen format created by the use of three cameras during filming and three projectors during screenings. (b) 3-D movies required that viewers wear simple, lightweight special glasses. A few such American movies were made and marketed between 1952 and 1954. (c) Huge and super wide-screen images were the era's most successful and enduring technological answer to TV. When shown in the theaters, *Ben-Hur* (1959), seen here, had an aspect ratio of 2.75:1, meaning the image's width was nearly three times greater than its height. (a–c) *The Museum of Modern Art/Film Stills Archive*

(Figure 11.16a). Because of the growing popularity of TV, the film industry even tried to lure customers into theaters with a few 3-D movies such as *Bwana Devil* (1952), with lions and spears seemingly hurling toward the audience, and *Dial M for Murder* (1954), a suspenseful movie about a man plotting his wife's murder (Figure 11.16b). By the end of the 1950s, Hollywood was presenting large and occasionally the widest of wide-screen images ever

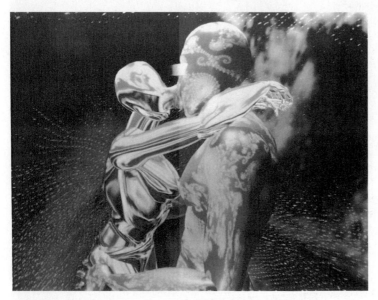

FIGURE 11.17 Computers used to depict virtual reality in movies
For *The Lawnmower Man* (1992) and occasional later movies such as *The Matrix* (1999), computers were used to create scenes of virtual reality, a computer-generated artificial world complete with changing imaginary environment and virtual people who interact with their environment and each other. At one point in *The Lawnmower Man*, a man and a woman in an advanced laboratory don virtual-reality headgear then see and seem to experience themselves as is shown here, as virtual people who change shape. Here the cybercouple are being affectionate and demonstrating in a new way the unifying force of love. *Gimel Everett; New Line Cinema*

shown commercially in the United States (Ultra-Panavision), as in the critical and popular success, *Ben-Hur* (1959, Figure 11.16c).

Ever since the 1990s, computers have been used to create effects with a verisimilitude previously impossible in live-action films. Computers can be used to change moving parts of images. In **morphing,** a transformation of one shape into another, sophisticated software can make something seem to transform into something else. In *Terminator 2: Judgment Day* (1991), for example, a cyborg transforms itself from a pool of liquid into its usual appearance as a man and at another time from its usual appearance into what looks like a police officer (see Figure 2.53 on p. 93).

Computers have many other uses for filmmakers. Digital manipulation can be used to eliminate part of a subject, such as part of a character's legs in *Forrest Gump* (1994). Computers were used to combine images to show Forrest Gump meeting and mingling with Presidents Nixon and Kennedy and to show characters in *Contact* (1997) interacting with President Clinton.[4] With computers, people can be placed in any setting, whether an actual location or a set constructed of building materials or of photographs stored in a computer. In *Contact* (1997), for instance, computers were used to move images of President Clinton from one place to another. Perhaps most impressively of all, computers can be used to create virtual realities—computer-generated worlds—with changing imaginary environments and virtual people who can interact and continuously change shape (be morphed) as in *The Lawnmower Man* (1992, Figure 11.17). Virtual

---

[4]"Through the Eyes of Forrest Gump" (1994), a documentary/promotional film, shows how the shot of Forrest meeting President Kennedy was a composite of altered footage of the president meeting with a football team in the White House and a shot of Forrest shaking hands with the air against a blue background. The film also explains how computers were used in the scenes of Lieutenant Dan without his legs, Forrest's championship Ping-Pong match, and that floating feather.

realities and other filmmaking effects possible only through computers were also used even more extensively and impressively in *The Matrix* (1999, see Figure 7.25 on p. 245).

It is not just visuals that have changed with the times. More recently, in the face of competition from cable and satellite, videotape, laser discs, DVDs, and CDs, theaters have countered yet again with superior sound systems, such as THX sound, DTS (Digital Theater Systems) six-track digital stereo, and Sony Dynamic Digital Sound.

CONTEXTS IN WHICH A FILM IS SEEN

So far, we have been examining some of the many ways that the contexts in which a film is made affect filmmakers and their films, and in turn film viewers. There is space here to introduce only briefly the idea that viewing environment and audience can also affect the way films are made and how viewers respond to them.

Many people now see more movies at home than in theaters. Since the 1960s, many filmmakers have known that their films would eventually be shown on TV screens, so they have composed their images with two screen shapes in mind: the **wide-screen film** shape most often used in theaters and the narrower shape of an analog TV screen (see Figure 1.30 on p. 35). Some filmmakers mindful of later TV audiences use fewer **long shots** and more close-ups than they would otherwise because the details of a long shot tend to get lost on analog TV; for the same reason, they might use more light. Since home viewing equipment can be relatively low priced and access to some form of the films and to refreshments much less expensive than in movie theaters, home viewing has vastly expanded the number of viewers. Viewers typically respond differently to a film seen at home than they do to one seen in a movie theater. Home presentation has many advantages over a theatrical showing—control over speed of presentation, continuity of presentation, replay, volume, tone, color, contrast, and so on—but it has many potential shortcomings as well. Home viewers may miss a visual or audio subtlety because it is difficult or impossible to discern on the viewing equipment (see, for example, Figure 12.8 on p. 417). Then, too, viewers are often more distracted and less caught up in the images and sounds at home than they are in a theater.

What were some of the main early viewing environments and audiences, and how did they indirectly influence filmmakers and the films they made? During the second decade of motion pictures (from about 1905 to 1915), most movies were seen in nickelodeons (Figure 11.18a). The interiors of nickelodeons tended to be plain and functional (not very decorative or even comfortable). The audiences were limited to perhaps a hundred or two, initially mostly recent immigrants and working-class viewers, many with only a

wide-screen film: Any film with an aspect ratio noticeably greater than 1.33:1 (shape wider than that of an analog TV screen).

long shot: Shot in which the subject is seen in its entirety, and much of its surroundings are visible.

shaky command of English. Nearly always, some form of musical accompaniment was provided, at least a piano or a piano and drums. More than a few nickelodeons provided "lecturers" to explain the films as they ran. As the nickelodeons grew popular, they quickly became part of the neighborhood scenery. Eileen Bowser's account of one city in 1908 is illustrative of the situation:

> In Indianapolis, for example, there were twenty-one nickelodeons and three ten-cent theaters in 1908, only three years after the first nickelodeon had appeared there. Each nickelodeon in this city gave a show consisting of one reel of film, which might contain two or three different subjects, and an illustrated song, with the show taking twenty to twenty-five minutes—"except when there is a crowd waiting, then it is speeded up to 15 to 17 minutes." The shows in Indianapolis were open from nine in the morning till eleven at night, which allowed

FIGURE 11.18 **Contexts in which a film is seen** ▶

(a) Nickelodeons were small storefront movie theaters popular in the United States from roughly 1905 to 1915. It is estimated that by 1910 there were already 10,000 of them, and most towns and urban neighborhoods had at least one. They were inexpensive to attend, accessible (though initially thought not very respectable), yet small and modest in environment and presentation. In the early years, their programs of short films lasted from twenty to thirty minutes. Seen here is the Cascade Theatre in New Castle, Pennsylvania, which was purchased by the Warner family in 1903. Sam Warner, seen on the left, sang to the audience during reel changes and intermissions, as was the usual practice in nickelodeons, and later was one of the four brothers founding Warner Bros. The small signs visible in this photograph include the information that the shows were "Refined Entertainment for ladies, gentlemen, and children," which assured would-be patrons that *this* theater was respectable. Others signs indicate that the pictures were changed twice a week; admission was always five cents; and performances were continuous. (b–c) A movie palace, the Brooklyn Paramount Theatre in 1928. When the Paramount Theatre opened on Flatbush Avenue in Brooklyn late in 1928, it was the second largest theater in New York City, complete with forty-one hundred plush upholstered seats and with ticket prices from approximately twenty-five cents to $1.25 depending on when one went and where one sat. Part of the sign on the side of the building says "Brooklyn Paramount Theatre, the last word in beauty, comfort, luxury, and entertainment." For years, the theater was used to show either movies or various live shows, such as rock 'n' roll stage shows. It was last used to show a movie in 1962. Like most of the ornate American movie palaces built in the 1920s and 1930s, it has not survived intact. Eventually parts of the building were incorporated into a building that is part of Long Island University. Now a gym floor covers the original stage and orchestra seating, and the auditorium's much-admired blue recessed dome is situated above a basketball court. *Sic transit gloria mundi.* (d) A huge screen in an IMAX theater. Although this screen is not as large as those for 3-D IMAX theaters, which are the equivalent of eight stories high, it extends beyond most viewers' peripheral vision. While watching a film in such a theater, viewers looking straight ahead see only the image and are caught up in it. With the marketing of large-screen digital TVs, perhaps IMAX will build more such theaters to lure people out of their homes and into theaters. History shows that with each major improvement in home viewing, the movie industry counters with an improvement in technology or luxury, or both. (a–c) *The Museum of Modern Art/Film Stills Archive;* (d) *Courtesy of IMAX Corporation*

a)

c)

b)

d)

about twenty to thirty shows each day. If you could afford ten cents, you could go to one of the three high-class theaters and get an evening of three or four reels of pictures with live entertainment consisting of illustrated songs, vaudeville acts, and slide lecturers lasting from one to one-and-a-half hours. By 1911, the number had increased to seventy-six motion-picture theaters alone, not including regular theaters that changed over to movies during the summer. However, only fifteen of the movie houses remained downtown in 1911, because of the high rents. (6)

Going to the nickelodeon was a modest experience easily accessible to the masses. Given the multiethnic and mostly uneducated audiences of the time, the limitations of the technology, and the nickelodeons' spartan accommodations, early filmmakers made short and intellectually undemanding films that they hoped would be entertaining and popular.

In the 1920s, after moviegoing had grown into a huge business in the United States and elsewhere, movie palaces were erected in various American cities, mostly in downtowns (Figure 11.18b and c): "The greatest of silent picture palaces was unquestionably the Roxy in New York, the 6,214 seat 'cathedral of the motion picture' . . . . Patrons who were not intimidated by a trip under the massive, five-story tall rotunda faced a squadron of ushers drilled by a retired Marine Corps captain. The statuary, the carpeting, the mural decorations, all worked together to create an effect of overwhelming grandeur, but the frame had grown far more important than any picture" (Koszarski 23, 25). Also adding to the experience was a large pipe organ used to accompany the films and fill the interludes. Compared with nickelodeons, the movie palaces cost more, attracted wealthier customers, and showed longer and more involved programs (including live variety acts). Such an environment encouraged moviegoers to think of movies and their venue as bigger than life, since the images and sounds were bigger and more involving than ever. The opulent and often exotic settings reflected by theater names such as the Egyptian, Chinese, Aztec, and Loew's Paradise also nurtured the feeling that moviegoing was an escape into a new world, a world of soft lights and music throughout the theater and huge moving images up on the screen. Such theaters could function as an opiate against the unreliable world outside. Venue, in short, could strongly affect viewer anticipation and response. Note the order in which the Brooklyn Paramount Theatre of 1928 touted its qualities: its "beauty, comfort, luxury, and entertainment" (Figure 11.18b). More than at any other time in movie history, the place where the movies were shown could be more exciting, more special than the movies themselves.

Something of the same experience was recaptured in the 1970s with the coming of IMAX theaters and films (Figure 11.18d). Like movie palaces, IMAX theaters seem special partly because they are generally available only in large cities. Like movie palaces, IMAX theaters provide the biggest image and sometimes the most enveloping sound available. Some IMAX theaters also provide the most satisfying 3-D experience yet achieved in movie history. Unlike the movie palaces, however, IMAX theaters in name and decoration are plain and functional. The system's screen can be up to approximately eight stories high and a hundred or so feet wide. For 3-D IMAX, viewers wear special glasses, and a subject in the extreme foreground can appear to be in the viewer's face or to move to the side of the viewer's head. The sense of three dimensionality is so convincing, it's hard not to duck—or at least flinch—as objects seem to hurl toward the audience or as the camera skims over the top of terrain. While viewing "Alaska: Spirit of the Wild" (1997) and many other IMAX films in three-dimensions in an Omnimax theater with its huge dome screen, viewers may feel queasy while seemingly looking straight down as an airplane flies over a vast territory. With no noticeable distortion, the accompanying eight-track sound system can vibrate the viewers' feet, armrests, and seat.

Although 3-D IMAX films have proven effective for short documentaries, it is not yet certain how amenable the system is to feature-length narrative films:

> Neither the rapid motion of humans or objects—save for a synesthetic zinger like the hurtle of a subway train in *Sea of Time*—nor the rapid editing of individual shots fits well into IMAX's formal protocols. At times, . . . directing in this format becomes an "engineering feat" instead of a creative endeavor. The IMAX camera weighs over four hundred pounds, takes twenty minutes to reload, and . . . holds only three minutes worth of stock. . . . At least for now, the stipulation to shoot slowfooted aquatic creatures that don't demand retakes hardly seems conducive to our roster of popular story types. Then again . . . (Arthur 81)

How widespread IMAX theaters become will be determined, as are all technological developments, by economic imperatives: to what extent filmgoers are willing to pay for a product made with the new technology.

Although many predicted a major drop in movie attendance with the growth of home videotape, movies via satellite, and with the growth of movie watching on DVDs and the Internet, theater attendance remains robust. It is likely to stay so because movie theaters can always provide technology and an environment that no home can match. In the latest development, many new movie theaters have extremely large screens and stadium seating. In such theaters, viewers can see all of the screen regardless of who sits in front of them; seats can be as large and comfortable as first-class seats on a U.S. airline, and there is no danger from your neighbors' elbows. The sound is also superior to any home system. Some of these theaters have seen attendance jump 300 percent. As of this writing, digital projection—with it ability to project large, sharp, unfaded, unscratched, and unwavering images—seems likely to gain in use in theaters. In short, compared with home viewing, movies in up-to-date theaters will always be superior in environment, image, and sound. As commentator J. C. Herz has written,

> The proliferation of small screens—televisions, computer monitors, L.C.D. cellular phone displays, personal digital assistants—only aggravates our desire for the huge screen in a plushly upholstered movie palace with three-dimensional symphonic sound. The more fractured information becomes, the more we long for an epic story that simply washes over us—and not over one of us at a time, but over all of us at once.

Many contexts for films are included in this book's chronology for 1895 to 2000, which includes columns on major world events, the arts, mass media, and films and videos (pp. 485–531).

Now that we have explored some of the factors that influence both the making of films and in turn the exhibition and viewing of them, we turn our attention in the next chapter to how viewers interact with the films themselves, including the meanings they find in them.[5]

SUMMARY

This chapter introduces five types of contexts in which a film has been made. The second part of the chapter briefly illustrates how the contexts in which the film is seen (theater and audience) can also influence filmmakers, the films they make, and viewer responses to the films.

Contexts in Which a Film Has Been Made

Filmmakers are subject to many influences, such as widespread attitudes in a society, censorship, filmic conventions, financing, and technological developments. Viewers who know about these and other contexts of a film can understand the film more completely.

SOCIETY AND POLITICS

■ Societal attitudes influence how filmmakers represent a subject. For example, before the late 1960s, homosexuals were usually shown obliquely and stereotypically in American movies, but with greater public tolerance

---

[5]For two examples that demonstrate the power of contextual and textual analyses, see Graeme Turner's analyses of *Butch Cassidy and the Sundance Kid* (1969) and *Desperately Seeking Susan* (1985) in his *Film as Social Practice* (3rd ed., 1999, pp. 188–206).

of homosexuality (and the latitude afforded by a ratings system) American movies since the late 1960s more frequently include gays and increasingly show them nonstereotypically. As is illustrated by some Tarzan movies, other subjects, such as certain popular stories, also change as societal attitudes do.

■ The political climate strongly affects how much freedom of expression filmmakers have and what political outlooks are likely to be explained or implied in their films.

CENSORSHIP

■ Censorship (written or implied) strongly influences the content of films.

■ In the United States from 1934 into the 1960s, most films were censored by an agency set up by the film producers and distributors to ensure that movies were suitable for viewers of all ages.

■ Often governments ban or censor a film as it is being made or after it is completed.

■ In many societies a rating system is devised that allows for a wide latitude of subjects but restricts some films to certain age groups.

ARTISTIC CONVENTIONS

■ Filmic conventions are techniques or content that audiences tend to accept without question.

■ Filmmakers may follow conventional practices. Or they may reject them, as in many westerns made since World War II.

■ Conventions may fall out of favor, and unconventional practices may catch on and become conventional.

■ Filmmaking conventions do not have inevitable and fixed meanings; usage, which varies over time, establishes their meanings.

FINANCIAL CONSTRAINTS

■ Since the amount of money available to filmmakers helps determine equipment, personnel available, settings, time to film, and distribution, financing is a crucial influence on the making of films and in turn viewer responses to them.

■ Generally, the greater the finances needed to make and promote a film, the greater the pressures to make a movie with such popular characteristics as chases, fights, explosions and other spectacular sights, romance or sex, and a happy ending.

- In general, the smaller the budget, the greater control filmmakers have over their work and the more individualistic it is likely to be.

Technological Developments

- New filmmaking technology may influence the types of films that are made.

- Advances in the technology of competing mass media and electronic entertainments, such as television, may influence the techniques filmmakers use, settings, and actions presented as well as the type of film exhibition used.

- Computers are now used to achieve effects with a verisimilitude previously impossible in live-action films, such as to change moving parts of the image, eliminate parts of a subject, combine images, place subjects in new settings, and create a virtual reality.

Contexts in Which a Film Is Seen

- The size, design, comfort, and accessibility of the viewing environment along with the types of audiences attending the showings affect the types of movies made and in turn how viewers respond to them.

WORKS CITED

Altman, Robert. Audio Commentary. *The Player* (DVD), New Line Home Video, 1997.

Arthur, Paul. "IMAX 3-D and the Myth of Total Cinema." *Film Comment* Jan./Feb. 1996: 78–81.

Berliner, Todd. "Hollywood Movie Dialogue and the 'Real Realism' of John Cassavetes." *Film Quarterly* 52.3 (Spring 1999): 2–16.

Bowser, Eileen. *The Transformation of Cinema, 1907–1915*. New York: Scribner's, 1990.

Broderick, Peter. "DIY = DVC." *Mediawatch '99*. Supplement to *Sight and Sound* 9.3 (March 1999): 6–9.

Cameron, Kenneth M. *Africa on Film: Beyond Black and White*. New York: Continuum, 1994.

Curry, Ramona. *Too Much of a Good Thing: Mae West as Cultural Icon*. Minneapolis: U of Minnesota P, 1996.

Hass, Nancy. "It's Synergy, Baby. Groovy! Yeah!" *New York Times on the Web*. 2 May 1999. <http://www.nytimes.com/library/film/050299film-sequel-synergy.html>.

Hayward, Susan. *Cinema Studies: The Key Concepts*. 2nd ed. London: Routledge, 2000.

Herz, J. C. "'Star Wars' World with a Sense of Humor." *New York Times on the Web.* 29 Oct. 1998. <http://www.nytimes.com/library/tech/98/10/circuits/game-theory/29game.html>.

———"What Is Art? That Can Mostly Depend on the Context." *New York Times on the Web.* 11 March 1999. <http://www.nytimes.com/library/tech/99/03/circuits/articles/11game.html>.

Jones, Chris. "Lesbian and Gay Cinema." *An Introduction to Film Studies.* 2nd ed. Ed. Jill Nelmes. London: Routledge, 1999. 307–44.

Katz, Susan Bullington. "A Conversation with Terry Zwigoff." *The Journal* [Writers Guild of America, West] Feb. 1996: 36–40.

Koszarski, Richard. *An Evening's Entertainment: The Age of the Silent Feature Picture, 1915–1928.* New York: Scribner's, 1990.

Krutnik, Frank. *In a Lonely Street: Film Noir, Genre, Masculinity.* London: Routledge, 1991.

Russo, Vito. *The Celluloid Closet: Homosexuality in the Movies.* Rev. ed. New York: Harper, 1987.

Sklar, Robert. *Movie-Made America: A Cultural History of American Movies.* Rev. and updated. New York: Random, 1994.

FOR FURTHER READING

Dyer, Richard. *Now You See It.* New York: Routledge, 1990. An examination of gay and lesbian films from 1919 to 1980.

History of the American Cinema. Ed. Charles Harpole. The University of California also publishes these books in paperback. Ten volumes are planned; forthcoming are volumes on the 1950s and 1960s. Seven are so far available:

Balio, Tino. *Grand Design: Hollywood as a Modern Business Enterprise,* 1930–1939. New York: Scribner's, 1993.

Bowser, Eileen. *The Transformation of Cinema, 1907–1915.* New York: Scribner's, 1990.

Cook, David A. *Lost Illusions: American Cinema in the Shadow of Watergate and Vietnam, 1970–1979.* New York: Scribner's, 2000.

Crafton, Donald C. *The Talkies: American Cinema's Transition to Sound, 1926–1931.* New York: Scribner's, 1997.

Koszarski, Richard. *An Evening's Entertainment: The Age of the Silent Feature Picture, 1915–1928.* New York: Scribner's, 1990.

Musser, Charles. *The Emergence of Cinema: The American Screen to 1907.* New York: Scribner's, 1990.

Schatz, Thomas. *Boom and Bust: The American Cinema in the 1940s.* New York: Scribner's, 1997.

Hollywood's Indian: The Portrayal of the Native American in Film. Ed. Peter C. Rollins and John E. O'Connor. Lexington: UP of Kentucky, 1998. A collection of essays exploring the changing representations of Native Americans in American movies.

Koch, Stephen. *Stargazer: The Life, World and Films of Andy Warhol.* 2nd ed. New York: Marion Boyars, 1991. Includes a filmography, organized chronologically, of the films Warhol made between 1963 and 1967.

Sklar, Robert. *Film: An International History of the Medium.* Englewood Cliffs, NJ: Prentice; New York: Abrams, 1993. Includes brief chronologies with columns for film, arts and sciences, and world events; bibliography; glossary; filmography; and an extensive assortment of photographs.

Thompson, Kristin, and David Bordwell. *Film History: An Introduction.* New York: McGraw, 1994. A comprehensive, one-volume survey.

Turner, Graeme. *Film as Social Practice.* 3rd ed. London: Routledge, 1999. A textbook that explains how movies can be understood not merely as artistic creations but as "representational forms and social practices of popular culture." To demonstrate the book's approaches, the last chapter, Applications, explains some possible analyses of two movies.

Wyatt, Justin. *High Concept: Movies and Marketing in Hollywood.* Austin: U of Texas P, 1995. An examination of the historical, institutional, and economic forces that influence the making of popular movies. Includes discussion of the functions of advertising, market research, film structure, and casting.

CHAPTER 12

Thinking about Films

As we see a film and think about it afterward, we respond in many complex ways. This chapter introduces two of the major ways viewers think about a film. They form expectations and hypotheses and modify them as the film proceeds. Viewers also often learn some explicit meanings and formulate implicit meanings. Those explicit and implicit meanings may be symptomatic of a group of people outside the film. The meanings viewers formulate are not universal and are shaped by many factors.

Terms in **boldface** are defined in the Illustrated Glossary beginning on page 539.

EXPECTATIONS AND INTERACTIONS

When I first showed *Smoke Signals* in Spokane to a largely Indian audience, we had to reshow it immediately because everyone had been talking so much and laughing so much. But when I showed it at the Nantucket Film Festival [in Massachusetts], it was very quiet during the showing. There was some laughter, but I don't think they saw the humor in it. There was certainly none of the raucous laughter of Indian groups watching the film. (Alexie)

If viewers are told beforehand that they are going to see a film entitled "Bambi Meets Godzilla" (1969), they begin to formulate expectations about the film. Some laugh at the mere mention of the title. When I asked students to write down their expectations for the film based on its title, some guessed that they were about to see a romance. As one wrote, "I expect a beautiful woman to be meeting some big, rugged guy." Others hypothesized a David and Goliath story: "Bambi is smarter than Godzilla and outwits him in the end." One student expected "a giant lizard chasing a baby deer around Tokyo." Various others expected Godzilla to fight Bambi: "I expect a gruesome tale of violence and bloodsport between two very different adversaries." Godzilla has a history of violence though Bambi does not, so right away we viewers are surprised by the matchup. If viewers know something about film history, they might assume that "Bambi Meets Godzilla" is about two different modes of filmmaking: Disney's high-budget color animation and the low-budget, black-and-white Japanese action films of the 1950s and 1960s. Before a film begins, even based on only a title, we viewers begin formulating expectations and hypotheses.

As "Bambi Meets Godzilla" begins, soothing music accompanies the basic animation of Bambi's grazing. Nothing happens for a while except from time to time Bambi stops grazing to look upward as more and more opening credits roll by. We viewers soon notice that Marv Newland did all the work on the film, including the "choreography" and "bambi's wardrobe." If they have not already done so, viewer expectations veer toward the comic.

Soon Godzilla's foot abruptly flattens Bambi as the sound shifts from the flute and strings music to a loud discordant chord (played on a piano?) that gradually starts fading out. Next, "the end" is **superimposed** and erased backward quickly a letter at a time, and we realize that the film has not met the viewers' usual expectation that a film show at least some of its story *after* the opening credits. Guess what? The film is still not over. There is yet another credit: "We gratefully acknowledge the city of Tokyo for their help in obtaining Godzilla for this film." While Godzilla's foot remains unmoving on the film's hapless costar, its toenails extend straight out then go limp and hang downward again, which is another unexpected and puzzling development in the plot. Has Godzilla experienced excitement followed by release? Is it merely twitchy or stretching or tired? Viewers cannot know the cause of the toenail movement or its significance. Finally, the image and chord fade out together as this ninety-second film ends.

The film's title and opening image create certain expectations, but viewers are quickly surprised. Few viewers will correctly anticipate the resulting developments: the timing and manner of Bambi's demise and the mysterious reaction of Godzilla's toenails. Nor are viewers likely to expect the prominence of the credits and their whimsy. The minimal story (Bambi eats; Bambi meets Godzilla; Godzilla remains standing and unmoving except for some toenails) happens behind the credits. Rarely have credits and a filmmaker's ego so (knowingly) been used to compete with story.

Normally, before we see a film, we know something about it. Usually we know its title and, if it is a movie with popular actors, know something about at least one of them. We may know something about the director and something about the types of films he or she tends to direct. We may have heard or seen a review or talked with a friend who's seen the film. We might even know the **genre,** or basic type of film we are to see, such as western, musical, science fiction, horror, or detective. If so, we will expect the film to conform to the basics of the genre. For example, if we are going to see a 1950s western, we expect to see a lawful man, usually of European descent, challenged by lawless European American men, Mexicans, or Native Americans. Normally, too, genres set parameters to a **narrative:** what is possible, what is not. Thus, if we know we are going to see a western, we do not expect alien invaders

superimposition: Two or more images photographed or printed on top of each other.

narrative: A series of unified consecutive events situated in one or more settings.

a)

b)

sixty minutes into the film, nor do we at any time expect the woman who works in the dance hall to dance the lambada or the macarena.

Our expectations may be shaped by other factors. The film's rating may lead us to expect sex and violence. Or we may have seen a **trailer,** which may include material not included in the movie; we may have seen a printed advertisement, visited the film's site on the Internet, read Internet reviews of a test screening of the film, seen the film promoted on a cable channel, or seen toy spin-offs or other product tie-ins, all of which created expectations— sometimes false ones. Consider a poster for *High Sierra* (1941) and one for *The Maltese Falcon* (1941, Figure 12.1). Although the poster for *The Maltese Falcon* is misleading, probably it did not hurt the film at the box office; but

trailer: A brief compilation film shown in movie theaters, before some videotaped movies, or on TV to advertise a movie or a video release.

a)

b)

FIGURE 12.2 **Publicity, expectations, and viewer responses**
(a) In *Four Weddings and a Funeral* (1994), Hugh Grant plays a boyish, reserved, charming, yet nervous and bumbling heterosexual. (b) In *An Awfully Big Adventure* (1995), Grant plays a sarcastic gay director of a theatrical group with whom an impressionable sixteen-year-old girl becomes infatuated. Before the film was publicized, its director warned that if *An Awfully Big Adventure* were marketed as the new film from the star and director of *Four Weddings and a Funeral*, "they'll kill it stone dead. . . . All the effort this time should go to altering expectations" (Maslin 11). (a) *Duncan Kenworthy; Gramercy Pictures*; (b) *Hilary Heath and Philip Hinchcliffe; Fine Line Features*

advertising that creates fundamentally false expectations can hurt a film's chances for commercial success. Advertising for a movie that is released shortly after an immensely popular film but features the star in a very different role can be especially tricky (Figure 12.2). Then, too, a distributor may have a film that garners excellent reviews but never find an effective way to market the film. In such cases distributors occasionally try to promote the film again at a later time—and again fail to attract large audiences. That was the experience of Warner Bros. in trying to market *The Little Princess* (1995) and Paramount in trying to market *Wonder Boys* (2000). Often the advertising for a film rouses interest and creates reasonable expectations, as was done by a famous poster for *Persona* suggesting a mystery about the film's dual subjects (1966, Figure 12.3).

From all these and other sources, we enter the theater or approach the video store rental counter with expectations: to be amused, amazed, mystified, inspired, aroused, frightened, or something else. Once the film begins, it shapes the viewer's expectations by its music or visuals or both. Theatrical showings of *Lawrence of Arabia* (1962), for example, begin with a blank screen and an overture of the film's music, thus giving a sampling of the moods to come. Much more often, music and visuals are used in tandem near the film's beginning. Consider the opening seconds of the superhero action movie *Spawn* (1997). First we see and hear a fiery explosion and briefly hear a (church?) bell ring faintly in the background. Sounds of wind and a chorus holding long notes are heard as we see a fiery round tunnel

FIGURE 12.3 **Publicity nurturing appropriate expectations** ▶
This poster for Ingmar Bergman's *Persona* (1966) nurtures appropriate
viewer expectations and does so almost exclusively by its visuals. On
one level the film is about two women who are as closely linked as the
parts of a puzzle. Both are also puzzling, so appropriately the puzzle's
two parts do not entirely mesh. The film is concerned with the women's
psychology and uses many close-ups of faces, as here and as in many
films directed by Bergman. *Ingmar Bergman; United Artists*

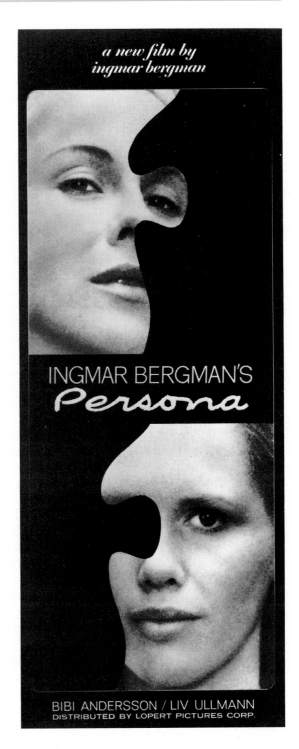

(seen later in the film as a gateway to hell); then the
narrator intones, "The battle between heaven and hell
has waged eternal, their armies fueled by souls harvested on earth. . . ." Shortly after the beginning of the
narration, a flying white dove is seen against the fiery
background; then a bright white, round shape like the
sun is seen behind the fire. Even without the narrator's
exposition, the film immediately encourages the viewer
to expect the central conflict of the story to come: fire
and destruction versus light and peace. As a narrative
film progresses, we also begin to interact with it as
readers interact with a written **text:**

> The literary text may be conceived of as a dynamic system
> of gaps. A reader who wishes . . . to . . . reconstruct . . .
> the fictive world and action [a text] projects, is neces-
> sarily compelled to pose and answer, throughout the
> reading-process, such questions as, What is happening
> or has happened, and why? What is the connection be-
> tween this **event** and the previous ones? What is the
> motivation of this or that character? To what extent does
> the logic of cause and effect correspond to that of every-
> day life? and so on. Most of the answers to these ques-
> tions, however, are not provided explicitly, fully and
> authoritatively (let alone immediately) by the text, but
> must be worked out by the reader himself on the basis of
> the implicit guidance it affords. . . . Some [gaps] can . . .
> be filled in almost automatically, while others require con-
> scious and laborious consideration; some can be filled in
> fully and definitely, others only partially and tentatively;
> some by a single [hypothesis], others by several (dif-
> ferent, conflicting, or even mutually exclusive) hypotheses.
> (Sternberg 50)

Throughout a film we interact with its images and
sounds: we fill in the gaps with our own inferences and

hypotheses. Without the attentive eyes and ears and active minds of the viewing audience, the film is incomplete—mere changing images and sounds. Viewers are not simply receptacles of a cascade of audio and visual information but collaborators and players with a wondrous, elaborate mechanism. The mental and emotional responses of viewers, which change in light of viewers' changing expectations and shifting questions and hypotheses, are the focus of viewer-response criticism.

If the film is to hold our attention, it must arouse viewer interest fairly quickly and from time to time renew that interest. In narrative films, story developments encourage us to consider possible consequences. We will get involved and be satisfied or frustrated in part by how well the film lives up to our changing expectations. We like to be manipulated, up to a point. People who enjoy horror films, for example, want to feel the tiny hairs on the back of their necks tingle—or at least they don't mind if they do. But viewers normally also crave variety, surprise, suspense, and some mental challenges. By the film's ending they like to think that they understand the film, more or less anticipated the major developments, or at least now see how developments could follow from earlier events, and viewers like to see unity and meaning in it all. There is much to experience in one viewing; later viewings of the same film usually reveal additional complexities, subtleties, meanings, and ambiguities. In analyzing a film, many viewers find it useful to consider many of the issues relating to expectations and interactions, including consistency, plausibility, predictability, surprise, and suspense.

For a few movies, seeing them again and again has become a more interactive and more communal experience than the usual film showing. The most popular of these cult favorites are *The Rocky Horror Picture Show* (1975) in the United States and elsewhere and *The Sound of Music* (1965), which was first shown in the sing-along mode in the United Kingdom and later on tour as "Sing-A-Long Sound of Music" in Canada, the United States, Australia, and other countries. Audiences know these cult films thoroughly and sing their songs at full volume in the theater. The films themselves create no surprises, but the film showings do: for instance, audience members volunteer supplementary sound effects, wisecracks, and cheers, hisses, boos, and other **vocals.** During *The Rocky Horror Picture Show* they may also throw objects at the screen or squirt water pistols. (The two-disc DVD of *Rocky Horror* has options that allow viewers to periodically see an audience's reactions to a showing of *Rocky Horror* and that encourage viewer participation.)

Digital filmmaking for theaters and the Internet also makes possible new alternatives to the usual interplay of expectations and interactions. *Time Code* (2000), which consists of four simultaneous uninterrupted **plotlines** shown on the quadrants of the movie screen (see Figure 8.10 on p. 277), requires viewers to decide which story line to interact with and for how long. And Internet films such as Amy Talkington's four-minute "The New Arrival"

vocal: Any sound made with the human voice, including speech, grunts, whimpers, screams, and countless other sounds.

plotline: A narrative or series of related events usually involving only a few characters or people and capable of functioning on its own as a story.

(2000) allow viewers to pan left or right around a 360-degree **filmic** world with potential action in every direction. In these and other films, the viewer has choices about where to interact with the story and for how long.

TYPES OF MEANINGS

> They watch moving shadows in dark caves together. Human females enjoy stories about one person dying slowly. The males prefer stories of many people dying quickly. (extraterrestrial narrator in *The Mating Habits of the Earthbound Human*, 1999)

We see a film; we think about it afterward; often we discuss it with others. Sometimes we read about others' reactions to the film. Often we generalize about the film. We may say, for example, that it glorifies violence or shows that wrongdoers end up suffering themselves. When we generalize about a film or a subject of the film or when the text does, we and the text are making **meanings;** we are explaining in general what we see as significant. In a fictional film, meanings are usually a viewer's generalizations about the characters' situations, personalities, ideas, and behavior. In a **documentary film,** meanings tend to be generalizations about the subjects represented in the film (for example, see Figure 9.2 on p. 302). In an **experimental film,** meanings are typically generalizations viewers make about film **conventions,** the experimental film's untraditional representation of its subjects, or the properties of the film medium itself (for example, see Figure 9.21 on p. 325). The meanings viewers construct may be shaped by many factors, including where and when they live and whatever **film theories** they apply.

Meaning may be divided into three types. An explicit meaning is a general verbal observation in a text (such as a film) about one or more of its subjects. An implicit meaning is a generalization viewers infer about a text or a subject in a text. A symptomatic meaning is a generalization about a text or part of a text that is the same as a belief or value of a group outside the film. The meaning is symptomatic of an outside group.[1]

Explicit Meanings

Explicit meanings are general verbal observations in a text about one or more of its subjects. In silent films, they may be conveyed by a subtitle or a **title card.** A sound film may use these forms of language and many other forms, such as a narrator, dialogue, or a monologue.

filmic: Characteristic of the film medium or appropriate to it, such as parallel editing or the combination of editing and a full range of vocals, silence, and music.

documentary film: A film whose representation of its subjects viewers are intended to accept primarily as factual.

experimental film: A film that rejects the conventions of mainstream movies and explores the possibilities of the film medium itself.

convention: In films and other texts, a frequently used technique or content that audiences accept as natural or typical.

film theory: A related and evolving structure of abstractions about the film medium.

title card: A card or thin sheet of clear plastic on which is written or printed information included in a film.

---

[1]For the terms *explicit meaning, implicit meaning,* and *symptomatic meaning,* I am indebted to David Bordwell's *Making Meaning: Inference and Rhetoric in the Interpretation of Cinema.*

In silent films, examples of explicit meaning are commonplace. A title card of the classic American film *Greed* (1925) reads: "First . . . chance had brought them face to face; now . . . mysterious instincts, as ungovernable as the winds of the heavens, were knitting their lives together." Another explicit meaning is found in a title card early in *Sunrise* (1927):

> For wherever the sun rises and sets . . .
> in the city's turmoil
> or
> under the open sky on the farm,
> life is much the same:
> sometimes bitter, sometimes sweet.

Yet another explicit meaning in a film from the silent era occurs at the end of *Metropolis* (1926): "Without the heart there can be no understanding between the hands and the mind."

In fictional films, explicit meanings are less common in sound films than in silent films, but they are by no means rare. In *Unforgiven* (1992), the Clint Eastwood character, William Munny, sometimes generalizes about one of the film's subjects, such as violence and killing. Near the end of the film, for example, he generalizes about killing people: "It's a hell of a thing killing a man. You take away all he's got and all he's ever gonna have." In narrative films, explicit meanings are generally not crucial to the plot. Munny's general statement, for example, could have been omitted without affecting the story.

A film's title may also reveal an explicit meaning. An animated film called "Technological Threat" (1988) shows that office workers may be replaced by more efficient anthropomorphic machines. There is also an explicit meaning in the title *Fatal Attraction* (1987): an attraction can be fatal or at least detrimental. A title may also misrepresent a story or understate a meaning. Mike Leigh's *Life Is Sweet* (1990)—about a husband and wife and their two very different grown twin daughters and three male friends—shows both sweetness and considerable emotional pain and could more accurately be characterized as bittersweet.

An explicit meaning is not necessarily comprehensive or persuasive; it is certainly not the final word on any subject. At the end of *King Kong* (1933), for example, one character says of Kong's fate, "It was beauty killed the beast." Many critics find that blame misplaced and that interpretation simplistic. In fictional films, meanings are usually not explicit but implied by **settings,** film **techniques,** actions, or other means. If a fictional or experimental film explains meanings too often or if the meanings are already apparent to viewers but they are told what meanings are intended, viewers may be annoyed that they were not allowed to discover the significance for themselves. General statements are commonplace, however, in documentary films, usually in the form of a **narrator,** interviews, subtitles, or title cards.

setting: The place where filmed action occurs.

technique: Any aspect of filmmaking, such as the choice of sets, lighting, sound effects, music, and editing.

narrator: A character, person, or unidentifiable voice in a film that provides commentary continuously or intermittently.

Implicit Meanings

An **implicit meaning** is a generalization a person makes about a film or other text or about a subject in a text, for example, about the implications of a narrative or the significance of a symbol. (For examples of implicit meanings in a documentary film, see the caption for Figure 9.2 on p. 302.) In this section, we will see how viewers can use awareness of cinematic techniques, symbols, and narratives or stories to develop implicit meanings.

CINEMATIC TECHNIQUES

As is explained and illustrated throughout Part One, the arrangement of the subjects within the **frame (composition)**, the lenses, lighting, camera distances and angles, sound mix, and many other aspects of filmmaking may all affect what meanings audiences detect.

Consider a **shot** from the original *Psycho* (1960) that shows a man sitting in a room (Figure 12.4). Setting, lighting, camera angle, and composition all help suggest that the human subject is strange, if not dangerous. How different the mood and meaning would be if the setting had been a knotty pine

FIGURE 12.4 **Mise en scène and cinematography creating meaning**
In a scene in *Psycho* (1960), a young woman talks with the motel manager in a room off the motel office. In the shot represented here—one of a dozen taken from the same camera position—setting, lighting, camera angle, and composition help create meaning. The stuffed bird seen above the painting of the nude woman is disquieting on a symbolic level, perhaps especially because that part of the image is balanced visually by the man on the right. The painting behind the man is of a naked woman seemingly menaced by two men. (Soon after this scene, viewers learn that behind that painting is a peephole through which the same young man will see the young woman undress in preparation for a shower.) Frame enlargement. *Alfred Hitchcock; Universal*

back wall with only a large frame containing a print of mountains, the lighting bright and even, the camera at an **eye-level angle,** and the man in the center of the frame. Then the man would not seem strange and certainly not dangerous.

Editing also influences meanings. As explained in Chapter 3, a shot can develop or undercut the meaning(s) of the preceding shot. Superimposition and **fast cutting** can also create meanings. The forty-two-second **montage** of Susan's opera career in *Citizen Kane* (1941) conveys an enormous amount of information, including the consequences of a man forcing a woman to do what she is ill equipped and reluctant to do.

Sounds that are selected, modified, and combined can also create or change meaning. During the 1987 Academy Awards ceremony, a clip from *The Sound of Music* showed Julie Andrews running around in the countryside as

shot (noun): An uninterrupted strip of exposed motion-picture film or videotape that presents a subject during an uninterrupted segment of time.

edit: To select and arrange the processed segments of photographed motion-picture film.

fast cutting: Editing characterized by many brief shots.

montage: A series of brief shots used to present a condensation of subjects and time.

a)   b)

FIGURE 12.5 **Obvious versus subtle representations**
(a) A still for *The Cabinet of Dr. Caligari* (1919) shows action that was staged for the benefit
of a still photographer. This image was used in publicizing the film but does not appear in it.
(b) A frame enlargement from the film shows what viewers see of the same murder represented
in (a): the victim and shadows. Many people think that a subtle presentation of a subject may be
more involving and thus more effective than an obvious presentation. *Decla-Bioscop; The Museum
of Modern Art/Circulating Film Library*

scene: A section of a narrative
film that gives the impression
of continuous action taking
place in continuous time and
space.

lap dissolve: A transition between shots in which one shot
begins to fade out as the next
shot fades in, overlapping the
first shot before replacing it.

viewers heard not the original sound track but sounds of an airplane engine
and machine-gun fire. Because of the sounds, viewers incorrectly (and humorously) inferred that she was under attack. In *What's Up, Tiger Lily?* (1966),
Woody Allen took a Japanese James Bond–type movie and redubbed it.
With the new sound track, the cast of characters now includes Wing Fat and
the sisters Terri and Suki Yaki, and the action centers on rivals trying to acquire
a famous egg salad recipe. Overlapping dialogue—as in some films directed by
Orson Welles and some directed by Robert Altman—suggests how people
may talk *at* but not *to* or *with* each other. **Scenes** with this use of sound suggest
that people may be together physically but isolated emotionally or spiritually.

Meaning in films, then, is always created or modified by the techniques
of cinema, though it is important to remember that a technique's meaning
can depend on place and time. As we saw in Chapter 3, in previous years
filmmakers tended to use **lap dissolves** to delete insignificant action and
time within a scene. Later in the history of cinema, lap dissolves usually
mean that the action changes to a different setting and a later time.

A subtle presentation may have more impact than an obvious presentation because viewers are forced to imagine what happens and help create
meaning. Similarly, many viewers believe that horror films and other violent
films are more expressive when they use shadows, sounds, and reaction
shots, not explicit violence (Figure 12.5).

Some viewers believe that erotic situations are sexier if restraint is used in the presentation. Sometimes a look can carry more erotic charge than caressing or kissing (Figure 12.6). And often the images that viewers imagine are more erotic than images on a screen. Novelist Leslie Epstein recounts that for her, "Perhaps the most erotic scene in all the sixties occurs in *Persona*. . . . Bibi Andersson tells the half-catatonic Liv Ullmann about the time she and a friend had been lying on a beach [sunbathing nude]. . . . Nothing [much] moves but the one actress's lips and the other's eyes" (289). In the film, the Bibi Andersson character's account begins as follows:

> Suddenly I saw two figures leaping about on the rocks above us who kept hiding and peeking. "There are two boys looking at us," I said to the girl. Her name was Katarina. "Let them look," she said, turning over on her back. It was such a strange feeling. I just lay there with my bottom in the air not a bit embarrassed. I felt very calm. Wasn't it funny? And Katarina was beside me with her big breasts and thighs. She just lay there giggling to herself. Then I saw that the boys had come closer and were staring at us. They were awfully young. Then the boldest of the two came over and squatted down beside Katarina and pretended to be busy with his foot and started to poke between his toes. I . . . I felt all funny. Suddenly I heard Katarina say: "Come here a minute." Then she helped him off with his jeans and shirt. Then he was on top of her. She showed him how and held him by his fanny. The other boy sat on the rock watching. I heard Katarina whisper and laugh. The boy's face was close to mine. It was all flushed and puffy. I turned over and said: "Won't you come to me too?" And Katarina said: "Yes, go to her now." So he left her and fell roughly on top of me and grabbed one of my breasts. It was over for me almost at once.

If the film instead showed a **flashback** of what happened, that section of the film would be less erotic for some viewers because instead of hearing once and briefly that the two boys were "awfully young," viewers would continuously see how young they are, and that would be troubling for some viewers who would interpret the scene as being about adults seducing children. For many viewers, then, the restrained presentation in *Persona* is more erotic than a more explicit rendition.

Near the end of *8½* (1963) is another example of less is more. After Guido, a

FIGURE 12.6 **Expressiveness of looks and gestures**
Looks and gestures alone (here as part of a flamenco) may convey romantic attraction or erotic tension or both, sometimes more powerfully than physical contact, as in *Carmen* (1983), directed by Carlos Saura. *Emiliano Piedra Productions; Orion Classics*

FIGURE 12.7 **Restraint and understatement**
Nothing but a Man (1964) has been much praised for the two main characters'
humanity and dignity and for the film's restraint in its presentation of its volatile
subjects. The film demonstrates that less may be more. *DuArt; New Video Group,
New York City*

medium shot: Shot in which
the subject and surroundings are
given about equal importance.

extreme long shot: Image in
which the subject appears to be
far from the camera.

distraught film director, has hidden
under a table at his nightmarish press
conference and pulled a pistol from
his pocket, we see a scene consisting
of only one shot: Guido's mother on a
beach turning and calling off-screen
"Guido. Guido. Where are you running to, you wretched boy?" We first
see her in **medium shot,** but as she
stops running and begins to call out,
the camera seems to race away from
her, and we end up seeing her in **extreme long shot,** her face no longer
discernible. In the next shot, we see
Guido under the table again, hear a
gun shot, and see his head drop.

In the six or so seconds before
Guido's fantasized death, we experience not the expected rush of images
and sounds from Guido's life, but one
brief, spare, evocative scene. We do
not even see young Guido. We see
only his mother being annoyed with
him because he is evidently running
away. By the end of the scene, Guido is presumably gone (in more than one
sense), and she has shrunk in size and importance. The scene displays great
restraint. Much more time, many more images, a much richer sound track
could have been used, but the muse whispered to Fellini, "Federico, less is
more."

Finally, we can see how less can be more by considering another film
that treats an emotionally charged subject with restraint. *Nothing but a Man*
(1964) shows an African American man in the 1960s South trying to get and
hold a job that allows him some dignity, marrying outside his class attempting to relate to an aloof father, trying to decide whether to take responsibility for a boy who may be his son, and coping with prejudice against African
Americans (Figure 12.7). The narrative is involving in part because it shows
the situations vividly and believably without explaining them in tiresome detail. For many viewers, it is off-putting for movies to explain their ideas, so
teachers and books implore future scriptwriters to "show, don't tell": don't
tell viewers anything that can be shown instead.

Subtle technique is not without risks. If the image or sound is too faint
or too fleeting, or both, or if viewers are otherwise engaged, they may miss a
significant detail, even on many later re-viewings. An example of excessive
subtlety is from *Citizen Kane*. After Susan's disastrous opera career, Kane in-

sists she persevere. Then comes the famous opera montage and the aftermath of Susan's suicide attempt. Just before Susan revives, an instrumental version of an aria that Susan had struggled with earlier in the narrative begins and plays faintly for about fifty seconds as she tells Kane she couldn't make him understand how she felt and how the audience simply didn't want her. As Kane says, "That's when you've got to fight 'em," the music stops.

The music is in a minor key and sounds as if it's played on a faraway calliope, the kind of music you may have heard to accompany a merry-go-round in an amusement park. The music is a subtle reminder of Susan's disastrous singing career: she was as ill-suited for singing opera as that calliope was to render an aria. The music may also remind us of the scene in which Kane imposes his will upon Susan and her reluctant opera coach; in that scene her voice cracks as she struggles to hit a high note in that same aria. However, the rendition after Susan's suicide attempt is so faint, few viewers ever hear it. It is so faint that I heard it only after many viewings over the years and then only on a laser videodisc version (no projector noise to contend with). Even after I told a class about the music and played the laser disc version for them, some did not hear it. Like so much of *Citizen Kane*, it's a brilliant touch, but, as occasionally happens in the film, it is too subtle.[2]

Another example of filmmakers being too subtle occurs early in another widely admired film, *The Searchers* (1956). Ethan Edwards hates Comanches because early in the film they kill his brother, Aaron, two of Aaron's three children, and, most important, Aaron's wife, for whom Ethan has more than perfunctory feelings (the film is restrained in suggesting why and how deeply). Understandably, critics seem not to have noticed that Comanches had also killed Ethan's mother. When Comanches are about to attack Aaron Edwards and his family, Aaron and his wife send their little daughter Debbie to hide by her grandmother's grave. Before Debbie sits in front of the tombstone, for six video frames (out of thirty per second) the following is legible:

> Here lies
> Mary Jane Edwards
> killed by
> Comanches
> May 12, 1852
> A good wife and mother
> In her 41st year.

If viewers noticed this detail, they could better understand Ethan's feelings about Comanches and his obsession to retrieve from them his sole surviving relative, his niece Debbie. But how many viewers read the tombstone since

---

[2]On the Criterion CAV laser disc version of *Citizen Kane*, the music can be heard on side 4, frames 20,200 and following. If the volume is turned up, the music is also audible on the 50th Anniversary VHS videotape from Turner Home Entertainment and on the DVD.

they have only a fifth of a second to do so and most will be preoccupied with the endangered little girl soon to appear in front of it?

Like all who hope to communicate effectively, regardless of the medium, mainstream filmmakers are challenged to have a clear sense of their audiences and not to insult them by being too obvious or lose them by being so subtle that audiences have no chance of getting the point, even during later re-viewings. For those who make texts, it is a judgment call, sometimes wisely made, sometimes not.

In these examples and elsewhere, the filmmakers may have known how demanding they were being when they used these subtle techniques. Perhaps filmmakers include them for those in the audience who are especially observant. Perhaps they include such subtleties for those who see the film more than once, as rewards for the faithful. Perhaps they include such touches for their own pleasure in being creative and sly. Then, too, possibly the filmmakers were unaware of how demanding they were being and simply goofed, which is possible even in otherwise brilliant films.

Sometimes viewers miss the significance of a technique because they watch a videotape version. Release prints of films shown in commercial theaters usually have detailed images. But when films are shown on an analog television monitor, the results are somewhat blurred and **grainy** (since video images have less definition than film images). The lighting is without subtle shades (**high contrast**), and in shadowed areas details tend to get lost because analog TV has far less range of tones than film; thus, many details in dark scenes are especially difficult to see. That is why films with many dark scenes—such as *The Third Man* (1949), the *Godfather* films, some of the *Batman* films since the late 1980s, and most **films noirs**—are frustrating to watch on analog television or videotape. Even in well-lit scenes, on an analog TV monitor viewers are likely to miss such significant details in *Citizen Kane* as the glass paperweight in Susan Alexander's apartment on the night Kane first meets her (Figure 12.8), the whiskey bottle he finds in her room in Xanadu after she leaves him, and, in *Psycho*, the fleeting triple superimposition of the film's last shot.

SYMBOLS

A **symbol** is anything perceptible that has significance or meaning beyond its usual meaning or function. Every society has certain public symbols: each society invests certain sounds and sights with widely understood meanings. In many societies, for example, a red traffic light symbolizes that people approaching it should stop. Painters, writers, filmmakers, and others who create works of the imagination may also create symbols (not always consciously). Depending on contexts, a sound, word (including a name), color, or representation of an object or action or person may function as a symbol. Viewers (or readers) do not perceive a symbol as merely performing its usual functions; they see it as also as conveying meaning.

grainy: Rough visual texture.

high contrast: Photographic image with few gradations between the darkest and lightest parts of the image.

film noir: A type of film first made in the United States during and after World War II, characterized by frequent scenes with dark, shadowy (low-key) lighting; (usually) urban settings; characters motivated by selfishness, greed, cruelty, ambition, and lust; and characters willing to lie, frame, double-cross, and kill or have others killed.

In *The Godfather* (1972), *The Godfather Part II* (1974), and *The Godfather Part III* (1990), doors or doorways do not always function simply as connections between rooms: they are sometimes symbols. In the last two shots of *The Godfather,* Michael's wife, Kay, sees him through an open door in his office surrounded by three of his men. One of them kisses Michael's hand and says "Don Corleone"—meaning that Michael is now the head of the Corleone family and its criminal business. The second man kisses Michael's hand and, at nearly the same time, the third man goes to the door and closes it. The film's final action obliterates Kay from Michael's and our view and, more important, blocks both Kay and the audience from further views of Michael's criminal life. Here, the door symbolizes how criminal activities must be carried on out of sight. Late in *The Godfather Part II,* Michael finds Kay, who is now estranged from him, sneaking a visit to their two children at the Corleone estate. After a tense, wordless, face-to-face

FIGURE 12.8 **Subtle visual clue**
In *Citizen Kane* (1941), this frame is from the second of three similar shots in Susan's room: notice the significant glass paperweight on the left side of her dresser. Subtle details such as this can be extremely difficult to see in a videotape or telecast analog version. Frame enlargement. *Orson Welles; RKO General Pictures*

confrontation of about thirty seconds—and many viewers may find that to be an enormous amount of silence in a film with dialogue—Michael shuts the door in Kay's uncertain, then pained face. Late in *The Godfather Part III,* it seems that Kay is about to be reconciled with Michael, and they are holding hands across a table. A man knocks on and opens twin doors leading into the room. In the background a woman weeps. The man backs up into the other room as Michael approaches and asks what's wrong. The man tells Michael that a long-term associate has been shot. As Michael and the man talk, Kay moves sideways to see Michael and the man better, bends slightly sideways, and moves forward to see and hear more clearly. Still with his back to Kay, Michael has put his hand on the man's arm, thereby evidently indicating to him to move sideways; they do so, in effect making it harder for Kay to see and hear. (Probably Michael thinks Kay would be trying to learn what is going on.) We hear Kay's voice saying "It never ends." After watching for a few more moments, she turns and walks out of the frame—no reconciliation after all. In all three movies, the door or doorway symbolizes the barrier that has come between Michael and his wife and reinforces an important meaning of the *Godfather* films: involvement in crime separates one from family.

The *Godfather* movies are rich in symbols. Another symbol occurs in *The Godfather* at the beginning and end of the scene where Luca Brasi (Vito's faithful henchman) is strangled to death, and the camera looks into the bar through a glass window with fish etched on it. Later, dead fish wrapped in Brasi's bulletproof vest are delivered to the Corleone compound, and a character explains that it is a Sicilian message that Luca "sleeps with the fishes" (is dead). Then viewers may realize that the etched fish seen briefly in the foreground as Luca is strangled functions as a symbol, not just part of the **mise en scène.**

Because so few viewers of *The Godfather* are likely to know the significance of the Sicilian message of fish, that symbol is explained. However, if we examine how symbols are used in stories, we will notice that like other vehicles of meaning they usually go unexplained and are subject to different interpretations. Objects functioning as symbols are usually shown more than once, are placed in prominent positions, are seen in important scenes, or are used under a combination of these conditions.

Sometimes symbols occur one after another or even one with another. The beginning of *Schindler's List* is in color. Soon we see a Jewish Sabbath candle go out (the film is now in black and white); then we see a wisp of smoke ascend from it. In the next shot, we have been instantly transported back in time, and we see a column of smoke and its source, a train engine. The candle's going out, the simultaneous transition from color to black and white, and the **match cut** from candle smoke to train smoke are all sym-

mise en scène: An image's setting, subject (usually people or characters), and composition (the arrangement of setting and subjects within the frame).

match cut: A transition between two shots in which an object or movement (or both) at the end of one shot closely resembles (or is identical to) an object or movement (or both) at the beginning of the next shot.

a)

b)

FIGURE 12.9 **Symbol concluding a documentary**
Crumb (1994), which was filmed in color, is about the life, work, and family of the satirical cartoonist Robert Crumb. (a) The penultimate shot in the documentary is of Charles, Robert's talented but suicidal brother, pulling down a window covering and darkening the room, followed by a rapid fade-out to black. (b) The film's final shot, a title card of white on black, informs us of Charles's fate; then the sentence in white fades out and leaves the screen black and blank. Frame enlargements. *Superior Pictures and Sony Pictures Classics; Sony Pictures Classics*

bolic. In countless myths and other narratives—including the Book of Genesis, ancient Greek tragedy, and Shakespearean plays—light is associated with life. Its extinction early in the film, before the story begins, not only suggests death but also compels viewers' attention. Often, draining something of its color suggests weakness and death. And a Sabbath prayer candle, which signifies both religious faith and memory of the departed, goes up in smoke to be replaced by a train, an object used in only one way in the film—to transport Jews to their deaths. Here, as in some poems and music, symbols can summon forth emotion and meaning without being entirely explicable.

Symbols may also be discovered in some experimental films and documentaries. The documentary *Crumb* (1994), for example, concludes with a shot of a man lowering a window covering and a title card announcing the man's suicide the year after he was filmed. The shutting out of light may symbolize the man's death (Figure 12.9). *Fast, Cheap & Out of Control* (1997) includes shots of a circus clown running around wildly as if trying to outrun a fake skeleton attached to the man's backside. In the context of the film, one may interpret the clown pursued by the skeleton as representing our shared human fate (Figure 12.10).

FIGURE 12.10 **Symbol opening a documentary**
In black and white, shots two through four of Errol Morris's *Fast, Cheap & Out of Control* (1997) show a clown screaming and running around a circus ring pursued by a skeleton attached to the clown's backside. The fourth shot, seen here, is in slow motion. Less than two minutes before the end of the film occur three more consecutive black-and-white shots of the clown and his mate. Because of the prominence given the shots and the film's melancholy tinge, the clown and skeleton might be seen as a symbol of the desperate and vain (and perhaps somewhat comic) attempts to elude the persistent pursuer of us all. Frame enlargement. *Errol Morris; Sony Pictures Classics*

NARRATIVES: MEANINGS AND UNCERTAIN MEANINGS

Viewers also detect meanings in narratives. Sometimes they notice general qualities of settings, such as the beauty but danger of nature in *Never Cry Wolf* (1983), a thoughtful adventure film set in rural Alaska. In *Never Cry Wolf*, *Lawrence of Arabia* (1962), *McCabe and Mrs. Miller* (1971), *Deliverance* (1972), *The Matrix* (1999), and many other films, setting affects how events unfold and helps reveal character and meaning. Setting is often used to reveal an occupant's personality or situation and to compare and contrast characters. One character's residence, for example, may be very different than another's, as in *Fight Club* (1999, Figure 12.11).

More often, viewers detect significance in behavior, the subject of narratives. Consider *The Last Emperor* (1987). Its subject is the life of the last Chinese emperor, from childhood to old age. One plausible meaning of the narrative is that someone who seems to have every comfort and material good may suffer from loneliness. Or consider *Waiting to Exhale* (1995). The main subjects are four single African American women and, secondarily, the

a)

b)

FIGURE 12.11 **Different residences symbolizing different situations and personalities**
(a) In *Fight Club* (1999), the Edward Norton character's condo "on the fifteenth floor of a filing cabinet for widows and young professionals" is full of furnishings in desaturated colors, clean, uncluttered, modern, and very consumerist. He narrates, "Like so many others, I had become a slave to the Ikea nesting instinct." Here part of his condo is seen with labeling from a catalog superimposed. (b) In contrast, the Brad Pitt character's residence, which was built to satisfy the needs of the film, is a dark, old, abandoned house without anything beyond the basics, well, often without even the basics: "The stairs were ready to collapse. . . . Nothing worked. Turning on one light meant another light in the house went out. . . . Every time it rained, we had to kill the power. . . . Rain trickled down through the plaster and the light fixtures. . . . Everywhere were rusted nails to snag your elbow on." Frame enlargements. *Ross Grayson Bell, Ceán Chaffin, and Art Linson; 20th Century-Fox*

men in their lives. Two of the film's narrative meanings are that men tend to let them down and that the friendships of women sustain them (Figure 12.12). Viewers also find meanings in narratives about living creatures with human qualities, such as extraterrestrials wanting to go home or the animals in *Homeward Bound: The Incredible Journey* (1993) and many other films.

A story, even a brief one, has multiple implicit meanings. "The String Bean" was made in France in 1962 and is seventeen minutes long. It has no dialogue, no printed words, no narration. All its scenes take place during daytime in a section of Paris. If you have not seen the film, take a moment to read the description on page 422.

A viewer might generalize that the film shows the aged selflessly aiding young life: the woman gives much time and attention to the plant, even after she has planted it in the park. The film shows the continuity of life, from planting to emergence to maturity and death and to the beginning of the next generation from the seeds of the previous one—in other words, from the conception of one generation to the conception of the next. The film also shows concern for more than survival of oneself. The woman not only works at her job but also nurtures young life: she seeks the water and sun needed for the plant to reach full maturity. The woman's fierce persistence and quiet care as she tries to ensure that life flourishes are perhaps the film's most subtle meanings.

a)   b)

FIGURE 12.12 **Women's strengths and men's shortcomings**
Waiting to Exhale (1995) shows four admirable women finding comfort in their friendships with one another as two of the four are treated badly by married men and later reject them; one eventually wins the neighborhood Prince Charming; and one is dumped by her husband but eventually wins the respect and love of a sensitive, noble man and a hefty divorce settlement from her husband. (a) Representative of the disappointing treatment by men is the scene where a man carries one of the women to her bed, dumps her on it like a sack of potatoes, then has sex with her selfishly. (b) Afterward, he is still oblivious to her feelings, and she pulls the sheet up tight under her chin, looks sideways at him, and gives him the look shown here. Frame enlargements. *Ezra Swerdlow and Deborah Schindler; 20th Century–Fox*

The outcome of her attempts is uncertain. Perhaps the fresh beans from the pod will grow more successfully than a bean from a package. But maybe a plant cannot grow to maturity in either confining city quarters or well-ordered parks. If so, the plant that would grow from the seeds the woman plants at the conclusion of the film will end up like the dried-out plant she found early in the film. What is important are the woman's patient efforts to help life begin, grow, and thrive. The film's final images are of rain (and the promise of growth) and of her waiting and watching.

"The String Bean" shows a realistic story: the settings are believable, and every event in it could have happened. Many movies are not realistic: they include settings or events that, given current human understanding, could not exist or occur. These nonrealistic or fantasy movies can be divided into two types. In one type, the unrealistic settings or events, or both, are soon obvious to viewers. Examples are *Godzilla* (1998), *The Matrix*, and *Crouching Tiger, Hidden Dragon* (2000). In *Crouching Tiger*, for example, the settings are realistic but many events are not. As is conventional in other Asian martial arts movies, four of the main characters in *Crouching Tiger* have the discipline, training, focus, and mental attitude to be able to fly through the air, fall great distances without harm, spiral upward through the air, skip up walls, bound over rooftops, and fight unbelievably long and well.

Plot Summary for "The String Bean"

An old woman sews purses in her room. She puts some beans in a pan, adds water, and places the pan on a counter; then she goes out.

The woman walks in a park then sits in the sun on a bench facing flowerbeds. Later she looks at colorful flowers in a shop window.

Near her building she spots a discarded pot with a dead plant in it. She wraps the pot in newspaper and walks away with it.

In her room, the woman pulls the dead plant from the pot and throws the plant away. She plants a bean she had originally taken from a package; then she sets the pot on the windowsill and waters it.

During the following days, she cares for the young bean plant, but it grows to only a certain height.

In a park, she sits on a bench, takes her plant from a tote bag, sets it in the sun, then sews (see figure, top). She gets up and puts the plant under a running sprinkler.

The woman works at the sewing machine again. She looks at the plant on the windowsill. It is still not growing.

The woman plants the bean plant behind a low hedge in the park (see figure, middle) and waters it; then she returns to a nearby bench, sits, and smiles.

The woman works in her room at her sewing machine and at various times visits the plant in the park. It thrives.

One day, the woman sees a gardener pull out her plant and throw it away. She goes to the plant, picks it up, and breaks off some bean pods.

Back in her room, the woman takes several beans from a pod and puts them in the pot she had taken in from the sill. She places the pot back on the sill as a gentle rain begins. She moves the pot so it catches some rain, closes the window, and watches the pot (see figure, bottom).

Narrative meanings in a short film
In "The String Bean" (1962), the woman nurtures a plant, sees it uprooted and discarded, and plants fresh seeds in hopes of growing another plant. Although the film is only seventeen minutes long, its plot suggests many meanings, including that an old person may want to stay in touch with nature and nurture young life. Frame enlargements. *Paul Claudon; Contemporary Films*

a)

b)

c)

FIGURE 12.13 **Realism and fantasy blended**

Stand by Me (1986) is about four boys who are unhappy at home and are united by the indifference or hostility of adults. (a) The boys are happy to go off on an adventure together because adults consistently mistreat them. One boy's father, we are told, held the boy's ear "to a stove and almost burned it off." Another boy's father gets drunk and beats his son. A third father, grieving over an older son whom he favored, alternates between indifference and criticism of his surviving son. We learn nothing about the father of the fourth boy (second from left), but by implication perhaps that father has been ineffective, too, because his son is insecure, awkward, and the target of much laughter. Even a woman teacher betrayed one of the boys. After the boy had stolen milk money then turned it over to her, she used the money to buy a new skirt and allowed the boy to suffer expulsion and a blotted reputation. (b) As in many movies, many dangers are packed into the film's brief story time. An example is when the boys are threatened by an onrushing train (presumably driven by an adult male), which doesn't brake and nearly runs down two of the boys on a bridge high above water. (c) One of the three examples in the movie where a boy cries in front of at least one of the other boys and is comforted by one of the boys. The story of *Stand by Me* suggests that these boys cannot trust the adult world and can find friendship and support only among peers. *Bruce A. Evans, Raynold Gideon, and Andrew Scheinman; Columbia*

The second group of fantasy films consists of films whose unrealistic aspects are not immediately apparent. These films include settings that audiences have no trouble believing in and situations that seem possible, but on reflection viewers realize that some of the events and often the resolution of the main characters' problems are more wish fulfillment than plausible action. These movies look true to life, but their events are not always true to life. They often attract audiences by including enjoyable and reassuring fantasies in a mostly "realistic" story. An example is *Stand by Me* (1986), a popular film with many teens and young adults (Figure 12.13). The movie's settings look authentic enough and so do many of the main character's actions, such as their bickering and insulting and bonding. But as in so many movies, more dangerous and exciting events are packed into a short time than most of us ever experience outside movie theaters (Figure 12.13b), as when one of the young boys has to point a gun at the older gang's leader to persuade the gang to leave the boys alone—this in a small town in 1959! Sometimes the boy who tends to act as the leader (on the left in Figure 12.13c) acts like a surrogate father, displaying wisdom and compassion well beyond his years. Most of the film's events considered individually are believable. However, the movie has so many events showing the dangers of adult males and the safety and reassurance of a small gang of young boys in so brief a **story time** (not even forty-eight hours, excluding the brief scenes of the adult Richard Dreyfuss character) that its story and the meanings implied by the story are not completely plausible.

story time: The amount of time represented in a film's narrative or story.

There are many other popular movies that seem realistic *while* you watch them, but you realize later that they incorporate quite implausible or even impossible events. *Double Jeopardy* (1999), which focuses on a woman who proves to be extraordinary, has a fairly high fantasy quotient and is in the tradition of Hitchcockian thrillers of a wronged person trying to set things right before the law catches up and intervenes (Figure 12.14). Much more often—both abroad and in the United States—films reenact popular male fantasies. Several films directed by Alfred Hitchcock—such as *The 39 Steps* (1935), *Saboteur* (1942), and *North by Northwest* (1959)—show a man displaying his resourcefulness, bravery, and appeal to women and eventually clearing himself of the wrongdoing he was falsely accused of early in the story by helping bring the guilty ones to justice. The producers of action movies, including the James Bond movies, have raked in truckloads of money by showing countless boys and men what they enjoy imagining themselves doing: dispatching tough guys and attracting an assortment of ravishing available women. In the late 1990s, a number of American movies enacted popular male adolescent fantasies. *There's Something about Mary* (1998), *Antz* (1998), *A Bug's Life* (1998), *American Pie* (1999), and *The Waterboy* (1998) all show geeky or insecure young males eventually winning an attractive female, quite implausibly. Most sexually explicit films enact common heterosexual male erotic fantasies: the women are attractive, available, and numerous; the men virile, usually dominant, and eventually unmistakably sexually satisfied.

FIGURE 12.14 Fantasy about a woman getting revenge and getting her son back
Double Jeopardy (1999) is a thriller about Libby, the Ashley Judd character. She is falsely imprisoned for murdering her husband, who had framed her for his murder and disappeared with their young son and another woman. After six years in prison, Libby, seen here in a final tête-à-tête with that errant husband, shows extraordinary poise, intelligence, resourcefulness, and athletic skill and grace. Some of the movie's scenes are rendered as much more fantasy than realism. For example, when Libby and her parole officer are trapped in a car that has run off a ferry and is submerged and sinking, Libby takes the man's gun, swims to the surface, struggles with the parole officer who surfaces near her, hits him in the head with his gun, then swims to shore and escapes. Much later, when she regains consciousness while imprisoned in a coffin, she uses a lighter and that gun again to shoot off the coffin's locks and escape. Although the movie received mostly middling to poor reviews, it was popular with many viewers, especially women, and during its first two weeks alone, grossed nearly $50 million at the box office. Frame enlargement. *Leonard Goldberg; Paramount*

Fantasies show life as audiences wish it to be. These films are not so much mirrors of life outside theaters as fun-house mirrors that briefly entertain viewers, often by showing them characters and situations that they can identify with and that make them feel heroic, powerful, rich, romantically desirable (Figures 12.15 and 12.16), or sexy (Figures 12.17 and 12.18).

Movies may also play upon viewers' fears and nightmares. Because many people distrust technology and the people who create and monitor it, movies such as *2001: A Space Odyssey* (1968), *Westworld* (1973), and *Jurassic Park* (1993) show technology failing but humans ultimately triumphing. Sometimes humans fail. *The Forbin Project* (1969, a.k.a. *Colossus: The Forbin Project*) cautions that if humans put complete trust in technology, it can become a Frankenstein monster that eventually dominates its creator. *The Matrix* carries the threat of supercomputers even further. Sometime in the twenty-first century, computers with artificial intelligence have created a new race of machines that use a form of fusion and human bodies that are grown and harvested as fuel to run the matrix, which is "a computer-generated dream world, built to keep us [humans] under control."

Some stories are told in such a way that the stories or parts of them are open to two or more interpretations of their meanings. They are ambiguous. An example is from a master of ambiguity, playwright and scriptwriter Harold Pinter. In *Betrayal* (1983), Jerry, a friend of a husband and wife who are having a party, confronts the wife in her own bedroom. After his passionate declaration of love, she calmly replies, "My husband is at the other side of that door." Does she mean "I'm not interested, and my husband may overhear you, and there could be trouble," or "I could be interested, but this is a poor time and place," or some other meaning? We cannot be certain. When the husband in *Betrayal*

FIGURE 12.15 Romantic identification
During this scene from *Gone with the Wind* (1939), many women viewers identify with Scarlett O'Hara and enjoy imagining being in Rhett Butler's/Clark Gable's arms and having his full attention. For years, American female viewers voted Clark Gable as the most appealing of all male movie stars. *Metro-Goldwyn-Mayer; Selznick International*

FIGURE 12.16 Frequent female romantic fantasy
In *Jules and Jim* (1961) two men, who are best friends, are in love with the same woman, and she determines the nature of her relationships with them and other men. As in many movies, one person attracts the attention of more than one member of the opposite sex and has power over them. *Films du Carrosse; Janus Films*

FIGURE 12.17 **Common female sexual fantasy** ▶
Fellini Satyricon (1969), which is set in ancient Rome, contains many scenes of cruel or commercial sex. It also has many scenes including homosexual sex. But in the part of the scene depicted here, one man kisses the woman tenderly then the other man does, then they kiss her again. As in many movies, one person proves sexually attractive to more than one person at the same time. *PEA; United Artists*

◀ FIGURE 12.18 **Common male sexual fantasy**
In *All That Jazz* (1979), Roy Scheider plays a fast-living, womanizing dancer/choreographer/director who does what many heterosexual males fantasize about: enjoy the attention and physical charms of sexually attractive women. *Robert Alan Arthur; 20th Century-Fox*

learns that his wife has been having an affair with his friend Jerry, he tells her that he has always rather liked Jerry better than her and that maybe he should have had an affair with Jerry himself. Does the husband mean it, or does he say it to hurt his wife, or both? In the play and film versions of *Betrayal* and many other contemporary texts, meaning and motive remain unknowable.

Sometimes an ambiguity may be peripheral to a narrative's main concerns. An example is the three brief references to the young girl's father in Jane Campion's *The Piano* (1993). The first time, the girl tells two women and her mother that her father was a German composer, but her mother is annoyed with that comment and quickly quiets her. Later, when the mother is not around, one of the two women asks the girl where her parents got married; the girl responds with a tale about the wedding ceremony, sees the disbelieving look on her listener's face, admits it was a lie, then names a location where they got married. Soon she also claims her father was killed by lightning (as we see a brief animated drawing of a man catch fire and burn up) and simultaneously her mother struck dumb. The woman seems to accept this last account. In a later scene, the mother nods to her daughter in agreement that the girl's father was a teacher, and in reply to the girl's question why they didn't marry she signs, "He became frightened and stopped listening."

What's to be made of all this? Probably the father was a teacher who would not marry the woman. Beyond that, it gets less certain. Perhaps the mother doesn't want the girl talking about the father (less chance of a slip-up about the girl's illegitimacy). Perhaps when the girl is asked about her father, she is afraid of revealing that her father never married her mother, so she tends to lie about him or to kill him off in her accounts so she won't have to talk about him anymore (or perhaps because she is angry at him for not marrying her mother). All the information about the father is presented so fleetingly and obliquely that his status is ambiguous, but audiences will probably not be troubled by the ambiguity, especially because the issue is touched on only briefly and is peripheral to the story's main concerns.

In other narratives, ambiguity is central. In *Reversal of Fortune* (1990), viewers cannot know whether the main character, Claus von Bülow, attempted to murder his wife or she attempted suicide. Near the end of the narrative, the defense lawyer has come to believe that the wife attempted suicide. His woman assistant concludes that Claus tried to kill his wife. Various scenes focusing on Claus drip with ambiguity, perhaps none more tantalizingly than the one in which he tells the defense lawyer, Dershowitz, the circumstances of finding his wife passed out on the bathroom floor. Next, Dershowitz and Claus arrive at Claus's chauffeur-driven car, and Claus starts to get in:

DERSHOWITZ: Yeah, but is it the truth?
CLAUS (*annoyed*): Of course.
DERSHOWITZ: But not the whole truth.
CLAUS (*more annoyed*): I don't know the whole truth. I don't know what happened to her.

[*Claus finishes getting into the car's backseat.*]

DERSHOWITZ: Wish I didn't believe you. You know it's very hard to trust someone you don't understand.

[*As Dershowitz pauses, Claus, his face now largely obscured by a shadow, turns to look at Dershowitz.*]

DERSHOWITZ (*continuing*): You're a very strange man.

[*Claus's face is still partially covered by a shadow.*]

CLAUS: You have no idea. [See Figure 12.19.]

FIGURE 12.19 **Ambiguous situation**
At the end of a scene from *Reversal of Fortune* (1990), Claus responds to the observation that he is a very strange man with "You have no idea," then pulls the door closed. His face is quickly obscured by the black car window as almost simultaneously his chauffeur begins to back the car out of the driveway. Here as in other scenes in the film, we cannot know Claus's meaning or nature. Perhaps he has tried to kill his wife. Perhaps he has killed others, as is rumored elsewhere in the film. Maybe he has engaged in deviant sexual behavior, as is also commented on elsewhere in the film. Perhaps Claus means "You'll never get to know me well" or something else. His meaning is elusive, but the shadow on his face and his ambiguous statement are ominous. Frame enlargement. *Edward R. Pressman and Oliver Stone; Warner Bros.*

FIGURE 12.20 **Ambiguous main character**
In *To Sleep with Anger* (1990), the character played by Danny Glover is hard to figure out—what he has done and what he is up to—but his visit to old friends is soon followed by one family problem after another. *SVS Films, Inc.; Samuel Goldwyn Co.*

FIGURE 12.21 **Source contributing to ambiguity**
In *Contact* (1997), James Woods plays a national security adviser and a prominent member of a presidential investigative committee who is quick to formulate theories and who comes across as anything but fair or scientific. Woods has a history of playing disreputable characters; for example, shortly before he acted in *Contact*, he played a racist murderer in *Ghosts of Mississippi* (1996). Ephraim Katz has written that Woods is "equally able to project villainousness or moral ambiguity" (1486). The skepticism voiced by the Woods character in *Contact* would be more credible if the role had been played by someone known for trustworthy characters, such as Tom Hanks. Frame enlargement. *Steve Starkey and Robert Zemeckis; Warner Bros.*

Ambiguity is also central in *To Sleep with Anger* (1990). We viewers cannot be certain about much of anything related to the visitor—his past actions, his motives, and the full extent of his influence on later developments—but after he comes to visit a family, the host family's problems multiply, as symbolically their well-kept backyard falls into disrepair and disorder (Figure 12.20).

Ambiguity may result when audiences are uncertain whether a major event occurred. In *Contact* (1997), there is uncertainty whether the main character's vast journey happened. Eyewitnesses and multiple cameras lead viewers to believe that it did not, but her video camera had nearly eighteen hours of elapsed tape, which is impossible for science to account for, and the main skeptic about the trip is untrustworthy (Figure 12.21). In *Reversal of Fortune, To Sleep with Anger, Contact,* and many other films of recent years, ambiguity is deliberate: key information is suggestive but also vague and indecisive or missing altogether.

Symptomatic Meanings: World → Film → Viewers

As we saw in Chapter 11, the widespread attitudes or beliefs of a large group may influence how filmmakers represent their subjects. It is not surprising then that a film's meanings, whether explicit or implicit, may be symptomatic of the society out of which the film emerged, and viewers aware of the widespread beliefs or values where and when a film was made often detect **symptomatic meanings** in the film.

Some meanings of *Unforgiven* are unthinkable in earlier westerns but coincide with popular beliefs in early 1990s America, especially the wrongness of many men's violent and unjust treatment of women and the cruel and unlawful behavior of some law enforcement officials. On the latter score, the film shows that upholders of the law may themselves lose control: the sheriff is so sadistic that when he becomes violent, the townspeople seem embarrassed by his excesses. It's police brutality, 1880s style. The videotape of part of the Rodney King beating by Los Angeles police officers was shown repeatedly on American TV nearly a year and a half before *Unforgiven* was first released in August 1992. That videotape excerpt increased American public awareness of potential police brutality and perhaps influenced some viewers' reactions to the film's sheriff, maybe especially late in *Unforgiven* when the sheriff beats and tortures a black man so mercilessly that he dies.

In the Japanese classic *The Seven Samurai* (1954), the samurai's defense of the farmers depends on coordinated, unified action; thus, when the individualistic Toshiro Mifune character goes off on his own and captures one of the brigands' rifles, the samurai leader reprimands him. The idea reinforced throughout the film—that in unity there is strength—is deeply symptomatic of Japanese society.

symptomatic meaning: Meaning stated or, much more often, suggested by a film or other text that is the same as the widespread belief or value of a group outside the film.

a)

b)

FIGURE 12.22 **Japanese and Western influences**
Shall We Dance? (1996) shows the story of a modern-day office worker in Tokyo who takes up ballroom dancing, a somewhat disreputable activity in the eyes of many Japanese. (a) Some scenes of the movie show behavior accepted as part of Japanese culture since the end of World War II: office workers in crowded commuter trains and office, for example. (b) The movie also includes Western behavior not yet widely considered acceptable and Japanese, such as ballroom dancing lessons and competitions. As a whole, the movie is symptomatic of the changing face of Japanese society and the resistance to accept (yet fascination with) Western behavior. Frame enlargements. *Shôji Masui and Yuji Ogata; Miramax*

Shall We Dance?—a 1996 Japanese film—was enormously popular in its home country. It was also a critical success, capturing all thirteen of the Japanese equivalents of the Academy Awards. (It could not qualify as best foreign film because to the Japanese the film is not foreign.) Probably part of the film's appeal to the Japanese is that many of its characters exhibit the mixed feelings the Japanese populace has toward Western lifestyles and values.

On the one hand, many Japanese cling to the values of the past, as is made clear by nearly all of the opening narration to the film version shown in the United States:

> In Japan, ballroom dance is regarded with much suspicion. In a country where married couples don't go out arm in arm, much less say "I love you" out loud intuitive understanding is everything. The idea that a husband and wife should embrace and dance in front of others is beyond embarrassing. However to go out dancing with someone else would be misunderstood and prove more shameful. Nonetheless, even for Japanese people, there is a secret wonder about the joys that dance can bring.

In *Shall We Dance?* the Japanese office worker and his exuberant, disguised coworker hide their unusual extracurricular activity from their fellow workers to avoid their disapproval (Figure 12.22a). The main character feels compelled to hide his dance lessons from even his wife. Dance halls had been considered questionable in Japan ever since the 1920s because men could buy alcoholic drinks and pay to dance with women who worked there. Even dance lessons were suspect. According to the film's director, Masayuki Suo, "Until recently, [dance] classes remained off-limits to people under 18" (Johnston 7).

On the other hand, *Shall We Dance?* shows the Japanese "secret wonder" about popular Western culture (Figure 12.22b). The influences of British and American cultures are especially strong. The film draws on the British tradition of ballroom dance competition. Part of the film is set in Blackpool, England, and while witnessing the Blackpool competition as a child, one of the dance instructors in *Shall We Dance?* had been inspired to become a dancer. American popular culture also plays an influence. "Shall We Dance?" is not only the film's title but also the last line of the film's dialogue (in English at that) and the name of the famous waltz that is heard several times in the film, including at its conclusion. That popular waltz (and song) derives from the Rodgers and Hammerstein stage musical *The King and I* (1951) and a film adaptation, *The King and I* (1956), which are also in part about differences between East and West. The film version of *The King and I* also inspired one of the dance instructors in *Shall We Dance?* to become a dancer.

With its characters' widespread adherence to traditional values yet attraction to popular Western culture, *Shall We Dance?* is symptomatic of 1996 Japanese society. The movie shows that dancing can bring pleasurable release from the boring, tiring, repetitive routines of the modern urban industrial world. To oversimplify a bit: the film shows that it can be beneficial for the earnest, hard-working Japanese to relax sometimes. The film is so in tune with its people and times that it attracted large audiences and in turn greatly spurred the growth of dance class enrollments and the acceptance of ballroom dancing in Japan.

In contrast to the emphasis on the group in Japanese films and the films of other countries, the emphasis in American films and other films from Western countries is much more typically on one person. Like so many popular movies, *Gladiator* (2000) demonstrates the extraordinary potential power of a dedicated, hard-working individual, even against staggering odds (Figure 12.23). The main character, Maximus—a Roman general chosen by the emperor Marcus Aurelius to be his successor— escapes execution, survives as a slave, and excels as a gladiator. Even in the one scene that best

FIGURE 12.23 Triumph of individualism
Like so many popular movies from Western societies, *Gladiator* (2000) extols the potential power of an individual, even in the face of tremendous adversity. Such movies excite large audiences and reassure them that one person can make a difference. Such a belief is a deeply ingrained component of American ideology. Here is seen the individual of the moment, actor Russell Crowe as Maximus, a general reduced to a gladiator trying to get his own personal vengeance and to set right the wrongs of the Roman power structure. Frame enlargement. *A Douglas Wick Production; DreamWorks; Universal*

shows the value of the group effort—the combat in which the gladiators coordinate their efforts and together defeat the opposing forces—one person (Maximus) organizes and rallies the others. Eventually, Maximus fulfills the wishes of Marcus Aurelius, ends the tyranny of the dictatorial successor (Marcus Aurelius's son Commodus), returns power to the Roman Senate and the people, avenges the murder of his wife and young son, and retains the love of Marcus Aurelius's beautiful and shrewd daughter (Lucilla). In his endeavors Maximus has the loyalty and help of others: Lucilla, Roman senators, Cicero (Maximus's assistant), and his own army, but the attempted coup against Commodus fails, and it is up to *one* man to make all the difference. Although Maximus is chained, imprisoned, and gravely wounded by Commodus, Maximus kills Commodus in the final showdown. Unlike the stories of many societies, such as the nations of Asia and Africa, *Gladiator* celebrates individuality, but then individuality and the freedom to make significant choices are integral to American and some other Western countries' sense of themselves, whether or not members of those societies are conscious of the pervasiveness and force of those **ideological** beliefs. For many viewers, these stories not only embody a society's beliefs but also inspire and reassure the society's members. A central meaning of *Gladiator*—an individual's actions can make a major difference—is symptomatic of the American and (less so) British societies that created the film.

For examples of types of viewer responses to one film, see pp. 434–36.

ideology: The influential underlying social and political beliefs of a society or social group.

INFLUENCES ON THE WAYS PEOPLE THINK ABOUT FILMS

> Cultural artifacts are not containers with immanent meanings, . . . variations among interpretations have historical bases for their differences, and . . . differences and change are . . . due to social, political, and economic conditions, as well as to constructed identities such as gender, sexual preference, race, ethnicity, class, and nationality. (Staiger xi)

In this section, we focus on a few extended examples to illustrate that people respond to films differently because of their own past experiences and their own ways of thinking. *Everyone's* responses to films are influenced by various factors. Perhaps you and one of your parents saw a film together, discussed it afterward, then decided that you had not seen the same film! Your differences in age, previous experiences, and ways of thinking led you to focus on different subjects in the film or to interpret the significance of certain aspects of the film differently. Maybe you were moved by the loss of love and life while watching *Titanic* (1997), whereas a man from a family of U.S. navy personnel was deeply moved by a different aspect of the film: the captain losing his ship. Even the same person experiencing the same text years later—whether *King Kong* or *King Lear*—usually sees different meanings. Sometimes a viewer will perceive two or more opposing meanings during the same viewing (one form of ambiguity). Many factors can influence the meanings a viewer formulates, such as the viewer's age, gender, sexual orientation, social class, religious and political beliefs, experience in general and experience of previous texts, and theories applied in analyzing texts. Let's consider three examples: the viewer's political views, sexual orientation, and application of film theories.

When *Titanic* was first screened, many American viewers and reviewers focused on the film's special effects and its psychological aspects, particularly its initial celebration of human achievement and its scenes of courtship, love, and loss. The movie was and still is enormously popular in China, too—but for different reasons. The Chinese are more focused on the film's social classes and particularly admire Jack (the Leonardo DiCaprio character) as a noble working-class man. At the time of the film's release in China, even the Chinese premier lauded the film for promoting "the correct class viewpoint because the hero Jack is a lower class figure" (Hessler).

Some film scholars have studied how the viewer's sexual orientation influences interpretations of certain films. Elizabeth Ellsworth studied *Personal Best* (1982) and describes its narrative as follows:

> *Personal Best* is . . . about two women athletes, Chris Cahill (Mariel Hemingway) and Tory Skinner (Patrice Donnelly), who meet at the 1976 Olympic Track Trials and become friends and lovers. They live together for three years, but after their male coach places them in direct competition with each other for a place on the Olympic Pentathlon team and hints that Tory is deliberately sabotaging Chris's training progress, they break up. Chris has an affair with a male Olympic swimmer, Denny. The two women meet again at the 1980 Olympic Track Trials. They reaffirm their friendship after Chris sacrifices her own chance to place first in the trials by buming out [*sic*, "bumming out" = wearing out] the lead runner early in the race so that Tory can place in the 800 meter event. Both women win a place in the 1980 Olympic team. (56)

Ellsworth studied reviews from both mainstream and lesbian publications. Her findings?

> Dominant reviewers consistently . . . [focused on] competition, coming of age, goal seeking. . . . [By way of contrast,] most lesbian feminist reviewers ignored large sections of narrative material focusing on heterosexual romance. . . . Some redefined "main characters" and "supporting characters" in order to elevate Patrice Donnelly as the film's star despite the publicity's promotion of Mariel Hemingway as star and the relative length of screen time each character occupied. Lesbian feminist reviewers consistently referred to Patrice Donnelly's performance as convincingly "lesbian" and pleasurable to identify with, reinterpreting Donnelly as the appropriate "object of desire" against the pressbook's [publicity's] and dominant media reviews [*sic*] contextualization of Mariel Hemingway as appropriate object of heterosexual desire. (53, 54)

The Truman Show (1998): Selected Responses

The Truman Show is about Truman Burbank, a young man who is unaware that he has lived his entire life on a gigantic television sound stage as the subject of a long-running, enormously popular TV show. As the story unfolds, Truman begins to question his life and rebel. These passages demonstrate some of the different types of responses possible.

EXPECTATIONS AND INTERACTIONS (VIEWER-RESPONSE CRITICISM)

The film starts out with a burst of information, running the delicious risk of disorienting us by providing more data than we can quite absorb. Its first shot is a tight close-up of a man in a beret who looks directly at the camera and goes to the heart of the matter. "We've become bored with watching actors giving us phony emotions. We're tired of pyrotechnics and special effects. While the world he inhabits is in some respects counterfeit, there is nothing faked about Truman. No script, no cue cards. It isn't always Shakespeare, but it's genuine. It's a life."

The speaker is Christof (Ed Harris), later described as the "televisionary" who created *The Truman Show*. . . .

. . . The film is savvy enough to dole out the ramifications and specifics of Truman's situation in artfully spaced doses. Only in bits and pieces do we find out the true dimension of what has been done to Truman, how it has all been managed.　—Kenneth Turan

EXPLICIT MEANINGS

There are only a few explicit meanings. Christof explains that "we accept the reality of the world with which we're presented," and he explains several explicit meanings near the end of the film, as when he says to Truman, "You were real. That's what made you so good to watch."
　—William H. Phillips

IMPLICIT MEANINGS

Cinematic Techniques

From the outset there's something strange about the place: The squeaky-clean tract houses could have been designed by Disney [see figure], the sunsets are so beautiful they're weird, and the town's inhabitants seem larger than life, as if they are characters, even caricatures.

Seahaven is a surreal version of America as America wishes it once was: paradise without the serpent.
　—Richard Rayner

Film noir . . . fifty years later . . . looks mannered, and we find no realism worthy of our trust. Every depiction of us needs to be ironic, cool, untouched by conviction or belief. . . . And as we looked for an image that embodied our detachment, our disaffection, we found it

Setting for *The Truman Show* (1998)
Truman Burbank lives out his life in the picture-perfect Seahaven, a gigantic enclosed TV studio. As seen here on a TV screen, Seahaven is incredibly clean, orderly, and light. Frame enlargement. *Scott Rudin Productions and Paramount; Paramount*

in the high-key, undifferentiated gloss of television—
a look for those who have given up on the Holy Ghost
of believing what they see.

Half a century after the ascendancy of film noir,
a new genre may be emerging. Call it film blanc, film
lumiere, film fluorescent, film flash, or film deadpan.
I like the latter two because they convey the instantaneous oneness of a kind of photography that bombs us
with light just to get a picture. It's the kind of light that
exists, like climate, on most TV sets and shows: a one-
dimensional lighting scheme without depth, shaping,
or character; a flood of light that lets you film without
having to pause; a light that, with only a little height-
ening, seems surreal, mad, glaring, and unsettling.

The Truman Show is bathed in such light. What
makes this so intriguing is the way it plays off our
dependence on and loathing of TV—as if TV had
become the base level of visible existence.

—David Thomson

Symbolic name in *The Truman Show* (1998)
Christof, the god of Truman's world, whose name rings of *Christ*, and who
commands the sun to rise and set, the sea to churn and calm. Frame enlargement. *Scott Rudin Productions and Paramount; Paramount*

Symbols

In a deft, ironic touch, even Truman Burbank's name
simultaneously evokes both reality (true-man) and
unreality (Burbank, Calif., of course, home to many
a TV and movie studio).   —Michael O'Sullivan

Christof (see second figure) symbolizes a strong-willed
TV director-writer with an increasingly unpredictable
subject, father figure to a rebellious son, tyrant whose
police force helps keep the subject ignorant and in
line, and god who restricts his subject's free will, nearly
kills him, and finally implores him to continue in his
role.   —William H. Phillips

Narrative Meanings

"The Truman Show" is a crowd pleaser that caters
to our horror of totalitarianism, our love of personal
freedom, our belief—justified or deluded—that knowledge is a powerful tool and that access to information
is a God-given right. I'm not sure if the movie is more
disturbing because Truman is a prisoner or because he has been lied to.   —Barbara Shulgasser

Pic trades in issues of personal liberty vs. author-
itarian control, safe happiness vs. the excitement
of chaos, manufactured emotions, the penetra-
tion of media to the point where privacy vanishes,
and the fascination of fabricated images over
plain sight.   —Todd McCarthy

For me, *The Truman Show* was about reality and
television, but also about deception and trust,
and control and ethics, and voyeurism, and movie-
watching, and corporate involvement in our daily
lives.   —Lise Carrigg

We're asked to believe that it took Truman 30
years to realize he was being watched—that he
hadn't noticed in all that time that everyone else
in his life was performing, colluding to protect
his innocence.

It's an outrageous conceit, but once we've sur-
rendered disbelief (and what great fable doesn't
require such a leap?), "The Truman Show" has a
lot to say about the way we live—about voyeurism

and lockstep consumerism, about media surveillance and lack of privacy.　　—Edward Guthmann

The captive of TV isn't Truman, it's the audience. Us. And our love of that captivity, the gobbling of show—fictional drama or news or sports or politics, but always shows—engulfs us. We used to go to theaters and films; now . . . TV comes to our homes, entwines us. . . . The shows don't have to be dramatic. . . . They need only be shows, life outside transmitted to the TV screen inside.　　—Stanley Kauffmann

Truman is living the universal fantasy, in a disease-, disaster-, war and stress-free environment whose minute-to-minute geniality is beamed on Prozac waves into homes around the world, calming the poor, the elderly, the lonely and the working classes with images of a life running its course in paradise.
　　—Jack Matthews

Its premise is a legitimate one: the shock and violent internal crisis undergone by an individual beginning to see his world for the first time, *really* see it, really see *through* it. A smiling face might suddenly suggest hidden malice, a cozy street complacency and even suffocation. This is not paranoia, but the beginning of knowledge.　　—David Walsh

SYMPTOMATIC MEANINGS:
WORLD ➜ FILM ➜ VIEWERS

Would anyone care to guess how many TV shows routinely violate the privacy of ordinary people—often by invitation? Add up the day-time talk tabloids, then factor in all the cops-in-action shows, the seemingly endless supply of the world's funniest home videos. What does this tell us about ourselves, and how we choose to spend our time?

　　At a certain level, this is the central question in . . . *The Truman Show*.　　—Stephan Magcosta

The accelerating blurring of news and entertainment, of real and simulated violence, of authentic history and landscape with screen and theme-park fictionalizations: they're all part of Truman's all too eerily familiar world. So is the passivity of an audience that, as Bill Gates has promised, will someday never have to leave its armchairs.　　—Frank Rich

WORKS CITED

Carrigg, Lise. "Lise reviews *The Truman Show*." 5 Aug. 1998. <http://www.girlson.com/film/navigation/loader.asp?story -http%3A%2F%2Fwww>.

Guthmann, Edward. "Remote Control Jim Carrey Is a Born TV Star in 'The Truman Show.'" *San Francisco Chronicle* 5 June 1998: C1.

Kauffmann, Stanley. "Caught in the Act." *New Republic* 29 June 1998: 22.

Magcosta, Stephan. "Must-See TV: *The Truman Show*." 18 July 1998. <http://seattlesquare.com/pandemonium/ featurestext/TheTrumanShow.htm>.

Matthews, Jack. "He Doesn't Know His World's a Stage." 18 July 1998. <http://www.newsday.com/movies/ rnmxz0d3.htm>.

McCarthy, Todd. "*The Truman Show*." 18 July 1998. <http://www.variety.com/filmrev/cfralso.asp?recordID =1117477427>.

O'Sullivan, Michael. "'Truman': A Surreally Big Show." *Washington Post* 5 June 1998, Weekend: N58.

Rayner, Richard. "*The Truman Show*." *Harper's Bazaar* June 1998: 92.

Rich, Frank. "Prime Time Live." *New York Times* 23 May 1998, national ed.: A25.

Shulgasser, Barbara. "Carrey Rings True in 'The Truman Show.'" *San Francisco Examiner* 5 June 1998. 27 May 2001. <http://www.sfgate.com/cgi-bin/article.cgi?file =/examiner/archive/1998/06/05/WEEKEND8781.dtl>.

Thomson, David. "*The Truman Show*." *Esquire* May 1998: 46.

Turan, Kenneth. "His Show of Shows." *Los Angeles Times* 5 June 1998, Calendar: F1.

Walsh, David. "*The Truman Show*: Further Signs of Life in Hollywood." *World Socialist Web Site* 15 June 1998. 27 May 2000. <http://wsws.org/arts/1998/jun1998/ tru-j15.shtml>.

In their interpretations of the film, lesbian feminist reviewers, however, go only so far in their interpretations: they "stopped short of rearranging the film's chronological order, severing or rearranging cause-effect relationships in the narrative and changing who does what in the narrative" (55).[3]

As film gained in popularity and status throughout the twentieth century, various thinkers developed different theories for understanding the film medium. *Film theory* can be defined as "an evolving body of concepts designed to account for the cinema in [some or] all its dimensions (aesthetic, social, psychological) for an interpretive community of scholars, critics, and interested spectators" (Stam 6). Different people with different backgrounds and different ways of thinking developed different film theories. The concepts constituting a theory are sometimes only loosely related, evolve over time, and lack universal acceptance. Not all theorists calling themselves feminist, for example, will agree what "feminist theory" or "feminist criticism" entails.

To help explain and analyze an individual film or group of films, a viewer might use concepts or ideas from one version of one film theory or different concepts from different theories. For example, a viewer with knowledge of Marxist theory (and Soviet ideology) could point out that Eisenstein's classic film (*Battleship*) *Potemkin* (1925) extols the masses in their struggles with the ruling class. Thus, the ship's officers are represented as cruel and indifferent to the sailors' plight (Figure 12.24). Like the ship's officers, the ship's priest also indirectly supports the oppressive status quo. Marxist theory can also be used to explain why *Potemkin* has no individual heroes because it celebrates the masses, not the individual.

Many types of theories have been drawn on to interpret films and explain the film medium. Formalist criticism, neoformalist criticism, cognitive film theory, and reader-response (or viewer-response) criticism all focus on the work and viewers' responses to qualities perceived in the work. Other approaches focus more on the relationship between the text and the world beyond it. Such contextual approaches include psychoanalytic criticism, Marxist criticism, feminist criticism, genre criticism, cultural studies, reception theory (which examines how historical conditions affect how groups interpret texts at different times and in different places), queer theory, and auteur theory.

Let us consider a theory that is very limited in its scope yet has nonetheless probably been more widely used than any other—**auteur theory,** the belief that some filmmakers, usually directors, function as the dominant creators of films and that the auteur's films embody recurrent structures, tech-

---

[3]For further illustrations of how sexual orientation may affect viewer responses to a film, including interpretations of meanings, see the documentary films *The Celluloid Closet* (1996) and "Jodie: An Icon" (1998) and Alexander Doty's book *Flaming Classics: Queering the Film Canon* (2000).

niques, and meanings. Let's look at an example of auteur theory applied to film analysis. By examining closely the films directed by Howard Hawks, critic Robin Wood helps his readers understand aspects of one film in the context of other Hawksian movies. Of the main woman character in the western *Rio Bravo* (1959), Wood writes,

> Feathers is the product of the union of her basic "type"—the saloon girl—and the Hawks woman, sturdy and independent yet sensitive and vulnerable, the equal of any man yet not in the least masculine. The tension between background (convention) and foreground (actual character) is nowhere more evident. We are very far here from the brash "entertainer" with a heart of gold who dies (more often than not) stopping a bullet intended for the hero. Angie Dickinson's marvelous performance gives us the perfect embodiment of the Hawksian woman, intelligent, resilient, and responsive. There is a continual sense of a woman who really grasps what is important to her. One is struck by the . . . beauty of a living individual responding spontaneously to every situation from a secure centre of self. It is not so much a matter of characterisation as the communication of a life-quality (a much rarer thing). What one most loves about Hawks, finally, is the aliveness of so many of his people. (42)

FIGURE 12.24　**Film as seen as Marxist story**
Eisenstein's (*Battleship*) *Potemkin* (1925) is set during the 1905 uprisings in Russia. Sailors on the *Potemkin* are so mistreated by their officers that they eventually revolt. Seen here is one of the Russian naval officers atop a piano firing a pistol at the rebelling sailors. In the background and on the right can be glimpsed a photograph of the reigning tsar, a reminder that the naval officer is part of the tsarist power structure oppressing the workers. Frame enlargement. *Goskino; The Museum of Modern Art/Circulating Film Library*

All applications of film theories have their advantages and limitations. The auteur approach works best with directors who exercise strong creative control, such as Hawks, Stanley Kubrick, Alfred Hitchcock, Ingmar Bergman, and Federico Fellini. Many movies, however—especially most American studio movies of the 1930s, 1940s, and 1950s and most animated feature films—are more the product of a studio or production company than any individual. Thus Warner Bros. movies were often about current social problems, such as organized urban crime during the prohibition era, and were presented in a way that viewers thought of as true-to-life. MGM movies tended to be lighter, both literally and figuratively, and include the upbeat, big-budget musicals. In recent years, the auteur theory for interpreting films has lost some of its popularity because critics and scholars have decided that the qualities shared by films of the same auteur are not always clearly only the auteur's contributions (see the last section of the Introduction, pp. 4–5) and not the only aspects to be considered in interpreting films. Then, too, since the birth of the auteur theory, film theorists have come to emphasize contexts other than additional films directed by the same person. Many film theorists now stress the types of contexts discussed in Chapter 11—for example, societal attitudes, political climate, and changes in filmmaking or media technology—as factors shaping a film's subjects and **style** and downplay the contributions of individual filmmakers.[4]

style: The way subjects are presented in a text, such as a film. Examples include black comedy, farce, magic realism, parody, and realism.

For a brief description of versions of two more of the many evolving film theories sometimes used by critics in analyzing films (Marxism and feminism), see the Web page for this book: <http://www.bedfordstmartins.com/phillips-film>.

As the examples on political views, sexual orientation, and applications of film theories demonstrate, meanings are not universal. This view is confirmed by scholar Barbara Klinger's study of the changing critical reception to films directed by Douglas Sirk—such as *Magnificent Obsession* (1954), *All That Heaven Allows* (1955), *Written on the Wind* (1957), *Tarnished Angels* (1958), and *Imitation of Life* (1959). Klinger discovered that different American groups operating at the same time—such as academics, review journalists, and star publicists—produce different meanings. She also found that more recent reviewers interpret Sirk's movies quite differently than did the reviewers in the 1950s; her findings illustrate that within the same group, people working at different times produce different meanings. After examining films directed by Sirk and reactions to them over a nearly forty-year period by different groups, Klinger concludes:

> There has been nothing stable about the meaning of his melodramas; they have been subject at every cultural turn to the particular use to which various institutions and social circumstances put them. In this process, meaning itself becomes something we cannot determine "once and for all," but a volatile, essentially cultural phenomenon that shifts with the winds of time. (159)

Even among viewers with similar backgrounds and similar outlooks and living at the same time, there are variations in meanings seen.

---

[4]For more information about the auteur theory and other applications of film theories that are used in film journals and advanced film courses, see J. Dudley Andrew's *The Major Film Theories: An Introduction*; Tim Bywater and Thomas Sobchack's *An Introduction to Film Criticism: Major Critical Approaches to Narrative Film*; Gerald Mast, Marshall Cohen, and Leo Braudy's *Film Theory and Criticism: Introductory Readings*; Bill Nichols, ed., *Movies and Methods*, vols. 1 and 2; R. Barton Palmer's *Introduction to the Cinematic Text: Methods and Approaches*; Robert Lapsley and Michael Westlake's *Film Theory: An Introduction*; and Robert Stam's *Film Theory: An Introduction*.

Although there are always varying interpretations of the same film, not all interpretations are based on salient textual details and are persuasively argued. All films establish broad parameters of meanings: a wide range of meanings is plausible, but some meanings are indefensible. If a viewer does not think carefully about the interpretation and support it with examples from the film and perhaps from outside the film (contexts), the meanings seen may be merely unsubstantiated opinions. In short, what is most illuminating and persuasive to readers and listeners are reasoned and supported arguments, not mere statements of beliefs.

In developing meanings and explaining them to others, viewers, readers, and listeners clarify their own understanding and communicate it, both deep-rooted human needs. Interpretations of meaning may not only illuminate films but also reveal both the interpreters—for example, their backgrounds, assumptions, priorities, or film theories they favor—and the historical time in which the text is being interpreted. Understanding meanings and how they are derived can help viewers realize when a film tries to unduly manipulate them—as in propagandistic films—or when a film demeans a gender, ethnic group, race, or nation. In societies where citizens need to be informed, critical of orthodoxy, yet tolerant of the diversity of people, ideas, and lifestyles, viewers benefit from training in discovering and questioning meanings in films and other texts.

SUMMARY

This chapter introduces two of the major ways viewers think about films. They form expectations and hypotheses and modify them as a film proceeds. Viewers also often learn some explicit meanings during the film showing and usually formulate implicit meanings. Those explicit and implicit meanings may be symptomatic of a large group outside the film. The implicit meanings every viewer formulates are not universal and are shaped by many factors.

Expectations and Interactions

■ As viewers watch a film, they interact with it, forming expectations, responding to clues set forth, guessing, readjusting their hypotheses, and consequently experiencing puzzlement or clarity and feeling excitement and pleasure or disappointment or boredom or something else.

Types of Meanings

■ As used in this book, *meaning* is an observation or generalization about a subject.

■ Unless a film includes some direct statement explaining its meanings, meanings are not inherent in a film. Mentally active people formulate most meanings.

EXPLICIT MEANINGS

■ Explicit meanings are verbal generalizations in a text about one or more of its subjects. They are included more often in documentary films than in fictional films or experimental films.

■ Fictional films that often include explicit meanings are frequently thought of as flawed, at least in Western societies, because generally modern audiences in the West expect movies to show, not tell or explain, their meanings.

■ An explicit meaning is not necessarily comprehensive or persuasive, and it is not the definitive word on any subject.

IMPLICIT MEANINGS

■ An implicit meaning is a generalization a viewer or reader makes about a text (such as a film) or a subject in a text.

■ A viewer may use awareness of cinematic techniques, symbols, and narratives to help formulate a film's implicit meanings.

■ As Part One of this book shows, a film's mise en scène, cinematography, editing, and sound can suggest meanings.

■ A technique may be used subtly and viewers required to be especially attentive in discovering its significance. However, a technique's significance may not be noticed if the technique is too subtle for the intended audience or if the version being seen and heard obscures important details.

■ Filmmakers and other makers of texts may create symbols: anything perceptible that has significance beyond its usual meaning or function. Usually symbols go unexplained within a film, and viewers interpret them variously, although not all interpretations are equally persuasive.

■ Narrative itself is a major source of implicit meanings because viewers often infer general implications from the story. For example, movies that include unrealistic events often present improbable though usually reassuring stories showing that people can overcome overwhelming adversity and achieve their goals.

■ A narrative or some aspect of it may be ambiguous: it may withhold significant information or provide conflicting information. Viewers may be unable to infer a story's meanings with much certainty, or the narrative or some aspect of it may be subject to two or more plausible interpretations.

SYMPTOMATIC MEANINGS: WORLD → FILM → VIEWERS

- Knowledge of the world outside the film helps viewers discover symptomatic meanings: explicit or implicit meanings that are the same as those of a group outside the film. For example, popular American movies are permeated with the message or implication that dedicated, industrious individuals can influence the outcome of important events. This meaning is symptomatic of much of American society.

Influences on the Ways People Think about Films

- The meanings a person perceives in a text may be influenced by many factors, such as the person's political views, sexual orientation, and application of film theories.

- Meanings are to some extent relative to time and place, but a film sets parameters to interpretation of meanings, and some interpretations are indefensible.

WORKS CITED

Alexie, Sherman (author, and scriptwriter of *Smoke Signals*). Telephone interview. 13 June 2000.

Bordwell, David. *Making Meaning: Inference and Rhetoric in the Interpretation of Cinema.* Cambridge: Harvard UP, 1989.

Ellsworth, Elizabeth. "Illicit Pleasures: Feminist Spectators and *Personal Best*." *Wide Angle* 8.2 (1986): 45–56; rpt. in *Issues in Feminist Film Criticism.* Ed. Patricia Erens. Bloomington: Indiana UP, 1990.

Epstein, Leslie. "The Movie on the Whorehouse Wall/*The Devil in Miss Jones*." *The Movie That Changed My Life.* Ed. David Rosenberg. New York: Viking, 1991.

Hessler, Peter. Interview. *Fresh Air.* National Public Radio. 5 Feb. 2001.

Katz, Ephraim. *The Film Encyclopedia.* 3rd ed. Rev. Fred Klein and Ronald Dean Nolen. New York: HarperCollins, 1998.

Johnston, Sheila. "Interview: Masayuki Suo." *The Observer* (England) 10 May 1998: 7+.

Klinger, Barbara. *Melodrama and Meaning: History, Culture, and the Films of Douglas Sirk.* Bloomington: Indiana UP, 1994.

Maslin, Janet. "Is It Unexpected? Is It Strange? It's Here." *New York Times* 28 Jan. 1995. national ed.: 11.

Staiger, Janet. *Interpreting Films: Studies in the Historical Reception of American Cinema.* Princeton: Princeton UP, 1992.

Stam, Robert. *Film Theory: An Introduction.* Malden, MA: Blackwell, 2000.

Sternberg, Meir. *Expositional Modes and Temporal Ordering in Fiction.* Baltimore: Johns Hopkins UP, 1978.

Wood, Robin. *Howard Hawks.* Garden City, NY: Doubleday, 1968.

FOR FURTHER READING

Although film theory helps us understand the film medium more completely, some recent examples are frustrating for students to read because of their involved sentence structure and the writers' heavy use of jargon. The books listed below, however, should prove accessible to many beginning film students.

Andrew, J. Dudley. *The Major Film Theories: An Introduction.* New York: Oxford UP, 1976. Includes an explanation of what film theory entails and a discussion of major film theories: early theorists, realist film theory, and contemporary French film theory.

Approaches to Popular Film. Ed. Joanne Hollows and Mark Janncovich. Manchester, UK: Manchester UP, 1995. Eight essays on different film theories for doing film analyses.

Bennett, Tony, and Janet Wollacott. *Bond and Beyond: The Political Career of a Popular Hero.* New York: Methuen, 1987. A study of the James Bond novels and films (to the late 1980s) showing in part how they have been read or interpreted differently at different times and different places.

BFI Film Classics and *BFI Modern Classics.* London: BFI. Two series of short books published by the British Film Institute, each devoted to one film and written by a film critic, film scholar, or novelist. Sample *BFI Film Classics* titles are for *Belle de jour, Blackmail,* and *Bonnie and Clyde.* Sample titles in the *BFI Modern Classics* series are *Blade Runner, Blue Velvet, Dead Man,* and *L'argent.*

Bywater, Tim, and Thomas Sobchack. *Introduction to Film Criticism: Major Critical Approaches to Narrative Film.* New York: Longman, 1989. Includes discussions of major ways to analyze films; sample student papers; a chronology of film reviewing, criticism, and theory; and a glossary.

Cambridge Film Handbooks. Ed. Andrew Horton. Cambridge, UK: Cambridge UP. A series of books, each focused on one film from a variety of theoretical, critical, and contextual perspectives and consisting of essays by film scholars and critics, a filmography, and a bibliography. Sample titles are *Bonnie and Clyde, Persona, The Wild Bunch, The Discreet Charm of the Bourgeoisie, Sherlock Jr., Tokyo Story, Do the Right Thing,* and the *Godfather* trilogy.

Carson, Diane, Linda Dittmar, and Janice R. Welsch, eds. *Multiple Voices in Feminist Film Criticism.* Minneapolis: U of Minnesota P, 1994. A collection of mostly theoretical essays, most for the advanced student.

Close Viewings: An Anthology of New Film Criticism. Ed. Peter Lehman. Tallahassee: Florida State UP, 1990. Part 1 emphasizes formal analysis; Part 2, cultural analysis; Part 3, an essay, applies many forms of criticism to one film, *The Searchers.*

Critical Dictionary of Film and Television Theory. Ed. Roberta Person and Philip Simpson. New York: Routledge, 2001. Includes over 400 entries from 500 to 3,000 words, each. Sample entries are for *continuity editing, film noir, mise-en-scene, narrative,* and *western.* Also included are suggestions for further reading, cross-references, and an index.

Film Theory Goes to the Movies: Cultural Analysis of Contemporary Film. Ed. Jim Collins, Hilary Radner, and Ava Preacher Collins. New York: Routledge, 1993. Interpretations of popular American movies in terms of issues in current film theories.

Greenberg, Harvey Roy. *Screen Memories: Hollywood Cinema on the Psychoanalytic Couch.* New York: Columbia UP, 1993. Film criticism from a psychoanalytic perspective.

Lane, Christina. *Feminist Hollywood: From* Born in Flames *to* Point Break. Detroit: Wayne State UP, 2000. Includes original interviews with women directors and close analyses of their films.

Miles, Margaret R. *Seeing and Believing: Religion and Values in the Movies.* Boston: Beacon, 1996. Examines what popular films of the 1980s and 1990s say and suggest about religion and values. Essays are divided into two parts: "Religion in Popular Film" and "Race, Gender, Sexuality, and Class in Popular Film."

The Political Companion to American Film. Ed. Gary Crowdus. Chicago: Lake View, 1994. Includes essays on filmmakers, genres, racial and ethnic representations, and social characterizations (such as politicians). Many essays discuss films' implicit and symptomatic political meanings (broadly defined). Includes a short bibliography after most of the essays.

Powers, Stephen, David J. Rothman, and Stanley Rothman. *Hollywood's America: Social and Political Themes in Motion Pictures.* Boulder, CO: Westview, 1996. The book combines an "extensive systematic content analysis . . . of social and political themes in [popular] motion pictures from 1946 to the present with the most detailed study ever conducted of the political views and personalities of a random sample of leaders in the motion picture industry." Includes many tables presenting the results of the research and an appendix entitled The Poverty of Film Theory.

Ray, Robert B. *A Certain Tendency of the Hollywood Cinema, 1930–1980.* Princeton, NJ: Princeton UP, 1985. In part, by analyzing such classic movies as *Casablanca, The Man Who Shot Liberty Valance, The Godfather,* and *Taxi Driver,* Ray explains and illustrates "the formal and thematic paradigms that commercially successful films in this country have consistently used."

Salt, Barry. *Film Style and Technology: History and Analysis.* 2nd ed. London: Starword, 1992. Both a critique of much of current film theory and a history of film technology and analysis of its impact on film style.

The St. James Women Filmmakers Encyclopedia: Women on the Other Side of the Camera. Ed. Amy L. Unterburger. Detroit: Visible Ink Press, 1999. More than 200 entries—each of which includes a short biography, filmography, and analysis—on female filmmakers, mainstream and independent, from around the world.

Tan, Ed S. *Emotion and the Structure of Narrative Film: Film as an Emotion Machine.* Mahwah, NJ: Erlbaum, 1996. A theoretical study of a largely neglected subject with emphasis on the traditional feature film. Sample chapter titles: The Psychological Functions of Film Viewing; Thematic Structures and Interest; and Character Structures, Empathy, and Interest.

Wood, Michael. *America in the Movies.* New York: Dell, 1975. Examines Hollywood movies from the end of the 1930s to the beginning of the 1960s as reassuring fantasies.

Other materials illustrating understanding films can be found on the Web site for this book: <http://www.bedfordstmartins.com/phillips-film>. For an extended example of how the concepts from Part Three can be applied to a film, see the following chapter.

CHAPTER 13

Understanding
The Player

*T*HE PLAYER CAME OUT IN 1992. It was written by Michael Tolkin, whose novel of the same title is the basis for the film, and directed by Robert Altman. This film is often used in introductory college film courses for many reasons. It is readily available on videotape, laser disc, and DVD; entertaining to watch; and displays many aspects of interest to filmmakers, film critics, and film scholars. Furthermore, *The Player* is a movie about the Hollywood movie industry, filled with references to earlier films and with direct and indirect commentaries on the Hollywood studio system.

DESCRIPTION

If you have not seen *The Player* recently or will not be seeing it, please read the following description at least twice.

The film, which is set in modern Hollywood, focuses on a film studio executive named Griffin Mill whose job entails listening to and approving brief summaries of stories to be made into movies. Griffin processes hundreds of pitches a week, but the studio can produce only twelve movies a year.

Viewers quickly learn three unrelated aspects of Griffin's situation: an unidentified screenwriter is threatening Griffin; rumor has it that an outsider named Larry Levy will be brought in to take over Griffin's position; and Griffin is involved romantically with a subordinate, a story editor named Bonnie Sherow (Figure 13.1).

After some hasty searching through office records, Griffin decides that the writer who has been threatening him is named David Kahane. That night, Griffin telephones Kahane from outside the writer's house. He sees Kahane's girlfriend, an artist named June Gudmundsdottir, answer the phone and is immediately attracted to her (Figure 13.2). June tells Griffin that Kahane went to a movie. Later Griffin finds Kahane at the movie theater and after-

FIGURE 13.1 **Main character's initial love interest**
Early in the film viewers see that Griffin Mill is romantically involved with a coworker, Bonnie Sherow. Here they are seen as she reads to him a particularly inept passage from a submitted screenplay. Frame enlargement. *Fine Line Features*

ward has drinks with him. The two men end up in a parking lot, tempers flare (Figure 13.3), and Griffin kills Kahane. Griffin makes the murder look like an interrupted robbery.

The next day, Griffin returns to his job and finds that Larry Levy has come to work at the studio. Later, Griffin also learns that the writer who had been threatening him is still alive. Griffin attends Kahane's funeral and soon begins to pursue Kahane's girlfriend romantically.

Because Griffin is a suspect in the murder, the police come to Griffin's office and interview him. After a producer and director pitch Griffin their plans for *Habeas Corpus*—a grim story likely to be a huge flop—Griffin "allows" Levy to take over championing the story in the hope that the movie will fail and Levy will be discredited (Figures 13.4).

The police summon Griffin to the police station, where Detective Avery's questions and methods fluster him (Figure 13.5). Later, Griffin and June slip off to a desert hideaway where at the conclusion of a romantic evening they become lovers. The next day, Griffin is called in for a police lineup, but the only eyewitness selects a police detective from among the possible suspects.

FIGURE 13.2 **Main character's new love interest**
From outside the writer's house and looking in, Mill sees a luminous vision in the night, an artist who always dresses in white and works in a shimmering silvery white studio. Soon he pursues her as he tries to cope with the threat of the police arresting him for murder, changes in studio personnel, his relationship with Bonnie, and a persistent and increasingly threatening postcard writer. Frame enlargement. *Fine Line Features*

FIGURE 13.3 **Mill and the writer, tempers flaring**
Mill finds a writer whom Mill assumed was writing the threatening postcards. The writer quickly gets angry at Mill, but Mill fails to calm the writer's anger. One thing to leads to another, and the two men face each other here, moments before the man pushes the car door against Mill knocking him backward and over a railing and Mill attacks back and kills the man. Frame enlargement. *Fine Line Features*

a) b)

FIGURE 13.4 A pitch to Mill and Levy's pitch to the studio head
(a) An intense director—holding Mill's leather-encased scissors in one hand and a fake grenade from Mill's desktop in the other—pitches the story for *Habeas Corpus* to Mill. Mill thinks the story would be a disaster as a movie, so he OKs it then plans to let Levy propose it to the studio head.
(b) Levy proposes the story of *Habeas Corpus* to the studio head as Mill waits behind clasped hands, probably enjoying that Levy is walking into the trap Mill set for him. Frame enlargements. *Fine Line Features*

A year later, the director of *Habeas Corpus* has included stars and a preposterous happy ending after all. After a screening at the studio, Bonnie Sherow points out the sellout the film has become, whereupon Levy fires her. Griffin now occupies the former studio head's office and is in charge of the studio. He and Levy are on good working terms. When Bonnie tries to make an emotional appeal to Griffin, he walks past her without looking at her and says she "will land on her feet."

In the final sequence, Griffin is cruising to his home in a Rolls-Royce convertible while listening to a pitch on his car phone. The speaker obliquely identifies himself as the writer who had been threatening Griffin and proposes a story about a movie executive who gets away with murder—in fact, the story of the movie that viewers have just seen. Griffin's main concern is that the movie executive gets away with the murder and lives hap-

FIGURE 13.5 Major threat to Mill's freedom and happiness
The main impediment to Mill's freedom and happiness is a clever police detective. She asks questions that catch Mill off-guard and interrogates him in an unorthodox manner (including twirling the tampon she holds in her hand here as she questions Mill). Frame enlargement. *Fine Line Features*

pily ever after married to the dead writer's girlfriend. The writer assures him that a green light will guarantee that outcome, and Griffin agrees. The writer proposes that the film be called *The Player*. Griffin arrives home and is greeted warmly by June, who is visibly pregnant.

UNDERSTANDING *THE PLAYER* THROUGH CONTEXTS

Any text is a product of its time and culture. Viewers who know some contexts of *The Player* can understand the film more completely than those who know only the film.

Society and Politics

Historically, Los Angeles fought for recognition amid aspersions that it was "sleepy," too much a part of the West to be considered a challenge to the East's position as the bastion of intellectual, financial, and social validity. The values that emerged and eventually grew to define Los Angeles are directly related to the emergence and eventual ascension to power of the movie industry. As a theatrical reviewer for the *Los Angeles Times* wrote in 1999, L.A. is "a city built on deception." The irony that Los Angeles has little to define itself other than its image is not lost on Angelenos. In fact, there is an air of pride rather than apology surrounding the statement. After all, it is a very large image.

The Player is L.A. on L.A. In this movie Los Angeles, unfiltered water is to be avoided, even though Los Angeles water has long been rated among the best-tasting and safest of all large American cities. Business contacts are generated at AA meetings; and Range Rovers are equipped with faxes. Success requires that people recognize one another but remain unencumbered by relationships or obligations. These elements help re-create the Los Angeles of the late 1980s and early 1990s.

Censorship

The Player was made free of Hollywood studio control; thus the director, writer, and actors enjoyed a wide range of freedom to present the subjects as they saw fit, including gently satirizing Hollywood studio filmmaking. The film is rated R—presumably for its partial nudity; a sex scene of heavy breathing and two sweaty, bobbing heads; vulgar language; and one scene of murderous violence. The rating also allowed its makers to roam a broad field. The film does not attract audiences because of its sex and violence. In truth, there is little. Its concerns and appeal lie elsewhere—with Hollywood-style deal making and people who make movies.

Artistic Conventions

The Player follows certain filmmaking conventions, except for the film's virtuoso opening shot, which runs more than eight minutes and is described in Table 3.1 (see p. 107). For instance, everyone, from principal characters to the studio mail carrier, is attractive. Some Angelenos would argue that that is true to life. It is, however, more an adherence to what viewers expect in movies (convention) than what is true of the gene pool in Los Angeles. All the "players" are white males. Women are portrayed as competent in a tough, competitive atmosphere, but they are not "players." The most sympathetic of them, Bonnie, gets fired and loses her footing. (That is not only adherence to film convention; it is part of the actual milieu that must be shown if the story is to be credible.) The main female character, June, is represented as a beacon in the night dressed in white whose radiance allows her to stand out even among the Beautiful People.

Financial Constraints

By 1991, director Robert Altman had been relatively successful both at the box office and in the reviewers' columns, but in the years before he made *The Player* he had not had a popular or critical success. He also had (and maintains) the reputation of being a Hollywood outsider. With its satiric story of Hollywood studio moviemaking, lack of big stars in big roles, and a low quotient of sex and violence, *The Player* had virtually no chance of attracting big audiences. So how did the film get funding? Keeping the satire amusing and good-natured (what Altman himself calls "tame" in the DVD commentary) probably helped. Although the concluding credits list a stunt coordinator, special effects, and set medic, the film has no costly special effects or dangerous action scenes, such as a car crash described in the source novel. Instead of filming in Mexico, as the novel indicated, some scenes were filmed at a desert resort during the off-season. Certainly, the relatively modest budget of approximately $8 million and the willingness of many actors, some of them stars, to be involved in an Altman film at minimal rates also helped make possible the funding and making of the film.

THINKING ABOUT *THE PLAYER*

The Player has multiple and unexpected story developments—especially the murder and the murderer escaping conviction. It also has many possible meanings. In the following pages, only a few examples will be pointed out, but others are sure to occur to anyone who has seen the film and thought about it.

Expectations and Interactions

Early in *The Player*, viewers read the title card "A Robert Altman Film." Those who have seen other Altman films—such as *M*A*S*H* (1970), *McCabe and Mrs. Miller* (1971), *The Long Goodbye* (1973), *Nashville* (1975),

Short Cuts (1993), *Ready to Wear* (1994), *Cookie's Fortune* (1999), and *Dr. T and the Women* (2000)—will immediately have certain expectations: satire; surprises; some complexity in characterizations, plot, or meanings; and a potential for a viewing experience that will linger in the mind after leaving the theater.

A film entitled *The Player* may pique a viewer's curiosity to see which meaning of the word will apply. By denotation, *player* has at least seven meanings about different types of people, including a person who engages in illegal activity. By connotation, the word can evoke shades of artifice, sleight of hand, and imposture. It may also suggest an elevated level of skill and competition.

In the opening shot, viewers discover immediately that they must process visual and verbal information at a demanding pace. We are going to get an insider's simultaneous, multichanneled view of Hollywood filmmakers at work. By reputation we know it to be a treacherous, illusory environment set in luxurious surroundings. By the film's conclusion we understand that Griffin Mill is a player. Larry Levy is a player. Bonnie is not. Levison was a player—then suddenly and inexplicably was not. The director of *Habeas Corpus* has been converted into one. *The Player* plays on our minds. We are encouraged to interact with it beginning with the title card "A Robert Altman Film" and ending with the film's final credits.

Types of Meanings

There are only a few explicit meanings in *The Player*. Probably the most noteworthy one is heard while Griffin explains to June what makes for a successful Hollywood movie, especially a happy ending. Generally, fictional films invite viewers to construct their own character attributes and motivations and the film's meanings. Otherwise, it would be like playing cards with all hands dealt face up.

The Player is rich in implicit meanings. The film's portrayal of film industry personnel confirms the industry's reputation: Hollywood threatens constancy in human relationships. *The Player* shows only one lasting alliance and that one (between Griffin and June) has the potential for survival only because she is completely and contentedly outside the movie industry (she does not even go to movies).

In *The Player* actors and talk of them are plentiful, and, of course, writers are prominent, appearing in the initial scenes and often thereafter. The film exposes the low esteem in which writers are held. We see this most clearly when Larry Levy proposes doing away with writers (expensive and unnecessary appendages) and suggests that the executives can create their own story lines from things as mundane as current newspaper headlines. Levy's next idea is to advocate production of *Habeas Corpus*, complete with unknown actors and unhappy ending. As pitched, beginning with the title, it is hard to imagine a less promising story for a commercial film. So after Levy's inauspicious start, what is his fate? Evidently when Griffin assumes control of the studio, Levy gets promoted to Griffin's old job. The continuity of the usual product is assured.

When Bonnie cries at the end of *The Player*, she violates a cardinal principle of the filmmaking industry: at work, emotions must be kept under control. Near the film's end, Griffin breezes past her without so much as a backward glance and says that she "will land on her feet." In contrast to Bonnie's emotions, recall Griffin's largely nonplussed demeanor when the studio's security chief questions him regarding Kahane's death. Remember Griffin's controlled response to each postcard. At one point he dismisses his secretary's suggestion that he involve studio security to help track down the threatening writer. Griffin knows he must not show fear if he is to remain a player, especially at this time when he believes that his job is in jeopardy.

Satire is the representation of human behavior that has as its aim the humorous criticism of the behavior. *The Player* is wide-ranging in its satiric targets. Writers are satirized for being so desperate and for wavering when they sense Mill's reluctance. Directors are satirized for selling out the integrity of a story for the sake of commercial success. Studio executives are shown as concerned more with profits than with creating quality products. Of course, the product of all these studio personnel—the studio movie—is parodied and satirized by the distracting presence of stars and the forced happy ending of *Habeas Corpus*.

As Chapter 12 reminds us, cinematic techniques create meaning and influence meanings conveyed by other aspects of a film. Beginning with the movie's first shot, the many shots of moving, fast-talking actors filmed by a moving camera or zooms lens (or both) contribute to the sense that people in the movie industry are an energetic group wrapped up in their work but not each other. Often scenes are filmed so that one character is walking away as another character walks alongside or behind, talking at rather than talking to each other—all the while without making eye contact. The film also relies heavily on eye-level camera placements; viewers get to see players at an interactive level. Here, as in other films, the filmmakers play to the belief that viewers have a right both to explore the world of people who wield enormous power and to be on an equal footing with them. Many scenes include an Altman trademark: overlapping dialogue. In their rush, characters speak without being entirely heard, and the cacophonous mixture of voices suggests that the attempt to be heard may be in vain. In such an environment, communication can be stressful, fragmentary, and incomplete.

Parts of *The Player*'s mise en scène suggest symbolic meanings. Mill's office is crammed with movie posters for *King Kong* (1933), *The Blue Angel* (1930), and six movies dealing with crime, especially murder: *Prison Shadows* (1936), *Hollywood Story* (1951), *Laura* (1944, Figure 13.6a), *Murder in the Big House* (1942, Figure 13.6b), *Prison Break* (1938, Figure 13.6b), and *M* (the 1951 remake). Many of the posters in Mill's office suggest that Mill's work involves

FIGURE 13.6 Symbolic Setting
(a–b) Most of the many movie posters in Mill's office are for films involving crime and punishment, an appropriate backdrop for a man who has committed murder and hopes to evade punishment. *Fine Line Features*

crimes and murder. By contrast, the office of the studio head has a poster for *Casablanca* (1942), whose subjects are romance, patriotism, and sacrifice.

Another component of the setting used to convey meaning is the cars. For most of the film Mill drives a black Range Rover—a status symbol for moneyed Angelenos and a vehicle that can comfortably accommodate actor Tim Robbins's six-foot five-inch frame. The studio head, Joel Levison, drives a black Mercedes, and Mill's rumored rival, Larry Levy, drives a black Mercedes convertible. Levy has the same tastes as the studio head and is a major player. In the film's last scenes, when Mill is now the studio head, he drives a Rolls-Royce convertible, an obvious symbol of his promotion. As in so many movies and in life, cars symbolize status and power.

Meaning is also suggested by another symbol: the main character's name. Hollywood is a griffin mill: a manufacturer of fabled creations. The product includes any number of chimerical masterpieces. But it likewise includes monstrosities. *Mill* has additional relevant meanings, including an institution or a business that makes a profit by turning out product without regard to quality, as in "diploma mill," a school that turns out graduates without regard to standards.

In its representation of the competition within and between companies, the use of consumer technology (such as cars, fax machines, and cell phones) in doing the work, and the immersion in work at the expense of personal connectiveness, *The Player* can be seen as symptomatic of much of life in late twentieth-century America.

As Chapter 12 illustrates, filmmakers decide how subtly to use techniques. Sometimes the expressive aspects of the settings—such as the movie posters—are seen only fleetingly. Another example of subtlety is a book glimpsed in Mill's secretary's desk as Mill begins his search for leads about the threatening writer. For less than a second, viewers have a chance to read the title of the book, *They Made Me a Criminal*, which is also the title of a 1939 movie. In an interview with Geoff Andrew, Altman implies that the postcard writer is the eulogizer at Kahane's funeral (187), and in the Criterion laser disc version of *The Player* (but not on the DVD), Tolkin says that the actor who plays the eulogizer was used for the telephone voice of the blackmailing writer at the film's end. Both characters use the phrase "some shit-bag producer." That detail is too subtle for nearly all viewers: the two speeches are brief, far apart, and the second is heard only as a telephone voice. Occasionally, though, significant details are not so much glimpsed as thrust into the viewers' faces, as when the camera zooms in on a movie poster or on a photograph of the cinematic master of mystery, murder, and suspense, director Alfred Hitchcock. Alert viewers have already understood the points about the poster and the photo.

Although *The Player* adheres to the basics of its source novel and screenplay, the film exemplifies Robert Altman's film work and could be a candidate for the auteurist approach. Like many Altman films, *The Player* relies heavily on satire without ever becoming venomous, and it is sometimes sprawling in terms of number of characters and intricacies of plot. Like other Altman films, there is also a heavy reliance on the moving camera, the zoom lens, and overlapping dialogue. A Marxist critic could point out how *The Player* shows that those in power exploit their workers and that the capitalist producers of images that support the status quo are themselves self-serving as they busily perpetuate stories of individuality and romance, not stories of collective group efforts for the good of society. A feminist critic could point out how June is largely constructed by males (writer and director), has no credible emotional core, and exists only to be beautiful, alluring, and eventually available to the hero. A feminist reading might also point out how complex and sympathetic Bonnie is. Furthermore, a feminist interpretation could point out how the film within the film, *Habeas Corpus*, is typical Hollywood fare created by men and concluding with the trite and condescending patriarchal episode of a male rescuing an imperiled female.

OTHERS' THOUGHTS ABOUT *THE PLAYER*

> INTERVIEWER: It was only on a later viewing that I noticed: The S in the studio motto MOVIES NOW MORE THAN EVER is made out of a strip of film that rears up like a cobra.
> ALTMAN: I hadn't thought of that, but you saw it and that's okay. Every time I make a movie, I then get to read the reviews and find out what I've done. ("The Movie You Saw" 173)

As is always the case with film viewers and reviewers, those who wrote about *The Player* responded differently and saw different meanings in the film. Below is a small sample of the published responses.

Expectations and Interactions
(Viewer-Response Criticism)

"There's a chill at the center of *The Player*. Altman gets us rooting for Griffin by subtle degrees—first, because his job is threatened; later, because he's in love and in trouble. But the movie needles us by degrees, too, by gradually exposing Griffin's corruption. If we're cheering Griffin on even though he's a cad (and worse), that makes us somehow accomplices in his perfidy. And, in the end, when he prevails while the nice but decidedly less glamorous folk around him tumble, Altman slathers on the triumphant music and sunshine in a way that may make us squirm. He's not letting anyone off the hook—not even the audience. After all, we're part of the system, too. We're the ones clamoring for '*Ghost* meets *The Manchurian Candidate*'; we're the ones drooling over Bruce [Willis] and Arnold [Schwarzenegger] and Julia [Roberts] and Mel [Gibson]. No one leaves *The Player* with a clear conscience" (Schiff 143).

Explicit Meanings

A few commentators quoted the film's most prominent explicit meaning, Mill's explanation to June about the ingredients of a successful Hollywood movie: "suspense, laughter, violence, hope, heart, nudity, sex, happy endings . . . mainly happy endings." Nearly always, *The Player* shows and suggests its meanings rather than state them, and as commentator Stephen Schiff observes, "Altman demonstrates all this [implicit meaning] without getting windy about it" (138).

Implicit Meanings

"*The Player* is about how the industry crushes the originality out of anyone who participates in it—any Player, be he writer, director, or production chief.

And that's because the Hollywood system makes it impossible to view the world afresh, to derive inspiration or even information from it" (Schiff 138).

"*The Player*" . . . satirizes Hollywood mores and mannerisms, but, at the same time, never truly disturbs its audience and can easily be enjoyed, absorbed, and promoted by the industry itself" (Quart).

"The film should captivate anyone with a taste for bold cinematics, unpredictable storytelling, and pitch-black humor aimed at the worthiest of targets: a self-involved and self-congratulatory industry that often gives lip-service to art while worshipping the bottom line" (Sterritt 14).

Symptomatic Meanings

"*The Player* does capture L.A. and today's Hollywood with chilling exactness. It's more than the way the details are right, things like the cars, the houses, the restaurants, even the mineral water. . . . Tolkin and Altman are also hip to the mind set of a completely self-absorbed, not to say amoral, business awash in frenzied round-the-clock schmoozing" (Turan).

In a 1992 interview with Geoff Andrew, Altman said that *The Player* is "*of* Hollywood, but it's not really just *about* Hollywood. Hollywood is a metaphor for our society, which is based on greed—take, take, take, and don't give anything back to the system; lie and cheat. So though the film is about the stupidity of Hollywood, it's also about the moral problems of our society at large" (185).

As with all films, the viewer's interactions with the film and the meanings the viewer formulates depend in part on the viewer and his or her contexts and ways of thinking.

WORKS CITED

Altman, Robert. Audio Commentary. *The Player* (DVD), New Line Home Video, 1997.

"The Movie You Saw Is the Movie We're Going to Make: Robert Altman Interviewed by Gavin Smith and Richard T. Jameson." *Film Comment* 28.3 (May–June 1992): 22–30; rpt. *Robert Altman Interviews*. Ed. David Sterritt. Jackson: UP of Mississippi, 2000: 163–81.

"The Player King." Robert Altman interviewed by Geoff Andrew. *Time Out* no. 1137 (June 3, 1992): 18–20; rpt. *Robert Altman Interviews*. Ed. David Sterritt. Jackson: UP of Mississippi, 2000: 182–87.

Quart, Leonard, and Alissa Quart. Review. *Cineaste* 19.2–3 (1992): 60 ff.

Schiff, Stephen. "Auteur! Auteur!" *Vanity Fair* 55.4 (April 1992): 136–43.

Sterritt, David. "A Movie That Pokes Fun at Movies." *Christian Science Monitor*. 10 Apr. 1992: 14.

Turan, Kenneth. Review. *Los Angeles Times*. 10 April 1992, Calendar: 1 ff.

Vicki Whitaker of Aztec, New Mexico, assisted me during preparation of the first edition of this chapter.

APPENDICES

Studying Films: Reading, Thinking, Researching, and Writing

WRITING ABOUT FILMS

No one ever has been able to give the exact measure of his needs, his concepts, or his sorrows. The human tongue is like a cracked cauldron on which we beat out tunes to set a bear dancing when we would make the stars weep with our melodies. (Flaubert 138)

To try to capture in speech the richness and nuances of human experience and thought can be frustrating. It is no easy task to capture them in writing, either, but writing can bring us closer to that goal than speech can. For understanding and communicating about something as complicated as our experiences of film, writing is indispensable.

Nearly everyone knows about the agony of committing words to paper. After all, the writer's job is to create clear and convincing prose that can be read without interruption, rereading, or puzzlement, often by a stranger, someone who knows nothing about the writer. It is no wonder effective writing requires much thinking and concentration and tends to be time-consuming.

Most writers find they work most efficiently if they don't work too long in a session and alternate periods of work with rest. They also know there's little time to do so the last few days before an assignment is due. Nearly all successful writers divide their work into steps because they know that most writing is too complicated to do well in one sitting or even two.

Prewriting

For convenience, I have divided writing into three major parts: prewriting, writing (the first complete draft), and rewriting. I say *for convenience* because writing is rarely a 1-2-3 process. It defies formulas and predictions. For example, some writers may organize their main points (prewrite), write a first draft, then realize the structure is wrong, reorganize their outline, and redo the draft before moving on to rewriting. Other writers develop an effective structure for their writing by writing draft after draft with no prewriting (but this is usually a time-consuming way to discover a useful structure).

A few people can write well by composing and rewriting one page or paragraph or sentence at a laborious time (they are sometimes called "bleeders"). Probably fewer still compose and revise in their heads, then write and revise slightly. If one of those two approaches works for you, fine, but they probably won't, and you will find it useful to divide and conquer your work.

Dividing your work into manageable steps and using the strategies explained here will improve your chances of writing well but do not guarantee it. Extensive previous practice in writing (and reading) and much work and persistence are also required.

Here is one of my favorite ways of getting some of my responses to a film into writing. As I view the film, I write a few notes. After the viewing, I sometimes write a brief description and always write observations (analysis). Next I reread and revise what I have written so far. The next day I rewrite my notes, select the main points, and arrange them in a brief outline.

These are the stages I sometimes go through before I write a first draft. They take time, but they help me gather my thoughts and arrange them. I'm not saying the first draft is then easy for me. Often it is not. But because of the prewriting, the first draft is always less difficult.

Before you write the first draft, consider the following questions:

■ Who are my readers?
■ What needs to be explained?
■ What does *not* need to be explained?
■ How do I want my readers to react to what I write?

Then try one or more of these steps:

1. Write and rewrite a thesis statement: a sentence or a few concise sentences that summarize the main and unifying idea of the planned essay and, ideally, explain the major parts and their arrangement.

2. Make an outline.

3. Write a "discovery" draft.

1.   THESIS STATEMENT   A thesis statement early in an essay—often at the end of the first paragraph or the beginning of the second—helps both writer and readers. The following thesis statement, for example, reveals the purpose and organization of the essay it helps introduce:

> Despite its reputation for faithfulness, a careful analysis reveals that the film [*The Dead*] is unlike Joyce's novella in three major ways. First, the adaptation expands the scope of the original narrative by adding new scenes. Second, the adaptation deletes important contextual elements from its literary source. Finally, the adaptation modifies significant dramatic elements in the literary source.

Occasionally you can formulate a thesis statement before making an outline or writing a first draft. Sometimes the thesis statement is so well thought out and detailed that you can write a first draft without first making an outline. Often, however, the thesis emerges more clearly as you work on an outline or a first or second draft. It usually takes time and effort to figure out what you are trying to say, and often you may start out to make a point and end up saying something else. For the essay to be unified and forceful, though, the thesis statement must eventually step forward and introduce itself or be implied in the introduction and explained in the essay itself. Few students can create a focused, clear, and persuasive essay without stating the thesis; without it, readers tend to get lost in a forest of words before emerging from page 2.

2. OUTLINE   Outlines are useful for most writers most of the time, especially in writing long essays and books or in writing about a new subject, but some successful writers never use them. Instead they think out the major points and their arrangement, jot notes, or write draft after draft. Sometimes a short outline, however, leads to a more detailed one that is a partial first draft.

3. DISCOVERY DRAFT   Some writers start to organize their material by rapidly writing a draft. Then they look at what they have written and perhaps underline the useful parts, perhaps rearrange its major points. Sometimes they toss out that draft and immediately write another one rapidly. For some writers it's a way to get something on paper and to start to discover what they have to say.

> In outlines and early drafts, leave wide margins on all four sides of the lines and double-space. Leave room to improve.

Writing

While writing the first draft, most writers find it best to focus on organization (what are the major parts and in what order should they be arranged?) and on examples (how can I illustrate my points to those who may misunderstand or disagree?). While writing the first draft, don't allow yourself to become sidetracked by spelling, punctuation, or even sentence structure. Like a sculptor, rough out the paragraphs; later, do the finishing work on the sentences and words. For most people, fussing over a spelling or a word, pausing to check a punctuation mark, or looking up a word or passage can halt their momentum and perhaps cause "writer's block," the inability to write anything.

In the first draft, try to see that your main points are arranged in a significant order and that they are explained and illustrated. Do not, as many poor writers do, try to rewrite while you write the first draft. Studies of writers show that few can write *and* rewrite well at the same time.

Rewriting and Rewriting: Some Strategies

What is written without effort is in general read without pleasure. (Samuel Johnson)

I never write five words but I correct seven. (Attributed to Dorothy Parker)

There are days when the result is so bad that no fewer than five revisions are required. In contrast, when I'm greatly inspired, only four revisions are needed. (John Kenneth Galbraith)

As you rewrite and rewrite, remember three indispensable guidelines:

1. *Studies show that few readers will remember—let alone be impressed by— more than five major points in a speech or essay.*

2. *Your goal should be to communicate—not impress.* Writers who try to impress their readers often stumble and look silly, waste their readers' time, and puzzle them. Consider, for example, this sentence: "Another major meaning of Orson Welles's film *Citizen Kane* is that Charles Foster Kane has an abiding and persistent hunger to be loved by others" (twenty-five words). The writer misuses one word (*abiding*) and tries too hard to impress, with wordiness, passive voice, and formal words. In contrast, the writer of the following sentence, one of my former students, was more concerned with communicating: "The third trait to note about Kane is his need for love" (twelve words). That sentence is short, is easy to understand, yet says much the same as its longer counterpart. Indeed, this second sentence is more specific: it indicates that the *third* point is next.

3. *If you focus on only one major point in each paragraph and explain it fully, with detailed examples, you will be understood, probably even appreciated.* If you jump from generalization to unrelated generalization, especially within the same paragraph, you will not be understood by your unfortunate readers.

SOME REWRITING TECHNIQUES   Because it is difficult to spot errors in what we write (we are better at spotting errors in what *others* write), we writers need to reread our drafts often and in different ways. Unfortunately, many writers, especially inexperienced ones, reread their drafts once—maybe twice if they want to be thorough!—and they seldom spot what to improve, so they make only a few minor changes, such as in spelling and the use of commas. One or more of the following strategies may help writers see more clearly what they have written so that they can rewrite and improve it:

1. After you finish the first or second draft, see if each paragraph explains one important point. Choose a paragraph at random, and read it at least twice (once aloud, once silently); underline the topic sentence or main point. (You may want to use a felt-tip pen so you can quickly spot each topic sentence later.) If a topic sentence is vague or misleading, rewrite it so it explains the main point of the paragraph. If the main point of the paragraph is not stated or clearly implied, write a topic sentence. If you have more than one important point in a paragraph, eliminate unimportant points and develop the main point, or explain each important point in its own paragraph.

   Next, select a different paragraph at random, and read it twice—once aloud and once silently. See that it has one major point and that it is fully and clearly explained. Proceed in this way until you have an underlined topic sentence for each paragraph. (Study your paragraphs out of order so that you can sneak up on what you wrote and see each paragraph for what it is.)

   Now that you have underlined the topic sentence of each paragraph, underline the main ideas of the essay with a double line; then read only the thesis statement and each topic sentence. If any topic sentences do not support the thesis or if the major points do not progress clearly, delete, add, or rearrange; then rewrite.

2. a. Reread your essay aloud at different speeds (rapidly one time, slowly the next). For many writers, reading a draft aloud—one time slowly, the next time rapidly—is the best way to spot weaknesses. They hear weaknesses they could not see.

   b. Read your essay aloud at different times (for instance, once after completing the first draft; once after a break; once more the next day).

   c. Reread your essay silently at different times looking for an aspect of writing that has given you trouble in the past—for instance, once for complicated, unclear sentences and once for wordiness. If you tend to write incomplete sentences, reread from the end of the essay to the beginning, a sentence at a time.

   d. Ask someone to read the draft aloud but without interruptions or commentary, perhaps as you close your eyes and listen (not recommended after lunch or late in the evening).

3. Another way to see what you have indeed written in each sentence is to read each sentence out of order. Pick up the latest draft; choose a sentence at random; read it twice (once aloud, once silently); then, if necessary, revise it. After you are finished with the sentence, place a check mark at the beginning of it; then repeat the process for every other sentence (out of order). You may be surprised how many weaknesses you can spot and eliminate using this method.

4. Are any sentences still not right? You've thought about them. You've put them aside. But you still frown as you read them. Imagine that you are with a friend, and say aloud what you mean; then write what you just said. Chances are you'll be much closer to writing what you meant all along.

5. Reread your essay and underline every general word; then consider replacing generalities with details from the film. Words like *good, great, wonderful, nice, interesting,* and *terrible* can be replaced by specific references to the film. "Vera Miles was great in *The Searchers*" neither communicates much nor convinces a reader who thought she was so-so. Instead, write a paragraph that includes examples from the film. Consider the following: "Vera Miles's Laurie is a complicated character. For example, she is not all patience and sweetness. In the scene where Martin is about to leave for the last time to rescue Debbie, Miles shows vehement and convincing frustration, wrinkling her brow and biting off her words." Although this second description is scarcely a full account of Vera Miles's performance, it is better than the original vague sentence.

   While you are checking word choices, make sure that when you describe action in a film, you use present-tense verbs. For instance, "The soldiers blow up the house" (not "blew up").

Getting Feedback

Only a few years ago, most college instructors would tell their students to "do all their own work." During recent years, however, research on writing has confirmed that feedback from others can help writers, and increasingly college instructors are encouraging their students to work in groups and otherwise get feedback from others. However, if you do not follow certain procedures, getting feedback can be of little use and can even be counterproductive.

Find at least one good reader: someone who can read and explain accurately what the reading means. (Unfortunately, such readers may be scarce.) Show the assignment to your readers, and ask them to read your paper carefully (and at least twice) and tell you (1) what they understand from it and (2) where the paper is unclear or incomplete, or both. Do not tell your readers beforehand what you intended to convey; let your writing speak for itself.

If your readers rate your writing as excellent, good, or whatever, disregard their evaluations. Your classmates and outside readers are in a weak position to evaluate (or grade) your work: they do not know well the course work out of which the assignment emerged and lack training, experience, and perspective to grade college-level writing (so do you). If you ignore this advice and take the evaluation of your writing by others seriously, you may end up frustrated and in an unnecessary confrontation with your instructor.

Finally, take others' feedback, and rewrite your paper to make it fulfill the assignment more successfully. Do not let readers rewrite for you. And do not let them dictate wording either. You rewrite (and rewrite) the parts that need improving.

Of course, any rewriting you do will be *your* responsibility. For example, if none of your readers notices an important omission from your paper, do not blame them. *You* failed to include the material. You're responsible.

If misused, feedback can hurt your writing. However, if you follow these guidelines, feedback can help you improve your writing, often considerably.

Before you run off that last draft, be sure to consult reference sources, especially a college dictionary. For example, you might want to look up words that you rarely use to make sure that you are indeed using them correctly. Remember that computer spelling checkers sometimes miss errors (for instance, when you wrote *it's* when you meant *its*). Remember, too, that computer grammar checkers often miss errors and, worse yet, are sometimes just plain wrong, as when they claim that a grammatical sentence is an incomplete sentence.

Most ineffective writers spend most of their time mired in the first draft, getting exhausted and demoralized by the ordeal. Effective writers, in contrast, tend to prewrite, divide the task into different work sessions, and spend much more time on rewriting than on writing the first draft.

Few writers do all the steps I suggest, nor do writers generally follow the same steps and same order of steps for every writing task. People are different, and writing is usually complicated. Let me repeat, too, that using the writing strategies I suggest will only improve your chances of writing well. Without extensive previous practice in reading critically and writing carefully, you will be limited in how well you can write, no matter what strategies you use. Similarly, even if you know the rules of a sport and follow them when you play it, you cannot play well unless you have worked hard and long at developing your skills. (Skillful coaches help, too.)

To write well about film requires much previous practice in reading and writing, practical strategies (such as some of those discussed in this essay), and patience and persistence. Writing well about anything you care about or enjoy, though, is well worth all the effort, for in writing and rewriting you think and learn, and you can communicate to others with more precision and permanence than you can any other way. When you write about a film or the film medium, you are unlikely to "make the stars weep" with your melodies, but by writing with care you can capture some of the magic.

The best writers have the satisfaction of knowing that people of distant times and places may learn from and enjoy their writing. What Carl Sagan said about ancient books applies as well to all writings that are preserved and read:

> One glance at . . . [a book] and you're inside the mind of another person, maybe somebody dead for thousands of years. Across the millennia an author is speaking clearly and silently inside your head, directly to you. Writing is perhaps the greatest of human inventions, binding together people who never knew each other, citizens of distant epochs. Books break the shackles of time. . . . If information were passed on merely by word of mouth, how little we should know of our own past. How slow would be our progress. Everything would depend on what we

had been told, on how accurate the account. Ancient learning might be revered, but in successive retellings it would become muddled and then lost. Books permit us to voyage through time, to tap the wisdom of our ancestors.

For sample student essays, see the Web site for this book: <http://www .bedfordstmartins.com/phillips-film>.

WRITING DEFINITIONS

An excellent way to gain a deeper understanding of what terms stand for is to write and rewrite definitions of them. To do so, indicate the category that the object or idea being defined belongs to and what differentiates it from other members of the same category. For example:

> **lap dissolve:** A transition between shots in which one shot begins to fade out as the next shot fades in, overlapping the first shot before replacing it.

Notice that a *lap dissolve* is not merely a transition between shots. It is, but so are *wipes, fade-outs, fade-ins,* and other transitions between shots. What distinguishes a lap dissolve from all the other transitions between shots is that one shot begins to fade out as the next shot fades in, overlapping the first shot before replacing it.

Do not begin a definition in either of these ways: "_____ is when . . ." or "_____ is where . . ."

Do not attempt to define a word or phrase by giving only a synonym, especially when dealing with an abstract word. For example, to write that an *evaluation* is an appraisal will not be clear to readers who have only a fuzzy notion about what *appraisal* means. After you indicate the category and what distinguishes the term in question from other members of the same category, you may want to include a synonym—but only after you have *defined* the term in question.

A final pointer: in your definitions use the same part of speech as the word being defined. Do not define *composition* as "arranging settings, lighting, and subjects (usually people and objects) within the frame," but as "the arrangement of settings, . . .": "Composition" (a noun) is a matter of "arrangement" (another noun). For more sample definitions, study some entries in the glossary.

IMPROVING READING COMPREHENSION

Different types of readings make different demands on readers. For example, for most of us, reading a letter from a friend is a simple and straightforward task, but reading a contract that will affect our emotional and financial well-being for years to come requires more elaborate reading techniques.

Unfortunately, regardless of the reading assignment, some students use the same, limited reading strategies. Learn to adapt your reading techniques to the task at hand. You probably won't have time to use all the following techniques, but for each important reading task preread, read, reread, and write. Don't just trust your memory and hope for the best.

Preread

These steps may take five to ten minutes, but they will help you get much more out of the reading the first time through:

- Consider the significance of the title.
- Consider the section of the book the reading selection is from. Examine the book's Table of Contents to see how the reading assignment fits into the book.
- Read the first paragraph (and perhaps the second) and the last paragraph to discover the main point and the conclusion.
- Examine the headings (to find out the major parts).
- Read the summary or abstract (if one is included).
- Read the study questions (if any are included).

Read

To discover the structure and purpose of the writing, during the first reading it is crucial that you read without long interruptions and keep your marks, comments, and questions brief:

- Mark important passages.
- Write brief notes in the margins, especially your descriptions of important points and any questions that come to mind.
- Draw lines between related or contrasted points.
- Circle key words (often they are repeated).
- Mark words you don't understand.

Reread

Many readers use far too few rereading strategies. Using them, however, helps them understand and remember the material in ways simply reading and quickly reviewing cannot:

- Reread passages you are still uncertain about, or reread the entire selection.
- Check a dictionary for words you still cannot figure out, and write the definitions in the margins.

- Study all marked passages; study your marginal notes, and rewrite and expand them as necessary.
- Study the summary (if one is included), *or* write a summary of the selection in your own words, *or* make an outline of the selection, *or* write the thesis sentence in your own words.
- Read the study questions and try to answer them, preferably in writing.

EXERCISES AND QUESTIONS

By using the following exercises and questions, you can learn more about individual films and about the film medium.

Exercises

The following exercises may help you become more aware of particular aspects of a film. For example, the sound track or part of it may be studied by listening to it repeatedly with the image turned off. Some of the following exercises may be applied to any film, and many of these exercises may be used with a videotape or DVD player. In home or classroom, time and resources limit the number of these exercises that can be used with a film. Probably most readers will want to read the following section quickly to get an idea of the kinds of exercises possible and at various times try out specific exercises. For convenience, the following exercises are divided into four kinds—viewing, listening, reading, and writing—though a number of them unavoidably overlap.

VIEWING

1. Run an excerpt with the sound off; then discuss what you have learned and how you have learned it. Rerun the same excerpt and discuss again what the visuals reveal.

2. View a scene with several other people; take notes; then discuss your observations with other viewers and note takers. Watch the next scene again while taking notes. Stop and discuss. Continue for several more scenes.

3. After you have seen a film, view its opening scene or section again. What moods and meanings does it convey? Next, view again the film's concluding scene or section. What moods and meanings does it suggest? In what ways are the opening and closing of the film related?

4. Rerun a scene or section (if possible in slow motion). Where do the filmmakers show more than they might have? Where is less shown than might have been (for instance, by moving the camera back, changing the lighting, using a lens that distorts the image, giving a sound for an object

rather than showing it, shortening a shot or omitting shots altogether)? Is the scene characterized by explicitness or restraint? To what effect?

5. Rerun an excerpt (if possible in slow motion). Explain what the camera angles and distances contribute.

6. Rerun a scene, probably more than once. Pay special attention to the lighting. How hard or soft is it? From what directions does the lighting come? What information is obscured or emphasized by the lighting? What mood is created or reinforced?

7. Rerun a short scene (if possible in slow motion). Explain how the duration of each shot, the arrangement of shots, and the transitions or connections between shots all influence the scene's impact. Run the scene yet again; perhaps make an outline of its shots. Review and revise your explanations.

8. View an important scene featuring one of the major characters, once with sound, once without. For the performer playing the major role, explain how face, body build, voice, and gestures all contribute to characterization. What other roles has the performer played that influence your response to this film?

9. View a scene that includes most of the major characters. Compare the scene with the comparable part of the script (preferably a cutting continuity script, which describes the finished film). Run the scene without sound; then run it without the picture but with sound. Discuss what the performers contribute to the scene.

10. Fast-forward through a video version or DVD, stopping only to examine the makeup and clothing of one of the major characters. What do they reveal about the character? Do they change significantly during the story? If so, how? What do the makeup and clothing reveal about the time and place of the story?

11. For a subtitled foreign-language film, view several scenes without reading the subtitles. What did you notice that you did not see during earlier viewings? What is the significance of those new details?

12. If you have access to a video player or DVD with freeze-frame option, freeze an expressive image; then discuss the importance of what was excluded from the frame and what was included. Next explain the significance of how objects are arranged within the frame.

Listening

1. Play a scene with sound only; then play the same scene with the picture only. Finally, play the scene with both sound and picture. Explain what the sound adds to the scene. *Or* run a scene with picture and sound;

discuss the sound; run the scene again with only the sound, and discuss the contribution of the sound.

    a. Discuss what the dialogue (what is said and how), sound effects, music, and silences all contribute to the impact of the scene.

    b. Try to identify as many different sounds as possible within the scene.

    c. Where are sounds faithful to their sources? Where are sounds distorted?

    d. How dense is the sound mix: is it made up of many or few sources blended together? Explain.

2. View a scene without the sound, and try to guess what sounds might accompany the images. Replay the scene with the sound then discuss. Play another scene without the image but with the sound track. Try to guess what images might accompany the sounds. Play sounds and images then discuss.

3. While watching a film, make notes about where music is used. Next play back the scenes where music is used, and discuss what the music contributes.

    a. Are any of the melodies or tunes repeated? If so, with or without variations?

    b. Is the music predominantly melodic or rhythmical?

    c. How do instrumentation, volume, tempo, and key affect the music?

    d. What information and mood does the music create during the opening credits?

    e. Is the music sometimes used to cover weaknesses in the film, such as inappropriate acting? If so, where?

4. For a short scene, make up a chart describing its visuals, vocals, sound effects, and music. See pp. 160–61.

Reading

1. Read one or more published outlines or synopses of the same film. Where are the descriptions accurate, clear, concise? Where do interpretations intrude? Where are evaluations made or implied? Discuss the usefulness and limitations of each outline or synopsis.

2. Read the fictional or dramatic source of the film, or at least a section of it. View the comparable section of the film. Reread the section of the fiction or play; then consider the following questions:

a. What are the major differences? In what sense are they "major"?

b. What are the major similarities? In what sense are they "major"?

c. What changes were made because of choices made by the filmmakers?

d. What changes had to be made because of differences between the media of fiction/drama and film?

3. View a scene or two of a film, and compare them to the similar section of the cutting continuity script, which describes the finished, released film. Where is the script accurate? Where is it inaccurate? What kinds of inaccuracies does it contain: interpretation, evaluation, vagueness, wrong facts, or what? In what ways is the script useful?

4. View a scene or two of the film, and compare them to the comparable section of the screenplay or shooting script (versions of the script used before and during the making of the film). In what ways does the finished film differ from the early versions of the script? How significant are the changes? See pp. 184–86.

5. Read carefully one or more reviews of the initial release of a film. Next compare and contrast your responses with those of the reviewers. Where do differences result from different backgrounds, perceptions, assumptions, and emphases?

6. After reading a review or analysis carefully and at least twice, consider the following questions:

a. Usually certain terms are used repeatedly or prominently in an essay. How clear are they? Are more examples needed to clarify the prominent terms? Are additional definitions necessary?

b. State the central and unifying idea: describe it as objectively as you can (without passing judgment on it). Is it stated directly (often at the beginning and/or conclusion)? Or is it left for the reader to infer? Finally, how persuasively is the thesis argued?

c. Is the argument or interpretation amply illustrated with specific, accurate, and relevant examples from the film?

d. Is the essay clearly organized? What are its major parts? Why are they arranged in the order they are in?

e. Does the analysis make any generalized statements not subject to proof? If so, what are they? What are some of the assumptions about the nature of the film medium that the writer makes? Are the assumptions (or premises) reasonable? Explain.

f. What does the analysis suggest about its author's personality and background? How do you know?

WRITING

1. Immediately after seeing a film, jot down a list of the images and sounds that come to mind. From the list select the most important ones; then explain why they are significant.

2. View a short scene at normal volume. As objectively as possible, describe the scene in writing: try to avoid making judgments (which reveal your approval or disapproval) and inferences (which show you making certain assumptions, which may not be correct). View the scene a second time, without the sound. Revise your description; perhaps divide it into shots. What aspects of the scene are especially difficult to capture in writing? Why?

3. Make an outline of a sequence or two of a narrative film. Try to describe the action as accurately, objectively, and concisely as possible. Later, formulate headings for the sequence(s) and justify them.

    a. What action is omitted that could have been shown?

    b. What action is shown in detail?

    c. What action is shown only briefly?

    d. What is emphasized by the film's selection and arrangement of scenes?

Though time-consuming, making an outline has many advantages. It helps you decide what is important in each scene; it helps you see which scenes are merely transitional; it makes you more aware of how individual scenes are connected to form a longer story. Making an outline also makes you more aware of when you are describing something and when inferences, interpretations, and evaluations slip in, and it teaches you that a film is more than its action and that much of the film experience is not easily captured in words.

For outlines of the scenes of *The Bicycle Thief* and of the sequences of *8½*, see the Web site for this book: <http://www.bedfordstmartins.com /phillips-film>.

4. Write and rewrite a one- or two-paragraph plot summary of a narrative film's major actions in the order they occur in the film. Review your draft; make the summary as accurate and clear as you can. (Assume that your reader has not seen the film.)

5. After you see a film, write an interpretation of an important scene; then view the scene again. How accurate and persuasive was your interpretation?

6. For a film based on a novel or short story, choose a scene from the fiction and adapt it into a scene for a film; then compare your adaptation of the scene with that of the filmmakers. (Satyajit Ray of India did this exercise before he became a film director.)

7. Choose some film terms that you have heard repeatedly but that are not included in the glossary of this book. (You may want to choose some terms you used in one of your essays or in class discussion.) Define each of the terms as accurately as you can. In your definitions, be sure to explain in what category the term belongs and what differentiates it from other members of the same category. For example, a projector is a machine (category) that makes possible the presentation of motion pictures on a reflective surface (kind of machine). Before you begin, you may need to review the guidelines for writing definitions (p. 466) and some of the definitions in the book's glossary, which begins on p. 539.

8. Make a set of study questions that apply to a film (and that are not merely adapted from the list of study questions given below). Try to formulate questions that draw attention to significant details and important issues. Also try to phrase your questions so that they do not encourage a particular answer (leading questions). Try to anticipate how your readers could misunderstand your questions and attempt to reword them to avoid this. Next arrange the questions in a meaningful order.

9. Imagine that someone who has never seen a particular film asks you what it is like. Write an interpretation of the film's major qualities. Before you begin writing, try to organize your thoughts and feelings, and in your interpretation try not to jump from detail to unrelated detail or, worse, generalization to unrelated and unillustrated generalization.

10. Look up a review of a film; then photocopy the review and study it. Write a summary of the review; then explain in writing how accurate and persuasive the review is. Why do you say so?

Questions

The following questions are intended to help viewers understand a film and their responses to it (and eventually the film medium). Not all the questions are appropriate for every film. For those questions most appropriate for the film being examined, please remember: In thinking out, discussing, and writing responses, be careful to stick with the issues the questions raise, to answer all parts of the questions, to explain the reasons for your answers, and to give specific examples from the film.

MISE EN SCÈNE

1. Are the settings realistic or nonrealistic? What settings are particularly expressive? What do the settings add to the film?

2. What are the film's major subjects? What actions and appearance are especially revealing?

3. In a fictional film, who is the protagonist or main character? Why do you say so? Describe the character's physical characteristics and personality.

4. What does the main character want? Does he or she succeed? Why or why not?

5. How does characterization function in the film?

   a. For the major characters, how is characterization revealed: actions, appearance, dialogue, thoughts (ideas, fantasies, dreams, hallucinations)? Which of these four methods of revealing characterization is used most often in the film? Which of the four methods is used least or not at all?

   b. How well do you get to know and understand the major characters? What information about them is revealed? What information about them is withheld?

6. How are the subjects arranged within the frame?

   a. Are significant subjects bunched up within the frame or spread apart? Are they in the center of the frame or off to a side?

   b. Are significant subjects arranged in such a way as to balance out the composition or to create an imbalance?

   c. In what ways do background and foreground subjects relate to each other?

CINEMATOGRAPHY

1. Are the images fine grain or rough grain? Are both looks used within the same film? What does the degree of graininess contribute to the film?

2. Does the film use "cool" or "warm" colors to achieve certain effects? Is color used in a symbolic way? Is color used to enhance mood? How lifelike is the color?

3. Notice any particularly expressive uses of light.

   a. Where is lighting used to support or create a particular mood? What mood?

   b. Where are shadows used to conceal information? To enhance mood? To reveal what a character is like or is feeling?

   c. If a certain kind of lighting is used repeatedly, describe it, and explain its effects.

4. For an especially significant part of the film, what camera distances are used? To what effect? Are many close-ups used in the film? Generally, does the camera stay back from the subjects and show much of the setting?

5. For some of the most significant shots in the film, what lens is used: wide-angle, normal, telephoto? With what consequences?

6. In the film, does the subject tend to be filmed in high, eye-level, or low angles? Where are camera angles especially significant or effective? Why do you say so?

7. Notice any especially expressive uses of camera placements.

   a. Where are point-of-view shots used? How often are they used? What effects do they have on your viewing experience?

   b. Where are camera placements used that make you feel like an outsider looking in on the action?

8. Characterize the camera movement.

   a. If the camera tends to remain stationary, what are the advantages and disadvantages of the stationary camera work?

   b. If moving camera shots are used, does the camera dolly or truck or move up and down through the air? Are Steadicam shots used? If so, to what effect? What is the effect of the camera movement or lack of movement?

9. Does the camera pan or tilt? Where and with what consequences?

EDITING

1. Generally, is the film's editing characterized by fast cutting or slow cutting? To what effect?

2. Does the editing tend to be smooth and unobtrusive or disruptive and obvious?

3. Where are shots joined for a particular effect, such as to stress similarities or differences or to create or enhance a mood?

4. Does the film use parallel editing? If so, where and to what effect?

5. Where is editing used to save time? To make viewers use their imaginations (for example, by use of a cutaway shot)?

SOUND

1. Where and why is offscreen sound used? Where is sound used to suggest the size of a location and the texture of the surfaces?

2. How frequently is dialogue used? Is the dialogue always distinct? Does it sometimes overlap? If so, with what consequences?

3. Where is silence used? What effect does it contribute?

4. Where is volume raised or lowered for effect?

5. Where is sound used between scenes to create a certain effect? What effect is created or supported?

6. Where is sound distorted? What does the distortion contribute?

7. Consider the film's music.

   a. Where is music used? For what purposes? Is the music always subordinated to the rest of the film, or is it sometimes dominant?

   b. What are the major melodies or tunes? Are they repeated? With or without variation?

   c. Is the music a part of the story itself, or is it played as complementary to the story (as in the case where we see characters in a lifeboat while we hear an orchestra)?

   d. Where does the music suggest a particular place or time or both?

   e. Where is music used to suggest what a character is feeling?

SOURCES FOR FICTIONAL FILMS

1. Is the film based on an original screenplay, or is it an adaptation of a source or sources?

2. Is the film based on written historical accounts? If so, how closely does the film follow the earlier accounts? Where does the film make changes for dramatic effect? Where does it make changes unnecessarily?

3. Is the film based on fiction? If so, how closely does the film follow the source fiction? Where does the film make changes for dramatic effect? Where does it make changes unnecessarily?

4. Is the film based on a play? If so, how closely does the film follow the source? Where does the film make changes for dramatic effect? Where does it make changes unnecessarily?

5. Is the film based on a TV show or series? If so, how closely does the film follow the source? Where does the film make changes for dramatic effect? Where does it make changes unnecessarily?

6. Is the film based on other films? If so, is the film a sequel or prequel? Does the film re-create, parody, or pay an homage to the earlier film(s)?

TYPES OF FICTIONAL FILMS

1. If the film is fictional, how may it be further classified—as classical Hollywood cinema, Italian neorealism, or some other kind? Why do you say so?

2. What major similarities and differences does the film have with earlier fictional films of the same genre or movement?

3. If the film is traditional in some ways but untraditional in others, explain.

4. If the film is a genre film, such as a western or horror film, consider the following questions.

   a. If the film is basically a traditional genre film, explain what major features it shares with most films of its genre.

   b. Is the film revisionist? If so, explain in what ways.

   c. Is the film a parody of earlier films of the same genre? In what ways does it imitate earlier films of the same genre? In what ways does it treat the subject(s) humorously? What conventions of the genre does the parody make fun of?

   d. Is the film a combination of genres? If so, explain which genres and which features of them.

NARRATIVE COMPONENTS OF FICTIONAL FILMS

1. How do conflicts function in the film?

   a. What are the major conflicts? How are they resolved?

   b. Do any of the characters have internal conflicts (such as uncertainty or guilt)?

   c. Are the film's most important conflicts between sharply distinguished good and evil, or are the most important conflicts more complex and subtle?

2. Consider the film's structure.

   a. What are the film's sequences (major groups of scenes)?

   b. Does the film have a chronological or nonchronological structure? What are the advantages of the choice?

   c. Does the film have more than one major plotline? If so, how are the different major plotlines related? See pp. 274–80.

3. In what sequences is the story time longer than the running time? Conversely, and much less commonly, in what sequences is the running time longer than the story time?

4. Consider the film's attitude toward its subjects.

    a. Usually films present their characters and their actions in such a manner that they encourage audience approval or disapproval. If the film presents certain behavior or attitudes in an approving manner, how does it do so?

    b. Which, if any, behavior or attitudes are satirized or made fun of? How strongly felt is the disapproval? How noticeable is the disapproval?

5. Are any untraditional styles, such as black comedy, being used? If so, what does the style contribute to the film?

ALTERNATIVES TO LIVE-ACTION FICTIONAL FILMS

1. If the film is a documentary, is it narrative or nonnarrative? Why do you say so?

2. What major types of sources are used in the documentary?

3. How accurate and reliable is the film? Are excerpts from interviews taken out of context? How do you know? Is editing used to criticize or praise a subject? If so, explain.

4. If the film is experimental, in what ways is it unlike classical Hollywood cinema?

5. For experimental films, what are the major types of sources (such as earlier films or the filmmaker's imagination)?

6. In what ways does the film surprise or frustrate you, or both?

7. If the film is a hybrid, what major types are combined? What expectations did you have early in the film and how were you surprised as the film progressed?

8. If the film is animation, what does the animation make possible that would be extremely difficult or impossible to achieve with live-action?

UNDERSTANDING FILMS THROUGH CONTEXTS

1. When and where was the film made? How do the times and places of its making affect how the film turned out? For example, did the political climate or widespread societal attitudes of the time preclude or restrict certain subjects or treatments?

2. Is the film a big-budget action film aimed at large audiences, a more modestly budgeted independent film, an inexpensive documentary or

experimental film, or some other type of film? Did limitations in the budget affect the way the film turned out? If so, how so?

3. Does the film follow filmic conventions or is it unconventional in its techniques and content?

4. What does the film convey to you about the history and culture of the society it depicts? How accurate are those representations? How do you know how trustworthy those representations are?

5. How does the film technology available when the film was made affect how the film turned out?

THINKING ABOUT FILMS

1. What were your expectations before the film began? What developments in the film required you to readjust your expectations and hypotheses as the film unspooled?

2. Where do cinematic techniques affect meanings?

3. Does the film sometimes use technique subtly and require attentive viewers and listeners? If so, where and with what consequences?

4. Is the film sometimes too subtle? If you were to see the film in a different format or version, what subtle techniques could be difficult or impossible to notice?

5. Does the film have any important symbols? How do you interpret them? Why?

6. Does the film include any explicit meanings? If so, what are they? Are they necessary?

7. What implicit meanings does the narrative itself suggest?

8. If you know the time and place the film was made, do you detect any symptomatic meanings in the film?

9. What are the film's major meanings?

   a. Are the meanings complex or simple? Ambiguous or clear?

   b. Do the meanings challenge the status quo or are they reassuring? Why do you say so?

10. What fantasies does the film reflect? What type of person would enjoy the movie's fantasies?

11. What meanings might other people (say a different ethnic group, gender, sexual orientation, or nationality) see in the film?

ANNOTATED BIBLIOGRAPHY

BOOKS

Annual Index to Motion Picture Credits. Beverly Hills, CA: Academy of Motion Picture Arts and Sciences. Production information and cast and crew credits for the films of the year provided by the producers and distributors or obtained from the files maintained by the Academy's library. Credits are searchable by craft, by name, or by film title.

Emmens, Carol A. *Short Stories on Film and Video.* 2nd ed. Littleton, CO: Libraries Unlimited, 1985. An alphabetical listing by authors of short stories adapted into films, usually short films. Supplied for each film are the title of short story, title of film, running time or number of reels, black-and-white or color designation, year, director, producer, cast, and a brief description of contents. Also includes indexes.

Enser's Filmed Books and Plays: A List of Books and Plays from Which Films Have Been Made, 1928–1991. Comp. Ellen Baskin and Mandy Hicken. Brookfield, VT: Ashgate, 1993. The main part of the book is an index arranged alphabetically by film titles, with brief information on each film and the name of the author of the source fiction or play. Also includes author and change of title indexes and information on made-for-TV movies and classic British television series.

Film Review Annual, 1981–. Ed. Jerome S. Ozer. Englewood, NJ: Film Review, 1982–. Reprints complete reviews of the feature films released in the United States during the previous year. Includes full credits, many different indexes, listings of major film awards.

The Focal Encyclopedia of Film and Television Techniques. Ed. Raymond Spottiswoode. New York: Hastings, 1969. Sixteen hundred entries by more than one hundred specialists on film and TV equipment and techniques.

Halliwell's Filmgoer's Companion. 12th ed. Ed. John Walker. New York: Harper, 1997. Thousands of entries on scriptwriters, actors, directors, and others; film terms; film movements; recurrent themes (or topics) in films; and some national cinemas. Also includes short quotations from actors, directors, and critics. For most people discussed, a selected list of films she or he worked on is also supplied.

The International Dictionary of Films and Filmmakers. Ed. Nicholas Thomas. 2nd ed. 5 vols. Chicago: St. James. Signed critical essays, bibliographies, and filmographies. Vol. 1: Films (1990); vol. 2: Directors (1991); vol. 3: Actors and Actresses (1992); vol. 4: Writers and Production Artists (including cinematographers, producers, editors, and designers) (1993); vol. 5: Title Index (1994).

Katz, Ephraim. *The Film Encyclopedia.* 4th ed. Rev. Fred Klein and Ronald Dean Nolen. New York: Harper, 2001. A comprehensive one-volume encyclopedia of world cinema. More than seven thousand entries on individual scriptwriters, producers, directors, and many others; studios and production companies; movements or styles of filmmaking; national cinemas; filmmaking personnel; and jargon and technical terms. For each person discussed, a selected list of films she or he worked on is also supplied.

Leff, Leonard J. *Film Plots: Scene-by-Scene Narrative Outlines for Feature Film Study.* 2 vols. Ann Arbor, MI: Pierian. Vol. 1: Scene-by-scene descriptions of sixty-seven films often studied or written about (1983); vol. 2: Descriptions of fifty more feature films (1988).

Leonard Maltin's Movie and Video Guide. New York: Signet. Appears yearly. Brief description and evaluation of thousands of feature films, theatrical and made-for-TV. Indicates which titles have been released on videotape, which on laser disc, and which on DVD.

For films made in a wide-screen process, indicates which process was used. Also indicates black-and-white titles available in a "computer-colored version."

Magill's Cinema Annual. Ed. Frank N. Magill. Englewood Cliffs, NJ: Salem Press. Published annually, beginning in 1982. For major films of the previous year and occasional older films, includes selected credits, synopsis of the narrative, essay review, and bibliography of reviews.

Pratt, Douglas. *Doug Pratt's DVD-Video Guide.* New York: Sag Harbor, 2000. Reviews 2,400 DVDs in detail, both for the artistic merit of the film and the technical merits of the DVD.

Sadoul, Georges. *Dictionary of Films.* Trans., ed., and updated Peter Morris. Berkeley: U of California P, 1972. Brief essays on approximately thirteen hundred films.

Selected Film Criticism. 7 vols. Ed. Anthony Slide. Metuchen, NJ: Scarecrow, 1982–1985. Reprints original reviews of feature-length and short films; one volume includes foreign films.

Slide, Anthony. *The New Historical Dictionary of the American Film Industry.* Lanham, MD: Scarecrow, 1998. More than 750 entries on film studios, production companies, distributors, technical innovations, film series (such as *The Thin Man*), industry terms, and organizations.

Subject Guide to Books in Print. New York: Bowker. Under "Moving-picture" and a noun (such as "direction") are listed appropriate books currently in print. Many cross-references. New edition every year.

The Video Source Book. Detroit: Gale. Published annually. Comprehensive information on programs available on videotape, (laser) videodisc, and DVD and on sources for rental or purchase.

Welch, Jeffrey Egan. *Literature and Film: An Annotated Bibliography, 1900–1977.* New York: Garland, 1981. Lists and annotates books and articles published in North America and Great Britain having to do with the relation between literature and films.

———. *Literature and Film: An Annotated Bibliography, 1978–1988.* New York: Garland, 1993. Lists and annotates books and articles published in North America and Great Britain having to do with the relation between literature and films.

The Women's Companion to International Film. Ed. Annette Kuhn and Susannah Radstone. London: Virago, 1990. Berkeley: U of California P, 1994. Approximately six hundred alphabetized entries, many including filmographies or bibliographies or both. Also includes an index of films directed, written, or produced by women.

INDEXES FOR PERIODICALS

Film Literature Index. Albany, NY: Film and Television Documentation Center. Published quarterly beginning in 1973. Indexes articles in more than three hundred international film and nonfilm periodicals. Entries are arranged alphabetically by author and subject (including film titles) and indicate the presence of filmography, credits, biography, and interviews.

Humanities Index. New York: Wilson. Published monthly beginning in 1974. At the end of each volume is a section on book reviews.

International Index to Film Periodicals: An Annotated Guide. New York: Bowker. Published annually beginning in 1972. Each volume lists articles and essays on film to appear during the past year in world film magazines. Some entries are annotated. Includes director and author indexes.

Readers' Guide to Periodical Literature. From 1910 to March 1977, film reviews are listed under Moving Picture Plays; after March 1977, film reviews are listed under Motion Picture Reviews. Since March 1976 (vol. 36), book review citations are listed at the end of each volume.

INDEXES FOR NEWSPAPERS

Los Angeles Times Index. Film reviews are listed under Motion Pictures.
New York Times Index. Film articles and reviews are listed under Motion Pictures.
The Times Index (London). Film reviews are listed under Films.

JOURNALS AND MAGAZINES

Because Web site addresses change so often, they are not included below but are available through the home page of this book at <http://www.bedfordstmartins.com/phillips-film>.

Because film journals and magazines so often change their coverage, place of publication, frequency of publication, even their names or subtitles, some of the following information may no longer be accurate. For more current information on most of the following publications, see the links to film publications on the Web site for this book: <http://www.bedfordstmartins.com/phillips-film>.

Afterimage: The Journal of Media Arts and Cultural Criticism. A journal of photography, independent film and video, alternative publishing and multimedia, and online communication. Published six times a year.
American Cinematographer. Includes many articles on the cinematography used in making particular movies, interviews with major cinematographers, and ads for such equipment as cranes, Steadicams, and cameras. Published monthly.
The American Historical Review. Beginning with vol. 96.4 (Oct. 1991), each October issue includes a section of films reviewed from a historian's perspective.
Big Reel (Dubuque, IA). Includes articles of interest to film and video collectors and hobbyists and ads for films (usually used, 16 mm); film equipment; various collectibles; photos, posters, and lobby cards; DVDs; videos; and video equipment.
Camera Obscura. Published three times a year. Focus on feminist perspectives on film, TV, and visual media. Each issue may include debates, essays, interviews, and summary pieces.
CineAction. Film criticism in terms of race, gender, sexual orientation, and politics. Published three times a year in Toronto since 1984.
Cineaste. Provides coverage of the art and politics of world cinema. Includes film reviews, book reviews, and interviews. A quarterly published without assistance from the film industry or any academic institution.
Cinema Journal. Published four times a year in cooperation with the Society for Cinema Studies, a professional association made up largely of college and university film teachers. Includes essays on a wide variety of subjects from diverse methodological perspectives.

Cinema Technology. Covers information of special interest to cinema managers, distributors, and projectionists. Published quarterly in London.

Film & History: An Interdisciplinary Journal of Film and Television Studies. Articles, film reviews, and book reviews. Published quarterly since 1970.

Film Comment. Published by the Film Society of Lincoln Center (New York). Articles, interviews, and book and film reviews.

Film Criticism. Articles, interviews, festival reports, and book reviews. Published three times a year at Allegheny College.

Film Culture: America's Independent Motion Picture Magazine. Articles on experimental films and filmmakers. Published irregularly.

Film History: An International Journal. Each issue includes articles on a special topic. Published quarterly.

Filmmaker: The Magazine of Independent Film. Published four times a year by the Independent Feature Project.

Film Quarterly. Interviews, discussion of film theory and film history, reviews of films and videos, and, especially in each summer issue, book reviews. Published since 1958 by the University of California Press.

Films in Review. Oldest film publication in the United States. Many short film reviews, longer articles on filmmakers, extensive obituaries. Now available only on the Web at <http://www.filmsinreview.com>.

The Independent Film & Video Monthly. Published ten times a year by the Foundation for Independent Video and Film (FIVF). Includes profiles of filmmakers, producers, and distributors; festival listings; information on new technology; coverage of political trends and legislation affecting independents; and reports from film festivals and markets.

International Documentary: The Magazine of the International Documentary Association is published ten times a year. Articles and departments, including information on premieres, funding, and festivals.

Journal of Film and Video. Quarterly published by the University Film and Video Association, which consists largely of filmmakers and university film teachers. Earlier known under the title *Journal of the University Film and Video Association.*

The Journal of Popular Film and Television (formerly *Journal of Popular Film*). Published quarterly. Articles on stars, directors, producers, studios, networks, genres, series, and other topics. Includes interviews, filmographies, bibliographies, and book reviews.

Jump Cut: A Review of Contemporary Media. Published irregularly since 1974. Recent perspectives on film, television, video and related media and cultural analysis. *Jump Cut* "is a nonsectarian left and feminist publication, open to a variety of left interpretations and to criticism which may not be explicitly left but which contributes to the development of a vigorous political media criticism."

Literature Film Quarterly. "Articles on individual movies, on different cinematic adaptations of a single literary work, on a director's style of adaptation, on theories of film adaptation, on the 'cinematic' qualities of authors or works, on the reciprocal influences between film and literature, on authors' attitudes toward film and film adaptations, on the role of the screenwriter, and on teaching of film." Also includes interviews, film reviews, and book reviews.

Monthly Film Bulletin. Detailed credits, summary of the story, and review of feature films and short films, contemporary and "retrospective." International coverage. Published from 1934 to April 1991. In May 1991, *Monthly Film Bulletin* merged with *Sight and Sound.*

MovieMaker. Published four times a year. Focuses on independent film and independent filmmakers.

Quarterly Review of Film and Video. Articles on production, history, theory, and reception, including the widest possible range of approaches and subjects plus book reviews and interviews.

Scenario: The Magazine of Screenwriting Art. Each quarterly issue includes complete (mostly recent) screenplays, interviews with the writers, articles on screenwriting, and short film scripts.

Sight and Sound. Published monthly by the British Film Institute. Articles, interviews, book reviews, and a review for each film released in the United Kingdom, each preceded by credits and a plot summary.

Sound & Vision. Published ten times a year with information on home theater, audio, video, multimedia, movies, and music. Test reports, evaluations, shopping tips, commentary, plus reviews of movies on DVD and music on CD.

Variety. A U.S. trade publication on the entertainment industry, including film reviews and many other types of information. Available in daily and weekly versions.

The Velvet Light Trap: A Critical Journal of Film and Television. Published twice a year by the Department of Radio-Television-Film at the University of Texas. Critical essays, especially on American film and TV.

Wide Angle. Published quarterly. Usually each issue stresses a single topic. Also includes interviews with filmmakers and book reviews.

Widescreen Review. Devoted exclusively to "widescreen digital surround home theatre experience." Includes reviews of widescreen DVD and of equipment, such as DVD players.

WORKS CITED

Flaubert, Gustave. *Madame Bovary.* Trans. Paul de Man. New York: Norton, 1965.

Sagan, Carl. "The Persistence of Memory." Program 11. *Cosmos.* PBS. The wording is from the television program, not the book based on the series.

A Chronology:
Film in Context
(1895–2000)

SOME FILM HISTORY BOOKS, such as those by Gerald Mast and Bruce Kawin and by David Cook, are mainly aesthetic histories: they stress the artistic achievements of films that scholars regard as significant or representative. Then there are industrial histories: studies that help us understand films as products of an industry. Other histories focus on film as one of the arts. Social histories emphasize how a society influences the films made, one of the topics discussed in Chapter 11. Sociological history focuses on how films influence viewers. There are many other types of histories of film, and increasingly historians blend different types of histories within the same written accounts because attempting to study films on their own makes for incomplete and misleading history. Dana Polan argues that films "are what they are because of the meanings given them by surrounding situations. A history of films is a history of films in history" (54).

In the last decade or so, scholars have focused much attention on how to study history ("historiography") and have concluded that there is no one history, only various histories. Jack Ellis, for example, entitled his useful book *A History of Film* because he is well aware that his is only one selection and interpretation of cinema. Douglas Gomery's *Movie History: A Survey* interweaves four approaches: aesthetics, technology, economics, and sociology. Kristin Thompson and David Bordwell's *Film History: An Introduction* is guided by three main concerns: the uses of the film medium over time; film production, distribution, and exhibition; and international trends in the film medium and the film market. Geoffrey Nowell-Smith coordinated the work of a group of international film scholars to create *The Oxford History of World Cinema*, which encompasses not just films but "the audience, the industry, and the people who work in it . . . and the mechanisms of regulation and control which determine which films audiences are encouraged to see and which they are not" (xix). The History of the American Cinema series, under the general editorship of Charles Harpole, uses four approaches to cinema history: aesthetic, technological, sociological, and economic.

The following chronology supplies information from four major sources. In the first column, arranged chronologically, are world events that have affected the lives of many people. The other columns are given over to the arts, including many works that were sources for films or were derived from films (column 2), developments in the mass media (column 3), and varied critically acclaimed films and videos, innovative films, and films and videos about filmmakers or films (column 4). Although a long and complicated chronology, it is woefully incomplete. Unavoidably, everyone who has studied history will have quarrels with parts of it.

Nevertheless, the chronology can be useful in a number of ways. You can read an entire column to get a sense of the order and occasionally the connections between similar types of events (for example, you might notice how conditions in Germany after World War I preceded the Nazis' rise to power). Or you can read all four columns one year at a time to get a sense of what happened in a particular year.

You can also use the chronology to place a film in other contexts. Imagine, for example, you are studying *Casablanca*, which was first shown in November 1942. From the chronology you can learn or be reminded about what else was happening before and during 1942. You might notice, for example, that Europe plunged into World War II in September 1939 and that the United States remained (officially) neutral for over two years (until the Japanese attacked Pearl Harbor in December 1941). On one level, *Casablanca* calls for Americans to put aside any inclination to isolationism and rally behind a traditional ally, the French, who at the time of the film's release were under German occupation. Once you consider when *Casablanca* was made, you can better understand its fervor in denouncing the Nazis, extolling the Free French, and criticizing the French government in Vichy that cooperated with the occupying Germans. The chronology can help you understand not only the times when a film was made but also the times a film is set in. For example, the information about events leading up to World War II can help you understand *Saving Private Ryan* (1998) more completely.

The year given for a film is the year it was first shown publicly. Sometimes different sources do not agree on a date. Whenever I have become aware of such discrepancies, I have tried to consult at least one additional authoritative source, but occasional inaccuracies may remain. When a film title in printed sources differs from the title in the film itself, I have used the title in the opening credits of the video or DVD version. Some films do not fit neatly into one of the three distinct categories of films used in this book (fictional, documentary, and experimental), but to save space I have listed fictional films first then labeled most of the rest *documentary* or *experimental*.

It is hoped that you will not use the chronology as your only historical source but will seek out more complete, coherent, and authoritative accounts, such as those cited following the chronology.

Two notes about film titles: throughout the chronology, as throughout the body of the book, film titles in quotation marks indicate films less than sixty minutes long. Titles in italics indicate films sixty or more minutes long. Parentheses included as part of a film's title indicate that the film is sometimes known by its longer title, sometimes by the shorter one (without the words in parentheses).

	World Events	Arts	Mass Media	Films and Videos
1895	Cuba fights for independence from Spain First U.S. automobile made for sale on a regular basis Roentgen discovers X-rays Invention of the diesel engine *Studies in Hysteria*, Sigmund Freud (book)	*The Red Badge of Courage*, Stephen Crane (fiction) *The Time Machine*, H. G. Wells (fiction) *The Importance of Being Earnest*, Oscar Wilde (play)	Lumière Brothers invent a portable motion-picture camera/projector to film short films and to show them publicly in Paris First U.S. demonstration of a motion picture shown on a screen, New York City Guglielmo Marconi sends and receives a radio signal	Lumière Brothers' first (and very brief) film, "Workers Leaving the Lumière Factory," is perhaps also the first documentary film Other Lumière films: "The Arrival of a Train at the Station" and "Feeding (the) Baby" "The Execution of Mary, Queen of Scots," Edison company
1896	Olympic games of ancient Greece reestablished Anti-imperialist violence in Africa: Ethiopian warriors defeat Italian soldiers and tribal rebellion erupts in Rhodesia Alaskan Gold Rush First "glider" flight	First major U.S. photography exhibition *Uncle Vanya*, Anton Chekhov (play) *Pont Boieldi in a Drizzle*, Camille Pissaro (painting)	Georges Méliès begins making short films Some U.S. vaudeville theaters include films in their programs Some newspapers give synopses of film programs but little criticism of them Some films are hand-painted with colors	"The Kiss," Edison "The Vanishing Lady," Georges Méliès "The Fairy in the Cabbage Patch," first film by the world's first female film director, Alice Guy-Blaché
1897	Discovery of the electron United States annexes Hawaii	*Dracula*, Bram Stoker (fiction)	Fire kills 140 people at a charity film showing in Paris	Fitzsimmons-Corbett boxing match filmed and shown in theaters
1898	Spanish-American War; Spain cedes Cuba, Puerto Rico, Guam, and the Philippines to the U.S.	*The Turn of the Screw*, Henry James (fiction) *The War of the Worlds*, Wells (fiction) "J'accuse," Émile Zola (letter)	First photograph taken with artificial light William Randolph Hearst epitomizes the ethics of "yellow journalism" with his comment: "You furnish the pictures, I'll furnish the war"	"Tearing Down the Spanish Flag" (a staged documentary and perhaps the first propaganda film) "Express Train on a Railway Cutting," Cecil Hepworth (documentary)

	World Events	Arts	Mass Media	Films and Videos
1899	Aspirin first marketed, as a prescribed drug U.S. goes to war with insurgents in the Philippines	*McTeague*, Frank Norris (fiction) "Maple Leaf Rag," Scott Joplin (music)	First magnetic recording of sound Marconi sends a wireless signal across the English Channel	"The Dreyfus Affair," Méliès (a film that re-creates a political scandal) "Cinderella," Méliès
1900	Boxer Rebellion in China, mainly against foreigners *The Interpretation of Dreams*, Freud (book) Max Planck proposes quantum theory of energy King Humbert I of Italy assassinated by anarchist Russia annexes Manchuria	*The Wonderful Wizard of Oz*, L. Frank Baum (fiction) *Sister Carrie*, Theodore Dreiser (fiction)	At about this time, Edison uses artificial light in his roof-top film studio in New York City Lumière Brothers use a 70-x-53 foot translucent screen at Paris World's Fair so 25,000 on both sides of the screen can see short films Kodak introduces the cheap, popular portable Brownie camera	"One Man Band," with Méliès himself playing the six band members and the conductor, Méliès
1901	Queen Victoria of England is succeeded by Edward VII Nobel Prizes first awarded President McKinley assassinated by anarchist Australian Commonwealth established	*Three Sisters*, Chekhov (play)	Marconi sends a radio signal from Wales to Newfoundland by tapping out "S" in Morse code First electric typewriter invented	"Queen Victoria's Funeral" (documentary)
1902	Boer War ends in South Africa Riots rage throughout southern Russia Aswan Dam finished in Egypt	*Heart of Darkness*, Joseph Conrad (fiction) *The Wings of the Dove*, James (fiction)	First Ealing studio is built, near London Pathé builds film studio in France First phonograph recording by Enrico Caruso	"A Trip to the Moon," Méliès "Coronation of Edward VII," Méliès (documentary re-creation)

	World Events	Arts	Mass Media	Films and Videos
1903	Scores of Jews murdered in Russia Ford Motor Company founded and begins new assembly-line system for car construction Wright brothers fly airplane	*Call of the Wild*, Jack London (fiction) *Man and Superman*, Bernard Shaw (play) Isadora Duncan pioneers modern dance (1903–1908)	Edwin S. Porter uses matte shots in "The Great Train Robbery" First radio message from U.S. to Britain	"The Great Train Robbery," "Life of an American Fireman," and "Uncle Tom's Cabin," all by Edwin S. Porter "La damnation de Faust," Méliès
1904	Theodore Roosevelt reelected president Russo-Japanese war Roosevelt Corollary added to Monroe Doctrine, asserts U.S. international policing rights	*Peter Pan*, J. M. Barrie (play) *The Cherry Orchard*, Chekhov (play)	A few nickelodeons—small storefront movie theaters showing programs of short films—open in U.S. Comic books, disk phonographs, and telephone answering machines are invented	"An Impossible Voyage," Méliès
1905	Police crush demonstration in St. Petersburg; general strike in Russia Russian sailors mutiny on battleship *Potemkin* Albert Einstein's theory of relativity	*The House of Mirth*, Edith Wharton (fiction) *Major Barbara*, Shaw (play) Fauvism and expressionism (artistic movements)	Pittsburgh theater is first to show films exclusively and regularly	"Rescued by Rover," Hepworth
1906	Britain launches the first large battleship, *Dreadnought* British Labour Party formed In India, Mahatma Gandhi begins campaign of nonviolent protest	*The Jungle*, Upton Sinclair (fiction) *Portrait of Gertrude Stein*, Pablo Picasso (painting)	Nearly 1,000 nickelodeons in the U.S. Movies are usually one reel (13–16 minutes for silent films) Victrola (record player) first marketed	"Dream of a Rarebit Fiend," Porter *The Story of the Kelly Gang*, Charles Tait (regarded as the first feature-length film)

	World Events	Arts	Mass Media	Films and Videos
1907	First completely synthetic plastic developed Ross Harrison grows human cells outside the body First blood test for syphilis	*The Playboy of the Western World*, John Millington Synge (play) Picasso's first cubist painting	Chicago creates its first film censorship board	"Ben Hur," Sidney Olcott
1908	Ford Motor Co. begins making the Model T Middle East oil boom begins in Persia	*A Room with a View*, E. M. Forster (fiction) Ashcan school of American realism (painting)	From 1908–1913, D. W. Griffith directs or supervises hundreds of short films at Biograph film production company	"The Adventures of Dollie," D. W. Griffith "The Last Days of Pompeii," Luigi Maggi
1909	Half of U.S. lives on farms or in small towns Congress passes the U.S. Copyright Law	The Italian book *Futurist Manifesto* exalts the beauty and dynamism of machines	At about this time, 35 mm becomes the standard film gauge throughout the world	"A Corner in Wheat" and "The Lonely Villa," Griffith
1910	Mexican civil war begins Portuguese monarchy ends after uprisings in Lisbon African American boxer Jack Johnson defeats white boxer Jim Jeffries, and race riots erupt throughout U.S.	*Howards End*, Forster (fiction) *The Dream*, Henri Rousseau (painting)	10,000 nickelodeons throughout the U.S. Film credits begin to identify U.S. actors First U.S. motion-picture newsreel exhibited Max Linder (France) writes, supervises, and performs in short comic movies	"A Child of the Ghetto," Griffith
1911	Mexican civil war ends First air flight across U.S. Indianapolis 500-mile auto race held for the first time	*Ethan Frome*, Wharton (fiction) *I and My Village*, Marc Chagall (painting)	The standard aspect ratio (4:3) is widely used in film showings	"The Battle" and "The Lonedale Operator," Griffith

	World Events	Arts	Mass Media	Films and Videos
1912	Revolution in China and abdication of the last Chinese emperor *Titanic* hits an iceberg and sinks on its maiden voyage; 1,500+ die 2,000 Turks killed by soldiers of the Balkan alliance	*Death in Venice*, Thomas Mann (fiction) *Tarzan of the Apes*, Edgar Rice Burroughs (fiction)	About 5 million see American movies daily Most American films now made in Los Angeles Universal Studios founded Wireless is useful when the sinking *Titanic* signals for help	"The Musketeers of Pig Alley," Griffith "Keystone Kops," Mack Sennett (series of short comic films) *Quo Vadis?*, Enrico Guazzoni (popular spectacle) *Queen Elizabeth*, Louis Mercanton and Henri Desfontaines
1913	Niels Bohr publishes his model of atomic structure Pancho Villa leads rebellion in northern Mexico; Mexican president deposed and killed in coup	First showing of avant-garde European art in the U.S. *Nude Descending a Staircase*, Marcel Duchamp (painting) *Rites of Spring*, Igor Stravinsky (music)	Olga Wohlbruck becomes the first German female filmmaker	*Judith of Bethulia*, Griffith "The Student of Prague," Stellan Rye and Paul Wagener
1914	World War I begins in Europe (1914–18) Panama Canal opens Term "birth control" coined	*Dubliners*, James Joyce (stories, including "The Dead")	In the U.S. the feature film becomes the norm Strand Theater, first movie palace, opens in New York	"Gertie the Dinosaur," Winsor McCay (series of short animated films) *Cabiria*, Giovanni Pastrone
1915	Germans use poison gas on western front German submarine sinks British liner *Lusitania*; approximately 1,200 die	*Of Human Bondage*, Somerset Maugham (fiction) *Metamorphosis*, Franz Kafka (fiction) New Orleans jazz is popular	First long-distance phone service established between New York and San Francisco	*The Birth of a Nation*, Griffith *The Cheat*, Cecil B. De Mille "The Tramp," Charles Chaplin *Les vampires*, Louis Feuillade (10-part series, 1915–16)

	World Events	**Arts**	**Mass Media**	**Films and Videos**
1916	Germans use gas against their enemies in the Battle of Verdun, which lasts from February to December Pancho Villa attacks the U.S., kills 14 Irish insurrection on Easter Day ("Bloody Sunday")	*A Portrait of the Artist as a Young Man*, Joyce (fiction) Dada (art and literary) movement founded in Zurich	Camera crane used for filming parts of *Intolerance* *The Art of the Moving Picture* by Vachel Lindsay and *The Photoplay: A Psychological Study* by Hugo Münsterberg are early and important books on film theory	*Intolerance*, Griffith *Civilization*, Thomas Ince "The Pawn Shop," "The Vagabond," and "The Rink," Chaplin *Her Defiance*, Cleo Madison
1917	Puerto Ricans granted U.S. citizenship Revolution in Russia; provisional government is formed; tsar abdicates U.S. enters World War I In Russia, Bolsheviks take control; later Vladimir Lenin becomes chief commissar	Symphony 1 ("Classical"), Sergei Prokofiev	UFA (major German film studio) formed Technicolor Corporation is founded; experimentation with color film continues First jazz recordings	"The Immigrant" and "Easy Street," Chaplin
1918	World War I ends Romanov royal family executed in Russia World influenza epidemic kills 20 million people	*The Magnificent Ambersons*, Booth Tarkington (fiction)	Warner Brothers Pictures incorporated by Harry, Albert, and Jack Warner During World War I, the U.S. film industry drastically increased its share of the world market	"Shoulder Arms," Chaplin *The Sinking of the* Lusitania, McCay (perhaps the first feature-length animated film) *Carmen*, Ernst Lubitsch
1919	U.S. states ratify prohibition amendment, which goes into effect in 1920 making the manufacture or consumption of alcohol illegal	*Winesburg, Ohio: A Group of Tales of Ohio Small Town Life*, Sherwood Anderson (fiction)	United Artists (distribution company) formed by Chaplin, Griffith, Mary Pickford, and Douglas Fairbanks RCA founded	*Broken Blossoms*, Griffith *Blind Husbands*, Erich von Stroheim *The Homesteader*, Oscar Micheaux (first feature film about U.S. blacks

	World Events	Arts	Mass Media	Films and Videos
1919 (cont.)	Civil war in Russia League of Nations founded Versailles peace treaty formally ends World War I	*Ten Days That Shook the World*, John Reed (nonfiction) Jazz arrives in Europe		written and directed by an African American) *The Cabinet of Dr. Caligari*, Robert Wiene *J'accuse*, Abel Gance (the "Griffith of Europe") *South: Ernest Shackleton and the Endurance Expedition*, Frank Hurley (documentary)
1920	Gandhi leads India's struggle for independence from Britain U.S. women get the vote Russian civil war ends	*Main Street*, Sinclair Lewis (fiction) *The Age of Innocence*, Wharton (fiction)	Lev Kuleshov founds workshop in Moscow and begins experimenting with editing U.S. films popular throughout much of the world KDKA in Pittsburgh offers regularly scheduled radio programs	*Way Down East*, Griffith *The Golem*, Paul Wegener and Henrik Galeen
1921	Adolf Hitler's storm troopers in Germany and Fascist blackshirts in Italy terrorize political opponents Irish Free State (excluding Northern Ireland) established	*Six Characters in Search of an Author*, Luigi Pirandello (play) *The Dream*, Max Beckmann (painting)	British Broadcasting Corp. (BBC) begins U.S. President Warren G. Harding makes first presidential radio address	*The Kid*, Chaplin's first feature *Orphans of the Storm*, Griffith *Destiny*, Fritz Lang "Rhythmus 21," Hans Richter (experimental)
1922	Benito Mussolini forms Fascist government in Italy USSR formed by various Soviet states Fuad I begins rule of Egypt Insulin isolated and used to save diabetes patients	*Ulysses*, Joyce (fiction) "The Wasteland," T. S. Eliot (poem) Beginnings of surrealist movement *Twittering Machine*, Paul Klee (watercolor and pen and ink)	New York Philharmonic radio concert	*Foolish Wives*, von Stroheim *Nosferatu*, F. W. Murnau *La roue*, Gance *Nanook of the North*, Robert Flaherty (documentary) *Witchcraft through the Ages*, Benjamin Christensen (experimental documentary)

	World Events	Arts	Mass Media	Films and Videos
1922 (cont.)	King Tutankhamen's tomb discovered in Egypt			*Kino-Pravda*, Dziga Vertov (creatively edited newsreels, 1922–25)
1923	In Germany, Hitler's attempted coup fails Former Mexican revolutionary Pancho Villa ambushed and killed by gunmen Massive earthquake kills 800,000 people in Japan	*St. Joan*, Shaw (play) "Stopping by Woods on a Snowy Evening," Robert Frost (poem)	Kodak produces first 16 mm movie film (black-and-white) Vladimir Zworykin develops television camera tube *Time* magazine begins	*Safety Last*, Sam Taylor and Fred Newmeyer (starring Harold Lloyd) *Our Hospitality*, Buster Keaton and Jack Blystone *The Ten Commandments*, De Mille "Retour à la raison," Man Ray (experimental)
1924	Lenin dies; struggle for succession begins in USSR American Indians given full U.S. citizenship by an act of Congress First winter Olympics held, in France Ottoman dynasty ends 600-year rule; modern state of Turkey formed	*A Passage to India*, Forster (fiction) *Juno and the Paycock*, Sean O'Casey (play) "Surrealist Manifesto" André Breton (essay) *Rhapsody in Blue*, George Gershwin (music)	M-G-M film studio formed 1.25 million radios in use in U.S. Introduction of the Moviola editing machine *Little Orphan Annie* comic strip begins Leica portable still camera invented in Germany	*Greed*, von Stroheim *The Last Laugh*, Murnau *Die Nibelungen*, Lang *(The Story of) Gösta Berling*, Mauritz Stiller *Strike*, Sergei Eisenstein "Entr'acte," René Clair (experimental) "Le ballet mécanique," Fernand Léger (experimental)
1925	Teacher John Scopes tried for violating Tennessee's anti-evolution statute Hitler publishes part of *Mein Kampf* (*My Struggle*) French build the Maginot Line for defense against an invasion	*The Great Gatsby*, F. Scott Fitzgerald (fiction) *The Trial*, Kafka (posthumous fiction) *Ralph 124C 41+*, Hugo Gernsback (science fiction) Art deco movement begins	Cinematographer Karl Struss uses colored makeup and color filters to depict the healing of lepers *Grand Ole Opry* radio show begins (eventually becomes longest continuously running radio show in the U.S.)	*The Gold Rush*, Chaplin *Ben Hur*, Fred Niblo *Body and Soul*, Micheaux (film debut of singer and actor Paul Robeson) *The Joyless Street*, G. W. Pabst *Variety*, E. A. Dupont *(Battleship) Potemkin*, Eisenstein

	World Events	Arts	Mass Media	Films and Videos
1926	New York–London telephone service begins Rocket launched by R. H. Goddard (U.S.) Emperor Hirohito comes to power in Japan Chiang Kai-shek takes control of the Chinese government	*The Sun Also Rises*, Ernest Hemingway (fiction) *Orphée*, Jean Cocteau (play) Harlem Renaissance begins	*Don Juan* made with Vitaphone: film plus synchronized music from disks *The Black Pirate:* one of the first films to use the two-color Technicolor process	*The General*, Keaton *Metropolis*, Lang *Mother*, V. I. Pudovkin *Faust*, Murnau
1927	Charles Lindbergh flies alone nonstop from New York to Paris German economy collapses Physicist Walter Heisenberg introduces his uncertainty principle Mao Zedong's Autumn Harvest Uprising is crushed by Chinese government	*To the Lighthouse*, Virginia Woolf (fiction) *Show Boat*, Jerome Kern and Oscar Hammerstein (musical) *Bird in Space*, Constantin Brancusi (sculpture) *Manhattan Bridge*, Edward Hopper (painting)	Warner Bros. releases *The Jazz Singer* using the Vitaphone sound system *Napoléon* (Abel Gance) includes triptych: wide-screen image made up of three synchronized standard images "To Build a Fire," experimental fiction by Claude Autant-Lara, first film to use anamorphic lenses developed by Henri Chrétien AM radio band created Sales of radio sets increase dramatically in U.S.	*Underworld*, Josef Von Sternberg (early gangster film) *Sunrise*, Murnau *Napoléon*, Gance *The Italian Straw Hat*, Clair *Bed and Sofa*, Abram Room *Berlin, Symphony of a Great City*, Walter Ruttmann (experimental documentary)
1928	German dirigible *Graf Zeppelin* makes first transatlantic crossing Penicillin, first antibiotic, discovered *The Oxford English Dictionary* published	*Lady Chatterley's Lover*, D. H. Lawrence (fiction) *Orlando*, Woolf (fiction) *Greta Garbo*, Edward Steichen (photograph)	First all-talking film, *The Lights of New York*, uses the Vitaphone sound system Feature films released on two rival sound-on-film systems, Movietone and Photophone	*The Circus*, Chaplin *The Crowd*, King Vidor *The Wind*, Victor Sjöström "Steamboat Willie," Walt Disney (first Mickey Mouse film released) *October*, a.k.a. *Ten Days That Shook the World*, Eisenstein

	World Events	Arts	Mass Media	Films and Videos
1928 (cont.)		*Three-Penny Opera,* Kurt Weill and Bertolt Brecht (musical)	Kodak introduces 16 mm color movie film First scheduled TV broadcast, in Schenectady, NY	*The Passion of Joan of Arc,* Carl Theodor Dreyer "Un chien andalou," Luis Buñuel (experimental) "The Seashell and the Clergyman," Germaine Dulac (experimental)
1929	U.S. stock prices plunge European economic crisis begins Josef Stalin becomes absolute ruler of USSR	*A Farewell to Arms,* Hemingway (fiction) *All Quiet on the Western Front,* Erich Maria Remarque (fiction) *A Room of One's Own,* Woolf (essay) Museum of Modern Art opens in New York	Sound film projector speed is standardized in U.S. at 24 frames per second Postdubbing (adding sound after filming) first used First Academy Awards ceremony held, for films for 1927–28 *Amos 'n' Andy* radio show debuts and quickly proves popular *Buck Rogers in the 25th Century* (sci-fi comic strip)	*Applause,* Rouben Mamoulian *Hallelujah!,* Vidor (first sound feature with all-black cast) *Blackmail,* Alfred Hitchcock (first British sound film) *Pandora's Box,* Pabst "Drifters," John Grierson (documentary) *Man with a Movie Camera,* Vertov (experimental documentary)
1930	Stalin orders collectivization of Soviet farms Major Indian cities in turmoil after Gandhi and some followers are arrested for leading campaign of civil disobedience against British rule of India	*The Maltese Falcon,* Dashiell Hammett (fiction) *Composition in Red, Yellow and Blue,* Piet Mondrian (painting)	U.S. production code for certifying movies is instituted but only loosely enforced Rear projection developed Worldwide, approximately 250 million people attend movies weekly 12 million U.S. homes have radios	*All Quiet on the Western Front,* Lewis Milestone *The Blue Angel,* Josef von Sternberg "The Blood of a Poet," Jean Cocteau (experimental)
1931	Cyclotron invented by Ernest Lawrence Big Bang theory	*The Persistence of Memory,* Salvador Dali (painting)	*Dick Tracy* comic strip begins	*City Lights* (includes sound effects and music but no dialogue), Chaplin

	World Events	Arts	Mass Media	Films and Videos
1931 (cont.)	U.S. unemployment is 16%, and over 800 banks close Japan occupies Manchuria	"The Star Spangled Banner" becomes U.S. national anthem	*Mädchen in Uniform*, by Leontine Sagan, early film with a lesbian character and an all-female cast.	*Frankenstein*, James Whale *Dracula*, Tod Browning *The Public Enemy*, William Wellman *M*, Lang
1932	First nuclear reaction U.S. unemployment: 24% Franklin D. Roosevelt elected U.S. president Neutron, a subatomic particle, is discovered	*Brave New World*, Aldous Huxley (fiction) *Mobiles*, Alexander Calder (mobile sculptures)	First international film festival: Venice Film Festival Technicolor three-color process first used, in the Disney cartoon "Flowers and Trees" Radio City Music Hall, a huge and opulent movie palace, opens in New York	*Scarface*, Howard Hawks *I Am a Fugitive from a Chain Gang*, Mervyn LeRoy *Trouble in Paradise*, Lubitsch *Dr. Jekyll and Mr. Hyde*, Mamoulian *À nous la liberté* (*Freedom for Us*), Clair
1933	Hitler appointed German chancellor Revolution in Spain spreads to the south of Spain Nazis erect their first concentration camp, and boycott of Jews begins in Germany First round-the-world airplane flight, by Wiley Post Prohibition ends in United States	*Shape of Things to Come*, Wells (fiction) *Blood Wedding*, Federico García Lorca (play) *Man at the Crossroads*, Diego Rivera (fresco for Rockefeller Center)	British Film Institute founded Nazis control German film industry World's first drive-in movie theater opens in Camden, New Jersey President Roosevelt uses radio for his Fireside Chats to the nation *The Lone Ranger* radio program debuts	*King Kong*, Ernest Schoedsack and Merian C. Cooper *Duck Soup*, Leo McCarey (starring Marx Bros.) *Gold Diggers of 1933*, LeRoy (with choreography by Busby Berkeley) "Lot in Sodom," James Watson and Melville Webber (experimental) "Zero for Conduct," Jean Vigo (experimental)
1934	Radar developed Stalin's purge of Soviet Communist Party begins Bank robbers Bonnie Parker and Clyde Barrow killed in police ambush	*The Postman Always Rings Twice*, James M. Cain (fiction) *The Children's Hour*, Lillian Hellman (play)	Production Code Administration seal of approval required for U.S. public film showings (1934–68)	*It Happened One Night*, Frank Capra *L'Atalante*, Vigo *Man of Aran*, Flaherty (documentary) "Composition in Blue," Oskar Fischinger (experimental)

	World Events	Arts	Mass Media	Films and Videos
1935	Germany begins massive military build-up Dust storms plague nearly half of the U.S. Italy invades Ethiopia Persia becomes the modern state of Iran Nuremberg Laws codify German anti-Semitism	*The Treasure of the Sierra Madre,* B. Traven (fiction) *Porgy and Bess,* Gershwin (opera) Popular songs: all five Irving Berlin songs from the film *Top Hat,* including "Cheek to Cheek"	Museum of Modern Art Film Library opens First three-color Technicolor feature film: *Becky Sharp,* directed by Mamoulian "The March of Time" newsreel series appears monthly in the nation's theaters, until 1951 FM radio developed Approximately 22 million U.S. homes have radios	*Mutiny on the Bounty,* Frank Lloyd *The Informer,* John Ford *Top Hat,* Mark Sandrich *The 39 Steps,* Hitchcock *Toni,* Jean Renoir *Triumph of the Will,* Leni Riefenstahl (Nazi-sponsored propaganda)
1936	Spanish civil war (1936–39) Mussolini and Hitler agree to Rome-Berlin Axis Jawaharlal Nehru becomes president of the Indian National Congress First Volkswagen ("people's car") built	Frank Lloyd Wright's Kaufmann House, Pennsylvania (architecture) "A Fine Romance" (popular song from the movie *Swing Time*)	La Cinémathèque Française (France's film archive) founded *Life* magazine begins publication	*Modern Times,* Chaplin *Swing Time,* George Stevens *Fury,* Lang "A Day in the Country," Renoir "The Plow That Broke the Plains," Pare Lorentz (documentary) *Olympia,* Riefenstahl (documentary)
1937	Stalin's purges result in millions of deaths and imprisonment in slave labor camps (1937–38) German warplanes bomb Guernica, Spain, killing hundreds of people, mostly civilians Japan invades China Italy withdraws from League of Nations	*Of Mice and Men,* John Steinbeck (fiction) *The Hobbit,* J. R. R. Tolkien (fiction) *The Cradle Will Rock,* Marc Blitzstein (opera) *Guernica,* Picasso (mural depicting results of German bombardment)	Henri Chrétien links two cameras with an anamorphic lens to produce an image 200 feet wide by 33 feet high for a Paris exhibition Crash of dirigible *Hindenburg* broadcast live in the U.S. on transcontinental radio	*A Star Is Born,* Wellman *Snow White and the Seven Dwarfs* (first Disney animated feature) *Grand Illusion,* Renoir

	World Events	Arts	Mass Media	Films and Videos
1938	Germany annexes Austria House Committee on Un-American Activities (HUAC) formed U.S. and Germany sever diplomatic relations	*Les parents terribles*, Cocteau (play) *Recumbent Figure*, Henry Moore (stone sculpture)	Orson Welles's radio broadcast of *The War of the Worlds* causes panic nationwide on Halloween *Superman* first appears, in Action Comics	*Bringing Up Baby*, Hawks *The Lady Vanishes*, Hitchcock *Alexander Nevsky*, Eisenstein
1939	Spanish civil war ends with Francisco Franco's forces victorious Pan-American Airlines begins scheduled flights between U.S. and Europe World War II begins when Germany invades Poland Ho Chi Minh creates the Viet Minh Party, which opposes French colonialism in Indochina	*The Big Sleep*, Raymond Chandler (fiction) *The Grapes of Wrath*, Steinbeck (fiction) *Alexander Nevsky*, Prokofiev (cantata based on his film score) "Over the Rainbow" (popular song from the movie *The Wizard of Oz*)	Hollywood studios produce 400 movies during the year National Film Board of Canada founded RCA demonstrates television at New York World's Fair First FM station begins operation, Alpine, New Jersey *Batman* first appears, in Detective Comics	*The Wizard of Oz*, Victor Fleming *Stagecoach*, Ford *Gone with the Wind*, Fleming (last director to work on the film) *Mr. Smith Goes to Washington*, Capra *The Rules of the Game*, Renoir
1940	Winston Churchill becomes prime minister of Britain Germans enter Paris Germans begin all-night air raids against London France divided into the occupied northern zone and the collaborative Vichy southern zone	*Farewell, My Lovely*, Chandler (fiction) *The Ox-Bow Incident*, Walter van Tilburg Clark (fiction) "When You Wish upon a Star" (popular song from the movie *Pinocchio*)	28½ million American homes have a radio Edward R. Murrow's radio broadcasts from London during German air raids Republican and Democratic National Conventions broadcast on radio First American TV network broadcast	*The Grapes of Wrath*, Ford *The Great Dictator*, Chaplin *His Girl Friday*, Hawks *The Bank Dick*, Eddie Cline (starring W. C. Fields) *Dance, Girl, Dance*, Dorothy Arzner *Fantasia* and *Pinocchio* (Disney animated features) *Jud Süss*, Veidt Harlan (influential Nazi anti-Semitic film)

	World Events	**Arts**	**Mass Media**	**Films and Videos**
1941	First jet airplane flies German armies invade Greece and Yugoslavia Germany invades Russia Japan bombs Pearl Harbor U.S. and Britain declare war on Japan Germany and Italy declare war on U.S.	*What Makes Sammy Run?*, Budd Schulberg (fiction) *Moonrise, Hernandez, New Mexico*, Ansel Adams (photograph)	NBC and CBS granted commercial TV licenses	*Citizen Kane*, first film directed by Orson Welles *The Maltese Falcon*, first film directed by John Huston *Sullivan's Travels*, Preston Sturges "Target for Tonight," Harry Watt (documentary)
1942	Germany begins killing Jews in gas chambers Japan invades the Philippines Heavy German air raids on London Fungus destroys Indian rice crops; 1.6 million die in famine	*The Stranger*, Albert Camus (fiction) *Nighthawks*, Hopper (painting)	In the U.S., radio is the main source of information about the war	*Casablanca*, Michael Curtiz *The Magnificent Ambersons*, Welles *To Be or Not To Be*, Lubitsch *Ossessione*, Luchino Visconti "The Battle of Midway," Ford (documentary) "Why We Fight," produced by Capra (series of seven wartime documentaries, 1942–45)
1943	Allied forces land in Sicily Mussolini dismissed as Italian premier Italy surrenders to Allies and declares war on Germany German forces fail to take Stalingrad after yearlong siege	*Oklahoma!*, Richard Rodgers and Oscar Hammerstein (musical)	*Perry Mason* radio series begins with Raymond Burr; later a TV series	*Shadow of a Doubt*, Hitchcock *The Ox-Bow Incident*, Wellman "Report from the Aleutians," Huston (documentary) *Fires Were Started*, Humphrey Jennings (documentary) "Meshes of the Afternoon," Maya Deren and Alexander Hammid (experimental)
1944	Allies land in northern France (D-Day) German V-2 rockets used against Britain Forces under the command of U.S. General	*The Glass Menagerie*, Tennessee Williams (play)	First general-purpose computer built, at Harvard University, funded in part by IBM	*Hail the Conquering Hero* and *The Miracle of Morgan's Creek*, Sturges *Double Indemnity*, Billy Wilder *Murder, My Sweet*, Edward Dmytryk

	World Events	Arts	Mass Media	Films and Videos
1944 (cont.)	Douglas MacArthur recapture the Philippines Roosevelt elected U.S. president for fourth term			*Laura*, Otto Preminger *Henry V*, Laurence Olivier "Memphis Belle," William Wyler (documentary)
1945	President Roosevelt dies unexpectedly U.N. charter signed in San Francisco War ends in Europe, 35 million killed, 6 million of whom were Jews U.S. drops two atomic bombs on Japan, and Japan surrenders Independent republic of Vietnam formed Nuremberg trials of Nazi war criminals begin	*Animal Farm*, George Orwell (fiction) *Carousel*, Rodgers and Hammerstein (musical) Beginnings of abstract expressionist movement in painting	*Meet the Press*, radio show 5,000 American homes have a TV set *Ebony*, first African American glossy magazine	*The Lost Weekend*, Wilder *Detour*, Edgar G. Ulmer *Open City* (a.k.a. *Rome, Open City*), Roberto Rossellini *Brief Encounter*, David Lean *Ivan the Terrible*, Eisenstein *Children of Paradise*, Marcel Carné (made in France during German occupation) "The Battle of San Pietro," Huston (documentary)
1946	Cold war between USSR and its allies and U.S. and its allies begins Juan Perón elected president of Argentina Philippine independence from the U.S., July 4 Nuremberg trials end French women get the vote France recognizes Vietnamese independence	*Zorba, the Greek*, Nikos Kazantzakis (fiction) *All the King's Men*, Robert Penn Warren (fiction) *Annie Get Your Gun*, Irving Berlin (musical)	Each week about 90 million Americans go to the movies, a record Cannes (France) Film Festival founded Sony Corporation founded in Japan	*My Darling Clementine*, Ford *The Killers*, Robert Siodmak *The Best Years of Our Lives*, Wyler *It's a Wonderful Life*, Capra *Beauty and the Beast*, Cocteau *Great Expectations*, Lean *Shoeshine*, Vittorio de Sica "Let There Be Light," Huston (documentary not released until many years later)

	World Events	Arts	Mass Media	Films and Videos
1947	India becomes independent of Britain Jackie Robinson first African American to play in major league baseball India is divided into India and Pakistan U.S. jet plane flies faster than sound	*A Streetcar Named Desire*, Williams (play) The Actor's Studio, which teaches Method acting, is founded	House Committee on Un-American Activities (HUAC) investigates possible Communist influence in Hollywood British Film Academy formed Regular TV news broadcasts begin in the U.S. Zoom lens developed, at first for use in TV	*Out of the Past*, Jacques Tourner *Crossfire*, Dmytryk *Monsieur Verdoux*, Chaplin *Odd Man Out*, Carol Reed "Fireworks," Kenneth Anger (experimental) "Motion Painting No. 1," Fischinger (experimental)
1948	Gandhi assassinated in India U.S. Congress passes Marshall Plan: economic assistance for rebuilding Europe Israel proclaimed a country Apartheid becomes governmental policy of South Africa USSR blocks all traffic between Berlin and the West; Western countries begin to airlift supplies into Berlin North Korea proclaims independence from Republic of Korea	*The Naked and the Dead*, Norman Mailer (fiction) *Cry, the Beloved Country*, Alan Paton (fiction) *The Loved One*, Evelyn Waugh ("black comedy" fiction) *Christina's World*, Andrew Wyeth (painting) *City Square*, Alberto Giacometti (bronze sculpture)	Drive-in theaters increase in popularity Hollywood Ten found guilty of contempt of Congress In "the Paramount case," U.S. Supreme Court rules the major Hollywood studios' control of production, distribution, and exhibition violates antitrust laws TV becoming a threat to the film industry Long-playing phonograph record introduced Transistor developed 135 million paperback books sold in U.S. during the year	*The Treasure of the Sierra Madre*, Huston *The Naked City*, Jules Dassin *Force of Evil*, Abraham Polonsky *The Lady from Shanghai*, Welles *Fort Apache*, Ford *The Red Shoes*, Michael Powell *Oliver Twist*, Lean *The Fallen Idol*, Reed *The Bicycle Thief* (a.k.a. *Bicycle Thieves*), De Sica *Les parents terribles*, Cocteau (film version of his own play of the same title)
1949	North Atlantic Treaty Organization (NATO) created, a collective defense alliance initially of twelve nations Berlin airlift ends USSR tests its first atomic bomb	*1984*, Orwell (fiction) *Death of a Salesman*, Arthur Miller (play) *South Pacific*, Rodgers and Hammerstein (musical)	1 million TV sets in U.S. *The Lone Ranger*, the first western TV series 45 rpm record introduced	*Gun Crazy*, Joseph H. Lewis *Pinky*, Elia Kazan *All the King's Men*, Robert Rossen *The Third Man*, Reed *Kind Hearts and Coronets*, Robert Hamer *Late Spring*, Yasujiro Ozu

	World Events	Arts	Mass Media	Films and Videos
1949 (cont.)	Chinese Communists come to power; Nationalists flee to the island of Formosa, later called Taiwan Republic of India begins	Zither music from the film *The Third Man* is popular		*The Quiet One*, Sidney Meyers (documentary) "Begone Dull Care," Norman McLaren (experimental)
1950	Senator Joseph McCarthy claims U.S. State Department is full of Communists North Korea invades South Korea, and Korean War begins Birth control pill developed	*The Third Man*, Graham Greene (fiction published after the film) *Guys and Dolls*, Abe Burrows and Frank Loesser (musical)	Live TV comedy show *Your Show of Shows* with Sid Caesar and Imogene Coca begins and runs until 1954 *The Jack Benny Show* (TV) begins *Peanuts* comic strip begins	*Sunset Boulevard*, Wilder *All about Eve*, Joseph L. Mankiewicz *Rashomon*, Akira Kurosawa *Los olvidados* (literally *The Forgotten Ones*, but sometimes known as *The Young and the Damned*), Buñuel *Diary of a Country Priest*, Robert Bresson
1951	Japanese women get the vote Organization of American States (OAS) founded Chinese Communists occupy Tibet Libya becomes an independent state with the help of the U.N.	*The Caine Mutiny*, Herman Wouk (fiction) *From Here to Eternity*, James Jones (fiction) *Catcher in the Rye*, J. D. Salinger (fiction) *The King and I*, Rodgers and Hammerstein (musical)	Second congressional hearing on possible Communist influence in Hollywood (1951–52) Nitrate-base film, used for most 35 mm movies, replaced with safety base films Color TV introduced in the U.S. TV shows *I Love Lucy* and *Today* begin	*The African Queen*, Huston *A Streetcar Named Desire*, Kazan *Strangers on a Train*, Hitchcock *The Lavender Hill Mob*, Charles Crichton *Forbidden Games*, René Clément
1952	Juan Batista seizes power in Cuba Coup in Egypt deposes king and leads to establishment of Egyptian Republic Puerto Rico becomes a U.S. commonwealth	*Invisible Man*, Ralph Ellison (fiction) *The Old Man and the Sea*, Hemingway (fiction) *Waiting for Godot*, Samuel Beckett (play)	A three-projector version of Cinerama is introduced with the travelogue *This Is Cinerama* *Bwana Devil* starts a brief craze for 3-D movies Eastman color film, easier to process and cheaper	*High Noon*, Fred Zinnemann *Singin' in the Rain*, Gene Kelly and Stanley Donen *Limelight*, Chaplin *Umberto D*, De Sica *Ikiru* (*To Live*), Kurosawa "Neighbours," McLaren (experimental fictional film)

	World Events	Arts	Mass Media	Films and Videos
1952 (cont.)	U.S. explodes first hydrogen bomb (General) Dwight D. Eisenhower elected president	"Do Not Forsake Me," from the film *High Noon* (popular song)	than Technicolor, is introduced and results in increased use of color in Hollywood films Handheld transistor radios marketed in the United States *Mad* magazine	
1953	Stalin dies Publication that DNA's double-helix structure can be deciphered Queen Elizabeth II of Great Britain crowned Korean War ends First humans scale Mt. Everest	*Fahrenheit 451*, Ray Bradbury (fiction) *Picnic*, William Inge (play) *The Crucible*, Miller (play) *Apples*, Georges Braque (painting)	U.S. theaters begin to show anamorphic movies Academy Awards ceremony first telecast *The Moon Is Blue* released without a Motion Picture Association of America seal Eisenhower's inauguration is broadcast live on TV *Playboy* begins publication	*Shane*, Stevens *The Band Wagon*, Vincent Minnelli *Peter Pan* (Disney animated feature) *Rififi*, Dassin *Mr. Hulot's Holiday*, Jacques Tati *Ugetsu* (*Monogatari*), Kenji Mizoguchi *Tokyo Story*, Ozu *Gate of Hell*, Teinosuke Kinugasa
1954	Polio vaccine discovered U.S. Supreme Court rules school segregation unconstitutional French defeated in Vietnam; Vietnam divided into North and South Senator Joseph McCarthy discredited and censured by U.S. Senate colleagues	*Invasion of the Body Snatchers*, Jack Finney (fiction) *Lord of the Flies*, William Golding (fiction) First volume of *The Lord of the Rings*, J. R. R. Tolkien (fiction)	*White Christmas* filmed in VistaVision, a nonanamorphic widescreen system Approximately half of American homes have a TV Army-McCarthy hearings carried live on TV First U.S. TV color telecast, Rose Bowl parade *The Tonight Show* (with Steve Allen) debuts on TV	*On the Waterfront*, Kazan *Rear Window*, Hitchcock *A Star is Born*, George Cukor *La Strada*, Federico Fellini *The Seven Samurai*, Kurosawa *Late Chrysanthemums*, Mikio Naruse *Godzilla*, Inoshiro Honda (science-fiction action)

	World Events	Arts	Mass Media	Films and Videos
1955	Civil war begins between North and South Vietnam Warsaw Pact signed by East European countries Blacks boycott segregated city buses in Montgomery, Alabama Coup overthrows the Perón regime in Argentina McDonald's and Kentucky Fried Chicken start first fast-food franchises	*Lolita*, Vladimir Nabokov (fiction) *The Diary of Anne Frank*, Albert Hackett and Frances Goodrich (play) *The Family of Man*, Steichen (photographic exhibit)	Filming from helicopters becomes more practicable Todd-AO (a nonanamorphic wide-screen) process used in film version of *Oklahoma!* Disneyland opens in California Highest-rated TV show (1955–56): *The $64,000 Question* (quiz show) *Alfred Hitchcock Presents*, TV show (1955–62)	*Rebel without a Cause*, Nicholas Ray *Night of the Hunter*, Charles Laughton *Smiles of a Summer Night*, Ingmar Bergman *Lola Montes*, Max Ophüls *Pather Panchali*, Satyajit Ray (first of three Apu films),
1956	Soviets crush Hungarian revolt Israel invades Sinai peninsula Fidel Castro leads revolution in Cuba (1956–59) Britain, Israel, and France invade Egypt when Egypt nationalizes Suez Canal	*Long Day's Journey into Night*, Eugene O'Neill (play) *Look Back in Anger*, John Osborne (play) *My Fair Lady*, Alan Jay Lerner and Frederick Loewe (musical)	Elvis Presley appears on *The Ed Sullivan Show* (TV) TV westerns are popular Singer Nat King Cole becomes the first African American to host a network TV show *The Huntley-Brinkley Report*, a TV news program, debuts	*The Searchers*, Ford *The Killing*, Stanley Kubrick *The Seventh Seal*, Bergman *A Man Escaped*, Bresson "The Red Balloon," Albert Lamorisse "Night and Fog," Alain Resnais (documentary)
1957	Martin Luther King Jr. and others found the Southern Christian Leadership Conference President Eisenhower sends troops to help desegregate the University of Arkansas Soviets launch *Sputnik*, first satellite to circle earth	*Doctor Zhivago*, Boris Pasternak (fiction) *On the Road*, Jack Kerouac (fiction) *The Cat in the Hat*, Dr. Seuss (fiction) *West Side Story*, Leonard Bernstein and Arthur Laurents (musical)	*Raintree County*, first film released in Ultra-Panavision 70 *Perry Mason* begins its nine-season run on TV *American Bandstand* (with Dick Clark) is first shown on national TV	*Paths of Glory*, Kubrick *A Face in the Crowd*, Kazan *The Sweet Smell of Success*, Alexander Mackendrick *Wild Strawberries*, Bergman *Throne of Blood*, Kurosawa "Two Men and a Wardrobe," Roman Polanski (experimental)

	World Events	Arts	Mass Media	Films and Videos
1957 (cont.)			Motown Records is founded and popular- izes the music style that bears the com- pany's name	"What's Opera, Doc?" Chuck Jones (animation) "A Chairy Tale," McLaren and Claude Jutra (experi- mental)
1958	European Common Market formed First successful launch of a U.S. satellite U.S. troops sent to inter- vene in Lebanese civil war General Charles de Gaulle becomes presi- dent of France's Fifth Republic	*Things Fall Apart,* Chinua Achebe (fiction) *The Birthday Party,* Harold Pinter (play) *A Raisin in the Sun,* Lorraine Hans- berry (play) *Numbers in Color,* Jasper Johns (painting)	More than 4,000 U.S. drive-in movie screens in operation Stereophonic LPs and phonographs come into use Most popular TV show (1958–59): the western *Gunsmoke*	*Touch of Evil,* Welles *Vertigo,* Hitchcock *Ashes and Diamonds,* Andrzej Wajda *Ivan, the Terrible, Part Two,* Eisenstein (completed in 1946) *Room at the Top,* Jack Clayton *The World of Apu,* Satyajit Ray "A Movie," Bruce Conner (experimental)
1959	After leading a successful revolution against the Cuban president, Cas- tro becomes premier of Cuba Yasir Arafat and others found Palestine Liber- ation Organization (PLO) Russia launches two monkeys into space Chinese suppress upris- ing in Tibet	*The Tin Drum,* Günter Grass (fiction) *Naked Lunch,* William Bur- roughs (fiction) "Happenings," multimedia events, first staged *Kind of Blue* (album by Miles Davis)	TV quiz show scandal *The Twilight Zone* TV show begins *Adventures in Good Music,* classical music radio program by Karl Haas, begins on a Detroit station Microchip is invented	*Ben-Hur,* Wyler *North by Northwest,* Hitchcock *Some Like It Hot,* Wilder *Imitation of Life,* Douglas Sirk *The 400 Blows,* François Truffaut's first feature *Breathless,* Jean-Luc Godard's first feature *Hiroshima, mon amour,* Resnais *Look Back in Anger,* Tony Richardson *Floating Weeds,* Ozu "Window Water Baby Moving," Stan Brakhage (experimental)
1960	FDA approves use of birth control pill Nigeria becomes an independent nation Laser invented	*To Kill a Mocking- bird,* Harper Lee (fiction) *Camelot,* Lerner and Loewe (musical)	*Echo 1,* the first communica- tions satellite, launched First TV debate between presidential candidates (Kennedy and Nixon)	*Psycho,* Hitchcock *Shadows,* John Cassavetes's first film as director *Saturday Night and Sunday Morning,* Karel Reisz

	World Events	Arts	Mass Media	Films and Videos
1960 (cont.)	South African government bans major anti-apartheid groups after protests turn violent Organization of the Petroleum Exporting Countries (OPEC) formed Wave of decolonization as France and Belgium give up African territories First Xerox photocopier John F. Kennedy elected president	Minimalist style in painting, sculpture, and music *Coltrane Plays the Blues* and *My Favorite Things* (albums by John Coltrane) Fluxus movement begins in New York and Germany (multimedia arts)	*Harvest of Shame*, TV documentary film on migrant farmworkers, Edward R. Murrow, commentator Approximately 100 million TVs in Europe and the U.S. The Twist dance craze influences songs, books, movies, and TV shows	*The Entertainer*, Richardson *L'avventura*, Michelangelo Antonioni *La dolce vita*, Fellini *Shoot the Piano Player*, Truffaut *Cruel Story of Youth*, Nagisa Oshima *Primary*, (Robert) Drew Associates (documentary)
1961	U.S. establishes Peace Corps USSR begins manned space flights U.S.-sponsored Bay of Pigs invasion of Cuba fails Communists build Berlin Wall to deter East Germans from fleeing to West	*Catch-22*, Joseph Heller (fiction) *The Moviegoer*, Walker Percy (fiction) Comic-strip and comic-frame paintings, Roy Lichtenstein	First live TV coverage of a presidential news conference *The Dick Van Dyke Show* begins on TV and runs five years	*West Side Story*, Robert Wise *Jules and Jim*, Truffaut *Last Year at Marienbad*, Resnais (experimental fiction) *Viridiana*, Buñuel *Chronicle of a Summer*, Jean Rouch and Edgar Morin (documentary) "Prelude: Dog Star Man," Brakhage (experimental)
1962	John Glenn is first American to orbit earth in a spacecraft Algeria wins independence from France U.S. and USSR in tense confrontation over Soviet missiles in Cuba U.N. troops enter the Congo to control civil war	*A Clockwork Orange*, Anthony Burgess (fiction) *The Death of Artemio Cruz*, Carlos Fuentes (fiction) *One Flew over the Cuckoo's Nest*, Ken Kesey (fiction) *The Thin Red Line*, Jones (fiction)	*The Alfred Hitchcock Hour*, TV show airs from 1962 to 1965 Johnny Carson becomes host of NBC's late night TV talk show, *The Tonight Show*, and remains host until 1992 Walter Cronkite becomes anchor (until 1981) of *CBS Evening News*	*The Man Who Shot Liberty Valance*, Ford *Dr. No*, Terence Young (first James Bond movie) *Lawrence of Arabia*, Lean *The Loneliness of the Long Distance Runner*, Richardson *Vivre sa vie (My Life to Live)*, Godard *Knife in the Water*, Polanski

	World Events	Arts	Mass Media	Films and Videos
1962 (cont.)	*Mariner 2* spacecraft sends back first close-up photos of another planet, Venus	*Who's Afraid of Virginia Woolf?*, Edward Albee (play)	*Telstar* satellite (for TV and telephone relays) launched Most popular TV show (1962–64): *The Beverly Hillbillies*	"An Occurrence at Owl Creek Bridge," Robert Enrico (experimental fiction) "La jetée," Chris Marker (experimental fiction) "Cosmic Ray," Conner (experimental)
1963	Alabama civil rights march results in beatings of blacks, arrest of Dr. Martin Luther King Jr., and the sending of federal troops Four black girls killed in bombing of Birmingham, Alabama, church President Kennedy assassinated and Lyndon Johnson becomes president By year's end, the U.S. has sent economic aid and 16,000 "advisers" to South Vietnam Kenya gains independence from British rule Artificial heart used for the first time	*The Feminine Mystique*, Betty Friedan (nonfiction) *Cinema*, George Segal (life-size sculpture) *Mona Lisa*, Andy Warhol (painting)	New York Film Festival established "Movietone News" last presented in U.S. movie theaters First movie multiplex built, in Kansas City Poll reveals TV is now the major source of news for most Americans TV networks expand evening news programs from 15 to 30 minutes Martin Luther King's "I have a dream" speech in Washington, D.C., is televised Unprecedented four-day TV coverage of President Kennedy's assassination and burial Audio cassettes used to play back music	*The Birds*, Hitchcock *Tom Jones*, Richardson *Billy Liar*, John Schlesinger *Dr. Strangelove: Or, How I Learned to Stop Worrying and Love the Bomb*, Kubrick *Lord of the Flies*, Peter Brook *8½*, Fellini *Dead Birds*, Robert Gardner (documentary) *7 Up*, Michael Apted (first in documentary series tracing lives of same small group of British citizens in seven-year increments) *Sleep*, Andy Warhol (experimental documentary) "Scorpio Rising," Anger (experimental) "Mothlight," Brakhage (experimental) "Christmas on Earth," Barbara Rubin (experimental)
1964	Martin Luther King Jr. wins Nobel Peace Prize Zambia (formerly Northern Rhodesia) becomes an independent nation	*The Woman in the Dunes*, Kobo Abe (fiction) *Little Big Man*, Thomas Berger (fiction)	Sports telecasts begin to use videotaped instant replay Beatles' first American TV appearance, on *The Ed Sullivan Show*	*Nothing but a Man*, Michael Roemer *A Hard Day's Night*, Richard Lester *The Gospel according to St. Matthew*, Pier Paolo Pasolini

	World Events	Arts	Mass Media	Films and Videos
1964 (cont.)	Following an attack on U.S. warships, Congress passes Gulf of Tonkin Resolution, which justifies U.S. military buildup in Vietnam Nelson Mandela sentenced to life in prison in South Africa The Civil Rights Act is passed in the United States Nikita Khrushchev is ousted from power in the USSR	*Fiddler on the Roof*, Jerry Bock and Sheldon Harnick (musical) *Jackie*, Andy Warhol (painting of Jackie Kennedy) First Moog (electronic) synthesizer "Raindrops Keep Falling on My Head," from the film *Butch Cassidy and the Sundance Kid* (popular song)	*Understanding Media: The Extensions of Man*, Marshall McLuhan (book)	*Woman in the Dunes*, Hiroshi Teshigahara *A Married Woman*, Godard *(The) Red Desert*, Antonioni *Point of Order*, Emile De Antonio (documentary) *A Stravinsky Portrait*, Richard Leacock (documentary) "Fuses," Carolee Schneemann (experimental 1964–67) *Dog Star Man*, Brakhage (experimental 1961–64)
1965	Malcolm X, a Black Muslim leader, murdered in New York In U.S., growing demonstrations against U.S. involvement in Vietnam The U.S. deploys Marines to the Dominican Republic First miniskirt appears	*The Autobiography of Malcolm X*, Alex Haley (nonfiction) Luis Valdez founds Teatro Campesino in California *Campbell's Soup Can*, Andy Warhol (painting)	Super-8 film introduced TV expands coverage of Vietnam War Eight-track tape player is introduced	*The Pawnbroker*, Sidney Lumet *Juliet of the Spirits*, Fellini *The Shop on Main Street*, Jan Kadár and Elmar Klos "The Dot and the Line," Jones (animation) "The War Game," Peter Watkins (fake documentary) *To Die in Madrid*, Frédéric Rossif (documentary) "The Sins of the Fleshpoids," Mike Kuchar (experimental)
1966	Cultural Revolution—led by Mao Zedong—begins in China (ends in 1971), resulting in terrorism, purges, destroyed art works, and restructuring of the education system Black Panther Party founded in Oakland, California	*The Last Picture Show*, Larry McMurtry (fiction) *Valley of the Dolls*, Jacqueline Susan (fiction) *In Cold Blood*, Truman Capote (nonfiction)	Color TV becomes popular in U.S. *Star Trek* begins its three-season run on TV *Mission Impossible*, TV adventure series, first airs and runs until 1973 William F. Buckley's *Firing Line* TV interview show first airs; runs until 2000	*Who's Afraid of Virginia Woolf?*, Mike Nichols *Blowup*, Antonioni *Persona*, Bergman *Closely Watched Trains*, Jiri Menzel *The Battle of Algiers*, Gillo Pontecorvo *La guerre est finie*, Resnais *Black Girl*, Ousmane Sembène

	World Events	Arts	Mass Media	Films and Videos
1966 (cont.)	National Organization for Women (NOW) formed By year's end, 389,000 U.S. troops in Vietnam France withdraws its troops from NATO Indira Ghandi becomes prime minister of India	*Cabaret*, John Kander and Fred Ebb (musical) *Sweet Charity*, Cy Coleman, Dorothy Fields, and Neil Simon (musical based on Fellini's film *The Nights of Cabiria*) *The State Hospital*, Edward Kienholz (mixed media) *Witness to Our Time*, Alfred Eisenstaedt (photographs)	*Amos 'n' Andy* reruns dropped from TV because of protests against the program's racial stereotypes *Sixteen in Webster Groves*, TV documentary "How the Grinch Stole Christmas," animation by Chuck Jones, first shown on TV	*The Chelsea Girls*, Warhol (experimental) *No. 4 (Bottoms)*, Yoko Ono (experimental documentary 1966–67) "Film in Which There Appear Sprocket Holes, Edge Lettering, Dirt Particles, Etc.," George Landow (a.k.a. Owen Land) (experimental) "The Flicker," Tony Conrad (experimental) "Lapis," James Whitney (experimental)
1967	Six-day war between Arab nations and Israel results in Israeli victory and acquisition of territory Thurgood Marshall, first African American Supreme Court justice First human heart transplant, in South Africa By year's end, more than 500,000 U.S. troops in Vietnam Five-year military dictatorship in Greece begins	*One Hundred Years of Solitude*, Gabriel García Márquez (fiction) *Rosencrantz and Guildenstern Are Dead*, Tom Stoppard (play) *The Great White Hope*, Howard Sackler (play) *Hair*, Gerome Ragni and Jim Rado (rock musical) First major rock festival, Monterey, California	American Film Institute founded *Rolling Stone* magazine founded *Ironsides* TV series, with Raymond Burr (1967–75) *The Carol Burnett Show*, TV show (1967–79)	*Bonnie and Clyde*, Arthur Penn *The Graduate*, Nichols *Weekend*, Godard *Playtime*, Tati *Belle de jour*, Buñuel *Accident*, Joseph Losey *Don't Look Back*, D. A. Pennebaker (documentary) *Portrait of Jason*, Shirley Clarke (documentary) *Titicut Follies*, first documentary by Frederick Wiseman "Quixote," Bruce Baillie (revised version; experimental documentary) "Wavelength," Michael Snow (experimental)
1968	Surprise Tet offensive demoralizes U.S. and South Vietnamese forces Martin Luther King Jr. assassinated	*2001: A Space Odyssey*, Arthur C. Clarke (fiction) *Black Rain*, Masuji Ibuse (fiction)	Motion Picture Association of America institutes four-part rating system Czech film movement ended by Soviet invasion of Czechoslovakia	*Faces*, Cassavetes *Night of the Living Dead*, first film by George Romero *2001: A Space Odyssey*, Kubrick *Once Upon a Time in the West*, Sergio Leone

	World Events	**Arts**	**Mass Media**	**Films and Videos**
1968 (cont.)	Senator Robert Kennedy assassinated Soviets invade Czechoslovakia and end its liberal policies Riots and police brutality outside the Democratic Convention in Chicago Richard Nixon elected president	*I Never Sang for My Father*, Robert Anderson (play)	*60 Minutes*, TV magazine news show, begins *Rowan and Martin's Laugh-In* features very short satiric pieces on TV (1968–73)	*Shame*, Bergman *Memories of Underdevelopment*, Tomás Gutiérrez Alea *David Holzman's Diary*, Jim McBride (fake documentary) *High School*, Frederick Wiseman (documentary) "Pas de deux," McLaren (experimental)
1969	Yasir Arafat becomes head of Palestine Liberation Organization (PLO) U.S. astronauts land on moon for the first time and return Woodstock (NY) music festival draws 500,000 Large U.S. demonstrations against Vietnam War continue Massacre of villagers in My Lai (Vietnam) by U.S. soldiers revealed American Gay Liberation movement begins with the Stonewall Inn riot in New York City	*Fat City*, Leonard Gardner (fiction) *The Godfather*, Mario Puzo (fiction; best-selling U.S. novel of the 1970s) *Portnoy's Complaint*, Philip Roth (fiction) *Slaughterhouse-Five*, Kurt Vonnegut Jr. (fiction)	Live TV broadcast from moon captivates the world's attention PBS begins broadcasting TV programs, including *Sesame Street*, which uses techniques of TV commercials to teach children basic language skills Most popular TV show (1969–70): *Rowan and Martin's Laugh-In*	*Midnight Cowboy*, Schlesinger *Medium Cool*, Haskell Wexler *The Wild Bunch*, Sam Peckinpah *I Am Joaquin*, Luis Valdez (possibly the first film written, produced, and directed by Latinos in the U.S.) *My Night at Maud's*, Eric Rohmer *If . . .*, Lindsay Anderson *Boy*, Oshima *Monterey Pop*, Pennebaker (early rock documentary) *Salesman*, Albert and David Maysles (documentary) *In the Year of the Pig*, De Antonio (documentary) *Tom, Tom, the Piper's Son*, Ken Jacobs (experimental) "Back and Forth," Snow (experimental)
1970	U.S. Supreme Court allows school busing to achieve integration U.S. and South Vietnamese troops enter Cambodia	*Deliverance*, James Dickey (fiction) *Spiral Jetty*, Robert Smithson (1,500-foot jetty, Great Salt Lake, Utah)	Rapid growth of film studies in U.S. colleges and universities IMAX ("image maximum"), extremely large screen film	*M*A*S*H*, Robert Altman *Patton*, Franklin Schaffner *The Great White Hope*, Martin Ritt *The Wild Child*, François Truffaut

	World Events	Arts	Mass Media	Films and Videos
1970 (cont.)	At Kent State University, Ohio National Guard members shoot at demonstrating students and kill four Massive student demonstrations against the Vietnam War close hundreds of U.S. colleges and universities Muammar al-Qaddafi comes to power in Libya Coup in Cambodia leaves it under oppressive military dictatorship		format, introduced at world's fair National Public Radio (NPR) begins broadcasting *The Phil Donahue Show* is first seen nationally on TV and runs until 1996 About 231 million TV sets used throughout the world *The Mary Tyler Moore Show* (TV sitcom) begins *Doonesbury* (satirical) comic strip begins	*Even Dwarfs Started Small,* Werner Herzog *Woodstock,* Michael Wadleigh (documentary) *The Sorrow and the Pity,* Marcel Ophüls (documentary) *Gimme Shelter,* Maysles Brothers (documentary) *Zorns Lemma,* Hollis Frampton (experimental) "Remedial Reading Comprehension," George Landow (a.k.a. Owen Land) (experimental) "Runs Good," Pat O'Neill (experimental) "Serene Velocity," Ernie Gehr (experimental)
1971	Saddam Hussein seizes power in Iraq Pakistan attacks India but is defeated in two-week war Bangladesh established as independent nation Failed coup attempt in China	*Maurice,* Forster (posthumous fiction) *Being There,* Jerzy (N.) Kosinski (fiction) *. . . And the Earth Did Not Devour Him,* Tomás Rivera (fiction)	Movie theater receipts are down sharply *Ms.* magazine founded to promote the women's movement Ban on TV cigarette advertising goes into effect *Masterpiece Theatre* begins on PBS, with Alistair Cooke as host Top U.S. TV show (1971–76): *All in the Family,* with Carroll O'Connor as Archie Bunker	*McCabe and Mrs. Miller,* Altman *The Last Picture Show,* Peter Bogdanovich *Sweet Sweetback's Badass Song,* Melvin Van Peebles *A Clockwork Orange,* Kubrick *Claire's Knee,* Rohmer *Walkabout,* Nicolas Roeg *The Conformist,* Bernardo Bertolucci "(nostalgia)," Frampton (experimental) "Kiri," Sakumi Hagiwara (experimental)
1972	White House announces the last U.S. ground combat units have left Vietnam	*Bless Me, Ultima,* Rudolfo A. Anaya (fiction)	*M*A*S*H* TV series, based on movie of the same title, begins and runs for 11 seasons	*The Godfather,* Francis Ford Coppola *Cabaret,* Bob Fosse *Fat City,* Huston

	World Events	Arts	Mass Media	Films and Videos
1972 (cont.)	Britain assumes direct control of Northern Ireland Men working for the Republican Party caught in the Watergate Hotel, Washington, D.C., breaking into the Democratic National Headquarters At Munich Olympics, terrorists invade Israeli compound and kill two; later developments lead to loss of more lives	*Story Show*, Laurie Anderson (multimedia performance) *Grease!*, Jim Jacobs and Warren Casey (musical) Christo wraps large section of Australian coastline in plastic sheeting	Home Box Office is first available through cable TV First International Festival of Women's Films is held in New York	*Deep Throat*, Gerard Damiano (first sexually explicit feature to gain U.S. national audience) *Frenzy*, Hitchcock *The Discreet Charm of the Bourgeoisie*, Buñuel *Last Tango in Paris*, Bertolucci *Aguirre, The Wrath of God*, Herzog *Cries and Whispers*, Bergman "Near the Big Chakra," Anne Severson (experimental documentary)
1973	U.S. Supreme court rules abortion is constitutional Vietnam cease-fire agreement signed; U.S. combat deaths: over 47,000 Salvador Allende, Marxist president of Chile, overthrown and reportedly commits suicide Amid scandal, Spiro T. Agnew resigns as U.S. vice president; Gerald Ford succeeds him During Yom Kippur, Egyptian and Syrian forces attack the Israeli-held Sinai Peninsula and Golan Heights	*Fear of Flying*, Erica Jong (fiction) *The Gulag Archipelago*, Aleksandr Solzhenitsyn (first volume of three-volume fiction) *Equus*, Peter Shaffer (play) Scott Joplin's ragtime music popular after its use in movie *The Sting*	Omnimax, huge dome screen for use with IMAX, developed Senate Watergate hearings broadcast on TV *An American Family*, 12-hour TV documentary series	*Mean Streets*, Martin Scorsese *American Graffiti*, George Lucas *Payday*, Daryl Duke *The Harder They Come*, Perry Henzell *Don't Look Now*, Roeg *Day for Night*, Truffaut *Fantastic Planet*, René Laloux (animated) *Spirit of the Beehive*, Victor Erice *Distant Thunder*, Satyajit Ray *Touki Bouki* (*The Journey of the Hyena*), Djibril Diop Mambety *No Lies*, Mitchell Block (fake documentary) "Three Transitions," Peter Campus (experimental videos)

	World Events	Arts	Mass Media	Films and Videos
1974	Nixon resigns presidency; Vice President Gerald Ford becomes president Ford pardons Nixon for possible criminal offenses committed while in office OPEC embargo causes oil shortages and serious economic problems in U.S. and elsewhere Turkish forces invade Cyprus; Greek forces mobilized to repel the invasion	*Jaws*, Peter Benchley (fiction) *Carrie*, Stephen King (fiction)	*Little House on the Prairie*, TV show (1974–83) *The Rockford Files*, TV show (1974–80) *Happy Days*, TV show (1974–84) *Prairie Home Companion* radio program with Garrison Keillor as host begins Word processors hit the U.S. market	*The Godfather, Part II* and *The Conversation*, Coppola *Chinatown*, Polanski *A Woman under the Influence*, Cassavetes *Amarcord*, Fellini *Scenes from a Marriage*, Bergman *Xala (Impotence)*, Sembène *Antonia: A Portrait of the Woman*, Jill Godmilow (documentary) *Film about a woman who . . .*, Yvonne Rainer (experimental) "Print Generation," J. J. Murphy (experimental) "8½ × 11," James Benning (experimental fiction)
1975	U.S. ends all involvement in Vietnam Soviet space probes transmit first pictures of Venus's surface Franco of Spain dies; Juan Carlos sworn in as king Khmer Rouge kill at least 1 million Cambodians (1975–79)	*Ragtime*, E. L. Doctorow (fiction) *American Buffalo*, David Mamet (play) *A Chorus Line*, James Kirkwood, Nicholas Dante, and Marvin Hamlisch (musical that opens in New York and runs 15 years)	Personal computers introduced Dolby film noise reduction system introduced *Saturday Night Live*, TV show, debuts Sony introduces Beta home videotape format	*Nashville*, Altman *Shampoo*, Hal Ashby *One Flew over the Cuckoo's Nest*, Milos Forman *Barry Lyndon*, Kubrick *The Rocky Horror Picture Show*, Jim Sharman *Picnic at Hanging Rock*, Peter Weir *The Mystery of Kaspar Hauser*, Herzog *The Story of Adele H.*, Truffaut *Jeanne Dielman*, Chantal Akerman (experimental documentary)
1976	Argentine military government begins "dirty war" against dissidents; tens of thousands disappear or are murdered or both	*The Woman Warrior*, Maxine Hong Kingston (fiction) *The Shining*, King (fiction)	Steadicam, a lightweight, portable mount for holding a motion-picture camera, first used in making a	*Taxi Driver*, Scorsese *Network*, Lumet *All the President's Men*, Alan J. Pakula *Face to Face*, Bergman

	World Events	Arts	Mass Media	Films and Videos
1976 (cont.)	Apple Computer company founded Two U.S. spacecraft land on Mars but find no signs of life Jimmy Carter elected president	*The Kiss of the Spider Woman*, Manuel Puig (fiction) *Roots*, Haley (nonfiction)	feature film (*Bound for Glory*) Louma (lightweight, modular, 25-foot) camera crane with remote-control camera head first used in filming a feature, *The Tenant* United States telecasts views from Mars worldwide *The McNeil-Lehrer Report* begins on PBS (TV)	*Seven Beauties*, Lina Wertmuller *In the Realm of the Senses*, Oshima *Harlan County U.S.A.*, Barbara Kopple (documentary) *Word Is Out*, Robert Epstein and Peter Adair (documentary) "Chulas fronteras," Les Blank (documentary) "Projection Instructions," Morgan Fisher (experimental)
1977	American space probes *Voyager 1* and *Voyager 2* are launched and two years later send back data and photographs of Jupiter Indira Ghandi of India arrested on charges of corruption President Carter pardons all Vietnam War draft evaders	Pompidou Center, Richard Rogers and Renzo Pieno (Paris architecture) Cindy Sherman begins her photographic series of herself in various movie roles	Eight-part TV dramatization of Alex Haley's book *Roots* is popular and critical success *The Lou Grant Show*, TV show (1977–82)	*Annie Hall*, Woody Allen *Star Wars*, Lucas *Equus*, Lumet *Close Encounters of the Third Kind*, Steven Spielberg *Providence*, Resnais *1900*, Bertolucci *Ceddo*, Sembène "Video Weavings," Stephen Beck (experimental video) "Turn to Your ~~Gods~~ Dogs," Richard Beveridge (experimental)
1978	In Nicaragua, Sandinista guerrilla war develops into a civil war that lasts until 1988 Vietnamese occupy Cambodia and end Khmer Rouge slaughter of Cambodians First "test-tube" baby born, in England	*Zoot Suit*, Valdez (play) *Betrayal*, Pinter (play) *Ain't Misbehavin'*, jazz musical celebrating the music of Fats Waller	120 million people see the U.S. TV movie *Holocaust* *Dallas*, TV show (1978–91) Laser videodisc players and videodiscs first marketed in U.S. 98% of all U.S. households have at least one television set	*The Deer Hunter*, Michael Cimino *Grease*, Randal Kleiser *Girlfriends*, Claudia Weill *Get Out Your Handkerchiefs*, Bertrand Blier *Autumn Sonata*, Bergman *The Marriage of Maria Braun*, Rainer Werner Fassbinder *Gates of Heaven*, Errol Morris (documentary)

	World Events	Arts	Mass Media	Films and Videos
1978 (cont.)	At Jonestown, Guyana, 909 American cultists commit suicide	Sound track albums for the movies *Saturday Night Fever* and *Grease* are popular	Gene Siskel and Roger Ebert first appear on a PBS film review show	"Daughter Rite," Michelle Citron (documentary)
1979	Shah of Iran forced into exile; new leader Ayatollah Khomeini Nuclear disaster averted at Three Mile Island, Pennsylvania Margaret Thatcher becomes first female British prime minister Sandinistas overthrow Nicaragua's President Somoza and establish Marxist government About 100 U.S. Embassy personnel taken hostage in Teheran, Iran Smallpox declared eradicated worldwide	*Sophie's Choice*, William Styron (fiction) *The Right Stuff*, Tom Wolfe (nonfiction) Spalding Gray begins to write and perform mostly autobiographical monologues *Evita*, Andrew Lloyd Webber and Tim Rice (musical)	Sony Walkman (portable audio cassette player) introduced in U.S. *The Far Side* comic strip begins *I Know Why the Caged Bird Sings*, TV adaptation of Maya Angelou's autobiography C-SPAN and ESPN cable networks founded	*Apocalypse Now*, Coppola *All That Jazz*, Bob Fosse *Breaking Away*, Peter Yates *Breaker Morant*, Bruce Beresford *My Brilliant Career*, Gillian Armstrong *Best Boy*, Ira Wohl (documentary) "Peliculas," Patrick Clancy (experimental) "Thriller," Sally Potter (experimental) "Hearts," Barbara Buckner (experimental video) "A Portrait of Light and Heat," Bill Viola (experimental video)
1980	USSR continues its invasion of Afghanistan Southern Rhodesia gains independence and becomes the republic of Zimbabwe Lech Walesa becomes leader of Polish trade union, Solidarity Iraq invades Iran, starting a war that lasts until 1988 and kills more than a million	*The Name of the Rose*, Umberto Eco (fiction) *Amadeus*, Shaffer (play)	*Cosmos* TV series with scientist and educator Carl Sagan on PBS Home dish antennas to receive TV signals from satellites begin to gain in popularity Cable News Network (CNN) begins U.S. TV networks begin to offer some captioning for hearing-impaired viewers	*Raging Bull*, Scorsese *Atlantic City*, Louis Malle *Melvin and Howard*, Jonathan Demme *The Empire Strikes Back*, Irvin Kershner *The Shining*, Kubrick *Berlin Alexanderplatz*, Fassbinder (TV miniseries later shown in theaters) *Moscow Does Not Believe in Tears*, Vladimir Menshev

	World Events	Arts	Mass Media	Films and Videos
1980 (cont.)	Mariel boat lift brings tens of thousands of Cubans to Florida Ronald Reagan elected president		First interactive videodisc: *How to Watch Pro Football*	*Kagemusha*, Kurosawa *Model*, Wiseman (documentary) (*The Life and Times of*) *Rosie the Riveter*, Connie Field (documentary)
1981	Iran releases remaining U.S. hostages First U.S. space shuttle successfully flown Scientists first identify AIDS Sandra Day O'Connor becomes first female U.S. Supreme Court justice Egyptian soldiers assassinate Egyptian President Anwar Sadat	*Sixty Stories*, Donald Barthelme (fiction) *A Soldier's Play*, Charles Fuller (play)	Walter Cronkite retires from regular TV broadcasting *Hill Street Blues*, TV show (1981–87) Highest-rated TV show (1981–82): *Dallas* MTV, a 24-hour-a-day music video channel, begins	*Zoot Suit*, Valdez (first Chicano Hollywood film) *Gallipoli*, Weir *Pixote*, Hector Babenco *Das Boot* (*The Boat*), Wolfgang Petersen *Céleste*, Percy Adlon *Mephisto*, Istvan Szabo "Ancient of Days," Viola (experimental videos, 1979–81)
1982	Argentina invades Falkland Islands, resulting in a war won by Britain Maya Lin's Vietnam Veterans' War Memorial with its 58,000 etched American names dedicated in Washington, D.C. First permanent implant of a mechanical heart in a human	*The Color Purple*, Alice Walker (fiction) *Cats*, Andrew Lloyd Webber and Trevor Nunn (musical that opens on Broadway) Popular songs: "Eye of the Tiger," from the film *Rocky III* and the "Chariots of Fire" melody from the film of the same title	28 million U.S. homes have cable TV *Cagney and Lacey*, TV show (1982–88) *Cheers*, TV show (1982–93) *USA Today*, newspaper available nationwide, begins publication Computer technology used to make images of settings and props for the film *Tron* Digital audio CDs first marketed	*Tootsie*, Sydney Pollack *E.T., the Extraterrestrial*, Spielberg *Blade Runner*, Ridley Scott *Fanny and Alexander*, Bergman *Night of the Shooting Stars*, Paola and Vittorio Taviani *Fitzcarraldo*, Herzog *Lola*, Fassbinder *Wend Kuuni* (*God's Gift*), Gaston Kaboré *Burden of Dreams*, Blank (documentary) "Reassemblage," Trinh T. Minh-ha (experimental documentary)

	World Events	Arts	Mass Media	Films and Videos
1983	President Reagan backs Contra rebels in their war with Marxist Nicaraguan government U.S. troops are sent into Grenada International introduction of highly addictive and destructive drug "crack cocaine"	American Telephone and Telegraph Building in New York City designed by Philip Johnson and John Burgee and regarded as an important postmodernist structure	*The Day After*, a TV movie about nuclear war, is seen by half of U.S. adults Final episode of TV show *M*A*S*H* seen by an estimated 50 million HBO begins producing feature films First civilian cellular phones hit the market	*El norte*, Gregory Nava *Betrayal*, David Jones *Local Hero*, Bill Forsyth *Entre nous*, Diane Kurys *Erendira*, Ruy Guerra *Koyaanisqatsi*, Godfrey Reggio (experimental documentary)
1984	Apple Macintosh computer first sold Indian army troops invade Sikh temple and kill 1,000 Sikh fundamentalists using the temple as a haven and headquarters Indian Prime Minister Indira Gandhi assassinated Ethiopia-Eritrea war, disease, and famine kill 1 million	*The Lover*, Marguerite Duras (fiction) *Love in the Time of Cholera*, García Márquez (fiction) *The Unbearable Lightness of Being*, Milan Kundera (fiction) *The House on Mango Street*, Sandra Cisneros (fiction) Sound track for *Purple Rain* is a huge success	PG-13 film rating begins *The Cosby Show*, TV show (1984–92) *Murder, She Wrote*, TV show (1984–96) U.S. Supreme Court rules that noncommercial private home videotaping of off-the-air programs is legal Criterion (company) releases *Citizen Kane* on laser videodisc	*Stranger Than Paradise*, Jim Jarmusch *This Is Spinal Tap*, Rob Reiner *Blood Simple*, Joel Coen *Frida*, Paul Leduc *Paris, Texas*, Wim Wenders *Yellow Earth*, Chen Kaige *The Times of Harvey Milk*, Robert Epstein (documentary) "In Heaven There Is No Beer?" Blank (documentary) *Marlene*, Maximillian Schell (documentary) "Thriller," Michael Jackson (video)
1985	Gorbachev becomes Soviet General Secretary Rock Hudson, movie star, dies of AIDS—first known celebrity to do so Gorbachev and Reagan meet for a summit in Geneva	*The Handmaid's Tale*, Margaret Atwood (fiction) *Black Robe*, Brian Moore (fiction) *Old Gringo*, Fuentes (fiction) *The Accidental Tourist*, Anne Tyler (fiction)	Home movie video revenues exceed those of theatrical revenues Sundance Film Festival founded by Robert Redford to promote independent films First 3-D IMAX film shown, in Japan	*Prizzi's Honor*, Huston *The Purple Rose of Cairo*, Allen *My Life as a Dog*, Lasse Hallström *Vagabond*, Agnès Varda *The Official Story*, Luis Puenzo *Ran*, Kurosawa

	World Events	Arts	Mass Media	Films and Videos
1985 (cont.)	Marxist Sandinistas gain control of Nicaragua; U.S. continues to support the Contra rebels The year is marked by terrorist hijackings, bombings, kidnappings, and murder, including at airports in Rome and Vienna	*Les liaisons dangereuses*, Christopher Hampton (play) *Fences*, August Wilson (play) *Biloxi Blues*, Neil Simon (play) *Les Miserables*, Alain Boublil and Claude-Michel Schönberg (musical)	*Desert Hearts*, first movie lesbian love story to obtain mainstream distribution First laser videodisc players and videodiscs both with digital sound	*Shoah*, Claude Lanzmann (documentary) *George Stevens: A Film Maker's Journey*, George Stevens Jr. (documentary) *The Man Who Envied Women*, Rainer (experimental) *Naked Spaces—Living Is Round*, Minh-ha (experimental documentary) "Standard Gauge," Fisher (experimental) "Roulement de billes" ("Rolling Balls"), Richard Barbeau (experimental video)
1986	U.S. space shuttle *Challenger* explodes shortly after lift-off killing entire crew Haitian dictator Jean-Claude Duvalier ousted by revolution and flees the country Corazon Aquino declared the winner of Philippine presidential election and President Ferdinand Marcos flees into exile Soviets orbit first long-term space station, *Mir* Nuclear accident at Chernobyl, Ukraine, pollutes Europe President Reagan admits that subordinates sold weapons illegally to Iran to raise money for Nicaraguan rebels 25,000 AIDS cases diagnosed in U.S.	*Paco's Story*, Larry Heinemann (fiction) *A Summons to Memphis*, Peter Taylor (fiction) *Phantom of the Opera*, Andrew Lloyd Webber and Charles Hart (musical)	Colorization of videos of older black-and-white films is controversial *L.A. Law*, TV show (1986–94) *The Oprah Winfrey Show*, TV talk show, begins Highest-rated TV show (1986–89): *The Cosby Show* *Calvin and Hobbes* comic strip begins Nintendo video game system hits U.S. market	*Blue Velvet*, David Lynch *Platoon*, Oliver Stone *True Stories*, David Byrne *Mona Lisa*, Neil Jordan *Tampopo*, Juzo Itami *Sherman's March*, Ross McElwee (documentary) *Mother Teresa*, Ann and Jeanette Petrie (documentary) *Rate It X*, Lucy Winer and Paula De Koenigsberg (documentary) *Private Practices: The Story of a Sex Surrogate*, Kirby Dick (documentary) "Street of Crocodiles," Timothy and Stephen Quay (experimental fiction) *Home of the Brave*, Laurie Anderson (documentary)

	World Events	Arts	Mass Media	Films and Videos
1987	World population: 5 billion Iran-Contra congressional report faults President Reagan Gorbachev and Reagan sign a treaty banning all short- and medium-range nuclear weapons in Europe	*The Bonfire of the Vanities*, Wolfe (fiction) *Beloved*, Toni Morrison (fiction) *Driving Miss Daisy*, Alfred Uhry (play) Sound track for *Dirty Dancing* is a huge hit	Home videotape rentals in U.S. continue to grow Iran-Contra congressional hearings televised live *Eyes on the Prize*, TV series on the civil rights movement, shown on PBS	*The Dead*, Huston *Full Metal Jacket*, Kubrick *The Last Emperor*, Bertolucci *Red Sorghum*, Zhang Yimou *A Taxing Woman*, Itami *Yeelen* (*Brightness*), Souleymane Cissé "Damned If You Don't," Su Friedrich (experimental fiction)
1988	Soviet troops begin retreat from Afghanistan UN mediates cease fire between Iran and Iraq; Iraq attacks rebelling Kurds Uprising by Palestinians in West Bank and Gaza Strip Crack cocaine increasingly used in U.S. cities Vice President George Bush elected president	*The Satanic Verses*, Salman Rushdie (fiction) (condemned by Muslim fundamentalists, who force Rushdie into hiding) *The Player*, Michael Tolkin (fiction) *The Heidi Chronicles*, Wendy Wasserstein (play) *Buster Keaton*, Jeff Koons (wood sculpture)	Morphing first used in making parts of a feature film, *Willow* *P.O.V.* series of documentary films begins on PBS *Roseanne*, TV show (1988–94) TNT cable network founded *Oxford English Dictionary* becomes available on CD-ROM Apple Macintosh with CD-ROM player can play music CDs	*The Unbearable Lightness of Being*, Philip Kaufman *The Last Temptation of Christ*, Scorsese *Dangerous Liaisons*, Stephen Frears *Little Vera*, Vasily Pichul *Saaraba* (*Utopia*), Amadou Seck *The Thin Blue Line*, Morris (documentary) *Comic Book Confidential*, Ron Mann (documentary) *Hotel Terminus, the Life and Times of Klaus Barbie*, Ophüls (documentary)
1989	In Czechoslovakia, large peaceful opposition to Soviet dominance Prodemocracy students occupy Tiananmen Square in Beijing; two months later, government uses tanks to disperse them; thousands believed killed Berlin Wall torn down	*The Mambo Kings Play Songs of Love*, Oscar Hijuelos (fiction) *The General in His Labyrinth*, García Márquez (fiction) *The Joy Luck Club*, Amy Tan (fiction) *When Harry Met Sally*, popular film sound track	U.S. National Film Registry established to recognize significant American films; the first group announced includes *Citizen Kane* and *Casablanca* Time, Inc. buys Warner Communications, creating the world's largest entertainment group	*Drugstore Cowboy*, Gus Van Sant *Mystery Train*, Jarmusch *Do the Right Thing*, Spike Lee *Sex, Lies, and Videotape*, Steven Soderbergh *The Little Mermaid* (Disney animation) *Lawrence of Arabia*, rereleased in revised and restored version *My Left Foot*, Jim Sheridan

	World Events	Arts	Mass Media	Films and Videos
1989 (cont.)	Playwright Vaclav Havel becomes president of Czechoslovakia		Most popular TV shows (1989–90): *Roseanne* and *The Cosby Show*	*Yaaba*, Idrissa Ouedraogo *Roger & Me*, Michael Moore (satirical documentary) "You Take Care Now," Ann Marie Fleming (experimental documentary)
1990	Mandela freed from prison in South Africa Yugoslavia moving toward split-up Boris Yeltsin resigns from Soviet Communist Party Iraq invades Kuwait; various diplomatic solutions sought Germany reunited Walesa elected Poland's president Haiti holds first democratic elections	*The Snapper*, Roddy Doyle (fiction) *Orphée*, Philip Glass (music) and Jean Cocteau (libretto, screenplay for his film of the same title) *Mo' Better Blues*, Branford Marsalis (music from film of same title)	NC-17 rating instituted; *Henry and June* first film so rated *The Civil War*, 11-hour TV documentary on PBS, directed by Ken Burns *Twin Peaks*, TV show directed by David Lynch *Billboard* announces that home video revenue is now twice that of theatrical box offices	*GoodFellas*, Scorsese *Reversal of Fortune*, Barbet Schroeder *To Sleep with Anger*, Charles Burnett *The Grifters*, Frears *Life Is Sweet*, Mike Leigh *Ju Dou*, Zhang *Tilaï*, Ouedraogo *Finzin (A Dance for the Heroes)*, Cheick Oumar Sissoko *Berkeley in the Sixties*, Mark Kitchell (documentary) *Paris Is Burning*, Jennie Livingston (documentary) *Privilege*, Rainer (experimental fiction)
1991	U.S. and its UN allies defeat Iraq in 100-hour battle and free Kuwait Rajiv Gandhi, prime minister of India, assassinated Boris Yeltsin elected president of Russia Bosnia and Herzegovina, parts of former Yugoslavia, wage civil war Coup against Gorbachev fails, Communist rule ends in the USSR, and cold war ends	*The Sweet Hereafter*, Russell Banks (fiction) *Lost in Yonkers*, Simon (play)	Morphing used in parts of *Terminator 2* to show the transformation of a character into various other characters Highest-rated TV show (1990–91): *Cheers*	*Europa, Europa*, Agnieszka Holland *Raise the Red Lantern*, Zhang *Sango Malo (The Village Teacher)*, Bassek ba Kobhio *Hearts of Darkness: A Filmmaker's Apocalypse*, Fax Bahr and George Hickenlooper (documentary) "First Comes Love," Friedrich (experimental documentary)

	World Events	Arts	Mass Media	Films and Videos
1992	Jury in Rodney King's state trial finds police defendants not guilty; parts of L.A. riot, leading to 58 dead and hundreds of millions of dollars in property damage USSR divides into 15 nations, including Russia Leader of the Peruvian terrorist group The Shining Path is arrested Thousands die in Muslim-Hindu conflict in India Bill Clinton elected president	*All the Pretty Horses*, Cormac McCarthy (fiction) *Angels in America*, Tony Kushner (two-part play) Sound track with Whitney Houston from *The Bodyguard* becomes best-selling sound track of all time	Johnny Carson retires as host of *The Tonight Show* (TV) and is replaced by Jay Leno Internet begins with the "Internet Society," a collection of 1 million linked host computers	*Unforgiven*, Clint Eastwood *The Player*, Altman *Reservoir Dogs*, Quentin Tarantino *Like Water for Chocolate*, Alfonso Arau *The Crying Game*, Jordan *Quartier Mozart*, Jean-Pierre Bekolo *Guelwaar*, Sembène *A Brief History of Time*, Morris (documentary) *Brother's Keeper*, Joe Berlinger and Bruce Sinofsky (documentary) "Women Who Made the Movies," Gwendolyn Foster and Wheeler Dixon (documentary) *Visions of Light: The Art of Cinematography*, Arnold Glassman, Todd McCarthy, and Stuart Samuels (documentary)
1993	Israel and PLO formally recognize each other Warring parties in former Yugoslavia persist despite outside diplomatic pressures Czechoslovakia divides into Czech Republic and Slovakia Bureau of Alcohol, Tobacco, and Firearms agents attempt to enter Branch Davidians compound in Waco, Texas; gunfights end in fatal fire	*Arcadia*, Stoppard (play set in 1809 and present) *Full Moon*, Bill Irwin and David Shiner (mime) *Marilyn*, Ezra Laderman (opera about Marilyn Monroe)	Last original *Cheers* episode draws record TV audience *The X-Files* first airs, on Fox Network	*Schindler's List*, Spielberg *Short Cuts*, Altman *The Ballad of Little Jo*, Maggie Greenwald *Orlando*, Potter *Naked*, Leigh *The Piano*, Jane Campion *Farewell My Concubine*, Chen *Thirty-Two Short Films about Glenn Gould*, François Girard (documentary) *The Wonderful, Horrible Life of Leni Riefenstahl*, Ray Müller (documentary) *Blue*, Derek Jarman (experimental)

	World Events	Arts	Mass Media	Films and Videos
1994	Civil wars in Yemen, Georgia (part of former USSR), and Rwanda Mandela elected president in first multiracial South African election Chechens seeking independence from Russia begin protracted guerrilla warfare U.S.-led occupation of Haiti leads to reinstatement of democratically elected president World Trade Center bombed in first foreign terrorist attack on U.S. soil Channel Tunnel (Chunnel) links Britain and France Mexican Indian guerrillas in southern state of Chiapas demand more land and self-rule; ruling party candidate assassinated and replaced by Ernesto Zedillo, later elected Mexican president	*Felicia's Journey*, William Trevor (fiction) *The Ice Storm*, Rick Moody (fiction) *Trainspotting*, Irvine Welsh (fiction) *The Hour We Knew Nothing of Each Other*, Peter Handke (100-minute wordless play with sound effects) *La belle et la bête*, Cocteau's film without sound track but with supertitles and live music composed by Philip Glass ("an opera for ensemble and film") *The Dangerous Liaisons*, Conrad Susa and Philip Littell (opera) Sound track for *The Lion King* is a huge hit Andy Warhol Museum opens in Pittsburgh	Steven Spielberg, Jeffrey Katzenberg, and David Geffen form Dreamworks SKG to produce theatrical films, animation, television programs, records, and interactive media Independent Film Channel offered on some cable systems (Short) IMAX 3-D films shown in U.S. (previously shown in Japan and Europe) More than 80% of all U.S. households have at least one VCR Marketing films first in video and perhaps later to theaters is a small trend DirectTV, Digital TV, offers multiple channels from a satellite Kodak introduces a digital imaging system in many U.S. stores, allowing customers to scan a photograph into the system, alter the image, and print out new copies Megaplexing of the U.S. begins when AMC Entertainment opens a megaplex in Dallas	*Pulp Fiction*, Tarantino *Vanya on 42nd Street*, Malle *Ed Wood*, Tim Burton *Natural Born Killers*, Stone *Exotica*, Atom Egoyan *Il Postino (The Postman)*, Michael Radford *Red*, Krzysztof Kieslowski *Burnt by the Sun*, Nikita Mikhalkov *To Live*, Zhang *Eat Drink Man Woman*, Ang Lee *The Lion King*, Disney animation *High School II*, Wiseman (documentary) *Crumb*, Terry Zwigoff (documentary) *The Troubles We've Seen*, Ophüls (documentary) *Hoop Dreams*, Steve James (documentary) *Carmen Miranda: Bananas Is My Business*, Helena Solberg (documentary) "A Great Day in Harlem," Jean Bach (documentary) "Cremaster 4," Matthew Barney (experimental)
1995	American astronauts dock with Russian space station *Mir* and work with cosmonauts	*Seven Guitars*, Wilson (play) *Rent*, Jonathan Larson (musical)	*Toy Story* is first feature film made entirely with computer animation	*A Little Princess*, Alfonso Cuarón *Welcome to the Dollhouse*, Todd Solondz

	World Events	Arts	Mass Media	Films and Videos
1995 (cont.)	Terrorists use gas in Japan and a bomb in Oklahoma City to kill civilians U.S.-brokered peace plan for Bosnia-Herzegovina agreed to by presidents of Serbia, Bosnia, and Croatia Yitzhak Rabin, Israeli prime minister, assassinated by right-wing Israeli radical	Untitled 8½-by-11-inch film stills, Cindy Sherman *24 Frames per Second*, Bill T. Jones, and Lyons Opera Ballet (dance homage to the Lumière Bros.)	Percentage of Americans reading a newspaper daily continues its decades-long decline Two studies show that the average American continues to spend more on books each year than on recorded music or home videos Disney and Capital Cities/ABC merge and form world's largest media company *Calvin and Hobbes* comic strip ends	*To Die For*, Van Sant *Richard III*, Richard Loncraine *Babe*, Chris Noonan *Hate*, Mathieu Kassovitz *Black is . . . Black ain't*, Marlon T. Riggs (documentary) *Orson Welles: The One-Man Band*, Vassili Silovic (documentary) *Theremin: An Electronic Odyssey*, Steven M. Martin (documentary) "A Cinema of Unease," Sam Neill and Judy Rymer (documentary on cinema of New Zealand) "Buried Secrets," Viola (experimental video and audio)
1996	Boris Yeltsin reelected president of Russia Chechens (in southern Russian republic) end uprising with temporary peace agreement War and famine in eastern Zaire kill massive numbers of people Suicide bombings by militant Muslims kill 61 in Israel, hamper peace talks, and contribute to election defeat of Israel's ruling party Unabomber captured and convicted after 17-year bombing spree Bomb explodes during Olympics in Atlanta, Georgia	*Angela's Ashes: A Memoir*, Frank McCourt (nonfiction) *The Tailor of Panama*, John Le Carré (fiction) *Selected Stories*, Alice Munro (fiction) *Ship Fever and Other Stories*, Andrea Barrett (fiction) *In the Beauty of the Lilies*, John Updike (fiction)	Sundance (independent) Channel offered on some cable and satellite systems *The Phil Donahue* [TV talk] *Show* ends Federal Communications Commission standards for digital TVs include wider screens and sharper pictures than analog TVs 45 million people using the Internet, two-thirds of them in North America	*Fargo*, Coen *The English Patient*, Anthony Minghella *Trainspotting*, Danny Boyle *Secrets & Lies*, Leigh *Breaking the Waves*, Lars von Trier *Prisoner of the Mountains*, Sergei Bodrov *Shall We Dance?*, Masayuki Suo *Hide and Seek*, Friedrich (fiction and documentary) *The Celluloid Closet*, Rob Epstein and Jeffrey Friedman (documentary) *A Personal Journey with Martin Scorsese through American Movies* (documentary) *The Devil Never Sleeps*, Lourdes Portillo (documentary)

	World Events	Arts	Mass Media	Films and Videos
1996 (cont.)				*Lumière and Company*, Sarah Moon (documentary of 40 films, each by a different director, each less than a minute long and shot on the Lumière Brothers' original 1895 camera) *Sergei Eisenstein: Autobiography*, Oleg Kovalov (documentary) "Trouble in the Image," O'Neill (experimental)
1997	China's top leader, Deng Xiaoping, dies Scottish embryologist announces sheep cloning Labor Party's Tony Blair becomes U.K. prime minister and ends 18 years of Conservative control Rebel forces capture the rest of Zaire; longtime dictator Mobutu Sese Seko flees into exile; country is renamed Democratic Republic of Congo or, later, Congo Britain returns control of Hong Kong to China, ending 156 years of British rule Unmanned *Pathfinder* lands on Mars; first mobile explorer of another planet sends data and photographs to earth	*How I Learned to Drive*, Paula Vogel (play) *The Lion King*, a Disney musical based on the film, opens on Broadway Sound track for *Titanic* is a huge success *Film Noir*, Carly Simon (CD)	*Star Wars* revised slightly, rereleased to theaters, and passes *E.T.* as highest-grossing movie in history (until *Titanic* appears in 1998) 413 movies released in the U.S., 125 more than in 1987 U.S. movie box office receipts set record Broadcast and cable networks begin using a four-part age-based rating system for most of their programs Digital videodiscs (DVDs) and DVD players first marketed in the U.S., but not all studios agree to market their films on them; most models also play music CDs NASA reports 45 million visit its computer sites daily for information about the *Pathfinder* exploration of Mars	*L.A. Confidential*, Curtis Hanson *The Ice Storm*, Ang Lee *Eve's Bayou*, Kasi Lemmons *The Apostle*, Robert Duvall *The Sweet Hereafter*, Egoyan *The Full Monty*, Peter Cattaneo *The Wings of the Dove*, Iain Softley *Will It Snow for Christmas?*, Sandrine Veysset *Life Is Beautiful*, Roberto Benigni *Taste of Cherry*, Abbas Kiarostami *Welcome Back, Mr. McDonald*, Koki Mitani *Princess Mononoke*, Hayao Miyazaki (animation) *Fast, Cheap & Out of Control*, Morris (documentary) *Public Housing*, Wiseman (documentary) *Waco: The Rules of Engagement*, William Gazecki (documentary)

	World Events	Arts	Mass Media	Films and Videos
1997 (cont.)	Algerian Islamic extremists continue to massacre civilians; more than 60,000 killed since 1992		Compaq introduces the PC theater: combination of computer and large-screen TV More than 31,000 movie screens in the U.S.	"2 or 3 Things but Nothing for Sure," Tina DiFeliciantonio and Jane C. Wagner (experimental documentary) "Bill Viola: Trilogy (Fire, Water, Breath)," (experimental installations)
1998	Ireland, Britain, and the U.S. broker peace settlement for Northern Ireland, which Irish voters later accept President Suharto of Indonesia is forced to step down after 32 years in power Asian economic crisis continues to worsen and to hurt world economies Terrorist bombs near U.S. embassies in Kenya and Tanzania kill 258 India and Pakistan, declared enemies, conduct independent nuclear tests	*Cloudsplitter: A Novel*, Banks *Hours*, Michael Cunningham (fiction) *Wit*, Margaret Edson (play) *Elaborate Lives: The Legend of Aida*, Tim Rice and Elton John (first Disney musical not based on a film)	*Titanic* passes *Star Wars* as the highest-grossing movie in history, but *Gone with the Wind* has sold more tickets *Seinfeld* TV show airs its last episode Adrian Lyne's version of *Lolita* is shown in the U.S.—first on Showtime Survey reveals that Internet use is up (an estimated 30 to 60 million users); TV- and VCR-watching and reading are all down Ticket sales for summer movies set U.S. record Four interactive movies released on DVD allow viewers to periodically choose plot developments Some high-definition television reception becomes available in more than 30 U.S. cities	*The Truman Show*, Weir *Happiness*, Solondz *Smoke Signals*, Chris Eyre *Touch of Evil* (1958) rereleased in a revised and restored version *Shakespeare in Love*, John Madden *Croupier*, Mike Hodges *Run Lola Run*, Tom Tykwer *Dreamlife of Angels*, Erick Zonca *Central Station*, Walter Salles *The Terrorist* (a.k.a. *Malli*), Santosh Sivan *Best Man*, Wohl (documentary sequel) *Wild Man Blues*, Kopple (documentary about Woody Allen) "Everest," David Breashears, Stephen Judson, and Greg MacGillivray (documentary, the most commercially successful film in IMAX history) *Divorce Iranian Style*, Kim Longinotto and Ziba Mir-Hosseini (documentary) *The Farm: Angola U.S.A.*, Liz Garbus, Jonathan Stack, and Wilbert Rideau (documentary)

	World Events	Arts	Mass Media	Films and Videos
1998 (cont.)				"Human Remains," Jay Rosenblatt (experimental documentary) "Mother and Son," Alexander Sokurov (experimental)
1999	President Clinton impeached by U.S. House of Representatives but acquitted by Senate King Abdullah succeeds King Hussein of Jordan NATO sends ground forces into former Yugoslavia to protect the ethic Albanian majority in Kosovo and bombs Serbia Earthquakes kill 21,000 in Turkey U.N. declares East Timor independent of Indonesia; pro-Indonesian forces attack the new nation U.S. turns control of Panama Canal over to Panama Russian President Boris Yeltsin resigns, succeeded by Vladimir Putin	*Interpreter of Maladies*, Jhumpa Lahiri (fiction) *A Star Called Henry*, Doyle (fiction) *Close Range: Wyoming Stories*, Annie Proulx (fiction) *Dinner with Friends*, Donald Margulies (play) *Betty's Summer Vacation*, Christopher Durang (play) *Songs and Stories from "Moby Dick,"* Laurie Anderson (stage multimedia production) Score for video reissue of the 1931 *Dracula*, Philip Glass *Jazz in Film*, Terence Blanchard (CD)	Highest summer movie revenues ever: $2.9 billion Nearly 91% of all American homes have a VCR; most have more than one *Big Brother* premieres in Europe, reality-based TV show features 9 people living under total surveillance for 100 days *The Sopranos*, TV show, is criticl and popular success Video game software sales reach $6.2 billion, $1.1 billion dollars less than domestic movie box office revenues DVD audio and super CD recorded audio formats become available 150 million Internet users worldwide; over half are in the U.S. Digital projection used to show *Star Wars: Episode I* on selected standard theatrical screens	*Boys Don't Cry*, Kimberly Peirce *American Beauty*, Sam Mendes *The Matrix*, Andy and Larry Wachowski "George Lucas in Love," Joe Nussbaum (first shown on Internet) *Felicia's Journey*, Egoyan *Titus*, Julie Taymor *Topsy-Turvy*, Leigh *American Movie*, Chris Smith (documentary) *Buena Vista Social Club*, Wenders (documentary) *Keeper of the Frame*, Mark McLaughlin (documentary on film preservation and restoration) *Hands on a Hard Body*, S. R. Bindler (documentary) *Mr. Death: The Rise and Fall of Fred A. Leuchter Jr.*, Morris (documentary) *Genghis Blues*, Roko Belic (documentary) *My Best Fiend: Klaus Kinski*, Herzog (documentary) *Cinéma Vérité*, Peter Wintonick (a documentary about the documentary) "Encounter in the Third Dimension," Ben Strassen (documentary about 3-D films)

	World Events	Arts	Mass Media	Films and Videos
1999 (cont.)			Silent American film classic *Greed* partially restored with inclusion of still photographs and premiered on Turner Classic Movies	"Negative Space," Christopher Petit (documentary) "Soliloquy," Shirin Neshat (film installation) "In Camera," Edward Stewart and Stephanie Smith (experimental) "Outer Space," Peter Tscherassky (experimental)
2000	Longtime Syrian president Hafez al-Assad dies; succeeded by his son Human genome, the entire genetic code for a human being, completely mapped in a rough draft Yugoslav President Milosevic steps down from office after domestic protests, general strikes, and international appeals More than a month after a close election, Texas governor George W. Bush declared U.S. president-elect	*Blonde: A Novel*, Joyce Carol Oates (fiction base on Marilyn Monroe) *Cats*, Weber and Nunn, longest-running Broadway production, closes after nearly 18 years run *Dead Man Walking*, Jake Heggie and Terrence McNally (opera) *Nighthawks*, Lynn Rosen (play based on Edward Hopper paintings)	Final original installment of *Peanuts* comic strip; thereafter past installments are reprinted First mass-market success in e-book format is Stephen King's *Riding the Bullet* *Life* magazine ceases publication "Quantum Project," first major film production developed exclusively for Internet distribution "The New Arrival," first film allowing viewers to navigate around characters and props, shown at Cannes and later on Internet "Dickson Experimental Sound Film" reunited with original, restored sound Museo Nationale del Cinema in Turin, Italy, opens, the world's biggest cinema museum	*You Can Count on Me*, Kenneth Lonergan *Memento*, Christopher Nolan *Gladiator*, Scott *State and Main*, David Mamet *Shadow of the Vampire*, E. Elias Merhige *Before Night Falls*, Julian Schnabel *Girlfight*, Karyn Kusama *George Washington*, David Gordon Green *The Claim*, Michael Winterbottom *Ratcatcher*, Lynn Ramsay *Amores perros*, Alejandro Gonzalez *Faithless*, Liv Ullmann *Aimee and Jaguar*, Max Fäberböck *Beau travail*, Claire Denis *Yi-Yi*, (a.k.a. *A One and a Two*), Edward Yang *In the Mood for Love*, Wong Kar-wai *Crouching Tiger, Hidden Dragon*, Ang Lee *Dark Days*, Marc Singer (documentary) *Divine Trash*, Steve Yeager (documentary)

	World Events	Arts	Mass Media	Films and Videos
2000 (cont.)			*Time Code*, one of first major feature films recorded entirely with digital technology More than 3,000 Internet radio stations More than half of all U.S. households have a computer U.S. has 37,000 movie theater screens Foreign cinema revenues now make up 55% of U.S. film industry income Modest, critically acclaimed films often earn much more in video than initial theatrical release; *Boys Don't Cry*, for example, takes in $3.7 million in the theaters but $17.5 million in 10 weeks of video rentals	*Calle 54*, Fernando Trueba (documentary) "The God of Day Had Gone Down upon Him," Brakhage (experimental) "Kyupi Kyupi I++," Kyupi Kyupi (a Japanese artists' collective) (experimental laserdisc)

SOURCES

Barnouw, Erik. *Tube of Plenty: The Evolution of American Television*. 2nd ed. New York: Oxford UP, 1990.

Beaver, Frank E. *Dictionary of Film Terms: The Aesthetic Companion to Film Analysis*. Rev. ed. New York: Twayne, 1994.

———. "An Outline of Film History." *Dictionary of Film Terms*. New York: McGraw-Hill, 1983.

Benét's Reader's Encyclopedia. 3rd ed. Ed. Katherine Baker Siepmann. New York: Harper, 1987.

Bohn, Thomas W., and Richard L. Stromgren. "A Film Chronology." *Light and Shadows: A History of Motion Pictures*. 3rd ed. Palo Alto: Mayfield, 1987. xiv–xlv.

Brooks, Tim, and Earle Marsh. *The Complete Directory to Prime Time Network and Cable TV Shows, 1946-Present*. 7th ed. New York : Ballantine Books, 1999.

Brownstone, David M., and Irene M. Franck. *Timelines of the Arts and Literature*. New York: Harper, 1994.

———. *Timelines of the Twentieth Century: A Chronology of 7,500 Key Events, Discoveries, and People That Shaped Our Century*. Boston: Little, Brown, 1996.

Bywater, Tim, and Thomas Sobchack. *Introduction to Film Criticism: Major Critical Approaches to Narrative Film*. New York: Longman, 1989.

Chronicle of the Twentieth Century. Ed. Clifton Daniel. New York: Dorling, 1995.

Cook, David. *A History of Narrative Film*. 3rd ed. New York: Norton, 1996.

Ellis, Jack C. *The Documentary Idea: A Critical History of English-Language Documentary Film and Video*. Englewood Cliffs, NJ: Prentice, 1989.

———. *A History of Film*. 4th ed. Boston: Allyn, 1995.

Gomery, Douglas. *Movie History: A Survey*. Belmont, CA: Wadsworth, 1991.

Greenspan, Karen. *The Timetables of Women's History: A Chronology of the Most Important People and Events in Women's History*. New York: Simon, 1994.

Grun, Bernard. *The Timetables of History: A Horizontal Linkage of People and Events*. 3rd ed. New York: Simon, 1991.

Hilliard, Robert L., and Michael C. Keith. *The Broadcast Century: A Biography of American Broadcasting*. Boston: Focal, 1992.

Kane, Joseph Nathan. *Famous First Facts: A Record of First Happenings, Discoveries, and Inventions in American History*. 5th ed. New York: Wilson, 1997.

Katz, Ephraim. *The Film Encyclopedia*. 3rd ed. Rev. Fred Klein and Ronald Dean Nolen. New York: Harper, 1998.

Mast, Gerald, and Bruce F. Kawin. *A Short History of the Movies* 7th ed. Boston: Allyn and Bacon, 2000.

McNeil, Alex. *Total Television: The Comprehensive Guide to Programming from 1948 to the Present*. New York: Penguin, 1996.

Monaco, James. *How to Read a Film: Movies, Media, Multimedia*. 3rd ed. New York: Oxford UP, 2000.

Nowell-Smith, Geoffrey, general ed. *The Oxford History of World Cinema*. Oxford: Oxford UP, 1996.

Ochoa, George, and Melinda Corey. *The Timeline Book of the Arts*. New York: Ballantine, 1995.

Polan, Dana. "History of the American Cinema." *Film Quarterly* 45.3 (Spring 1992): 54–57.

Rood, Karen L. *American Culture after World War II*. Detroit: Gale, 1994. Pages xix–xxx consist of two timelines, works and events.

Samuelson, D. "Equipment Inventions That Have Changed the Way Films Are Made." *American Cinematographer* 75.8 (1994): 74, 76.

Sklar, Robert. *Film: An International History of the Medium*. Englewood Cliffs, NJ: Prentice; New York: Abrams, 1993.

Strauss, William, and Neil Howe. *Generations: The History of America's Future, 1584–2069*. New York: Morrow, 1991.

Thompson, Kristin, and David Bordwell. *Film History: An Introduction*. New York: McGraw, 1994.

Winston, Brian. "Z for Zoetrope." *Sight and Sound* July 1998: 28–30.

Other Sources

Various issues of *Billboard*, the *Los Angeles Times*, the *New York Times*, and the *World Almanac*.

On the Web: many newspapers, magazines, and journals accessed via Nexis; information on the Internet Movie Database (IMD); and reviews accessed via Movie Review Query Engine (MRQE).

How to Read Film Credits

Most movies now run a long list of credits at the end identifying the many people who worked on the film. But did you ever wonder what a gaffer does, or a best boy, or a grip? To help you appreciate all the work involved in making a typical movie, the closing credits from *The Player* are reprinted here along with brief explanations of the terms that a typical viewer might not know.

The chapters of this book explain the roles of the professionals with the high-profile jobs: producers, directors, cinematographers, editors, writers, composers, designers, and actors. In *The Player*, these people are identified in the opening credits. (In many older films, the entire crew is listed in the opening credits, but that is now rare.) The closing credits, listed here, identify all the actors and everyone else associated with the production but not listed at the film's beginning.

A caution: Film credits do not always indicate accurately who did what. Some job titles are largely ceremonial, favors to friends, supporters, or movie executives with a lot of clout. Two films may use a different term to indicate the same type of work. Then, too, some job titles are simply vague, and others (such as *construction coordinator* and *construction foreman*, and *promotion* and *publicity*) are synonymous or overlapping. All these caveats aside, most of the titles and descriptions here accurately describe who did what. Although you cannot always know what certain producers do, you can be certain what a Foley artist and a dolly grip do.

CLOSING CREDITS FOR *THE PLAYER*

CAST

These actors have major roles and appear in several scenes. Except for Sydney Pollack's name, their names also appear in the opening credits.

Griffin Mill	TIM ROBBINS
June Gudmundsdottir	GRETA SCACCHI
Walter Stuckel	FRED WARD
Detective Avery	WHOOPI GOLDBERG
Larry Levy	PETER GALLAGHER
Joel Levison	BRION JAMES
Bonnie Sherow	CYNTHIA STEVENSON
David Kahane	VINCENT D'ONOFRIO
Andy Civella	DEAN STOCKWELL
Tom Oakley	RICHARD E. GRANT
Dick Mellen	SYDNEY POLLACK
Detective DeLongpre	LYLE LOVETT
Celia	DINA MERRILL
Jan	ANGELA HALL

These actors have minor roles. Most of them appear in only one scene.

Sandy	LEAH AYRES
Jimmy Chase	PAUL HEWITT
Reg Goldman	RANDALL BATINKOFF
Steve Reeves	JEREMY PIVEN
Whitney Gersh	GINA GERSHON
Frank Murphy	FRANK BARHYDT
Marty Grossman	MIKE E. KAPLAN
Gar Girard	KEVIN SCANNELL
Witness	MARGERY BOND
Detective Broom	SUSAN EMSHWILLER
Phil	BRIAN BROPHY
Eric Schecter	MICHAEL TOLKIN
Carl Schecter	STEPHEN TOLKIN
Natalie	NATALIE STRONG
Waiter	PETE KOCH
Trixie	PAMELA BOWEN
Rocco	JEFF WESTON

AS THEMSELVES

These are all of the sixty-five cameos—brief roles played by well-known people.

STEVE ALLEN	MAXINE JOHN-JAMES
RICHARD ANDERSON	SALLY KELLERMAN
RENE AUBERJONOIS	SALLY KIRKLAND
HARRY BELAFONTE	JACK LEMMON
SHARI BELAFONTE	MARLEE MATLIN
KAREN BLACK	ANDIE MacDOWELL
MICHAEL BOWEN	MALCOLM McDOWELL
GARY BUSEY	JAYNE MEADOWS
ROBERT CARRADINE	MARTIN MULL

CHARLES CHAMPLIN	JENNIFER NASH
CHER	NICK NOLTE
JAMES COBURN	ALEXANDRA POWERS
CATHY LEE CROSBY	BERT REMSEN
JOHN CUSACK	GUY REMSEN
BRAD DAVIS	PATRICIA RESNICK
PAUL DOOLEY	BURT REYNOLDS
THEREZA ELLIS	JACK RILEY
PETER FALK	JULIA ROBERTS
FELICIA FARR	MIMI ROGERS
KASIA FIGURA	ANNIE ROSS
LOUISE FLETCHER	ALAN RUDOLPH
DENNIS FRANZ	JILL ST. JOHN
TERI GARR	SUSAN SARANDON
LEEZA GIBBONS	ADAM SIMON
SCOTT GLENN	ROD STEIGER
JEFF GOLDBLUM	JOAN TEWKESBURY
ELLIOTT GOULD	BRIAN TOCHI
JOEL GREY	LILY TOMLIN
DAVID ALAN GRIER	ROBERT WAGNER
BUCK HENRY	RAY WALSTON
ANJELICA HUSTON	BRUCE WILLIS
KATHY IRELAND	MARVIN YOUNG
STEVE JAMES	

These are all of the sixty-five cameos—brief roles played by well-known people.

Works closely with the producer(s) on artistic and financial matters. Unlike some "producers," the associate producer has day-to-day involvement with the making of the film.

The director's assistants; typically they keep track of scheduling, manage crowd scenes, supervise rehearsals, and prepare call sheets and production reports.

Manages the production crew and the business arrangements for each day's shooting, such as housing, meals, transportation, and payroll.

Associate Producer — DAVID LEVY

Unit Production Manager — TOM UDELL

First Assistant Director — ALLAN NICHOLS

Second Assistant Director — CC BARNES

Responsible for the business and administrative aspects of making a film; assisted by the associate producer.

A.k.a. Production Manager. Supervises and coordinates all business and technical matters.

Often the film editor is listed only in the opening credits. For *The Player*, the opening credits list Geraldine Peroni as the editor; thus, this listing is a puzzle. Perhaps the credit here should have read "Assistant Film Editor." Or perhaps Maysie Hoy edited only the clip from *Habeas Corpus*, the film-within-the-film in *The Player*.

Film Editor — MAYSIE HOY

Production Executives — CLAUDIA LEWIS, PAMELA HEDLEY

Production Supervisor — JIM CHESNEY

Decides how to decorate the indoor sets with furniture, props, art, and so on.

Creates the look of the film and runs the art department; ultimately responsible for all the visuals in the film, including architecture, locations, sets, decor, props, costumes, and makeup.

Art Director — JERRY FLEMING

Set Decorator — SUSAN EMSHWILLER

Leadman — PETER BORCK

Location Manager — JACK KNEY

Finds locations for shooting and negotiates for their use.

The camera crew; they maintain the equipment, load the film, and use a clapboard or comparable electronic device to mark the beginning of each take.

In *The Player*, one scene occurs in a karaoke bar, where videos are playing in the background. This person made those videos.

First Assistant Camera — ROBERT REED ALTMAN

Second Assistant Camera — CARY McKRYSTAL

Third Assistant Camera — CRAIG FINETTI

Karaoke Videos — LARRY "DOC" KARMAN

The editor's assistants; they splice the film, maintain the editing equipment, and keep records.

Assistant Editor
Second Assistant Editor
Apprentice Editor

A. MICHELLE PAGE
ALISA HALE
DYLAN TICHENOR

Responsible for the final sound track; supervises the mixer, ADR (automated dialogue replacement) editor, dialogue editor, sound effects editor, music editor, and assistant sound editor.

Supervising Sound Editor
Dialogue Editors

MICHAEL REDBOURN
JOSEPH HOLSEN
ED LACHMANN
KEN BURTON
BILL WARD

Edits the music to make sure it complements the film's action and the other elements of the sound track.

Sound Effects Editor
Assistant Sound Editor

Music Editor
Music Scoring Mixer
Orchestration By

BILL BERNSTEIN
JOHN VIGRAN
THOMAS PASATIERI

Blends and balances the tracks of the various film scores.

Arranges the score for the parts of the orchestra.

Postproduction technicians who mix vocals, sound effects, music, and silence to produce the master sound track.

Re-Recording Mixers

MATTHEW IADAROLA
STANLEY KASTNER
RICH GOOCH
JOHN POST
PAUL HOLTZBORN
BOB DESCHAINE
DAVID JOBE

Sound specialists who use various objects to simulate and record sound effects while synchronizing them with their corresponding movie images.

Records sound during shooting; reports to the production sound mixer.

Recordist
Foley Artists

Foley Mixer
Foley Recordist

Mixes the sound produced during shooting to get the desired combination of vocals, sound effects, and ambient sound.

Production Sound Mixer
Boom Operator
Cable Puller

JOHN PRITCHETT, C.A.S.
JOEL SHRYACK
EMILY SMITH-BAKER

Sound technician who operates the boom, a pole with a microphone at one end.

Protects the cables and wires of the sound equipment from damage and the production crew from injuries from the cables and wires.

Gaffer
Best Boy Electric
Electricians

DON MUCHOW
ANDREW DAY
ROBERT BRUCE
VAL DE SALVO
TOM McGRATH
CHRIS REDDISH
ANTHONY T. MARRA II
MICHAEL J. FAHEY
WAYNE STROUD

The head electrician, assisted by the best boy electric. Supervises the electricians, who are responsible for supplying current and lights on the set.

Manages the grips, or stagehands, who set up and move equipment and props. Assisted by the best boy grip.

Key Grip
Best Boy Grip
Dolly Grip

Moves the dolly during shooting.

Stagehands or crew workers.

Grips

KEVIN FAHEY
SCOTT "EL GATO" HOLLANDER
TIM NASH

Obtains the costumes and takes care of them during filming. Assisted by the wardrobe assistants.

Wardrobe Supervisor
Wardrobe Assistants

LYDIA TANJI
ANGELA BILLOWS
VICKI BRINKKORD
DEBORAH LARSEN
SCOTT WILLIAMS
SYDNEY COOPER

Arranges the actors' hair.

In *The Player*, the character June is an artist, and her artworks are seen in her house. This person created that art.

Runs the makeup department; applies the makeup to the actors.

Make-Up Artist
Hairdresser
June's Artwork

Oversees acquisition and maintenance of all props. → Property Master — JAMES MONROE

Assistant Property Master — JULIE HEUER

Get the set ready for filming and disassemble it after filming. ⌐ Set Dressers — MATTHEW ALTMAN, JOHN BUCKLIN, DAVID RONAN, JIM SAMSON

Swing Gang — DANIEL ROTHENBERG, MARIO PEREZ

Assistant Location Manager — PAUL BOYDSTON

The member of the construction crew who paints the sets. — Scenic Painter — JOHN BEAUVAIS → Painter — RICKY RIGGS

Construction Coordinator — LOREN CORNEY
Construction Foreman — PAT MAURER

Build the sets, furniture, props, and camera tracks. → Carpenters — CHRIS MARNEUS, DARRYL LEE, KENNETH FUNK, THOMAS CALLOWAY, JOHN EVANS, JUSTIN KRITZER

Supervise the construction crew, who make the sets.

Responsible for coordinating the visual elements of the film (other than the camera work). → Art Department Coordinator — MICHELE GUASTELLO

Keeps track of all expenditures during production and supervises payment of salaries and bills. Assisted by the assistant accountant. →

Production Coordinator — CYNTHIA HILL ← An administrator in charge of communication, correspondence, travel, accommodations, and bill paying. Assisted by the assistant coordinator and the production secretary.

Assistant Coordinator — BETSY CHASSE
Production Secretary — STACY COHEN
Production Accountant — KIMBERLY EDWARDS SHAPIRO
Assistant Accountant — CHERYL KURK
Avenue Financial Representative — SHERI HALFON ← Avenue Pictures was a small film production company. Its chairman at the time *The Player* was produced was Carey Brokaw, who served as executive producer of *The Player*.
Additional Accounting Service — JUDY GELETKO
Post-Production Accountant — CATHERINE WEBB

Personal assistants, who help the director and producers. ⌐ Assistant to Robert Altman — JIM McLINDON
Assistants to Cary Brokaw — ROBIN HAGE, DANIELLE KNIGHT

Sandcastle 5 Productions, Inc., is a small film and TV production company closely associated with Robert Altman. ⌐ Assistant to Nick Wechsler — ALISON BALIAN
Sandcastle 5 Representative — CELIA CONVERSE
Production Assistants — ANGIE BONNER, JOHN BROWN III, SIGNE CORRIERE, STEVE DAY, KELLY HOUSEHOLDER

Run errands for the director and assist him or her in various other small ways.

Keeps a log of the details in each shot to make sure continuity is maintained from shot to shot. → Script Supervisor — CAROLE STARKES

Plans, arranges, and supervises the stunts.

Stunt Coordinator — GREG WALKER ←
Special Effects — JOHN HARTIGAN ← The department responsible for the shots unobtainable by live-action cinematography.

Handles the animals on the set; in *The Player*, a rattlesnake appears twice. → Animal Trainer — JIM BROCKETT

Still Photographer — LOREY SEBASTIAN ← Takes photographs for publicity and advertising.

Set Medic — TOM MOORE

Responsible for maintaining and operating all vehicles.

Drive the vehicles that transport equipment and personnel.

Perform odd jobs, such as getting coffee and snacks for the cast and crew. ⟶

Hires the actors who speak no lines and do not stand out as individuals.

Lab person who adjusts the color of the negative as needed, often in coordination with the cinematographer.

Designs the words that appear on the screen (such as the credits).

This organization, here a Japanese-based bank, lent the producers money to produce the film.

Publicizes the film through advertising and other publicity.

Arranges publicity events, such as interviews and appearances.

Transportation Coordinator	DEREK RASER
Transport Captain	"J. T." THAYER
Drivers	CHRISTOPHER ARMSTRONG
	RON CHESNEY
	STEVE EARLE
	DON FEENEY
	D. J. GARDINER
	GREG WILLIS
Caterer	RICK BRAININ CATERING
Craft Service	STUART McCAULEY
	ANDREA BERTY
Extras Casting	MAGIC CASTING
Location Security	ARTIS SECURITY
Negative Cutter	BOB HART
Color By	DELUXE ®
Color Timer	MICHAEL STANWICK
Titles & Opticals By	MERCER TITLE & OPTICAL
Title Design	DAN PERRI
Legal Services	SINCLAIR TENNENBAUM & Co.
	WYMAN & ISAACS
Financing Provided By	THE DAIWA BANK LTD.
Completion Bond	FILM FINANCES, INC.
Promotions Arranged By	ANDREW VARELA
Publicity By	CLEIN + WHITE INC.
Title Painting By	CHARLES BRAGG

Maintains security for scenes shot on location.

Cuts and splices the negative to make it match the final edited version of the film.

Uses an optical printer or perhaps a computer to create the words that appear on the screen.

The company responsible for drawing up the contract between the producers and the financiers that guarantees the film will be completed at a set time and within a set budget.

SPECIAL THANKS TO

PATRICK MURRAY	SUZANNE GOLDMAN	MIMI RABINOWITZ
RANDY HONAKER	TOYOKO NEZU	MORGAN ENTREKIN
LUIS ESTEVEZ	REEBOK	GEOWORKS
BASELINE	MARK EISEN	BALLY

These people or companies donated products or services or allowed the filmmakers to use certain locations. For *The Player*, companies such as Reebok, Bally, and Range Rover may have paid a fee for product placement.

GERALD GREENBACH & TWO BUNCH PALMS
BOB FLICK & ENTERTAINMENT TONIGHT
STEVE TROMBATORE & ALL PAYMENTS
RANGE ROVER OF NORTH AMERICA
MARCHON/MARCOLIN EYE WEAR
SPINNEYBECK/DESIGN AMERICA
HARRY WINSTON JEWELERS
L.A. MARATHON

These people or companies donated products or services or allowed the filmmakers to use certain locations. For *The Player*, companies such as Reebok, Bally, and Range Rover may have paid a fee for product placement.

THE LOS ANGELES COUNTY MUSEUM OF ART
JANIS DINWIDDIE
JULIE JOHNSTON
RON HAVER
THE LES HOOPER ORCHESTRA

THE BICYCLE THIEF
© RICHARD FEINER & CO., INC.

These are copyright acknowledgments, required whenever a film uses material that someone else claims copyright to.

"SNAKE" & "DRUMS OF KYOTO"
© Lia-Mann Music
Written & Performed By
KURT NEUMANN

"TEMA PARA JOBIM"
© Mulligan Publishing Co., Inc.
Music by GERRY MULLIGAN
Lyrics by JOYCE
Performed by JOYCE
MILTON NASCIMENTO
Courtesy of Estudio Pointer Ltda.
& RCA Electronica Ltda.

"PRECIOUS"
Written by LES HOOPER
© Chesford Music Publications

ENTERTAINMENT TONIGHT
Theme by
MICHAEL MARK
Published by ADDAX MUSIC CO. INC.

Re-Recording Facilities
SKYWALKER SOUND
A division of LucasArts Entertainment Company

This film recorded digitally in a THX Sound System Theatre.

RECORDED IN
ULTRA-STEREO

SOURCES

IMDb Film Glossary (Internet Movie Database Web site): <http://us.imdb.com/Glossary>. Accessed 14 June 2001.

Katz, Ephraim. *The Film Encyclopedia*. 3rd ed. Revised by Fred Klein and Ronald Dean Nolen. New York: Harper, 1998.

Konigsberg, Ira. *The Complete Film Dictionary*. 2nd ed. New York: Penguin, 1997.

Law, Jonathan, et al., eds. *Cassell Companion to Cinema*. 2nd ed. London: Cassell, 1997.

Oakey, Virginia. *Dictionary of Film and Television Terms*. New York: Barnes, 1983.

Singleton, Ralph S., and James A. Conrad. *Filmmaker's Dictionary*. 2nd ed. Beverly Hills, CA: Lone Eagle, 2000.

Illustrated Glossary

IN THIS GLOSSARY I HAVE TRIED TO DEFINE and explain the main terms used in the book. The number in parentheses at the end of an entry indicates where that term is discussed most extensively in the text. For additional terms or other explanations of the terms included in this glossary, see Robert Atkins's *ArtSpeak: A Guide to Contemporary Ideas, Movements, and Buzzwords, 1945 to the Present*, 2nd ed. (1997); Steve Blandford, Barry Keith Grant, and Jim Hillier's *The Film Studies Dictionary* (2001); Susan Hayward's *Cinema Studies: The Key Concepts*, 2nd ed. (2000); Kevin Jackson's *The Language of Cinema* (1998); Ira Konigsberg's *The Complete Film Dictionary*, 2nd ed. (1997); and Gerald Prince's *Dictionary of Narratology* (1987). Various glossaries of film terms, especially terms used in film production, also appear on the Web. For sample sources, see the Web page for this book: <http://www.bedfordstmartins.com/phillips-film>.

ambient sound: The pervading sound atmosphere of a place that people tend not to notice. In a woods, for example, ambient sound may consist mainly of trees moving in the breeze and insects heard at a low volume.

anamorphic lens: A lens that squeezes a wide image onto a film frame in the camera, making everything look tall and thin. On a projector, an anamorphic lens expands the image, returning it to its original wide shape (usually nearly two and a half times wider than its height). Many movies from the 1950s to the 1980s and some since then have been filmed and projected with anamorphic lenses. See also **CinemaScope**. (33)

animation: See **stop-motion cinematography**.

animatronic: A puppet likeness of a human, creature, or animal whose movements are directed by electronic, mechanical, or radio-controlled devices.

aperture: (1) The adjustable opening in the camera lens that permits the operator to regulate how much light passes through the lens to the film. The size of the

aperture helps determine depth of field. (2) The rectangular opening in a motion-picture projector that helps determine the size and shape of light sent from the projector to the screen. The size and shape of the projected image may be further changed by the use of an aperture plate in front of the projector's standard aperture.

aperture plate: (1) A small metal plate with a rectangular opening that is used in cameras to determine the shape and area of the light reaching the film. (2) A small metal plate with a rectangular opening used in front of a projector's aperture or opening to help determine the shape and area of the light reaching the screen. Both camera and projector aperture plates may be changed to create different aspect ratios.

aspect ratio: The proportion of the width to the height of the image on a TV or movie screen or on the individual frames of the film. The most common aspect ratio for nontheatrical film showings is 1.33:1 (4:3); that is also the approximate aspect ratio of analog TV screens. Currently, most movies shown in American theaters have an aspect ratio of 1.85:1. The aspect ratio has nothing to do with the size or area of the image; rather it indicates the shape (width in proportion to height) of film images. (31)

1.85:1
The aspect ratio used for
most U.S. theatrical showings
since the 1960s

---

asynchronous sound: A sound from a source on-screen that precedes or follows its source, such as words that are not synchronized with lip movements. (165)

auteur ("oh TOUR") theory: The belief that some filmmakers—usually directors though sometimes producers, writers, or actors—function as the dominant creators of films and that the auteur's films embody recurrent subjects, techniques, and meanings. (437)

avant-garde film: See **experimental film.**

backlight or **backlighting:** Lighting from behind the subject. If used alone or if the backlighting is the strongest light used, the subject's identity may be obscured. Used in combination with other lighting, backlighting may help set the subject off from the background. (66)

bird's-eye view: A camera angle achieved when the camera films the subject from directly overhead. (83)

black comedy: A narrative style that shows the humorous possibilities of subjects often considered off-limits to comedy, such as warfare, murder, death, and illness. Black comedies are often also satiric. Examples of films using black comedy are *The Ladykillers* (especially the five deaths and disposal of the five bodies that are treated comically toward the end of the film); *Kind Hearts and Coronets; Dr. Strangelove: Or, How I Learned to Stop Worrying and Love the Bomb; Catch-22; Monty Python and the Holy Grail; Life of Brian;* and *To Die For.* (290)

boom: See **crane.**

bridge (music): Music used to link two or more scenes. Often used to enhance continuity.

cameo: A brief role in a narrative entertainment—such as a TV show or film (fictional or occasionally documentary)—performed by a well-known person, usually a famous actor, whose name is often not included in the credits or publicity. Cameos may also be played by famous people playing themselves or by insiders in the film community—a type of cinematic in-joke. (26)

canted framing: See **Dutch angle.**

catchlight: The light from one or more sources that is visible in the pupils of a subject's eyes. By examining the catchlight, one can often discover the number and direction of some or all of the light sources. (66)

cel: A thin sheet of clear plastic on which images are painted for use in making some animated films. To produce some animated films, a series of cels is superimposed on a painted background then each finished image is photographed.

celluloid: (1) Short for cellulose nitrate, film stock used until the early 1950s. The nitrate-based films could produce high-quality images but were subject to decomposition and combustion (illustrated by the projection room fire in the Italian film *Cinema paradiso*). (2) Any transparent material used as the base for motion-picture film. (3) Synonym for movie, as in "celluloid heroes."

character actor: An actor who tends to specialize in well-defined secondary roles. Dennis Hopper, for example, is a character actor who has largely made a career of playing unstable secondary characters. (23)

cinéma noir: See **film noir.**

CinemaScope: A wide-screen process introduced in 1953 made possible by filming and projecting with anamorphic lenses.

cinematic: See **filmic.**

cinematographer: The person responsible for the motion-picture photography during the making of a film. Often called *director of photography* (DP).

cinematography: Motion-picture photography, including technical and artistic concern with such matters as choice of film stock, lighting, choice and use of lenses, camera distance and angle, and camera movement. (Chapter 2)

cinéma-vérité: Literally, "film truth." A type and style of documentary filmmaking developed in France during the early 1960s the aim of which was to capture events as they happened. To this end, cinéma-vérité filmmakers used unobtrusive lightweight equipment to film and to record sound on location. Similar to direct cinema arising at about the same time in the United States, although the French

filmmakers were likely to question their subjects during filming. Practitioners of cinéma-vérité include Jean Rouch, Chris Marker, and Marcel Ophüls (as in his monumental *The Sorrow and the Pity*). See **direct cinema.** (313)

Cinerama: A wide-screen process involving the use of three synchronized projectors showing three contiguous images on a wide, curved screen. Cinerama was first used commercially in the early 1950s and was available only in selected theaters in large cities. (390)

classical Hollywood cinema: Films that show one or more distinct characters facing a succession of problems while trying to reach their goal or goals; these films tend to hide the manner of their making by using continuity editing and other unobtrusive filmmaking techniques. (224)

close-up: An image in which the subject fills most of the frame and little of the surroundings is shown. When the subject is someone's upper body, the close-up normally reveals the entire head and perhaps some of the shoulders. Close-ups are used to direct viewers' attention to texture or a detail or, probably most often, the expressions on a person's face. (78)

closure: A sense of resolution or completion at the end of a narrative. A story that has closure leaves its audience with no major unanswered questions about the consequences of the narrative's most significant events. (274)

compilation film: A film made by editing together clips from other films. Sometimes used in creating a documentary film—as in *Point of Order, To Die in Madrid,* and *The Atomic Café*—or an experimental film, as in Bruce Conner's "A Movie." (309, 319)

composition: The arrangement of settings, lighting, and subjects (usually people and objects) within the frame. Composition can be an extremely expressive aspect of filmmaking. (31)

continuity (editing): Film editing that maintains a sense of uninterrupted time and action and continuous setting within each scene of a narrative film. (115)

contrast: In photography and cinematography, the difference between the lightest and darkest parts of an image. Low-contrast images show little difference between the intensity of the lightest part of the image and that of the darkest part. In high-contrast images, the dark parts are very dark and the light parts very light.

convention: In films and other texts, a frequently used technique or content that audiences accept as natural or typical. For example, it is a convention that movie audiences are allowed to hear both sides of a telephone conversation even if they see only one of the conversationalists; it is also a convention that westerns include showdowns and shootouts. As the authors of *The Film Studies Dictionary* point out, "conventions function as an implied agreement between makers and consumers to accept certain artificialities." (383)

crane: A mechanical device used to move a camera through space above the ground or to position it at a place in the air. A shot taken from a crane gives the camera operator many options: different distances and angles from the subject, different heights from the surface, and fluid changes in distance and angle from the subject. (89)

cross-cut: In editing, to alternate between subjects or events occurring at different settings and often presumably transpiring at the same time. See **parallel editing.**

cut: (1) The most common transition between shots, made by splicing or joining the end of one shot to the beginning of the following shot. When the two shots are projected, the transition from the first shot to the next appears to be instantaneous. (2) A version of an edited film, as in "director's cut," meaning the version the director intended. (3) To edit or edited, as in "They cut the movie in four months." (4) To sever or splice film while editing. (109)

cutaway (shot): A shot that briefly interrupts the visual presentation of a subject to show something else. Used in many ways, such as to reveal what a character is thinking, show reactions, maintain continuity, avoid showing sex or violence, or allow a passage of time. In *The Dead*, for example, viewers see the beginning of a dinner, a cutaway to the street outside, then the dinner table again where the guests have finished eating.

cutting continuity (script): A script that describes a finished film. Often contains detailed technical information, such as shot and scene divisions, descriptions of settings and events, dialogue, camera angles and distances, sometimes even the duration of shots and transitions between them. Extremely useful for studying a film, especially a foreign-language film, because any dialogue is usually translated more completely and more accurately than in the film's subtitles. See **screenplay** and **shooting script.** (183 footnote)

dailies: The positive prints usually made from a day's filming (exposed negatives). The director, cinematographer, and perhaps editor usually check the dailies to see if the recently filmed shots are satisfactory and if additional takes or shots are needed.

deep focus: A term used widely by film critics to indicate photography in which subjects near the camera, those in the distant background, and those in between

are all in sharp focus. Achieved in photography by use of wide-angle lenses or small lens aperture or both. In low illumination, fast lenses and fast film stock also help create deep focus. Filmmakers are likely to use the phrase *great depth of field* rather than *deep focus*. Opposite of **shallow focus**. (74)

depth of field: The distances in front of the camera in which all objects are in focus.

desaturated color: Drained, subdued color approaching a neutral gray. Often used to create or enhance an effect, as throughout Werner Herzog's *Nosferatu the Vampyre* and Tim Burton's *Sleepy Hollow*. Opposite of **saturated color**. (62)

designer or **production designer:** The person responsible for much of what is photographed in a movie, including architecture, locations, sets, costumes, makeup, and hairstyles.

diffuser: (1) Material such as spun glass, granulated or grooved glass, or a silk or thin nylon stocking placed in front of the camera lens to soften the image's resolution. (2) Translucent material such as silk or spun glass placed in front of a light source to create soft light. (75)

direct cinema: A type and style of documentary film developed in the United States during the 1960s in which actions are recorded as they happen, without rehearsal, using a portable 16 mm camera with a zoom lens and portable magnetic sound recording equipment. Editing is minimal, and usually narration and interviews are avoided. Similar to cinéma-vérité, which developed in France at about the same time, though direct cinema attempted to be less directive and intrusive. Used by such American documentary filmmakers as Robert Drew and Richard Leacock, Albert and David Maysles, Donn Pennebaker, and Frederick Wiseman and an in-

fluence on some fictional filmmakers, such as John Cassavetes. See **cinema-vérité**. (311)

director of photography (DP): See **cinematographer**.

dissolve: See **lap dissolve**.

docudrama: A film that re-creates and dramatizes occurrences from history, often recent history, by blending fact and fiction. The term is usually applied to TV movies that purport to be factual recreations of newsworthy people or occurrences.

documentary film: A film whose representation of its subjects viewers are intended to accept primarily as factual. A documentary film may present a story (be a narrative film), or it may not. (299)

Dolby sound: Trade name for a system that reduces noise on optical and magnetic sound tracks.

dolly: (1) A wheeled platform most often used to move a motion-picture camera and its operator around while filming. (2) To film while the camera is mounted on a moving dolly or wheeled platform. See **track,** definition 1. (88)

dominant cinema: See **classical Hollywood cinema**.

dub: (1) To add sound after the film has been shot. Sometimes used to supplement sounds that were recorded during filming. (2) To replace certain sounds, for example, to substitute native speaking voices for the original voices of a foreign-language film.

Dutch angle: A camera angle in which the vertical and horizontal lines of the film's image appear at an angle to the vertical and horizontal lines of the film's frame. For example, in a Dutch angle shot, the vertical lines of a door frame will appear slanted. Often used to suggest disorientation by the film's subjects or to disorient viewers or both. (83)

edit: To select and arrange the processed segments of photographed motion-picture film. Editors, often in collaboration with directors, determine which shots to include, what is the most effective take (version) of each shot, the arrangement and duration of shots, and transitions between them. To edit a film is sometimes called "to cut a film." (Chapter 3)

effect: See **sound effect** and **special effect.**

emulsion: A clear gelatin substance containing a thin layer of tiny light-sensitive particles (grains) that make up a photographic image. The emulsion and a clear, flexible base are the two main components of a piece of film. (55)

episodic plot: Story structure in which some scenes have no necessary or probable relation to each other; many scenes could be switched without strongly affecting the overall story or audience response. Episodic plots are used in *Nashville*, *Clerks*, and occasional other films. Such stories may be unified by means other than character and action, such as setting.

establishing shot: A shot, usually a long shot or extreme long shot, used at the beginning of a scene to "establish" or show where and sometimes when the events that are to follow take place.

event: In a narrative or story, either an *action* by a character or person or a *happening* (a change brought about by a force other than a person or character). Settings, subjects, and events are the basic components of a narrative. (262)

experimental film: A film that rejects the conventions of mainstream movies and explores the possibilities of the film medium itself. Probably the best-known experimental film is "Un chien andalou," a surrealist creation by director Luis Buñuel and the artist Salvador Dali. (317)

explicit meaning: A general verbal observation in a text about one or more of its subjects. In films, explicit meanings may be revealed, for example, by a narrator, a character's monologue or dialogue, a title card, a subtitle, a sign, or a newspaper headline. See **implicit meaning** and **meaning.** (409)

exposition: Information supplied within a narrative about characters (or people in a narrative documentary) and about events that supposedly transpired before the earliest event in the plot. Exposition is intended to help the audience better understand the characters or people and make sense of the plot. (271)

expressionism: A style of art, literature, drama, and film used to convey not external reality in a believable way but emotions in striking, stylized ways. As Ira Konigsberg says, in film this goal "was accomplished through distorted and exaggerated settings, heavy and dramatic shadows, unnatural space in composition, oblique angles, curved or nonparallel lines, a mobile and subjective camera, unnatural costumes and makeup, and stylized acting" (126). One of the first examples of film expressionism is *The Cabinet of Dr. Caligari* (above).

exterior: A scene filmed outdoors or on a set that looks like the outdoors.

extreme close-up: An image that shows only a detail and largely or completely excludes the background. If the subject is someone's face, only part of it is visible. (78)

extreme long shot: Image in which the subject appears to be far from the camera. If a person is the subject, the entire body will be visible (if not obstructed by some intervening object) but very small in the frame, and much of the surroundings will be visible. Usually used only outdoors, often to establish the setting of the following action. (77)

eye-level angle: A camera angle that creates the effect of the audience being on the same level as the subject. (84)

eyeline match: A transition between shots in which the first shot shows a person or animal looking at something offscreen, and the following shot shows what was being looked at from the approximate angle suggested by the previous shot. (115)

fabula: A term used by the Russian Formalist school of literary theory and some later film theorists to mean the mental chronological reconstruction of the events of a nonchronological narrative. See also **plot**. (284)

fade-in: Optical effect in which the image changes by degrees from darkness (usually black) to illumination. Frequently used at the beginning of a film and sometimes at the beginning of a sequence.

fade-out: Optical effect in which the image changes by degrees from illumination to darkness (usually black). Sometimes used at the conclusion of a sequence and at the end of a film as a gradual exit from its world.

fade-out, fade-in: A transition between shots in which a shot changes by degrees from illumination to darkness (usually to black); then, after a pause, the image changes from darkness to illumination (usually a new image). Sometimes used to indicate the passage of time. (109)

fake documentary: A film that purports to be a documentary film and seems to be one until viewers learn otherwise after the film has ended. Examples are *David Holzman's Diary* and *The Blair Witch Project*, which seem to be documentaries until viewers can figure out from the final credits that the films are fictional after all. See **mock documentary**. (339)

fast cutting: Editing characterized by many brief shots, sometimes shots less than a second long. Most recent American action movies, music videos, and trailers have extensive fast cutting. Opposite of **slow cutting**. (128)

fast film (stock): Film stock that requires relatively little light for capturing images. Fast film, especially before the last decade or so, has tended to produce grainy images. Opposite of **slow film (stock)**. (57)

fast lens: A lens that is efficient at transmitting light and thus transmits more light than a slow lens used in the same circumstances.

fast motion: Motion in which the action depicted on the screen occurs more rapidly than its real-life counterpart, as when the cowboys in early 1920s films seem to ride horses faster than any yet seen by people outside movie theaters. Achieved whenever the projector runs significantly faster than the speed at which the camera filmed, for example when the projector runs at 24 frames per second and the camera filmed at 14 frames per second. Opposite of **slow motion.**

feature (film): A fictional film that is at least sixty minutes long.

fill light: A soft light used to fill in unlit areas of the subject or to soften any shadows or lines made by other, brighter lights. (66)

film continuity: See **cutting continuity (script).**

filmic: Characteristic of the film medium or appropriate to it, such as parallel editing or the combination of editing and a full range of vocals, silence, and music. For example, a novel or play with many short scenes or frequent shifts between two locales (similar to parallel editing in a film) may be called filmic.

film noir ("film nwahr"): Literally, "black film." A type of film first made in the United States during and after World War II, characterized by frequent scenes with dark, shadowy (low-key) lighting; (usually) urban settings; characters motivated by selfishness, greed, cruelty, ambition, and lust; and characters willing to lie, frame, double-cross, and kill or have others killed. The moods of such films tend to be embittered, depressed, cynical, or fatalistic and their plots compressed and convoluted. Examples are *Murder, My Sweet; Out of the Past;* and *Touch of Evil* (below). (235)

film stock: Unexposed and unprocessed motion-picture film. Sometimes called *raw stock*. (55)

film theory: A related and evolving structure of abstractions about the film medium. As Dudley Andrew has pointed out in his *Major Film Theories*, a film theory often includes considerations of the properties of the film medium, its techniques, its forms, and its purposes and value. (437)

filter: A sheet of transparent plastic or glass either in a color or a shade of gray attached before or behind the camera lens to change the quality of light reaching the film.

final cut: The last version of an edited film.

fine cut: A late version of an edited film, though perhaps not yet the final cut. See **rough cut.**

fisheye lens: An extreme wide-angle lens that captures nearly 180 degrees of the area before the camera and causes much curvature of the image, especially near the edges. (72)

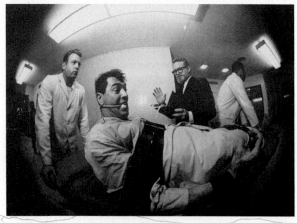

flashback: A shot or a few shots, a brief scene, or (rarely) a sequence that interrupts a film narrative to show earlier events. (281)

flashforward: A shot, scene, or sequence—though usually only a shot or two—that interrupts a film narrative to show events that happen in the future. For example, *GoodFellas* begins with a few scenes that occur again late in an otherwise chronological narrative. Flashforwards are rarely used, though examples are found in *Don't Look Now* and *Heavenly Creatures*. (280)

Foley artist: Sound specialist who uses various objects such as different types of floor surfaces (usually in a Foley studio) to simulate sounds and synchronize them with their corresponding movie images. (150)

footage: A length of exposed motion-picture film, as in "They had enough footage to complete the film."

form: See **structure.**

form cut: See **match cut.**

frame: (1) A separate, individual photograph on a strip of motion-picture film. (2) The borders of the projected film or TV set or monitor. (3) To position the camera in such a way that the subject is kept within the borders of the image. (105)

frame enlargement: A photograph of an individual frame from a motion picture, blown up (enlarged) to reveal its details. Used in some publications, including this one, to illustrate certain features of a film or the film medium. Not to be confused with publicity still, which usually refers to a posed photograph taken for promotional purposes with a still camera during the making of a film. (412 right)

freeze frame: A projected yet unmoving motion-picture image, which looks like a still photograph, achieved by having the film laboratory reprint the same frame or two repeatedly. Sometimes used at the end of a film; often used at the conclusion of TV sitcoms. Used, for example, in *Tom Jones* and *GoodFellas*. Many videotape, videodisc, and DVD players also make it possible to freeze a frame.

French new wave (cinema): See **new wave (cinema).**

gauge: In filmmaking and film studies, the width of a film, as in "The gauge of most theatrical films is 35 mm." (57)

genre ("ZHAHN ruh"): A commonly recognized group of fictional films that share settings, subjects, or events (and sometimes techniques) and that change over time. Western, science fiction, horror, gangster, musical, and screwball comedy are sample film genres. (226)

grain: One of the many tiny light-sensitive particles embedded in gelatin that is attached to a clear, flexible film base (celluloid). After the film is exposed to light and developed, many grains make up a film's finished images. (55)

graininess: Rough visual texture, as in "That film stock produces excessive graininess." In a film, graininess is caused when individual particles clump together in the film emulsion. Graininess also results if a film is magnified excessively during projection, as when a 16 mm print is used to fill up a large screen intended for 35 mm films. (61)

grainy: See **graininess.**

happening: As defined by some narrative theorists, a change brought about by a force other than a person or character, for example, the fox running in front of a pickup truck and causing an accident, which in turn leads to further actions in *A Simple Plan*. In narratives, happenings and actions by characters or persons constitute events.

hard light: Light that has not been diffused or reflected before illuminating the subject. On subjects illuminated by hard light, shadows are sharp-edged and surface details are more noticeable than with soft light. Examples: midday sunlight on a clear day or unreflected and focused light from a spotlight. Opposite of **soft light.** (65)

high angle: A view of a subject from above, created by positioning the camera above the subject. (83)

high contrast: Photographic image with few gradations between the darkest and lightest parts of the image. Black-and-white high-contrast photos are made up mostly of blacks and whites with few shades of gray. Opposite of **low contrast.** (341)

high-key lighting: A high level of illumination on the subject. With high-key lighting, the bright frontal key lighting on the subject prevents dark shadows. Often used to create or enhance a cheerful mood, as in many stage and movie musicals. Opposite of **low-key lighting.** (68)

homage (in French and in film studies, pronounced "oh MAZH"): In film studies, a tribute to an earlier text (such as a film) or part of one, for example, by including part of an earlier film, re-creating parts of it, or respectfully imitating aspects of it. French new wave films often contain homages, especially to American movies. An homage may also be to a director's films. For example, sometimes entire films, such as some directed by Brian De Palma, are seen as homages to films directed by Alfred Hitchcock. (214)

hybrid film: A film that is not exclusively fictional, documentary, or experimental but instead shares characteristics of two or all three of the major film types. An example is *David Holzman's Diary*, which contains aspects of fiction, documentary, and experimental films. (336)

ideology: A frequently used term with different meanings in different contexts. Here, *ideology* means the influential underlying social and political beliefs of a society or social group. Often these beliefs are unexamined by the group's members and are assumed to be true and not the product of the group's way of thinking. For example, part of the ideology of the United States is the belief that individuals can influence major events in a significant way. This aspect of American ideology is often conveyed by popular American movies. See also **symptomatic meaning.** (432)

implicit meaning: A generalization a viewer or reader makes about a text (such as a film) or subject in a text. An implicit meaning, for example, may be a viewer's generalization about the implications of a narrative or the significance of a symbol. See also **meaning.** (411)

independent film: (1) Film made without support or input from the dominant, established film industry. Usually an independent film is made without costly stars, director, and writer(s) and thus has a budget far below a big studio-backed movie. Sometimes called an *indie*. (2) In some publications, the phrase is used as an alternative to *experimental film*. (252, 256)

installation art: An art exhibit or ensemble, which is usually shown in a museum of modern or contemporary art, integrating various objects or arts, such as video images, a bed, and recorded voices (333)

intercut: See **cross-cut.**

intercutting: See **parallel editing.**

interior: A scene filmed indoors, either in an existing building or one constructed for the occasion.

intertextuality: The relation of one text (such as a film) to another (such as a journalistic article, play, or another film). Intertextuality includes such forms as translation, citation, imitation, and extension. Allusion, homage, parody, remake, prequel, sequel, and compilation film are examples of intertextuality in films. (209)

intertitle (card): See **title card.**

iris-in: An optical effect usually functioning as a transition between shots in which the image is initially dark, then a widening opening—often a circle or an oval—reveals more and more of the next image, usually until it is fully revealed. (114)

iris-out: An optical effect usually functioning as a transition between shots in which the image is closed out as a constricting opening—usually a circle or an oval—closes down on it. Normally the iris-out ends with the image fully obliterated.

iris shot: Shot in which part of the frame is masked or obscured, often leaving the remaining image in a circular or an oval shape. The iris shot was widely used in films directed by D. W. Griffith, Sergei Eisenstein, and Abel Gance and in many other early films but is rarely used today except as an homage. (32)

Italian neorealism: See **neorealism.**

jump cut: A transition between shots that causes a jarring or even shocking shift in space, time, or action. A jump cut may be used to shorten the depiction of an event or to disorient viewers, or both. It sometimes results unintentionally from careless editing or missing footage (above). Opposite of **continuity editing.** (109)

key light: (1) The main light in a shot. (2) The lighting instrument used to create the main and brightest light falling on the subject. (66)

lap dissolve: A transition between shots in which one shot begins to fade out as the next shot fades in, overlapping the first shot before replacing it. Usually used between scenes or sequences to suggest a change of setting or a later time or both. Also frequently known as a *dissolve*, but *lap dissolve* better conveys what happens: (over)lapping (by the second shot) and dissolving (of the first). (109)

leader: A piece of clear or opaque motion-picture film of any color that usually precedes and concludes a reel of film. It is used to decrease the chances of damage to the film print during shipment and projection, to carry information about the reel of film, and to thread a projector. It has even been included in some experimental films, as in Bruce Conner's "A Movie." (320b and g)

letterbox format: A videotape, videodisc, and DVD format that retains the film's original theatrical widescreen aspect ratio by not using a portion of the top and bottom of the analog TV or monitor screen. (35)

limbo: An indistinct setting that seems to extend to infinity. In such a setting, the background may be all white (as in most shots in George Lucas's *THX 1138*), all black, or all the same color. Also called *limbo background* or *limbo set*. (10)

location: Any place other than a film studio that is used for filming. For example, the Monument Valley region in Utah and Arizona was a location for the 1939 John Ford *Stagecoach* and other westerns, and *Schindler's List* was filmed on location in Poland, not on studio sets built to resemble Poland. See **set**.

long lens: See **telephoto lens**.

long shot: Shot in which the subject is seen in its entirety, and much of its surroundings are visible. Not to be confused with **long take**. (77)

long take: A shot of long duration, as in the opening of *Touch of Evil*, *Halloween*, *The Player*, *Boogie Nights*, and *Snake Eyes*. Not to be confused with **long shot**.

loose framing: An image in which the main subject has ample space and does not seem hemmed in by the edges of the frame and the background. Such framing can be used to give a sense of the subject's freedom of movement or of its being lost in or engulfed by its environment. Opposite of **tight framing**. (13)

loose shot: See **loose framing**.

low angle: A view of the subject as seen from below eye level. (84)

low contrast: Photographic image with many gradations between darkest and lightest parts of the image. In black-and-white film, low-contrast images have many shades of gray. Opposite of **high contrast**. (171)

low-key lighting: Lighting with predominant dark tones, often deep dark tones. By using little frontal fill lighting, the filmmakers can immerse parts of the image in shadows. Often used to contribute to a dramatic or mysterious effect, as in many detective and crime films and in many horror films. Opposite of **high-key lighting**. (68)

magic realism: A style in which occasional improbable or impossible events are included in an otherwise realistic story. For example, in *Like Water for Chocolate* the food one character prepares causes those who eat it to feel as she felt as she prepared it. (292)

masking: A technique used to block out part of an image (usually) temporarily. Normally used to block out

extraneous details and focus viewer attention, to elongate or widen the viewed image, or to censor certain details. Used more often in silent films than in sound films.

master-scene format: A screenplay that describes and often numbers scenes but does not break them down into shots. A film script in the master-scene format includes descriptions of setting and action and any dialogue but usually excludes instructions about the making of the film, such as indications about the camera setups. (185)

master shot: A shot, usually made with an unmoving camera, that records an entire scene, usually in a long shot. Parts of the master shot plus other shots of the same scene may be used as the final version of the scene, or the entire master shot may be used.

match cut: A transition between two shots in which an object or movement (or both) at the end of one shot closely resembles (or is identical to) an object or movement (or both) at the beginning of the next shot. (109)

meaning: An observation or general statement about a subject. Meaning in films may be explicit, a general verbal observation in a text about one or more of its subjects; implicit, a generalization a viewer makes about a film or subject in the film; or symptomatic, an explicit or implicit meaning that coincides with the belief of a large group of people outside the film. (409)

medium close-up: Image in which the subject fills most of the frame, though not as much as in a close-up. When the subject is a person, the medium close-up usually reveals the head and shoulders. As with the close-up, the medium close-up is often used to direct viewer attention to a part of something or to show facial expressions in detail. (78)

medium shot: Shot in which the subject and surroundings are given about equal importance. When the subject is a person, he or she is usually seen from the knees or waist up. (77)

Method acting: Acting in which the performer studies the background of a character in depth, immerses himself or herself in the role, and creates emotion in part by thinking of emotional situations from his or her own life that resemble those of the character. (23)

mise en scène ("meez ahn sen," with a nasalized second syllable): French for "staging." An image's setting, subject (usually people or characters), and composition (the arrangement of setting and subjects within the frame). (Chapter 1)

mix: (1) To select sounds from sound tracks of music, dialogue, and sound effects; adjust their volumes; and combine them into a composite sound track. (2) A final composite sound track consisting of a blend of other sound tracks.

mock documentary: A fictional film that parodies or amusingly imitates documentary films. Because mock documentaries have some documentary characteristics—such as interviews, handheld cameras, and the absence of stars—viewers at first may think they are seeing a documentary but soon realize the film is an extended joke. Examples of mock documentaries are *This Is Spinal Tap*, purportedly a documentary about an inept, aging heavy metal band, and *Fear of a Black Hat*, supposedly a documentary film about the problems confronted by a rap group. See also **fake documentary.** (211, 339)

montage ("mon TAZH"): From the French *monter*, to assemble. (1) A series of brief shots used to present a condensation of subjects and time. *The Third Man*, for example, begins with a montage about the political and social conditions in Vienna after the ending of World War II. (2) A type of editing used in some 1920s Soviet films (as in [*Battleship*] *Potemkin* and *October*) and advocated by some Soviet film theorists, such as the director Sergei Eisenstein. In films using this type of editing, the aim is not so much to promote the invisible continuity of a narrative favored in classical Hollywood cinema as to suggest meanings from the dynamic juxtaposition of many carefully selected details. (3) Editing, especially in European usage. (131)

morphing: (1) The alteration of a film image by degrees by use of sophisticated computer software and multiple advanced computers. As Kevin Jackson has written, "Thanks to morphing, the director of live-action films can now achieve the kind of wild images previously reserved for the animator" (161). Used increasingly since 1988 in TV commercials and feature films, as in *Spawn* and *X-Men*. (2) The changing of the shape of a subject. (93)

narration: Commentary in a film about a subject in the film or some other topic, usually from someone off-screen. Occasionally the narration comes from a person on-screen, as in *Zoot Suit*, where the action sometimes freezes briefly as the character played by Edward James Olmos steps out of character and comments on some aspect of the story or the times of the story. Narration may be used off and on throughout a film or only occasionally. Sometimes it us used only at the film's beginning or ending, or both. Narration is sometimes used in documentary films and TV commercials, fictional films, and experimental films.

narrative: A series of unified consecutive events situated in one or more settings. A narrative may be fictional or factual or a blend of the two. Its events may be arranged chronologically or nonchronologically. (262)

narrative closure: See **closure.**

narrative documentary: A film that presents mainly a factual narrative or story. Examples are *Hearts of Darkness, Hoop Dreams,* and *Genghis Blues.* See **docudrama.** (302)

narrator: A character, person, or unidentifiable voice in a film that provides commentary continuously or intermittently. As in written fiction, a narrator is not necessarily a reliable source for information.

negative: (1) Unexposed film stock used to record negative images. (2) Film (other than reversal film) that has been exposed but not yet processed or developed. (3) Excluding reversal film, film that has been exposed and processed. It is normally then used to make (positive) prints for projection but is occasionally used in part of a finished film. In such films, negative footage is sometimes used to suggest death, as near the ending of *Gladiator*, where negative images suggest the main character's loss of consciousness and approaching death. In black-and-white negatives, the light and dark areas are reversed. In color photography and cinematography, the colors of the negative image are complementary to those of the subject photographed. (316)

neorealism: As a film movement in Italy during and after World War II, neorealist films are a mixture of imaginary and factual occurrences usually located in real settings and showing ordinary and believable characters caught up in difficult social and economic conditions, such as poverty and unemployment. Other characteristics of this "new realism" are a heavy but not exclusive reliance on nonprofessional actors, use of available lighting, chronological narratives, few close-ups, straightforward camera angles and other unobtrusive filmmaking techniques, and natural dialogue that includes a range of dialects. Probably the best-known neorealist film is *The Bicycle Thief* (also known as *Bicycle Thieves*). (246)

new wave (cinema): A diverse group of French fictional films made in the late 1950s and early 1960s in reaction to the carefully scripted products of the French film industry and as explorations of more current subjects sometimes rendered with untraditional techniques. Like cinéma-vérité, some new wave films were shot on location with portable, handheld equipment and fast film stock. Often new wave films include homages and surprising or whimsical moments. Examples of French new wave cinema are the early feature films of Truffaut (such as *The 400 Blows* and, more so, *Shoot the Piano Player*), Godard (*Breathless*), and Claude Chabrol (*Handsome Serge*). (248)

nickelodeon: Literally, "five-cents theater." A small, modest storefront converted into a movie theater, popular in the United States from 1905 to roughly 1915. The successor to one-person peephole machines and the forerunner of large, elaborate, and more comfortable movie theaters that were sometimes called *movie palaces*. (393)

nitrate: See **celluloid,** definition 1.

nonfiction film: See **documentary film.**

nonnarrative documentary: A film that presents mainly factual information without using a narrative or story. Examples abound, such as Frederick Wiseman's *High School II* and *Public Housing*, many TV commercials, and many industrial and training films. See **documentary film.** (301)

normal lens: A camera lens that provides the least distortion of image and movement. The normal lens—50 mm on a 35 mm camera—comes closest to approximating the perceptions of the human eye. (73)

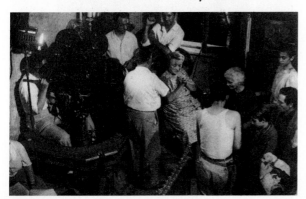

nouvelle vague: Literally "new wave." See **new wave (cinema).**

objective camera: Camera placement that allows the viewer to see the subject approximately as an outsider would, not as someone in the film sees it. Opposite of **point-of-view shot.**

offscreen: The area beyond the frame line, which has many possible uses. For example, someone may look offscreen at someone else; a shadow may be cast into the frame by something offscreen; or a sound may be heard from offscreen. See **offscreen sound.**

offscreen sound: Sound that does not derive from any on-screen source, such as an unseen dog barking or music that is not made by anyone within the frame. (163)

on-screen sound: Sound that derives from an on-screen source, such as someone viewers see and hear sneezing. (163)

optical effect: Special effect usually made with an optical printer or computer. Examples are lap dissolves, wipes, and freeze frames.

optical printer: A device consisting of a camera and one or more projectors used to reproduce images or parts of images from already processed film. It can be used to make a lap dissolve, wipe, and many other optical effects.

outtake: A take (version of a shot) not included in a film's final version, although occasionally outtakes are included during the ending credits, especially in a comedy, as in *The Nutty Professor* (1996). During editing, often shots or even whole scenes or entire sequences are deleted because the film is running too long or the material is not functioning as the filmmakers had envisioned.

pace: A viewer's sense of a subject (such as narrative developments or factual information) being presented rapidly or slowly. A highly subjective experience that is influenced by many aspects in a film, such as the film's editing (fast cutting or slow cutting) and the frequency of the introduction of new and significant subjects. (128)

panning: Filming while a movie camera is pivoted horizontally on a stationary base (often a tripod). Used frequently to show the vastness of a setting, such as a sea, plain, mountain range, outer space, or the inside of an immense hangar. The term derives from the word *panoramic* because with this movement the camera shows an extensive area. When the camera pans too rapidly and the resultant images are blurred, the camera movement is called a *swish pan.* (86)

parallel editing: Editing that alternates between two or more subjects, often suggesting that different events are related to each other or are occurring simultaneously. Parallel editing may also be used to depict subjects or events from different times or eras (as in D. W. Griffith's *Intolerance*). See **cross-cut.** (124)

parody: (1) An amusing imitation of human behavior or of a text, part of a text, or groups of texts. For example, a parody may be of a famous narrative, part of a narrative, or genre. Examples of film parodies are *Rocky Horror Picture Show*, a musical parody of horror movies, and *Spaceballs*, a parody of sci-fi movies, especially of *Star Wars*. (2) To imitate human behavior or a text or part of one in an amusing way. (210)

perspective: As used by painters, photographers, and cinematographers, the relative size and apparent distances between objects in a photographic image. (81)

pixillation: Rapid, jerky stop-motion cinematography that usually uses people in rigid poses or real objects as the subject of each frame and that makes possible the appear-

ance of new types of movement, such as a person gliding around a level lawn on one rigid leg. (343)

plot: The structure (selection and arrangement) of a narrative's events. (284)

plotline: A narrative or series of related events usually involving only a few characters or people and capable of functioning on its own as a brief story. Short films tend to have one plotline, but many feature films combine two or more. (274)

point-of-view shot: Camera placement at the approximate position of a character or person (or occasionally an animal) that gives a view similar to what that creature would see. Opposite of **objective camera.** (85)

pop art: An art movement begun in the United States and Britain in the 1950s and extending into the 1960s whose subjects were everyday objects—such as soup cans, clothespins, comic strips, graphic print ads, or celebrity images—that were represented archetypically, whimsically, ironically or in a combination of these ways.

p.o.v. shot: See **point-of-view shot.**

prequel: A narrative film that shows a story that happens before the story of an earlier film. For example, *Butch Cassidy and the Sundance Kid* came out in 1969; ten years later the prequel *Butch and Sundance: The Early Days* was made. (215)

preview (of a coming attraction): See **trailer.**

producer: A person in charge of the business and administrative aspects of making a film. The (main) producer's job typically includes acquiring rights to the script and hiring the personnel to make the film. Sometimes producers influence the filmmaking process, for example, by changing directors or insisting on changes in the script, filming, or editing. Producers may be known under a variety of titles, such as executive producer and assistant producer; the nature of their involvement (if any) remains obscure to those outside the production.

production: The making of a film or video, which typically involves three stages: preproduction (which in a large production may include planning, budgeting, scripting, designing and building sets, and casting); production (filming or taping); and postproduction (which includes editing, preparing and mixing sound, and making the credits).

production still: See **publicity still.**

product placement: The practice of including commercial products or services, such as Coca-Cola cans or a particular airline, in films so that viewers can notice them. Makers of movies often make agreements with companies to display their products or services in exchange for money or, much more often, goods, services (such as airline tickets or hotel accommodations), or promotion of the movie. (49)

product plug: See **product placement.**

publicity still: A posed photograph taken with a still camera, usually during production, to help publicize a film. (412 left)

pull focus: See **rack focus.**

rack focus: Changing the sharpness of focus during a shot from foreground to background or vice versa. (44)

reaction shot: A shot, usually of a face, that shows someone or occasionally an animal reacting to an event. Used frequently in films to intensify a situation and to cue viewers how to react. (122)

reel: (1) A metal or plastic spool to hold film. (2) One thousand feet of 35 mm motion-picture film stored on a reel. Since the speed of projection was not standardized before the late 1920s, early films were measured in terms of the number of reels. For example, the 1925 version of *Les Misérables* reputedly consisted of thirty-two reels (each reel could take from thirteen to sixteen minutes to project). Today, a 35 mm reel of sound film takes approximately eleven minutes to project if the film has leader attached to it or ten minutes if it has no leader.

reflexive: See **self-reflexive.**

revisionist: Referring to a new or revised interpretation or representation of a subject (such as history, a narrative, or genre). *Unforgiven* is a revisionist western, for example, in that most of the film is critical of violence and killing. Opposite of **conventional.** (229)

rough cut: An early version (usually the first complete or nearly complete version) of an edited film. See **fine cut.**

running time: The time that elapses when a film is projected. The running time of most feature films is 80 to 120 minutes. (286)

rushes: See **dailies.**

satire: A representation of human behavior that has as its aim the humorous criticism of the behavior shown. In attempting to reach this goal, satirists often use irony or styles such as parody or black comedy. The tone of a satire may be tolerant amusement, bitter indignation, or somewhere in between.

saturated color: Intense, vivid, or brilliant color. Opposite of **desaturated color.** (62)

scanned print: A version of a film made in the standard aspect ratio from an original anamorphic film. In making a scanned print, a technician—not the film's editor or director—decides which part of the width of the original anamorphic image to show at each moment of the film or video. (32)

scene: A section of a narrative film that gives the impression of continuous action taking place in continuous time and space. Most feature films are made up of many scenes—often one hundred or more—as are narrative documentary films, such as *Hearts of Darkness, Hoop Dreams,* and *Genghis Blues.* (106)

scope lens: See **anamorphic lens.**

screenplay: The earliest version of a script, a script written before filming begins. Usually a finished film varies considerably from the original screenplay. See **shooting script** and **cutting continuity.**

self-reflexive: Characteristic of a text, such as a novel or film, to refer to or comment on itself or its medium. For example, a self-reflexive narrative film may include a character interrupting the story to speak to the camera or audience about the story. Examples of self-reflexiveness are found in Luigi Pirandello's play *Six Characters in Search of an Author,* John Fowles's novel *The French Lieutenant's Woman,* and the films *Man with a Movie Camera, Tom Jones, Persona,* and various movies directed by Mel Brooks, such as *Silent Movie.* Many experimental films are self-reflexive at times, as are occasional documentary films. As the authors of *The Film Studies Dictionary* point out, self-reflexive cinema "has

generally been seen as consciously opposed to mainstream cinema's realistic illusion, which hides processes and conventions from immediate view" (197). (253)

sequence: A series of related consecutive scenes, perceived as a major unit of a narrative film, such as the Sicilian sequence in *The Godfather.* A sequence may be analogous to a chapter in a novel or an act in a play. (106)

serial: From the 1910s until the early 1950s, a low-budget action film divided into chapters or installments, one of which was shown each week in downtown and neighborhood movie theaters. Typically serials featured extensive fast-paced action, danger to the heroes, romance, and obvious cheap special effects. Villains often wore bizarre costumes, and the stories were often set in exotic locales. Usually, each chapter or installment ended with an unresolved problem. For example, one or more of the main characters was placed in mortal danger or seemed to be killed. Serials have influenced the *Star Wars* films, the series of *Raiders* films, and other action movies.

set: A constructed setting where action is filmed; it can be indoors or outdoors. See **location.**

setting: The place where filmed action occurs. It is either a set, which has been built for use in a film, or a location, which is any place other than one built for use in a movie. Setting is often used to indicate a period and to reveal or enhance the film's style, characters, mood, and meanings. (9)

shallow focus: A term used widely by film teachers and scholars to indicate photography with sharp focus in only a short distance between the foreground and the background, for example, between ten and fifteen feet in front of the camera. Achieved in photography by using a long or telephoto lens or a large lens aperture, or both.

The technique is often used to deemphasize the background and focus attention on the subject in the foreground. Filmmakers often use the terms *restricted depth of field* or *shallow depth of field* rather than *shallow focus*, the term favored by film teachers and scholars. Opposite of **deep focus.** (74)

shooting script: The version of the script used by the filmmakers during filming. Because usually many changes are made during filming and editing, the finished film typically varies considerably from the shooting script. See **screenplay** and **cutting continuity.**

short film: Variously defined, but usually regarded as a film of less than sixty minutes. (269)

short lens: See **wide-angle lens.**

short subject: See **short film.**

shot: (1) An uninterrupted strip of exposed motion-picture film or videotape that presents a subject, perhaps even a blank screen, during an uninterrupted segment of time. (2) Filmed, as in "they shot the movie in seven weeks." (105)

simulated documentary: See **fake documentary.**

slow cutting: Edited film characterized by frequent lengthy shots. Most of the early films directed by Michelangelo Antonioni and *2001: A Space Odyssey*, for example, have extensive slow cutting, as does the experimental film "(nostalgia)." Opposite of **fast cutting.** (128)

slow film (stock): Film stock that requires a large camera aperture or bright light for appropriate re-creation of images. Slow film produces images with fine grain and sharp detail. Opposite of **fast film (stock).** (57)

slow motion: Motion in which the action depicted on the screen is slower than its real-life counterpart, as when people are seen running slowly. Achieved whenever the projector runs at an appreciably slower speed than the speed at which the camera filmed. Opposite of **fast motion.**

socialist realism: A Soviet doctrine and style in force from the mid-1930s to the 1980s that decreed that all Soviet texts, including films, must promote communism and the working class and must be "realistic" (actually an idealized depiction of the working class) so as to be understandable to working people. (375)

soft light: (1) Light that somewhat obscures surface details and creates shadows that are soft-edged. Soft light has been reflected off something else before illuminating the subject. It is available during the so-called magic hour, the time after sunset but before dark or the time of increasing light before sunrise. Another source of soft light is the light emitted through a frosted lightbulb then reflected off or through a cloth lampshade. Opposite of **hard light.** (2) A type of open-faced lamp that creates soft or diffused light. (65)

sound dissolve: A transition in which a sound begins to fade out as the next sound fades in and overlaps the first sound before replacing it. (157)

sound effect: A sound in film other than vocals or music. Three examples of sound effects are a door slamming, a dog barking, and thunder. (148)

sound stage: A permanent enclosed area for shooting film and recording sound. A sound stage is especially useful because its controlled environment allows for filming and sound recording without unwanted sights and sounds.

Soviet montage: See **montage,** definition 2.

special effect: Shot unobtainable by live-action cinematography. Includes split screen (one subject in part of the image, another subject in another part of the image); most superimpositions; freeze frame; and many others.

spoof: See **parody.**

staged documentary: See **fake documentary.**

standard aspect ratio: For an image on a screen or on the film itself, the ratio of the width to the height is 4:3 or 1.33:1. Until the 1950s the usual shape of motion-picture screens throughout the world, and the approximate shape of analog TV screens. (31)

Steadicam: A lightweight and portable mount for holding a movie camera that provides for relatively steady camera movements during handheld shots. Especially useful for filming in rugged terrain or tight quarters. (90)

still: See **publicity still.**

stock footage: Footage stored for possible duplication and use in other films. Often stock footage is of subjects and locations difficult, impossible, or costly to film anew, such as warfare or the Paris background in the flashback sequence of *Casablanca*.

stop-motion cinematography: The process of filming a subject for only one or a few frames, stopping the camera and changing something in the image, filming again, and

repeating this process many times. May be used to create a continuous movement, as in most animated films, or rapid, discontinuous or jumpy movement, as in pixillation. See **time-lapse cinematography.** (344)

story: See **narrative.**

storyboard: A series of drawings (or occasionally photographs) of each shot of a planned film or video story, often accompanied by brief descriptions or notes. (186)

story time: The amount of time represented in a film's narrative or story. For example, if a film's earliest scene occurs on a Sunday and its latest scene takes place on the following Friday, then the story time is six days. Nearly always the story time for a movie is much longer than its running time. (286)

straight cut: See **cut,** definition 1.

structure: The selection and arrangement of the parts of a whole. In a narrative film, structure can be thought of as the selection and arrangement of scenes or sequences. In other films, structure refers to the selection and arrangement of discernible parts. In a nonnarrative documentary film, for example, the structure might consist of the selection and arrangement of interviews and film clips. (264)

style: The way subjects are presented in a text, such as a film. Styles for films or parts of films include abstract, black comedy, expressionism, farce, magic realism, parody, realism, and socialist realism. Style is sometimes contrasted with content, though many theorists argue that the two are not exclusive but symbiotic. (290)

subjective camera: See **point-of-view shot.**

superimposition: Two or more images photographed or printed on top of each other. Can be achieved in the camera during filming or, more often, by using an optical printer or computer. At the beginning of many movies, the credits are superimposed on the opening action.

During a lap dissolve, one image is momentarily super-imposed on another. Sometimes, as in several scenes in *Drugstore Cowboy*, two or more shots are superimposed to suggest a character's emotional or physical instability. The technique is often used in experimental films, as in Carolee Schneemann's "Fuses," but rarely in documentary films. (117)

surrealism: A movement in 1920s and 1930s European art, drama, literature, and film in which an attempt was made to portray or interpret the workings of the subconscious mind as manifested in dreams. Surrealism is characterized by an irrational, noncontextual arrangement of subjects. The surrealist movement has been especially influential on some experimental filmmakers, such as Luis Buñuel ("Un Chien Andalou" and *L'Age d'Or*) and Jean Cocteau, especially his "The Blood of a Poet." It has also influenced some music videos.

swish pan: (1) Filming while a movie camera is pivoted horizontally so rapidly on a stationary base that the resultant filmed images are blurred. (2) The blurred images that result from pivoting a movie camera horizontally too rapidly during filming. Used as a shot, within a shot; or as a transition between shots. (87)

symbol: Anything perceptible that has significance or meaning beyond its usual meaning or function. Depending on the contexts, a sound, object, person, word (including a name), color, action, or something else perceived by the senses may all function as symbols. In *Citizen Kane*, for example, many viewers believe the glass paperweight that Kane drops at the beginning of the film and that is seen two other times is not simply an object serving its usual functions but also a symbol that suggests meanings. (416)

symptomatic meaning: Meaning stated or, much more often, suggested by a film or other text that is the same as the widespread belief or value of a group outside the film. For example, *Fatal Attraction*, which first appeared in 1987, suggests that casual sex can be dangerous, even deadly. This implied message is symptomatic of the growing concerns in late 1980s America about casual sex and the spread of AIDS and other sexually transmitted diseases. See **ideology** and **meaning.** (429)

take: A version of a shot. Directors often call for additional takes because of some mistake or imperfection in the original take. Different takes of each shot are usually made in shooting theatrical films. One of the major jobs of the editor is to select the most effective take of each shot to be used in the finished film.

(film) technique: Any aspect of filmmaking, such as the choice of sets, lighting, sound effects, music, and editing. How well techniques are selected and used is a strong determinant of a film's content, style, and impact.

telephoto lens: A lens that makes all subjects in an image appear closer to the camera and to each other than is the case with a normal lens. With its long barrel, a telephoto lens resembles a telescope. Not to be confused with a zoom lens, which is capable of varying by degrees from telephoto range to normal, sometimes even to wide-angle range, while the camera is filming. (73)

text: Something that people produce or modify to communicate meaning. Examples are a film, photograph, painting, newspaper article, opera, and T-shirt with a message.

theme: See **meaning.**

THX sound: A multispeaker sound system developed by Lucasfilm and used in selected movie theaters to increase frequency range, audience coverage, and dialogue intelligibility while decreasing low bass distortion.

tight framing: A shot in which there is little visible space around the main subjects for example, the main subjects are near the edges of the frame and a wall behind

them is nearby. Uses for such framing include giving a sense of the subject's confinement or lack of mobility. Opposite of **loose framing.** (14)

tilting: A movie camera pivoting vertically during filming, usually while the camera is attached to a stationary base, such as a tripod. Often used as a way of gradually revealing information, as when we first see someone's shoes, then the camera tilts up to reveal the wearer. This is done memorably near the beginning of Hitchcock's *Strangers on a Train.* See also **panning.**

time-lapse cinematography: The process of filming the same subject one frame at a time at regularly spaced intervals, for example, one frame every thirty minutes or one frame every twenty-four hours. When the processed film is projected at normal speed, any change that was photographed is much accelerated, perhaps even blurred. Can be used to show quickly the changes of a long process, such as the building of a house or the budding of a flower, or for some other purpose, as in the experimental documentary *Koyaanisqatsi* (below), in which time-lapse cinematography was used to suggest the rapidity of modern urban life. See **stop-motion cinematography.**

tinting: The process of dyeing a film with color. Sometimes used before the adoption of color film stock in the late 1930s. In such movies, often each scene or sequence would be tinted one color. For example, blue was often used for night scenes or scenes set in the cold, and red for scenes of violence, danger, passion, or heat. (61)

title card: A card or thin sheet of clear plastic on which is written or printed information included in a film. Before the late 1920s, title cards were used to supply credits,

> **In October of 1994, three student filmmakers disappeared in the woods near Burkittsville, Maryland while shooting a documentary.**
>
> **A year later their footage was found.**

exposition, dialogue, thoughts, descriptions of actions not shown, the numbered parts of a movie, and other types of information. Since the late 1920s, they have been used less often but they are seen, for example, in the 1995 *Richard III* and *The Blair Witch Project;* in some documentary films, such as *The Thin Blue Line, Hearts of Darkness,* and *Hoop Dreams;* and in occasional experimental films.

track: (1) To film while the camera is being moved around. Sometimes the camera is mounted on a cart set on tracks; sometimes it is handheld, and the camera operator moves or is moved about in a wheelchair or on roller skates or by some other means. In some publications, *to track* and *to dolly* are used interchangeably. (2) A film sound track, a narrow band on the film that contains recorded optical, magnetic, or digital sound. (58)

trailer: A brief compilation film shown in movie theaters, before some videotaped movies, or on TV to advertise a movie or a video release.

treatment: A condensed written description of the content of a proposed film, often written in paragraphs and without dialogue.

underground film: See **experimental film.**

vocal: Any sound made with the human voice, including speech, grunts, whimpers, screams, and countless other sounds. Along with silence, music, and sound effects, one of the components of the typical film sound track. (144)

voice-over: See **narration.**

wide-angle lens: A camera lens (significantly shorter than 50 mm on a 35 mm camera) that makes all subjects in an image appear farther from the camera and from each other than is the case with a normal lens. The wide-angle lens also renders subjects at all distances from the

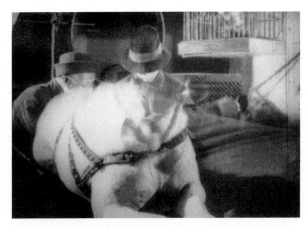

camera in sharp focus and captures more of the sides of the image than is possible with a normal lens, though at the cost of some distortion. (73)

wide-screen film: Any film with an aspect ratio noticeably greater than 1.33:1 (a shape wider than that of an analog TV screen). Most current films shown in U.S. commercial theaters have a wide-screen aspect ratio of 1.85:1. Wide-screen film formats have been tried since nearly the beginning of cinema but have been used in most theaters only since the 1950s. (31)

wipe: A transition between shots, usually between scenes, in which it appears that one shot is pushed off the screen by the next shot. Many kinds of wipes are possible; perhaps the most common is a vertical line (sharp or blurred) that moves across the frame from one side to the other, seemingly "wiping away" a shot and replacing it with the next one. (111)

zip pan: See **swish pan.**

zoom: To use a zoom lens to cause the image of the subject to either increase in size as the area being filmed seems to decrease (zoom in) or to decrease in size as the area being filmed seems to increase (zoom out).

zoom lens: A camera lens with variable focal lengths; thus it can be adjusted by degrees during a shot so that the size of the subject and the area being filmed change. During filming, the lens may assume the properties of a telephoto lens, normal lens, wide-angle lens. Zooming in or zooming out from the subject approximates tracking or dollying toward or away from it. Since the 1960s, the zoom lens has often been used in documentary filmmaking and in making many other films. For example, throughout nearly all of the experimental film "Wavelength," the movie camera imperceptibly zooms in on a photograph on the background wall.

Acknowledgments

Front Cover Photos, from left to right:
Traffic: Photofest
Crouching Tiger, Hidden Dragon: Photofest
Crooklyn: Photofest

Back Cover Photos, from left to right:
Bride of Frankenstein: Photofest
Run, Lola, Run: Photofest
The Third Man: Library of Congress

Text Illustrations (in addition to individual captions):
Jon Jonik. Copyright © 1989 Jon Jonik/Cartoonists & Writers Syndicate. <www.cartoonweb
.com.> Reprinted by permission.
Gary Larson. THE FAR SIDE © 1991 FARWORKS, INC. Used by permission. All
rights reserved.
Wiley Miller. NON SEQUITUR © 1999 Wiley Miller. Distributed by Universal Press
Syndicate. Reprinted with permission. All rights reserved.

Index

Page numbers in **boldface** type refer to the longest discussion of a topic; page numbers in *italic* type refer to illustrations or captions. Numbers within parentheses are usually dates of films.

563